MUSORGSKY
AND HIS CIRCLE

MUSORGSKY
AND HIS CIRCLE

A Russian Musical Adventure

STEPHEN WALSH

ALFRED A. KNOPF · NEW YORK · 2013

Library of Congress Cataloging-in-Publication Data
Walsh, Stephen, [date]
Musorgsky and his circle : a Russian musical adventure /
by Stephen Walsh.
pages cm
ISBN 978-0-307-27244-7 (hardcover)
1. Mussorgsky, Modest Petrovich, 1839–1881. 2. Moguchaia kuchka
(Group of composers) 3. Composers—Russia—Biography. 4. Music—
Russia—19th century—History and criticism. 5. Music—Russia—20th
century—History and criticism. 6. Nationalism in music. I. Title.
ML390.W175 2013
780.92—dc23
[B]   2013004600

Jacket images: (center) Modest Musorgsky from
The Granger Collection, NY; (corners, clockwise)
Nikolai Rimsky-Korsakov, Alexander Borodin, César Cui,
and Mily Balakirev from DeA Picture Library /
The Granger Collection, NY
Jacket design by Peter Mendelsund

Manufactured in the United States of America
First Edition

For Anthony Powers

It is strange to remember those thoughts and to try to catch

The underground whispers of music beneath the years

—HENRY REED

Contents

Preface

The story of nineteenth-century Russian nationalism is one of the most fascinating and colorful in music history, and the music the nationalists wrote is some of the most popular and original in the entire classical repertoire. Moreover, it connects directly with the social and political history of the period, because the composers were responding specifically to ideas about society and the relationship between society and art that were central to Russian thought in the century between the end of the Napoleonic Wars and the 1917 revolutions.

Yet despite this rich texture of significance, there are few essential books specifically on the subject. The only book in English on the *kuchka* as a whole is an enjoyable but essentially anecdotal account by the Russian historian Mikhail Zetlin which is stronger on atmosphere than ideas or music. There are standard, if old-fashioned, biographies of Borodin and Balakirev, and some excellent lives of Musorgsky, including David Brown's Master Musicians volume, a short study by Caryl Emerson, and two at one time indispensable but now antique books by Gerald Abraham and Michel Calvocoressi. The academic literature is strong but specialized, much preoccupied with source materials, textual variants, issues of style, the correcting of supposed historical misunderstandings, and general questions such as realism and ethnography. To the best of my knowledge, no musically literate general study that is both scholarly and readable exists.

My book is an attempt to meet those rather stiff criteria. The case for such a study is certainly unanswerable. When one considers the vast literature on Wagner and Verdi, the poverty of what is available on the *kuchka* is shameful. One doesn't have to claim that any of the Five are in the same league as those two masters to argue that their work and ideas merit closer attention than they have so far received. Leaving aside the indisputable fact that Musorgsky's *Boris Godunov* is among the greatest and most original of all nineteenth-century operas, that the work of Borodin and Rimsky-Korsakov includes music adored by people who could not name its composer, and that Musorgsky's songs are as remarkable in their way as any in the German tradition, the intellectual and aesthetic context of these composers' lives and work is alone well worth studying.

Their existence as an authentic group—meeting several times a week, discussing one another's work in progress, arguing about the goals of art—coincided roughly with the 1860s, which were a time of intellectual ferment following the emancipation of the serfs in 1861. Genuine creative collectives of this type are rare in music, probably because music doesn't usually deal with discussable ideas. For the *kuchka* it was crucial that their mentor was a nonmusician, the art historian Vladimir Stasov, a follower of the literary critic Vissarion Belinsky, who had argued that it was the task of art to reflect the realities of social and political life and the task of the critic to interpret art in that spirit. Stasov, who had known Glinka—the "father figure" of Russian music—concocted his own set of values as to how such ideas might be adapted to a specifically nationalist music, and he did his best to impose them on his musical circle, with the help of the composer Mily Balakirev, the strongest personality in the group.

The group's amateurism is often held against it, and it's true that their failure to produce regular, completed scores was at least partly due to their lack of the discipline and technical know-how that come from proper study. The fact that they mostly had other jobs obviously didn't help. Borodin, a musical genius, was also a vocational research chemist. Musorgsky was the younger son of landowners impoverished by the Emancipation, who was forced by sheer necessity into civil-service drudgery. Only Rimsky-Korsakov, who started out as a naval cadet, managed to square the circle by accepting a professorship in the Conservatoire in 1871. As a result he turned himself into a productive and disciplined musical worker who passed on his reformed work ethic to pupils like Glazunov and (especially) Stravinsky.

But that wasn't all that he, and the *kuchka* as a whole, passed on. Not only was their music part of the stylistic environment from which Stravinsky emerged, but it also had a profound influence on the two most important French composers of the turn of the century, Debussy and Ravel; and things Debussy found in Musorgsky inspired innovations that passed into the work of Messiaen and from there to Boulez and others of the postwar generation. Musorgsky's *Boris Godunov, Pictures from an Exhibition, Night on Bald Mountain,* his many songs, and the problematical unfinished opera *Khovanshchina* are monuments to one of

the most independent-minded of all composers. Borodin's two completed symphonies, two string quartets, and the operatic torso *Prince
Igor* reveal a more conventional but brilliant talent dissipated by divided
loyalties. The steadier, less remarkable, but still individual work of
Rimsky-Korsakov, and occasional flashes of brilliance in Balakirev's
piano music and his symphonic poem *Tamara,* round out this strange
but intriguing picture. Only the fifth member, Cui, a crucial figure
within the group, left no music of lasting significance, even though
there are works of his, as I try to show, that don't deserve the near-total
oblivion to which posterity has consigned them.

The emergence of this curious and somewhat quarrelsome bunch of
semitrained composers from a musical environment previously dominated (like the other arts in pre-Napoleonic Russia) by foreigners, is
a strangely moving and absorbing episode in music history. In trying
to bring it to life for the general reader I have been heavily dependent
on existing published material, as will be evident from my endnotes
and bibliography. To a large extent the book is a work of synthesis,
thickly colored, though, by critical ideas of my own for which no one
else can conceivably be blamed. Some thanks are due, nevertheless.
Natalya Braginskaya, of the St. Petersburg Conservatory, helped me
on matters to do with Russian language and accentuation and, along
with her husband, Dmitry, was a warm and attentive host to me and
my wife during our visit to St. Petersburg for the Rimsky-Korsakov
Conference there in March 2010. I was also greatly helped on this
visit and subsequently by Larisa Miller, chief music archivist of the St.
Petersburg Conservatory. The conference itself was a huge stimulus;
thanks to Lidia Ader, hard-working and efficient organizer, for inviting us. We Westerners still mostly read only horrors about Russia in
our newspapers. It's a pleasure to emphasize the amazing friendliness
and generosity of real Russians when one visits their country these
days.

At home I have had invaluable archival help from, especially, Dr.
Nicolas Bell, curator of Music Collections at the British Library; from
the staff of Cardiff University Music Library; and from Alison Harvey
of the Special Collections division of the university's Arts and Social
Studies Library. I had useful and interesting conversations about
Rimsky-Korsakov with John Nelson during his year in Cardiff on an
Erasmus doctoral exchange. The extensive, if curiously erratic, Russian holdings of the London Library filled many potential gaps, and the
library staff were unfailingly calm and efficient in helping me dig them
out. My own department, Cardiff University School of Music, sup-

ported me as ever with research funds. Andrew Maby gave me hours of his time on technical support. I should like particularly to thank Chuck Elliott, for his support, patience, and strong editorial help on this and previous projects.

My darling wife, Mary, has as ever endured it all with no more protest than was necessary to keep me focused. Above all her advice has been a vital corrective to the hermetic tendencies of university-funded and -refereed research. Now she has to read the book to prove that it has worked.

MUSORGSKY
AND HIS CIRCLE

CHAPTER I

Arrivals

M ily Alexeyevich Balakirev—eighteen years old, of medium height, thick-set, and with a youthful beard already framing a noticeably ample, rounded head—arrived in St. Petersburg for the first time in his life late in November 1855* He was travelling with his patron, Alexander Ulïbïshev, a scholarly, music-loving Nizhny-Novgorod landowner who had taken young Mily under his wing four years before, paid for his piano lessons, and given him the run of his exceptionally well-equipped music library. The boy was one of those young musicians who seem from time to time to spring up from nowhere, almost out of nothing. His mother had played the piano and taught Mily what she could. But she had died when he was ten years old, after a summer visit to Moscow for the boy to have piano lessons with Alexander Dubuque, a pupil of the great John Field.

As for Mily's father, not much was to be expected from that quarter. Alexey Konstantinovich Balakirev was a minor civil servant in Nizhny-Novgorod. But he was by no means a dull, steady, mildly corrupt citizen of the kind most often to be found in such provincial government posts at that time. On the contrary, he was a difficult, quarrelsome man, quick-tempered and intolerant, and all too ready to make enemies among his colleagues and employers. In course of time Mily would be called on to pull strings for his father in precisely the way that a father might normally be expected to pull strings for his son.

---

* Note: All dates are Old Style.

Yet the young man had evidently come to St. Petersburg with Alexey Konstaninovich's blessing, since, however slight his father's interest in music, he at least had the wit to see that Mily's talent represented the family's best chance of swimming out of the provincial backwater to which his own limitations had confined it.

Mily, decidedly, had talent. His mother must have recognized it, or had it forcefully pointed out to her, or she would hardly have transported them both two hundred and fifty miles, long before the country's first significant public railway, for three months of what must have been expensive lessons with a distinguished teacher. The child's gift was that of a keyboard prodigy, whose significance in the 1840s was perhaps comparable to that of a promising young footballer in our own day. But there can have been few in Nizhny-Novgorod who were capable of penetrating the musical extent of that gift, a full century before the founding of the city's conservatory. You were a good pianist? Excellent, you would give concerts and make a lot of money. The idea that precocious brilliance on an instrument might conceal or breed some kind of creative genius—whatever that might be—was unlikely to have struck any but the most speculative thinkers among the music lovers of the great east-facing commercial city on the Volga. And who could blame them? Even in west-facing St. Petersburg in 1855 there was no conservatory, no music college, few professional concerts, no institution of any kind that might encourage a musically gifted teenager to explore his abilities outside the narrow corridor of tried and trusted instrumental method. Public music making in the capital was still dominated by foreigners and under the administrative control of more or less nonmusical bureaucrats. Russian musicians were scarcely taken seriously.

All the same, it was an interesting time for a gifted young man to arrive in St. Petersburg. Nicholas I, the most reactionary scion of the autocratic Romanov dynasty so far, had died in February 1855, and his son Alexander II was already being seen as the white hope of those who regarded the reform of Russia's social and political institutions as an essential concomitant of her longed-for economic, moral, and cultural liberalization. By chance that same year, a Ukrainian-born Russian composer and virtuoso pianist by the name of Anton Rubinstein had launched a critique of the condition and character of Russian music in the Viennese journal *Blätter für Musik, Theater und Kunst*. The main motif of the article was the inadequacy of a national music based exclusively on folk song, but it underpinned this thesis by noting public neglect of native music and the lack of proper professional musical training in Russia. Rubinstein himself had been an infant prodigy, had been carted round Europe in the early 1840s as a child phenomenon, and had then spent two years studying music theory in Berlin. His own music understandably owed nothing to folk sources, Russian or otherwise, but was at its best a well-formed branch of the German instrumental school dominated at the time by Mendelssohn.

Of course, Rubinstein's remarks had gone down badly in St. Petersburg. But however vague his grasp of the essence of Russian folk music, it could hardly be denied that there were few if any Russian composers able to compete in terms of professional expertise with the foreigners whose music still dominated the boards of the main (Italian) opera house on what is now Teatral'naya Ploshad'—Theatre Square. Most Russian opera at least up to the 1830s had been of the Singspiel or vaudeville type, made up of simple folkish songs interspersed with dialogue. A handful of composers had studied in Italy and come back writing music of an essentially Italian cut. But that would naturally have supported Rubinstein's point about the desirability of a cosmopolitan attitude to style and technique.

As for orchestral music by Russian composers, there was hardly any at all and none of real substance, for the good reason that there were still, in 1855, no established concert series or symphony orchestras anywhere in Russia. Such orchestral concerts as were given took place only in Lent, when theatrical performances were banned, and they not unnaturally tended to include Western repertoire, probably in mediocre, pickup performances. Instrumental chamber music existed, but essentially for amateur performers in rural or aristocratic drawing rooms. No Russian had composed anything remotely on the scale or in the intellectual manner of the classical Viennese string quartet. No groups existed in St. Petersburg or Moscow that would attempt to play such music.

The most characteristic genres of Russian music in the twenties and thirties were the sacred concertos of Dmitry Bortnyansky, eighteenth-century in style but unlike the classical church music of the West in being for voices alone (since instruments were not allowed in the Orthodox Church), and the drawing-room songs with piano composed in large numbers and to Russian texts by gifted dilettantes such as the three Alexanders, Alyabyev, Gurilyov, and Dargomïzhsky. For the most part the aim of these composers' romances (as Russians call the lyrical song) was to provide a shapely, metrically regular tune with a simple, unobtrusive accompaniment—an 1820s equivalent, perhaps, of a modern guitar chord sequence. There would be the occa-

sional imitation folk song; and here and there the music would take
on a freer, more declamatory character, as in some ancient ballad of a
bardic singer accompanying himself on the harp. A fine example of this
ballad type is Dargomïzhsky's early setting of Lermontov's "Tuchki
nebesnïya" (Heavenly Clouds) (1841–2), in which the poet, exiled to
the Caucasus, compares himself to the clouds driven southward by
the north wind. Very occasionally something in a poem will prompt
mildly daring harmony, as in the same composer's setting of Pushkin's
"Vostochnïy romans' " (Eastern Romance) (1852), where the opening words—"You were born to arouse the poet's imagination"—pro-
voke some risky chords, but not, alas, a very inspiring melody. These
are nevertheless superior examples of what Richard Taruskin once
called the "urban *style russe*," an idiom much cultivated by Russian
songwriters of the twenties, thirties, and forties, in which authentic
or quasi-authentic folk songs had their faces washed and their hair
combed to make them suitable company for nicely brought-up young
ladies.[1]

The one person whose music challenged Rubinstein's melancholy
diagnosis was Mikhail Glinka, the composer of two works that had
seemed to set new standards for Russian opera but which, at the time
of Balakirev's arrival in St. Petersburg, were languishing, performed
poorly or not at all, unpublished and to a large extent unappreciated.
In 1855 Glinka was fifty-one years old and had more or less abandoned composition in favor of socializing, disillusioned by the comparative failure of his second opera, *Ruslan and Lyudmila,* in 1842 and
by the shoddy, inattentive revivals of his first, *A Life for the Tsar* (1836),
since then. He was like Chulkaturin, the hero of Turgenev's recent
short story "The Diary of a Superfluous Man." By birth a *dvoryanin,*
a member of the minor land-owning gentry, he had grown up in an
environment where it was possible to cultivate an intensely musical,
artistic nature, but out of the question to put it into any kind of professional practice. Glinka could perform music at home or on his uncle's
estate to his heart's content; he could even write songs or piano music
or chamber works for the kinds of mixed group that might assemble on
such occasions. But it would be little more than a hobby. "No doubt I
was occupied with music," he records in his *Memoirs* for the summer of
1826, "but I really don't know what I accomplished." "Did I compose
anything in Naples?" he asks himself later. "I don't remember."[2] Having neither the need nor the opportunity to embark on a career, and
being—like many of his class—an instinctive valetudinarian, he had
gone abroad on medical advice at the age of twenty-five, spent three

and a half years in Italy, and another five months in Berlin studying harmony and counterpoint with the great Siegfried Dehn, before returning to his family home in Novospasskoye, near Smolensk, in May 1834, two months after his father's death.

It was at this point that Glinka's musical career, and with it the whole history of Russian music, took a decisive turn. The American scholar Lynn Sargeant began a fascinating recent study of the social context of Russian musical life by insisting that "Russia was hardly a silent world in the first half of the nineteenth century," and that "although prominent composers of European fame were slow to emerge, Russian musical life was dynamic and successful, meeting the needs and expectations of its participants and the public."[3] But that "although" is just the point. It was not simple mythmaking that prompted virtually all Russian composers in the second half of the century to regard Glinka as the starting point of a Russian music that would be accepted abroad as a significant tributary of the muddy river of great art. "Dynamic and successful," perhaps, but only to the extent that "the needs and expectations" were limited and untutored. To this day, not a single work by any other Russian composer of Glinka's generation or earlier has entered even the fringes of the repertoire abroad. Glinka's own work from before his return to Russia, mainly hybrid chamber music and songs, remains little known farther west. No less strikingly, this music, though occasionally of superior quality, had relatively little impact on the work even of his compatriots. It was his two operas, together with a handful of brilliant late orchestral miniatures, that suddenly, almost out of the blue, created the launching pad for that adorable, eccentric repertoire of masterpieces and near-masterpieces that we now think of as the very essence of Russian romantic music. More surprisingly, perhaps, it was precisely that repertoire, with all its oddities and unorthodoxies and inspired gaucheries, that provided one vital resource for the new music of the twentieth century, music that was far from gauche, sometimes far from adorable, too, but that knew its own mind and method, and that eventually swelled into an alternative mainstream flowing from a source remote from that of the classical symphonic and operatic tradition.

In this strange history, a major role—perhaps *the* major role—was played by the subject of the present book, the group of composers known in the West as the Five and in Russia as the *moguchaya kuchka,* the Mighty Little Heap (sometimes less accurately translated as the Mighty Handful). As with most such artistic circles, the origins and membership of the *kuchka* were a good deal less clearly defined than history has tended to imply. The name originated in 1867 in a review by the group's intellectual guru, the musically trained art historian and critic Vladimir Stasov, of a concert that included music by only two members of the history-book *kuchka*—Balakirev and Rimsky-Korsakov—alongside works by Glinka and Dargomïzhsky. It was evidently meant to give the sense of a commando unit of Russian composers forcing themselves on the attention of an unsuspecting world. But it was studiedly nonspecific. No doubt Stasov would have included the other three of the Five—Borodin, Cui, and Musorgsky—if they had had pieces in the concert. But then he might have included other circle members too—Nikolay Lodïzhensky, Apollon Gusakovsky, and others—on the same grounds. His object was to locate a new tendency in Russian music starting with Glinka, flowing through the somewhat younger Dargomïzhsky into the work of a burgeoning group of composers still in their twenties or early thirties. The *kuchka* was simply his image for this tendency.

In fact, by 1867, as we shall see, the group was more than a decade old, and was already starting to show signs of disintegration as a coherent aesthetic unit, though its members stayed friends and the circle as such continued to meet. As one might expect, this was roughly at the moment when the various composers were beginning to emerge as clearly profiled personalities, and the profession of ideals was being replaced by strong and individual acts of creation. Indeed, it is by no means easy at this stage to identify in their music exactly what it is that makes them a unified group, as distinct from "outsiders" like Tchaikovsky or Alexander Serov or even Anton Rubinstein himself. Perhaps it was nothing more than the spirit of the stockade, combined with a sense of loyalty to some notional set of principles, often betrayed in practice, in their work as in their lives. Even if one singles out particular attributes that can be traced back to the common source of Glinka, they are rarely if ever unique to the *kuchka*: Tchaikovsky and Serov, for instance, owed as much as they did to the composer of *A Life for the Tsar*. The kuchkist César Cui, on the other hand, owed relatively little to him. Moreover, they often disagreed sharply over the relative value of Glinka's works. Stasov disliked *A Life for the Tsar* because its hero was a doglike peasant who sacrificed his life pointlessly to shore up a corrupt tyranny; Musorgsky and Rimsky-Korsakov admired it because it gave them musical and dramatic clues for their own work. Stasov defended *Ruslan and Lyudmila* because it wasn't *A Life for the Tsar* and Glinka had nevertheless to be idolized; but the composers of the circle loved it for its sheer fertility of idea, its fearless mixing of styles, its magic and fantasy, and its astonishing originality of sound and texture. They forgave its dramatic absurdity, rambling narrative, and vague characterization, things it shared with Russian fairy tales and that set it apart from the orderly dramas of the Western tradition they were so anxious to reject.

Glinka, then, was an icon, part image, part symbol. No doubt the image explained the symbol. Glinka's music, especially his operas, was so much more powerful and brilliant than anything previously composed by a Russian that it was inevitable to regard it as a starting point. What else was there? Bortnyansky, Catterino Cavos, Yevstigney Fomin, Alexey Verstovsky, Alyabyev, Gurilyov: relentlessly parochial, derivative, even amateurish figures, not fit for starting anything more exciting than a church service or a coffee morning. Glinka towered as far above such composers as Beethoven had towered above the Spohrs and Hummels and Clementis of his day. It was even tempting to regard him as practically the equal of Beethoven; at least his impact on the Russian composers who followed him was in some ways comparable to the impact of Beethoven on his German successors. He was at once a model and a touchstone; the very concept "Russian composer" seemed to depend on his authority. Above all, he was a source not shared by Western composers, a signpost that pointed away from the Italo-Germanic school tradition into regions inaccessible to them.

Glinka is therefore a necessary starting point for us, too, if we hope to get under the creative skin of his successors, and especially of the *kuchka*. There will be other starting points, not all of them musical. None of them will explain the phenomenon of the *kuchka*. They will merely help locate it.

Alexander Ulïbïshev was acquainted with Glinka by correspondence, though it seems unlikely that they had ever met. A dozen years before bringing Balakirev to St. Petersburg, he had published a three-volume biographical and analytical study of Mozart, and he had sent a copy to Glinka a few months after the premiere of *Ruslan and Lyudmila*. It was thus perfectly in the normal order of things for him to take his young protégé to call on the great composer. Mily of course knew Glinka's music. He had even composed a piano fantasy, in the manner of Liszt, on themes from *A Life for the Tsar*. He knew and admired *Kamarinskaya* and the so-called *Jota aragonesa,* the first of two Spanish overtures, of which the second was the *Souvenir d'une nuit d'été à Madrid.* And he knew *Ruslan* (but perhaps admired it somewhat less).

The two "Nizhegorodskies" arrived at Glinka's apartment one evening in late December 1855, in the middle of a supper party the composer was giving for a group of friends, including Dargomïzhsky and Dargomïzhsky's sister Sophia and her husband. Glinka's own much younger sister, Lyudmila Shestakova, was also present, and she described the occasion. It was Christmas, and the atmosphere was convivial. Glinka asked Balakirev to play something, and he, with consummate tact, sat down and played his own arrangement of the trio from the final scene of act I of *A Life for the Tsar.* "My brother listened very attentively," Shestakova reported, "and afterward they talked about music together for a long time." It transpired that the two composers, thirty-three years apart in age, had many musical opinions in common, and by no means in every case opinions of which Ulïbïshev will have approved. On Russian music especially they found common ground: on the role of folk music, on orchestral writing, on form, aesthetics, and interpretation. Glinka, for all his authority as the doyen of Russian music, was inclined to be agreeable and a shade languid in conversation, while Balakirev, just turned nineteen, provincial and inexperienced, spoke with the confidence and certainty of untroubled youth. They were as if on an equal footing. "Balakirev," Glinka told his sister, "is the first man in whom I have found views so closely approaching my own on everything concerning music. . . . He will in time become a second Glinka."[4]

A few weeks after this meeting, Ulïbïshev returned to Nizhny-Novgorod, leaving Balakirev to his own devices in the capital. Of course they remained in close touch, and Ulïbïshev continued to support the young man financially, until quite suddenly a year later he died and the patronage ceased. By that time, Balakirev had made a handful of concert appearances, and some influential acquaintances. At Glinka's he had met Stasov and Alexander Serov, one of the most feared music critics in St. Petersburg. At a soirée of the university inspector Fitztum von Eckstedt he had befriended César Cui, a twenty-one-year-old student at the Academy of Military Engineering. But like his father he was a poor networker; and he detested concert giving. "I have to use all my will-power to play or conduct an orchestra in public," he once wrote, "not of course without injury to my nature. It always struck me as horrible that if you write something, there's no other way of hearing it than in a concert. It's like telling a policeman all your most secret inner impulses. I feel morally defiled after every such public act."[5]

Thus Balakirev, poor and unknown, rejected the one means that might have gained him money and status in a capital city that, it must sometimes have seemed, understood little else. At this moment he could easily have faded back into oblivion. That he did not do so was a triumph of personality as much as of talent; but above all it was a feat of historical opportunism such as can only happen at the most inauspicious times and in the least favorable places.

CHAPTER 2

The Father Figure

Until the first production of *A Life for the Tsar,* in November 1836, Glinka's work had been strictly that of a dilettante. To call it amateurish would be to miss the point; among his early compositions are works of real brilliance and expertise. But—with the possible exception of a few songs—they are historically indolent, say nothing new or particularly personal, and merely confirm the essentially salonesque character of the culture for which they were conceived. In Italy he had rubbed shoulders with the famous composers of the day, including Donizetti and Bellini, had heard and to some extent imitated their music, but had at last begun to feel artistically homesick, fed up with his own aesthetic neutrality and with the facile lingua franca of the music that was all around him in one Italian opera house after another. "All the pieces I had composed to please the inhabitants of Milan," he wrote near the end of his life, "had only convinced me that I was not following my own way and that I truthfully could not become an Italian. Longing for home led me, step by step, to think of composing like a Russian."[1] What that might mean, of course, remained to be seen. It was something for which no theory existed, but which, like all solutions to great problems, awaited the consideration of a unique practitioner of genius.

Glinka's immediate answer, when he arrived back in Russia, was to plan an opera with a specifically Russian plot, but not the kind of comic or picaresque-folksy subject that had dominated the vaudeville repertoire. Instead the composer's choice fell on the historical tragedy of the peasant Ivan Susanin, a serf of the future first Romanov tsar, Mikhail Fyodorovich, who at the time of Mikhail's election as tsar in 1613 was supposed to have saved his master from a murderous band of Polish and Cossack marauders by losing them in a deep forest, sacrificing his own life in the process.

Glinka himself was by no means a political animal. The subject seems to have been pressed on him by the writer Vasily Zhukovsky as an alternative to his own romantic short story "Mar'ina Roshcha," for which Glinka had already started composing music. If so, Zhukovsky was probably being opportunistic on Glinka's account. For the past eight years he had been tutor to the young tsarevich (the future Tsar Alexander II), and he was certainly well briefed on the concept of *Pravoslaviye, Samoderzhaviye, Narodnost'*—Orthodoxy, Autocracy, Nationality—which had been promulgated a year or two earlier by the minister of education, Sergey Uvarov, as an approved ideological basis for what Uvarov called "the education of the people." The doctrine of Official Nationality, as it came to be known, was essentially a clever device for harnessing the dangerous energy of progressive national consciousness that had grown out of the defeat of Napoleon in 1812, had infected especially the aristocratic and intellectual classes of Russian society, and had culminated in the Decembrist putsch against the new tsar, Nicholas I, in December 1825. In the Glinka libretto, largely written by the tsarevich's secretary, Baron Georgy Rosen, Susanin at first greets the Polish soldiers (Roman Catholics, of course) by inviting them to his daughter's wedding; but when they rudely brush this aside and insist on his showing them the way to Moscow, he changes his tune (literally) and, to a melody plainly colored by Russian Orthodox chant, loftily proclaims that "our native land is great and holy! . . . The road to Moscow is not for foreigners." "I have no fear of death," he adds, adopting the folk tune that had begun the opera as an apostrophe to the Russian motherland: "I will lay down my life for Holy Russia!"

It would be hard to imagine a situation or characterization that more thoroughly reflected the three terms of Official Nationality. What might have been a good deal less obvious was what kind of music would suit it in the same way. One might idly suppose that some combination of folk song and Orthodox chant would meet the case. But even if such an outlandish concept had occurred to Glinka, it's hard to see how he could have implemented it on the scale required. Genuine folk tunes, such as had been collected, arranged, and published by Nikolay Lvov and Ivan Prach in 1790, were essentially compact, limited musical objects, ideal for adapting to the needs of comic vaudevilles (rather in the manner of *The Beggar's Opera* in London a century earlier), but hardly adequate to the broad canvas and heightened tone of a grand historical drama. As for the music of the Orthodox liturgy, its beauties and limitations may seem familiar to anyone who has stood through any part of a Russian service; but in fact this form of setting was not widely known in the 1830s, which were still dominated liturgically by the Bortnyansky style of unaccompanied classical harmony.

From the start Glinka seems to have planned *Ivan Susanin* (as it was originally called) as a musical drama without dialogue, something that, as a matter of fact, no Russian composer had attempted before, even though the operatic repertoire in St. Petersburg in the twenties and thirties offered plenty of foreign models: Glinka records seeing Cherubini's rescue opera *Les Deux Journées* and Méhul's biblical *Joseph,* among other French works. Later, in Germany, he saw Beethoven's *Fidelio,* Weber's *Der Freischütz,* Spohr's *Faust,* and Cherubini's *Médée* (which, however, he could neither understand nor remember). In Italy, he had become intimate with the local version of the unbroken-music formula: aria, ensemble, recitative. In Milan he had attended the premieres of Donizetti's *Anna Bolena* and Bellini's *La sonnambula,* theatrically powerful works that at times vary and extend the formula in the direction of seamless musical narrative. He may have wearied of the Italian and French styles, but when it came to operatic modelling on a tragic scale they were what he knew. On the other hand, he had no particular reason to feel restricted by them. His studies with Dehn in Berlin on the way home read now like the dreaded curriculum of a first-year university music student. He spent the five months harmonizing Bach chorales and writing fugues, essentially Teutonic disciplines not much cultivated in the opera houses of Italy, but a valuable resource to a Russian composer seeking to assemble the elements of his musical experience into a new and individual style of his own.

A composer naturally composes out of his own head, without necessarily weighing up the ingredients that have gone to form his particular mode of expression. He writes what he feels with the largely unconscious help of what he knows. But Glinka's situation was peculiar. Not only was he attempting a work on a vastly bigger scale than anything he himself had written before, but he was composing something that was completely outside the framework of what his audience would expect. Foreign touring operatic companies were a familiar part of the St. Petersburg landscape, and since their repertoire was in general contemporary, Petersburg audiences were reasonably au courant with the styles of opera being turned out in Paris, Italy, and Germany. Glinka could hardly evade such models, which were equally part of his own mental furniture. Yet at the same time he had to Russify them, both for the benefit of his subject matter and for the good of his soul. The Susanin story, after all, is about the rejection of foreign intrusion. Its operatic treatment had at least to seem to reject it too.

Glinka's solution to this problem was to have profound consequences for the entire course of Russian music in the nineteenth century. To some extent this was because of the specifically Russian elements that he worked into his score. They gave it, of course, an identity that set it apart from any previous grand opera, known or unknown to Russian audiences. Specifically, they marked it out from a work like Verstovsky's *Askold's Tomb* (*Askol'dova molgíva*), a romantic opera with dialogue which had enjoyed a spectacularly successful premiere a year or so before, but which now seems lightweight and derivative and largely devoid of noticeable Russianisms.[2] Crucially, Glinka's opera did this without drastically disrupting the genre itself. So *A Life for the Tsar* is not some weird ethnic concoction derived from the tribal rituals of northern Muscovy, but a tragic opera recognizably in the traditions that Glinka had absorbed from France, Italy, and Germany, based on the formulae of recitative, arioso, aria, ensemble, and chorus, though without directly resembling any one particular composer or work.

The overture starts, after a couple of peremptory gestures, with a slow introduction based on an oboe tune in Taruskin's "urban *style russe*," in which, in this case, "the Russian folk melos [has] been put through an Italianate refinery."[3] It then quickly reverts to type with a sparkling allegro in sonata form, complete with fugal development, such as might suit an opera by Weber or Spohr. The curtain goes up on a scene of peasant life, as it does, for example, in Weber's *Der Freischütz* and Rossini's *William Tell*. And like those composers, Glinka takes the opportunity provided by country people enjoying themselves to localize his story, while also, unlike them, localizing his music. A troop of partisan fighters against the invading Poles arrives in Domnino and are fêted by the villagers. One of the soldiers intones an apostrophe to the motherland, like a precentor giving the tune (*zapev*), and is answered in solemn harmony by the other partisans; then the village women enter to a sprightly dance tune, which again might be, and isn't, an authentic song of welcome. But Glinka next does something extremely peculiar: he combines the two tunes in a complicated imitative texture that sounds like a brilliant solution to an exercise set by Dehn, and certainly nothing like anything ever heard in a Muscovy village. It's true that the peasants of Glinka's day, and no doubt Mikhail Romanov's too, had a way of singing in polyphony, but it was a particular kind of polyphony, in which the different parts were variants of the same tune, freely individualized without regard to any rules of combination. (Musicologists call this heterophony.)[4] Glinka's chorus is very learned and regulated by comparison, but also, it must be said, a dazzlingly effective way of treating folk material in a formal context.

This hybridization of what seem like folk materials continues, one way and another, for the rest of the work. Susanin's daughter, Antonida, whose wedding has been postponed by her ultra-royalist father pending Romanov's election, sings an exquisite lament in a cross between Italian bel canto and what Russian ethnomusicologists call *protyazhnaya pesnya* (extended song), in the manner of a highly ornate vocal elegy. The second part of her aria is a quick cabaletta, like Violetta's "Sempre libera" in *La traviata,* but again with folk-song coloring: Antonida is, after all, a peasant girl, albeit with coquetries of her own, which are hinted at by distinctly unfolkish touches in the melody and rhythm. Susanin, on the other hand, enters to an actual folk tune, which Glinka had heard sung by a coachman in Luga.[5] But the superbly convincing offstage song of the boatmen bringing Antonida's betrothed with news of Romanov's election is apparently Glinka's own work, studiously fitted out with authentic details, like the melodic fall at the end of the third phrase and the persistent uncertainty whether—in Western harmonic language—we are in C major or A minor.[6] Glinka typically doesn't scruple to romanticize the approaching chorus with a double-speed "balalaika" (in fact string pizzicato) accompaniment, which contrasts the expectancy of the villagers with the stately progress of the oarsmen and their momentous news.

To what extent Glinka had thought out this brilliant fusion of operatic convention with identifiable Russianisms, to what extent it emerged as an ad hoc solution to the self-imposed problem of writing a Western kind of grand opera in Russian and on a Russian subject, is hard to say. One element, at least, was preplanned, and it is by no means the most convincing. At the Polish court (act 2), and later when the Polish soldiers enter Susanin's hut and haul him off as a guide to Romanov's whereabouts, the hated foreigners are portrayed entirely through Polish dance music: a polonaise, a krakowiak, a mazurka—a device that both depersonalizes them (all Poles are the same) and, of course, ridicules them (nothing but a bunch of dancers). By contrast, the Russians are individually characterized and their emotions explored: Antonida, as we have seen; Susanin confronting the Poles, at first with feigned innocence ("Oh, sirs! How should we know where the tsar is pleased to stay? We live out here in the wilds"), then with an air of dignified reproach, and finally with lofty refusal. Glinka hits off each of these moods with amazing musical precision for a composer of such limited theatrical experience, portraying Susanin as a man of simple but stubborn loyalty and courage, an ideal model for a doctrine that wants to represent the authentic Russian soul as inextricably bound up with trust in the autocracy. In the deep wintry forest of the final act, realizing that the Poles are beginning to see through his deception, Susanin achieves a kind of tragic grandeur while never for a moment stepping out of character. The square phraseology, stepwise melody, and static D-minor harmony of his lament are those of the simple-hearted hero, no more than lightly touched by the pathos of all those Bellinian Aminas and Normas whom Glinka had fled Italy partly in order to escape. At the end, in place of the cabaletta that would hardly have suited either the man or the situation (but which an Italian audience would nevertheless have expected), Susanin sadly remembers his loved ones in fragments of their music: Antonida's cavatina, Sobinin's announcement of the new tsar, the adopted orphan Vanya's song.

The final hybrid in A Life for the Tsar is the epilogue in Red Square, in which the people greet Mikhail Romanov (unseen, because it was not permitted to represent the tsar onstage). For this scene Glinka devised a Russianized version of the choral hymns of triumph that conventionally ended the rescue operas he knew, such as Les Deux Journées and Fidelio, basing himself on the modernized and in fact Westernized Russian choral style of the late seventeenth century known as kant.[7] It's a style that masquerades as antique harmonized chant and was in fact accepted as such by nineteenth-century Russia, though its connection with the ancient and to a large extent forgotten znamenny chant of the Orthodox Church was negligible. As we shall see, it was part of Glinka's genius to serve as a musical mythmaker, an inventor of genres and styles that would subsequently be accepted as the acme of authentic Russianness. This triumphal chorus, much imitated in later operas, might stand as a symbol of his paternity as a whole.

A Life for the Tsar was received with enthusiasm on its first performance in St. Petersburg's newly restored Bolshoi Theatre on 27 November 1836. People went around singing tunes from it, and Glinka became famous overnight. But it was perhaps inevitable that press reviewers should attempt to see beyond the work's immediate appeal and position it as the start of a new era in Russian music. The music critic of the Severnaya pchela (Northern Bee), Prince Vladimir Odoyevsky, reviewed the opera in millennial terms: "How can I convey the astonishment of true lovers of music when, from the first act onwards, it became clear that this opera was going to provide an answer to a question which is of vital importance to the arts in general and to the arts in Russia in particular—namely that of the very existence of Russian opera, Russian music and, ultimately, the existence of national music." And he added: "Glinka's music has brought to light what people have long sought and not found in Europe—a new element in art. This is the dawn of a new age in the history of the arts—the age of Russian music."[8] Glinka's friend Nikolay Melgunov, who had in the past expressed sophisticated views on the possible character of a Russian national opera, was delighted that Glinka "has not confined himself to a more or less close imitation of folk-song; no, he has studied deeply the repertoire of Russian songs ... [and] has opened up a whole system of Russian melody and harmony, founded upon the very music of the people, and in no way resembling the music of any prevailing schools."[9]

The expectation was naturally that Glinka would follow up *A Life for the Tsar* with another opera in the Russian national spirit. But even in the hour of his triumph Glinka was incapable of behaving like a professional composer. Soon after the premiere he began tinkering with an idea for an opera based on an early narrative poem of Pushkin, *Ruslan and Lyudmila.* Of all Pushkin's tales apart from the verse novel *Yevgeny Onegin, Ruslan* is by far the longest and most diffuse; and like all the fairy tales of the master it is a subtly ironic work which treats the bardic tradition as an opportunity for satire as well as mimicry, and as a pretext for digressions on issues of style and genre. To distill a coherent operatic plot from it would have tested a Boito or a Hofmannsthal, whereas Glinka never managed to settle on a librettist at all. In his *Memoirs* he claims to have intended to map out a scenario with Pushkin himself, whom he knew well, but the poet's death in a duel in January 1837 put paid to that idea. Some time later, at a soirée at which Glinka had played some of the music he had already written for *Ruslan,* another poet, Konstantin Bakhturin, "undertook to make a plan for the opera, and sketched it out in half an hour, while drunk, and—how about this?—the opera was written according to that plan!"[10] In due course various other writers chipped in with individual numbers while Glinka pottered along composing his music whether or not relevant text was to hand. Few operas of significance can have been compiled in such a haphazard way. But *Ruslan's* significance, luckily, does not hang on its coherence.

Pushkin's poem tells of the Kievan knight Ruslan and his young bride, the princess Lyudmila, who is abducted from their marriage bed by the evil dwarf Chernomor. Furious at Ruslan's inattentiveness, Lyudmila's father promises her hand and half his kingdom to whoever finds her and brings her back. What follows is in some respects a parody of those Russian fairy stories in which the hero is sent on some seemingly impossible quest and is subjected to an increasingly elaborate and improbable series of obstructions and misfortunes at the hands of assorted wizards, hags, giants, rival suitors, and fabulous monsters before returning safely with his prize. Bakhturin's scenario necessarily cuts out a good deal of incident and simplifies the order of events, but in all essentials it follows Pushkin's narrative—which is to say that it makes no serious attempt to rationalize its haphazard dramaturgy, or to remedy its psychological vacuity. In the opera, Lyudmila is abducted from the actual wedding feast (so no blame attaches to Ruslan); the number of rival suitors is reduced from three to two; and two of the most fantastic elements—Chernomor's magic hat, which Lyudmila steals and puts on to avoid recapture, and the killing and resuscitation of Ruslan—are omitted. But Glinka retains the giant severed head of Chernomor's brother, which Ruslan encounters on an old battlefield and which—in proto-Wagnerian fashion—reveals to him the magic sword with which he will defeat Chernomor; and he keeps Chernomor's long beard, to which Ruslan clings as they fly through the air and then cuts off, thereby destroying the dwarf's power.

For those who had seen A Life for the Tsar as a landmark in the search for an authentically Russian style of opera, Ruslan and Lyudmila might well have seemed a retrograde step. It lacked almost all the features that had defined its predecessor as specifically and contemporaneously Russian. Instead of a realistic drama based on true history it offered a silly, dramatically inert and implausible fairy tale, acted out by pasteboard characters devoid of moral stature and helpless in the face of magic and fate. Of political or national signification there was no obvious trace. And as for the music, it abandoned almost completely the folk models that had so invigorated the earlier opera. Apparently only two melodies have folk origins, neither of them Slavonic: the main theme of the wizard Finn's ballad, which Glinka had taken down from a coachman near Imatra, in Finland, in 1829; and the theme of the Persian chorus in the magic castle of the enchantress Naina, which he got from a Persian embassy official that same year. On the face of it, Ruslan diverges much less than A Life for the Tsar from the Franco-Italian manner that had still underpinned the latter work. For instance, Lyudmila's cavatina, and especially her subsequent cabaletta, are noticeably more Bellinian than Antonida's. One could nearly, if not quite, say of

Ruslan that had the young Wagner decided in 1833 to base his first opera on the Pushkin tale (instead of on a fairy play by Gozzi), it might not have come out as an essentially different style of work from Glinka's.

Nevertheless *Ruslan* was to prove fully the equal of its companion in the effect it had on Glinka's Russian successors. "Nothing glaringly new appears anywhere," Alfred Swan wrote of it, "but the sum-total of musical speech is the result of Glinka's taste, measure, and proportion, imbued, moreover, with the hidden accents of the old Russian heritage . . . There is not a single formation here that one could not find in the romantic armoury, yet the whole effect is a revelation."[11] Swan perhaps underrates the force of some of Glinka's eccentricities. No Western composer would have risked the interminable prophecies of Bayan (the ballad singer) at the very start of proceedings, or Finn's extended life story at the beginning of act 2. But these studiously monotonous presentations embody something peculiarly Eastern and antique that Glinka must have intended to suggest far-off, immutable truths, even while, musically, they contain no single phrase that Schubert or Rossini could not have written. Later in the first act there is a rough unison chorus in praise of Lel, the Slav god of love, in a highly unusual five-four time and with harsh accents, building up to the moment when the lights suddenly go out and Lyudmila is whisked away by a pair of shadowy monsters. Glinka famously marks this, and all subsequent apparitions of Chernomor or his henchmen, with a loud descending whole-tone scale, a scale that, being completely symmetrical, disrupts our sense of musical gravity and hints therefore at the suspension of the normal laws of musical nature.

What such details indicate is a deeply idiosyncratic attitude to conventional language. This has sometimes been put down to a lack of technical expertise on Glinka's part; but a better explanation might be that, in the search for an individual native manner with no specifically native conventions to support him, he was forced to adopt a pragmatic, opportunistic approach to whatever materials came to hand. Being both brilliantly talented and, it seems, shameless, he consequently made discoveries about quite simple music that nobody else had made. The Persian chorus is a good example of his invention of an idiom out of entirely commonplace materials. The borrowed melody itself is by any standards unremarkable; its obvious features are a downbeat start and a feminine ending on every phrase, combined with a lullingly repetitive rhythm and bland, unvarying harmony tending, though, toward the relative minor key (C-sharp minor here in the key of E major)—an effect that somehow suggests vaguely improper consequences (Ratmir, one of the rival suitors, is being lured into Naina's castle by young girls).

Perhaps, though, the single most notable example of Glinka's fearlessness in the treatment of convention is his orchestration. His actual orchestra is normal, apart from a few exotic extras (such as the glass harmonica that tinkles away seductively in Chernomor's garden as his flower maidens tempt Lyudmila with magical food), and the onstage wind band, whose precise constitution Glinka in fact fails to specify.[12] What is far from normal is Glinka's style of orchestration. In essence the theatre orchestra he inherited was a fairly stereotyped affair; the Italian composers of his day used it almost exclusively as functional support for the singers—string-based, with the occasional woodwind solo, plus stage instruments as required. French opera was more adventurous, partly under the influence of the band music that had held sway during the revolution. But the chief models in 1840 for an uninhibited treatment of the orchestra as a total resource were Beethoven, especially his "Choral" Symphony, and Berlioz, whose *Symphonie fantastique,* with its extravagant wind scoring and elaborate instructions for the brass and percussion instruments, Glinka in point of fact cannot yet have known.[13] Here, too, Glinka's own procedures suggest a pragmatic approach. Given the distinct sections of the standard orchestra—the strings (bowed and plucked), the woodwinds, the brass, the percussion—why not treat them as a set of equal possibilities, especially in an opera of strange encounters and evil magic? Why limit oneself to the blend and balance of the classical orchestra? Why not invent sonorities to go with the bizarre characters and fantastic incidents that serve in place of a coherent or plausible narrative? So, for Chernomor's entrance, Glinka chooses the harsh, unblended sounds of the stage wind band, alternating with the glitter of high woodwinds, bells, and pizzicato strings. The "Turkish" dancers enter to a rich texture of low strings answered by full orchestra dominated, once again, by wind instruments. The "Arab" dance is in fact a waltz scored initially for strings in triple octaves, a sumptuous sonority much exploited later by Tchaikovsky but which seems to have been Glinka's invention. Countless other details show Glinka using the orchestra as an imaginative resource scarcely less versatile than melody, harmony, or rhythm. Bayan's gusli—the Russian peasant zither—is represented by piano and harp, a brilliantly successful effect (and probably the first use of the piano as an orchestral instrument rather than as a soloist with orchestra). The suitor Ratmir, a Khazar prince from the northeastern Caucasus, is accompanied in his aria by a cor anglais, whose sultry tones suggest some kind of Middle Eastern shawm. Page after page is dominated by wind instruments, solo or in groups, in defiance of the classical convention of string-based sonorities. When the strings are fully employed, they are often doing strange things, as in the spectacular coda of the lezghinka, the last of the Oriental dances, where the alternation of natural harmonics (harmonics played on the open strings) with rapid woodwind scales creates an effect of a frenzied improvisation by a rustic band barely in control.

Ruslan opened at the Bolshoi Theatre in St. Petersburg on 27 November 1842 (the sixth anniversary of the premiere of *A Life for the Tsar*), to a mixed reception. "Some there are," one critic wrote,

> who find in Mr. Glinka's opera a lot that will guarantee the composer immortality in a hundred years' time; others, not wanting to wait so long, are bestowing on him a wreath of immortality here and now; a third group unreservedly call the piece a failure and find nothing in the least remarkable in it; a fourth group—the coolest—maintain that there is much merit in the opera, but also many defects, and that the excess of lyricism in the music and complete lack of dramatic movement in the libretto are a great hindrance to its success, rendering it even tedious to the majority taste—which, however, is quite unjust. In a word, opinions of *Ruslan and Lyudmila* vary widely; but everyone who saw the opera agrees that M. I. Glinka is a highly gifted composer.[14]

The first-night audience was certainly cool; but this was as much as anything due to a weak cast, including an inexperienced understudy as Ratmir—musically (with Lyudmila) the biggest part in the opera, despite its title. At the final curtain, Glinka "turned to General Dubelt in the director's box and said, 'They seem to be hissing. Shall I take a curtain call?' 'Certainly, go ahead,' replied the General. 'Christ suffered more than you.' "[15] Later performances, though, went better, and the opera stayed in repertory in St. Petersburg, then Moscow, until 1848, after which it was not heard complete anywhere in Russia during Glinka's lifetime.

He never again attempted an opera. Perhaps he was disheartened by the fate of the two he had written; but more likely he was unable to muster the necessary creative energy. Often in poor health, he travelled a good deal, composed only spasmodically; and the works he managed to complete were almost always in response to chance impressions and devised in a manner that studiously avoided the complexities of large-scale working. At one point he started a symphony based on

Gogol's *Taras Bulba*. He sketched parts of the exposition of a first movement in C minor, "but since I didn't have the energy or the desire at
the time to work my way out of the German rut in the development,
I dropped the whole thing."[16] A few songs and piano pieces survive
to remind us of the easy talent of the salon master; and with them, a
handful of short orchestral pieces, two of which, in particular, were
to have an impact on Russian music far beyond their undoubted but
self-limited virtues. These two works, *Kamarinskaya* and *Recuerdos de Cas-
tilla* (later expanded into the *Souvenir d'une nuit d'été à Madrid*), were both
composed in 1848 in Warsaw, where Glinka was stranded for several
months without a passport. Both are entirely based on folk tunes: *Kamarinskaya* on a well-known Russian dance tune of that name elaborated
in combination with a wedding song, "Izza gor, gor vïsokikh" (From
behind the mountains, the high mountains); the *Souvenir* on four tunes
Glinka had picked up on a visit to Spain three years earlier. Neither
work develops its material in any conventional way. Their brilliance
is entirely due to the composer's coloristic genius and his flair for a
kind of musical montage which, like many of his orchestral sounds,
was essentially his own invention. Almost casually he seems to have
discovered a method of composing with folk tunes that would provide
a technical manual for later, no doubt greater, composers. The curiously cinematic musical footage of the *Souvenir* might have been (may
actually have been) in Debussy's mind as he composed his *Ibéria* some
sixty years later. And the constantly varied orchestral and harmonic
colorings of *Kamarinskaya* would in due course prompt Tchaikovsky to
the hyperbolic judgment that

> *merely in passing,* not in the least setting out to compose something sur-
> passing on a simple theme, a playful trifle—this man (out of nothing)
> gives us a short work in which every bar is the product of great creative
> power. Almost fifty years have passed since then; many Russian sym-
> phonic works have been written; it is possible to state that there exists
> a pure Russian symphonic school. And what is the result? All of it is in
> the *Kamarinskaya,* in the same way as the whole oak is in the *acorn*! And
> long will Russian composers borrow from this rich source, for much
> time and much strength is needed in order to drain all of its richness.[17]

CHAPTER 3

The Lawyer-Critic

It was in the nature of St. Petersburg intellectual life that it took shape through groups of like-minded doers and thinkers: what the French called *cénacles*—literary or artistic circles. The tendency was far from unique to Russia, but it flourished there particularly, no doubt, because of the heavy censorship under Nicholas I, which forced writers and artists to keep their most adventurous ideas under lock and key, behind closed doors.

For musicians, though, the situation was a little different. For them the discussion of ideas had never been central to their activity as artists, and certainly not to their practical function as performers; then, as now, they would talk technique, or else avoid the subject altogether. But for Russian musicians in the 1840s and '50s technique was something of a nonsubject, since their knowledge of it was sketchy and they had no institutional context in which to acquire or share it. Balakirev's pianistic brilliance seems to have been a natural flair, like the ability to hit a ball with good timing or shoot straight at a moving target. It went in his case with an exceptional musical memory and an acute aural sense (what musicians call a good ear). He was a marvellous improviser at the piano, and an instinctive judge of musical good form, in both the literal and the metaphorical senses. But he had little theoretical knowledge and hardly any language in which to explain his judgments. He could only demonstrate. And this would prove a crucial feature of his relations with the other musicians who gradually came into his orbit in his first years in St. Petersburg.

Among these musicians, Vladimir Stasov was an altogether distinct case. A Petersburger by birth, he had been an early pupil at the Imperial School of Jurisprudence, which he had entered at the age of twelve in 1836, a year or so after the school's foundation. In spite of its name, this was not strictly a school of law, but a feeder school for the highly centralized imperial civil service, which was virtually the only civilian institution in Russia that provided employment for members of the *dvoryanin* class, to which the Stasov family, like the Glinkas, belonged. One might suppose that a school of this kind would be run along strictly pragmatic lines, with a view to producing methodical, unimaginative, above all subservient administrators and bureaucrats. But this was not entirely the case. The school's founder, Prince Peter of Oldenburg (a nephew of Nicholas I), was a passionate music lover and insisted that every pupil study an instrument and participate in timetabled musicmaking that, in intensity and possibly even quality, would hardly disgrace a modern specialist school. The headmaster, Semyon Poshman, was himself an amateur musician. The best foreign teachers were engaged. Stasov studied the piano with the great German pianist-composer Adolf Henselt, and it seems probable—to judge from his later correspondence with Balakirev—that he also learned a certain amount of theory, either from Henselt or from the school's music teacher, a Finn by the name of Karel, who papered the walls of the music room with portraits of the great composers, and who possessed a small but well-ordered library of music books, including histories and theoretical treatises, to which he allowed his pupils access.

Stasov had no more ambition to become a professional musician than he had to become a civil servant. He was rather like a boy in an English cathedral-choir school, absorbing music and acquiring a solid education out of a need that was not his. The Stasovs tended more toward the visual arts. Vladimir's father, Vasily Stasov, was the most famous Russian architect of his day—designer of the Preobrazhensky and Izmaylovsky cathedrals in St. Petersburg, and restorer of the eighteenth-century palace on the Fontanka that housed the School of Jurisprudence. Vladimir had himself wanted to go to the Academy of Arts, but never afterward regretted his parents' decision in favor of the law school. He became and remained almost pathologically hostile to the teaching of the fine arts, a cast of mind little challenged on the Fontanka, where painting and sculpture were barely even mentioned and art teaching was limited to a few slapdash drawing classes. In any case, Stasov was not much of a practitioner; his bent was more toward history and criticism. Above all he was a voracious reader. As a schoolboy he was already reading widely in recent critical literature on art and music as well as in literature itself, both Russian and foreign. Some of this reading was simply the normal educated mental furniture of the day, if not necessarily that of the average fourteen- or fifteen-year-old. Vladimir and his friends of course read Pushkin and wept at his death; they pored over the Lermontov poems in the monthly *Otechestvennïye zapiski* (*Notes of the Fatherland*); and they devoured Gogol's *Dead Souls* when it came out in 1842 and went about talking Gogolese to one another. Vladimir himself, a good linguist from childhood, read Hugo and Dumas (*père*), also probably Shakespeare, in French, Hoffmann and Jean Paul in German, Walter Scott and Fenimore Cooper in Russian translation.

Perhaps more significant than his acquaintance with these fashionable literary heroes of the early nineteenth century was his growing enthusiasm for the critical literature about their work. This was something more than the mere casual interest in the arts that prompts modern educated man to turn to the reviews section of the daily newspaper. Stasov was growing up in a new age of critical exegesis on a grand scale, whose leading exponents were starting to exert an influence far beyond the subject matter they took as their starting point. In Paris, Charles-Augustin Sainte-Beuve was evolving what he called *critiques et portraits littéraires,* extended articles that fused biography and criticism into integrated, pamphlet-sized studies of individual authors or major historical figures. Heinrich Heine was reporting at length for German readers on music and art in Paris. In St. Petersburg, Vissarion Belinsky was beginning, in the mid-thirties, the long series of articles and reviews that would transform the whole philosophical perception of the relation between literature and society. Stasov was certainly reading Heine's reviews in the volumes of *Der Salon* (which were banned in Russia) by the early 1840s. Heine's writing about the arts is that of a *literatus,* an observant, sharp-witted wordsmith, capable of hitting off the feeling and atmosphere of a painting or a symphony without posturing or aestheticizing, but also without any pretense at technical expertise. Or rather, he understands technical details as an astute observer understands them, as an aspect of the surface through which he experiences the image or the sound. "In no other picture in the Salon," he writes about Delacroix's *Liberty Leading the People,* "has the colour sunk in so much as in Delacroix's July Revolution. Nevertheless, this very absence of varnish and of shining surface, together with the smoke and dust which envelop the figures like a grey cobweb, these sun-dried colours which seem to thirst for a drop of water, all this seems to stamp the picture with truthfulness, reality, originality."[1] And on music criticism: "Nothing is more inadequate than the theory of Music. Undeniably it has laws, laws mathematically determined. These laws, however, are not music, but the conditions thereof; just as the art of design and the theory of colours, or even the palette and the pencil, are not painting but the means necessary thereto. The essence of music is revelation; it permits of no analysis, and true musical criticism is an experimental science."[2]

Stasov was struck, he later recalled, by the depth and clarity of Heine's perceptions, even though "he understood little about the technique of art and had absolutely nothing in common with specialist critics."[3] This was one important aspect of the new criticism: its ability to bridge the chasm, so rarely crossed in the past, between art as métier and art as signification. All the same, there remained something of the dilettante about Heine as a critic. When all was said and done, he was expatiating on something that, as he tacitly admitted, he only partially understood. With Belinsky the case was completely different. Belinsky was a writer writing about writers. Though not himself a creative artist—neither poet, novelist, nor playwright—he understood the nature of their materials, and was brilliantly equipped to carry out the particular hermeneutical program that he himself devised and that required the close analysis of, in particular, stories, novels, and poems in terms of their concealed psychological, social, and political meanings. We are so used today to the idea of the novel as a simulacrum of our life and times and the book review as an exposé of that relationship that it can be hard to imagine a time when such things were the exception rather than the rule. Art as social commentary was essentially a by-product of romanticism, and criticism of it in those terms followed hard on its heels. In music one might compare a Handel opera about ancient Rome with Mozart's *Marriage of Figaro*, which twists an old convention into sharp social satire. Beethoven's obvious sense that music could—perhaps should—be at least partly understood as psychological narrative was picked up by E. T. A. Hoffmann, himself a composer, in reviews that drew a clear distinction between process and connotation. But for Belinsky even this much interpretation would have seemed not much better than idle speculation. For him a work of art was not only a reflection of the world into which it was born, but had a positive duty to seek to make that world a better, more humane place. Of course Belinsky's world, the St. Petersburg of the 1830s and '40s (he died in 1848, a few days before his thirty-seventh birthday), was a grim, distressing place even by the not very high standards of contemporary Europe, and it was the sheer awfulness, inhumanity, unfreedom, and brute authoritarianism of Russia under Nicholas I that drove Belinsky to his essentially moralistic, didactic understanding of art as an encrypted mechanism for social and political change. Stasov tells us that Belinsky's monthly articles in *Notes of the Fatherland* did more for his and his fellow pupils' education than all their classes, courses, written work, and exams put together. "The huge influence of Belinsky," he concludes, "was by no means confined to the literary aspect; he nurtured character, he hacked away, at a stroke, the patriarchal prejudices with which the whole of Russia had hitherto lived their lives."[4]

Belinsky's particular impact took various forms. His conviction that art should above all reflect the reality of life as it was experienced by the ordinary individual—the Truth, however unpalatable—emerged comparatively late in his bumpy intellectual career. It is expressed with typically violent clarity and energy for the first time in a series of letters he wrote to his friend the writer Vasily Botkin in 1841, and more temperately in an essay written that same year but published posthumously: "Art," he wrote there, "is the *immediate* contemplation of truth, or a thinking in *images*."[5] For a time before that he had been in the grip of a barely less violent pro-Hegelian idealism which had seduced him into an objective—that is, passive—acceptance of reality; Hegel, he confesses to Botkin, "has turned the realities of life into ghosts clasping bony hands and dancing in the air above the cemetery."[6] But even before his brief Hegelian digression, he was writing criticism that penetrated with extraordinary originality and imaginative force into the psychological texture of the works under review. His long articles on Pushkin, for instance, the first of which date from before the poet's death in 1837, not only helped set up Pushkin's reputation as the founding father of modern Russian literature, but set a standard for the close reading of texts that has rarely been surpassed since.

To some extent one has to separate Belinsky's philosophy from his day-to-day critical activities. It was characteristic of the Russian situation in the thirties that thinking people looked to Western ideas and either accepted or rejected them (often with equal violence) in the quest for a social or political theory able to resolve the confusions of life under their own massively inert autocracy. They took what they thought they needed from German idealism, from French utopian socialism, and from English utilitarianism, not to mention Western political and economic systems. Not surprisingly the path through this jungle of ideas was sometimes tortuous and unclear; in the undergrowth, you could never be sure whom you would meet—friend or foe, even supposing you would know which was which. By temperament, Belinsky was always a Westernizer: that is, a progressive who argued for the remodernization of Russian society along the Western European lines initiated in the early eighteenth century by Peter the Great. He was an admirer of Tsar Peter. He opposed the mystical leanings of the Slavophiles, with their faith in the spiritual values of old Russia, the Orthodox Church, and the Russian peasant in his muddy baste shoes; yet he remained an ardent patriot, a strong believer in the concept of nationality (*natsional'nost'*—the quality of this rather than that ethnic group) as against the misty, hard-to-define *narodnost'*, with its undertones of popularism, nationalism, and the black earth. Then in the forties he moved toward socialism, or at least a social consciousness too individualistic to align itself readily with the new communism (though not so much as to prevent his coming, through selective reading, to be regarded as a father figure by all subsequent fellow travellers, up to and including the Soviets).

Through all these twists and turns, he remained at heart a believer in art as truth and in criticism as the revelation and elucidation of that truth. Interpretation naturally brought into play the preferences and biases of the critic. But Belinsky was not essentially a propagandist; he never argued for the appropriation of art as a vehicle for ideology. The truth of a book or a poem was innate. For Stasov, this was perhaps the most striking lesson Belinsky taught. "Up to now all criticism in the arts has consisted of saying: this is good, this is bad, this is not appropriate, here are such-and-such mistakes of costume, here such-and-such of proportion, etc. For this kind of criticism no talent is needed, only a certain measure of *training and study*, so anyone . . . could produce this kind of criticism. But what should we demand of artistic creation, what are the arts for? They don't exist for their parts but in order to create *a whole*, united in one point, and the product of all its parts, all its elements. . . . Every genuine work of art consequently bears within itself its *meaning* and *intention*; to reveal the one and the other for humanity is the purpose of criticism."[7] No doubt Stasov was also attracted by other aspects of Belinsky's thought and personality. His individualism must have appealed to the young student trying to balance intense artistic enthusiasms with the dry study of the imperial system of law and administration. Stasov was equally receptive to Belinsky's social consciousness post-1840. This is not to say that he was or ever had been politically minded in any strong sense. In Nicholas I's Russia almost any social thinking, even that of the deeply traditionalist Slavophiles, lay in the direction of emancipation and liberalization; it was hardly possible to think about politics without desiring the end of serfdom, a system as economically debilitating as it was humanly degrading, or the purging of the country's rigid, inefficient, and corrupt state bureaucracy. For the young Stasov, widely read in German, French, and English as well as Russian literature, it was natural in any case to look outward, which in the nature of things meant to think progressively, even if your reading was Fichte and Schelling. The breadth of Belinsky's thought chimed with the breadth of Stasov's literacy. Above all, the self-assured, quick-tongued, strong-willed law student was surely impressed by Belinsky's eloquence, his polemical brilliance, his boldness in the assertion of heterodox opinions, and, not least, his fierce combativeness.

Stasov emerged from the School of Jurisprudence in 1843 an educated, cultivated nineteen-year-old, well read, with highly developed, if perhaps unduly emphatic, musical and artistic tastes and a broad knowledge of European (including Russian) literature and thought. At school he had certainly spent more time on music and art and reading than on jurisprudence. His closest friend there (until he left the school in 1840) had been another, somewhat older musician, Alexander Serov, and most of their musical experiences—though by no means all their likes and dislikes—had been shared. Serov was an enthusiast for German music, including Weber and Meyerbeer, while Stasov's tastes in that direction still stopped generally with Bach and late Beethoven, though he had, and retained, a passion for Schumann. Perhaps influenced by his attachment to Italian painting, he leaned also in the direction of the music of that country—but less, at first, that of the Renaissance than that of the recent operatic composers, Rossini, Donizetti, Bellini. For both of them, Chopin was a genius, Liszt a mere showman, an empty purveyor of spectacular but vapid roulades and arpeggios, artistically of no serious account. They had not, of course, heard him play. When they did hear him, at his first St. Petersburg concert in 1842, they were instantly smitten, not so much by his virtuosity as by his sheer artistic presence and power, even though he played only transcriptions and operatic fantasies, presented in the manner of a prizefighter from a stage erected in the middle of the Hall of the Assembly of the Nobles. "After the concert," Stasov noted, "Serov and I were like madmen. We exchanged only a few words and then rushed home to write each other as quickly as possible of our impressions, our dreams, our ecstasy . . . We were delirious, like lovers! And no wonder. We had never in our lives heard anything like this; we had never

been in the presence of such a brilliant, passionate, demonic temperament . . . Liszt's playing was absolutely overwhelming."[8]

Stasov wrote a review of the concert but was unable to get it accepted
for publication. He was desperate, he wrote later, to make people
understand Liszt's artistic importance, just as, a year or two before,
he had written an article on Karl Bryullov's large-scale pencil sketch
for the *Apostles* mosaic in St. Isaac's Cathedral, whose lack of popular
recognition infuriated him (the expression is his own, and characteristic). This too remained in his drawer. Not till 1847 was he able to
get a substantial article accepted by a public print: a lengthy, opinion-
ated, but compulsively readable survey of the musical events of the
year, published in Belinsky's old paper, *Notes of the Fatherland*.[9] But one
could hardly survive on occasional journalism, and like many writers
and artists in nineteenth-century Russia Stasov was forced on leaving
the School of Jurisprudence to take precisely the kind of government
post for which the school was supposed to be a preparation. From 1843
to 1851 he worked successively in the Senate Boundary Department,
the Department of Heraldry, and the Ministry of Justice. Needless
to say, these were routine jobs within a bureaucratic system that neither encouraged nor rewarded personal initiative. But they left Stasov time to pursue his artistic enthusiasms more or less as he liked.
He haunted the Hermitage Museum, with its vast collection of paintings, prints, and sculpture; he wheedled his way into the office of the
curator of engravings, Nikolay Utkin, who was at that very moment
cataloguing the Warsaw collection, confiscated at the time of the 1830
Polish rising, and may well have been astonished at the expertise of
this nineteen-year-old boy (who had pored over the Parisian *Annales du
musée* since childhood). He also began to frequent the Imperial Public
Library, an institution that, then as now, was very much more than
its name might suggest to an Anglo-Saxon bookworm. The library
was not only a major repository for books, including the Voltaire and
Diderot collections acquired by Catherine the Great and nearly half a
million volumes appropriated from Poland's Zaluski Library. It also
held quantities of manuscripts, paintings, and artworks, all more or less
chaotically organized, largely uncatalogued, and in an appalling state
of repair. From Stasov's point of view there was little question of serious study in such conditions; but here too he was energetic in making
contacts that were to prove important later on, both for his ideas about
art and for his eventual job prospects.

In 1851 he was taken on as a travelling secretary by the hugely rich
Russian expatriate industrialist Prince Anatoly Demidov, whose estate

at San Donato, near Florence, housed an outstanding library and a magnificent art collection. The three years Stasov spent abroad with Demidov, mainly in Italy, were crucial in rounding out his knowledge of Renaissance painting and architecture in particular. They also cemented his confidence in his own taste and judgment in artistic matters, however unorthodox or, at times, doctrinaire. An extraordinary letter survives which he wrote to his aunt Anna Suchkova, his mother's sister, in 1852, describing in exhaustive detail, and with unconcealed pride, his project of refitting the Catholic chapel at San Donato in Russian Orthodox style, "*not*," he hastens to assure her, "because it makes any difference *to me*—to me it's really all one, as you know—but because I'm in the habit of getting everything (even very small things) as right as possible and as they *ought* in fact to be, if I can only get my hands on them."[10]

On their way to Italy, they had passed through London at the time of the Great Exhibition; and they were in Paris for part of the summer or autumn of 1851. Here, according to Stasov's Soviet biographers, he was in touch with (unspecified) revolutionary activists and attended socialist meetings.[11] Whether or not he did so might be doubted. For Soviet critics it was always of course important to assert the political credentials of those of whom, on general grounds, they approved, and Stasov would plainly qualify in this respect, if only in view of his debt to Belinsky and, later, Nikolay Chernïshevsky, left-wing thinkers whose views on art influenced him. On political questions, however, his position was less clear-cut. As a free-thinking agnostic, he had little sympathy with the hyper-Orthodox Slavophiles, but nevertheless shared some of their ideas about history and was attracted by the imagery they inspired. He approved of Herzen's friend Vadim Kel'siyev's later attempt to draw a connection between revolutionary socialism and the Old Believers. "Both in pagan and Christian times," he enthused to Balakirev in a long letter about Kel'siyev, "the real Russia was in its soul and its nature democratic."[12] But this was probably as much an aesthetic as a political response, and one that to some extent reflected the confusion of radical thinking among the intelligentsia in the fifties and sixties. If Stasov had actually attended revolutionary meetings in early-fifties Paris, he would certainly have been watched and probably apprehended as soon as he returned to Russia. Nothing of the kind seems to have happened to him, at least on this occasion.

Demidov and Stasov left Italy for Russia in the spring of 1854, on the way taking in Vienna, where Stasov saw Wagner's *Lohengrin* for the first time. This was another of those formative experiences the effects of which remained with him for the rest of his life, largely unmoderated by the passage of time. Like many of his antipathies, his loathing of Wagner seems to have been prompted as much by circumstantial factors as by a direct response to the music. He evidently took against what he later called "Wagner's incoherent, mystical and moralizing plots,"[13] and possibly also against his writings, with their interminable, self-important theorizing that seemed to have nothing whatsoever to do with such works (and there were as yet not many of them) as had actually reached the stage. Still basking in the glow of Italian art, he may well have been repelled by the slow Germanic heaviness and ponderous symbolism of *Lohengrin,* with its "knights [Stasov is generalizing] who appear from somewhere out of the sky and go back there just because here on earth they are asked who exactly they are."[14] In Italy he had met Rossini, and found in him "an artistic soul of beautiful simplicity"; he had had access to the huge collection of Italian polyphonic motets and madrigals in the collection of Abbé Francesco Santini, "pure veins of gold, silver and whole cliffs of diamonds and emeralds."[15] Now reading an article by Liszt in praise of Wagner (we don't know which one), he turned momentarily against his great hero of the previous decade and planned a riposte which he intended to submit to Franz Brendel, editor of the *Neue Zeitschrift für Musik.* Perhaps fortunately for future relations with Liszt, the article was never written. But Stasov's anti-Wagnerism survived as one of several important negative elements in the dogmas that were to have such a powerful influence on Russian music of the next decade and a half.

At the time of his return to St. Petersburg, Stasov was thirty years old and badly in need of paid work. For reasons that are not wholly clear, the association with Demidov came to an end. He was still technically single, though before Italy his life had been complicated by a series of love affairs and at least two illegitimate daughters. In another sense, it's true, his life was secure. The Stasovs were an extremely close-knit family, lived under the same roof (or, to be exact, roofs, since they also shared a dacha at Pargolovo, ten miles to the north of St. Petersburg), and even half-resented the occasional marriage of one of their number. When his brother Dmitry married in 1861, Vladimir wrote in a fury to Balakirev:

> In half a year or a year he'll be a completely different person, and we simply won't recognize him. He'll acquire a totally new circle, be surrounded by other people, and he'll take on their smell, their tastes and coloring. But what must be must be. I'm just a bit annoyed that he

doesn't mind enough being separated from our family; I know that he's deeply in love with his wife now, and I also know that it's impossible for us all to go on living together forever in some kind of Noah's Ark—yet a break is a break, and arguments don't help . . . This wedding of Mitya's I regard as much the same as a death in the family.[16]

This was to have future resonances, also, for a family of a different kind. But for all the Stasovs, money was in short supply. Vladimir pulled strings as best he could with ministry contacts. Nothing was forthcoming. He went back to the public library, now gradually being transformed under the hands of its hyper-efficient but liberal-minded new director, Baron Modest Korff; and there, sure enough, he soon established a contact that led to a series of tasks that, in turn, led in due course to a post. Stasov's work began in 1855 with an unpaid commission to catalogue the library's huge Rossica section. With typical thoroughness he not only did this, but in the process evolved an appropriate cataloguing system while reading many of the books as he went along. Korff quite soon realized, as Utkin and Demidov had done, that he had an extraordinary talent on his hands, and by the end of 1856 had arranged for Stasov to be appointed his full-time personal assistant. Thus this young man whose enthusiasm for art in the broadest sense outstripped all considerations of personal advancement, official rank, or any of the normal status symbols on the career ladder of the imperial civil service, had for the third time in his life struck lucky. Just as hardly any school in tsarist Russia would have vouchsafed the intellectual freedoms of the School of Jurisprudence, just as his service with Demidov had brought him into contact at exactly the right time with a range of artistic experience scarcely available at home, so now he found in Korff a rare superior of a liberal turn of mind, indulgent of his broad and sometimes wayward interests, and responsive to his astounding intellectual energy.

While he was thus simultaneously setting up his library career and broadening his artistic knowledge, Stasov was by no means neglecting his musical interests. He had eventually met Glinka, through Serov, in 1849, and had begun to attend his musical soirées that spring. But these had come to an end in the autumn when Glinka went abroad, and by the time he returned to St. Petersburg in 1851 Stasov was in Italy. Now, in 1854, Stasov again became a Glinka "brother," as the great composer liked to call his musical intimates, in the manner of a secret society plotting against the neglect of his music in the capital at large. The circle was small and somewhat dilettante in flavor. Apart from Vladimir

Stasov and his lawyer brother, Dmitry, it included Serov, by this time an active and influential music critic; Dargomïzhsky; another composer, Nikolay Borozdin; the music publisher Constant Villebois; and assorted amateur-musician friends of Glinka's. Vasily Sobol'shchikov, the director of the public library's art department and a decent pianist, would sometimes appear; and even Korff himself would turn up with his entire family. There would be string quartets and two-piano arrangements of orchestral pieces and operatic excerpts, including from Glinka, sometimes played eight-handed, more often four-. It was the kind of music making that reflected the very low density of professional music in St. Petersburg in the 1850s. There being no established series of orchestral concerts, the best way to get to know orchestral music was in salon transcriptions. Chamber music remained an almost exclusively amateur pastime, in spite of the decidedly unamateur character of recent repertoire such as the late Beethoven quartets, which were nevertheless attempted at Glinka's soirées (the master himself on viola). As for Glinka's operas, almost the only way to hear them properly performed in the mid-fifties was in piano or ensemble arrangements and occasional recital excerpts. There was talk of Glinka and Vladimir Stasov starting a concert society with the composer as chairman. But the idea, if it was ever more than a conversation topic, was interrupted by Glinka's departure for Berlin in April 1856, and terminated by his death nine months later.

Stasov's meeting with Balakirev in Glinka's drawing room a few weeks before that departure was to prove a profoundly symbolic moment for Russian music. Whatever might be thought of Glinka in world terms (and Stasov was a qualified admirer), he was indisputably the first native Russian composer whose work could be offered in all seriousness as worthy of the attention of foreign musicians. Berlioz had written of *Ruslan and Lyudmila* that its composer might "with good reason claim a place among the outstanding composers of his time."[17] Liszt regarded *Ruslan* as a masterpiece. Now here together at its composer's fireside were two of the most alert musical and artistic minds of their generation in Russia, thinkers and doers in sharp contrast with the dilettante atmosphere that had hitherto reigned in even the best St. Petersburg musical circles. Stasov, though in no sense a professional musician, brought to music, alongside a burning passion, a deep knowledge not only of the repertoire as understood at the time but also of the historical evolution of the art form, information he had picked up as a kind of spin-off from his scholarly and professional study of the history of art. Probably no practicing musician of his day would have got as much as he did out of his visit to Abbé Santini in Rome. According to Gerald Abraham, he paid from his own pocket to have some four hundred of the manuscripts in Santini's collection hand copied, with a view not to performance but to study.[18] He was well informed about folk music, plainchant, and the music of the Orthodox Church, was musician enough to discuss these things on a technical level, and historian enough to locate them in their aesthetic and historical context. He also knew how to advocate their incorporation in modern art music. He was a born systematizer and a natural taxonomist; he had as well, it must be admitted, the dogmatic cast of mind to go with those talents. He had read everything of importance on the philosophy of art, and was gradually, if tortuously, evolving in his own mind a philosophy of Russian music adapted mutatis mutandis from the recent literary theories of nonmusicians such as Belinsky. He was politically just leftist enough to see art in the progressive, sociological light that seemed to be demanded by the spirit of the times, but not leftist enough to find himself being transported—like so many of his predecessors and contemporaries—to Siberia or the Caucasus.

Balakirev was his perfect foil. A performer of consummate brilliance who disliked performing, he had to turn his musical energies in other directions. One of them would be composition. But this, too, would only partly satisfy him; and instead, in order to fill the creative gap, he would turn himself into a mentor of other composers, even though he quite lacked the technical knowledge (lacked it, indeed, more than Stasov) to teach them in any conventional meaning of the term. But this, too, may have been fortuitous, since, lacking the expertise himself, he was in no position to force it on others. Thus the character of what emerged from this conjunction of strong personalities was something very different from anything that might have been preconceived as the necessary environment for the creation of a new Russian music. It subsisted, to put it crudely, on talent and on ancestor worship, backed up by philosophy. We should hardly be surprised if the results had little in common with the academic tradition of Western music.

CHAPTER 4

The Officer and the Doctor

One day in the early autumn of 1856 two young men, a guards officer and a house surgeon, found themselves on duty together in the orderly room of the Second Army Hospital in St. Petersburg. The officer was seventeen years old, of medium height and somewhat plain looking, but very proud of himself in his new dark-green Preobrazhensky Regiment uniform, his hair waved and pomaded, his hands manicured, a picture of slightly exaggerated elegance and refinement. The medical orderly's dress and manner were more relaxed and matter-of-fact. He was five or six years older than the officer, tall and slim, already a graduate with distinction from the Medical-Surgical Academy, and he observed his colleague's teenage posturing with a certain amused detachment.

They were both bored by the duty routine, which demanded their presence but for the most part gave them nothing to do with it, and they quickly fell into conversation. It soon turned out that they had more in common than appearances might have suggested. Above all, they were both passionate musicians, pianists; and it transpired that they would be meeting again that very evening at the house of the hospital's chief medical officer, who was in the habit of arranging soirées for his daughter. In the evening the medical orderly observed his young colleague more critically: his "refined, aristocratic manners, conversation the same, speaking somewhat through his teeth: interspersed with French phrases, rather flowery. Some traces of foppishness, but very moderate. Unusually polite and well-bred. The ladies made a fuss of him. He sat down at the piano and, raising his hands coquettishly, played excerpts from *Trovatore, Traviata,* etc., very sweetly, gracefully, and so forth, while around him buzzed a chorus of 'charmant, délicieux.' "[1]

This young dandy with the smart uniform and the courtly manners was Modest Petrovich Musorgsky. His medical colleague was Alexander Porfiryevich Borodin. Musorgsky was the younger son of the owner of a large estate at Karevo, in the province of Pskov, 250 miles to the south of St. Petersburg, where Modest had been born on 9 March 1839. When he was ten, his parents had brought him and his older brother, Filaret, to the capital and enrolled them in the Petropavlovsk secondary school, from where they had passed, after a year in the Komarov preparatory school, into the Cadet School of Guards Ensigns. At the time of his meeting with Borodin, Modest had recently graduated from the Cadet School to the Preobrazhensky reserves, but was transferred back when the reserves were disbanded in October. The Cadet School could hardly have been more unlike the School of Jurisprudence. There was a rigid hierarchy among the cadets, comparable to the fagging system that survived in English schools well into the twentieth century. Junior cadets were routinely subjected to brutal humiliations of one kind and another by their seniors, and were flogged if they fell short of requirements. The senior cadets spent much of their leisure time in hard drinking and womanizing, activities that were regarded as an essential part of the formation of a proper guards officer. The cultivation of intellectual or artistic pursuits was definitely not on their agenda. Modest's predilection for history and philosophy is supposed to have prompted the school's director, General Alexander Sutgof, to inquire: "What kind of an officer will you turn out to be, *mon cher?*"

To some extent, no doubt, this philistinism was a pose. Sutgof was himself well educated, a decent linguist and historian, and at least respectful of art. Ever since his arrival in St. Petersburg, Musorgsky had taken piano lessons with Anton Herke, a pupil of Stasov's teacher Henselt; but Sutgof's daughter also took lessons with Herke, which Musorgsky himself—according to his brother—attended and sometimes participated in. In any case a good pianist is a useful adjunct to a dancing, drinking culture, and a musician who is prepared to sit down and play or sing on demand will always be popular with even the rowdiest—perhaps especially with the rowdiest—revellers. As a young teenager Musorgsky was already showing a talent for quick adaptation to the musical needs of those around him, a talent that would soon stand him in good stead in social circles very different from those of the Preobrazhensky Guards. But facility can be a dangerous gift; it encourages people to use you for their own ends, and at the same time discourages hard learning and application. And Musorgsky was unquestionably facile. He could play at sight or by ear; he could transpose into different keys; he could sing well to his own accompaniment, without, perhaps, a voice of any great distinction but with a gift for characterization and mimicry that more than made up for the lack of particular vocal beauty or bravura. He was fond of improvising at the keyboard and could do so in a variety of styles, like an accomplished café pianist. But he had actually composed, in the sense of writing down on paper, practically nothing. Of all the polkas and waltzes he must have bashed out for the delectation of his fellow cadets, only one survives, the mysteriously titled "Porte-Enseigne" Polka, which we possess because it was published, in 1852, when Musorgsky was thirteen, apparently on his father's initiative. But this piece, though faceless, is so polished in execution as to be mildly suspect. It must surely have been tidied up and written down either by his father or by Herke, even if we need not take literally Nikolay Kompaneysky's memory that the young Modest had not "the slightest idea of how to put down his thoughts on paper or of the most elementary rules of music."[2]

It is hard to see through these various poses and disputed memories in order to form a reliable picture of this unusual guards officer's character. Reminiscences of famous people tend to be colored by the memoirist's knowledge of their mature achievements and of how they were subsequently regarded. Musorgsky himself reports having been well enough taught the piano by his mother at Karevo to be able to play short pieces by Liszt when he was seven and a concerto by John Field by the time he was nine. Herke, according to Kompaneysky, insisted on an exclusively German repertoire, which at that time was hardly a serious limitation, even if it excluded everything Russian—of which, after all, there was little of significance outside opera and song. Musorgsky tells us that his first piano improvisations were inspired by the Russian fairy tales told him by his *nyanya* at Karevo, a suitable enough inspiration for the later dedicated nationalist. But in the main, the young man's intellectual orientation was probably German, not only in music but also in philosophy. Like many Russian children of his class, Musorgsky had had a German governess and could read and speak German well; at the Petropavlovsk school, too, the teachers were predominantly German, and lessons were in that language. So it was natural that if drawn to philosophy, he would read mainly the German idealists whose work had dominated Russian thought since the 1820s, and he would read them in the original. What he read, specifically, we do not know, but we can speculate that it would have included Schelling, probably Fichte, perhaps also Hegel, because these were the writers fashionable in Russian intellectual circles. Whether he derived anything from them at that time, beyond the sense of being in the intellectual swim, is questionable. By the time he was himself producing work detectably related to particular intellectual tendencies, they were of a diametrically opposite thrust. But insofar as the creative impulse was beginning to stir in him, the philosophy of art implicit in the work of Herder or Schelling would have led him toward a concept of individualism, the original, the eccentric, even the disagreeable, that in a sense fitted in with something of which, it's true, no German pedagogue could possibly have approved: the rejection of conventional schooling.

The truth about the young officer with whom Borodin shared a hospital orderly room that autumn day of 1856 is that he was as yet an inchoate personality, not fully formed, and still essentially unsure of himself. The posturing and polished manners, the affected speech and the litter of French phrases, were a mask concealing something more awkward, less approachable. His music making at this time, too, was a kind of uniform: insider wear for an outsider personality. At the time Borodin saw only the surface; and for many people Musorgsky would remain a superficial, or at best enigmatic, character, too easily influenced by other, more forceful minds, too weakly rooted in his own. If his music would in due course prove this view profoundly false, his life would lend it all too much support.

Apart from their shared musical enthusiasm, he and Borodin will have found little immediately in common. Or perhaps their personalities complemented one another. Where Musorgsky made a somewhat immature, self-conscious impression, the five-years-older Borodin seemed an altogether more integrated, mature, well-adjusted personality. Where Musorgsky had no clear vocation, Borodin could have laid claim to two. As a musician he was not only a decent pianist and a passable cellist, but already a talented composer with a variety of works to his credit. Admittedly, they were a curious miscellany: a handful of songs in the lyrical, sentimental manner of the Russian romance composers, Alyabyev and Gurilyov, but with accompaniments that included a part for cello; three or four chamber works in the style of Haydn or Mendelssohn; and some juvenilia for piano. Several of these works were incomplete, partly no doubt because Borodin was writing in a purely amateur environment with no particular compulsion toward performance, but above all for a reason that would plague his music for the rest of his life: the overpowering demands of his other, entirely professional vocation, that of a research chemist and university teacher. He had already, in his early teens, set up a miniature laboratory in his room at home, and by the time he met Musorgsky he had completed a six-year course in natural science, anatomy, and chemistry at the Medical-Surgical Academy and was about to embark on a doctoral dissertation with the pithy title: *On the Analogy of Arsenic Acid with Phosphoric Acid in Chemical and Toxicological Behavior.*

At that time their meeting had every appearance of a passing encounter, repeated two or three times, then terminated by a parting of their ways. Borodin went abroad for several months as part of his doctoral research, and when he returned to Russia in late 1857 he was for a time preoccupied with his dissertation and his work as assistant professor at the academy. They met again only toward the end of 1859, in the house of a colleague of Borodin's, by which time Musorgsky had resigned from the guards in order to dedicate himself entirely to music. He was now moving in quite new musical circles, and his views were beginning to reflect these new influences. There was a dogmatic force to his opinions that particularly struck Borodin. Mendelssohn, still to some extent Borodin's hero, was to be regarded with condescension. When their host invited them to play Mendelssohn's A-minor symphony in a four-hand piano arrangement, Musorgsky made a show of reluctance before agreeing on condition that he "be spared the andante, which is not at all symphonic, but one of the *Lieder ohne Worte* arranged for orchestra, or something of the kind."[3] On the other hand, he talked enthusiastically about Schumann, a composer new to Borodin, and played some extracts from the Third Symphony, after which he played a scherzo of his own with what he called an "Oriental" trio section (probably his orchestral scherzo in B-flat, composed the previous year, whose middle section has a drone bass somewhat in Glinka's *Ruslan* style). All this had a great effect on the impressionable Borodin. "I was dreadfully astonished," he recorded much later, "at what were, for me, unheard-of new elements in the music. I won't say that they even particularly pleased me at first; rather they somewhat puzzled me by their novelty. But after listening for a while more attentively, I began gradually to savour it."[4]

Soon after this second encounter, Borodin again went abroad to pursue his scientific research, basing himself in Heidelberg, but working also in Rotterdam, Paris, and, eventually, Pisa. Musorgsky's own life in the months that followed their first meeting was listless and unfocused. He performed his duties as a guards officer conscientiously, but—by his own admission when applying for his discharge in 1858—had no special commissions, undertook nothing on his own initiative, and gained no particular merit.[5] Military service simply did not interest him. In the summer of 1857 he took four months' extended leave in the country, probably at Karevo, no doubt on the pretext of family business. His musical activities seem to have been equally desultory. He tinkered with one or two brief compositions. There is a song, "Where Art Thou, Little Star?", composed in April and once regarded as a prophetic treatment of the ornate Russian folk style known as *protyazhnaya*—the "drawn out" style—until it was proved by Richard Taruskin that the supposed original was in fact a later revision of a more conventional setting in the manner of Gurilyov or Alyabyev.[6] Six months later Musorgsky wrote a short piano piece enigmatically titled "Souvenir d'enfance," perhaps based on something he had composed as a child, but otherwise devoid of obviously infantile features. The suave melody is vaguely suggestive of Glinka's "Oriental" manner (as in the Persian chorus of *Ruslan*), with the same sense of going nowhere in particular. Musorgsky underpins it for much of the time with a bass pedal, an unvarying low B which clashes with the changing harmonies in the right hand, a favorite and convenient device that he probably took over from his piano improvisations.[7]

Two years later he described himself as having been, at this time, "under the weight of a severe illness, which came on with great force during my time in the country. This was mysticism—mixed up with cynical thoughts about the Deity."[8] What on earth did he mean? A glimmer of light dawns in a reminiscence of a few months later. Here he describes his previous condition as nervous irritation, brought on only partly, he claims without a flicker of embarrassment, by masturbation, "but chiefly this: youth, excessive enthusiasm, a terrible, irresistible desire for omniscience, exaggerated critical and idealistic introspection that amounted to the embodiment of a dream in images and actions."[9] Almost as striking as the symptoms is his willingness to analyze them in such candid and painful detail. A problem with introspection can be the anxiety it creates about the validity of one's own existence. Is this "I" that I observe a possible, plausible concept compared with the well-formed, well-motivated, well-adjusted individuals whom I meet every day, with their settled functions and useful talents, whether they be peasants going about their rural tasks, or clever intellectuals thinking lucid, humane thoughts, or artists or politicians, or just ordinary, friendly people who relate so well to one another and into whose presence I intrude like a two-headed monster

or a bearded lady? On the other hand there is that nagging consciousness that I am in fact a special individual with something unusual to
contribute, which, however, I am signally, emphatically, not contribut-
ing. This condition, intensely characteristic of Russians of the minor
aristocracy in the early-to-middle decades of the nineteenth century,
had been named and brilliantly described only a few years earlier by
Turgenev in his "Diary of a Superfluous Man." "During the course of
my life," the superfluous man, Chulkaturin, laments,

> I was constantly finding my place taken, perhaps because I did not look
> for my place where I should have done. I was apprehensive, reserved,
> and irritable, like all sickly people. Moreover, probably owing to exces-
> sive self-consciousness, perhaps as the result of the generally unfor-
> tunate cast of my personality, there existed between my thoughts and
> feelings, and the expression of those feelings and thoughts, a sort of
> inexplicable, irrational, and utterly insuperable barrier; and whenever
> I made up my mind to overcome this obstacle by force, to break down
> this barrier, my gestures, the expression of my face, my whole being,
> took on an appearance of painful constraint. I not only seemed, I posi-
> tively became unnatural and affected. I was conscious of this myself,
> and hastened to shrink back into myself. Then a terrible commotion
> was set up within me. I analysed myself to the last thread, compared
> myself with others, recalled the slightest glances, smiles, words of the
> people to whom I had tried to open myself out, put the worst construc-
> tion on everything, laughed vindictively at my own pretensions to "be
> like every one else,"—and suddenly, in the midst of my laughter, col-
> lapsed utterly into gloom, sank into absurd dejection, and then began
> again as before—went round and round, in fact, like a squirrel on its
> wheel. Whole days were spent in this harassing, fruitless exercise. Well
> now, tell me, if you please, to whom and for what is such a man of use?
> Why did this happen to me? what was the reason of this trivial fretting
> at myself?—who knows? who can tell?[10]

Chulkaturin has been diagnosed with a terminal illness, so writes
about himself in the past tense. Musorgsky is merely facing a blank
future, without purpose or ambition. He returns from the country to
his military duties in October and his condition worsens. He becomes
morbidly oversensitive and touchy in his relations with other people,
and broods on death and the afterlife. As the younger son, he has nothing to do with the family estates, yet the Russian system offers him no
alternatives outside the army, the church, or the civil service. Unlike

Stasov, he has no driving enthusiasm that marks out an unconventional alternative route. At the age of eighteen, his world is adrift.

At this low point in his young existence, Musorgsky made an acquaintance that would change his entire life. Through one of his musical Preobrazhensky friends, Fyodor Vanlyarsky, he met the composer Alexander Dargomïzhsky, and was invited to attend musical soirées at his apartment. At that precise moment, the autumn of 1857, Dargomïzhsky was perhaps the most prominent living Russian composer. Glinka had been dead nine months;[11] Alexey Verstovsky's opera *Gromoboy* had recently been staged in Moscow, but nothing new by the composer of *Askold's Tomb* had been heard in St. Petersburg for almost two decades; Alexander Gurilyov had composed some excellent songs, but little else. Dargomïzhsky was also the composer of many fine and interesting songs; but most importantly he had written two operas, of which the second, *Rusalka,* premiered with modest success in St. Petersburg in May 1856, but assumed an almost iconic significance in the critical press, particularly thanks to a huge, admiring ten-part review by Stasov's old school friend Serov in the *Muzïkal'nïy i teatral'nïy vestnik.*

On the face of it, *Rusalka* was a conventional romantic-folk opera about a miller's daughter who turns into a mermaid and drags her unfaithful lover to the bottom of the river Dnieper. Much of the music was cast in the standard operatic genre forms of chorus, aria, duet, trio, with simple, charming melodies, uncomplicated rhythms, and plain, effective scoring. What excited Serov was something else of which, it seems, Dargomïzhsky was only half aware: the unusually close relationship between his music and the text of Pushkin's verse play. Of course he realized that in adapting the play as a libretto, he had stayed as close as possible to the original text, sometimes even setting Pushkin's exact lines. What he seems not to have grasped was the comparative novelty of his own technique at those points where the original verse was set to a kind of free-flowing dramatic recitative in which the music shaped itself round the natural declamation of the words as if the singer were—albeit in a heightened style—actually speaking the play. Serov had been reading the operatic treatises of Wagner (though he had not yet seen any of his operas), and had absorbed his theories about fluid word setting and the derivation of the musical ideas from the vocal-poetic line. Oddly enough, Serov was skeptical about Wagner's insistence that music, poetry, and stage setting should be on an equal footing; and yet he now praises precisely those parts of *Rusalka* where the music is most subservient to the text. He enthuses about the scene in which the Miller, driven mad by the loss of his daughter and believing himself to be a raven, encounters her lover, the Prince, on the river bank and demands her restitution. The conversational nature of the discourse is reflected in an informal succession of orchestral ideas, sometimes doubling the words, sometimes picking up their intonation, but hardly proceeding thematically at all. None of this is exactly revolutionary; but it does introduce to Russian music a technique that would in due course have consequences unforeseen and unforeseeable at the time. Not the least remarkable thing about it is Serov's influence in drawing Dargomïzhsky's attention to his own achievement. "Late last night," the composer wrote to the critic, "I read your analysis of the duet between the miller and the prince. I thank you with all my heart not so much for your praise as for the uncommonly deep penetration of my innermost and even unconscious thoughts. In truth I had never thought that my duet was so successful . . ."[12]

Whether or not Musorgsky saw *Rusalka* during its run of performances in 1856 we don't know. Stasov says not: Glinka's two operas and *Rusalka*, he assures us, were unknown to the young guards officer.[13] Yet if Musorgsky had entered Dargomïzhsky's home in November or December 1857 unable to discuss—and preferably praise—his host's latest opera, he could well have been poorly received, since Dargomïzhsky was profoundly aggrieved at what he saw as the work's inadequate reception and extremely touchy about Glinka's (as he considered it) inflated reputation. He would grumble incessantly at the injustices to which he was subjected. Had not the most important critic in Russia praised *Rusalka* to the skies? Had he not identified in it progressive elements that even the great Glinka had not thought of? But where was the official recognition? *Rusalka* received a handful of performances but was soon withdrawn. Nobody but Serov seemed aware of its significance. Well, he, Alexander Sergeyevich Dargomïzhsky, would soldier on nonetheless. "I do not deceive myself," he wrote to the singer Lyubov Karmalina just at the time of Musorgsky's appearance in his circle, "my artistic situation in Petersburg is unenviable. The majority of our music-lovers and newspaper hacks do not recognize any inspiration in me. Their routine attitude looks for melodies that flatter the ear, which I do not seek out. I have no intention of lowering music to a pastime for their sake. I want sound to express the word directly. I want truth."[14]

Regardless of official St. Petersburg, Dargomïzhsky had assumed the mantle of chief musical progressive from the composer of *Ruslan and Lyudmila*. His soirées were dominated by excerpts from the Glinka operas and from *Rusalka*, especially, no doubt, the famous Miller's song, the Prince's lyrical cavatina from the third act, and perhaps also the "realist" dialogue discussed by Serov, all of which Dargomïzhsky himself would sing and accompany, not beautifully but to vivid dramatic effect. It was Musorgsky's first experience of an environment in which music was taken seriously, not just as a vehicle for entertainment or display, but as a subject for debate and the airing of ideas. One of the regular guests was Mily Balakirev, a mere two years older than Musorgsky, not only a spectacularly gifted pianist but a talkative young man with strong opinions about music which he was prepared to back up with arguments. Another was César Cui, the young engineering graduate from Vilnius whom Balakirev had met at Glinka's with Ulïbïshev. Cui, like Musorgsky, was an army officer, a military engineer. But he was a composer as well. He had already written a handful of songs and piano pieces, and was now starting an opera based on Pushkin's narrative poem *Kavkazskiy Plennik'* (*A Prisoner of the Caucasus*).

The mere attempt at such a project with no expertise beyond a familiarity with fortifications and high explosives must have struck Musorgsky, who had written nothing more than three minutes long, as impressively, absurdly ambitious. Even Balakirev, who in musical accomplishment was far above either of them, was working on nothing more pretentious than an orchestral overture on three Russian folk songs; and it may have been as part of a discussion of the problems involved in writing even a short work for orchestra that Balakirev offered to give Musorgsky informal instruction in composition. He will have explained—as he did later to Stasov—that he was not competent to teach Musorgsky music theory; that his teaching would take the form of practical demonstration and explanation through a close study of great works. On this basis the two young musicians began meeting frequently almost at once, early in December 1857.

Balakirev had now been in St. Petersburg for two years, but, though chronically short of money, he had made no serious attempt to secure pupils, and his sessions with Musorgsky—who was by no means without resources—were always given without payment. The arrangement reflected Balakirev's purity of soul at least as much as any lack of qualification, though in truth the one kind of teaching for which he certainly was qualified—piano lessons—was probably the one kind Musorgsky neither needed nor wanted. From the start the basis of Balakirev's pedagogy was an overpowering confidence in the rightness of his own musical judgment. To put it bluntly, he was bossy and intolerant; he had the power of instant opinion, what he decided was to be regarded as absolute truth, and from such positions he rarely if ever deviated.

He was, admittedly, often right. In the deeply provincial atmosphere of fifties St. Petersburg, with its dominant Italian opera and a local musical culture mainly centered on vaudeville (ballad opera) and private soirées, Balakirev's insistence on the study of great works, his ruthless rejection of the tawdry and second-rate, his intensely critical attitude to what went on in Petersburg music, were vastly stimulating as attitudes even if the judgments they led to were sometimes quirky or frankly prejudiced.

They met initially, it seems, at Balakirev's apartment. But one of the first instructions he issued was that Musorgsky, who was living with his mother and brother, should acquire a decent piano of his own; and a new Becker was duly delivered to the apartment in Grebetsky Ulitsa, beyond the Fontanka, a few days before Christmas. Subsequent lessons were often at the Musorgsky apartment. They were frequent but sometimes had to be cancelled because of Musorgsky's guard duties, a situation that no doubt brought to a head his growing sense that music and soldiering didn't mix and led directly to his application for discharge in the spring of 1858. By early July, when the discharge came through, and Balakirev departed to spend the summer in Nizhny-Novgorod, they had established a firm way of working. They would play through four-hand piano versions of works by the great classical composers, Mozart, Haydn, Beethoven, and Schubert; older masters such as Bach and Handel, and, where available, recent works by Berlioz, Liszt, and Schumann. According to a much later recollection of Balakirev's, Musorgsky was by this time familiar with the important works of Glinka and Dargomïzhsky (presumably thanks to their prominent role in the Dargomïzhsky evenings).[15] So these were passed by. We know that at one of their early lessons they played Beethoven's Second Symphony. Later Balakirev introduced Musorgsky to the symphonies of Schumann; in one of Modest's first letters to Nizhny-Novgorod in July he reports that he and his brother have been playing the first two symphonies, and, as we saw, he would later regale Borodin with the Third Symphony, a work at that time less than ten years old. We can take it, finally, that his condescending attitude to Mendelssohn on that occasion was likewise a deep bow in the direction of Balakirev.

These so-called lessons must have been astonishing sessions from a musical point of view. Musorgsky, we know, was a talented pianist and an excellent sight reader; Balakirev was an authentic virtuoso. It was just at this time, in February 1858, that he played Beethoven's "Emperor" Concerto for Tsar Alexander II and his brother Grand Duke Constantine at the so-called Petersburg Concert Society. But

as to what Balakirev said about the music, we are reduced to speculation. His teaching method is described somewhat satirically by
Rimsky-Korsakov in his memoirs (we have to bear in mind that by this
time Rimsky-Korsakov had himself been a conservatory professor for
more than thirty-five years):

> At that time, under the influence of Schumann's works, the gift for
> melody was in disfavour. . . . Nearly all the basic ideas of Beethoven's
> symphonies were considered weak; Chopin's melodies, sweet and
> lady-like; Mendelssohn's, sour and bourgeois. However, the themes of
> Bach's fugues were undoubtedly respected. . . . In the majority of cases a
> piece was judged by its separate elements: it would be said: the first four
> bars were excellent, the next eight weak, the ensuing melody good for
> nothing, the transition from it to the next phrase beautiful, and so on.
> A work was never considered as a whole in its aesthetic significance.[16]

Balakirev himself later told Calvocoressi that he "explained to
[Musorgsky] the various forms of composition." But this would have
been strictly impossible without the theoretical knowledge he denied
possessing. Classical form depends on a subtle and complex interaction
between harmony, counterpoint, rhythm, and phrase structure. It cannot simply be described in terms of this brick, then that brick, as one
might describe a wall while ignoring the gravitational mechanics that
hold it together or push it apart. Balakirev may have pointed out thematic connections; or he may simply have drawn attention to remarkable details and tried to explain why they were remarkable. Why is
the E-flat-major chord that opens the "Emperor" Concerto different
from the E-flat chords that open the "Eroica" Symphony or the ones
that introduce Schumann's "Rhenish" Symphony? Fussing about such
details can seem terribly pedantic to the layman in search of a quick
program-note; but it lies at the core of the process whereby the genius
constantly renews a seemingly outworn musical language. Or did Balakirev justify his prejudices on the basis of generalities? Beethoven: a
revolutionary in the scale and grandeur of his writing; Mendelssohn:
weak, effeminate, academic; Berlioz: uninhibited by textbook rules;
Liszt: empty bravura but an instinctive innovator; Wagner: a German
gasbag. His teaching seems to have been a strange blend of pedantry
and sweeping generalization, leavened, one might suppose, with sharp
perceptions of the sort that only the intensely musical mind is capable
of making.

The pedantry comes out in the tasks he sets Musorgsky by way of homework. First of all he has to compose an allegro, presumably for piano two or four hands, and evidently in sonata form. This is a project not at all to Musorgsky's liking, and by the end of February he is in open revolt and talking about "this allegro that's boring me sick." Later, Balakirev sets him to arrange the Persian chorus from act 3 of *Ruslan and Lyudmila* for piano duet. This takes him four or five days, after which he spends a couple of days orchestrating his own song "Where Art Thou, Little Star?" In between he thinks of writing incidental music for Sophocles' *Oedipus the King,* and by early July has actually composed all or part of an overture. Yet there remains something desultory about these projects. César Cui, who, having finished his first opera, is already planning his second, jokes to Balakirev that "Modest probably, as usual, thinks for half the day about what he will do tomorrow and the other half about what he did yesterday,"[17] Modest's own word for this tendency is "distractedness" (*rasseyannost'*)—an inability to concentrate on one thing at a time.[18] With Mily out of the way in Moscow and Nizhny-Novgorod, he writes two more songs in the romance style of Gurilyov: "Tell Me Why, Dearest Maiden" ("Otchego, skazhi, dusha devitsa") and "The Heart's Desire" ("Zhelaniye serdtsa"—a Russian setting of Heine's poem "Meines Herzens Schnsucht"), he starts, and perhaps completes, a piano sonata in E-flat, and starts, but probably does not complete, another in F-sharp minor. Not a scrap of either sonata survives (unless, of course, they were plundered for subsequent works), apart from three themes of the E-flat that Musorgsky wrote into his August letter to Balakirev. Finally, in the autumn, he composes two more scherzos, one (in B-flat) for orchestra, the other (in C-sharp minor) for piano, and makes a transcription of Glinka's *Souvenir d'une nuit d'été à Madrid* for piano duet.

These works, such as survive, show talent but little individuality. The series of scherzos (there was one in the E-flat sonata as well) suggests that Balakirev was urging him to write quick music, or at least music with a consistent impulse. The songs are restrained in tempo but are kept moving by rhythmic ostinatos: "Tell Me Why" is a slow waltz with a running quaver accompaniment; "The Heart's Desire" is in duple time, also with even quavers, but with a middle section in the style of a slow pavane. One might suppose that Balakirev gave him models. "Tell Me Why," as Taruskin has pointed out, is probably modelled on a song by Gurilyov, "A Maiden's Sorrow" ("Grust' devushki"), which starts with the same words and is also a slowish waltz. The C-sharp-minor scherzo, likewise, sounds like a take on Schubert's F-minor *Moment musical.* Balakirev probably made more specific contributions as well. The

C-sharp-minor piece exists in two versions, both dated 1858, the second of which looks very much like a piano arrangement of an orchestral score. So Balakirev perhaps instructed Musorgsky to orchestrate the original, and at the same time indicated the need for revisions, including notably the addition of a coda based on the music of the middle section. Balakirev's biographer Edward Garden has suggested that the master himself may have written all or some of this coda himself. In any case, the revision certainly reflects his sense of formal balance and growth. In the first version the A-B-A form ends crudely with an exact replica of the first A section; the second version modifies the repeat and then adds the slow coda, which clinches the piece in an unexpected but organic way. The thinking is classical, of course, and Musorgsky never organized his mature forms in anything like this fashion. But he did learn the lesson that good form is not something preplanned but an end product: a result, not an ingredient.

None of these works would be seriously worth discussing if it were not for the light they shed on Musorgsky's early development out of practically nothing, and for what they tell us (or at least imply) about Balakirev's teaching. The whole process has an extremely creaky look to anyone who has studied music at all systematically. But it worked for Musorgsky. Balakirev could not remedy the defects in his pupil's character, but he could confront him with works of genius, and Musorgsky was quick to understand what he needed, and to reject what he did not. In his teacher's absence, but no doubt at his behest, he studied Gluck's reform operas, Mozart's Requiem, and various Beethoven sonatas that were new to him (including one or both of the op. 27 sonatas "Quasi una fantasia"). Balakirev's precepts did not stop with music. It was probably at his suggestion that they read Byron's *Manfred* together, and perhaps also Herzen's novel *Who Is to Blame?* (*Kto vinovat?*). "How I would like to be Manfred!" Musorgsky had blurted out one day as they walked together down Sadovaya Ulitsa. "I was a complete child at the time," he later confessed, "and it seems that fate was kind enough to fulfil my wish—I was literally 'manfredized,' my soul slew my body. Now I have to take every kind of antidote."[19] Since "manfredization"—self-identification with Byron's guilt-wracked but unrepentant Romantic hero—was more or less epidemic among Russian writers and artists of the period, it is as easy to understand why the nineteen-year-old Musorgsky would be infected as it is to understand why his (almost) twenty-one-year-old self would see the need of an antidote. But one still cannot tell from his music what form he thought it would take.

CHAPTER 5

On Aesthetics and Being Russian

The year before Musorgsky's meeting with Borodin, a twenty-seven year-old postgraduate student at St. Petersburg University had published his master's dissertation under the title *The Aesthetic Relations of Art to Reality.*

Nikolay Chernïshevsky was the son of an Orthodox priest in Saratov, on the lower Volga five hundred miles southeast of Moscow. His father, however, must have been exceptionally broadminded, not to say well educated, by the usual standards of the provincial Russian priesthood, for by the time Nikolay reached St. Petersburg in 1846, after four years in the seminary at Saratov, he not only was well enough taught to enroll as a student in the university's Faculty of History and Philology but was able to abandon his religious studies with his parents' consent.

Whether they would have agreed so readily had they foreseen the precise direction his studies would take is an open question. Before long he was immersed in the literature of the French utopian socialists, Fourier, Saint-Simon, Proudhon, and company; had worked his way through the German idealist philosophers, from Hegel to Schelling and eventually Feuerbach; at which point he abandoned his Christian faith altogether and became a confirmed believer in the anthropological theory of man as the arbiter of his own destiny and the proper focus of his own spiritual aspirations. At the same time he was moving more and more toward a radical, even revolutionary, politics. In the late forties he had flirted with the (by modern standards) moderately leftist Petrashevsky group, but not so much as to be involved in the mock execution and Siberian exile to which the group's members, including the young Dostoyevsky, were subjected in 1849. Nevertheless, by the time his *Aesthetic Relations* was published in 1855, he was already well to the left politically. That year he became literary editor of Belinsky's old journal, *Sovremennik* (*The Contemporary*) and began to contribute articles that shifted Belinsky's emphasis on socially and psychologically directed interpretation toward a more specifically political radicalism. The idea that it was the essential task of literature—and by extension, art in general—to prepare and promote the demise of Russian autocracy emerges clearly for the first time in these writings: Belinsky, for all his radicalism, had never argued for the subjection of literature to any such political program. In 1857, when Chernïshevsky handed over the editorship to his twenty-one-year-old colleague Nikolay Dobrolyubov, he was passing the torch to an extreme advocate of this point of view, and at the same time associating it unequivocally with the politics of revolution and nihilism.

There is as yet hardly anything political in the *Aesthetic Relations*. What the book does suggest is a certain hard-nosed materialism that goes perfectly well with the political activist's determination to get things done. It spends a good deal of time refuting Hegel's view of art as the perfection of a beauty that in the physical world is invariably tainted or ephemeral. It argues that, on the contrary, reality is always more beautiful than art, which can never be more than a pale copy. How, Chernïshevsky asks, can a copy be more beautiful than the original? How can the artist imagine more beautiful faces and bodies than the ones he himself has seen? How can the imagined rose match the perfection of the real flower? Art is transient, whereas nature is constantly self-renewing. Beauty in art is lifeless and monotonous, while beauty in the real world is alive and forever changing. Beauty in art demands an effort of the imagination, whereas beauty in life is instantly, spontaneously recognizable and comprehensible. Even literature (poetry and prose), which Chernïshevsky considers the least problematical art form, tends to be "feeble, incomplete and indefinite" in its imagery, compared with the corresponding images in reality. It's true that the written word is more informative than the other arts; it can describe character and ideas and can tell a complex story. But all these things are present in reality as well. The writer can, certainly, use rhetorical effects to enhance this or that detail. But this leads to exaggeration and a corresponding tendency to oversimplify. Novels in general, he grumbles, are stilted in dialogue and artificial in motivation; they also pander to certain weaknesses in man that deny reality:

the need for characters to be good or bad, the need for happy endings or for the tragic hero to come to a sticky end, the love of tear-jerking sentimentality.

Chernïshevsky is no musician, and like most thinkers who apply their ideas arbitrarily to music he soon runs into difficulties on this terrain. Obviously music is not, except in special cases, imitative of reality; so it can hardly be reckoned as inferior on that count. But if music is not a product of the search for beauty such as is found in the world around us, what is it? Chernïshevsky, writer that he is, finds his answer in the art of singing—that is, music explained by words. Singing, he suggests, is not about beauty but about the expression of feeling. A singer sings as a dog howls or a child cries. This may seem evasive, since the singer, of course, is not on the face of it the same person as the composer: not, that is, the creator, but the middleman. But Chernïshevsky gets round this problem by designating folk song as the most authentic kind of vocal music, far superior, in his book, to what he calls the "artificial" singing of opera or the art song; and folk music, as everyone knows, is not, strictly speaking, composed at all, but just grows, like a plant or a tree. In this sense, he concludes, singing (or if one insists, vocal music) is not really a fine art like painting or poetry at all, but a useful art, like plowing or carpentry. This is clearly very convenient for his general argument, because it allows him to regard a certain type of music as a phenomenon of nature—an aspect of reality—while art music is implicitly denounced as a feeble (and useless) copy of this phenomenon. Instrumental music began as accompaniment to singing; later it achieved independence, partly because of the limitations of the human voice. But it remains a poor imitation of singing, just as art singing remains a poor substitute for singing "as a work of Nature."

It hardly seems necessary to dwell on the fallacies in this argument. Chernïshevsky knows perfectly well that art is not solely, or even mainly, concerned with beauty in the conventional sense, but deals with man's consciousness of the world around him, something that, by definition, the world cannot know. What he seems to be feeling his way toward is a theory of art that, so to speak, keeps its feet firmly planted on the ground, and rejects the abstract Hegelian concepts of beauty and universals in favor of individualism, particularism, and a sense of the world in which it is objects and people that determine our emotional and aesthetic responses.[1] His mistake, perhaps, is to oversimplify. Here and there he seems genuinely to be arguing that art as such is an irrelevancy. Turgenev famously read the book in this sense: "In his eyes," he remarked, "art is only what he calls a surrogate for reality, for life, and is essentially only fit for the immature. Whichever way you look at it, this idea is the basis of everything for him. And in my view it's rubbish."[2] At times one can find oneself wondering whether Chernïshevsky has ever looked closely at a Rembrandt portrait or listened attentively to a Bach suite or a Beethoven string quartet. He seems impervious to the idea that art might itself represent a reality transfigured by the imaginative powers of genius, just as, on a more commonplace level, dreams and fantasy transform but in no way ignore our experience of day-to-day existence. In particular, his ideas about music may seem hardly worth more than a passing glance. Yet at other times it seems perfectly clear that when he talks about life, he means something other than base matter. "True life," he says, "is the life of the heart and mind." "Beauty is life: beautiful is that being in which we see life as it should be according to our conceptions; beautiful is the object which expresses life, or reminds us of life."[3]

Chernïshevsky's monograph, though only a master's thesis, seems to have been studied with some attention at least by the artistic community of the mid-fifties. Whether Vladimir Stasov read it at the time is less certain. In an autobiographical note written in old age, he names Belinsky, Chernïshevsky, and the nihilist Dmitry Pisarev as his guides.[4] But leaving aside the question of memory, it remains unclear at what stage the guidance took effect, and through which works. All three wrote about literature and aesthetics, Stasov's field of interest. Chernïshevsky later also published an influential novel. But both he and Pisarev were more notable as political radicals, and both spent a significant part of their adult life (Pisarev's was short) in either prison or exile. Both were hugely admired by Lenin, and came to be seen as prophets of revolution. Accordingly, Stasov's self-association with these two was seized on by his Soviet biographers and treated as confirmation of his "correct" proto-Marxist views. He was said, for instance, to have "perceived in Chernïshevsky the authentic leader of the revolutionary democratic movement of the sixties and to have valued his teaching as the most forward-looking of his time." "Stasov," the same biography goes on, "particularly valued Chernïshevsky's demand that art make a judgment about life, stamping everything with those social appearances and forms which stifled and crippled the people, at the same time asserting progressive democratic ideals." And he called for "the active participation of art in the struggle for the emancipation of the people and for historical progress, [and] placed art at the service of the emancipation movement."[5]

Stasov's émigré Russian biographer, the Washington-based Sovietologist Yuri Olkhovsky, is understandably dismissive of such claims. "In the USSR," he points out, "Chernïshevsky's views are considered the apex of Russian pre-Marxist materialist socio-philosophical and aesthetic thought. When one also considers that Vladimir Lenin based many of his ideas on the writings of Chernïshevsky one begins to realize that Belinsky carries much less significance with Soviet ideologists than does Chernïshevsky."[6] Olkhovsky goes so far as to doubt whether Stasov actually ever read anything by Chernïshevsky, while accepting that he was familiar with his ideas. This might seem to be carrying skepticism to unnecessary lengths. That Stasov read Chernïshevsky's novel *What Is to Be Done?* (*Shto delat'?*) when it came out in 1863 is practically certain, since Balakirev praises it in a letter to him of April that year without naming it. But Stasov was in any case a voracious reader of books and articles about art, and would no more have ignored an important writer on aesthetics in the fifties than, as a teenager, he would have overlooked the latest major essay by Belinsky in *Sovremennik*. Even Olkhovsky concedes that he probably read Chernïshevsky's series of "Sketches of the Gogol Period in Russian Literature" in *Sovremennik* in 1856, since Stasov himself had an article in one of the relevant issues. Perhaps one can assume that Stasov was well acquainted with Chernïshevsky's work at this time without any need to impose on him its author's subsequent political tendencies one way or the other.

The point is that Stasov was not, at bottom, a political thinker at all. He was uninterested in revolution or "the emancipation of the people" as political goals, though he was in favor of any kind of social reform that he thought would benefit art. So, like many intelligent people who spend little time worrying about political issues as such, he could be profoundly inconsistent in his views. Like most of his generation, he loathed the restrictions placed on art and literature by the whole apparatus of autocracy. He liked the idea of Russia's ancient democratic institutions, from the village commune (*obshchina*) up to the supposed elective democracy of medieval Novgorod. But he was much less enthusiastic about the apparatus of modern democracy, which ultimately gave power to committees of the ignorant and the uncultivated. In modern terms he was what might, clumsily, be called an elitist. He was essentially interested only in the first-rate, was generally contemptuous of the second-rate, and had no discernible interest in popular or demotic art, such as may have existed in nineteenth-century Russia. His great aesthetic awakening had been through the masterpieces of Western music and literature and Western—especially Italian and French—painting. Except in some recent literature and architecture and perhaps the operas of Glinka, Russian art had little to offer that was even remotely comparable, and this was something Stasov regretted and began in the fifties to hope to alter. Under the influence of Belinsky and Chernïshevsky, it seemed natural to pursue this goal in terms of the content of art rather than its style or method. If significant art was to be understood as a direct reflection of the society by and for which it was made, then Russianness was best achieved through Russian subject matter; and if the significance of Russian art was to be gauged according to its contribution to an awareness of that society and its problems, then the best subject matter would be, as Belinsky had written in 1834, the "faithful portrayal of scenes of Russian life."[7] Not that there was anything particularly new about that idea. Literate Russians knew and admired the work of Dickens and Balzac. Gogol's *Dead Souls* had brilliantly caricatured the absurdity and corruptness of the serf economy. Alexander Herzen's novel *Who Is to Blame?* had used the rigid structure of Russian society to frame a love story that presented misery and confusion as what seemed the inevitable outcome of emotional emancipation. But on the whole the Russian novel as social critique was still in its infancy in 1859, the year of Ivan Goncharov's *Oblomov* and Turgenev's *Nest of Gentlefolk,* and the year after Alexey Pisemsky's *Thousand Souls.* As for painting—Stasov's home ground—it had barely ventured beyond the idealized peasantry of Alexey Venetsianov's *Threshing Floor* (1822) and the vivid theatricality of Bryullov's *Last Day of Pompeii* (1833), painted in any case in Italy.

The question of realism in painting and storytelling only had to be posed for its solution to be self-evident, at least in theory. But with music, as Chernïshevsky had already discovered, it was another matter. Singing as a natural phenomenon like the wind and the rain was one thing. But how could you talk about realism in a Beethoven symphony or string quartet? You could argue for historical subject matter or social realism in opera, within certain obvious limitations imposed by the conventions of the medium. You could talk about pictorialism in songs or choruses: the turning mill wheel and babbling brook in Schubert's *Schöne Müllerin,* the Resurrection in Bach's B-minor Mass. But such imagery was only comprehensible through the words, conventionalized into music. Music on its own could only paint pictures by trivializing itself, through onomatopoeia or that curious process of mental substitution whereby we understand the movement from left to right on the piano as "rising," or repeated musical figures as "machines." None of this added up to music in any but the most peripheral sense.

For Stasov, one solution to the problem lay in the concept of program music. Again there was nothing very new about this idea. Obvious orchestral examples like Beethoven's "Pastoral" Symphony and Berlioz's *Symphonie fantastique* were either known or known about (though Berlioz's hybrid, part-vocal *Roméo et Juliette* symphony was better known than the *Fantastique* in St. Petersburg). But Stasov, no doubt with Belinsky's criticism in mind, wanted to go beyond the overt intentions of such works and decipher programs in instrumental works that were to all outward appearances purely abstract. "What are the majority of Beethoven's overtures," he wrote much later, "what are certain parts of his last quartets, what are many of his sonatas, what are all Beethoven's symphonies starting with the Third, if not 'program music'?"[8] He read A. B. Marx's book on Beethoven the minute it appeared in late 1858 and was delighted, he told Balakirev, to find that Marx shared his opinion that "the finale of the Third Symphony depicts a *crowd* of people, a popular festival, in which diverse groups succeed one another: now ordinary people, now soldiers, now women, now children—and all against the background of some rural landscape."[9] Yet even before reading Marx he had detected at least the essence of a narrative in Schumann's Piano Quintet, a work to which—unlike the "Eroica" Symphony—the composer himself attached no hint of a program. "Have you noticed," he asked Balakirev, "how one musical detail governs nearly everything in it? It's the *scale*—explicit or implicit." He gives several music examples, and then: "It seems to me that this procession of scales, this constant *upward motion* is not accidental, but must serve as the expression of some kind of 'striving,' some spiritual or mental impulse. From the first time I heard this quintet (or almost-symphony), it struck me that there is some program here. The main role in this program is played by 'striving.' "[10]

How much Stasov had read of the recent German literature on program music and its association with the progressive wing of new music in that country is hard to establish. The fact that he laid hands on Marx's *Beethoven* so soon after its publication suggests that he will also have perused Franz Brendel's *History of Music in Italy, Germany and France*, first published in 1852 and a key text on the linking of program music with the "Music of the Future," as Wagner was calling it, or the "New German School," as Brendel dubbed the somewhat arbitrary (and not very German) grouping of Berlioz, Liszt, and Wagner himself. The point was that treating music as portraiture or depiction or narrative freed it from the stereotyped requirements of classical form and harmony and opened up new vistas of musical sound and sense. For Brendel the climax of this process was the recent symphonic poems of

Liszt. Berlioz was brilliant, but too wedded to what Brendel called "the poetic idea," not musical enough in his thinking. Wagner was still the composer of *Tannhäuser* and *Lohengrin* and the author of a series of provocative theoretical essays about opera whose musical outcome was as yet unknown. But Liszt was the very model of a composer who derived new, autonomous musical forms from literary or pictorial subject matter, and filled them with music that was vivid, daring, and original.

For Stasov, the idea of free form went with another tendency that he wanted to promote in Russian music: a healthy distaste for theory and the authority of the academy. There was a strong element of sour grapes about this. Since there was no such thing as a conservatory of music in Russia, the only way for a Russian musician to acquire any kind of advanced musical training was to study abroad—in Germany, France, or Italy. And this would inevitably impose a procedural straitjacket and Western colorings that would be hard to reconcile, Stasov thought, with the Russian spirit. Glinka, admittedly, had studied counterpoint with Dehn in Berlin. But he was at some pains in his *Memoirs* to play down the importance of such things. The director of the Milan Conservatory had tormented him, he said, with the intricacies of counterpoint, "but my lively fantasy could not be subjected to such dry and unpoetical work, and I soon gave up my lessons with him." "Subsequently," Stasov reports, "Dargomïzhsky too mastered precisely the same thing very quickly . . . [and] later on Dargomïzhsky's successors and colleagues did not, like the Germans, expend long years pointlessly, but learned it very quickly and easily, like any other grammar."[11]

Stasov himself probably knew enough about music theory, and certainly, by the 1880s, enough about the composers in question, to know that this assessment was simply untrue. He knew all about the difficulties they had had finishing works, the lack of formal and technical sophistication, the short-windedness and lack of intellectual thrust, in much Russian music of the fifties and sixties. It simply did not suit his book to admit it. No doubt Glinka was right that too much counterpoint could stanch the imagination; but the right amount could just as well release it. Everything depended on the teaching. But since there were no reputable Russian composition teachers in the 1850s or early 1860s, it might well have been that the heavy hand of imported pedagogues would have crushed the fragile flower of native genius at that time. At any rate it would probably not have fitted the particular materials and subject matter that Stasov already had in mind as appropriate to an emerging national music.

Thus Stasov's objection to systematic theoretical study in music

automatically conjured up Belinsky's observation that "*absolute* nationality is only within the reach of men who are free from extraneous foreign influences."[12] Music theory was essentially a German invention;
so the rejection of theory was anti-German, and furthermore implied
a rejection of the dominant German musical culture, notwithstanding
Stasov's huge admiration for individual manifestations of that culture,
just as Belinsky, for all his love of Western literature, saw that in order
to create an identity of its own Russian literature had to separate itself
from the overpowering influence of the French and English novel. But
there was an important difference. For Belinsky, the insistence on a
national literature was linked to the idea of social and political reform,
but the connection was somewhat ambiguous. "Though nationality,"
he wrote in 1841, "is intimately associated with historical development
and the social forms of the nation, these two things are not one and the
same thing; . . . both Peter the Great's reforms and the Europeanism
he introduced in no way changed, nor could they change, our nationality, but only reanimated it with the spirit of a new and richer life
and provided it with a boundless sphere for manifestation and activity."[13] Belinsky draws a distinction between the Russian word *narodnost'*, which he takes to mean nationality in the sense of a prelapsarian,
ethnically integrated people, and the loan word *natsional'nost*, which he
understands in the greatly enriched sense of the nation at large, "the
conglomerate body of all social estates and conditions."

> There may be yet no nation in the *people,* but the nation has a people.
> The songs of Kirsha Danilov [an eighteenth-century itinerant musi-
> cian and folk-song collector] possess *narodnost;* the poetry of Pushkin
> is national . . . *Narodnost'* . . . presupposes something static, permanently
> established, not moving forward; it represents only what is actually
> present in the people in its given state. Nationality, on the contrary,
> contains not only what was and is, but what will be or can be. National-
> ity, in its evolution, draws together the extreme opposites which, to all
> intents and purposes, could not be foreseen or foretold.[14]

Narodnost', for all its coherence and purity, was the frozen condition
of Russia before Peter the Great came along and thawed it into a flowing river with tributaries, confluences, and, at the far end, the great
wide ocean.

Stasov might have agreed with Belinsky's historical analysis,
but he would not have been so interested in his outcomes. For him
narodnost' possessed a cultural authenticity that far outweighed any

associations with social or political backwardness. Like the Slavo-philes, he saw some kind of salvation in the uniqueness—the essential non-Europeanness—of pre-Petrine Russia, though his emphasis was more on folklore and peasant culture than on the Orthodox Church, which for the Slavophiles was the focus of the distinction they drew between the communal spirit of old Russia and the growing material-ism and individualism of the West. Stasov, in fact, was agnostic, and his interest in the Russian church and the Russian soul was primarily aesthetic. He would talk about the "flesh-and-bone inmost character of the Russian people [*narod*]," through which "one grows and draws strength."[15] He took a deep interest in the church modes—the various scales of the sung liturgy—and explained them to Balakirev, pointing out their differences and the fact that they occur also in Russian folk music. Excited by the possibilities they offer a modern composer, he urges Balakirev to get to know them through use rather than study. "Imagine," he writes, "what new ammunition you would bring back here [Balakirev is in Nizhny-Novgorod]. Instead of the two scales new music possesses [major and minor] . . . you'd suddenly have a whole eight!! What a new source of melody and harmony!"[16]

Stasov was also becoming obsessed with Russian folklore, not because it provided a model for social reform but because it embodied a spirit that was fundamentally unlike and unrelated to anything in the Western tradition: a spirit purely Russian in character and origin. In fact he was slow to bring this point of view into focus. In a long memorial article on Glinka spread over three issues of the *Russkiy vestnik* in 1857, he had argued that *A Life for the Tsar* was specifically weakened by its reliance on folk models, when the essence of nationality "is con-tained not in melodies, but in the general character, in the *sum total of conditions*—diverse and wide-ranging."[17] But this, as Taruskin explains, was part of a highly tendentious polemic in favor of *Ruslan and Lyudmila,* and particularly in praise of that work's many dramatic absurdities and irrelevancies, which happened to suit Stasov's current idea that oper-atic verisimilitude—the pretense that traditional opera had anything to do with realism—was dead. The idea was no more than a tempo-rary convenience. Quite soon he is trying to interest Balakirev in the ancient tale of the merchant Sadko, who descends to the seabed and marries the Sea King's daughter, but whose gusli (psaltery) playing at their wedding inspires such frenzied dancing that a great storm blows up, the Sea Kingdom comes to an end, and Sadko has to return to his real wife in his native Novgorod. Stasov is excited by the tortuous detail and bizarre situations of this story, and rages correspondingly against the "unbearable vulgarity" of all those sailors' songs, shepherds' songs, and yeomen's songs in Wagner, Haydn, and Félicien David. "It might," he concedes, "be a pendant to Gluck's *Orfeo,* but with a totally different subject and in a Russian mold."

> Anyone who wants to grasp Russian art, ancient Russian life, must start by putting out of his mind the wish to seek out with us anything resembling the Greek Olympus or the Greek gods, Neptune and company. With us everything is different, a quite different tone, different situations, different characters, different background, different scenery. Neptune in an izba! Neptune and the dance of the Sea King! Neptune a lover of gusli music! How unlike the Greek temper all this is, how it all goes against the habits and tastes of the European public, and of our apelike public as well! And meanwhile what new, fresh, colorful, succulent themes. What tableaux of Russian nature on the island of the Sea King, what themes of pagan antiquity, of ancient worship, of our ancient life, at the start, on the ship, then at the wedding feast, people and gods all together. And finally, at the very end, a tableau of old Novgorod and the river Volkhov a marvellous subject, it seems to me![18]

The point about the people and gods reflects the pre-Petrine structure described also by Belinsky, but productively superseded, in his view, by Peter the Great. Before Peter, he explains, "the wedding of the lowliest village muzhik was the same as that of the greatest boyar: the difference was merely a matter of abundance of viands, costliness of clothing—in short, the importance and sum of expenditure. The same knout hung over both the muzhik and the boyar, for whom it was misfortune but not dishonor. The serf easily understood his master, the boyar, without the slightest strain on his intelligence; the boyar understood his serf without need of coming down to his intellection. The same corn brandy cheered the hearts of both . . ."[19] Peter the Great was a hero because he had breathed life into this dead system, and given it the potential for reform, even if the present situation was disagreeable. But Stasov's liberalism was skin deep, apolitical. He was attracted by what he saw as the egalitarian aspects of mythic Russia, but what he really loved was its authentic Russianness, its whiff of ancient ritual and magic, its fairy-tale colorfulness, and that rambling irrationality that comes with the additive nature of old folk tales. This was the essence of *narodnost',* and it was *narodnost',* if he was completely honest, that made his blood tingle, however much he might side with reformist *natsional'nost* in his mind, his conversation and his friendships.

The fascination with folk myth and ritual led naturally to another of Stasov's illiberal proccupations, what one might call the Oriental connection. In *Ruslan and Lyudmila,* his preferred Glinka opera, the base setting is Kievan Rus; but when Ruslan and his fellow suitors set off in search of the abducted Lyudmila, they implicitly head east—that is, into strange lands where magic is commonplace and good and evil wage perpetual war through the lives of anyone foolhardy enough to travel that route. Of course, "east" has to be understood metaphorically. It could embrace any of those territories Russia had annexed since 1800, including the Caucasus (to the south), much of central Asia to the east of the Caspian Sea, even Finland to the northwest. It was an Orient of the mind, but nonetheless potent for that. Its general character was in fact Islamic rather than Chinese, its climate hot and sultry, conducive to enchanted sleep and sensual abandon, an enticing but dangerous place of unreason and forgetfulness. Stasov, though, took a scholarly view of these unbookish attributes. Russian culture, he argued, was essentially Asiatic in origin: its language, its clothes, its customs, its architecture, its utensils, its ornaments, even its stories and bardic poems, its melodies and its harmonies—all came from the East, whether from central Asia, from India or Persia, from the Ottoman Empire, or from Byzantium.[20]

The argument, with all its obvious flaws and biases (Stasov knew nothing about Eastern harmony; the Russian language is a hybrid of Eastern and Western elements, and its alphabet is Greek) was no doubt a considered deduction from his knowledge of Eastern art. Its application to music was a great deal more speculative, and not in itself very useful. But it gave him an extra peg on which to hang his hostility to German music, a music as remote from the exotic East as one might suppose it possible to find. The East, by comparison, belonged to Russia. To a Russian the Orient was at the same time strange and familiar. He looked across his eastern (or, preferably, southern) border and there it was, beckoning, yet veiled and mysterious, girt with high mountains and washed by the dark sea, geographical features that, as a matter of fact, were unknown to most Russians. No wonder so many Russian writers had evoked these fringes of the empire: Pushkin in his *Prisoner of the Caucasus* and his verse tales *Tsar Saltan* and *The Golden Cockerel;* Lermontov in *A Hero of Our Time;* Tolstoy, just recently, in his *Sevastopol Sketches.* These authors, admittedly, were describing or evoking; they were not mimicking. Stasov in effect wanted Russian music to absorb Oriental elements, just as, he later hyperbolically claimed, "every truly talented European architect, sculptor, and painter has tried to reproduce the unique forms of the East." Only music, he grumbled, had dragged its heels. The *alla turca* episodes in Mozart and Beethoven were little more than gestures, of no real significance. It would be the task of the new generation of Russian composers to create a new idiom that incorporated orientalism as an organic element in a recognizably national musical language, folk-song-based, taking its subject matter from Russian history or myth, tales of the East, or the reality of Russian life. It was a task only Russians could perform; and nothing a conservatory could offer would help them perform it.

CHAPTER 6

New Institutions

In the same year that Chernïshevsky published his influential master's thesis, Anton Rubinstein's article "Die Componisten Russland's"—"The Composers of Russia"—came out in the Viennese *Blätter für Musik, Theater und Kunst.* The title was bland enough, and to tell the truth the article amounted to not much more than a brisk survey of the provincial scene in St. Petersburg, with lists of composers and brief outlines of work, all almost entirely unknown even to specialists outside Russia itself. It was, however, read or at least reported in Russia; and it caused trouble.

Rubinstein himself was Russian in a slightly complicated sense. His parents were converted Jews who lived in a Ukrainian-speaking part of Transdniestria, on the Russian side of the river Dniestr which at that time divided the tsarist empire from Romanian-speaking Bessarabia. The region was in the so-called Pale of Settlement, the mainly non-Russian fringe to which Jews in the empire had been confined by law since 1791. However, having converted while Anton was still an infant, the Rubinsteins were no longer trapped in the Pale, and they moved to Moscow in about 1834, when he was four or five years old. There he took piano lessons, progressed with barely credible rapidity, and was soon touring Europe as a child prodigy in the company of his teacher, Alexander Villoing. For most of the nine years from 1839 to 1848 he lived abroad, in Paris, Berlin, and Vienna. He met Liszt, Chopin, Mendelssohn, Meyerbeer. In Berlin he studied theory with Glinka's old teacher, Siegfried Dehn, and he only returned to Russia in 1848 in order to escape the widespread revolutions in the West that year.

The next six years in St. Petersburg were crucial for Rubinstein in establishing himself as a virtuoso pianist and composer. He was patronized by Nicholas I's widowed sister-in-law, Grand Duchess Yelena Pavlovna; he had several operas staged, conducted the first performance of his "Ocean" Symphony, and appeared many times as a solo pianist. By the time he left St. Petersburg for a European concert tour in 1854, his reputation in Russia, at least as a pianist and conductor, was absolutely secure. His music, admittedly, had made less of an impact. It was fluent, competent, but not strikingly individual, and it always made the greatest effect when he himself played it. It must have been his inability to make solid progress as a composer with the Russian public and critics that, among other things, nourished his sense of dissatisfaction with the St. Petersburg musical scene as a whole. And yet the Viennese article did not dwell on such matters, but instead attempted an assessment of the composers working in Russia and of the creative issues raised by their best work. And it was precisely here that he gave what was no doubt unintentional offense.

The first part of the article confines itself to a general account of Russian musical life and its underpinnings, as Rubinstein understood them. Wherever you go in Russia, he assures his readers, you hear music—sung or played, and accompanying all kinds of activity, work or leisure. As for music as an art, he credits Catherine the Great with the setting-up of the first music schools (the empress Anne had in fact preceded her in this). He fails to mention that these early schools were essentially training grounds for court singers, and were certainly not designed to provide any sort of theoretical grounding. Catherine sent Russian musicians abroad to study, most significantly the young Dmitry Bortnyansky, who studied in Italy, then returned; was appointed Kapellmeister to the Imperial Court Chapel; and composed a large number of mass and psalm settings and motets which became the staple of the Orthodox repertoire and eventually, together with the work of his successor as Kapellmeister, Fyodor Lvov, acquired a monopoly under which, by Rubinstein's day, it was illegal to replace their church music with music by other composers.

In Orthodox services, he explains, musical instruments were not permitted, and the composers had at their disposal only a four-part choir. Within these limitations, and with his Western training, Bortnyansky was able to produce much beautiful music in an essentially simple, pure idiom, even if his works could hardly measure up to the great masterpieces of the Roman Catholic liturgy. Rubinstein here raises the question of Russian folk song. Distinctive though it is, he finds in it a certain monotony, a persistent lugubriousness and melancholy that infect every aspect of its melody and rhythm. As material for an entire opera, this is scarcely endurable, especially for foreign audiences, who have no interest in the issues that might impel a Russian composer to base his music on folk materials.

No composers are named at this point. But Rubinstein begins the second part of the article, published two weeks later, with the claim that "Glinka was the first to have and carry out the bold but unfortunate idea of composing a national opera." Both Glinka's operas, he maintains, suffer from the monotony this entails on his view of folk song, and he claims that Glinka was aware of the problem and tried to mitigate it by introducing national elements from elsewhere: Polish dances in *A Life for the Tsar,* Orientalisms of one kind or another in *Ruslan and Lyudmila.* Unfortunately this merely added a new monotony to the old, since it still involved whole scenes limited to the chosen style of the moment. Rubinstein is at pains to soften these remarks by praising Glinka as "not only one of the most important Russian composers, but as deserving of an honorable place among the finest foreign masters." Turning to Glinka's songs, he calls him "the Russian Schubert, [who] turned Russian song into an art form, and was not content to send out into the world a more or less suitable word setting with simple arpeggio accompaniments"—as had been the standard convention for drawing-room songs. And Glinka's *Kamarinskaya,* he suggests (without naming it), is "among the most beautiful and the richest products of either Russian or non-Russian music." Thus a minor, if delightful, orchestral piece is elevated above the two great operas that had made their composer a beacon for all subsequent Russian composers.

"There is folk music and folk dance," Rubinstein asserts by way of summary of this aspect of his article, "but folk opera there strictly speaking is not." The typical emotional elements of opera are common to everyone in the world, and the musical setting of these universal feelings must have a world tone, not a folk tone. A sharp distinction emerges only between Western and Eastern music, thanks to differences of climate, religion, social customs, and other general influences. "Just as one wouldn't try to write a Malayan or Japanese opera but an Oriental one, so one shouldn't write an English, French, or Russian one, but a European one (speaking only about the musical aspect)."[1]

It seems unlikely that Glinka ever read Rubinstein's article, but he certainly read a report of it in the German-language *St. Petersburger*

Zeitung by the composer-critic Karl Friedrich Berthold. Berthold had seized on what he saw as an attack on *A Life for the Tsar* in particular, and used it as a basis for refuting Rubinstein's argument about the limitations of folk material in general. Precisely because of the authenticity they derive from their national character, he argued, "they acquire . . . a universal character, and thanks to their style and originality they belong to world history and become immortal." Berthold meanwhile ignored the fact that the rest of the *Blätter* article had been broadly positive about Russian music. Thus Rubinstein's apparently sincere attempt to introduce his German readers to what he saw as the best of his fellow countrymen's work was received in the Russian capital as a straightforward attack. Glinka told his friend Vasily Engelhardt that "the yid Rubinstein has taken it on himself to tell Germany about our music and has written an article in which he does us all dirty and handles my old woman *A Life for the Tsar* rather insolently."[1] Glinka, as we saw, was touchy about his first opera on account of the poor quality of its recent revivals, and no doubt he communicated his reaction not only to Engelhardt, but to the other members of his musical circle, who already included Vladimir Stasov and would also within a matter of weeks include Mily Balakirev.

Rubinstein does little more than hint at musical conditions in Russia. He notes that opera in St. Petersburg is dominated by Italian Opera; and who can complain, he asks, when this brings the greatest singers and the best music to the capital? Still, it was undeniably hard on Russian composers, neglected by an Italophile public and having in consequence to make do with a third-rate opera company. Of course there were bright young talents emerging; but they were not writing operas, and few of them were composing instrumental music, "partly because the public has little understanding of this kind of music, partly because the necessary educational apparatus is not available anywhere in the country." He could well have added that in any case there were few concerts at which such music might be played. Concerts happened mainly in Lent, when the theatres were closed by law and the orchestral players from the opera houses were therefore temporarily available. And there was one final grievance which Rubinstein spared his probably uncomprehending Viennese readership. Musicians in Russia were denied the status of Free Artist, in a country where all social and political relationships were defined by rank (or *chin,* to use the technical Russian word); they did not, like distinguished practitioners of other arts, receive the privileges that went with status, such as tax benefits and exemption from military service. In fact, musicians were not recognized at all within the bureaucratic system. Elsewhere Rubinstein recounts a painful experience of his own in St. Petersburg, in which an official at Kazan Cathedral insisted on registering him as "son of a merchant of the second guild" (the middle of the three merchant ranks) at a time when he was world-famous as a pianist and among the most professionally successful Russian artists in any sphere.[3]

Although the Vienna article skirts these issues, we know that they rankled with its author. In St. Petersburg in the early fifties he had already been contemplating ways of remedying them. In October 1852, he had written to his mother that he was at work on a plan for a music academy: "The plan is ready and today I shall give it to the Grand Duchess who will hand it to the tsar. This may have great consequences for the future of music in Russia and also for me."[4] Rubinstein had worked his plan out in considerable detail, basing it on his knowledge of the conservatories in Paris and Vienna and the Academy of Music in Berlin. But his timing was bad; Nicholas I was less open than ever to new ideas of a liberal character, and in any case he was increasingly distracted by the political tensions that would lead, in a matter of months, to the outbreak of the Crimean War. Toward the end of his three-year European concert tour, Rubinstein spent the winter of 1856–7 in Nice with Yelena Pavlovna discussing the problem. "The idea of a Russian musical society and a conservatory was born there," he wrote in his autobiography. "Yelena Pavlovna became interested in it as well."[5] In 1858 he returned to Russia and began, with her political and financial support, to put his ideas into practice.

Since his departure three years before, the country had undergone a sea change. Nicholas I had died in February 1855 and had been succeeded by his son, Alexander II, who was widely expected (on admittedly somewhat flimsy evidence) to be a more liberal tsar. In fact Alexander's first task was to try to win the Crimean War, which had been dragging on, for the most part disastrously for Russia, since 1853; and then, when it became clear that winning it was impossible, to bring it to an end. The Treaty of Paris was signed in March 1856. Thereafter, Alexander was able to turn his attention to the by now pressing need for land reform, with particular emphasis on the abolition of serfdom and the modernization of the rural economy and the politics that went with it. Obviously there was liberal thinking behind these moves, even if the main motive was to improve efficiency and discourage rebellion; and to some extent they brought with them a more open, receptive atmosphere in society at large. Even so, it was necessary to tread warily in seeking to establish new institutions in such a habitually conservative environment. Rubinstein's tactic, which seems to have been suggested by his friend Vasily Kologrivov, was to represent his new musical society as a revived version of the former Symphonic Society, which had put on the occasional orchestral concert in the time of Nicholas I. With a renewed charter to organize concerts, it would be a mere formality to transform them into regular events. And by including "the development of music education" among the "revived" society's principal aims, the ground would be laid for the new conservatory that it had for so long been Rubinstein's real dream to found in St. Petersburg.

After a good deal of lobbying and much energetic fund-raising by a board of directors which included Vladimir Stasov's lawyer brother Dmitry, the Russian Musical Society (RMS) finally opened its first season in November 1859 with a series of ten symphonic concerts in the Hall of the Assembly of the Nobles. The importance of this venture can hardly be overstated. Orchestral concerts in the capital had been a rarity. The Imperial Theatres held a monopoly on musical performances during the opera season, and it seems that Rubinstein was only able to evade the theatre directorate's embargo through the influence of Yelena Pavlovna, which also enabled him to draw on the best players from the opera orchestras and to assemble a concert orchestra superior to anything previously heard in St. Petersburg. For the first time, Petersburgers could hear the classics of the Western repertoire in performances worthy of the name. But Rubinstein also had the tact to include music by Russian composers in every program, even though the historic lack of concerts meant that the native repertoire of such things was decidedly thin. He played Glinka and Dargomïzhsky, Musorgsky (Scherzo in B-flat), and Cui (Scherzo in F, op. 1). And naturally he included his own music, in the form of the G-major Piano Concerto (no. 3). But many of the Russian offerings were not much more than tokens, sops to Cerberus. It was a situation that precisely illustrated the problem that his other great project was eventually designed to solve.

The new conservatory remained Rubinstein's prime goal; but here he began to face more serious opposition. His initial proposal for what he grandly but sycophantically labelled the Imperial Music School was rejected out of hand by the Ministry of Education on the grounds, more or less, that it was not needed. Stung by this characteristically obtuse bureaucratic response, he launched once more into print. This time his article appeared in the Russian-language newspaper *Vek,* and took the form of a direct attack on the basic conditions of Russian music. At its core lay an extended grumble at the state of affairs whereby the refusal of official status to musicians meant that only the gentry could afford to cultivate music at all. Anyone else with musical aspirations had first to find himself some gainful employment outside music, and this necessity would rob him of the time and energy to devote to music the concentrated effort without which it was idle to expect worthwhile artistic results. Rubinstein makes no attempt to conceal his profound contempt for the amateurism that dominates the Russian musical scene as a result. The amateur is a mere dabbler who never masters the rudiments of the art he pretends to cultivate. He imagines that if he writes a single romance, however primitive and inept, he can call himself a composer. He will set himself up as musical celebrity, write the same song over and over again, and "start to contend that only melody has value in music, and that everything else is German pedantry; and he will end up composing an opera."

> There are, it is true, amateurs who study musical theory, but here too they do not behave like true artists. They value not the rules but the exceptions; and having assimilated these exceptions they never give them up. Thus, in some work by a great composer we can, for example, come across a chord progression of an unusual kind. The amateur will take this and turn it into a rule for himself and will write only unusual harmonies, without taking into consideration the fact that where the great composer was concerned this harmony was the result of the overflowing of his inspiration, a cry of despair or ecstasy, and the logical consequence of the whole composition.

Many amateurs want to study, he continues, but cannot afford to do so. In any case, since Russians are musically untaught and music is not a viable profession, Russian teachers hardly exist, which means that the would-be student must be able to speak French or German.

> But what can be done to remedy this sad situation? I shall tell you: the only answer is to establish a conservatory.
>
> People will argue that great geniuses have rarely come out of conservatories; I agree, but who can deny that good musicians come out of conservatories, and that is precisely what is essential in our enormous country. The conservatory will never prevent a genius from developing outside it, and, meanwhile, each year the conservatory will provide Russian teachers of music, Russian orchestral musicians and Russian singers of both sexes who will work in the manner of someone who sees his art as his livelihood, the key to social respect, a means of becoming

famous, a way of giving himself up completely to his divine calling, and as a person who respects himself and his art ought to work.[6]

Rubinstein mentioned no names: it was more a case of "if the cap fits . . ." And it certainly did fit quite a few heads. Anyone could recognize the Alyabyevs and the Gurilyovs in the gibe about single-romance composers. And as for the songwriter who contends that rules of harmony are German pedantry and ends up writing an opera, could that be Dargomïzhsky, or even (perish the thought) Glinka? Then there were the amateur geniuses who made a career out of weird harmonies: there were plenty of candidates for this accolade, some of whom, like Cui and Musorgsky, had already had works played by the RMS. In a way this was the most damaging barb, since it tore at the very idea of a specifically Russian kind of originality, one that would break away from textbook rules and classical formulae and create a completely new language. For Vladimir Stasov it was altogether too much. "The fact is," he told Balakirev, "that Anton has written the piece out of jealousy of Russia and out of sheer bloody-mindedness, and to my mind it will do terrible harm. I'd like—if only it were still somehow possible—to put a stop to this or at least force those who scurry around like busy ants and try to push logs pointed out to them by the genius maestro to think what they're about."[7] His public reply had just appeared in *Severnaya pchela* (Northern Bee), and it would lay the ground for a quarrel that would infect Russian musical life for the next thirty years.[8]

Stasov's article starts with a sneer that was to become standard with the *kuchka* where Rubinstein was concerned. Rubinstein, he asserts, "is a foreigner with no understanding either of the demands of our national character or of the historical course of our art." Rubinstein was, of course, a Russian citizen by birth, but ethnically a Jew whose mother tongue was probably either Ukrainian or Yiddish. Stasov seems to be echoing the routine anti-Semitic argument (put most recently and notoriously by Wagner in his *Judaism in Music*) that Jews are acquainted with European languages and cultures only as something learned rather than innate, and are therefore incapable of anything but a superficial understanding of their inner workings. Stasov wants to argue, on the other hand, that what Rubinstein condemns as amateurism is in reality the natural Russian distaste for the stultifying effects of Western academicism. The weaker form of amateurism he complains of is no different from dilettantism anywhere; it can produce bad results or good, but in neither case does it do significant harm. The question is, would sending musicians off to conservatories and offering them civic status achieve anything better? The offer of status would surely act as a bait to all kinds of riffraff to get themselves a qualification and a better life, without achieving anything useful in terms of art. After all, Stasov suggests, "our men of letters were never given any ranks or titles, and yet a deeply national literature has grown up and thriven in our country." As for conservatories, is Rubinstein unaware of the opinion widely held in Europe that such institutions "serve only as breeding grounds for talentless people and aid the establishment in art of harmful ideas and tastes"? As a matter of fact, Russia was long ago flooded with foreign music teachers, and if academic tuition were the solution to the problems Rubinstein perceives, they would have been solved a long time ago.

It was true that Rubinstein tended to view the Russian scene from the point of view of a musician thoroughly well trained in Western orthodoxies and instinctively suspicious of the deviant behavior of Russian composers whose sole ambition seemed to be to assert their difference from everyone else at no matter what cost to their artistry. We know that he had little time for a maverick Westerner like Berlioz or even Wagner, and admired Liszt as a pianist and great human being more than as a composer. Still, with all allowance made, it is hard to take seriously Stasov's general arguments about the evils of study and the virtues of creative instinct. It might well be that in the particular cases of Stasov's close composer friends, study of the kind recommended by Rubinstein was something of an irrelevance. Rubinstein himself acknowledges that genius is an exception to which the academy has no answer. But what about all the other musicians, the performers, the writers, the teachers, even the useful minor composers? Stasov's example from literature is somewhat disingenuous, since writers can learn their trade in ordinary university courses, or simply by practicing it, while writing as a profession involves a much less complicated support apparatus, except perhaps in the theatre—and even acting, however skilled, hardly calls for the same depth of training as musical performance (or the same number of trainees). The infrastructure simply is not comparable. As for Stasov's theory that Western Europe was turning against the musical academy, this looks like an invention ad hoc. The Paris Conservatory remained the mecca for aspiring French musicians, even those like Berlioz himself or, half a century later, Debussy who affected to despise its precepts. The Vienna Conservatory would soon number Mahler and Wolf among its students, Bruckner among its teachers. And Stasov ignores the whole question of expense and language, insignificant to people of his class, but crucial to the vast, less privileged majority to which Jews like Rubinstein himself belonged.

However tendentious Stasov's criticisms, they were echoed by others. Balakirev of course was of precisely the same opinion. Musorgsky read the *Vek* article on the train to Moscow and grumbled to Balakirev especially about Rubinstein's views on amateurism.

> He says that in Russia there are not and never have been musician-artists, but there have been and are *musician-amateurs;* he bases his argument on this, that the genuine artist works for glory and money, and not for anything else, and then he clinches his argument saying that it is impossible to call anyone an artist and proclaim him a talent who has written less than three or four good things during his lifetime. What prerogatives does Rubinstein have for such narrowness glory and *money and quantity rather than quality.*[9]

This, too, distorted Rubinstein's argument, which was in essence that the amateur who has no need to compose (or perform or teach) for a living will become a dilettante who works spasmodically and never entirely masters his craft: money is not a test of quality but a necessary condition, and quantity its natural concomitant. But it is easy to see that for Musorgsky, still an uncertain pupil with vague ideas about composition but little or no technical knowledge, the article represented something of a threat. Very different was the case of Stasov's old school friend Alexander Serov, by now an experienced and outspoken music critic, but also a would-be composer who had never made any serious attempt to offer his work to the public gaze, apparently precisely because of the conditions of Russian musical life that Rubinstein was describing.

Serov remained silent about Rubinstein's *Vek* article, but instead used the opening of a new venture called the Free Music School (FMS) just over a year later as the occasion for a vicious attack on the RMS and its founder. The FMS was the brainchild of a conductor by the name of Gavriyil Lomakin, who had built his reputation as director of the private choir of Count Dmitry Sheremetev, but had had the idea of using choral training as a framework for basic music teaching. This was an utterly different concept from that of the conservatory, and may even have been suggested to Lomakin by the prominent opponents of Rubinstein specifically as a counterthrust to that institution. Balakirev, for one, was certainly involved in the plan from an early stage, lending ideas and conducting the school's orchestra. Lomakin was in charge of the choral training. In any large amateur chorus most of the singers are musically untrained enthusiasts who read music with difficulty if at all, but who love making music in the only way available to the untaught, by singing. They present an obvious opportunity for elementary instruction in music theory, sight singing, and those other ancillary terrors of childhood instrument lessons which grown-ups, on the other hand, welcome with the desperate enthusiasm of those who have discovered late the profound joys of self-improvement. Lomakin was evidently a talented choral conductor and a gifted communicator, and he quickly established the school's concerts as major musical events in the St. Petersburg calendar, and its day and evening classes as a magnet for the would-be amateur musicians of the second and third ages in Russia.

The FMS opened its doors in April 1862, and Serov seized on it at once as a pretext for a brutal onslaught against Rubinstein. His argument, in a nutshell, was that while the RMS was an essentially bogus institution imposed on the supine Russians by an incompetent but well-connected foreign virtuoso, Lomakin's choral concerts (pre-FMS) were an authentic expression of the Russian spirit, amateur only in the very best sense, "gathered together and guided by that great master of his craft, the Russian conductor, without any outside help." In the same way the new conservatory, due to open in September, was portrayed in the most lurid colors by comparison with the Free Music School.

> Russia itself cannot expect anything but positive harm from this institution, as from everything built upon lies, deceit, ignorance, narrow-mindedness and selfishness ... We, I repeat, could have seen all this, and, perhaps, we do see and realize it, but ... we doze on in our Slavonic apathy. Our "Yankels," however, are not slumbering. On the contrary, they keep all musical activity in both St. Petersburg and Moscow under continual siege. Soon, with the founding of the conservatory they desired for themselves as the future breeding-ground for talentless musical civil servants, they begin to throw their weight around in the province they have acquired in a thoroughly despotic manner, trying to crush any musical talent in Russia that does not spring from within their own Yankel ranks. Out of a hatred of all that is Russian, they are doing all they can to nip in the bud any true and natural development of Russian musical talent.[10]

Yankel is the Jewish innkeeper and money lender in Gogol's *Taras Bulba*, who, when asked to help Taras Bulba rescue his son from the

Poles, thinks first of the price on Bulba's head, but tries "to suppress within him that everlasting obsession with money which winds like a worm around the soul of every Jew." Serov is alleging that Rubinstein's motive in founding the conservatory is greed and self-interest. But the suggestion is as preposterous as the allegation that Rubinstein is hostile to "Russian talent." In reality the conservatory was so short of the necessary funds in the months before it opened that Rubinstein and his supporters had to go cap in hand to potential sponsors and were practically reduced to collecting money in the streets. During the five years of his early directorship, he contributed substantial sums of money from his own pocket to support indigent students. Meanwhile, his intensive teaching and administrative load often obstructed his own more lucrative career as a performer and composer. As for his supposed anti-Russianness, if Rubinstein had wanted to block Russian talent, he would hardly have wasted time and energy on a conservatory in the Russian capital, the interminable battles with ignorant autocrats and self-important civil servants, and the abuse to which he was subjected by a largely malevolent press.

Serov, distinguished critic though he was undoubtedly capable of being, was partly motivated where Rubinstein was concerned by jealousy, partly by plain anti-Semitism, partly by personal disappointment. The fact that Rubinstein was a Jew certainly made his successes harder to stomach. Here was this foreigner, as Serov, like Stasov, chose to regard him, starting an artistically successful concert series, composing, performing, and conducting with brilliance, founding and running a conservatory; and Serov, a leading Petersburg music critic with aspirations to compose, was not even consulted, not invited to sit on the board of either organization, and meanwhile, under the conditions of Russian musical life, could barely scrape a living from his own public activities. His bitterness is perhaps understandable. What is more striking to the modern reader is the candor with which it is expressed. There is little attempt to conceal his malice, little attempt to argue his point of view in a coherent or rational way, not the slightest pretense at objectivity or fair-mindedness. As a result, the genuine arguments against Rubinstein go largely unarticulated. He was himself an autocrat and an authoritarian. He antagonized colleagues and supporters by his insistence on getting his own way in every detail, by his bullying micromanagement and reluctance to delegate. His own music, though attractive and well written, was devoid of individuality, but served willy-nilly as a model of the kind of good practice that had previously been beyond the reach of untaught Russian composers. Rubinstein, as we saw, was no progressive; he disliked the modern trends in Western music and certainly did not encourage their emulation by his students. His touchstone was Mendelssohn, dead fifteen years and, inconveniently, a fellow Jew. It was by no means ideal in Russian eyes to have such a figure alone guiding the minds, as well as the method, of the most naturally talented and impressionable of their young musicians.

Stasov, unlike Serov, was motivated not by malice but by dogma. Personally he seems to have stayed on reasonable terms with Rubinstein, and he was certainly above Serov's crude ad hominem anti-Semitism. Calling Rubinstein a foreigner was for him a device for positioning the conservatory outside his definition of what was truly Russian, and if that involved a measure of generalized anti-Semitism, well, so be it. Just at this moment he was at the height of his enthusiasm for ancient Rus, its myths and its music. His passion for the Sadko story coincides precisely with his attack on Rubinstein and his defense of the Russian amateur. A few months later he is criticizing Glinka for his dependence on certain harmonic clichés picked up from his study with Dehn in Berlin, but praising him for his grasp of the old Russian *skazki* (tales), greater, he claims, than even Pushkin's or Lermontov's. It is precisely this passion, this desperate aesthetic partisanship, that he maintains Serov lacks: Serov's opinions are influenced by events, personal relationships, popular taste. There was some truth in this. For instance, Serov supported the FMS against the conservatory; but soon afterward, when he realized that Balakirev was involved with Lomakin, he turned against the FMS as well, having fallen out with Balakirev a year or so earlier over the latter's opinion of his opera *Judith*. This inability to detach ideology from personal hostility, common enough at all times and in all places, was endemic in the small world of sixties St. Petersburg.

Rubinstein survived as director of the conservatory until 1867, when he resigned over the refusal of the political authorities to guarantee him the degree of control he demanded, in what he still regarded as a personal fiefdom. At the same time he relinquished the directorship of the RMS. The circle were beside themselves with delight. "The Petersburg conservatory is falling apart," Musorgsky wrote to Balakirev, who was conducting in Prague. "General-of-music Tupinstein has quarrelled with the conservatory clique and intends to resign—the poor professors have lost heart and you can now see them on the streets in sackcloth, with cheap penitential cigars (in place of candles) in their teeth (hands) and their heads strewn with ashes (from these cigars)—the heart contracts when you meet them."[11] At the conservatory Rubinstein was succeeded by Nikolay Zaremba, another theorist detested by the circle. The new conductor of the RMS, however, was none other than Balakirev, an appointment that apparently had Rubinstein's support and may even have been his recommendation.

CHAPTER 7

First Steps

Modest Musorgsky's studies with Balakirev had pursued their unconventional course. On the one hand he was a dutiful, acquiescent pupil, ready to accept his master's superiority in all things musical, intellectual, and psychological, though the master was barely two years his senior. On the other hand, the need to assert his own identity was becoming more urgent. Reading between the lines of a complicatedly self-analytical letter he wrote to Balakirev in October 1859, one detects echoes of disagreements about which Musorgsky felt a certain compunction, as if they reflected unresolved confusions in his own character. They had been arguing, most recently, about Christ and the Mosaic law of "eye for eye, tooth for tooth," and evidently the discussion had become heated, since Musorgsky felt constrained to write an explanatory letter as soon as he got home in the small hours. The next day, he wrote again, assuring Balakirev of his deference while excusing his occasional fractiousness. "I must explain my conduct towards you from the very start of our acquaintance.—At first I recognized your priority; in our arguments, I saw the greater clarity and stability in your point of view. And however furious I sometimes became both with myself and with you, I had to admit the truth. From this it's clear that my self-esteem provoked me into a stubborn persistence both in argument and in my general relations with you."[1] Musorgsky is, naturally, apologizing for what the authoritarian Balakirev must have seen as a lack of due respect. But others could recognize the virtues of this trait. "How skillful he was," Vladimir Stasov's daughter Sofia Fortunato recalled, "at defending his own convictions while respecting the views of others!"[2] Later, as we shall see, he would mellow to the point where the respect would sometimes submerge the convictions altogether.

Argument, no doubt, was one thing, artistic direction quite another. Musorgsky was wearying of the scherzos and allegros that Balakirev had set him, and instead was following his example in a more constructive way. At some time in the late spring of 1858, Stasov had suggested to Balakirev that he compose incidental music for the forthcoming production of Shakespeare's *King Lear* at the Alexandrinsky Theatre; and although, despite Stasov's promptings, no commission came from the theatre and there was never in any case much hope that Balakirev would finish in time for the play's opening that December, he nevertheless worked away at the score, starting with an entr'acte before act 5, then continuing somewhat laboriously with the overture. Musorgsky must have known about this project; in a letter to Stasov from Nizhny-Novgorod in July 1858, partly about the *King Lear* idea, Balakirev specifically suggests Musorgsky as one of the people to whom their correspondence can be shown.[3] And it was precisely at this time that Musorgsky embarked on his overture to Sophocles' *Oedipus*, another famous play about a dispossessed king.

No such overture has ever surfaced, though Musorgsky had it complete in his head and played it to Stasov that same July.[4] Six months later, however, he finished a chorus which he labelled "Scene in the Temple from the tragedy *Oedipus in Athens*." This chorus survives in several versions, was eventually reused by Musorgsky in his first opera, *Salammbô,* and can reasonably be considered the earliest work that in any way—however slight—foreshadows the composer of *Boris Godunov* and *Khovanshchina*.[5] Exactly what sort of work it was meant to be, though, is by no means clear. The earliest manuscript includes stage directions, which might suggest an opera, or possibly choral music for inclusion in the play; but there is no specific correspondence with either of Sophocles' Oedipus dramas, except to the extent that Oedipus's children Antigone and Polynices appear, as in *Oedipus at Colonus*. It might simply be that, having started out with the idea of writing incidental music, Musorgsky found himself drawn into the subject quite independently, and without any practical association. The stage directions disappear from the later manuscripts, which probably reflects his vagueness about which Oedipus play the music was actually meant for. *Oedipus in Athens,* as Gerald Abraham was the first to point out, is a play by the Alexandran playwright Vladislav Ozerov (1804). Yet the second version of the chorus expressly identifies the tragedy in question as

"*Oedipus*, by Sophocles," while the third version refers only to a "Chorus of the People, from *Oedipus*." Thirteen years later Musorgsky described the work to Lyudmila Shestakova as "music for Sophocles' tragedy *Oedipus*: a chorus in the temple of the Eumenides, before the entrance of Oedipus." By that time, perhaps, it no longer mattered much either way.

Whatever its intention, two things can be said about this three-minute chorus. In style, it entirely lacks individuality; even to place it as the work of a Russian composer would be difficult if it weren't for the text in that language. It might be music from an early Verdi opera; and indeed the stage directions are more suggestive of the Old Testament paganism of, say, *Nabucco*, with its high priests, ritual sacrifices, and terror-struck crowds, than the structured, dignified intensity of Greek theatre. The people are assembling in the temple in a mood of anxious expectancy; a sacrifice is taking place. Oedipus and his children appear and "the people recoil in horror. The high priest enters holding a ritual sword and attended by two other priests. A muffled thunderclap. The people are rooted to the spot . . ." Oedipus's death is redemptive, as in Sophocles, but his blood, in the sung text, is innocent, unlike that of the play's "doer of dreadful deeds."

Conventional though it is in idiom, the chorus reveals a decided talent for dramatic portraiture in music. The crowd's anxiety is caught in the hushed, panting unison of the opening phrase and the sudden crescendo of terror; the ending is subdued and prayerful, but ruffled by a single detail—the sharpened fourth degree (B-natural instead of the routine B-flat) which robs the harmony of its natural closure and leaves suspended the final question, "Will innocent blood save us?" With an acute instinct for situation, Musorgsky avoids peroration, but ends quickly, as if to say that silence is the most powerful response to public despair. This vivid sense of theatre and dramatic psychology was something Musorgsky could hardly have learned from Balakirev, who had no more experience of music for the stage than he had himself. At the very moment that Musorgsky was completing the first version of his Oedipus chorus, in January 1859, Balakirev was struggling with his overture to *King Lear*, having already composed only the short entr'acte, material from which was providing the basis for the overture. Three more entr'actes and a processional would follow in the course of 1860 and early 1861. But the production meanwhile had long since come and gone, and Balakirev's score was destined never to be played in any theatre during his lifetime.

It is not, in any case, a stagey score. Apart from the processional, which accompanies Lear's first entrance in act 1 (somewhat eccentrically in triple time), and the music for Lear's awakening in act 4, the overture and entr'actes are all apparently curtain music, and their models—more or less overt—are mainly symphonic. Above all they are foreign: specifically German, and in one case English, or at least fantasy-English. For his own overture, Balakirev had plainly been studying the symphonies and theatre overtures of Schumann. He and Musorgsky had played them many a time four-hands, and the scores had all been available for several years. On occasion the modelling is so close, even down to the orchestration, that one might well suppose one was listening to a lost work of the Leipzig master, except that Balakirev's writing is squarer and more repetitive, more dependent on imitation and sequential repetition. Of any debt to Glinka there is little trace. Instead the perhaps surprising image of the despised Mendelssohn pops up here and there, in the shape of his incidental music to *A Midsummer Night's Dream*. For some reason—perhaps the Shakespeare connection—this work was an exception to Balakirev's usually condescending attitude to Mendelssohn. Or maybe he simply found it a convenient model for his own Shakespeare music, however different the context. At one point in the entr'acte to act 3 the debt comes close to actual borrowing, in the puckish folk tune Balakirev attaches to the Fool, which seems to derive directly from Mendelssohn's rustic tune for the mechanicals at the end of his intermezzo. It turns out, however, that the situation is rather more complicated than that.

Vladimir Stasov had the occasional habit of writing Balakirev long letters full of excitement about his latest musical discoveries. One such letter, about scalic melodies in Schumann's Piano Quintet, has already been discussed. But this was only one part of an epic communication prompted, as it happened, by Stasov's interest in the *King Lear* project. Having offered to put in his oar with the Alexandrinsky management, he starts suggesting actual themes for Balakirev's score. He copies into the letter a tune which he calls "a very ancient English song, to the music of which English peasants in Gloucestershire to this day sing some kind of ballad about the Anglo-Norman invasion of England, in an English so old as to be now almost entirely incomprehensible." Next he turns to "a clown's song for Shakespeare's *As You Like It*" that he claims "was used for this purpose in the English theatre in Shakespeare's own lifetime." The tune, which he quotes, turns out to be a close cousin to the Mendelssohn theme—so close, in fact, that a German music critic had speculated "that Mendelssohn must have got to know this song at the time of his English trip and made use of it for his *Midsummer Night's Dream.*" Finally Stasov quotes a third, more lyrical tune that he again claims (not very plausibly in this case) to have served as music for the fairies in Shakespeare's day. "I hope you like it," he prompts. This time, however, Balakirev does not take the hint, but prefers a more wistful "English theme" which he seems to have found for himself, and which he composes very beautifully into the "soft music" that accompanies Lear's awakening in Cordelia's tent in act 4 of the play.⁶

Taken as a whole, this is an accomplished and attractive score which certainly deserves to be better known. But, like Musorgsky's *Oedipus,* it is largely devoid of any discernibly Russian profile. Even when Balakirev incorporates folk material, it is not Russian, and the treatment has a generic character which stays close to the harmonic textbook with a few decorative modal attachments. In fact the curious thing about this act 4 music is how closely it anticipates the lyrical manner of the English ruralist composers of the Vaughan Williams generation and after—curious, of course, because Balakirev was writing music for an English play in a Kentish setting, albeit that of a French encampment, and because Vaughan Williams was not even born for another dozen years. This is perhaps the one real invention in the whole work. Otherwise one has to bear in mind that, notwithstanding his air of authority in the presence of his young colleagues, Balakirev was still himself only in his early twenties, with an unformed style and a limited compositional technique to go with it. His previous work, apart from a breezy (but not very Spanish) Overture on a Spanish March Theme and a scrappy, medleylike Overture on Three Russian Songs, either had been for his own instrument or had at least included the piano in a significant role. Hardly any of it was noticeably personal. An early one-movement piano concerto in F-sharp minor, composed during his first year in St. Petersburg and given a single performance at a university concert in February 1856, had subsequently vanished into a bottom drawer; a piano sonata in B-flat minor from the same period had drawn on folk material for its first movement but was otherwise heavily indebted to Liszt. Neither work came out in print in Balakirev's lifetime. Instead, his first published music was a set of twelve songs composed in the interstices of work on *King Lear,* settings of lyric poems by Lermontov, Alexey Koltsov, and the like. They are likeable but unambitious pieces in the romance style of Alyabyev and Gurilyov, a style that brings folk simplicity into the drawing room and attaches to it a certain mild emotional intensity that today might be called "attitude." At this stage Balakirev writes on the whole more interestingly for piano than for voice. He almost entirely avoids the melismatic writing that Russian composers associated with the "drawn out" style of the *protyazhnaya* which allowed the Slav passion to flow, and instead composes one note to each syllable, as in genuine folk songs and nursery songs. Not one of these works could be said to propose a new direction for Russian music. At best they announce a talented young composer who might translate the European tendencies of the forties into a solid, interesting local equivalent.

The *King Lear* Overture was played for the first time by an orchestra at a university concert in November 1859, but must have been run through before that, at Balakirev's or Cui's, in the four-hand piano transcription Musorgsky made as soon as it was finished in September. The three young composers were often together these evenings, at least during the long spring and winter months, with Stasov and other friends; and it had become a routine to present their latest pieces of work, or work in progress, for one another's approval, or disapproval, as the case might be. Sometimes we know how they reacted; often we don't. Musorgsky had played his *Oedipus* prelude at Stasov's, and reported to Balakirev (who had not been present) that Stasov had liked it.[7] Unfortunately he seems to have improvised, or played from memory, and never to have written the music down. The chorus, of course, we have, but we don't know when or if he played it, and if so, what the reaction was.[8] One evening in February 1859 there was a major event of this kind. A handwritten poster survives announcing a private performance, at the house of Cui's new parents-in-law, of Gogol's play *Tyazhbe* (*The Lawsuit*) and a one-act comic opera by Cui himself called *Sin' Mandarina* (*The Mandarin's Son*). The cast is listed. Cui's young wife, Malvina Bamberg, played the soprano lead, Yedi, the innkeeper's daughter who (as in Smetana's not-yet-written *Bartered Bride*) is being forced to marry against her will but ends up with the man she loves when he turns out to be the long-lost son of the local mandarin. Musorgsky sang the part of the mandarin, according to Stasov, "with such vitality and gaiety, with such skill and comedy of voice and diction, attitude and movement, that he made the whole company of friends and colleagues roar with laughter."[9]

It was Cui's second opera. At the time of his first meeting with Musorgsky, as we saw, he had been writing a romantic opera based on Pushkin's narrative poem *A Prisoner of the Caucasus,* and he had completed the two-act score in 1858 and submitted it for consideration by the Imperial Theatres directorate. It had even got as far as a run-through, but had then been rejected, supposedly on the grounds of inept orchestration.[10] Meanwhile, he had composed *The Mandarin's Son* to a libretto by Viktor Krïlov, a far less ambitious piece made up of musical numbers separated by spoken dialogue, in the manner of German comic Singspiels such as Weber's *Abu Hassan* or the opéras comiques of Auber. The music shows talent but, as one might expect, little individuality. Yedi and her lover, the servant Muri, sing a pretty waltz duet of a mildly Gounodesque cut (exactly a month before the Paris premiere of *Faust*); there is an effective rage song for the Osmin figure Zay-Sang, who has a contract to marry Yedi, and attractive arias for Yedi and for the mandarin, lamenting the loss of his son. But there are few musical surprises, except perhaps of the undesirable kind: where Orientalisms might be expected, for instance, Cui produces a polonaise (for the innkeeper's duet with the mandarin) and a polka (for the final quintet). The mandarin is announced, for no obvious reason, by a sprightly (and rather likable) march already heard at the start of the overture. From this *jeu d'esprit* by an untrained twenty-four-year-old one might well have predicted a successful future as a composer of light opera, if hardly as a member of a deviant avant-garde group of Russian nationalists. *A Prisoner of the Caucasus,* though, is a somewhat more interesting case.

Exactly what had prompted the twenty-two-year-old fortifications graduate to embark on a tragic opera on this scale is a matter for conjecture. Perhaps it was the example of Dargomïzhsky's *Rusalka,* also based on a narrative poem by Pushkin, which had been premiered in St. Petersburg the year before. The libretto, again apparently by Krïlov (but not credited in the published score), incorporates one or two parts of Pushkin's text verbatim and adapts other parts, while generally keeping fairly close to the original narrative outline. There is nothing supernatural or magical in the poem, unlike in *Rusalka;* but instead Pushkin, who was on holiday in the Crimea (and much the same age as Cui) when he wrote it, richly evokes the atmosphere of those parts of the southern empire where ethnic Russia confronts the alien and by implication barbarian cultures of the annexed territories. The setting is a Circassian camp in the Caucasus, at a time of tribal warfare against the neighboring Cossacks. A Russian prisoner is dragged in amid wild rejoicing, exhausted and barely conscious. In the course of the poem he is befriended by a beautiful Circassian girl, who brings him food and drink and nurses him back to health. She eventually declares her love for him, but he tells her he is in love with a Russian girl in his home country and cannot reciprocate her feelings. In the end, she engineers his escape; suddenly he implores her to leave with him; she refuses, then seems to agree; but then, as he swims across the river to freedom, she throws herself into it and drowns.

For Cui, one big problem with this tale was the need to flesh out the situation and the main characters and invent new ones to populate his stage. He gives the girl a name, Fatima; a companion called Mar'yam; a father, Kazenbek; and a worthy but uncomprehending princely betrothed, Abubekar. We learn rather little about the Prisoner, who alone remains nameless, and his Russian girl is mentioned only in the final duet with Fatima, so that Fatima's reluctance to escape with him is hard to understand. Nevertheless, in the opera she does not do so, but stays behind and, when confronted by the enraged Circassians, stabs herself.[11] Not surprisingly, Cui was unable really to capture the poem's atmosphere, which is to some extent a function of Pushkin's ironic detachment from his characters but intense involvement in the world in which they live and move: the beauty of the Caucasian landscape, the tedium of the Prisoner's life, the daily activities of his captors. The libretto is more or less a conventional East-meets-West melodrama, not very well motivated, and with only brief glimmers of exotic local color. The characters are wooden, the musical design stereotyped. It sets no agenda; its "Orientalism" is limited to a few augmented seconds and fourths and some stamping choral rhythms; its realism is pasteboard; its Russianness negligible. In its original two-act form it must also have seemed pretty short-winded, proceeding in a rush from the capture of the Prisoner halfway through act 1 to Fatima's wedding ceremony and her final scene with him in the second act. In 1881 Cui added an entirely new second act and the Circassian dances in what thus became act 3, and at the same time he revised the whole score, above all the orchestration, for publication, so that a clear picture of his achievement of 1857 is now by no means easy to make out.

All the same, for a first opera it must have shown talent. Today it is more or less routine to write Cui off as a rank amateur who, moreover, lacked the individual genius of his circle colleagues. But this judgment, like many of its kind, is nearly always made in convenient ignorance of his work. *A Prisoner of the Caucasus* is certainly not a score of strong personality (how could it be?), nor is it to any measurable extent innovative or even eccentric, in the way that Glinka's operas are innovative and eccentric. In fact, like *King Lear,* it is surprisingly free of Glinka-isms of any kind. One recurring motif for Kazenbek makes prominent melodic use of the flattened sixth degree, a quasi-exoticism Glinka cultivated (Cui's 1881 second act has more of this kind of thing). But in general the music's virtues are more discreet. In style and method it belongs broadly to the tradition of German romantic opera, transferred to a sub-Russian locale. Fatima has a highly singable D-minor aria reject-ing her arranged marriage, with a brief cabaletta ending entirely from Italian stock; and for the newly captured Prisoner (tenor) there is an eloquent lament preceded by a particularly attractive F-sharp-major quartet in which he bids farewell to his freedom in a musical idiom perhaps a shade too redolent of opera buffa but unquestionably tune-ful, even hummable, in its way. In fact Cui's lyrical writing for the voice is always one of his strong suits. His phrasing, it's true, is square, and usually at the service of a strict verse meter modelled on, when not actually taken from, Pushkin, who here—as elsewhere—uses meter partly as a distancing device, something not readily available to a com-poser of tragic opera. One might describe Cui's work as a salon tragedy: agreeable, well made, at times touching, but by no means equal to the psychological and emotional range of its source. To be fair, it was nei-ther the first nor the last Pushkin opera of which that would be true.

Taking these various dramatic or quasi-dramatic works of the young Russian proto-radicals as a whole, the striking thing is how lit-tle they deviate from the best Western models. That they show talent is beyond question. They even, on a certain level, show expertise; at least, the conventional image of rank incompetence is not borne out by these scores, any more than by countless other works of twenty- and twenty-two-year-old composers not famous for their lifelong ineptitude. A similar picture emerges from the smaller, less ambitious works of the time. Between 1857 and 1861 Cui composed a number of songs—a set of three romances, op. 3, and a set of six, op. 5, settings of Lermontov, Pushkin, Krïlov, and others. Like much in the operas, they are sensitively written for voice, in a style that recalls the sim-pler lieder of Schumann, rhythmically and harmonically unambitious, mainly syllabic settings that stay close to the poetic meter and seldom venture anything strikingly individual, either in the word setting or in the accompaniment. This is music that serves an amateur market, and serves it well enough: neither inept nor in the least degree ground-breaking, not even noticeably Russian, in the sense that Balakirev's songs are Russian.

Musorgsky, too, was spending some of his time composing songs that reflect an acquaintance with the German repertoire. But some-thing about these pieces, few though they are, hints at wider musical horizons and a particular gift for visualizing situations, even through mediocre poetry. He was still making keyboard transcriptions for Balakirev: the andante from Beethoven's C-major "Razumovsky" Quartet; his teacher's *King Lear* Overture. And he was writing piano pieces of his own, promisingly titled ("Ein Kinderscherz" and "Impromptu passionné"), but little better than salon music in effect. But with words at his disposal, his music is starting to respond in an altogether more vivid way. Koltsov's "Veselïy chas" ("The Happy Hour") is set as a rough drinking song, perhaps unremarkable as music, but strikingly graphic in its imagery: the clinking glasses in the piano introduction; the *subito fortissimo* on "Give the singing all you've got, lads" ("Gromkiye pesni gran'te, druz'ya"); and not least the bibulous profundity of the "tomorrow we die" middle section, in the mellow key of the flat submediant (F major in the key of A). His only other 1859 song, "The Leaves Rustled Sadly" ("List'ya shumeli unïlo"), is arresting musically as well as pictorially. In Alexey Pleshcheyev's poem, an unnamed freedom fighter is being buried, mourned only by the leaves. (Pleshcheyev was a member of the Petrashevsky group, and spent ten years in exile in Siberia.)[12] Once again, Musorgsky pictures the scene: the gloomy oak wood, lit only by the moon; the exaggerated weight of the foliage; the somber, elegiac cantilena of the bass voice. Musically, there is not much here that Musorgsky could not have found in, say, late Schubert. But the intensity of the imagery is Russian: not only the dark, remorseless lyricism of the vocal writing, but the heavy, tocsin-like piano part, which tolls on at the end, long after the singer has departed with the other dutiful mourners. This is not yet realism in Chernïshevsky's sense, or in the sense that Musorgsky himself came to understand it. The motivic approach to scene painting is essentially German. But the painterly response, if not yet original in musical terms, is individual and to some extent prophetic.

A young composer who could write as well as this (he was still only twenty) might have been expected to advance rapidly toward more substantial and original work. But it was precisely at this point that the fault lines in Musorgsky's character, aggravated by the circumstances of his life, began seriously to interfere with his composing. His relations with Balakirev, as we saw, were becoming a problem. From what we know of his work during 1860 and 1861, we can deduce that Balakirev was still leaning on him to practice instrumental writing and orchestration. He was (or at least said he was) finishing off the F-sharp-minor piano sonata begun in 1859 but apparently now lost without trace. He composed an allegro in C major for piano duet, imagining—as Balakirev reported in December 1860 to their pianist friend Avdotya Zakharina—that "he has already accomplished a great deal for art in general and Russian art in particular."[13] The point is that Musorgsky had just dutifully announced to his teacher his intention "to work at voice leading [part writing], beginning with three voices; and I shall achieve something worthwhile and to the point; it's a good stimulant for me to think that there's something nonsensical about my harmony, which must not be and that's that."[14] Soon, on a visit to Moscow in January 1861, he is composing a symphony in D, and by the sixteenth he is telling Balakirev that the scherzo—"a big symphonic one"—is finished apart from the second trio (even though, in his December letter, he has pleaded to be let off writing scherzos). An andante in F-sharp minor is planned. The symphony is still hanging around in 1862, but not a note of it survives, apart perhaps from a four-bar fragment in B major (the supposed key of the scherzo), which Musorgsky wrote into his 13 January letter to Balakirev but did not specifically identify.

If these were Musorgsky's only blanks in the early sixties, one might be tempted to blame Balakirev for bullying him into didactic projects that did not suit him, taking advantage of his compliant nature and tendency to self-denigration. But there is a good deal else besides. During the summer of 1860 he composed a pair of choruses for his *Oedipus* project and began to plan what he called "a whole act on Bald Mountain (from Mengden's drama *The Witch*), a witches' sabbath, separate episodes of sorcerers, a solemn march for all this nastiness, a finale—the glorification of the sabbath which with Mengden is embodied in the master of the whole festival on Bald Mountain." He also wrote a vocal quartet called "Lord of My Days." These are obviously suggestive projects, which probably had nothing to do with Balakirev. But as far as is known for certain, not a note of them survives, either. Gerald Abraham speculated, on good intuition but without hard evidence, that the *Oedipus* choruses subsequently found their way, along with the temple scene, into *Salammbô*. As for the Bald Mountain, the idea in all its detail is so close to what would eventually be Musorgsky's most brilliant orchestral score that it is hard to think of it as an essentially different piece. It looks, though, as if this would have been a vocal work, perhaps even incidental or staged music.[15] In fact the subject—or something very like it—had come up two Christmases before, in a discussion between the Musorgsky brothers, Balakirev, and one or two others, on the possibility of turning Gogol's story "St. John's Eve" into a three-act opera.[16] As before, the visualization is striking, almost as if Musorgsky found it easy to picture the kind of work he would like to write, but as yet had no idea how to write it. A programmatic model for the idea might have been the finale of Berlioz's *Symphonie fantastique*.

But that would hardly have been a useful model musically for a Russian composer of Musorgsky's inexperience.

For the best part of three years, then, he wrote hardly anything of significance, and almost nothing that he was prepared to keep and put his name to. In 1862 he composed literally nothing apart from whatever he may have added to the ill-fated symphony, together with a piano-duet transcription of Beethoven's op. 130 string quartet. He even withheld the *Oedipus* temple chorus from a possible performance by the RMS in the winter of 1860–61, telling Dmitry Stasov, who was on the RMS committee, that the chorus was too quick and short to stand alone, and boasting to Balakirev that he had thereby cocked a snook at Rubinstein. It appears that he was nervous about the effect of the piece, and unwilling to expose himself to the ridicule of his political enemies. But this fear, if fear it was, was merely one manifestation of a general malaise that was evidently infecting every aspect of his life.

Musorgsky, as we saw in chapter 3, had been experiencing the perturbations of what he himself analyzed in retrospect as delayed adolescence. In his letters to Balakirev he describes the symptoms with disconcerting candor. But he is vague about the causes, perhaps because, like most adolescents, he is not sure what they are. Modern scholarship has been less reticent. Musorgsky has been flatly labelled sexless, homosexual, masochistic, and even, rather disappointingly, a discreet heterosexual. There is in fact very little evidence for any of these diagnoses.[17] Of homosexuality in his known behavior there is not the slightest trace, and one can only attribute this assumption to a certain modern tendency to regard sexual discretion as more or less conclusive evidence of what one is no longer allowed to call deviance. By far the most probable thing is that he was an uneasy heterosexual nervous of physical commitment. He seems to have been attractive to young women, but tended to erect a wall of polite badinage against any threat of direct emotional involvement in that quarter. He was clearly more comfortable with older, preferably married women, and the resulting sense of security perhaps occasionally landed him in mildly disturbing situations before he had time to put up the necessary barriers.

Something of the sort happened in the late spring and early summer of 1859, when he spent several weeks of May and June at the manorial estate of his friend Stepan Shilovsky and his wife, Maria, at the village of Glebovo, near Voskresensk on the Moscow River. Maria Shilovskaya was an amateur singer who had Dargomïzhsky as a teacher and liked to invite musicians for extended stays on the estate. Before her marriage, according to the editors of *The Musorgsky Reader,* she had pursued "a lurid career as salon singer, during which she dabbled in composing and exercised other less specialised talents which had earned her the distinction of 'the most charming woman of her time.' "[18] The implication, of course, is that she fluttered her eyelashes at Musorgsky and that he, nine years younger and vastly less experienced, duly succumbed. In fact no such conclusion can be drawn even from between the lines of his correspondence of the time. In a letter to Balakirev he describes his journey to Glebovo and he paints a vivid but unnuanced picture of the place itself. The house is luxuriously situated on a hill overlooking the home farm and surrounded by a kind of English park, "all very splendid, as you'd expect, since Shilovsky is stinking rich." "The host and hostess are very nice," he adds, "and Shilovskaya is entirely attentive to her guests."[19] There is a house choir rehearsing Bortnyansky and choruses from *A Life for the Tsar,* a performance of which is planned with Shilovskaya as (presumably) Antonida and Konstantin Lyadov conducting. Musorgsky is going to work with them.

Did Shilovskaya really set her cap at him, now or later, and did he respond? (The reverse interpretation, one feels, would be inconceivable.) The evidence is circumstantial, to put it mildly. Less than two years later, Vladimir Stasov wrote to Balakirev asking him to persuade Musorgsky "to go straight to Maria, fall on his knees before her, weep, tear his hair, climb inside her skirt, do something nice to her: only force her *by hook or by crook* to summon [Konstantin] Lyadov and compel him to give the third entr'acte of *Ruslan.*"[20] This assumption of influence is in a curious way more suggestive than the actual reality, since it implies a reputation. Musorgsky himself had just written to Balakirev, reminding him that "I was once stuck, not musically, but morally—I crawled out; but you'll learn one day how things were—if ever our conversation should touch on it—it had something to do with a woman."[21] Was that woman Maria Shilovskaya? And was Musorgsky thinking of her when, years later, he compared the viselike grip of Darwin's *Descent of Man* (which he was reading at the time) to that of a passionate lover?

> If a strong, passionate and loving woman clasps the man she loves firmly in her arms, he will recognize violence, but will have no wish to tear himself away from her embrace, because this violence is "over the border of bliss," because from this violence, "youthful blood bursts into flame." I am not ashamed of the comparison: however much you may twist and flirt with the truth, anyone who has experienced love in all its

freedom and power has *lived* and will remember that *he has lived beautifully,* and will not cast a shadow on his former bliss.[22]

The next summer (1860) Musorgsky was again at Glebovo, and for a much longer stay. He arrived there at the end of May, travelling by train via Moscow, and he seems not to have left until mid-September. It was on this visit that he tinkered with the Mengden project and composed the extra choruses for *Oedipus.* But otherwise we know very little about how he passed the long Russian summer in the quiet, dull Muscovy countryside. Probably he also composed the romance "Shto vam slova lyubvi?" (words by Alexander Ammosov), which is dedicated to Maria Shilovskaya.

> *What are words of love to you?*
> *You call it delirium.*
> *What are my tears to you?*
> *Tears, too, you won't understand.*

The music begins in agitation, but switches halfway through to a mood of dreamy reflection, with repeated chords reminiscent of the Schumann of "Die Lotosblume." The poet now addresses a third party: "I love her alone, as I love my life, as I love the light." Back in St. Petersburg, Musorgsky reported to Balakirev that he had been ill for most of the summer, "so that I could devote myself to music only at brief intervals; most of the time from May to August my brain was weak and highly irritated." Quite often throughout his life he refers to nervous ailments, without being clear that any clinical condition is involved. On this particular occasion it would be easy to interpret his mental state as an inability to concentrate on his work because of some emotional or even sexual distraction. But in the end this can only be speculation.

Whatever the cause of Musorgsky's mental troubles, they were taken seriously by his friends. Eventually Balakirev wrote him a heart-to-heart letter chiding him for preferring the company of what Balakirev called "limited personalities."[23] Musorgsky was in Moscow at the time, staying at the Shilovskys' house in the Degtyarni *pereulok,* but probably in their absence, since he was sharing it with a friend called Shchukarov, who seems to be one of the characters Balakirev had complained about. He had evidently not spared Musorgsky's feelings; "heated and hasty" is how Musorgsky describes his letter. "As to my being swamped," he replies, "and having to be pulled out of the swamp, I say only this—if I have talent—I will not be swamped as long as my brain is stimulated." But another passage sounds a more ominous note: "As to my preference for *limited personalities,* that calls for only one answer: 'tell me who you love, and I'll tell you who you are.' And so logically—I, too, must be limited." His friends, he insists, are cultivated and intelligent. But then so too were the friends who, one day, would bring him down.

CHAPTER 8

The Third Rome:
The Clerk and the Midshipman

On his way home from Glebovo in June 1859, Musorgsky had paid a brief visit to Moscow. It was his first acquaintance with the ancient capital, which his friend Nikolay Borozdin, an amateur composer and legal clerk who lived there, had nicknamed Jericho in honor of its sheer antiquity. On a visit a year before, Balakirev had described the city in lyrical terms. "In my soul," he had told Stasov, "were born many beautiful feelings which I can't describe to you. Here I felt with pride that I am *Russian*."[1] Now Musorgsky seems to echo Balakirev's letter, as if Stasov had shown it to him. "Even as I approached Jericho," he writes, "I noticed its originality, how its belfries and cupolas reeked of antiquity, ... The wonderful Kremlin—I approached it with involuntary reverence. Red Square, in which have happened so many remarkable and chaotic events ... this is holy antiquity ... I climbed the bell tower of Ivan the Great with its wonderful view of Moscow ..." But he is touched by the squalor as much as by the splendor: "Such beggars and swindlers as the world has never brought forth ... In general Moscow transported me to another world—an ancient world (a world which, though filthy, for some reason has an agreeable effect on me) ... You know that I was a cosmopolite, but now there's some kind of rebirth: everything Russian is close to me."[2]

Moscow was the third Rome, the self-styled spiritual capital of Orthodoxy ever since the fall of Constantinople in 1453. Everything that Peter the Great had tried to root out of Russian life had its home here: the power of the church, the backwardness and barbarity, the solemn, slow existence, the cultural provincialism, the whiff of Asia and the East. It was the deliberate burning of old wooden Moscow that had destroyed Napoleon. To a large extent Moscow was and remained the deepest symbol of Russianness, even for those whose lives were fixed in St. Petersburg. "There is a part of Moscow in us all," Pushkin's friend Filipp Vigel wrote, "and no Russian can expunge Moscow."[3] Above all, Moscow was the spiritual home of the Slavophiles, the group of philosophers who rejected the view that Russia's salvation lay in modelling itself industrially, economically, and culturally on Western Europe, and argued that, on the contrary, she should cleave to her own traditions—the traditions of the Orthodox Church and ancient rural institutions such as the village-commune, the *obshchina*. In Moscow, the Slavophiles felt closer to the Russian soil, closer to the collective, conciliar spirit that their leading thinker, Alexis Khomyakov, had labelled *sobornost*, and remote from the materialism, rationalism, and individualism that they perceived in Western society and that for Russians was symbolized by West-facing, Western-planned St. Petersburg.

Stasov's interest in old Russia had been emerging gradually in recent years. Much later, when he was writing a history of the artistic movements of the time, he wanted to give the impression that by the early 1860s "an independent and original, profoundly national school had already come into being with us."[4] In support of this contention, however, he could only cite a motley repertoire of early works—Balakirev's Overture on Three Russian Themes and his *King Lear* Overture, his and Cui's early songs, the scherzos of Musorgsky and Cui that Rubinstein conducted in the first season of the RMS: a collection neither independent nor profound, and mostly devoid of any recognizably "national" character at all.

In truth, the concept of a Russian school was still in its infancy in 1860. Glinka's operas hardly amounted to a definition of anything so specific, and in any case there was disagreement as to precisely what they represented; Stasov himself had difficulty making up his mind about them. In his Glinka biography, written in some haste immediately after the composer's death in 1857, he played down the national element in *A Life for the Tsar*. In the thirties, he argued,

> it was thought that in order to invest his work with national character, an artist had to put into it, as in a new setting, something that already existed among the people, born of their spontaneous creative instinct. People wanted and demanded the impossible: the amalgamation of old materials with a new art; they forgot that the old materials belonged to

their own specific time and that a new art that had already succeeded in working out its own forms, also needed new materials.[5]

It would be hard to conceive a more thorough refutation of his later view that "in order to be national, in order to express the spirit and soul of a nation, [music] must be directed at the very roots of the people's life." "Russian musicians," he now insisted, "are no longer outsiders, but are 'at home' in that world from which our folk melodies, indeed all Slavic melodies, emerged into the light, and therefore they are able to use them freely, to have them appear in all the truth and strength of their coloring, personality, and character. Glinka's achievement is now widely known and recognized. He blazed a new trail; he created a national opera in forms that exist nowhere else in Europe."[6] But this trail was barely perceptible in 1860. What else was there? Dargomïzhsky's *Esmeralda* had been a grand opera in the manner of Meyerbeer, and had in any case vanished without trace. His *Rusalka* had folk elements and some novel word treatments, but had made few waves; and since then he had sulked and completed nothing for the stage.

In Balakirev's and Musorgsky's response to Moscow one senses, rather, a new revelation, something that on a certain level took them by surprise. In Balakirev's case, at least, it went with his current reading. Like many educated Russians in the late 1850s, he was engrossed in the volumes of Sergey Solovyov's vast *History of Russia from the Most Ancient Times,* which had been coming out annually since 1851. Solovyov, in his turn, was acting in part as a corrective and expansion of Nikolay Karamzin's incomplete twelve-volume history, with its emphasis on great men as the driving force. Balakirev and Stasov had been discussing Solovyov, in particular an article of his, "The Manners, Customs, and Religion of the Slavs, Especially in the East, in Pagan Times," just before Balakirev embarked on a trip down the Volga collecting folk songs in the summer of 1860. The idea that Russia's true nature was to be sought in the study of its people and their way of life was coming into focus and taking on a new intensity just at a time when the need for a special artistic direction was becoming more and more urgent.

Russian historiography before Karamzin had been effectively nonexistent, and his work made an electrifying impact on his fellow countrymen's sense of themselves as Russians, just when that consciousness was at its most suggestive after the defeat of Napoleon in 1812. Karamzin was to a significant degree an "official" historian. He saw the history of Russia substantially in terms of the tsars; but at the same time he assembled a huge store of background information about the Russian people, so that the idea of an ethnographically based history was already latent in his work, even when not fully realized. Under the conditions of autocracy that survived at least until the death of Nicholas I in 1855, the idea that historians might take an interest in the ordinary life of the peasantry inevitably took on a political coloring. So when intellectuals like Balakirev and Stasov discussed the work of Solovyov or his historian contemporaries Nikolay Kostomarov or Konstantin Kavelin, they would end up talking about the historical role of the people, their political institutions, and, naturally enough, their art. In Kostomarov, for example, they encountered the distinction between what he called the "Two Russian Nationalities," the Great Russians and the Little Russians (Ukrainians), and the parallel distinction between what Kostomarov saw as the centralizing, statist instincts of the Russians and the tendency of the Ukrainians toward local institutions, the *veche* (or popular assembly), and the supposedly democratic structure of the federated cities of Kievan Rus.

Perhaps it was some such impulse that sent Balakirev along the Volga from Nizhny-Novgorod in May 1860, the first of several summer trips that led eventually to the publication of a collection of folk-song arrangements in 1866. We know very little about this Volga journey, because his letters have all disappeared. But his descriptions of later (noncollecting) trips up the Don from Rostov (1862) and to the Caucasus (1863) suggest that he not only persuaded the locals to sing to him, but took a general interest in their way of life. "I went to the bazaar," he wrote to his friend Alexander Arseniev from Rostov, "sought out Ukrainians and chatted with them . . . I tried hard to find out about their lives; in general I wanted to get inside them and discover what this people is like."[7] One pictures the young composer, notebook in hand, asking fashionable sixties questions about the local produce, agricultural methods and forms of distribution, the types of local government, the means of transport. This would obviously have called for a friendly, open manner. But privately Balakirev regarded a lot of what he saw with a certain metropolitan distaste. "What a shame," he tells Stasov, " that this huge expanse of the very best soil, with the Don, belongs to such abominations as the Don Cossacks, the nastiest of the Great Russian tribes." "They are even," he adds provocatively, "mostly Old Believers." He compares the "bright, healthy minds" of the Russians, their "multi-talentedness" and "sense of honor" with the laziness and stupidity of the Ukrainians.[8] It was a judgment all too easily reversed. A year or two later the Russians have become "inept (if clever), ugly, dishonorable, even base." "I looked at them," he admits, "through rose-tinted spectacles."[9] But in truth Balakirev was not a natural lover of humanity, and the liberal, man-of-the-sixties image very soon fell away.

Balakirev was by no means the first collector to sally forth into the Russian countryside, note down rustic songs from the mouths of the peasantry, and publish the result in a performable edition with piano accompaniment. In fact the melodies in his Overture on Three Russian Themes had all been taken from published collections, only one of them recent. In this respect, of course, the Russians were not essentially different from Western collectors in the late eighteenth and early nineteenth centuries, who published so-called folk songs in the form of drawing-room songs which combined the ethnic characteristics of the original tunes with elements of contemporary urban high-art style. Recent scholarship has shown how this style sometimes fed back into folk practice, to the extent that the ethnic and the urban became almost impossible to disentangle.[10] In the 1860s, however, such transcriptions were starting to be regarded as corruptions of the "pure" music of the ancient Russian peasantry, and it may well be that Balakirev, fresh from his experience of old Moscow and his reading of Solovyov, went collecting at least partly with the idea of rediscovering the "natural" idiom of this music. As we shall see, his own method of transcription certainly suggests some such intention, however remote the settings may still be from anything that could be called authentic folk music.

Neither Balakirev's nor, for that matter, Stasov's enthusiasm for the music and mythology of old Russia had much to do with liberal politics, though the two were easily confused. The Slavophiles had also been interested in such things, and their politics were in most respects profoundly conservative.[11] They had rejected the rationalism and individualism of the West, which, they argued, had undermined the spiritual integrity of society, damaged Russia (through the Petrine reforms), and broken the connection between modern life and native culture and tradition. They despised the Roman Catholic Church for what they saw as its argumentative, syllogistic character and the constant upheavals this engendered; and they cleaved to the Orthodox Church as a guarantor of moral, spiritual, and intellectual stability within an autocratic monarchy. Of course there was a good deal of fantasy in all this. They managed to overlook the repressive aspects of such a society, even though they were surrounded and occasionally victimized by them. They talked about the "natural, untrammelled development of Russian society under the aegis of the Orthodox Church,"[12] and they ventilated their ideas about the empire's administrative structure by dividing it notionally between what they called "state business" (*gos-udarego delo*) and "land business" (*zemskoye delo*).

It was at this point that they in some measure dovetailed with liberal thinking. The agency for *zemskoye delo* was the *obshchina,* the ancient institution of the village commune, which acted as a local collective, organizing the distribution of land, the payment of taxes, and other essential matters of village administration. While the Slavophiles loved the *obshchina* as a symbol of Russian social stability and its unbroken connection with the soil, the liberals and proto-socialists from the Westernizing side were also drawn to it as a model for collective landholding which cut out the bourgeois concept of private ownership and profit. The most trenchant expression of this overlap was given by Alexander Herzen, an early socialist thinker twice exiled for his political views and eventually self-exiled to Paris and then (from 1852) London, where he founded and edited a left-wing journal called *The Bell* (*Kolokol*). Of all Russian socialists, Herzen was the most humane and the most critical, in the best sense, in his thinking. He had been on friendly terms with Slavophiles like Khomyakov and Konstantin Aksakov, but he was uncompromising in his analysis of their philosophy. As he wrote in his autobiography:

> They took the return to the people in a very crude sense ... accepting the people as something complete and finished. They supposed that sharing the prejudices of the people meant being at one with them, that it was a great act of humility to sacrifice their own reason instead of developing reason in the people ... To go back to the village, to the workmen's guild, to the meeting of the *mir* [*obshchina*], to the Cossack system is a different matter; but we must return to them not in order that they may be fixed fast in immovable Asiatic crystallisations, but to develop and set free the elements on which they were founded, to purify them from all that is extraneous and distorting, from the proud flesh with which they are overgrown.

"The Novgorod bell," he added, "which used to call the citizens to their ancient moot was merely melted into a cannon by Peter but had been taken down from the belfry by Ivan III; serfdom was only confirmed by the census under Peter but had been introduced by Boris Godunov ..."[13] Not all these distortions of the spirit were the fault of Peter the Great.

Stasov was and remained an admirer of Herzen, a fact that argues—without quite proving—watertight liberal credentials. The

difficulty here, once more, is the Soviet habit of exaggerating the socialist leanings of its cultural heroes, together with a not unnatural tendency of the aging Stasov to play up his past relations with great men.
So, for instance, A. K. Lebedev and A. V. Solodovnikov, writing in the
1970s, lay some emphasis on the mutual regard of the two writers at
the time of their meeting in London in 1862, whereas Stasov's niece
Varvara Komarova-Stasova, in the long and detailed biography of her
uncle that she published under the nom de plume Vladimir Karenin in
1927, before Stalin got his claws into Russian intellectual life, mentions
Herzen only in passing.[14] Arriving in London in early August, Stasov
wrote to Herzen proposing to call on him, and Herzen replied, warmly
inviting him, but warning that he and therefore his visitors were under
tsarist surveillance. Stasov nevertheless visited Herzen on two or three
occasions, they talked about art and society, and on his way back to
St. Petersburg Stasov was duly searched at the Russian border and his
books and papers confiscated. "At that time," he told his niece, "I was
as good as in love with him . . . [and] Herzen was also very fond of me
and told me that he *valued me highly.*"[15] Yet one searches Herzen's collected writings in vain for significant references to Stasov, and he is not
mentioned at all in the seven volumes of Herzen's autobiography. "The
friendship," the Herzen scholar Aileen Kelly suggested to me, "seems
to have been largely in Stasov's mind."[16]

Slavophiles and Westernizers alike, though for different reasons,
yearned for the abolition of serfdom, and at last, on 19 February 1861,
it came. For landless gentry such as Stasov, Balakirev, and Cui, the
practical consequences of emancipation, in the short term at least,
were negligible; it merely pleased them on emotional and intellectual
grounds. But for Modest Musorgsky the effects were more serious. His
father had died in 1853, but his mother was still living on the family estate at Karevo, and he and his brother were entirely dependent
on the income it produced. By the emancipation decree, all serfs were
immediately freed from the authority of their landlords, which meant
that they could no longer be forced to work the land, two-thirds of
which remained the property of the estate, while the remaining third
was made available to the former serfs for purchase backed by government mortgages of eighty percent of the value. As regards ready money,
this was all very well. But from the point of view of management it was
nothing short of a disaster. Henceforth all labor had to be paid for and
all rents accounted for. The kinds of bookkeeping chaos satirized by

Gogol in *Dead Souls* would from now on lead to actual destitution, and yet many—perhaps most—landlords had not the slightest idea how to organize such matters on a coherent basis. And it seems unlikely that the peasantry did much to help by, for instance, volunteering prompt payment or efficient, productive labor.

Musorgsky's life suddenly became a round of meetings to do with the need to put Karevo on a sound business footing. The summer of 1861 was almost certainly spent there. On several occasions in the spring and autumn, he was forced to cancel social plans because of what he called "our business." Most of the donkey work was done by his elder brother, but Modest was unable to escape altogether, as is apparent from his letters of two summers later from the nearby city of Toropetz, where he was helping in the final settlement at the end of the two-year transition period. "I had thought to busy myself with worthwhile things," he writes to Cui,

> but here one conducts investigations, makes enquiries, and trails around various police and nonpolice authorities . . . And what land-owners we have here or in our place! what planters! They're happy at the opening of a club in town, and practically every day they assemble there to *make a racket.* It starts with *speeches, statements to the Gentlemen of the Nobility,* and nearly always ends practically in blows, with the police called . . . And all this happens at assemblies of gentry, and you meet these people every day, and every day they pester you with tears in their eyes about their *lost rights,* their *utter ruin* . . . moanings and groanings and scandal![17]

Meanwhile, he informs Balakirev that "the peasants are much more capable than the landlords in the running of self-government—at meetings they bring their business straight to the point, and *in their own way* discuss their interests efficiently; but the landowners quarrel at their meetings, and take offence—and the purpose and business of the meeting go out of the window."[18]

Filaret Musorgsky was not one of the quarrelsome landlords, but seems to have acted in a calm and fair-minded way toward his former serfs. Even before emancipation he and Modest had freed one of their house serfs, with his entire family, and given them twenty-two *desyatin* (about sixty acres) of good quality land rent-free.[19] Filaret was clearly a good manager, but even so it was almost impossible for him and his brother to obey the law and emerge with sufficient means to maintain themselves and their mother in the kind of comfort previously taken for granted by landowning gentry of their class. "My affairs are bad," Modest wrote to Balakirev from Toropetz, "very bad!"

> I, great sinner that I am, run around the estates, and come gradually to the conclusion that it's impossible to live on the income from *those people,* and that one must definitely enter on a career in the service, in order to feed and pamper my delicate body. This I shall do in Peter[sburg], that is, I'll enter the service.[20]

Early in December 1863 he duly started work as a clerk in the Central Engineering Department of the Ministry of Communications, with the civil rank of *kollezhskiy sekretar'* (collegiate secretary); and for the rest of his life, with brief interruptions, until his final dismissal from the service sixteen years later, the composer of *Boris Godunov* occupied a more or less lowly desk in this or that ministry department, filling in forms, checking inventories, filing documents, writing out reports. Admittedly the civil-service regime was reasonably relaxed, partly no doubt because, since the centralized imperial system offered few if any alternative outlets for intelligent enterprise, it was heavily overstaffed with indigent intellectuals and dispossessed landowners like Musorgsky himself. Such individuals were not expected to show initiative or enterprise, but had merely to put in a daily appearance, maneuver a pen around pieces of paper for a set number of hours, and resist the temptation to make themselves disagreeable. Curiously enough, Musorgsky seems to have managed this deadening combination fairly well, perhaps aided by the goodwill of superiors aware of his unusual talent. But it certainly did not help him in the troublesome task of composing music with a still undeveloped technique, and it did not protect him from the ravages of a temperament too easily distracted—as he himself had admitted—from the lonely terrors of creative work by night.

One Sunday evening in the autumn of 1861 a seventeen-year-old naval cadet appeared for the first time at a soirée in Balakirev's apartment, introduced by his piano teacher, the French pianist Théodore Canille. The cadet's name was Nikolay Rimsky-Korsakov, and he brought with him—apparently on Canille's insistence—some pieces of music he himself had composed. There were piano pieces, a scherzo and a nocturne, and there was something else that aroused Balakirev's pedagogical enthusiasm: fragments of a symphony in E-flat minor that Rimsky-Korsakov had been writing under Canille's tutelage. About the piano pieces we know nothing; they have not survived. But the symphony exists, and thanks to Rimsky-Korsakov's own memoirs we know quite a lot about its origins and how it evolved from the fragments that the young composer took with him to the Balakirev soirée. The key itself is puzzling. Why compose your first orchestral work in so remote a key, a key with six flats, hard for most instruments to play, hard to write, hard to read? The curious thing is that it was Balakirev who liked extreme flat-side and sharp-side keys and urged them on his pupils. Both his own piano sonatas are in B-flat minor (five flats), and a disproportionate number of his smaller piano pieces inhabit remote tonalities at one or other end of the spectrum. On the other hand, perhaps significantly, his own First Symphony, composed in the mid-sixties, is in C major (no flats or sharps) and his (late) Second Symphony is in D minor (one flat). As a brilliant pianist, Balakirev could feel the "color" of the black notes under his fingers, but he was enough of a practical musician not to wish such preferences onto an orchestra.

The young cadet was neither a brilliant pianist nor an experienced practical musician. We have his own word for this. Under Canille his keyboard technique had advanced only somewhat laboriously, and as for any compositional method, that was a complete blank. "I had no idea about counterpoint; in harmony I did not even know the fundamental rule of leading the seventh downward, did not know the names of the chords. Gathering a few fragments from the Glinka, Beethoven, and Schumann that I played, I concocted, with considerable labor, something thin and elementary."[21] Undeterred by such trivial considerations, Balakirev at once set him to composing his symphony in an orderly fashion, starting with the first movement, then proceeding to the scherzo and finale. At the soirées, meanwhile, he imbibed Balakirev's authoritative, if sometimes surprising, opinions on the music of composers whose work he had just been starting to get to know in the months before his introduction to the circle. He observed with some astonishment Balakirev's idiosyncratic method of critical analysis. "A work was never considered as a whole in its aesthetic significance," he reports:

> The new compositions with which Balakirev acquainted his circle were invariably played by him in fragments, bar by bar, and even piecemeal: first the end, then the beginning, which usually produced a strange impression on an outside listener who happened to find himself in the circle. A pupil like me had to show Balakirev the plan of a composition in its embryo, if only in the shape of its first four or eight bars. Balakirev

would quickly make corrections, indicating how such an embryo had
to be remade; he would criticize it, would praise and extol the first two
bars, but would abuse the next two, make fun of them, and try to make
the author disgusted with them.[22]

In this way the first movement of the symphony got written, partly in
response to suggestions by Balakirev, partly no doubt with his direct
participation. Rimsky-Korsakov had little idea how to orchestrate what
he had composed, but Balakirev helped him with that, too, and soon
Rimsky-Korsakov was handling this mysterious discipline with some
ease. "In the opinion of Balakirev and others," he tells us, "I proved to
have a gift for instrumentation."[23]

Nothing in the boy's background had prepared him for the intensely
artistic yet wayward atmosphere at Balakirev's Saturdays. His father
was a retired civil governor living in the town of Tikhvin, a hundred
miles or so to the east of St. Petersburg. His mother came from a
family of landowners in Oryol, south of Moscow, the region of Turgenev's Sportsman's Sketches. They were elderly parents (Nikolay had
a brother twenty two years his senior). And on the whole they were
conventional, "people of the 1820s," Nikolay calls them, "who rarely
came into contact with the literary and artistic life of those times."[24]
Music played a part in their lives, but was not regarded as a suitable
or secure profession—quite rightly, of course, at least in Russia at that
time. Something, however, was necessary, as Rimsky-Korsakov senior
had been impoverished, his son informs us, by "crooked friends who
traded estates with him to their advantage, borrowed money from
him, and so forth."[25] It so happened that an uncle, Nikolay Petrovich
Rimsky-Korsakov, had been a distinguished naval commander and
that young Nikolay's elder brother, Voyin, had followed his uncle into
the navy and become an excellent sailor in his own right. So what more
natural than that Nikolay should go to sea in his turn? At the time of
his meeting with Balakirev he was about to graduate from the Naval
School as midshipman, after which he would set off on what was called
a "practice" cruise: a long practice, though, lasting between two and
three years. Given the choice, Nikolay would have forgone this pleasure, and with it any prospect of a naval career. But his brother would
not hear of it. What evidence was there, in his mediocre piano playing and the one or two insignificant compositions, of any conceivable
career in music—a career that, in any case, was scarcely on offer in St.
Petersburg? And Nikolay never afterward held this against his brother.
He admitted to Voyin that "Mama very much dislikes this career, and

it's the same with my associating with Balakirev and the others."[26] And later he wrote that Voyin "was a thousand times right to regard me as a dilettante: I was one."[27]

The young midshipman sailed away on his world cruise in the middle of October 1862, less than a year after joining the Balakirev circle. But no sooner was one lost than another was found. In September Musorgsky's old medical acquaintance Alexander Borodin at last returned from his foreign travels, and in December he accepted a full-time academic post as adjunct professor at the St. Petersburg Academy of Physicians. From his time in Germany and Italy, Borodin brought back several new instrumental works (again mostly incomplete) and a wife, a pianist by the name of Yekaterina Sergeyevna, née Protopopova. Yekaterina was a beautiful woman and an excellent musician (Borodin had been astonished to discover that she had perfect pitch); but she was to prove a difficult wife—what amounted to a third vocation for the already hard-pressed chemist-composer. She not only suffered from tuberculosis and chronic asthma, which eventually compelled her to live for half of every year in the drier climate of her native Moscow, but she was also an incurable insomniac with neurotic tendencies that required her loving husband to share her sleepless nights. In these circumstances her extended absences were something of a relief for him in his already doubly charged existence; and since he wrote to her in Moscow every two or three days—long, newsy, candid, sharply observant letters, which survive and have been published in extenso—they were also hugely valuable to historians of this period in Russian life and music.

Borodin was already twenty-nine, three years older than Balakirev, when they met in the apartment of Balakirev's doctor, Sergey Botkin, an old cello-playing friend of Borodin's. On discovering that Borodin was himself a musician, Balakirev naturally invited him to his next soirée, and there Borodin once again ran into Musorgsky, as well as presumably meeting Cui and Stasov for the first time. As usual there was a great deal of music. Musorgsky and Balakirev played the finale of Rimsky-Korsakov's symphony, and Borodin "was struck by the brilliance, the intelligence and energy of the performance, as well as by the beauty of the piece." No doubt they astonished him by informing him that its composer was an eighteen-year-old midshipman at that moment afloat somewhere on the North Sea. "And do you by any chance write music?" Musorgsky perhaps asked, recalling their earlier discussions about other people's music. Borodin must have confessed that he did, then found himself nervously backpedaling when pressed to go to the piano and play something of his own. "I was terribly ashamed," he later recalled, "and flatly refused."[28]

What might he have played them? There was in fact plenty of choice, since, although the majority of his instrumental works were in one way or another incomplete, it was in most cases whole movements, or at least sections, rather than parts or endings, that were missing. Borodin had not had Balakirev's habit of sketching out movements which he then played from memory and which remained unwritten, often for decades. A few weeks before, Balakirev had played his three-movement E-flat piano concerto to Rimsky-Korsakov, who had banged his fist on the table and confidently asserted that it was "better than *Lear*."[29] But only the first movement existed on paper; the other two were preserved, if at all, only in their composer's head, from which they may or may not have emerged in the same form whenever he sat down to play them.[30] Borodin, by contrast, had at his disposal, and written down, most of a four-movement string quintet in F minor, composed when he was twenty, two movements of a string trio in G (for two violins and cello), three whole movements of a D-major piano trio, a couple of movements for string sextet, a recent piano quintet in C minor, and much of a three-movement cello sonata in B minor, as well as several attractive songs. Unlike his new Balakirev friends, he had played chamber music all his adult life, and had even learned the cello in order to participate in string groups. The string quintet, for instance, has two cello parts (like Schubert's quintet and unlike Mozart's) and even some solo writing for cello. The songs also have parts for cello as well as piano. In Heidelberg, Borodin soon took up with chamber-music-loving friends, and wrote more for their use. But he was lazy about dotting his i's and crossing his t's; after all, nobody else was going to play his music, still less publish it. And he had many other things on his mind. So neither trio ever acquired a finale, and the sextet lacked both a finale and probably the final section of its slow movement. The piano quintet, composed during the summer (and possibly intended as an orchestral work),[31] was supposedly complete, though its three movements were strangely balanced: a folksy andante and scherzo, with a finale longer than the other two movements combined. What survived of most of these scores, in any case, was fully performable. Only the cello sonata was to some extent fragmentary.

Taken as a whole, these scores are the work of an intensely gifted "natural," apparently able to write beautifully in the received style of the classical and early romantic music that he and his friends played, week in, week out, in their private sessions. The hand of Mendelssohn lies over them, but lightly, without any sense of facile imitation. On the contrary, an individual voice can often be heard, in the form of a gift for melody neither quite Germanic nor yet identifiably Russian, but easy and personal. For instance, the odd idea of basing his cello sonata on the fugue theme from Bach's G-minor solo-violin sonata (overheard from the next-door flat in Heidelberg) is that of a composer both conscious of tradition and uninhibited by it; in fact, of all these early chamber works, it is the sonata that contains the most Borodinesque tunes.[32] There is also, in the ensemble pieces, a feeling for instrumental writing due surely to the experience of playing masterpieces of the genre, whether well or badly, evening after evening. What perhaps comes less readily at this stage is the concept of organic design: the idea of sonata forms that work through harmonic tension and release. Borodin's forms are well enough made but stereotyped, pattern-based—hardly surprising in a composer who had never studied, never worked at composition under critical scrutiny. Yet his music always moves, dances, seldom lingers or gets stuck in musical blind alleyways. Only in a country like 1850s Russia, where the very idea of native instrumental music was like palm trees in Greenland, could so talented a composer have reached his late twenties without, it seems, ever seriously considering a career in music.

CHAPTER 9

Wagner and His Acolyte

A few days before Christmas 1862 Mily Balakirev celebrated his twenty-sixth birthday. There was a good deal to celebrate. In the past year he had collected two new acolytes and had set them to work, in his inimitable fashion, composing symphonies. Under his tutelage young Rimsky-Korsakov had composed most of three movements of his E-flat-minor symphony before sailing off on his world cruise, and was now battling with a slow movement based on a Russian folk song called "The Tartar Captivity," given him by Balakirev. Borodin, having previously written nothing but songs and chamber music, had embarked on a symphony in E-flat major, and by the end of the year had already composed enough of the first movement to be able to play it to his wife in Moscow. Meanwhile, Musorgsky struggled on with the D-major symphony he supposedly had been writing for two whole years, to the exclusion of everything else apart from orchestration exercises and piano transcriptions of Beethoven string quartets.

At this stage of their careers, these symphony projects might have seemed like a high wall between the composers and their future. Rimsky-Korsakov's would be four years in the writing, Borodin's five, and during this time they composed practically nothing else. Musorgsky's symphony was soon abandoned altogether, and he never thereafter attempted anything remotely classical in form or genre. Instead, some time early in 1863, he composed a mildly eccentric piano piece which he christened, perhaps ironically, "Intermezzo in modo classico." Years later he told Stasov that the title reflected his "musical preoccupations at that time," referring presumably to his attempts at composing a symphony.[1] In fact there are grounds for speculating that the intermezzo may have been a product of those attempts. Cui wrote to Rimsky-Korsakov that "Modinka has uttered some kind of musical monster—supposedly a trio to his scherzo . . . Liturgical chants of interminable length and the usual Modinka pedals etc., all unclear, strange, clumsy and in no way a trio."[2] This could well be a description of the intermezzo, whose main theme, many times repeated, is a chantlike unison melody somewhat in the style of the "Song of the Volga Boatmen," and which certainly does use pedal effects, so far as is possible on the piano. A few weeks later Musorgsky himself told Balakirev that he planned to orchestrate the intermezzo "and leave it as a separate piece." It would have made an odd trio in its original form; but then Musorgsky would probably have written an odd symphony if he had ever got round to finishing one.

He did eventually orchestrate the intermezzo in 1867, greatly extending it and providing it with a trio section of its own. At the same time (or so one suspects) he supplied Stasov with an account of the work's origins which seems to apply to the extended form more than to the original—a fact that obviously calls in question its strict accuracy. In the winter of 1861, Stasov reported, Musorgsky had been in the country with his mother:

> And one beautiful, sunny winter day—a holiday—he saw a whole crowd of peasants crossing the fields and plunging heavily through the snowdrifts; many of them fell down in the snow and then extricated themselves with some difficulty. "This," said Mussorgsky, "was at one and the same time beautiful and picturesque and serious and amusing. And suddenly in the distance appeared a crowd of young women, coming with songs and laughter along a level pathway. This picture flashed into my head in a musical form and unexpectedly there shaped itself the first 'stepping up and down' melody *à la Bach*; the jolly, laughing women presented themselves to me in the shape of a melody from which I then made the middle part or *Trio*."[3]

This incident, if it really happened, probably took place in March 1862, and not at Karevo, but at the village of Volok, several miles to the north of Toropetz, where Musorgsky was staying with his distant cousin Natalya Kushelova. He was there for his health, and was taken for sturdy walks through waist-deep snowdrifts by the German tutor of his hostess's children, who considered that Musorgsky's "semi-stupor," as he called it, was "due to bad circulation" and that his organism needed "constant stimuli until *it gets stronger.*"[4] Perhaps the more detailed picture he painted for Stasov's benefit was an embroidered memory of these walks. In any case its scenic character is noteworthy, and of course makes a jest of the "in modo classico" (which may be why he changed the "classico" to "antico" for the orchestral version). Rather, it looks forward to the vivid sketches in *Pictures from an Exhibition,* composed more than a decade later. Even the piano writing anticipates that work: heavy and slightly awkward, like that of "Bydlo" or "The Old Castle." Musorgsky was an accomplished pianist, so his sometimes antipianistic way of writing for the instrument must have been conscious, a way perhaps of bypassing "automatic" keyboard technique in pursuit of the strong visual image. This assumes, of course, that he had a picture in his mind when he first composed the piece as opposed to when he revised it, which is by no means certain.[5]

The chief musical excitement in St. Petersburg in the late winter of 1863 was the arrival of Richard Wagner in February to conduct a series of concerts of his own music, together with four symphonies by Beethoven. Between mid-February and early April he gave no less than six concerts in the capital, plus three in Moscow, with programs made up of excerpts from all his mature operas thus far, apart from *Das Rheingold.*[6] Wagner's music was scarcely known at all in Russia; not one of his operas had been staged there, and only a few excerpts had figured on concert programs. But he was notorious for his involvement in the Dresden rising of 1849 and, among thinking, German-speaking musicians, for his theoretical essays on opera *The Artwork of the Future,* and *Opera and Drama,* and for the connection of the theatre with revolutionary politics.

All this meant, needless to say, that he arrived in St. Petersburg as something of a celebrity; but it also meant that battle lines tended to be drawn up around him on any basis except that of his music. Among the prominent musicians in St. Petersburg in 1863, only Anton Rubinstein and Alexander Serov could be said to have had sufficient knowledge of Wagner's operas to express an informed opinion, and even they knew next to nothing of the music dramas that, so to speak, explained the theories, for the good reason that not one of them had yet been staged. Rubinstein, in any case, was broadly hostile to such of Wagner's music as he knew. Serov, on the other hand, had become a fervent Wagnerite after hearing a run of performances of *Tannhäuser* in Germany in 1858 and a single *Lohengrin* in Weimar in 1859. But Serov's advocacy was a mixed blessing in St. Petersburg in the early 1860s, and for the Balakirev circle, in particular, it confirmed their worst fears about Wagner, whom they already instinctively disliked for his theorizing and his Germanness. They made studiously little of his concerts. Cui and Balakirev attended the first one and Cui reported to Rimsky-Korsakov that Wagner was "*a marvellous conductor*" and that Balakirev had become a better conductor for having heard him.[7] Cui also wrote a review of the concert, his first essay at criticism, but it was not published and has not survived.[8] Neither Musorgsky nor Borodin seems to have attended any of the concerts; at least their respective correspondence is silent on the subject. As for Stasov, it's hard to believe he will have stayed away completely from an event that he must have known to be of importance, whatever his views on Wagner's music, of which he had some knowledge, having heard *Lohengrin* in Vienna in 1854. A month or so after Wagner's departure he expressed the opinion, in a letter to Balakirev, that "Wagner hasn't the slightest gift for recitative," but that he was "a purely orchestral, symphonic composer, in the fullest sense of the word. He doesn't know about voices, and doesn't want to know. To him they're just a flavoring and a pretext."[9] He would hardly have written in such terms without having taken the opportunity to hear Wagner's recent music. But the letter in question was mainly an attack on Serov, in the person of his opera *Judith,* which had just had its premiere at the Maryinsky. And for Stasov, above all, Serov had become a major obstacle to balanced judgment on anything to do with contemporary music in general and Russian music in particular.

The whole background to the relations between Serov, Stasov, and the Balakirev circle is complicated by personal factors which are now hard to disentangle and still harder to understand. Serov and Stasov had been fellow pupils and intimate friends with many musical tastes in common. Until the late fifties they remained on good terms, and Serov was often at musical evenings attended by Stasov, Cui, and Balakirev, and to all appearances shared their views on Russian music, the relative merits of the classical and early romantic masters, and the desirability or otherwise of formal teaching. The first sign of a rift came after Glinka's death in 1857, when Stasov published a long obituary article in the *Russkiy vestnik* including a virulent attack on *A Life for the Tsar* and a profoundly tendentious defense of *Ruslan and Lyudmila,* in conscious rejection of the standard opinion that *A Life for the Tsar* was a masterpiece of national art and *Ruslan* an unfortunate digression.[10] Eighteen months later, *Ruslan* was at last revived after an absence from the stage of fifteen years, and Serov seized the opportunity to reverse Stasov's judgment and ostentatiously praise *A Life for the Tsar* at the expense of *Ruslan,* which he called "a conglomeration of individual strokes of genius and brilliant, profound musical beauties, somehow strung upon one of the most pitiful libretti in the world."[11] In his turn, Stasov soon responded in a long letter to the *Russkiy vestnik* with a fresh assault on *A Life for the Tsar.*[12] And so it went on, into the 1860s, with Serov ridiculing Stasov and his friends as "Ruslanists," and on beyond Serov's death in 1871, with Stasov, who outlived Serov by thirty-five years, continuing to offer posterity his personal opinion of his former friend and enemy, couched in terms that assured the reader that he was giving his victim the benefit of every possible doubt, but could not in the end, and in all conscience, help denouncing him. Serov, he wrote,

> was a composer but also a music critic. In both spheres he displayed considerable gifts, wide learning, maturity, force, and brilliance. But in both he lacked the most important, highest qualities. His compositional gift was second-rate and lacked an individual character; his critical gift was devoid of all depth and solidity: his chief trait was a perpetual instability and changeability in his convictions. As a result neither his musical nor his critical works have left any strong trace, and they cannot have any influence on the future destiny of Russian music. They did, on the other hand, exert an especially strong influence in their day.[13]

Russian musical society was by no means alone in nineteenth-century Europe in mapping its artistic judgments onto its personal or intellectual vendettas. But it was certainly an extreme case. One has to remember what a small place St. Petersburg was musically in the 1850s and '60s, and how little it offered the aspiring composer or would-be critic. Every scrap of recognition had to be fought over like dead mice in an alley of starving cats. Add to this the desperate need of Russian musicians to assert their existence at the heart of a community that for a century and a half had taken it for granted that foreign music was the only sort worth considering, and it is hardly surprising that their quarrels sometimes grew vicious and their disagreements absolute. One thinks of Herzen's description of Belinsky, how

> when he felt stung, when his cherished convictions were called in question, when the muscles of his cheeks began to quiver and his voice to burst out: then he was worth seeing: he pounced upon his opponent like a panther, he tore him to pieces, made him a ridiculous, a piteous object, and incidentally developed his own thought with unusual power

and poetry. The dispute would often end in blood, which flowed from the sick man's throat; pale, gasping, with his eyes fixed on the man with whom he was speaking, he would lift his handkerchief to his mouth with shaking hand and stop—deeply mortified, crushed by his physical weakness.[14]

In Serov's case, no doubt, the blood was metaphorical. But metaphorically, it flowed.

By any standards, Serov was a difficult, quarrelsome man with an unhappy tendency to antagonize those with whom he came into close contact. Stasov, on the other hand, could be obstinate and contrary, only too ready to fight his corner no matter how irrational or untenable his position. It was an unfortunate match. The Glinka quarrel was typical of their relish for controversy for its own sake, but it need not have been terminal. Even Serov's conversion to the Wagner cause in 1858 and his passionate Wagnerism thereafter might not have wrecked their personal friendship had it not been for two incidents, one musical, the other apparently not, which drove an immovable stake into its heart.

About the (presumably) nonmusical incident, only vague, uncertain details are known. There are tantalizing hints in Stasov's letters. Early in May 1858 he sent Balakirev a note that "on Thursday, while I was at your place, Alex Nikol [Serov] did something as a result of which Mitya [Dmitry Stasov] has broken with him conclusively, and with the rest of his family, who were also apparently involved. How loathesome and disagreeable this all is! Maybe you too will cease to be pure, bright, beautiful and noble."[15] And almost two years later: "Serov has sent another disgusting letter, not mentioning me personally, but clearly with the aim of abusing Mitya . . . To think that the first cause of all this nastiness is Sophia Nik[olayevna Serova] and that without her everything could have been different and Al Nik's becoming a complete scoundrel might even have been put off for a long time."[16] Sophia was Serov's sister, a former mistress of Vladimir Stasov and the mother of his daughter, Nadezhda. But that was long ago. Whatever it was that the Serovs had said or done, Balakirev naturally sided with Stasov, and when Serov nevertheless showed him the first act of his new opera in 1861, he made only dismissive comments on the orchestration and an offhand compliment on the act's soft, quiet ending, one of Serov's subtlest touches. For Serov this was the last straw, as Balakirev no doubt intended it to be, and from that time on the die was cast. It was Stasov, though, who was the more implacable of the two former friends. At the funeral of Serov's mother in 1865, Serov offered Stasov his hand and asked for their former good relations to be restored. Stasov refused.

Under these circumstances, it was hardly likely that the Balakirev circle would greet *Judith* with anything but ostentatious contempt. Who, after all, was this composer? Nothing but a jumped-up music critic, and a Wagnerite to boot, an apostle, therefore, of German music and the much-heralded, much-ridiculed Music of the Future—the *Zukunftsmusik.* He was something far worse than a Ruslanist: he was a Zukunftist, and an inept and insincere one at that, as was very clear to the young masters of the Balakirev salon. "This *Wagners Kindchen* in all its five-act life," Musorgsky reported to Balakirev, who was away in the Caucasus and had missed the premiere, "doesn't offer a single place that touches you deeply, nor one scenic episode that gives pause for thought. What's more the libretto is extremely bad, the declamation pitiful, un-Russian; only the orchestration is interesting in places, though sometimes too complicated."[17] To Stasov, it seemed that Serov's was "the consciously constructed nature of a man in whom nothing is genuine, but in whom each thread is bent to the taste of the masses." He was "some kind of unusual glove that fits absolutely any hand."[18]

Genuine or not, Serov was not quite entirely new to composition. For a long time he had cherished an ambition to write operas, and had in fact pondered a number of subjects and even composed substantial chunks of music, but had apparently destroyed virtually everything, including "almost three acts" of an opera on Gogol's story "May Night" ("Mayskaya noch' "). It seems clear that the basic problem with his previous works had been what Taruskin calls "his utter lack of practical skill."[19] As for *May Night,* Serov was "dissatisfied with his work from the point of view of its style, in which the influence, now of Glinka, now of the German classical models, was too noticeable."[20] Later his work as a music critic took him away from composition for several years. But the desire never left him, and evidently his Damascene conversion to Wagner in 1858 merely intensified it. He again began looking for suitable subjects, and late in 1860 he found one, in the unlikely shape of an Italian play, by Paolo Giacometti, on the Apocryphal story of Judith and Holofernes.

Serov had been writing about issues connected with musical drama for some time even before he had read Wagner's theories, let alone seen or heard any of his operas. In 1851 he had used a long and profoundly hostile obituary essay on Gaspare Spontini as the pretext for a lengthy disquisition on the proper relationship between music and the other elements of opera, especially the libretto. "In initiating *musical* drama," he asserted, "Gluck was the first to grasp that its main principles were the same as *spoken* drama, that musical drama must above all be *drama*."[21] But in practice Gluck had been trapped by the conventions of the eighteenth century, things like the deus ex machina, Greek heroes in powdered wigs, and so forth, and since then opera had become a slave to public taste. In Paris, supposedly the world center of musical drama, every opera had to have a ballet, irrespective of its subject; even Weber's *Der Freischütz* was provided with a ballet when it was staged in the French capital. As for the so-called grand opera (works like Meyerbeer's *Le Prophète* or Auber's *L'Enfant prodigue*), these were merely an excuse for the kind of noisy bacchanalia beloved of the unmusical French, five acts of allsorts, with dancing, horses, camels, and spectacular effects like the electrically lit sun in *Le Prophète*. For Serov, the true province of music for the stage lay not in such things, "but in deep psychology, in conversation between the hearts of the dramatis personae and the hearts of the audience, in emotion, in uprushes of feeling, now passionate, now tender, in a word, in everything that makes up the *life of the heart*."[22]

When he read Wagner's *Oper und Drama* soon afterward, he must quickly have realized that they differed on the question of the relation between words and music, since the implication of Serov's view is that the text must in the end defer to the dramatic needs and pace of the music, whereas for the Wagner of the theoretical writings text and music were on an absolutely equal footing. When Serov discovered that Wagner solved this problem by invariably writing his own libretti, he was impressed, but recognized that for him this would never be possible, since he completely lacked the power of versification. For *Judith,* he initially planned to stick to the language of the play, with the help of an Italian librettist, then changed his mind and wrote a detailed prose draft of his own in Russian, partly based on the German play by Christian Friedrich Hebbel, which he then instructed a new librettist, D. I. Lobanov, to turn into verse. Meanwhile, he was composing the music on the basis of nothing more specific than his own prose scenario, hence without the text to which it would eventually be sung. As Taruskin points out, this was near enough to what Glinka had done with *Ruslan,* a work Serov himself had excoriated not least for the shambles of its libretto.[23]

In all these circumstances, the astonishing thing about *Judith* is not that it got past the fussy and conservative selection committees of the Imperial Theatres, but that having done so, it turned out to be such a fine and interesting piece of work. This was recognized at the time, but then for some reason forgotten to the point where it became acceptable to dismiss Serov as a figure of purely historical significance without troubling to acquaint oneself with his work—which admittedly was not easy, as the music was long out of print, performances nonexistent, and recordings nearly so. Audiences, of course, react to what they hear, historians rather to what they read. So *Judith* has tended to be thought of as an inferior example of sub-Wagneriana, though it resembles Wagner's pre-*Ring* operas only in certain general aspects, most notably its vocal writing and orchestration, and some details of harmony. Its more superficially obvious ancestors are precisely the works that Serov had attacked in his Spontini obituary: the five-act grand operas, with dancing (Serov has ballets in both his third and his fourth acts), camels on the stage, noisy, spectacular choruses, and, of course, a happy ending with at least implied divine intervention. "So you see," he wrote to a friend, "it has come to five acts—*grand opéra en forme en 5 actes, avec deux divertissements!!*—by *Robert-le-Diable*'s recipe, or *La Juive*'s or the *Huguenots*'!! Precisely: whatever you mock the most you end up doing yourself!"[24]

To some extent this is unjust. *Judith* does go in for mass effects, but they are by no means entirely meretricious. The largely choral, oratorio-like first act has authentic power and moments of genuine solemnity, notably in the hymnlike passage in which the renegade Assyrian Achior describes to the besieged Jews how he tried to explain their God to the Assyrian commander, Holofernes (Judith repeats this music when she talks to Holofernes about Achior in act 3). The solo scenes are also musically impressive, even if the actual characterization is rudimentary and the word setting—unsurprisingly in view of Serov's method of composition—clumsy at best. Above all, Serov's musical idiom owes much less to the Paris school than might be supposed from a description of the type of work *Judith* is. Meyerbeer, though a German from Berlin, derived his vocal style from Italian bel canto, translated into the picturesque idiom that was the postrevolutionary version of the French *ballet de cour.* Serov's writing for voice is closer to German romantic opera, a mixture of expressive arioso and long-line lyricism, much like Weber's *Der Freischütz* and Wagner's *Tannhäuser,* which, as we saw, Serov had recently heard several times in Germany. The general discourse, too, is Germanic, through-composed up to a point, but with the movement breaks still showing (which is also partly true of *Tannhäuser*), and with some touches that a German composer might not have imagined, such as the quiet ending of the first act, a detail of which Serov was proud and which the Balakirev circle admired, and the slightly wan Orientalism of the Assyrian dances and coarse splendor of Holofernes's march, all too obviously indebted to the Glinka of *Ruslan and Lyudmila.*

Two things stand out about *Judith.* On the one hand it is a predictable kind of opera for its time and place, a Russification of an up-to-date operatic genre handled with some expertise by a composer who had spent a lot of time in the theatre and understood its needs. On the other hand its power is crude, partly perhaps deliberately so, partly no doubt as a result of Serov's lack of experience and learned technique. Like Cui, he at times lapses into a metric word-setting that maps the music onto a foursquare poetic scansion: a kind of musical doggerel. His orchestration, too, is rough, primitive, but often effective; in particular his writing for brass has a boldness that again suggests Wagner, but also occasionally recalls his own complaint against Spontini's "weakness for brass instruments."[25] One thing *Judith* is not is a "dialogue" opera, like those parts of Dargomïzhsky's *Rusalka* Serov had raved about a mere four years before starting work on his own opera. There is recitative of every kind: unaccompanied, secco (with orchestral chords), accompanied, arioso (like the Dutchman's monologue in Wagner's opera, or Tannhäuser's Rome Narration). But there is hardly any attempt at musical prose—at folding the music round the natural contours of the words. Serov, of course, disagreed with Wagner about the equal status of music and text. But in any case the way *Judith* was composed—the music often *before* the text—ruled that kind of matchmaking out. All of which only goes to remind us of the gulf between theory and practice; even Wagner, in some ways the most theoretical composer of all, rarely sticks to his own prescriptions in practice. Serov, a critic more than a theorist, hardly seems to have tried.

Whatever its faults, *Judith* was a huge event in the generally featureless operatic life of early-sixties St. Petersburg. Musorgsky went to the premiere on May 16 with Vladimir Stasov, and reported to Balakirev—away in the Caucasus—that "*Judith* is the first seriously worked-out opera on the Russian stage since *Rusalka.*" In fact his account (June 10) is so long and detailed, and with such relatively precise musical quotations, that it looks as if he heard the work several times before writing. His report, it's true, is largely, studiously negative. The overture is "uninteresting, chaotic, but with intentions not, however, fulfilled"; the declamation is "laughable"; Avra's duet with Judith, imploring her "not to go to Holofernes," is "of extremely poor quality"; Holofernes's first scene with Judith is "so bad and untalented that it's not worth expanding on," and so forth. But between the lines are some intriguing positives. Musorgsky praises the orchestration in a number of passages, and admits to finding the quiet end of act I beautiful and truthful. The scene of Holofernes's decapitation is "melodramatic, but very effective." And Serov's musical dramaturgy excites his professional interest. Quoting the start of act I—a somber phrase in E minor "which depicts the state of the people lying exhausted on the stage"—he criticizes Serov's failure to develop the theme:

> I would have carried it on, I would have added some juice [a favourite image of Musorgsky's] and on the development, on the motions of this phrase, I would have built the elder's recitative.—One mustn't forget what's onstage: exhausted by thirst, the Jews lie there in silent disarray, and Serov has forgotten to think about them—he needed the people later for some kind of superbly rubbishy *fugato.* The concept of having the chorus stay silent is truthful, but Serov hasn't controlled it. The idea of the people gets lost in the orchestra, but if he had managed it differently—it would have turned out new and interesting.[26]

Later he muses on the scene of Holofernes's drunken delirium and his attempted seduction of Judith. "The third and fourth acts," he grumbles, "show Serov's complete lack of talent and passion. . . . Holofernes is as drunk as the devil and starts hallucinating . . . What a broad field for a musician, a carousing sensualist-despot,—how interesting it could have been to set the hallucination scene in the orchestra.—There's nothing of this,—only a banal French melodrama with howling Wagnerian violins."

Musorgsky must have kept quiet about these matters at the first performance, to judge by Stasov's remarks about him to Balakirev in a letter written the next morning. Stasov is desperate to discuss the new opera with Balakirev, but has to put it all into long letters, this one and the next, two months later. And why is this such an obsession? Because he, too, recognizes that, however hateful Serov might be personally to him and however suspect his talent, there are qualities in *Judith* that can't be denied and that turn him from a mere poseur into an issue. It shows talent, after all, to be able to hold the attention of a diffuse and indifferent public for five long acts on an unfashionable subject. Of course, it's all effects, like Meyerbeer, all external, nothing inward. But that's precisely what's so worrying. Serov will have influence, where (the no less hated) Wagner will not. Yet Musorgsky, while seeming to agree, expressed "not a single thought, not one word out of a genuine depth of understanding, or a deeply excited, agitated heart. With him everything was flabby, colorless. It seems to me he's a complete idiot."[27]

The other possible explanation—that Musorgsky thought better of the work than he dared admit—seems not to have occurred to Stasov.

Balakirev responded in kind from Pyatigorsk.[28] He remembered the first act of *Judith* from the time Serov had sent it to him, and even remembered some of the themes well enough to quote them back to Stasov. It was more like an oratorio than an opera, he recalled, and all very derivative: he mentions Berlioz, Méhul, Cherubini, even Handel—a fine assortment to add to Stasov's pet hates, Meyerbeer and Halévy. Balakirev himself was far away from such concerns. He had been travelling through Georgia in the company of Old Believers, finding nourishment in "the many-talented, generous nature of our muzhiks and the fine, honest faces of the Circassians," and enjoying the sight of Mount Elbrus, "the brilliant stars, the cliffs and crags, the snowy mountains and grandiose precipices of the Caucasus—this is what I'm living for at present." He had watched Circassian dancing to a kind of balalaika music that reminded him of Russian and Spanish folk song. And probably—though he doesn't mention it—he had been listening to what Pushkin had called "the sad songs of Georgia," with their strange ornamental melodies and their suggestion of an Oriental languor. Either while still in the Caucasus or soon after his return to St. Petersburg at the end of the summer, he composed his own setting of Pushkin's famous poem, which had actually been written to fit a Georgian folk tune sung to him by a pupil of Glinka's. Balakirev's "Georgian Song" ("Gruzinskaya pesnya") is an exquisite, perhaps idealized lament in his favorite B-flat minor, full of decorative roulades in the piano accompaniment and free-flowing melismas with alternately flattened and sharpened sevenths in the voice: a kind of blueprint, as it turned out, for the "Oriental" style soon to be cultivated by the circle as a whole.

The contrast between this minor masterpiece and the bland, syllabic little songs Balakirev was otherwise mostly writing is startling to say the least. Lermontov settings such as "Why?" ("Otchego?") and "If I Hear Your Voice" ("Slïshu li golos tvoy") are still like piano miniatures with added voice. For Lermontov's version of Byron's Hebrew melody "My Soul Is Dark" he found a dramatic gesture for the poem's "Oh! quickly string the harp / I yet can brook to hear," very different from the somewhat impassive Schumann setting (which he surely knew), yet curiously Schumannesque in style overall. By far his best Lermontov song is the sinister "Song of the Golden Fish" ("Pesnya zolotoy rïbki"), in which a mermaid lures a child to the bottom of the sea with a lullaby of haunting, ineffable beauty. Here Balakirev has clearly been inspired by the concept of the voice, this expressive weapon that can convey two or three meanings at once—the plain sense of the words, the loving tone of the voice, and the hint of evil or at least coercion that can lie in this or that inflection, this or that harmony. Balakirev's biographer Edward Garden regards this, with only mild exaggeration, as "among the world's greatest songs"; it would surely be much better known if it weren't for the impenetrability, for most singers, of the Russian language and especially the Cyrillic script.

While Balakirev was exploring the scenery and culture of the Caucasus, Musorgsky had disappeared, as we have already seen, to the family estate at Karevo. The final arrangements of the emancipation were under way. And meanwhile he, too, was writing songs, either because the business distractions were too great to allow concentrated work on anything more substantial ("Thanks to the bailiff," he told Cui, "my brain is at the police station"),[29] or because, having abandoned the symphony he had spent the last two years not composing, he simply lacked a project that demanded his full attention. In his case, the poetry book fell open at Goethe, and specifically at one of the Harper's songs in *Wilhelm Meister*: "An die Thüren will ich schleichen" ("Song of the Old Man," "Pesn' startsa"). Then, after a brief return to his romance style in Vasily Kurochkin's "But If I Could Only Meet You" ("No yesli bï s toboyu ya vstretitsya mogla"), he too turned to Byron, and composed his "Song of Saul Before His Last Battle" ("Tsar' Saul," translated by Pavel Kozlov).

Just as Balakirev's Georgian song opened up new musical territory in the Orient of the Russian mind, so Musorgsky's settings of Goethe and Byron conjured up a vivid dramatic landscape, part theatrical, part psychological, that may have surprised even the composer himself. Goethe's Harper, blind and tortured by guilt as he creeps from door to door begging for food, suggested to him both an image and an action. "A beggar," he wrote pointedly to Cui, "can sing my music with a clear conscience" (whatever sin he may have committed, that is, within the virtual frame of the song).[30] As with Balakirev, Schumann stands somewhere behind this music. His own beautiful setting of the poem has the same plodding gait and the same way of leading the bass voice attentively along a pathway marked out by the piano. But Musorgsky's song has a religious tinge, a mendicant spirituality, that Schumann's lacks, and that seems to arise from the modal character of the melody, which is pure aeolian (A to A on the white keys of the piano, though Musorgsky has it characteristically black, in E-flat minor). Even the piano strays from the mode in only five of the song's thirty-five bars.

The penitential flavor is emphasized by the chantlike vocal line and by the accompaniment's pseudo-chorale, ending, after a brief coda (another Schumann touch), on a mysterious, inconclusive seventh chord, deep in the piano.

The Byron poem inspires a portrait of quite a different kind. This is the biblical Saul—brusque, arbitrary, violent, but facing death with unflinching heroism—and Musorgsky portrays him with a certain grudging admiration for the sheer ferocity of a warrior who can instruct his commanders to slaughter him in case of defeat.[31] The 1863 setting is in fact a rougher, less refined version than the one now usually sung, which is a revision from the late sixties (to a different translation by Kozlov). It has more daring harmony, more jagged phrasing, and a bigger, longer piano part. The opening is typical: the original version has a five-bar piano introduction made up of a pair of bars in four-four time followed by three bars in three-four, with a trumpet fanfare and a claxon of whole-tone chords, whereas the revision gets rid of the claxon and the three-four bars and hurries into the running quaver figure that accompanies the voice entry. In the original, too, the setting of the first two words, "O vozhdi!" (Byron's "Warriors and chiefs!"), is detached from the rest of the line, making it more imperious, more stagey. In revising the song, Musorgsky seems to have slightly lost his nerve (or given in to his publisher)[32] and smoothed out the effect, while judiciously shortening the song as a whole. Later still he orchestrated the revised version. But the original is somehow, in its rough-and-ready way, more exciting.[33]

It is hard to escape the impression with this song that Musorgsky still has Serov's music for Holofernes running through his head. Admittedly his King Saul is a tenor or high baritone (high A-flats in the key of E-flat minor, which become F-sharps in the revised version in C-sharp minor). But the character portraits have many points in common. The fanfares that introduce the bass Holofernes's "Pobednaya truba" ("Victorious trumpet of our glory everywhere") in act 3 of *Judith* are much the same as the ones that announce Saul's speech to his generals, complete with following dissonance, which Serov, characteristically, resolves in conventional fashion but Musorgsky, no less typically, leaves hanging, unresolved. Both commanders then launch into strident, warlike marches, melodically and rhythmically similar, but in harmony always strikingly different, since Serov rarely if ever strays from the textbook while Musorgsky studiously ignores the rules and instead treats the accompaniment as a suitable backcloth to Saul's heroic but unruly directives.

One might speculate that Musorgsky was influenced, in this wild portrait of arbitrary power, by Mikhail Sariotti's notorious performance as Holofernes—a blueprint for the ranting, histrionic Russian basses of the Chaliapin era and beyond. But if so, the model for Musorgsky's Harper surely lay elsewhere, in the lyric bass epitomized by the great Osip Petrov, Glinka's first Susanin.[34] In any case, both styles would soon prove essential, when Musorgsky himself began to contemplate music for the stage.

CHAPTER 10

An African Priestess and a Scottish Bride

Musorgsky returned to St. Petersburg in September 1863, and moved into a large apartment by the Kokushkin Bridge over the Griboyedova Canal, a short step from the Haymarket (Sennaya ploshad'). The apartment was rented by three brothers by the name of Loginov, and shared with two other friends, a certain Nikolay Lobkovsky, and Nikolay Levashov, a friend of Musorgsky's from their Cadet School days. They all lived commune-style, taking their cue from Chernïshevsky's novel *What Is to Be Done?* (*Shto delat'?*), which had come out early that year and was being devoured by intellectual Petersburg.

The novel is more or less a tract, today barely readable, about the new progressive society for which Chernïshevsky had been laying the ground in his political and philosophical writings since the mid-fifties—writings that had landed him the previous year in the Peter and Paul Fortress. *What Is to Be Done?* was written there. Like the novel's heroine, Vera Pavlovna Rozalsky, and her husband, Dmitry Sergeyich Lopukhov, each of the Loginovs and their three tenants had his own room, and was permitted to enter anyone else's only with that person's permission. There was a common room for evening social activities: reading, music making, conversation. Needless to say, the form was little more than a pose, as shallow as the liberal pretensions of the professional classes in all ages. Musorgsky, after all, never in his entire life owned or rented an apartment of his own, but always shared, with his mother, his brother, or one or other friend, imposed upon or otherwise. To what extent the Loginov arrangement was essentially any different is hard now to discern. None of the other essential Chernïshevsky elements (Vera Pavlovna sets up a sewing collective, switches husbands, behaves in every way like a rational New Woman in relationships with a succession of rational New Men, etc., etc.) seem to have had any relevance to the Loginov commune.

Until quite recently, since the collapse of the Soviet Union, the area around the Sennaya Ploshad', along Sadovaya Ulitsa and the Griboyedova Canal, was one of the tormented quarters of St. Petersburg. On Sadovaya, the pavé was so unstable that the tram lines would become buckled and unusable, leaving the poor would-be passengers unsure whether their tram would ever arrive, and if so, precisely where. The piles of rubble from partly demolished houses made side streets virtually impassable, and in the courtyards the debris created lakes of water or ice that one negotiated at one's peril. The square itself, no longer a haymarket, had become a perennial building site from which there emerged only gradually a complicated network of modern shops and kiosks and, eventually, a grand new metro station. In Musorgsky's day this was the territory, precisely, of the student Raskolnikov, the hero of Dostoyevsky's *Crime and Punishment,* who occupied a miserable room in a large tenement on Stolyarniya Pereulok, just up from the Kokushkin Bridge, from where he walked the 730 paces to the fourth-floor apartment of the old moneylender Alyona Ivanovna and murdered her with a hatchet stolen from the porter's lodge of his own house.

Dostoyevsky began *Crime and Punishment* just after Musorgsky moved out of the Loginov apartment in May 1865. But the novelist had been practically a neighbor of the commune, on Malaya Meschanskaya (now Kaznacheyskaya) Ulitsa, and must often have been seen about the streets and bars of the locality. His recent books were very probably on the commune's reading list, especially *The House of the Dead,* which had come out in book form only in 1862. But the communards did not confine themselves to Russian literature, nor to the social realism in which Russian authors were, in the wake of Belinsky and Chernïshevsky, at that time specializing. A recent French novel that was read by all of them at the very start of their communal life was Gustave Flaubert's *Salammbô,* which had been published in France less than a year before and had already appeared in Russian translation, in two issues of *Notes of the Fatherland,* in the summer of 1863. *Salammbô* specifically lifted them out of the squalor and degradation of the Sennaya and deposited them in the heat and turmoil of Carthage in the third century B.C., at the time of the revolt of the mercenaries unpaid by Hamilcar at the end of the First Punic War. The exotic tale of the priestess Salammbô and the theft of the sacred veil from the Temple of Moloch by the mercenary leader Mathô seems to have struck a chord with these understimulated young men. But Musorgsky in particular responded with startling alacrity, and was soon at work on an operatic version of the novel. By mid-December he had composed an entire scene, including the theft of the veil, in piano score. He had already been working at the Ministry of Communications (Central Engineering Department) for two whole weeks.

By his standards, this was a spectacular burst of creative energy. Methodical it was not. He evidently started work without any clear overall plan, without a proper scenario, and certainly without a libretto, which as a matter of fact never did get written as a whole, by him or anyone else. His approach seems to have been much the same as with "King Saul," only on a larger scale. He pictured the scene as an isolated tableau and imagined the music to go with it. Here is Salammbô alone in the temple, guarding the veil; she strews flowers before the image of the goddess Tanit and the sacred lotus, then falls asleep while an off-stage chorus intones a prayer to Tanit; Mathô and his servant Spendius appear in the darkness; Mathô is overwhelmed by Salammbô's beauty, but snatches the veil and makes off with it, pursued by the imprecations of Salammbô, the other priestesses, soldiers, and people. This might, perhaps, have sufficed as a twenty-five-minute concert cantata. But in fact Musorgsky always intended more, as we know from Balakirev's report to Rimsky-Korsakov, the day before the completion of the temple scene, that "Musorgsky also wants to write an opera based on *Salammbô*." Balakirev was himself contemplating an opera, on the Firebird legend; and Cui, too, was deep into his next opera, based on Heine's tragedy *William Ratcliff,* an excerpt from which had already been programmed by Rubinstein at an RMS concert early in the year. Cui's two colleagues, he informed Rimsky-Korsakov from the steepling heights of his own experience, "are venturing to write operas. About Musorgsky I shall say nothing, but Balakirev will need spurring on." What Balakirev needed most of all was a libretto. Several versions would be rejected; only a few fragments would ever be composed.

For Musorgsky the real question was exactly what kind of opera he might venture to write. His model, plainly, was still *Judith.* Like Serov's opera, *Salammbô* had a besieging army, priests, and barbaric rituals; it had a devout heroine who goes in disguise to the tent of the enemy commander (in this case to retrieve the temple veil); it had an exotic, "Oriental" flavor, big crowds, animals, blood, and cruelty. For an experienced theatre composer, it might have been an inspiring blend of the public and the private, the wide screen and the dark interior. Flaubert's novel opens with a vivid description of the chaotic scenes at the mercenaries' victory banquet in Hamilcar's gardens at Megara. Later there are spectacular battles and blood-curdling massacres, an atrocious episode (recounted with unashamed relish) in which the Carthaginians sacrifice their children to Moloch while the mercenaries attack the city walls, and a general atmosphere of barbaric splendor and violence presented in the most horribly graphic detail. To do such scenes operatic justice would have needed the Meyerbeer of *Les Huguenots* or the Auber of *La Muette de Portici*. Musorgsky avoided them from the start, and instead went straight to the story's narrative core, offering a portrait of Salammbô as priestess that is both charming in a decorative, filigree kind of way and at the same time largely devoid of individuality or personal character. The choral hymn to Tanit that follows is similarly beautiful but static. Things liven up modestly with the arrival of Mathô and Spendius and the theft of the veil; but their stay is brief, and Mathô's eye contact with Salammbô little more than the casual observation of a pretty girl in church. In fact the most dynamic part of the whole scene is the final chorus of horror and pursuit, which turns out to be an adapted version of the *Oedipus* temple chorus of four or five years before.

For some weeks after the completion of this scene, Musorgsky seems to have put the opera to one side. He must have been distracted by his duties at the ministry—on one occasion he put off visiting Balakirev because he was too busy, on another he pleaded his old trouble "nervous irritation" as a pretext for avoiding Alexey Lvov's *Undine* at the Maryinsky. He then took up a Koltsov poem, "Winds Are Blowing, Wild Winds" ("Duyut vetrï, vetrï buynïye"), and turned it into a rambling but vivid song for bass that, in its elemental power and somber colorings, already touches areas of experience well outside those of the conventional romance. Like the "Old Man's Song," much of it is modal, the source, perhaps, of that curiously implacable quality which is becoming a Musorgsky fingerprint; at the same time the piano octaves lend a sweeping energy that might be the meteorological equivalent of King Saul's "Mine be the doom." Most interesting of all is Musorgsky's willingness to throw in disruptive details that defy the textbook yet are obviously not a product of ignorance or incompetence. A striking example comes at the very end of the song, where, after a regulation plagal cadence in C-sharp major, the piano adds a loud F-sharp–G-sharp, like some mocking echo of the last two chords, or a door left banging by the passing gale.

Effects of this kind may have been details remembered from improvised performances. Musorgsky often played and sang his songs at circle gatherings, and there is plenty of evidence that he, like Balakirev,
sometimes made them up as he went along, either because they were
not yet written down or simply because he felt entitled to change them
as the mood took him. This might be partly why "King Saul" exists in
two distinct versions, though, as we saw, the simplification of the later
version might have been due to the publisher Bessel's intervention. A
better example is the Pushkin song "Night" ("Noch' "), which Musorgsky first wrote down in April 1864, two weeks or so after "Winds Are
Blowing," and which survives in two significantly different versions of
more or less equal intricacy, constructed on the same basic framework
(and apparently in the same year). Various details suggest an improvisation.[1] The tremolando piano chords that dominate the opening in
both versions are an accompanist's cliché for a troubled mood (picking up Pushkin's "disturbs the latter silence/Of the dark night"), while
the frequent changes of figuration sound like impromptu reactions to
the changing verbal imagery: languid quaver triplets for "beside my
bed/A mournful candle burns," rippling semiquaver triplets for "my
words, / Mingling and murmuring/Flow," and so forth. Finally, the
puzzling fact that Musorgsky revamped Pushkin's poem in the second
version of the song, making it more verbose while leaving out some of
the imagery (including the mournful candle), suggests a routine impatience with the artwork as an untouchable icon. Changing Pushkin,
incidentally, was extremely *mal vu* in sixties (and later) Petersburg. It
would get Musorgsky into trouble again, on a more famous and much
more notable occasion.

Having completed "Night" in its original version, he returned to
Salammbô, and turned his attention to the problem of the choral scenes.
The first thing he composed was a thumping "War Song of the Libyans" ("Voyevaya pesn' liviytsev") for male chorus, which may or may
not have been intended as part of the wild festivities in Hamilcar's
garden—supposedly act 1 of the opera—or might just as well have served
for the mercenaries' siege of Carthage in (presumably) the first scene
of act 2. According to Stasov, the main theme was a Jewish melody that
Musorgsky had overheard sung in the courtyard of his house "during
a prayer session of a Jewish neighbor."[2] Musorgsky never got round to
indicating the exact placement of this fine, suitably barbaric number,
and one half-suspects that he composed it without any very clear idea
about where it would go. One other set piece, which he wrote a few
months later, the "Song of the Balearic Islander" ("Pesn' baleyartsa"),

is also usually assumed, on the authority of Pavel Lamm, to have been intended for the first act, though the only Balearic song in the novel is sung later in the story by the mercenary chief Zauxas after he has slit the throat of a Carthaginian guard and drunk his blood. But Musorgsky's version is a love song, "In the embrace of a young girl . . . I forget the clash of swords," quasi-Oriental in character (for some reason), and rather too obviously indebted to the chorus of Holofernes' odalisques in act 3 of *Judith,* with its sultry cor anglais and harp.

Neither of these pieces helped in the least solve the crucial problem of *Salammbô* as an operatic subject: how to animate the crowd and battle sequences as a context for the rather thin love story at its center. They were detachable items, not entwined with the drama in any way. Musorgsky later included the Balearic song in the collection of his early songs under the title *Youthful Years* (*Yunïye godï*), the bound auto·graph manuscript of which turned up in Paris around 1908.[3] As for the "War Song," this was subjected to a series of revisions and expansions, the last of them as late as 1877 and under a completely different title, *Jesus Navin,* by which time it existed purely as a concert piece for solo voice, chorus, and orchestra. Meanwhile he made serious assaults on two complete scenes of his putative scenario: the scene in the Temple of Moloch after the theft of the veil, the priests and people calling on the god to avenge them but fearful of his anger against them, the brief thunderstorm that confirms at first their fears and then their hopes, and Salammbô's resolve to go to Mathô's tent and steal back the veil (Musorgsky labelled this act 3, scene 1); and a scene for Mathô in prison before his torture and execution (act 4, scene 1), an episode entirely invented by Musorgsky.

These are substantial stretches of continuous music, a good three-quarters of an hour in total, and much of it so good that Musorgsky later found it worthwhile to adapt it—sometimes without substantial alteration—for an opera with an utterly different plot and setting, *Boris Godunov.* In the temple scene, the people's lamentations are set as a kind of Orthodox hymn in block harmony, while the Chief Priest bemoans the fate of Carthage to music that will later describe Boris's guilty fear of the "right hand of the dread judge on the criminal soul."[4] One can suggest that this whole situation has its origins in the Hebrew scenes of *Judith.* One can point out that Musorgsky's grumbles to Balakirev about the lack of action in those scenes, and about Serov's use of Christian musical idioms for Jewish prayers ("It's about time to stop converting Jews to Christianity or Catholicizing them"),[5] could just as well be levelled at *Salammbô,* which converts bloody, child-sacrificing pagans to Russian Orthodoxy and is also distinctly short on action. But the fact remains that Musorgsky's music for this scene explores territory unsuspected by Serov, territory outside the normal boundaries of harmonic and textural good behavior that even Serov, despite his lack of formal training, knew how to respect, but did not know how to disrespect.

Musorgsky's style here can be traced back, somewhat speculatively, to certain primary ingredients that seem to have struck deep into his imagination. Some of them have already been mentioned: Orthodox chant as a way of thinking about melody; modal harmony, which "traps" the harmony within specific fields out of which it has to be "forced" into new fields, without the smooth grammar that regulates conventional modulation from key to key. Curiously enough, this approach to harmony, though restrictive in some ways, is liberating in others. It allows dissonance to be treated as a modal element, part of the field, rather than as some kind of deviance that has to be justified and corrected ("prepared and resolved," in textbook parlance). It doesn't encourage the kind of rich contrapuntal developments of the German classical tradition from Bach to Beethoven (and on, eventually, to the as yet inadequately known Wagner), which, like long sentences and paragraphs in a written or spoken language, depend on a complex grammar for their coherence; it does encourage vivid dramatic and poetic contrasts, a quality of ritual, powerful effects of mass, a sense of the roughness and color of life. One symptom of this approach is the prominence of unison writing and parallel chords, not only in the chorus, but also in the accompaniment (Musorgsky did not orchestrate this scene); another is the bursts of temper, as when the people take up the priests' "Smite our insolent enemies with thunderbolts of deadly arrows" or in the ensuing thunderstorm, where the intervention of supernatural forces is marked by violent whole-tone harmonies (as in the abduction scene of *Ruslan and Lyudmila*) and rushing chromatic scales.

So much of this music is striking and individual that its lack of real dramatic effect is at first puzzling. The explanation probably lies in Musorgsky's failure to vary the pace of the scene, which crawls along, more or less in the querulous vein of the opening, and mostly in slow or moderate tempo, with a single burst of allegro for Salammbô's decision to retrieve the veil and the chorus's brief attempt to dissuade her. The other obvious failure is Salammbô herself: ever the stately mezzo-soprano priestess, never the vulnerable, sensuous, but inexperienced girl who will later (in a scene Musorgsky did not set) succumb to Mathô in his tent, not entirely in the calculating spirit of Judith. The treatment of Mathô himself, in the prison scene, is superficially more ambitious. Musorgsky gives him a long monologue which amounts to a summary of all the events in the novel that he had presumably by this time (November 1864) despaired of ever including in a stageable opera. Once again the writing is highly unconventional and individual, and once again it fails to catch fire. Mathô, like Ruslan, is a rather ponderous bass, far from the image of the dashing commander who, with the stolen veil in his hands, risks capture for the look in Salammbô's eyes and the touch of her sweet lips. Worse, we know nothing about his mind, because his actions, like Salammbô's, have no context. He remains a wooden statue in a dungeon, like Florestan without the advantage of Beethoven. Musorgsky could perhaps have remedied this by composing the necessary earlier scenes, better still by composing them first. In fact he never composed them at all.

By the end of 1864 he must have realized *Salammbô* was going nowhere. He wrote only one more scene—another set piece—a chorus of priestesses before Salammbô's death from grief at the sight of Mathô's horrible torture and death: another invention of his. That was in February 1866; soon afterward he revised and orchestrated the "War Song," and he also at some point orchestrated the Balearic song and the prison scene. After that, the work went into a drawer, to be plundered as necessary for future scores. Occasionally he would play excerpts at Balakirev's or Cui's evenings. "These fragments," Rimsky-Korsakov tells us, "prompted on the one hand the highest approval for the beauty of their themes and ideas, on the other hand the most severe reproof for disorderliness and muddle."[6] But Musorgsky must long have known that *Salammbô* was a wrong direction for him; that, as he told Nikolay Kompaneysky, "there is enough of the East in *Judith*. Art is no game. Time is valuable."[7] He had in fact already begun to explore a landscape much nearer home.

During the previous winter, Balakirev had composed a Second Overture on Russian Themes, basing himself this time mainly on tunes from his own as yet unpublished collection of *Russian National Songs* (there are three tunes from the collection; a fourth appears to be original). This is a more sophisticated piece than its predecessor, though it suffers, like most quasi-symphonic treatments of folk tunes, from the too obvious boundary between the actual melodies and the working to which they are subjected. Above all, it goes beyond the simple repetitive design of Glinka's *Kamarinskaya* or Balakirev's own first overture. It was performed almost immediately, in a Free Music School concert on 6 April 1864, conducted by Balakirev himself, and again four weeks later in an RMS concert under Rubinstein, and Musorgsky must surely have attended both. In any case, he will certainly have been aware of Balakirev's collection and probably knew some of the arrangements. In setting them for voice and piano, Balakirev had gone out of his way to respect the tunes' modal character, keeping the accompaniments mostly spare and unobtrusive, rather than dressing them up as richly textured and harmonized salon romances. He had also paid attention to their occasionally freewheeling metric and decorative patterns, and avoided routinely cramming them into rigid three- or four-beat bars and four-bar phrases. The general effect is to bring out certain peculiarities of the folk style that tended to get smoothed out in conventional arrangements: peculiarities of melody and rhythm (like those of ecclesiastical chant) which didn't fit in with standard academic procedures.

Perhaps it was in response to such things, as well as to the overture itself, that Musorgsky composed his song "Kalistratushka" that May, and labelled it "Étude in folk style" ("Etyud v narodnom stile"). The song is a setting of a pseudo-folk poem by Nekrasov about a young man who fulfills his mother's prediction of a happy life while his wife slaves away and dresses in rags. As a genuine folk song, this kind of story would have been told to one short tune with many verses (there are several of the kind in the Balakirev collection). Musorgsky treats it artily by varying the melody and tone to fit the changing moods, rather as if the singer were telling the story by way of a chain of related melodies.

Some of these melodies, however, derive fairly candidly from tunes in the collection. The singer's first theme is close to Balakirev no. 1 ("Ne bïlo vetru"), which is also the first theme of the overture, while the second theme of the song is not quite so close to no. 2 ("Poydu, Poydu," also in the overture) but with an obvious family resemblance. After that, the song drifts away from the collection, but never so far as to lose kinship. Here and there Musorgsky imitates the *protyazh-naya pesnya*—the metrically fluid lyrical peasant style in which individual words are "drawn out" over several melody notes, and the meter reflects the sung phrase, rather than the other way round. The first line of the setting is of this kind: a seven-beat bar (for the two syllables of "nado"—"over"), followed by two six-four bars and a four-four for the seven syllables of "mnoy pevala matushka" ("Mama sang [over] me"). In general the melodic style is like an extended version of folk song, modal but with chromatic colorings and some leaps unlikely in authentic folk singing. The fall of a whole tone at the end of the first phrase is highly idiomatic, however (it even has a technical name: *peremennost',* "mutability").[8] In general one might be listening to a folk musician with a developed mind but his roots still in his village soil. It was a style that Musorgsky, who was not much interested in folksy arrangements as such, soon learned to put to higher use.

While Musorgsky had been doing battle with Carthage, César Cui had also been at work on a new opera, set in Scotland. In fact his idea for an operatic version of Heine's *William Ratcliff* went back to 1861. But his method of working was barely more systematic than Musorgsky's. According to Richard Taruskin, the author of the best English-language study of this opera, Cui began with the first scene of Heine's second act (a tavern scene), and only turned to the opening act some time in 1862, then left the final (short) scene of this act unwritten, and instead at some time in 1863 set to work on the opening of the last act, and so forth.[9] At the time in 1864 when Musorgsky was struggling with *Salammbô*, Cui was writing the crucial scene in his act 2 in which Ratcliff, having murdered his beloved's two previous bridegrooms, confronts but fails to dispatch the third. Then, like his young friend, Cui seems to have shelved the project—not, however, out of any waning of enthusiasm or conviction, but simply because the need to supplement his income as a fortifications instructor had become too pressing to be denied. "Since the salary I received," he wrote later,

> was insufficient for subsistence, my wife and I opened a preparatory boarding school for youths wishing to enter the Engineering Academy, and, with the exception of languages, I took it upon myself to give instruction in all subjects. Even the summer with its holidays was not free. On the contrary, this was the most feverish preexamination time. Besides, one had to bring the boarders up, not just instruct them. So we were together at all times, as if one big family, eating, living in the country, taking walks, boating, and so on, all together. It is understandable that in such conditions I could write only in snatches, and I wrote the opera not sequentially, in order, from first scene to last, but in separate scenes from various acts, whatever I was most interested in at a given moment.[10]

As if the school were not enough to keep the wolf from the door, Cui also started taking on work as a writer on music for the *Sanktpeterburgskiye vedomosti* (*St. Petersburg Gazette*), at first on an occasional basis (one or two long articles a month, starting in March 1864), later as a regular reviewer. It hardly seems surprising that, for a time, composition took a backseat, even if—as Taruskin points out—Cui did not need the excuse of a busy life to justify a spasmodic approach to creative work. He had worked the same way ever since graduating in 1857, and so, for that matter, in their various circumstances, had Balakirev and Musorgsky.[11] Taruskin calls it a habit; others have put it down to sheer amateurishness. But part of the trouble, at least, may have been a lack of clear artistic direction, in circumstances where it would have been morally, if not technically, easy to tag along with the German or French mainstream, but where there was a conscious aesthetic need to find a Russian alternative. Cui did eventually—unlike Musorgsky—finish his opera. He returned to it in earnest in 1867 and 1868, and it was staged at the Maryinsky Theatre under the youthful Eduard Nápravník in February 1869. And the finished product tends to support the "mainstream" argument, because, with all its considerable virtues and by no means inconsiderable character, *William Ratcliff* is very far from establishing a Russian alternative, in style, in technique, or in content.

A German play about Scotland hardly looks like an attempt at anything of the sort, even with a libretto in Russian (adapted by Cui himself from the translation by Alexey Pleshcheyev, the radical poet of Musorgsky's rustling leaves). Heine's early tragedy (1822) taps into the romantic spirit of Scott's recent *Waverley* novels and *The Bride of Lammermoor,* but with a Macbethian image of Scotland as a country of wild, gloomy mountains, crazed aristocrats, melancholy ballads, and cackling witches. William Ratcliff, rejected by Mary, the daughter of the laird MacGregor, has twice murdered her betrotheds as she waited at the altar, and now intends to kill a third, whose wedding is in progress as the curtain rises. But Ratcliff himself is wounded in the ensuing fight, and when he presents himself, pale and distraught, in Mary's bedchamber, she suddenly realizes her love for him. There is, though, a sinister backcloth to these events. William's father had loved Mary's mother but had been killed by her jealous father. As William enters the bedchamber, Mary's nurse is relating the old story, and William, who has himself had visions of a mysterious couple reaching out their arms to one another, is suddenly transformed into an agent of revenge. He draws his sword and kills Mary, her father, and himself.

From the start, Cui approached this terrifying story in the spirit of German romantic opera—Weber, Marschner, the Schumann of *Genoveva*—leaving out the social ironies (Douglas, the latest bridegroom, talking wearily about London life) and the genre detail (the thieving innkeeper teaching his little boy the Lord's Prayer), and setting the violent action in a more or less conventional operatic frame. A lot of what he composed first—the act 2 tavern scene and act 1 wedding—is chorus, of the kind that would have attracted Wagner's anathema against "scenery that has learned to march and sing." But for the dramatic action he gradually evolves a through-composed, quasi-symphonic style of which Wagner might rather have approved, whatever he would have thought of Cui's technical mastery, which is reasonably adequate to the tasks he sets himself but looks distinctly thin beside such contemporary masterpieces as *Tristan und Isolde* or even Verdi's *Forza del destino,* which had its first performance in St. Peters-burg in November 1862 when Cui was probably at work on his act 1. Like Wagner (whose music he encountered for the first time in the St. Petersburg concerts of early 1863), Cui uses leitmotifs, of a sort, to bind the musical drama, though never with the richness or intricacy of Wagner. In one or two cases, the motives serve as important recurrent themes, developed in the orchestra as well as the voices; mostly they are simple reminiscence motives, reminders of one person or situation in the context of another—a device of some importance in an opera so heavily dependent on the narration of past events.

It's hard for us now to be sure about the effect of *William Ratcliff* in the theatre, since performances in recent years (or in the West at any time) have been nonexistent. The music itself is interesting, some-times strong and atmospheric, certainly better than the work's total neglect would suggest; it is easy to understand Tchaikovsky's remark to Balakirev, before he had actually heard a performance (if he ever did), that "I look through Cui's opera every day and am delighted. I didn't expect that this opera would be so remarkably good."[12] We may even appreciate the importance attached to it by the Balakirev circle, who were desperate to succeed in opera (not least because St. Petersburg concert life was so limited) but had still achieved practically nothing in the field. What is less easy to accept is the work's iconic status as an example of what Taruskin, in his chapter heading, calls (perhaps ironically) " 'Kuchkism' in Practice." If by "kuchkism" we understand what Stasov, Balakirev, and company, saw as the defining attributes of an identifiably Russian style, then *William Ratcliff* is scarcely kuchkist at all. In the single respect that it seeks to create a close bond between the words and the music, so that the latter is heard as an emanation of the former, it might seem to reflect (of all people) Serov's analysis of those scenes in Dargomïzhsky's *Rusalka* where the music is tightly mapped onto the contours of Pushkin's own verse, an idea that became impor-tant for the *kuchka* later on. It frequently, though by no means always, sets Pleshcheyev's Russian as it stands. But the rhythmic and accentual patterns are in fact largely conventional, and sometimes, as Taruskin has shown, even violate natural Russian prosody. The few cases where Cui achieves a naturalistic effect are offset by many pages dominated by the normal artifices of early romantic opera.

The most kuchkist thing about *William Ratcliff*, truth to tell, is the haphazard way in which it was composed. Cui certainly had no doctrinaire Russianist intentions, or he would hardly have chosen a subject so spiritually and geographically remote, one in which the only ethnic or exotic colorings would be the occasional Scotch snap and a single, mildly incongruous, Scottish folk song, "Tibbie Fowler o' the Glen," supplied by Stasov and set by Cui as a chorus of (presumably) gentry at Douglas's wedding feast. There is a nod to Glinka's *Ruslan* in the whole-tone passage in which MacGregor describes the nonappearance of Mary's first two bridegrooms, Macdonald and Duncan, at *their* weddings. But all in all, *Ratcliff* is a less candidly Russian piece of work than *Judith,* which imitates Glinka more overtly, is partly through-composed, uses leitmotifs, and sets the Russian language no worse. The irony is that, after he had abandoned work on his opera toward the end of 1864, one of Cui's first acts in his new role of music critic was to publish a belated denunciation of Serov's, cast in a mold that one recognizes from Rimsky-Korsakov's description of Balakirev's analytical method, praising this or that brief passage, damning others, and generally lurching from praise to blame like a music examiner marking each category of performance out of ten. "The general impression which *Judith* makes on the spectator," he grumbles at the end, "is a painful one. Weariness sets in from Act II on and, constantly intensifying, weighs upon you right to the very end of the opera." And yet "Mr Serov's labours have produced a work which is worthy of respect and remark, standing prominently and sharply apart from the voluminous trash which is being written both abroad and here in Russia."[13] When *William Ratcliff* finally reached the stage, Serov wasted no time getting his own back. "A real artist," he began his *Golos* review, "is *always* a critic, but from this it does not follow that any old musical reporter can become a real artist by merely wishing it . . . Art takes its revenge on those who slander it"—which amounted, as Taruskin observes, to "casting an enormous boulder at his own glass house."[14]

Thus, as 1864 drew to a close, the Balakirev circle had arrived at a mature phase which, many years later, its youngest member would find all too easy to satirize from the safety of a professorial chair at the St. Petersburg Conservatory. "Thirty years have passed by now,"

Rimsky-Korsakov wrote in 1897, "since the days when Stasov would write that in eighteen-sixty-so-and-so the Russian school displayed a lively activity: [Nikolay] Lodïzhensky [briefly a member of the circle in the sixties] wrote one romance, Borodin got an idea for something, Balakirev is planning to rework something, and so on."[15] Cui was shelving one opera, Musorgsky another; Borodin was still tinkering with his symphony in E-flat (last year the slow movement, this year the scherzo), Rimsky-Korsakov—on the high seas—with his in E-flat minor; and Balakirev had himself embarked on a large-scale symphony in C which, as it turned out, he would only finish thirty-three years later, in the very year of Rimsky-Korsakov's reminiscence. At their musical evenings they duly came and went. Musorgsky in particular would vanish for weeks on end, then reappear inexplicably; but whether these motions reflected intensities of composition, duties at the ministry, or socio-emotional fickleness, nobody quite knew. These days he was close to some friends called the Opochinins—brother and sister—and spent time with them that was discreetly resented by Balakirev ("Modinka," he muttered to Cui, "is probably sitting on a leash at the Opochinins' in a store-room").[16] Modinka may even have been in love with the somewhat older Nadezhda Opochinina, the dedicatee of "Night," among several other works of his.

A certain pattern had been set, one that would adjust itself from time to time as allegiances changed or the ordinary necessities of life began to interfere with its intellectual bohemianism. Like most artistic *cénacles*, it would last until its members emerged fully formed and no longer desired its protection, and thereafter would survive essentially only in the historical imagination.

CHAPTER II

Home Is the Sailor

M usorgsky had had a month's leave from the ministry at the end of 1864 in order to visit his mother at Karevo; though only fifty years old, she was evidently tired and ailing, a widow for more than a decade, and old before her time. Modest was composing a setting of "Molitva," Lermontov's prayer to the Mother of God for a young child, but dedicated by the composer to his own mother: "Not for my own pilgrim soul do I pray, but for an innocent in the cold world. Surround her with the happiness she deserves, give her caring companions, bright youth and a calm old age, peace to a guileless heart, the peace of hope." Alas on 17 March, not long after the simple, pious song was completed, Yuliya Ivanovna passed away, and her son was left to compose her epitaph, a sadly undistinguished little piano piece called "Nyanya i ya" ("Nanny and Me"), nostalgically subtitled "From Memories of Childhood."

A few weeks after his mother's death, Musorgsky moved out of the commune that had been his home for the past twenty months, and moved into his brother's family apartment on the Kryukov Canal. He had been suffering from one of his periodic bouts of nervous trouble, and it seems that it was his sister-in-law, Tatyana Pavlovna, who persuaded him, somewhat against his will, to come and live with them.[1] Then, when the family went for the summer to a farmhouse at a village called Minkino, near Luga, a hundred or so miles south of St. Petersburg, he naturally went with them. Here, amid the flat, marshy farmland on the banks of the river Oredezh, he composed two more not very exciting piano pieces: "Rêverie," based on a theme by Vyacheslav Loginov, one of the three commune brothers, and a bland A-minor scherzo, "La Capricieuse," on a rather shapeless six-note theme by a piano pupil of Balakirev's. The only curious thing about such music is that a composer of Musorgsky's talent should have bothered to write it at all, unless it was as a dutiful gesture to the friends whose themes it borrows. A song, "The Outcast Woman" ("Otverzhennaya"), is more interesting, if only because of certain facts about the choice and treatment of the poem, which is the work of a noted revolutionary, Ivan Holz-Miller, recently deported to Siberia. The song itself is not remotely revolutionary, but it does suggest a dawning enthusiasm for the portrayal of the socially deprived, in this case a raddled old prostitute. Musorgsky subtitled it "An Experiment in Recitative," which might lead one to expect a very flexible, perhaps dramatic approach to verbal meter and accentuation. In fact the experiment goes the other way, and the setting is both entirely syllabic (one note to each syllable) and largely undifferentiated in its note values, so that the strong Russian tonic accent is reduced to a pattern of discreet metric stresses. Above all, there is neither anger nor distaste in the observation of misery, merely a kind of amiable detachment, like that of a tour guide pointing out some less than salubrious aspect of an otherwise agreeable town.

Characteristically, Musorgsky seems to have composed little else at Minkino that summer, though he later described to Stasov an experience he had while there that eventually gave rise to an altogether more poignant study in human wretchedness.

> One day [Stasov reports] he was standing by the window and was startled by a commotion that was taking place before his eyes. An unfortunate simpleton was making a declaration of love to a young girl he liked, was begging her, while ashamed of his own ugliness and wretched condition; he himself understood that nothing existed for him in the world, least of all the happiness of love. Musorgsky was profoundly struck; the bizarre figure and the whole scene imprinted themselves on his mind; they instantly conjured up distinctive forms and sounds for the embodiment of the images that had so disturbed him.[2]

But a whole year would go by before Musorgsky composed "Darling Savishna," and instead he wrote a quite different song of misfortune, a setting of the lullaby in Ostrovsky's play *The Voyevoda*. An old man rocks his grandson to sleep in some kind of pre-Chekhovian frame of mind: there is misery on this earth, but "your little soul flies in the heavens." And Musorgsky's "Lullaby" reflects the contrast: somber and stoical at first, then smiling and drowsy toward the end. In fact the performance directions he attached to the first version of the song (but for some reason removed when he revised and shortened it four or five years later) indicate that the grandfather himself is struggling to stay awake and does in the end fall asleep, so that the radiance of the final page amounts to dream versus reality. The music develops the idiom of the "Old Man's Song" from a purely modal (Dorian) B-flat minor, rather dark, through strange, drifting chromatics, toward a hesitant, not quite convinced B-flat major. As in the Goethe song, a liturgical note is apparent. Much of the melody is like ornamented plainchant, now and then thrown into disarray by the contemplation of toil: "disagreeable, alien, back-breaking, everlasting, cruel, punishing." Meanwhile, the harmony frequently evades the normal processes of tonal accompaniment, either by simply doubling the voice or by doubling it with parallel chords or, less eccentrically, through conventional chord sequences in root position. The effect of all this is to undermine one of the most crucial foundations of tonal harmony: the independent movement of the different parts. Whether Musorgsky was consciously feeling his way toward a new kind of expression, or was simply following an intuition uninhibited by any undue reverence for convention, the fact remains that this song, beautiful, touching and individual as it is, points discreetly along a path no one before him had travelled.

Musorgsky returned to St. Petersburg from Minkino in September, and that same month young Rimsky-Korsakov, now a world-travelled twenty-one-year-old, finally arrived back in the capital from the island fortress of Kronstadt, where he had spent the summer helping decommission the cruise clipper. Music had not featured prominently on the voyage, but he had managed to complete his symphony, partly under instruction by letter from Balakirev, who, as we saw, had provided him with a Russian folk tune called "The Tartar Captivity" ("Tatarski polon") to use as the main theme of the as yet unwritten slow movement, and then sent him corrections, which Rimsky-Korsakov dutifully incorporated. He initially wrote the movement, he tells us in his autobiography, while anchored off Gravesend at the start of 1863.[3] After this the symphony went into storage until his return to St. Petersburg, at which point the scherzo—composed before his departure—still lacked a trio. Balakirev was soon bullying him to write one and to reorchestrate the whole work. Once again, Rimsky-Korsakov did as he was told, and as a reward Balakirev actually conducted the symphony in an FMS concert that December, the first public performance of any work by the young naval officer, who astonished the audience, Cui reported in his review, by appearing in uniform to take his bow.[4]

Many years later Rimsky-Korsakov made a fairly drastic revision of the whole work, including a substantial recomposition of the finale. But while the final version is tighter and more accomplished, it cannot be said that it is better or more individual. On the contrary, he seems to have had a natural feeling for symphonic writing of a certain kind from the start, unlike Musorgsky, who tended to struggle with received conventions; and in following strong models, he often found personal turns of melody and harmony that still, at this distance, identify the music as his even when it lacks any striking originality. The first movement is typical. The slow introduction might belong to a lost symphony by Schumann, and the influence survives into the allegro, whose main theme is a bleak descendant of the main theme of the "Spring" Symphony. But the way Rimsky-Korsakov boxes his movement into clearly delineated sections rounded off by well-behaved passages of motivic development, all without in any way sacrificing momentum or interest, is entirely Russian, studentlike perhaps, except that one finds it also in some of the very greatest, most sophisticated symphonies of that tradition (most famously Tchaikovsky's "Pathétique" and Stravinsky's Symphony in Three Movements).

Cui at once drew attention to the Schumann influence, noting, for instance, the resemblance of the trio (the last music to be composed) to the equivalent section in the scherzo of Schumann's Overture, Scherzo, and Finale. But he also rightly insisted on Glinka as a countermodel, though his suggestion that Glinka (who wrote little or no symphonic music) was the stronger influence is an exaggeration with an obvious ideological motive. The traces of Glinka are mainly confined to orchestral coloring and a few chromatic twists of melody and harmony: moments here and there where the music suddenly, inexplicably, changes from sounding German to sounding—well, Russian. But Cui was understandably on the lookout for a non-German white hope, and he readily saw it in this skillful, talented, but not in the least challenging new symphony by a composer who, as a matter of fact, had written practically nothing else. Rimsky-Korsakov's music had all the virtues of what one already knew, with a few individual quirks, a seemingly effortless brilliance, and the beauty of being homegrown. It lacked the disadvantage of extreme originality, something with which Russian critics and to a lesser extent Russian audiences—much like their colleagues in every other country—have always had difficulty.

Rimsky-Korsakov had quickly re-established contact with the Balakirev circle, and had once more become a regular at their evenings. Balakirev had already had some unknown degree of input into the symphony, and he and Musorgsky had played it through, four-hands, at one of his musical evenings in November. At Balakirev's, too, the young midshipman met Borodin for the first time, and despite the eleven-year difference in their ages they got on well and were soon close friends. Borodin was now ensconced in a ground-floor flat in the Academy of Physicians (where he was a professor) at the northern end of the Liteiney Bridge over the Neva, and had settled into the bizarre combination of professional and domestic circumstances that would plague him for the rest of his life and, in all probability, help bring on his early death. His biographer Serge Dianin, whose mother was Borodin's adopted daughter and who was himself born in the academy apartment, provides a hair-raising description of the apartment itself.

> The flat was quite spacious but not convenient as it was scattered around among official premises: the kitchen was in the basement, and those parts of the flat that were on the ground floor were separated by a corridor with doors opening on to laboratories and offices, for which reason there was a constant scurry of students and employees. There were plenty of other inconveniences. There was no quiet, secluded place for Alexander Porfir'yevich to work at home; and he did not even at that time have a private laboratory of his own, such as he managed to fix up somewhat later.[5]

Rimsky-Korsakov, who had himself moved into a bed-sitter on Vasilevsky Island, took to visiting Borodin at the academy, and occasionally stayed the night. Sometimes other members of the circle would be there as well. They would talk about music, and Borodin would show them the drafts of his own symphony, at least three movements of which existed in various stages of incompleteness (the first movement complete enough to have been given a play-through by the composer and Canille at a soirée early in 1865). Borodin, Rimsky-Korsakov reports,

> was an exceedingly warm and cultivated man, agreeable company, witty and original. When I visited him, I would often find him at work in the laboratory next to his apartment. When he sat over his retorts full of some colorless gas and distilled it through a tube from one vessel to

another, I would tell him that he was transfusing from the empty to the emptier. Having finished his work, he would go with me to his apartment, and we would get down to musical activities or conversation, in the midst of which he would jump up and run back to the laboratory to make sure nothing had burnt out or boiled over there, meanwhile filling the corridor with improbable sequences of ninths or sevenths.[6]

Borodin's placid temperament was the one thing that enabled him to survive the circumstances of his working and married life for as long as he did. As a professor, he had to reconcile his research activities, like any modern university lecturer, with a heavy teaching load and a demanding administrative schedule. His wife, Yekaterina, charmed everyone she met and, according to Rimsky-Korsakov, "worshipped her husband's [musical] talent." But she did little to foster it. During her long absences in Moscow, visiting her mother or her doctors, her husband lived a bachelor life in St. Petersburg, trying his best to hold back the tidal waves of disorganization and overwork. When she returned to St. Petersburg, she would often have one or more relations to stay in their already dysfunctional flat. All this, Dianin remarks with cool understatement, "made things awkward for the Borodins, and they sometimes actually suffered privation, since they felt obliged to help all those in need." To make matters worse, the insomniac Yekaterina would sit up half the night and keep her husband up as well. Not surprisingly, composition tended to stagnate. "Music," he wrote homerically to Balakirev on one occasion, "is asleep; Apollo's altar is extinguished; the ashes on it have grown cold; the muses are weeping, while around them the urns fill with tears, the tears spill over the brim and mingle into streams, and the streams babble and sadly announce my cooling towards art for today."[7] On this particular occasion he blamed the goose that Cui had given him for supper the day before. But the situation was, alas, of more or less daily occurrence.

Meanwhile, the industrious Serov had composed a second opera and had it staged at the Maryinsky toward the end of October 1865. *Rogneda* seems to have been an attempt to create an authentic Russian music drama on the basis of a plot derived from the ancient chronicles of Kievan Rus and with a substantial infusion of simple melodies either taken from published Russian folk collections or imitations thereof. The rambling scenario, partly based on episodes in Mikhail Zagoskin's novel *Askold's Tomb* (which Zagoskin had himself turned into a libretto for the Verstovsky opera of that name), revolves round the conversion to Christianity of the founder of the Kievan state, Prince Vladimir

Sviatoslavich, as the somewhat confusing result of his rescue from a marauding bear by a young Christian, Ruald, and a failed attempt on his life by his wife, Rogneda, acting on instructions from the High Priest of the pagan god Perun. Serov had fallen in with the so-called *pochvenniki,* a splinter group of Russophile thinkers who shared the Slavophile belief that the future for Russia lay in the study of its own native history and culture (the *pochva,* or soil). In its own peculiar way, *Rogneda* was a kind of remake of *Judith* in terms of the emergence of the Russian nation: its location at the frontier between paganism and true religion, its confrontation of antique heroism and idealism (distorted or otherwise) with the earthy reality of the common people, its origin in a theory of what sort of opera it was necessary for a Russian composer to write at that moment, when the air was rent with competing social and political manifestos of this or that kind, none of which had any obvious chance of fulfillment in the foreseeable future.

All this comes out musically in *Rogneda* as a tapestry of somewhat startling contrasts. The actual plot, which is thinly spread over the five acts, is conveyed in reasonably conventional terms: a lot of fluid recitative and arioso, post-*Lohengrin,* rich (if that's the word) in standard-issue chromatic harmony dominated by the diminished seventh chord—the nineteenth century's musical equivalent of the shock-horror bubble in a 1950s comic strip. On the other hand, the lengthy genre scenes—the dances and jester's songs, the choruses of pilgrims, the hunters' drinking songs—adopt a self-consciously naïve, folkish, even primitive manner, diatonic and repetitive to the point of tedium, almost studiously avoiding musical interest in any previously known sense of the term. It appears that Serov's intention was to bring to the grand-operatic stage a lofty version of *Askold's Tomb.* Richard Taruskin has shown how closely Serov's analysis of Verstovsky's opera can be mapped almost item by item onto *Rogneda,* and also the extent to which the apostrophizing of what was not much more than a better class of vaudeville was partly a way of playing down Glinka's status as the founding father of Russian opera.[8] Stasov was, of course, outraged. Long before *Rogneda* reached the stage he was spitting fire in Balakirev's direction:

A friend of Serov's has related to me some of his recent pronouncements, which I simply can hardly believe. For instance, Serov has (apparently) stated in his lectures and countless times in conversation that there's no Russian music at all in Glinka, only some Russian themes, but with foreign workmanship: for instance, *Kamarinskaya* and the greater part of *Ruslan;* that if only Verstovsky could have been given Glinka's talent and musical education, he would have been a much more Russian musician, and would have shown what our national music ought to be. But since none of this has yet been done by anybody, it will have to be and will be revealed in *Rogneda* what a true national Russian music ought to be, not just in its themes but in its spirit, its atmosphere, its workmanship and its smallest details. In this sense, naturally, the "Dance of the Skomorokhi" serves as an indictment and a corrective to *Kamarinskaya*. It seems to me that this is all a consequence of Serov's lecherous cohabitation with the *pochvenniki* at [the journal] *Epokha*.[9]

The biggest concern for the Balakirev circle was precisely the extent to which *Rogneda* did or did not point the way to the authentic Russian opera of the future. They had, of course, absolutely no interest in Serov being the pioneer in this respect, however good or bad his music. But needless to say, they all went to see his new work, and one way or another they reacted. According to Rimsky-Korsakov, the official line was mockery, and damning with the faint praise of agreeing to admire one or two insignificant episodes. Musorgsky sneered loftily at this "well-educated musician who in a Russian epic poem made Perun a high priest and planted pilgrims in the Kievan forest. And as regards the connection between music and history, he came out below Verstovsky: at Vladimir's feast he started up a modern tavern song and made the girls dance, exactly as if Vladimir were Holofernes."[10] Cui naturally seized on the opportunity to have a go at Serov in his *Sanktpeterburgskiye vedomosti* review, satirizing the plot and ridiculing its pretensions as drama. "Not a single act goes by without all manner of artifice: witches, high priests, hunters, dogs, horses, death scenes, processions, dances, dreams, moonlight—what isn't there in this opera! These effects can be wonderful if they proceed from the subject itself. But if the subject be fashioned to seek out these effects as if by compulsion, then this is hardly art."[11]

But Rimsky-Korsakov admitted long afterward that "*Rogneda* interested me a lot, and I liked a good deal of it, for instance the sorceress, the chorus of sacrifice to the idol, the chorus in the banqueting hall, the dance of the *skomorokhi,* the hunt prelude, the chorus in 7/4, the finale, and many other bits": that is, precisely the things that Cui had made fun of. "I dared not," he went on, "confess all this in the Balakirev circle, and even, as someone sincerely devoted to the ideas of the circle, ran the opera down in front of acquaintances . . . I remember how this astonished my brother, who liked *Rogneda*."[12] He even owned up to having incorporated ideas from Serov's opera in works of his own. Specifically, he mentions a triplet figuration in his second symphony, *Antar;* but Taruskin spots a number of other minor borrowings, including the start of Rimsky-Korsakov's *Sadko* (the symphonic poem, soon to be composed), an obvious echo of the curtain music at the very start of Serov's opera.[13] Musorgsky also grumbled to his friend about a phrase in *Sadko* that reminded him of the witch's music in *Rogneda,* and begged him to change it (he didn't).[14]

One can reasonably surmise that what chiefly annoyed the circle about *Rogneda* was how close it actually came to their own preferred creative direction, which, however, they themselves had not yet clearly identified. Serov's occasional use of folk song, and more especially his invention and treatment of folkish themes, were a sight too close for comfort to their father figure, Glinka—Serov's own disclaimers notwithstanding. And though there was not much that was "realistic" in the opera's subject matter—it was really the same old fake medievalism as in countless romantic operas, from Weber's *Euryanthe* through Meyerbeer and Schumann to Wagner's *Tannhäuser* and *Lohengrin*—there was undoubtedly something in the handling, especially of the genre choruses, that brought ordinary people to life, whatever might be thought about the quality of Serov's musical material. This was one aspect of his *pochvennichestvo.* The other aspect, no less impressive—or disturbing, depending on your point of view—was the way he used all this quasi-populist material in the service of an "elevated" theme, the founding of the Christian Kievan state against the tide of sorcery, paganism, and other assorted villainies. Of course there was nothing very new about such things in world opera. But it was profoundly annoying to the Balakirev circle, who had scarcely a complete opera to their collective name, to be upstaged in this respect by a composer-critic whom, for reasons not entirely connected with his music, they had elected to despise.

The annoyance soon came out in a satirical operetta by the kindliest member of the circle. A year or so after the Serov premiere, Viktor Krïlov (the librettist of Cui's operas) invited Borodin to supply the music for an operatic farce called *The Bogatyrs* (*Bogatïri*—the heroic knights of Russian mythology), to be staged at the Bolshoi Theatre in Moscow in the autumn of 1867. But because, as usual, Borodin had no prospect of composing a complete score of his own in time, he put together what amounts to an elaborate montage of borrowings from *Rogneda* itself, candidly satirical in intention, from Meyerbeer, Rossini, and Verdi, and from the operettas of Offenbach, bound together by a certain amount of authentic Borodin, and wrapped round a plot only mildly more ludicrous than that of *Rogneda* itself. *The Bogatyrs* received only one performance (on 6 November 1867), has never been published, and survives only in manuscript form in the notoriously tight-fisted archives of the Maryinsky Theatre. But even for that single Moscow audience, it seems that the parody was largely impenetrable; or rather, as Dianin suggests, they failed to grasp the work's satirical intention, but "saw in it simply a collection of rehashes of their favourite tunes," which of course made them unwitting participants in what was being satirized. Today only half of the tunes, and of course none of the Serov, would be recognized at all.[15]

The one composer in their group who had any kind of a reputation as an operatic composer, Alexander Dargomïzhsky, had been keeping a comparatively low profile since his disappointment over *Rusalka* almost ten years before. He had still kept up his own musical evenings, but they were mainly for his students, and Stasov and Balakirev had stopped going to them. Then, at the very end of 1865, *Rusalka* was at last revived, and in the shadow of *Rogneda* it suddenly became a talking point among the circle. As against the popular realism of Serov's opera, they could set the conversational realism of Dargomïzhsky's, which, by a delicious irony, had actually been pointed out to its composer by Serov himself. As one critic put it, somewhat fancifully, the two composers were "inspired by the same ideal, they strive for truth in art and its cleansing from the coarse materialism that, alas, so firmly reigns in our time."[16] Cui reviewed *Rusalka* in the *Vedomosti,* and took a slightly different line. "In *Rogneda*," he pointed out, "we encounter a tasteless overload of mere external effect under the emblem of so-called 'organic drama,' [while] in *Rusalka* there is simple, truthful, stupendous drama without any emblems." Then, to counter any suggestion that he might be exaggerating a little, he added that while Dargomïzhsky was at his best in recitative and declamatory music, he was "much weaker in the choruses and pure-musical numbers, which demand the development of musical thought and mastery of form which, generally speaking, have not been given to [him]."[17] A few days after the review came out, Dargomïzhsky appeared at Stasov's birthday party, and at once got into an argument with him about the orchestral interludes in the arias in *Rusalka,* which for some reason Stasov disliked. Dargomïzhsky, who was perhaps understandably touchy about the fate of his chef d'oeuvre, sat down at the piano and played one of the interludes, then got up, "irritably closed the piano and put an end to the discussion, as if to say: 'If you can't appreciate this, there's no use talking to you.' "[18]

Despite this encounter, Dargomïzhsky began to turn up more often at the circle's musical evenings, which now included regular Mondays at the house of Glinka's sister, Lyudmila Shestakova, who had emerged from a sort of purdah prompted by the death of her young daughter Olga in 1863. She was also at Stasov's birthday party early in January, and there met Musorgsky, Rimsky-Korsakov, and possibly also Cui for the first time. At first she seems to have confined her invitations to musicians (rather oddly, since music was by no means the only entertainment: cards were also regularly played). At any rate Stasov was not initially on the guest list, and had to ask to be included. At Balakirev's request she also began to invite Borodin. So it was that under the somewhat matronly guidance of the "aunt figure" of Russian music, the circle finally achieved the rounded form, with one or two outcrops, under which it has gone down in history as that unlikely phenomenon, a coherent aesthetic grouping of like-minded artists: the *moguchaya kuchka* (Mighty Little Heap) or, simply, the Five.

No such coherence, admittedly, would have been apparent to anyone casually surveying the recent work or work in hand of the group's members at the start of 1866. You might have come away from one of their evenings thinking of them as a symphonic tendency. Rimsky-Korsakov's First had just been performed, Borodin was showing off fragments of his symphony in E-flat, and Balakirev had the big first movement of his C-major symphony in a fairly advanced state, though apparently languishing and probably tucked away in some drawer. Much symphonic music was played in four-hand arrangements. Or you might have associated them with opera: Cui was well on with *William Ratcliff,* Balakirev was toying with (though hardly composing) his *Firebird,* and Musorgsky had not yet given up on *Salammbô.* The trouble was, of course, that as ever most of these works were in a seriously incomplete state. At the evenings there would be songs. Rimsky-Korsakov recalled a certain S. I. Zotova (sister of the well-known soprano, and friend of Balakirev's, Lyubov Karmalina) singing Balakirev's "Song of the Golden Fish." Perhaps she also sang one or two of his more recent songs, none of them quite on the same level, or recent songs by Dargomïzhsky, who had spent some of the time while he was sulking over *Rusalka* composing romances, including a fine, dramatic setting of Kurochkin's "The Old Corporal" ("Starïy kapral' "—a translation from the French of Pierre-Jean de Béranger), a harmonically adventurous one of Zhukovsky's "Paladin," and a lively one of the Spanish romance from Pushkin's little play *The Stone Guest* (*Kamennïy gost'*). He had also composed a pair of short, brightly scored but musically unsophisticated orchestral fantasies (*Baba-Yaga* and *Kazachok:* a third piece, *Finnish Fantasy,* was still incomplete). But none of this added up to much of an artistic manifesto, even if you included the handful of songs Musorgsky had managed to write in the past year.

To discover their tendency as a group you would have had to listen to what they said at least as much as what they played or sang. And even then you would have had to see past their personal animosities, which encouraged them to ridicule work that was in fact consistent with their own professed aspirations. By rights they ought to have welcomed *Rogneda* as a serious attempt at a specifically Russian opera, and a remarkable achievement for a composer of such limited experience. Instead they made fun of it because they could not abide its author and were frankly jealous of his success. In the same way, their musical preferences in general were so much at the beck and call of their prejudices that it would have been hard to form a clear sense of the criteria behind them: why, for instance, Schumann was to be admired but Mendelssohn not, Berlioz but not Wagner, and so forth. The clear exposition of *kuchka* principles that one now finds in dictionaries and history books was cooked up by Stasov some years later, long after the group had ceased to exist as such. At the time you would have had to sift them out of a good deal of intellectual dross. The abiding distaste for academic learning and systematic study would certainly have been evident; jokes at the expense of Rubinstein and his conservatory were standard currency. A broad enthusiasm for Russian history and mythology would have been apparent, especially when Stasov was present, or the historian Vladimir Nikolsky, who started frequenting Lyudmila's evenings in 1866. But exactly what that might mean in artistic terms was still far from clear: what, after all, had *William Ratcliff* and *Salammbô* to do with being Russian? That year, however, the mists did begin to part a little, and artistic direction started, fitfully, to take the place of scattered prejudice.

Balakirev had been putting together the songs he had collected on his trips along the Volga in the early sixties with a view to their publication by the firm of August Johansen later in 1866. Like previous collectors, he was arranging the tunes for voice and piano, but he was plainly conscious of the need for a fresh approach to the kind of harmony and texture that would go with tunes that, in their natural state, would have had either no accompaniment or a simple rhythm or drone. The old collections (notably those of Lvov/Prach, Daniyil Kashin, and Danilov, which we know he studied, because he asked Stasov to get them for him from the public library) had treated folk tunes as if they were normal "composed" songs in need of conventional barring and harmonization in the style of the day, like the Haydn and Beethoven arrangements of Scottish folk songs for George Thomson. By contrast Balakirev, as we saw in the last chapter, was looking for a style of accompaniment that would match the innate character of the tunes. This meant writing piano parts that kept to the mode set by each tune, without the passing chromatic inflections and the standard cadences one takes for granted in classical tonal music; it sometimes meant irregular barrings to match a song's variable meter—something that a classical composer would have ironed out into a regular pattern of twos, threes, or fours; and it occasionally meant reducing the accompaniment to a held chord or a single line (though Balakirev does now and then provide a more pianistic accompaniment, with picturesque figuration and short piano introduction). On occasion, he would play his arrangements at the evenings, and no doubt talk about his approach. And when the songs came out in December, Cui wrote a long review which discussed the whole issue of folk-song transcription and tried to explain the extent to which Balakirev had superseded his predecessors in the matter of idiom. Even Serov, who published a huge three-part article on the subject in *Muzïkal'nïy sezon* (1869–71), praised Balakirev as the first editor to adopt "a sensible, clear (if not yet critical) view of the matter," though he then, characteristically, lurched from praise to blame and back again, adding that "the theoretical principle worked out by others is put into practice by Mr. Balakirev, and to some extent successfully. We see at once that Mr. Balakirev's collection, as a *collection,* is quite poor and is shot through with crude blunders of every kind—but, as a first step on a new path, it's a highly remarkable effort."[19]

Where that new path would lead neither Serov nor anyone else could have said. It is even unclear whether he was thinking of new artistic directions, or simply of a more authentic, scholarly approach to the collecting and taxonomy of folk songs. Rimsky-Korsakov was inspired by evenings spent with Balakirev listening to the new transcriptions and discussing the method by which they were made, but his immediate creative response was simply to compose an Overture on Russian Themes of his own, a well-scored but compositionally primitive copy of Balakirev's overtures. Nobody seems yet to have had any serious idea of evolving a radical musical style derived from the principles that lay behind the arrangements. It was merely one step up from a set of songs with piano to a medley of tunes for the orchestra.

While all this was going on, Dargomïzhsky was letting slip information about a quite different project of his own, at least partly inspired, it seems, by the unexpected success of the *Rusalka* revival, and perhaps especially by Cui's observations about that work in his *Vedomosti* review. The first mention of the idea of setting Pushkin's *Stone Guest* word-for-word as an opera comes in a letter to Lyubov Karmalina in July 1866. But he certainly talked about it at the Balakirev or Shestakova evenings in January, since at the end of that month Balakirev sent a note to Stasov grumbling that Dargomïzhsky had chosen to attend a performance of *Ruslan* when he "would do better to spend the day with us, and play us his *Don Juan*."[20] And barely four months later, Stasov wrote back enthusiastically that *The Stone Guest* was almost finished.[21] Needless to say it was nowhere near finished; in fact it never did quite get finished. More likely, Dargomïzhsky had talked about the idea, and perhaps played one or two fragments, with such newfound warmth and energy that his friends simply could not wait to hear what the work would be like as a whole. Stasov was completely convinced, Balakirev less so. "I don't doubt," he had said, "that a *Don Juan* by him will contain some unusual things, but I'm also convinced that in its essence what ought to be inevitably won't be."[22] In any case it was to be almost another two years before any substantial work on the project took place.

Dargomïzhsky later claimed that he had been thinking about Pushkin's famous short play as a possible subject since about 1863, but had "shrunk from so colossal a task."[23] Whether this was the same project as Stasov mentioned in a letter to Balakirev in August of that year is hard to know. As in 1866, there was a Serov connection. "One good thing about *Judith*," Stasov wrote, "Dargo was so hooked by it that it has forced him to get down sooner to the (comic) opera about which he's merely been chattering for so long."[24] Could this have been the Pushkin opera, and if so, what might that tell us about Dargomïzhsky's original idea of the work? Unlike its historical predecessors (including even Mozart's *Don Giovanni*), the play is not a comedy, either in fact or in genre, though it has its sardonic aspects, notably in the character of Leporello. Pushkin called his four short plays, of which *The Stone Guest* is in fact the longest, "little tragedies," while as always in his work there are generous pinches of irony in the mixture. In any case, Dargo obviously did not get down to it. "If you see Dargomïzhsky," Balakirev instructed Stasov in May 1865, "give him my regards and praise him to the skies, and he will then compose."[25]

What chiefly excited them about *The Stone Guest*, when it really did start to get written, was the idea of setting the play more or less as it stood, with the attendant idea that the words would to some extent control the flow of the music, and would be, both intellectually and artistically, at least its equal. This was a new kind of response to Chernïshevsky's insistence that art should above all aspire to reality: not the realism of action, certainly not the realism of the soil—*pochvennik* or otherwise—but the realism of speech and gesture; no arias or detachable numbers at all (except where the action itself required one, as with Laura's song in scene 2), and no vocalizing, no elaborate cadenzas, no melisma, simply one note per syllable of text throughout, exactly as we speak. Here was something so close to the Russian language as such, so remote from textbook formulae, so uncompromisingly "real," that it quickly and easily took its place in the Stasovian agenda. What the music would actually be like remained to be seen. But that it would be new and astonishing, and above all Russian, they did not doubt.

CHAPTER 12

Life Studies

The circle were in raptures about Dargomïzhsky's idea, but they made little immediate attempt to copy it. Rimsky-Korsakov had been inspired by Zotova's singing of Balakirev's "Song of the Golden Fish" to compose a series of songs of his own, and—as one would expect of settings inspired by a beautiful romance and a fine voice—his songs responded to the voice, not in the spirit of Chernïshevsky's description of singing as "like conversation . . . a product of practical life and not of art,"[1] but as a vehicle for lyrical melody in the tradition of the salon romance of Alyabyev, Glinka, and indeed Dargomïzhsky himself.

The dozen or so songs that Rimsky-Korsakov composed during 1866 break no new ground in these ways. It's true that his settings are mainly syllabic and respect the rhythms and scansions of the poetry, which is more or less what Dargomïzhsky was claiming to be doing with Pushkin's verse play. All the same, they remain "art" songs in the usual sense. The accompaniments are stereotyped, so to speak, from images in the poems, rather than commenting anecdotally on the words from line to line. Lev Mey's "Cradle Song" ("Kolïbel'naya pesnya," from his play *Pskovïtyanka*) is supplied with a continuous rocking accompaniment; Heine's "Aus meinen Tränen" ("Iz slyoz moikh," in the recently published translation by Mikhailov) gets delicate semiquaver figures in the treble suggestive of the "fragrant flowers springing from my tears"; Nikolay Shcherbina's "Southern Night" ("Yuzhnaya noch' ") has harp arpeggios; Koltsov's "Eastern Romance" ("Vostochnïy romans") has standard Orientalisms; and so forth. These are resourceful, not to say beautiful, well-written songs, and remarkably accomplished for such an inexperienced composer. But in genre they are conventional; they strive, not for novelty, but for excellence, and occasionally, within certain limitations, they achieve it.

Even Musorgsky spent the early part of the year composing rather run-of-the-mill romances, or working in desultory fashion on *Salammbô*. His settings of Pleshcheyev and Heine from this time are agreeable and expressive in a sociable kind of way;[2] one can imagine their soulful chromatic thirds and sixths provoking gasps of appreciation at Shestakova's evenings. But the most interesting things about the Heine song, "Zhelaniye" ("Desire"), are that Stasov disliked it, and that it carries a bizarre and alas unexplained dedication "to Nadezhda Petrovna Opochinina in memory of her judgment on me"—two items of information that are possibly connected, since Musorgsky may for a time have been in love with Opochinina, and the attachment (whatever it was) was regarded with mild disfavor by Balakirev and very likely also by Stasov. Ruminating on the surprising failure of this song, composed as it was "at a moment of particular excitement, at night on 15–16 April, as indicated in a note on the original manuscript" and with the aforementioned dedication, he points out that Musorgsky's earlier "Impromptu passionné" (likewise, though Stasov fails to mention it, dedicated to Opochinina) was similarly written in a state of excitement, aroused by the love scene between Beltov and Lyuba in Herzen's novel *Who Is to Blame?*, but also "turned out very insignificant."[3]

Stasov is hinting that Musorgsky's supposed passion for Opochinina got in the way of his creative inspiration in both cases, separated though they were by a six-and-a-half-year gap. Admittedly, the "Impromptu passionné" is far from being Musorgsky's only feeble piano piece, and one could also argue that "Zhelaniye," though conventional, is by no means the failure Stasov claims. Nevertheless the claim itself is significant, because it probably reflects what was being said in the Balakirev circle: that Musorgsky's feelings for Opochinina were more than platonic, that in general his emotional attachments were suspect or unsuitable, and that they were bad for his music. Stasov himself, who had affairs and daughters but never married, hated his friends' romantic involvements, and sometimes reacted badly to their marriages. "Marrying young," he would say, "is like going to bed too early. You wake up in the middle of the night."[4] He was annoyed by Cui's marriage at the age of twenty-three, and grumbled to Balakirev that "we'll have to say goodbye to him until such time as he and Matilda quarrel and part company, which of course can't fail to happen."[5] And as we saw, he overreacted spectacularly to his brother Dmitry's marriage in 1861. Where Musorgsky was concerned, however, he need not have worried on this particular score. The threat to his genius would come from a very different quarter.

Only a few days after the Opochinina incident, whatever it was, he was writing to Balakirev in an entirely positive spirit about two quite separate projects.[6] One of them was a revised version of the "War Song of the Libyans" in *Salammbô,* which he called a "new little piece," though it did not substantially differ from the original of two years before, except that he now produced an orchestral score. The other was a still older project in a new form, which Musorgsky referred to as "the witches." This harked back to his old idea of a dramatic scene drawn from a play called *The Witch* by Mengden; in fact it looks as if he may have been working from the original sketch plan which he had outlined in a letter to Balakirev in September 1860, so similar is that plan to the eventual form of *St. John's Night on Bald Mountain (Ivanova noch' na Lïsoy gore),* though there is no evidence of any music for the Mengden project. A much more direct inspiration was probably Anton Herke's performance of Liszt's piano-orchestral *Totentanz* at an RMS concert under Rubinstein in March 1866, apparently its Russian premiere.[7] There are no witches in Liszt, but plenty of diabolism and rattling of bones; and the musical evidence that Musorgsky was impressed by Liszt's frenetic variations on the *Dies irae* plainchant is irresistible.[8]

How soon did he hit on the astounding opening of *St. John's Night on Bald Mountain,* so utterly unlike anything in Russian music up to that time? There are no intermediate dates in the manuscript, but the evidence of his April letter to Balakirev is that he already had a good idea of what he later called "the assembly of the witches" at the start of the piece, but was having trouble with the next section, "the devils" (*poco meno mosso*) and Satan's cortège (*irruente, senza fretta*). That year he spent the summer months at a dacha in Pavlovsk; but in mid-August he was again writing to Balakirev and wanting to take the train back to St. Petersburg, a journey of an hour or so, to talk to him about what he was still calling "the witches." However, soon after that he was again writing songs, including two or three of his most original to date. So it's tempting to conclude that at this point he was again stuck on the orchestral work and instead vented his mischief making, so to speak, on a medium with which he was more at home and in which he knew how to go against convention in a creative way.

His first diversion was a brilliant voice-and-piano setting of an episode from Taras Shevchenko's epic poem *Haydamaki:* an old man sings and dances a fast "Gopak" to his own accompaniment on the Ukrainian lute (*kobza*), in the form of a *naigrïsh,* a kind of nonstop dance with varied repeats of a basic melody and rhythm, somewhat in the manner of Glinka's *Kamarinskaya.* This is by far Musorgsky's most folkish piece of writing to date; both tune and rhythm have a rough, authentic flavor, with harmonic discolorations and wild strummings: "A potom vsyo chok da chok, vsyo chok da chok!"—"Then it's cheers and more cheers, and still more cheers!" The singer/narrator steps into the different characters: the old man himself, tipsy and somewhat rowdy; the shrewish wife who hauls him out of the pub and sends him off to fetch millet, then reminds him slyly how as a young girl she used to throw her apron front over the windowsill and nod at every passing Semyon and Ivan while making lace.

This is some way away from the comfortable folk-song arrangements in the Balakirev and Rimsky-Korsakov overtures, and very far indeed from anything in their songs. One might speculate that Musorgsky was still to some extent mentally in the world of satanic revelry, even that Balakirev may have suggested writing a dance-song as a study for the orchestral work. The similarities are certainly worth noting. The *naigrïsh* quality is of course common to the two works, as is the harmonic freedom. The song answers the question, how do you keep a fast dance going for a significant length of time without monotony? The simple folk-song idea in "Gopak" (each two-bar phrase repeated) may well have suggested a way of treating the problematical "devils," starting square and easy but becoming more and more tipsy-delirious, with added half-bars for the diabolical equivalent of the old wife's shouts of "Vot kak!" and "Vot shto!" ("That's how!" and "That's what!"), which in turn suggest the dancer's cries of "Goy!" ("Hey!") at the start and finish of the song. There are even thematic parallels. For instance, the rising quaver melody at the wife's "Kol' zhenilsya, satana" ("Since you're married, you Satan") is a clear foretaste of the clarinet-and-bassoon theme, *poco accelerando,* in Satan's cortège on Bald Mountain. Of course, these satanic elements in the song are comic. But Musorgsky also saw comedy in his witches' sabbath, as we learn from a description he gave to Rimsky-Korsakov after the work was finished.[9]

After composing "Gopak" at the end of August, he made his own setting of Heine's "Aus meinen Tränen," more Schumannesque than Rimsky-Korsakov's with many repeated chords (but far longer and more elaborate than Schumann's own laconic little song in *Dichterliebe*), then at last turned his attention to the sad episode he had observed from his window at Minkino the summer before. "Darling Savishna"

("Svetik Savishna") is his first serious attempt at a musical portrait "from life." "Life" in this case, however, was something different from Dargomïzhsky's idea of a vocal line controlled by the prosody of the spoken language; or rather, it was such a special case of that idea as to suggest a completely different intention. In Musorgsky's memory, at least, the simpleton ("Vanya-of-God," people called him) regaled Savishna in the manner of a crazed automaton, in rapid, even phrases, scarcely taking breath, pleading, urging, nagging, bullying. Savishna, one supposes, was trying to escape; perhaps Vanya-of-God was clutching her arm, or perhaps she merely stood her ground and laughed at him. This is a slice of life not only in time but in space; the camera is on the speaker, with his interlocutor outside the frame. What is remarkable, and in due course typical of Musorgsky, is that one so vividly imagines the scene; this almost eidetic property of his vocal music is something we shall encounter again and again.

Musically, "Darling Savishna" is an extreme example of the adaptation of the folk manner to a special artistic need. Vanya-of-God, being an idiot, sings in five-four time throughout, and every bar is rhythmically identical, five even crotchets in unbroken, fairly quick tempo without any rests—a primitive example of a device later called "monometrics" by Igor Stravinsky. The only rhythmic variation is in the piano part, which splits the second crotchet of every bar (including the introduction, and the postlude except for the very last bar) into two quavers. Melodically, the song is a string of variations on the five-beat figure of the first bar, as if Vanya were all the time repeating himself but with changing degrees of urgency. The overall form, too, is by no means random. In effect there are four verses in an A-B-B-A design, the A sections in the Dorian mode on D, the B sections switching to Dorian on F, a move to the dark side for the two verses that refer to Vanya's miserable state, while the outer verses are mainly about his love for Savishna. The simplicity of this whole scheme is not the least touching thing about the song, completely devoid as it is of the remotest hint of sentimentality or condescension. The scene is observed, and the observer passes by. Vanya moves out of earshot, but, for all we know, his pleadings continue.

Back in St. Petersburg in September, Musorgsky developed this genre-painting technique in two further scenes "from life": "Oh, You Drunken Sot!" ("Akh tï, p'yanaya teterya!") and "The Seminarian" ("Seminarist"). Both are studies in one or another form of human depravity, based on texts (one would hesitate to call them poems) composed, like "Darling Savishna," by Musorgsky himself. The drunkard

in the first song was apparently the historian he had met at Lyudmila's, Vladimir Nikolsky, who had quickly become a close friend, with
the mysterious but typically Stasovian nickname "Pakhomich." In the
song, he arrives home at dawn, drunk and incapable, and is threatened
by his wife with the oven prongs. No doubt the story grew with the telling, but it was always meant to be a private joke. We know this because,
whereas Musorgsky went to immense lengths to have "The Seminarian" printed after it was banned by the censor in 1870—even publishing it in Germany, then having copies smuggled back into Russia by
friends—he never seems to have taken any step toward publishing the
Pakhomich satire, which remained unknown until it was discovered
and brought out by Andrey Rimsky-Korsakov in 1926.

Just as the style of "Savishna" was set by the idea of the gabbling
simpleton, so "Oh, You Drunken Sot!" takes its cue from the relentless
patter of the nagging wife, eight quavers to the allegro bar with monotonous regularity except when she rises to a climax of rhetorical fury,
at which point crotchets are required (or perhaps these are moments
when Pakhomich tries unsuccessfully to get a word in edgeways). The
melodic style is a highly individual blend of nursery rhyme and awkward distortions bred, presumably, by the stress of the situation. But
by far the most intriguing aspect of the whole song is the piano part,
which if anything gets even crosser than Mrs. Pakhomich, is littered
with *sforzando* accents on unexpected beats, and is soon breaking out
into harmonies that very likely gave the straitlaced César Cui a nervous fit.

Musorgsky's technique is simple but brilliantly effective. His harmonies are framed by "correct" preparations and resolutions. For instance,
the opening D minor is set up by a perfectly legitimate cadence, though
the piano texture is mildly unorthodox; the song ends in the right key,
and so forth. But in between the harmonies become increasingly wayward, partly following the voice, partly exploring avenues of their own,
directed as much as anything, one suspects, by the shape and position
of the hands on the keyboard. Eventually, at the point where the wife
rages against Pakhomich for abandoning his children, the piano hammers out a stack of white-note discords over a dominant, then tonic,
pedal, in a superb ecstasy of recrimination that only a pianist could
devise.

Whether or not Musorgsky thought of this kind of writing as a
study for larger, perhaps theatrical, works, we shall never know. But
it certainly served that purpose. Several aspects of this particular
song reappear in his opera *Boris Godunov,* including some of its actual

music, another piece of evidence that he had no intention of publishing the song. Halfway through, the wife leaves off scolding and becomes pleading and tearful: "Have I not begged you, Pakhomich; have I not reproached you, my dear?" Here the female voice is doubled in the bass by the piano left hand, and perhaps it was this sudden darkening that suggested reusing the music for the scene where the dying Boris warns his son against the machinations of the boyars. "Don't trust the slanders of the seditious boyars," he urges, suddenly animated; "keep an eye on their secret dealings with Lithuania." And now the voice itself is in the bass, no longer comically tearful but minatory and grimly foreboding.

Within a few days of completing "Oh, You Drunken Sot!" Musorgsky composed "The Seminarian," again on a text of his own perhaps derived, like "Darling Savishna," from personal observation. A young novice is reciting the list of third-declension-masculine Latin nouns ("Panis, piscis, crinis, finis / Ignis, lapis, pulvis, cinis," and so on); but his thoughts are rather on the feminine, in the shapely form of Styoshka, the daughter of Father Semyon. The good father caught him the other day making eyes at Styoshka, slapped his cheek three times, and punished him with this wretched Latin. "That's what happened to me," he concludes, "in tasting the fruits of love in the Lord's house."

The text, accordingly, is macaronic: the Latin nouns, in the form of a verse mnemonic, alternate with the novice's deviant thoughts in Russian. And Musorgsky naturally makes the contrast musical as well: a rapid mechanical patter on one or two notes for the Latin, a much bolder, folk-song-like melody for the wandering thoughts, which are never allowed, however, to break the fixed tempo. It's as if what the listener "sees," in that vivid Musorgskian way, is the novice with his head bowed continuously over his grammar book, while the music takes us inside his head and reveals what he is actually thinking. And as in the Pakhomich song, the piano has its own wandering thoughts, harmonies that sometimes behave themselves, sometimes stray. We are, of course, in church; so the harmony (as in the Goethe setting the year before) is churchy, with block chords in root position, like the harmonized chant of the Orthodox liturgy, even, or perhaps especially, when the novice is thinking about Styoshka's breasts and his ardent desire to kiss every part of her body. Briefly, when Father Semyon delivers his slaps, the chords are jolted into a whole-tone configuration, as if the music itself were momentarily stunned by the blows. Here and there, as before, Musorgsky has the piano and voice in unison or with parallel chords, as if deliberately to avoid conventional harmonization. And at the end he creates a dissolve by means of a falling chromatic scale, fading out, as it were, on the novice still reciting his nouns.

After presumably trying the song out at Balakirev's or Shestakova's, Musorgsky decided it was too long and made changes and substantial cuts before submitting it to the censorship, who rejected it, the composer told Stasov, "because of the Seminarian's concluding confession that he 'had happened to receive temptation from the devil in the Lord's house.' "[10] The odd thing about this supposed reason, which may have been guesswork on Musorgsky's part, is that the original ending of the song (as quoted above) had a much milder form of confession to exactly the same music, with no mention of the devil or temptation. Furthermore, it's clear from the Stasov letter that it was the copies printed in Leipzig that got into trouble with the censor and were eventually allowed to be brought in only as a limited edition of ten, for distribution to named individuals. Yet the censor must already have banned the song in its revised form (or German publication would have been unnecessary). If so simple a change might have enabled the song to be cleared for publication in Russia, one wonders why Musorgsky didn't think—or choose—to make it.

A more interesting question arising out of these three brilliant life studies is what Musorgsky actually thought he was about in writing them. In the normal way such questions hardly need to be asked of music. But with this kind of originality, in this kind of context, they pop up unbidden. Obviously Musorgsky had begun to be fascinated by the relationship between the visual and the musical—the seen and the heard. But that was hardly anything new: song, to look no further, had routinely depended on the connection, whether it was Beethoven on his hillside in *An die ferne Geliebte* sending messages to his distant beloved, or Schubert's wanderer communing with the brook in *Die schöne Müllerin,* or even the humble "Ash Grove" or "Sumer Is Icumen In." But these are mostly conceits (of the pathetic-fallacy variety), or they are conventional settings of texts that happen to have a strong visual content, or they are onomatopoeia of one kind or another. With Musorgsky there seems to be a new kind of intention. For one thing, he nearly always begins with some particular turn of speech—the idiot pleading, the housewife nagging, the novice reciting—and from this he fleshes out an entire scene, never losing contact with the original idea, and insisting that the music maintain that contact as well. Certain things follow from this approach. The most obvious is the informal character of much of the writing, its lack of subservience to standard textbook formulae, its contempt for the normal rules of balance, linkage, and closure. For Musorgsky the precision of the image starts to take precedence over beauty of form or elegance of expression. Melody becomes a function of situation and psychology, not a lyrical essence in its own right. Beauty goes out of the window; realism, that much abused, much misrepresented concept, comes in.

Not that Musorgsky was impervious to the beautiful. Toward the end of 1866, he made a somber but powerful setting of another passage from Shevchenko's *Haydamaki*, Prince Yarema's invocation of the river Dnieper before leading the Cossacks into battle against the Poles. Here the composer adopts the formal structure and idiom of a Ukrainian *bilina*, or ballad song, with a slow invocatory introduction and conclusion (based on an actual Ukrainian folk song) and a *risoluto* middle section colored by strange melodic leaps: augmented (in place of perfect) fourths, alternating minor and major seconds, and minor sevenths in place of octaves. The whole character of the setting is "epic"—sturdy melody, square-cut rhythm and phrasing—yet curiously subdued, especially the accompaniment, which seldom rises above pianissimo even when the voice is forte. It's as if heard from a great distance, a distance that the singer, however, can arch across through some magic of personality, like the voice-over on a film soundtrack.

A good deal has been written about what one scholar has called "Musorgsky's realist aesthetics,"[11] but in fact there is little evidence in his correspondence before 1867 of any clearly conceptualized interest in realism as an aesthetic goal. Composers rarely indeed theorize in advance of their work (Wagner is a massive exception, but an exception nonetheless). No doubt they had all read their Chernïshevsky; but as for applying his very limited ideas about music to their own work, they seem barely even to have discussed the matter. Stasov, as we saw in chapter 2, had taken on board Belinsky's idea of art as "the *immediate* contemplation of truth, or a thinking in *images*,"[12] but at the time he had interpreted it as a recipe for criticism, not creative work. Even Dargomïzhsky had only found out about the artistic "truth" he was now going on about from Serov's review of *Rusalka*. It may well be that Musorgsky's 1866 songs owed most to the fact, precisely, that Dargomïzhsky was at that moment so full of his *Stone Guest* experiment. But when he subtitles "The Seminarian" "A Picture from Nature" ("kartinka s naturï"), we have surely to understand this as ironic, or at the very least as hanging on a double sense of the word "nature": not only, that is, the real world untainted by man, but that part of our inner selves that drives us to act against the normal assumptions of civilized life.

If Musorgsky was not riding any aesthetic hobbyhorses in these songs, he was most certainly not riding any sociopolitical ones. When Richard Hoops describes the composer's pictures of folk life (*narodnïye kartínki*) as "songs of social criticism," he is begging a huge question about the motivation and subject matter behind these pieces.[13] Hoops quotes Stasov's remark about "the aching feeling of indignation and pain" that Musorgsky, and the painter Vasily Perov (with whom Stasov was comparing him), were supposed to have felt about "what they saw in the world around them," without pointing out that the notoriously revisionist Stasov was writing in 1883, two years after Musorgsky's death. In fact very few of Musorgsky's songs have a political angle, even though their subject matter is often the life of the poor and deprived, who, after all, constituted the vast majority of the population of Russia in the late 1860s. Exactly what radical social message can be extracted from "Darling Savishna," "Oh, You Drunken Sot!" and "The Seminarian" is hard to imagine, yet this does not prevent Hoops from describing them, by clear implication, as "realistic genre scenes that take a sharply critical or satirical attitude towards social inequities."[14]

The truth is that Musorgsky, like Stasov, was not essentially a political animal at all. He supported emancipation in theory (like nearly all his class), though it harmed him in practice, and he was shocked by the behavior of his fellow landowners at the time of the emancipation. He was a humane man. But none of this turned him into a political radical. Certainly he was fascinated by the quirkish and picaresque aspects of Russian street life. Not surprisingly, he found the rough and ragged types, the dirty children and gnarled workers that he encountered in the city and the countryside, more interesting and amusing as artistic subject matter than the comfortable bourgeoisie and minor aristocracy with whom he passed his time socially and professionally. No doubt in his kindlier moments he wished their lives could be better. But what he really loved about them was precisely those things that, for them, made life unendurable; and it was out of this conflict that he would in due course devise his greatest works.

While Musorgsky was busy studying deviant corners of the Russian character, Balakirev had been casting his gaze outward in the direction of his brother Slavs. Lyudmila Shestakova had asked him to go to Prague to supervise the productions of her brother's operas, and he had duly set off early in June 1866 and arrived in the Czech capital on about the 12th. It was unfortunate timing. Two days later the

Austro-Prussian War broke out, the Prussians advanced on Prague, and Balakirev was suddenly transformed into a refugee. But before leaving Prague, he witnessed the arrival by train after train of large numbers of wounded Czech soldiers; he observed the waves of popular sympathy for these fellow Slavs injured by German guns—some of it, he was touched to discover, transferred to him as another fellow Slav—and in the end, as he wrote to his father, he was "abandoning with sadness a city that in the course of two days has become no less dear to me than St. Petersburg and Moscow."[15]

These two days had had an artistic as well as emotional outcome. He had had discussions about the possibility of staging the Glinka operas, and he must have convinced the directorate of the Provisional Theatre, and in particular its conductor Jan Nepomuk Maýr, that these works were of sufficient merit to justify production on the Czech national stage, since some time before his return to Prague at the end of the year *A Life for the Tsar* was actually presented there under the theatre's newly appointed chief conductor, Bedřich Smetana. When Balakirev arrived back in Prague just before Christmas, this production was the first thing he saw. But if two days had been long enough to trumpet the work's virtues, they clearly had not been long enough to elucidate its character. "At last I've seen *A Life for the Tsar* here," he wrote to Lyudmila. "What a horror it was! I haven't quite come to my senses yet. The overture was so-so. But the curtain rises and oh! Horror, what costumes. The peasants were waving some kind of peaked caps and wore overcoats with white buttons, and they had beards, but not Russian ones, Jewish ones!"[16]

Balakirev was convinced that the production had been sabotaged by Smetana, who (the singers informed him) "deliberately gave them the wrong tempi in performance in order to put them off." Smetana was supposed to be in league with the large local Polish community (whom Balakirev might have forgiven for disliking a work in which Poles are so roundly demonized) and was said to be organizing a claque "in order to hiss *A Life for the Tsar* off the stage" when it was eventually revived. "Smetana and I," he added for Lyudmila's benefit, "are no longer on speaking terms. We only bow to one another."[17]

Exactly what took place between the two composer-conductors is by no means clear, but it seems unlikely that the difficulties were quite as one-sided as Balakirev makes out. As we have seen, he was himself a notably authoritarian character, and may well have rubbed the recently appointed Smetana the wrong way. Probably, as John Clapham suggests, he made no attempt to conceal his irritation at the way *A Life for the Tsar* had been performed.[18] He may also have failed at first to take sufficient account of local ethnic and political issues, the touchiness of recently emancipated Czech nationalism, Smetana's equivocal position as a German-speaking Czech whose own music had a reputation for awkward modernism, and the conservatism of the German-language press. On the other hand, Smetana does seem to have behaved toward his Russian guest in a bizarrely inhospitable way, the climax of which was the mysterious disappearance of the vocal score of *Ruslan and Lyudmila* just before a crucial rehearsal—a piece of sabotage, if such it was, that failed dismally, since Balakirev was able to accompany the entire run-through from memory.

Whatever Balakirev's troubles with the Provisional Theatre directorate, and whatever his endless difficulties with the musicians (spelled out in laborious detail in a letter to Cui),[19] *Ruslan* enjoyed something of a triumph when it finally opened on 4/16 February. "You can't imagine," he wrote to Stasov, "what a stunning effect the whole of *Ruslan* produces without Lyadov's emasculations."[20] The first act provoked audible cries from the parterre, and afterward they were singing Bayan's song in the streets. Even the German press were friendly, though Balakirev was quick to attribute this to their desperate desire not to diverge from the popular view. And this time even the production pleased him. "The curtain went up," he reported to Lyudmila, " and I myself was staggered. Before my eyes, real Russian costumes and décor, not at all badly done."[21] (Had there been no dress rehearsal?) Altogether he conducted *Ruslan* four times, each time with undiminished success; and after the third performance the directorate persuaded him to conduct *A Life for the Tsar,* which he had to prepare on a single rehearsal, a previous one having been cancelled because nobody turned up. Not surprisingly, the performance was wretched, but nobody seems to have minded, so pro-Glinka had they all become as a result of *Ruslan.* And Balakirev was the proud recipient, he told Stasov, of two wreaths from the public "as the representative of Glinka and Russian music."[22]

He came away from Prague in mid-February full of warm thoughts about the Czech people ("Slavs through and through," he said: don't judge them by their newspapers), but with no illusions about the place of Russia in the wider European world. The Polish papers in Prague had alleged that the Glinka operas had only been put on thanks to a fifty-thousand-ruble backhander from the Russian government. "But I won't enlarge on that," he told Stasov,

> since all those things one constantly comes across in foreign countries are double dutch to you. Your naïve childish view of these matters,

which with time fossilize into senility, prevent you from seeing things as they really are, and for that reason you view everything through a cosmopolitan pince-nez. But I don't yet despair of you. Judging by what's going on in Europe, we should expect frightful upheavals, which will soon pose the question: Russia—to be or not to be.[23]

Within weeks of Balakirev's return from Prague, the whole question of Russia's identity, both within its own multi-ethnic empire and in the wider European context, was brought sharply into focus by the All-Russian Ethnographic Exhibition (Vserossiiskaya etnograficheskaya vïstavka), held in the Manezh, the former Alexandrine riding school, in Moscow from April to June 1867.

> Entering the Manezh, the visitor was transported into a virtual Empire, a symbolic space defined by the diversity of its inhabitants. From the Aleuts of Alaska to the Mazurs of Central Poland, the peoples of the Empire were laid out like tiles in a mosaic depicting Russia's vast expanse and human variation. Over 300 mannequins, meticulously rendered to convey characteristic physical features, constituted the focal point of the exhibition. Divided into almost sixty national and regional groups, the mannequins were adorned in genuine native costumes and surrounded by artifacts of everyday life, most sent directly from the regions by local enthusiasts.[24]

In recognition of this event, and no doubt with his recent Czech experiences in mind, Balakirev put on a "Pan-Slav" concert of the FMS at the Duma in St. Petersburg in the middle of May. His own contribution was an overture on Czech themes that he had assembled in Prague; and he also persuaded Rimsky-Korsakov to write a new work for the occasion, his Fantasia on Serbian Themes, composed in a hurry on themes supplied (needless to say) by Balakirev. In addition the program included Glinka's *Kamarinskaya*, Dargomïzhsky's *Kazachok*, some arias from the operas of Moniuszko (representing Poland), and Liszt's Hungarian Fantasy, which for the purposes of the Pan-Slav concert was deemed to be actually based on Slovak themes. Balakirev's overture is an attractive, well-made piece rather along the lines of his Russian overtures, but the Rimsky-Korsakov is a more basic piece of writing, dependent for its effect on spectacular scoring (which the composer polished up a good deal when he revised the work twenty years later).

Stasov spent most of his review in the *Sanktpeterburgskiye vedomosti* describing the scene, with its colorful drapes and flags, its rows of Slav visitors, its warm, appreciative atmosphere. When the more important Slav delegates arrived late from a dinner with the minister of public enlightenment, they were greeted by waves of applause and shouts of welcome, which only died down after they had solemnly bowed to the audience. Stasov was nevertheless particularly concerned to end on a note that drew attention to the importance of the Russian contribution, which he may perhaps have thought would have surprised some of the visitors, and in so doing he unwittingly gave the Balakirev circle a sobriquet that stuck.

"We conclude our remarks," he wrote, "with a wish: may God grant that our Slav guests never forget today's concert, and may God grant that they forever preserve the memory of what poetry, taste, talent, and skill reside in a small but already mighty heap (*moguchaya kuchka*) of Russian musicians."[25] The *kuchka* they became, and have remained.

CHAPTER 13

Symphonic Pictures and an Abstract

No one would dispute that Glinka really was a remarkable musician who was prevented by circumstances, both inner and outer, from becoming the founder of the Russian opera; but no, that's not good enough! He must at once be promoted to a commander-in-chief, a lord marshal of music, and other nations must be put in their place: they, if you please, have nothing like it. And one is immediately told of some "mighty" home-grown genius whose works are merely a pitiful imitation of second-rate foreign composers—second-rate ones are the easiest to imitate. Nothing like it, indeed! Oh, poor silly barbarians, who don't understand what tradition in art means, and who imagine that artists are something like the strong man Rappo: "A foreigner," they say, "can lift only thirteen stone with one hand, and our man lifts twenty-six!"[1]

Ivan Turgenev had just published his novel *Smoke* (*Dïm*) when he attended a concert of the Free Music School in the Assembly of the Nobles in St. Petersburg on 6 March 1867, and met Vladimir Stasov for the first time. Stasov remembered Turgenev's reaction. "What terrible music! It's sheer nothingness, sheer ordinariness. It's not worth coming to Russia for such a 'Russian school'! They'll play you that kind of stuff anywhere you like: in Germany, in France, at any concert . . . and no one will pay the slightest attention . . . But here immediately it's all great works, an original Russian school! Russian, original!"[2] And after the concert he wrote to Pauline Viardot: "This evening I went to a grand concert of Russian music of the future, for that too exists.

But it's absolutely pitiful, devoid of ideas or originality. It's nothing but a bad copy of what's done in Germany. And along with it a presumptuousness bolstered by all the lack of civilization that marks us out. Everyone is thrown into the same bag: Rossini, Mozart, and even Beethoven . . . Come! It's pitiful!"[3]

To some extent, Turgenev was merely expressing the grown-up opinion of the sophisticated Westernizer who spent half his life in France and Germany and the other half on his country estate in Russia, with only an occasional, brief descent on St. Petersburg or Moscow. It was the view also of his alter ego, Sozont Ivanich Potugin, in *Smoke.* He had, all the same, struck unlucky. The March FMS concert had originally been planned to include music from Glinka's operas, but it had had to be withdrawn at short notice on the insistence of the publisher, Fyodor Stellovsky, because Balakirev declined to pay a fee. This weakened an already scrappy program, which included a Fantasy on Russian Folk Themes by the FMS's founder, Gavriyil Lomakin; a chorus of nuns from Boris Fitingof-Shel's opera *The Demon;* and a chorus by Nikolay Afanas'yev—works that Cui, in his review of the concert, described as "so bad that it's not even worth talking about them."[4] The fugal chorus from *A Life for the Tsar* was replaced by a women's chorus from Dargomïzhsky's unfinished opera *Rogdana,* and the dances from *Ruslan* by Balakirev's *King Lear* Overture. Then there was a Bach chorus, Berlioz's *Carnaval romain* Overture, and a new chorus by Musorgsky, "The Destruction of Sennacherib" ("Porazheniye Sennakheriba"), a free setting of part of the Byron poem. By any standards, the program ended up a mess. But above all the sheer provincialism of the attitudes it embodied was shown up—even allowing for natural bias—by the fact that Cui felt able to praise the Balakirev overture at the expense of *Carnaval romain,* which he found "effective and interesting" but ultimately not very good. No wonder Turgenev was bewildered by the image of this New Russian School.

Compared to his recent songs, Musorgsky's chorus is conventional but well made and highly singable. Cui found it similar to the Assyrian music in *Judith,* adding waspishly that "if it were included in *Judith,* it would become its crowning glory and virtually its best number."[5] But he found fault with the slow hymnlike setting of the verse about the angel of death, comparing it to a Jewish chorale—an error of style or taste, exactly which is unclear. (Musorgsky seems in any case to have agreed with this criticism, and completely rewrote the middle section, including the text, when he revised the chorus six years later.) One can reasonably see "The Destruction of Sennacherib" as a dry run for

the choruses in *Boris Godunov* and *Khovanshchina*: the work of a composer
with an instinctive feeling for the musical impulse of a crowd of people. But it barely hints at the psychological tension of those operas; the
sheer terror of that famous opening line, "The Assyrian came down
like the wolf on the fold," is matched only by a brisk, mildly uneasy
march in E-flat minor, with the central chorale in B major/G-sharp
minor—keys that may have warmed Balakirev's heart, but were insuf-
ficient to turn the piece into a beacon of what Turgenev was ridiculing
as "the Russian music of the future."

Of course, nobody would seriously expect a six-minute choral work
to be much more than bread-and-butter music. The real answer to Turgenev had to come through large-scale orchestral or theatrical works,
but as usual with the Balakirev circle there was little sign of anything
of the sort on the public platform. As ever, there was no shortage of
ideas. Rimsky-Korsakov had written part (or possibly all) of an allegro
in B minor and a scherzo in E flat intended for a Second Symphony,
in B minor; Cui had composed about half of his opera *William Ratcliff*;
and Balakirev had yet again shelved his own *Firebird* opera as well as his
C-major symphony, but had for some time been talking about a symphonic poem he was planning to base on Lermontov's poem *Tamara*.[6]
He was in the habit of playing excerpts or even just the themes of
works-in-progress at circle evenings. Rimsky-Korsakov remembered
him playing melodies he had brought back from the Caucasus three
or four years before, including a tune by the name of "Islamey." And
that winter of 1866–7 he often (again according to Rimsky-Korsakov)
played substantial chunks of *Tamara*, apparently improvising the music,
with nothing written down.[7] There had been another Lermontov plan,
a program symphony called *Mtsyri*, based on a longer poem by the great
writer, but this too had died the death.[8] Whether or not any music
from *Mtsyri* found its way into *Tamara* is a matter for conjecture.

The one significant work that was now complete, though still
unknown to anyone outside the circle, was the E-flat symphony that
Borodin had been writing for the past five years. Exactly when he finished it is uncertain, but it was probably during the Christmas holidays at the end of 1866. An undated letter to Balakirev from about
that time announces the work's completion, and invites him to act as
its "godfather"—meaning, no doubt, to come round and look the score
over. "I am free every day," Borodin announces uncharacteristically,
from which Dianin (editing the correspondence) craftily deduces that
it was holiday time.[9] Balakirev later told Stasov that "each bar [of the
symphony] was examined and criticised by me,"[10] but this was probably

an exaggeration, since Borodin these days (like Balakirev himself) was not in the habit of writing his music down systematically, but tended to mull it over, play sections extempore and not necessarily in their eventual sequence, and only write up at his infrequent moments of leisure or when ill in bed. Their relationship was emphatically not like Balakirev's with Musorgsky, if only because Borodin was so rarely free from other cares.

There is nevertheless something of the journeyman about this First Symphony, which starts off, like Rimsky-Korsakov's symphony and Musorgsky's chorus, in the Balakirevan key of E-flat minor, before settling more conventionally in the major. And as with Rimsky-Korsakov, there is a goody-goody aspect to the form, with every section, every key correctly placed, plenty of motivic dialoguing between instruments, thematic links between movements, smooth transitions, and so forth. Here too the hand of Schumann lies at times rather heavily, especially on the finale, whose main theme is a little too obvious a variant of a favorite pattern in the German master's symphonies (first movement of no. 1, finales of nos. 3 and 4). The clear intention seems to have been to write as well as possible on the basis of certain models and with certain precepts always in mind. Under the circumstances, it's amazing how well Borodin survived these restrictions.

He did so, as is evident from the start of the symphony, by sheer talent. The essential energy of Borodin's imagination comes out at the start of the allegro section of the first movement, where the syncopated main theme triggers conflicting patterns of threes and twos which he sometimes contains within the basic three-four time by an unambiguous rhythmic accompaniment, but sometimes allows to drift into six-eight (two long beats instead of three). Borodin obviously liked these strong rhythmic characters. The second subject makes an issue of the crotchet pulse, with heavy string downbows on each beat, a physical process for the players which involves retaking (carrying the bow back to the heel) on every stroke, and guarantees a degree of violence in the execution. (A well-known parallel case is the second subject of Beethoven's *Egmont* Overture: the rhythm itself is similar.) In the finale the first subject and its extension may be derivative, but the second theme is again rhythmically idiosyncratic, with half-bar accents which effectively redivide the four-beat bars into out-of-phase fours and eights. The idea is slightly self-conscious and looks like a studied attempt to complicate a perfectly regular melody. But this proves all the more, of course, how aware Borodin was of the possibilities of rhythmic experiment.

The scherzo second movement suggests one source for this idea. The sparkling, deftly scored main theme, obviously indebted to Berlioz's "Queen Mab," is essentially regular in its patterning. But the trio is quite another matter. Here the model is folk song, and the irregular meter characteristic of the *protyazhnaya*. Each of the first two phrases is extended by one beat in the form of an extra upbeat to the next phrase. The third phrase is shortened by one beat, while the fourth phrase is unmodified in the first statement (oboe) but shortened by a beat the second time round (flute). These may seem trivial modifications, but the device has such remarkable consequences in later Russian music that its occasional appearance in the music of the sixties is well worth noting. The lyrical main theme of the andante third movement is rather ordinary by comparison. Though not without some individual touches (especially the little quasi-Oriental twiddles), it perhaps doesn't quite deserve the buildup Borodin gives it to a grand peroration, which again may have been suggested by Berlioz's *Roméo et Juliette*.

With *Tamara* the difficulty is to know exactly how much was composed (if only in the sense of improvised) by Balakirev at this period. Rimsky talks about "a significant part of *Tamara*" having been improvised in 1866–7, but he does not say which parts.[11] Twelve years later, after Balakirev had for three years or so been working again on the sketches, Stasov told Borodin that "a few days ago Balakirev played us the whole of *Tamara,* straight through, with big new inserts and a wonderfully poetic introduction depicting a deserted landscape and the quiet noise of a river. This is incomparable! Now all that are needed are the last brush-strokes, and the orchestration."[12] So the long and highly original opening—the first four or five minutes of the finished work—was only added in the late seventies. By the same token, though, it's obvious that the main allegro, which Rimsky-Korsakov said was based on a melody he and Balakirev had heard played on balalaikas by guards at the royal barracks in Shpalernaya Ulitsa, was already known to Stasov and had probably always been part of the work since its early improvisations. As for the other insertions, it seems idle to speculate what they might have been. *Tamara* is by its nature an episodic work, to the extent that it picks up the elements of Lermontov's sinister vignette of the Caucasian princess—"beautiful as a celestial angel, treacherous and evil as a demon"—who lures travellers into her tower in the gorge of the river Terek, and after a night of passionate love has them murdered and their bodies thrown into the river. Quite informally constructed, the work is a kind of free fantasy on a pair of themes representing Tamara herself, varied, so to speak, from the lure, through the passion, to the death and disposal. One can well imagine Balakirev sketching ever more colorful images of this situation and splicing them into the work. But the composition is so skillful that the chronology of the process is virtually impossible to reconstruct in hindsight.

This question is of more than academic interest, because *Tamara* was a key work for the *kuchka,* and plainly influenced them long before it was even so much as written down. In a sense Balakirev invented a whole musical vocabulary for a particular kind of sensuous so-called Orientalism. (The Terek gorge in fact lies due south of Balakirev's birthplace, Nizhny-Novgorod, and Lermontov was a native of Moscow.) You have only to compare *Tamara* with Rimsky-Korsakov's much better-known *Sheherazade,* written after the eventual first performance of Balakirev's symphonic poem in 1883, to grasp the extent of the debt. Not only several of Rimsky-Korsakov's themes, but also rhythmic, instrumental, and decorative ideas, are unashamedly copied from *Tamara,* which in turn owes something to Glinka's *Ruslan,* at least for the concept of an exotic Eastern music, if not for much of its detail. Mostly these ideas are not "Oriental" at all, but merely stand for that aspect of the East which frightens or entices Westerners, that aspect which is "mysterious" because civilized in ways of which the West is ignorant. Musically this might mean strange chromatic melodies like the oboe second subject of *Tamara,* or it might be a matter of instrumental coloring, like the wheedling high bassoon (figure 4 in the first subject, repeat of the second subject), or the soft tambourine accompaniment to that same oboe and bassoon melody. It might be the wild "Scythian" compound rhythms that dominate the main allegro music almost from start to finish. All these features reappear, sometimes not much altered, in *Sheherazade;* but not only there. Borodin also knew how to adapt them to his own needs; and they can be traced through Russian music up to *The Rite of Spring* and even beyond.

Most of these elements (though obviously not the orchestral coloring) will have been present in Balakirev's improvisations of the late sixties. We can test this because they are already partly present in the virtuoso piano work (*Islamey*) that he wrote soon afterward and whose main themes Rimsky-Korsakov recalls being part of Balakirev's keyboard repertoire when *Tamara* was first on the stocks. In other words, they were very much in the air at circle gatherings in 1867. What might not have been apparent at that time was exactly how Balakirev would meld these elements into a coherent whole. After all, the question of large-scale form had usually come back to sonata modelling of one kind or another, which was all very well for a symphony or an overture, but might not suit a program work like *Tamara,* which had a narrative basis that was bound, in the end, to influence the musical design, particularly if your hero was Liszt, whose symphonic poems are models of sui generis form controlled, if not by an actual story, at least by concepts derived from one. It seems to have taken Balakirev fifteen years to solve this problem by means of a complex and carefully thought-out mechanism of tempo transitions (a technique later known as metric modulation). For instance, at the point where the first allegro theme (the doomed traveller) subsides into the seductive music for Tamara herself, Balakirev works a neat transition, from a bar of twelve quavers (four units) to one of six crotchets with a triplet subdivision, which maintains a rhythmic link with the allegro while reining in its tempo in a structured way. Scene change without loss of momentum is brilliantly engineered. But since, in its uncodified form, this is essentially an improvisatory technique—a way of passing smoothly from one thing to another—it may well be that Balakirev was experimenting with these types of continuity as he sat at the piano in his apartment, or at Cui's or Shestakova's, in 1867. The evidence of *Islamey,* again, is that he was.

While *Tamara* remained in a half-formed state, Musorgsky was back at work on his witches. Early in the year he had been sick with influenza and an attack of his old nervous fever. Then at the end of April, for reasons not precisely known, he lost his job at the ministry (it says something about the Russian imperial civil service that his dismissal came only four months after he had been promoted in the table of ranks from collegiate secretary to titular counselor). It left him, of course, more dependent than ever on his brother, with whom he was still living, and with whom he returned to Minkino in June. But even with Filaret's support he found himself unable to live a normal life in the capital, and after a brief return to St. Petersburg in August, he was forced to leave again for Minkino, and there he spent the entire two months of September and October. "My means have shrunk, it's true," he wrote in reply to an anxious letter from Balakirev,

> but not so far as to deprive me conclusively of the possibility of independent existence. Accustomed as I've been to a life of ease and a certain amount of luxury, the future seemed to me, in my present circumstances, not completely settled, and it's no wonder that I made a sour face; at first blush anyone would do the same in my place.—I can well understand the alarm that shows in your friendly letter and I am more convinced than I can say of its genuineness.—But it's precisely in

the interests of sincerity that I do not ask, but implore you to calm yourself on my account and calm all those dear to me, since their fear for
me places an unbearably heavy weight on me, and my situation doesn't
merit it.—It's all the more painful for me in that more than anything
I fear deception. Believe me, my dear Mily, that living in a family and
having got used to it these last two years, rather spoilt in the family
than restricted in it, and entirely settled in my domestic way of life, I
had to consider well how to behave with reduced means.—After serious
discussion of the matter and an arithmetical calculation of my finances
I came to the conclusion that the shortfall deprives me of the possibility of living in Peter from the beginning of October (as I wanted) and
commands me to skip this month of the Peter budget . . . As regards a
job, if I bothered with that I'd be looking for a fixed post (as being more
secure), but one can only think of such a thing after the New Year, since
in all ministries there are cut-backs and upheavals up to New Year . . . [13]

In the event it would be more than a year before he was able to secure
a new post, in the Forestry Department. Meanwhile he was free to
compose.

His first task at Minkino was to complete *St. John's Night on Bald Mountain,* as the witches piece was to be called. Exactly how much of it he
took with him to the country is in fact far from certain. He had, as
we saw, written the first section a year before, but on the other hand
he tells Rimsky-Korsakov, early in July 1867, that the score is finished
and that he has written it in a fortnight of mid-June, directly into fair
copy without drafts and "without sketches of any kind." The wording is mildly ambiguous: for instance, he says "wrote" (*napisal*), which
might conceivably mean "wrote up," rather than "composed" (*sochinil*);
and the absence of sketches might simply mean the absence of orchestration sketches. But all this is rather laborious, and it seems reasonable
to conclude that he essentially composed most of the piece straight into
orchestral score in those two weeks, "not sleeping at night and finishing the work precisely on St. John's Eve" (23 June).[14]

None of these details would be of any importance if it were not for the
fact that he had previously composed virtually nothing of significance
for orchestra. What there was of *Salammbô* was largely unscored, and
probably the same was true of the symphony he had been composing for
Balakirev. He had scored up his various choruses—*Oedipus,* "The Libyans," "Sennacherib"; he had composed the nondescript B-flat scherzo
(no doubt orchestrated with Balakirev's help); and he had orchestrated
his "Little Star" song. Now he was writing a twelve-minute orches-

tral work of a particularly colorful type, and composing it straight into score, rather than as a piano piece that he would then orchestrate. It would hardly have been surprising if the result had been a complete failure, a prime example of the ineptitudes catalogued with such clinical ruthlessness by Rimsky-Korsakov long after Musorgsky's death: "absurd, incoherent harmonies, ugly voice-leading, sometimes strikingly illogical modulation, sometimes a depressing absence of any, unsuccessful instrumentation of orchestral pieces, in general a certain impertinent self-satisfied dilettantism, at times moments of technical adroitness and skill but more often complete technical feebleness."[15] Of all the Musorgsky works Rimsky-Korsakov edited, *St. John's Night on Bald Mountain* was the one he subjected to the most radical recomposition. His edition, compounded of elements of the 1867 score and two later versions Musorgsky made to insert in theatre works that were themselves never completed, was for nearly a hundred years the only one known to concert audiences; and when Musorgsky's own original score was performed for the first time in the 1970s, the general reaction was that Rimsky-Korsakov's judgment had not been far wrong.

It would certainly be hard to deny that the original symphonic poem—or "intermedia," as Musorgsky initially described it on the manuscript title page, then crossed the word out in thick pencil—is a flawed work, somewhat unvaried in character and, in its conclusion, decidedly perfunctory. The problem of structure is better solved in the version he made as a choral intermezzo in the opera *Sorochintsï Fair,* which ends beautifully with the chiming of morning bells and the rising sun breaking through clouds, an ending Rimsky-Korsakov adapted for his own version, whereas Musorgsky was content to conclude his intermedia, as Berlioz had done his *Symphonie fantastique,* with the witches' sabbath itself, but without quite finding and controlling the necessary additional frenzy to overtop that of the preceding music. After finishing the score, he described the program to Rimsky-Korsakov: the witches assembling, Satan's arrival and cortège, the glorification of Satan, and finally the sabbath itself. He also discussed the music at some length, even giving details of the key structure (perhaps in a studentish desire to demonstrate his credentials), and including a pair of music examples which in fact show that the work as completed in June was subsequently revised, since neither of the quoted passages appears in the surviving manuscript. This may have been due to negative remarks by Balakirev, who, as we learn from Musorgsky's September letter, had reacted "evasively" to the work and apparently criticized its design and tried to get his young colleague to modify it. "Whether or not you agree, my friend, to perform my witches," Musorgsky responded, "that is, whether or not I hear them, I will not change anything in the general plan and treatment, closely connected with the contents of the scene, and executed sincerely, without sham or imitation."[16] Balakirev did not conduct the work, and Musorgsky never heard a note of it.

In view of the inferior works he *was* prepared to conduct, one wonders what it was about the piece that turned Balakirev against it. Unsatisfactory the form might be; but the music contains so much that is brilliant and original that one is forced to the conclusion that he was simply too disconcerted by it to want to risk it in the public arena. From start to finish the writing is utterly fearless. Musorgsky had plainly been impressed by the sheer diabolism of Liszt's writing in the *Totentanz,* and at the same time by the way he explores this property by means of a set of variations which, so to speak, excuse him from the need to constantly invent new material—never, after all, Liszt's strongest point. *St. John's Night on Bald Mountain* is in the same way a set of variations on a group of themes which sprout new elements while never straying far from the controlling material of the opening pages. But Musorgsky's variation technique is superbly promiscuous. He keeps coming up with new ways of playing with his material, no doubt thinking of the witches and their sexual pranks (*shashni*)[17] without too much concern for formal process. The variations in scoring and texture also recall Glinka's *Kamarinskaya* method. But Glinka never attempted an orchestral work on quite this scale, nor did he monkey with convention to anything like the same extent.

Musorgsky's originality is best measured against the changes Rimsky-Korsakov saw fit to make, not so much to the work's structure (which he unquestionably improved) as to its detail. The ferocity of Musorgsky's opening, complete with timpani tuned eccentrically to the adjacent pitches G-sharp, A, and B-flat and horns growling away on their bottom A, is partly sacrificed by Rimsky-Korsakov in the interests, one assumes, of good conservatory practice; and in general Rimsky's scoring favors well-behaved family groupings over Musorgsky's stark, Glinka-esque spotlighting of tearaway subsections. For instance, the wild staccato countertheme at bar 13 of the original (bar 12 in Rimsky), which Musorgsky allocates to flutes, oboes, cornets, and trumpets, is completely revamped by Rimsky-Korsakov for woodwind and strings (with bass drum), a "better" solution in every respect except the crucial one of the graphic effect required. In general, the Rimsky-Korsakov of 1886 nearly always plumps for the best scoring from the "brilliance" chapter of the orchestration manual, whereas

Musorgsky, as he told Balakirev, always had the specific picture in his mind's ear, and wrote the sounds he saw.

Much the same applies to the main parameters of the music, especially its melody and harmony. In essence, Musorgsky's variation technique, like Glinka's, is based on the idea of continuous modified repetition. But whereas Glinka had tended to operate within the normal constraints of tonal grammar, keeping the shape of the tune while varying the harmony and texture, Musorgsky tinkers with the melody, adopts a freewheeling approach to countermelody (the "underneath" parts), and often seems to let the harmony go hang. A good example of this is his treatment of the folk-song-derived second theme at figure 4 in the original score, letter B in the Rimsky-Korsakov version. Musorgsky continually tweaks this melody, changing flats to naturals, naturals to sharps, apparently at random, like a schoolboy trying his cap at different angles just for the fun of it. He also extends bars from four to six beats, presumably to accommodate the witches' shrieks, like the shouts of "Vot kak!" and "Vot shto!" in the Shevchenko "Gopak." Such procedures are beyond Rimsky-Korsakov's comprehension, and he invariably "corrects" the accidentals to fit the tonal context and the bar lengths to fit a regular scheme. But Musorgsky hasn't bothered too much about the tonal context, either. At one point, nine bars after figure 5, he has the melody going against two countermelodies, one rising chromatically, the other falling chromatically at half-speed, and the "harmony," such as it is, held together by a pedal (repeated) D on horns and cornets. Rimsky-Korsakov simplifies the passage by cutting out one of the countermelodies and making sure the pedal notes move toward a logical closure, with clear G-minor harmonies for the end of the passage (letter E; figure 6 in the original). All this is a big improvement, if what you want is an orderly design that broadly does what it's told. If, however, what you want is a musical image of a *disorderly* saturnalia, then Musorgsky hardly needs improving. In such cases genius is practically incapable of error; it has its own rules of which, to misquote Pascal, the rules know nothing.[18]

At the time, long before he became a conservatory professor, Rimsky-Korsakov was a good deal more sympathetic to Musorgsky's symphonic poem, which admittedly he knew only from the composer's own description and memories of early play-throughs of the opening pages. Their exchange is revealing. "In the general process of composition," Musorgsky had written, "I've done a lot that's new, for instance in the *filthy glorification* there's a bit for which César [Cui] will dispatch me to the Conservatory" (here he quoted half a dozen bars not found in the eventual score); later he described a sequence for which "they would expel me from the Conservatory to which César will have banished me." He talked about his (extensive) use of what he called "a *chemical scale*," by which he meant Glinka's whole-tone scale, used here especially for dissolves from one scene to the next. And he concluded: "In my view *St. John's Night* is bound to make a good impression on a thinking musician for what's new in it . . . Let's agree that I'm not going to start redoing it; with whatever defects it was born, with them it will live, if it will live."[19] "The glorification of Satan," Rimsky-Korsakov replied, "must certainly be most filthy, and for that reason all kinds of harmonic and melodic filth are permissible and fitting, and no grounds for sending you to the conservatory. The conservatories will of course be horrified by you, but then they themselves can't compose anything decent."[20]

In the past few months, these two youngest members of the circle had drawn closer together, and were freely exchanging information about their work. With the symphonic poem finished, Musorgsky was now orchestrating his "Intermezzo in modo classico" and composing the new middle section which was supposed to represent the young girls singing and laughing in the snow. "The piece itself," he assures Rimsky-Korsakov (without saying a word about the alleged program), "is nothing but a tribute to the Germans," a remark which suggests some mild embarrassment at the music's conventional idiom by comparison with *St. John's Night*.[21] Hastily he moves on to set out a new plan for an orchestral work about Podebrad, the fourteenth-century Hussite leader and regent of Bohemia (another stab at the Germans, in the shape of the Holy Roman Empire and the German king of Bohemia whom Podebrad ousted); he describes the music in some detail and quotes several themes, before passing on to discuss Rimsky-Korsakov's own latest orchestral project.

This is the long-delayed fulfillment of Stasov's old idea of a work based on the legend of the Novgorod gusli-playing merchant Sadko. Stasov, as we saw, had originally pressed this story on to Balakirev, who had eventually passed it on to Musorgsky, who seems to have thought about it for a while, then lost interest and proposed it to Rimsky-Korsakov. This pass-the-parcel aspect of the *kuchka* was the reverse side of their dependence on each other's opinion of their work; it reflected both their lack of confidence in their own ability to complete large-scale projects and their willingness to abandon or at least shelve work—as Musorgsky had just done—of which the others disapproved. But Rimsky-Korsakov was perhaps the least afflicted in this way, and he was rapidly becoming the one member of the circle who could decide to write a work, then get on with writing it, and then quickly get it performed. Admittedly he was not much less addicted to revision than Musorgsky (his *Sadko* tone poem, for instance, exists in three different versions); but this was largely due to his becoming a conservatory professor at the age of twenty-seven, after which he tended to view the sins of his youth with a certain pedagogical severity—a severity he also applied, as we have just seen, to the work of his deceased colleagues.

The twelve-minute *Sadko* illustrates his growing self-assurance. He started writing it at the end of June 1867 at his brother's house near Viborg, in Finland (at that time a *guberniya* of the tsarist empire), and despite having to spend a whole month on a naval cruise in the Gulf of Finland, he completed the full score at the end of September. By the second week of July he is able to describe the first two sections to Musorgsky in laborious detail, with the same rather self-satisfied cataloguing of key schemes and scale formations, orchestration, and several music examples.[22] At the start of the work (in Balakirev's beloved D-flat major), Sadko has already been thrown into the sea from the becalmed ship, and is floating on a plank on the rolling waves. Very soon, however, he is being dragged down to the seabed so that he can play his gusli at the wedding of the Sea King's daughter. We picture the swell of the sea, graphically portrayed in the gently rotating string figures, then the moment of supernatural intervention and Sadko spiraling down, down into the deep waters, where a decorous wedding feast is in progress, *scherzando* in D major, with flowing limbs and fluttering eyelashes. The composer goes on to outline his intentions for the rest of the work. Sadko's gusli playing (D-flat major again) sets off a vigorous trepak which soon becomes so violent that it triggers a storm that sinks many ships. At the climax, Sadko is to be visited by St. Nicholas, the patron saint of sailors, and asked to stop playing and break his gusli. Rimsky-Korsakov has a "church theme" ready for this moment (he quotes it). But Musorgsky takes against the theme and begs his friend to change it.[23] Finally, the St. Nicholas idea is abandoned; after all, Rimsky admits, "Sadko himself could have the sense to smash the gusli . . . And Nikolay would spoil the impression of the dance with his church theme, and indeed his appearance in the midst of the pagan world is somewhat ridiculous"[24] (though it is exactly what happens in the original *bilina*).

The composer is at pains to describe the technical devices involved in all this.[25] At first the waves rise and fall in terms of both the melodic figuration and the harmonic motion; and when Sadko descends to the ocean floor, the music carries him down another of those "chemical" scales, like the whole-tone scale of Lyudmila's abduction or Musorg-sky's witches, but this time a more complicated affair of alternating tones and semitones, eight notes to the octave instead of seven—hence its modern name, the octatonic scale (Rimsky-Korsakov called it the *gamma ton-poluton,* the "tone-semitone scale"). As with Glinka, the idea is one of dissolution and disorientation. The whole-tone scale, lacking the semitones which point us toward the keynote, is effectively atonal, musically weightless and directionless. Rimsky-Korsakov's scale, on the other hand, has an equal number of whole tones and semitones, equally distributed, so that the semitones point us in four possible directions. It sacrifices weightlessness in favor of complexity. We are in a square room with a door in the middle of each wall, all or none of which may lead us to our unknown destination. Rimsky-Korsakov seems already to have understood that this kind of pattern had har-monic possibilities not offered by the whole-tone scale, which is, so to speak, a room without any doors. Harmony comes from a sense of direction, however ambiguous; and for direction we require choice, and criteria for choosing.

Like Musorgsky, Rimsky-Korsakov was consciously indebted to Liszt for many aspects of *Sadko.* Images of water abound in Liszt's music, especially flowing water as something at once mobile and unchanging. The discarded idea of St. Nicholas visiting Sadko on the seabed irresistibly recalls Liszt's "St. Francis of Paola Walking on the Waves." But the most striking derivation is the technical one. Octa-tonic scales crop up here and there well before Liszt (Taruskin found them in Scarlatti and Bach),[26] but Liszt seems to have been the first to employ them in any systematic way. In his memoirs, Rimsky-Korsakov acknowledges his debt to *Ce qu'on entend sur la montagne,* the first of Liszt's symphonic poems, where octatonics are prominent, though he avoids mentioning the scale, but merely refers to one of its properties: namely, that it lends itself to harmonic motion by descending minor thirds. He also incidentally itemizes a number of other allusions, including Bala-kirev's "Song of the Golden Fish," Dargomïzhsky's *Rusalka,* and Liszt's First *Mephisto* Waltz.[27] Reading all this is rather like eavesdropping on a confessional. The aging master is quite hard on his youthful work: he finds it derivative, unbalanced, and short-winded, but he praises the freshness of the material and "the orchestral coloring, caught by some miracle, in spite of my impressive ignorance in the matter of orchestra-tion." The whole impression is that if the young midshipman had had the advantage of tuition by Professor Rimsky-Korsakov, all would have been well; and of course the same applied to Musorgsky.

Whatever its technical novelty, virtues, and defects, *Sadko* is not a work that makes great waves outside its own subject matter. Like his symphony, but in a more individual manner, it achieves what it sets out to achieve attractively and with a certain elegance of surface and style, some of which comes from a revision of 1892. It quite lacks the roughness of *St. John's Night on Bald Mountain,* but it also lacks the sheer thrill of that work, its sense of adventure and danger. A better work it undoubtedly is, but a more limited one. When Balakirev conducted its first performance in an RMS concert on 9 December 1867, it was well received, at least, by an audience not always noted for its receptiveness to radical masterpieces. Rimsky-Korsakov's talent was clearly of the kind that wore its individuality lightly, the sort that adapted itself well and quickly to known idioms and methods, while adding just enough flavor of personality to mark him out as a composer above the common herd. Balakirev, according to Rimsky's own typically candid memoir, "paid my work a certain tribute of patronizing and encouraging admiration, but characterized my compositorial nature as female and in need of impregnation by alien musical ideas."[28] For once the guru may not have been entirely wrong.

CHAPTER 14

A French Guest and a Stone One

Balakirev's appearance on the rostrum of the previously scorned RMS was the outcome of a swift succession of events that shone a bright light on the parish-pump world of St. Petersburg music.

Rubinstein's resignation in the summer of 1867 both as director of the conservatory and as conductor of the RMS was not strictly a surprise; he had been muttering for some time about political interference in the management of the conservatory and had been openly talking about leaving at least since January. But while the Balakirev circle chortled among themselves about his imminent departure, nobody in any official position seems to have believed he would go, and no provision was made for a replacement until he announced in July, from Germany, that he had no intention of returning to the Russian capital that autumn.[1] There at once ensued a scurrying in the rafters of power that precisely illustrated Rubinstein's reason for resigning. The RMS board, of which Dargomïzhsky was president and which included Dmitry Stasov and Rubinstein's friend Vasily Kologrivov among its directors, came down in favor of appointing Balakirev to conduct the RMS concerts in the coming season. But alas, their decision was subject to the approval of Grand Duchess Yelena Pavlovna, who admittedly was a mere amateur musician herself but who happened to have recently heard Balakirev conduct, in her opinion, rather badly at an FMS concert, and was unwilling to allow him more than four of the winter concerts. For the rest, she insisted on the appointment of an internationally famous musician to conduct, suggesting to Prince Dmitri Obolensky, the vice-president of the RMS, that "in this way we would satisfy the public's eagerness for novelty and make it easier to forget Rubinstein's absence."[2]

For Balakirev to take the RMS baton at all must at first have seemed a bitter pill. He disliked Rubinstein as a musician, disliked his choice of repertoire, disliked the whole past image of the RMS. The idea of sharing that particular rostrum with some foreign dignitary would hardly have sweetened the medicine for this unblushing xenophobe. On the other hand, he desperately needed the money. And of course the opportunity to promote the music of his own circle was too good to resist. Accordingly he accepted the post, such as it was, on the condition that he would have choice of repertoire for the concerts he himself was conducting; and at the same time he expressed a strong preference on the subject of celebrities from overseas. The choice might well have fallen on Liszt. In fact it was decided to invite Berlioz, and this, according to Rimsky-Korsakov, was on Balakirev's insistence.[3] For the *kuchka*, Berlioz was the supreme living icon of modern music, a genius who had beaten the Germans at their own game, who wrote brilliant symphonies that broke free of academic forms, dramatic works that did not pretend to be Wagnerian music dramas, vocal works of a lightness and fantasy that no German could match. As an original master of the orchestra he was the nearest thing to Glinka in Western Europe. And he was an outstanding conductor, especially of his own music, which, for all its notoriety, and despite the impact of his previous visit to Russia in the 1840s, was far from well known in the empire.

Berlioz duly arrived in St. Petersburg in mid-November 1867 and stayed until mid-February, with a brief side trip to Moscow in the first half of January. In St. Petersburg he conducted six concerts in all, based mainly on his own music, Beethoven, and Gluck. "Hector Berlioz," Rimsky-Korsakov wrote in his autobiography, "came to us already an old man; alert when conducting, but weighed down by illness and therefore absolutely indifferent in his attitude to Russian music and Russian musicians."[4] This memoir, written nearly forty years after the event, perhaps reflects a certain desire to play down the imagined importance of the New Russian School, as Stasov called them, in the eyes of the sophisticated world. But David Cairns has shown that it was quite untrue. Old and ailing Berlioz certainly was, but he was evidently rejuvenated by his contact with this new and enthusiastic audience, and by the stimulus of conducting once again music that was so close to his heart. The orchestras he found excellent, and far better acquainted with his music than he had feared, and he was thrilled by his own reception, which inspired him, he wrote, to "conduct as I have perhaps never conducted before."[5] It seems clear that he spent time with the young Russian musicians. He rehearsed the conservatory choir painstakingly with Balakirev, who had charge of it as one of his new duties. Some at least of them attended a birthday dinner given for him by the RMS on 11 December. And from time to time Berlioz received visitors in his apartment in the Mikhailovsky Palace. Stasov found him in bed a few days before the dinner, "a real corpse, moaning and wheezing, ripe for instant burial." But at other times the great composer was in better form. His visitors certainly included Cui and Borodin, possibly Musorgsky and Rimsky-Korsakov.[6] And of course they went to his concerts. Cui reviewed them at length in the *Vedomosti,* and, while characteristically grumbling at some of the repertoire ("three very weak pieces by Mozart"; Beethoven's "Pastoral," which "has by now lost much of its freshness and novelty and perhaps counts as the least successful of Beethoven's symphonies"), nevertheless praised Berlioz's conducting to the skies.

> The highest stage of artistic development—a stage to which even the most happily regulated natures very seldom rise—is simplicity. This priceless quality Berlioz possesses in the highest degree. What is most striking of all in his performances is the complete lack of affectation or exaggeration alongside the most refined, varied, colorful communication of nuance. There is nobody who would respect someone else's ideas more religiously than Berlioz; nobody more angered by the cutting, alteration, distortion of the concept or expression in the work of others, no conductor who would perform more faithfully, with greater understanding of a work's spirit, or more complete preservation of all the author's nuances ... And what simplicity of manner, what sobriety, yet at the same time what wonderful precision of gesture, what modesty! When after his performance of the first piece the audience called Berlioz out with loud cries, he came out and with a charming gesture indicated that the credit for the performance belonged to the orchestra, not to him. Of all the conductors Petersburg has heard, there is no doubt that Berlioz is the greatest ...[7]

Amid all this kerfuffle, Balakirev's own series of four concerts inevitably sounded a subdued note. As a conductor, it seems that he possessed many of the virtues Cui praised in Berlioz:

> Simplicity, precise observation of all the composer's indications, not permitting any sort of exaggeration, undue emphasis or inappropriate hurrying up or slowing down ... There was no false expression, pre-

tentiousness or artificiality about him. His tempi were correct, exact, unexceptionable. But his performances were never dry or lifeless. The warmth of his nature was transmitted to his performances without detracting from their high artistic value.[8]

His programs, though, were an idiosyncratic blend of works by Russian composers (nearly half the items)—such as had enraged Turgenev earlier in the year—and works by Western composers who happened to meet with Balakirev's highly selective approval. So there was Beethoven but no trace of Haydn, Mozart, or anything earlier, Schumann but no Mendelssohn or Schubert, Liszt but no Wagner apart from the early and uncharacteristic *Faust* Overture, which for some reason Balakirev admired. The Russian pieces were the usual motley array, including excerpts from *Ruslan* and Dargomïzhsky's *Rusalka,* songs by Glinka and Balakirev himself, and the two "star" works from the Slavic concert, Rimsky-Korsakov's hastily written Fantasia on Serbian Themes and Balakirev's Overture on Czech Themes.

In this company, *Sadko* shone out as a significant and substantial novelty. For Cui (who was not always generous to his *kuchka* colleagues in print), it showed that "Korsakov's talent is maturing and strengthening rapidly; in less than two years he has given us four beautiful orchestral works, of which the most recent, *Sadko,* is noticeably superior to the others and occupies a highly prominent place among contemporary symphonic compositions."[9] Even Serov praised Rimsky-Korsakov's material and his handling of the orchestra ("a boundless wealth of what is not just common-Slavonic but also *truly Russian* . . . the composer's palette sparkles with distinctive, original richness"), but then proceeded to devote the rest of a longish review to an attack on the young composer for having selected one episode from the Sadko legend instead of composing the entire *bïlina*—a bizarre complaint, one might think, from the composer of *Judith.*[10] Meanwhile the recently appointed, ultra-conservative music critic of *Golos,* Alexander Famintsïn, used the *Sadko* concert as a pretext for a broadside against so-called nationalist music in general and the Balakirev circle in particular. "Many people," he wrote, "seem to think that we already have Russian instrumental music and even call it 'national.' But is music national just because it uses as themes for composition trivial dance tunes that automatically remind one of disgusting scenes in front of a saloon? . . . If that is 'nationalism,' then we can indeed boast of Russian national instrumental music, since we have quite a few *trepak* dances of various kinds in this form."[11] Balakirev's Czech overture and Rimsky-Korsakov's *Sadko* both include trepaks.

Famintsïn was himself a (Leipzig) conservatory-trained music historian, a professor of history and aesthetics at the St. Petersburg Conservatory, and a composer in his own right. When Balakirev's appointment to the RMS had been announced in September, Famintsïn had referred to him in *Golos* as "a young and very talented composer and conductor," but this may have been at least partly because he hoped to persuade the talented conductor to program his recently composed incidental music to Schiller's *William Tell*. He also treated Balakirev's Czech overture with caution in his review of the December concert. Balakirev did duly conduct Famintsïn's work two months later in a private RMS tryout that also included a scrappy run-through of Borodin's E-flat symphony. But the good professor's remarks about the new Russian music were too much for Musorgsky, who promptly penned a musical lampoon in the form of a song to a specially composed text which he called "The Classicist—Concerning a Number of Musical Articlets by Mr. Famintsïn" ("Klassik—po povodu nekotorïkh muzïkal'nïkh stateyek g-na Famintsïna").

As a professional colleague and de facto ally of Rubinstein, Famintsïn naturally opposed what he saw as the dilettantism of the New Russian School, along with the modernism that Rubinstein himself rejected in the composers of the so-called New German School, including Wagner and Liszt. But what sort of music did he like? Musorgsky had his own answer. "I am simple," he has Famintsïn declare, "I am lucid, I am modest, polite, I am beauteous . . . a pure classicist." The music has the hesitant charm of a diffident visitor stepping into an eighteenth-century drawing room, until the song's middle section, where courtesy turns to rage against "the newest devices" and "all innovations," especially (the accompaniment reminds us) the ones in Rimsky-Korsakov's *Sadko*. "The Classicist" is not a great song, but nor is it quite a failure. The tease against Famintsïn is of course as meaningless now as the place occupied by that personage in history; but to some extent the satire is generic—a neat, wittily crafted send-up of those (still to be found) who believe that music came to an end with Beethoven, or who wish it had.

One of the reasons why Musorgsky was able to hit off the self-conscious purist so accurately was that he himself had been composing a series of studies based on the comedy of simplicity and the childlike. They followed on from the tragic humor (as he saw it) of the simpleton in "Savishna," the novice in "The Seminarian," and the husband in "Oh, You Drunken Sot!" Even the romance-like "Yevreyskaya pesnya" ("Jewish Song"), a setting of a very free paraphrase of the opening verses of chapter 2 of the Song of Solomon, preserves a kind of languorous purity, with its suggestion of a harp accompanying an antique folk melody colored by apparently random chromatics. Mey's poem tweaks the biblical text into a dialogue between male and female lovers, which surely can't be why Musorgsky, who was still dependent on his brother and sister-in-law for the roof over his head and (presumably) the food and drink in his stomach, dedicated this exquisite song to them.

"Jewish Song" had been composed in June 1867, just after the Musorgskys had arrived at Minkino, and just before the composer finished off *St. John's Night on Bald Mountain*. The rest of the summer had produced exactly three songs, but they are of an originality of style and precision of aim and method that belie any suggestion of slow or lazy working. All three are studies in monometrics—composition in single, unvaried rhythmic units, as for the simpleton's patter in "Darling Savishna." Here, though, the simpleton is replaced by children and peasants, and his mindless desperation turns into the ritual incantations beloved of the very young and those whose lives are governed by nature and routine. Thus the magpie in "Chattering Magpie" ("Strekotun'ya beloboka") is turned initially into a pretext for a game of mimicry, while in "Mushrooming" ("Po gribï") a mechanical counting rhythm serves as conveyor belt for a petulant tirade against some temporary enemies of the young girl doing the collecting.

The magpie song, for all its childish tone (and its subtitle: "shutka," "A Joke"), is a subtle and intricate piece of work. The text is a fusion of two quite separate poems by Pushkin, done in such a way as to create ambiguities of meaning that Musorgsky then uses as a basis for musical cross-cutting. Pushkin's eight-line fragment about the magpie already throws together seemingly unrelated images: a bird by the gate, a prophecy of guests, an imagined bell, dawn light silvering the snowy earth (perhaps he intended to expand the poem into a coherent narrative, though in fact the rhyming scheme works well as it is). The other poem ("Kolokol'chiki zvenyat," "Little Bells Are Ringing") picks up the bells, adds a drummer, a crowd of people, and a little Gypsy girl, who jumps up and down waving a handkerchief. It seems that for Musorgsky this array of images was like an additive folk poem whose incoherences were simply an aspect of the palimpsest of history; but at the same time, the linkages are suggestive. The people are (let's say) the expected guests; the Gypsy girl is the magpie, who also jumps up and down, foretells the future, and pronounces herself a songster.

The music reflects this pattern of sequitur and non sequitur. The magpie chatter (staccato quavers) is soon colored by bell sounds (semiquavers) high on the piano; but as rosy dawn gleams on the snow, the sounds glow like church bells, in even crotchets that are then taken up by the bells of the second poem, and run through like a steady chime until the final couplet, at which point the music augments into a solemn peroration to the Gypsy girl's "I'm a songster, I'm a singer, I'm a mistress of fortunetelling." The whole is then repeated (with one abridgment). There is something mysterious about this linking of mundane observation to church bells, like the deification of folk wisdom. It was essentially a Slavophile idea: the divine to be sought in the lives of rural folk. But it took a Musorgsky—no Slavophile, no more than a routine Christian if one at all, but an artist without baggage—to realize its particular musical potential.

Mey's "Mushrooming" is more obviously coherent. The girl gathering the mushrooms is young, but not too young to marry, and it seems that she plans to poison her parents-in-law, her husband's grandfather (presumably), and finally her husband, lying down beside him in her widowhood. But Musorgsky typically sees this not as a drama but as a character study. Clearly the girl is not going to kill anyone, she is merely in a rage about some domestic tiff, and vents her fury by thinking poison while actually picking edible. This is the only possible sense of the music's relentless joviality, discolored here and there by sinister chromatic harmonies as the girl mutters dark threats and (one imagines) snaps off the mushrooms with unnecessary vehemence. As usual with Musorgsky, the vagrant harmony is expressive rather than grammatical, enhancing the picture of a girl who is spirited but no murderess. She will go home and cook a perfectly palatable supper, and the song ends with the same bouncy offbeat rhythm with which it began.

The last of these late-summer songs is a setting of a poem by Koltsov called "Pirushka" ("Little Feast," or, perhaps better, "Peasant Feast"). Musorgsky subtitled this "rasskaz" ("Story"), but once again the focus is less on narrative than on the painting of a scene. Guests (a current preoccupation of his, for perhaps obvious reasons) arrive, are solemnly led into the house and, after praying before the icon, are served home-brewed bitters and strong beer in home-carved ladles. The song is like a genre painting by Perov: the rich simplicity of the scene, the image of hospitality as a devout ceremony, the charm of the host and hostess and of their daughter as she dispenses honey "with maidenly kindness"—for all these details Musorgsky finds a music that captures their integrity and timeless dignity.

That he was proud of the song is shown by the fact that he not only mentioned it in a letter to Rimsky-Korsakov but quoted its main theme and described it as specifically Russian. Rimsky-Korsakov, in response, refused to judge the piece "until I can hear the whole song."

Yet in a sense the whole song—"its whole *chic*," as Musorgsky described it—is already present in the theme, with its solemn eleven-beat tread (a constant six-plus-five) and, once more, unbroken crotchet rhythm, which places a duty on the singer to maintain the pulse and not add stray half-beats at the end of each phrase, since the point about the steady flow and the irrational beat count is to deny the usual tendency of music to advance from A to B via some kind of climax and a rhetorical close. Musorgsky's feast neither climaxes nor ends in the normal sense. It merely comes to a halt on a plagal (Amen) cadence, as the guests depart, as calmly as they arrived.

Back in St. Petersburg in December and January, he composed another five songs, four of which (including "The Classicist") are life studies in the same sense as the summer pieces. "The Ragamuffin" ("Ozornik"), unlike the earlier songs, sets a text (again one could hardly call it a poem) by Musorgsky himself, in which the lines or half-lines are for the most part pentasyllabic, and because the subject is a naughty little boy making fun of an old crone, the music comes out as a rapid childish incantation mainly in five-four time. This is an extension of the idea of "Darling Savishna," with its obsessive, infantile fives, and "The Little Feast," whose sixes and fives had also been the result of a strict syllabic setting of the poem's couplets. But just as, in verbal play, a child will deliberately distort the normal accents of speech in order to preserve a mechanical pattern, so Musorgsky's urchin sometimes misaccentuates the fives, routinely dividing them as two-plus-three, regardless of where the natural accent falls, or extending unaccented syllables to make an apparently random six-beat bar. The setting of the text, that is, is governed by the picture the composer wants to paint.

The same is true, in a rather different sense, in "Sirotka" ("The Orphan"), also to a text by the composer. A homeless, starving boy pleads for alms from a well-to-do passer-by, and the whole song is dominated (almost in the manner of a baroque *Affekt*) by the strongly downbeated dactylic rhythm of the first phrase: "*Barin moy, mílen'kiy*"—"*Please*, good sir, *please* be kind." This accent, already strong in Russian as in English, is intensified by the child's desperation, which Musorgsky stresses not only through the persistent rhythmic motive, but with dynamic emphases in almost every bar—either forte downbeats or piano downbeats followed by hairpin crescendos and decrescendos. The result is a musical picture of quite extraordinary vividness and poignancy. A few years later Turgenev was present at a soirée of the great operatic bass Osip Petrov, at which his wife, Anna, sang "The Orphan," and Turgenev, by his own report to Pauline Viardot, was "moved to tears."[12]

By contrast, "The Billy Goat" ("Kozyol") is more in the nature of a charade, the sort of thing one can imagine Musorgsky having improvised on the spot. Yet again the text is his own, but now there is a brief narrative—a little ironic comedy that might, fifty years later, have served as a revue sketch. The composer subtitled it "Svetskaya skazochka"—"A Society Tale." A girl goes walking in the fields "to show herself off" (delicate, tripping melody in A major), but meets a horrid old billy goat (grumpy C-sharp minor), runs away and hides in the bushes (A major again, but quicker and with a scurrying semiquaver figure in the piano); soon, though, the girl marries (delicate A-major music as at the start), and whom does she marry? Naturally, a grumpy C-sharp-minor old goat of a moneybags. And of course she doesn't once run away, but cozies up to him, swearing fidelity, etc., etc. (tripping A-major finish). Musically the song is trivial to a degree, but Musorgsky brings it off by the sheer pithiness of the treatment, like that of a comic strip.

The single exception to these life studies is the little romance "Along the Don a Garden Is in Bloom" ("Po-nad Donom sad tsvetyot"), to another poem by Koltsov. Strictly speaking, it is a romance that partakes of the composer's realist method. Again there is a girl out for a walk, along the garden path outside the poet's window. But the song is more about her feelings than her appearance, and it is the empathy that makes the romance: the delicacy of her step, her lovelorn sighs, the hint that she is watering the flowers with her feelings. This is an increasingly rare glimpse of what Rimsky-Korsakov regarded as "that ideal side of [Musorgsky's] talent which he himself subsequently trampled in the mire," and which "lacked a suitably crystalline transparency of finish and graceful form . . . But when in spite of his prejudices, he did manage a beautiful and flowing succession, how happy he was! I witnessed this more than once."[13]

Rimsky-Korsakov was naturally prejudiced by the fact that his own bent was precisely in the direction he was regretting the rarity of in Musorgsky. His own songs of this period are romances of exquisite refinement and entirely conventional character, like the fluid setting of the Pushkin lyric "My Voice for You Is Sweet and Languorous" ("Moy golos dlya tebya"), one of the four songs published in 1867 as opus 7, or the languid Orientalisms of the Lermontov romance, "Like the Sky Your Glance Shines" ("Kak nebesa, tvoy vzor blistayet"), in the same set. It would be a mistake, nevertheless, to see this lyrical quality in Rimsky-Korsakov as necessarily hostile to any kind of radical thinking.

· · ·

"Dargomïzhsky commissions me to invite you to his place on Wednesday evening (the 1st May): they will *sing* all he's composed of *Don Juan* so far."[14]

Stasov's emphasis on the word "sing" (*pet*) in his note to Balakirev might suggest that previous samplings of *The Stone Guest* had been more in the nature of piano fragments, perhaps with the voiceless Dargomïzhsky groaning the parts; or it might just be a mildly ironic joke about the work's speech-melody idea. It seems probable, in fact, that not much actual music had been on offer at all, but that the circle's knowledge of the work was largely through conversation about the underlying idea. In January 1868 Dargomïzhsky wrote to his friend Konstantin Velyaminov that "I am now returning again to *The Stone Guest*," adding that "it has given great delight not only to the Cui-Balakirev circle, but also to [his musician friends] the Purgolds and [the singer Yulia] Platonova."[15] But how much of it they had actually heard at that stage remains a mystery.

Dargomïzhsky's health had taken a severe turn for the worse, and it may well have been his realization that his heart disease was slowly killing him that lent urgency to the task of composing the opera he had been talking about for so long. Between late January and early April he wrote most of what became the first act (the first two of Pushkin's four scenes). "Despite my grave condition," he informed Lyubov Karmalina, "I have started up my swansong; I am writing *The Stone Guest*. It's a strange thing. My nervous state calls forth one idea after another. There is hardly any effort on my part. In two months I have written as much as would formerly have taken me a whole year . . . Of course, this work will not be for the many, but my own musical circle is pleased with my labors."[16]

In fact there had been at least one serious run-through of a significant part of the work at Dargomïzhsky's apartment early in March. This was a performance of the second tableau, most of which is a dialogue between Laura (Pushkin's Donna Elvira equivalent) and her lover, Don Carlos. The May run-through to which Stasov invited Balakirev will have included the first two tableaux, at least as far as Don Juan's entry in scene 2 and the fatal duel with Don Carlos that ends the scene.

Up to this time, Dargomïzhsky had been a regular guest at Shestakova's evenings, but otherwise had tended, according to Rimsky-Korsakov, to surround himself "with admirers consisting of amateurs or musicians notably his inferiors."[17] The implication, not openly stated by Rimsky-Korsakov, is that Dargomïzhsky had preferred not to have his failure to produce worthwhile work since *Rusalka* exposed by association with the highly critical aspirants of the Balakirev circle. They could, as we know, be ruthless in their assessment of each other's activities. When Dargomïzhsky's old opera-ballet *The Triumph of Bacchus* (*Torzhestvo Vakkha*) had recently been premiered without success in Moscow, Musorgsky had positively gloated over its failure in a letter to Balakirev.[18] But now that *The Stone Guest* was making rapid progress, to distant shouts of approval from the *kuchka,* its composer began to feel the confidence to display his work and to discuss it openly in their company. He accordingly dumped most of his old amateur admirers, and instead once more invited Balakirev, Stasov, and the rest of their circle. Of his own former associates, only two sisters survived: Nadezhda Purgold, a gifted pianist, a pupil of Musorgsky's teacher Anton Herke, and her elder sister, Alexandra, a fine, talented mezzo-soprano.

Dargomïzhsky was destined never to hear his last opera performed on the stage or with orchestra. But the renditions with piano must have been highly theatrical in their own way. "It would scarcely be possible," Stasov wrote later, "for anyone to hear the great works of Dargomïzhsky in the theatre in such a perfect performance."[19] The composer himself would croak the part of Don Juan "in the hoarse voice of an old man,"[20] but with vivid dramatic effect; Musorgsky took the roles of Leporello and Don Carlos, Alexandra (Sasha) Purgold sang Laura and Donna Anna, Velyaminov sang the small bass parts—the Monk in scene 1 and the Commander in the final scene. Nadezhda (Nadya) Purgold was invariably the pianist, "our dear little orchestra," as she came to be known. These would not have been occasions for connoisseurs of the voice. Musorgsky was himself a decent singer with a pleasant baritone; but his main talent in this department was as a vocal actor. His qualities reflected those of his most characteristic songs. He had an ability to personify the role he was singing with a comic or tragic wit and precision that could reduce his audience to laughter or tears or sometimes both at once. Sasha Purgold likewise was at her best in character roles. She had, Stasov recalled, "little talent for the performance of formal operatic arias, but on the other hand was inimitable in the realistic and lively declamation of all those musical works where the foreground quality was their genuine truth-to-life, realism, the ardor of the soul, or comedy and humor."[21]

Dargomïzhsky's writing served these talents well. Starting with the idea of setting Pushkin's little play more or less word for word, he adopted a style that entirely avoided conventional vocalisms. Instead the vocal lines are a compromise between the contours of speech and the lyrical requirements of singing. They nearly always respect the natural accents of the spoken Russian, and they never lapse into any kind of vocal display: there is no melisma, no roulades or cadenzas, and few extremes of vocal range. So for example, though the part of Don Juan is written for a tenor, it hardly ever strays outside the range defined by the treble clef: low D to high G—an extremely limited tessitura for an operatic tenor. The same goes, mutatis mutandis, for the other roles. But this (obviously deliberate) restriction on the singer's natural athleticism is matched by the syllabic setting of the text, which in the same way restricts any tendency to expressive vocalization. The music, like Pushkin's verse, moves along in steady, even values, without the variety of rhythm and pulse that composers usually, with good reason, impose on the texts they set. The writing leaves the singer free to nuance the words in marginal ways. But it allows hardly any room for the sorts of expressive freedom to which opera singers are accustomed, while at the same time it denies them the liberties of timing that an actor takes for granted. On the face of it, *The Stone Guest* has all the disadvantages of music and of speech, and none of the advantages of either of them.

The obvious question is: what did Dargomïzhsky think he would achieve by setting Pushkin's play in this consciously restricted way? His watchword, as he had told Karmalina, was "truth"; but it was truth defined in a highly specialized way, defined, that is, in terms of the spoken word, which might not seem the most obvious criterion for judging the truth value of music. One might as well assess the "truth" of the spoken word according to its musicality, which would plainly be ridiculous. Musorgsky, who was as excited as any of the *kuchka* about the idea behind *The Stone Guest,* had actually been working on a somewhat different assumption, that music could take us to the heart of an individual or a situation by isolating some particular aspect of speech or sound and turning it into a musical motive: the breathless declarations of the simpleton, the mindless declensions of the novice, the pleading dactyls of the orphan, the vengeful mutterings of the mushroom picker. All these were treated, in the end, as musical material. Of course, there were other aspects to what amounted, with Dargomïzhsky, to a concept of operatic reform. Like Gluck and Wagner before him (Wagner's theories were known, his relevant works not yet), he wanted to do away with the artificialities of traditional opera: the vocal display, the big arias, the huge galumphing choruses sung by Wagner's "scenery that has learned to march and sing." He wanted the music to be wedded to the text in a way that would fully justify the old label of the Florentine

Camerata: *dramma per musica*. But he was also influenced by Chernï-shevsky's theory of art as an aspiration to the condition of reality. He thought that by making the music as much like the spoken text as was consistent with its still being music, he would be producing something more real and hence, by definition, artistically superior.

The argument is hard to sustain in the face of the work itself. *The Stone Guest* is musically a frustrating piece of work, neither as radical nor as sterile as the theorizing that surrounded it might lead one to expect. Taruskin quotes Paul Henry Lang on the subject: in both *Rusalka* and *The Stone Guest,* Lang asserts, "the purely musical element is totally submerged in abstract dramaturgical doctrines and the lyric drama emerges as a forbidding new *stile recitativo* of arid monotony, even though this recitative occasionally reaches remarkable pregnancy."[22] But Lang had probably heard neither work. There is very little that is forbidding about *The Stone Guest*. As Taruskin shows, its prevailing tone is lyrical, and if its music is indeed sometimes monotonous, this has nothing to do with aridity, everything to do with the simple limitations of expressive range that Dargomïzhsky imposed on himself. If he had been a greater composer, he might have produced something startling out of his root concept, if only by sometimes ignoring it, as Wagner had done when working on *The Ring* a decade before. In fact what he produced was a minor, though by no means worthless, score, to some extent trapped by its concept. As we shall see, it cost a greater composer a good deal of effort to release the artistic potential in this idea, by teaching himself how to forget it.

CHAPTER 15

A Child and an Aborted Wedding

That March evening at Dargomïzhsky's, the Purgold sisters observed Musorgsky closely. It was their first meeting and, according to Nadya, they had previously known nothing at all about him, which, if true, argues that Dargomïzhsky had not been promoting the Balakirev circle among his own set. Her recollection was not unduly flattering. "Musorgsky's personality was so original," she wrote,

> that once you had met him, it was impossible to forget him. He was of medium height, well-built; he had elegant hands, beautiful, shapely wavy hair, quite large, slightly protruding light-gray eyes. But his facial features were not at all attractive, particularly his nose, which was always rather red, as he explained, because it had once got frostbitten at a parade. Musorgsky's eyes were not at all expressive, one could even say they were almost like tin. In general his face was not very mobile or expressive, as if it were hiding some enigma. In conversation Musorgsky would never raise his voice, but would rather lower his speech almost to a whisper. His manners were refined, aristocratic, and one saw in him a well-bred man of the world.[1]

But Musorgsky's personality "impressed both my sister and me. No wonder: he was so interesting, so original, talented and mysterious." Sasha Purgold, in particular, was struck; in fact she fell in love with the elusive young man. But though herself pretty and talented, she seems never to have got through his emotional guard. Soon Nadya would note in her diary that Sasha "sees only coldness in the man who might inspire passion in her if only he would show a little more interest in her. Not seeing what she would like to see in him, she exaggerates, and refers to his attitude as almost hatred, and says that he doesn't even like her singing, and that his visits are not for her sake."[2] Then: "I still can't quite understand his relation to Sasha. Anyway it seems to me that she interests him, and that he sees her as a puzzling, original, capricious but powerful nature. But whether he is able to be attracted by her, to fall in love with her, I don't know. He is an egotist, a terrific egotist!"[3]

The reflex explanation of this impenetrability has been, as we saw, that Musorgsky was homosexual. But the evidence for this is thin. Everything about Nadya's description suggests, rather, sexual repression, and this is borne out, surely, by his lifelong preference for older, often married women, and otherwise in general for male company. The sisters' nickname for him was "Yumor" ("Humor"—they called Rimsky-Korsakov "Iskrennost',"—"Sincerity"), which might suggest, in the circumstances, that he was in the habit of parrying sentimental engagement with flippancy. "He has his own kind of brain," Nadya recorded, "original and very witty. But he sometimes misuses this wit. This may be either a pose, to show that he is not like other people, or it may be just the way he is. The former is more believable . . ."[4] There was something about Musorgsky's use of language that seemed to reinforce this idea of his protecting his true feelings behind a shield of artifice. "Simple, commonplace words repelled him. He even contrived to change and mangle surnames. The style of his letters was unusually original and piquant; the wit, humor, and precision of his epithets sparkled so much. In the last years of his life, this originality of style was already becoming mannered . . . [and] incidentally, by then this mannerism and unnaturalness sometimes manifested themselves not only in his letters but in his entire way of behaving."[5]

Not the least striking thing about this unmistakably convoluted quality in Musorgsky's letters is that it went with an intense and growing interest in the natural properties of ordinary Russian speech. Up to now he had been painting portraits that treated speech habits as an aspect of some particular situation: the simpleton or the orphan pleading, the novice reciting, the ragamuffin taunting. The idea of setting words in general according to the contours of ordinary speech must have been suggested by Dargomïzhsky's approach in The Stone Guest. And yet this was not exactly what Dargomïzhsky was doing. Pushkin's play, after all, is written in (admittedly blank) verse, and the composer's task—or at least what Dargomïzhsky saw as his task—was to find a lyrical equivalent of reciting it. The text is set word for word as it stands, but hardly as if it were normal conversation. Musorgsky, having sung the music and no doubt discussed the philosophy with its composer, comes to a slightly different conclusion. He will take a prose text, if necessary written by himself, and try genuinely to capture its precise nuances in a form that will be music only in the sense that each syllable will be represented by a single pitch, whereas in speech the pitch is normally in constant motion within the syllable. You can try this out for yourself. Say the simplest phrase: "I've lost my ticket"; "There's a man at the door"; "What's the time?" The pitches will be indefinable, whatever expression you adopt. The minute you try to hold the pitch on each syllable, you will be singing, and this applies however terrible your singing voice. Musorgsky, it seems, now made up his mind to get as close as possible to speech in that sense without actually quitting the territory of song. The consequences of what might seem an almost frivolous decision were to prove, in due course, momentous.

From the start the idea seems to have been connected in his mind with children. Perhaps the discovery was accidental. A week or two after the Dargomïzhsky evening he made a setting of a bitter little lullaby by Nikolai Nekrasov, "Yeryomushka's Lullaby" ("Kolïbel'naya Yeryomushki"), in which the rocking of an orphan's cradle is accompanied by worldly advice about getting on in life by sucking up to the right people. Soon afterward he wrote two more songs about children, a setting of a tiny poem by Mey called "Children's Song" ("Detskaya pesenka": perhaps "Nursery Song"), and a more elaborate piece to a text by Musorgsky himself, "With Nyanya" ("S nyaney"), in which a small boy pesters his *nyanya* to tell him stories. This latter song and the Nekrasov lullaby were written down in the same notebook and dedicated "to the great teacher of musical truth, Alexander Sergeyevich Dargomïzhsky."

Musorgsky loved children and was at ease with them. While inclined to keep grown-ups, especially emotionally demanding ones, at arm's length, with children he could relax and talk to them in their own language. Dmitry Stasov's daughter Varvara remembered him well from this time.

> He often came to our house, either in town, or at the dacha in Zamanilovka, near Pargolovo, and since he didn't *pretend* with us and didn't talk to us in that artificial language that grown-ups normally talk with children in houses where they are friends of the parents, we not only quickly became attached to him but even began to consider him one

of us . . . With me, as the oldest, Musorgsky often talked about "serious matters." Thus he was the first to explain to me that the stars were divided into different constellations and that many individual stars, like the constellations, had their own names . . . We children were not in the least afraid of him and would often run to him with all our nonsense and even for "judgment" on some of our "dramatic conflicts."[6]

Musorgsky would sing and play children's songs to them. Varvara recalled how they would laugh "to see a grown-up at the piano singing such 'songs' as were usually sung by our nannies . . . But it was only later that we realized the difference between 'the songs a child invents' and art songs." It may be, though, that Musorgsky himself was inclined to blur this distinction. The world of the romance, with its roses and nightingales, its sighs and tears, its rustling leaves and rippling brooks, was no longer of much interest to him; but in turning to children for his subject matter, he was very far from playing down life's earnestness. On the contrary, it must have been the essential seriousness of children that made it easy for him to identify with them. It wasn't a case of escaping into the frivolous. The point about children was not that they were silly or funny, though they often were; the point was that they were natural, unforced. Observing them brought one close to a reality of behavior and feeling untainted by drawing-room manners or sophisticated passions. They were a ready-made starting point for the art of the truthful.

What was needed was a reversal of point of view. "Yeryomushka's Lullaby" is still a grown-up's song—still, that is, a lullaby, colored by anxious fears *for* the child, untouched by the child's own fears. "Detskaya pesenka" seems, by contrast, to be a genuine child's song, almost a nursery rhyme. A raspberry bush grew in the garden; the sun warms it, the rain cherishes it. Naninka grew up in the tower; Daddy loves her, Mummy cherishes her (the parallelism, and the shift of tense, are characteristic of folk poetry). But though the song is charming, there remains a touch of artifice in its simplicity, symbolized, in a way, by its ending on an unresolved seventh chord which, in this context, feels like a rhetorical gesture. It was only in the third of these songs, "With Nyanya," that Musorgsky entered convincingly into the child's mind and created a miniature drama whose scenario and music seem to be entirely controlled by childish logic. He must have realized that he had taken a significant step in this song, since he soon added more in the same vein and published them all as a cycle called *Detskaya* (*The Nursery*).[7]

Everyone has had or had to look after a child like the one in "With Nyanya." Tell me, he (or possibly she) pleads, the story about the horrid bogeyman, the one who dragged children into the forest and chewed their bones. Was it because they'd been rude to their *nyanya* and disobeyed their daddy and mummy? No, don't tell me that story. Tell me the one about the tsar with a limp and the tsaritsa who always had a bad cold and every time she sneezed it smashed the windows.

Each of Musorgsky's previous children's songs, like his character songs in general, had hinged on one crucial pattern of speech, from which the music took its core thematic material. Now the technique is subtly different. Somewhere behind the composer's text is an unstated genre scene; the *nyanya* is perhaps making the bed or cooking supper, while the child plays with his toys or does a painting. Meanwhile, his demand to be told a story is no more than surface chatter, since *nyanya* evidently is not telling him a story and probably is not intending to. So the character of the song comes, not from an essential activity, but from an inessential one. It's as if Musorgsky were suggesting that, when you come down to it, true reality is made up of trivial or unimportant things. Reality in the grander sense, like Berlioz's "March to the Scaffold" or Lyudmila's abduction, or in the symbolic sense, like Schubert's rejected lover in a winter landscape or Beethoven's distant beloved on his hillside, was all very well for a certain kind of formal, stylized composition. But if you wanted to get at the essence of humanity, you had to catch it in its day-to-day off moments, and this meant listening to its unreflecting speech, its chitchat, its bread-and-butter language, since we reveal ourselves most fully when we are thinking least about ourselves.

Hence the little boy prattling away about stories. Naturally his chatter is formless and erratic, since his mind is half on some other activity. But for Musorgsky this is precisely where its interest lies. He wants his music to reflect the child's fickleness of mind, his in-and-out focus, as expressed in the varying pace and emphases of his speech. So: "Rasska*zhi* mne, nyanyushka, rasska*zhi* mne, milaya [*tell* me, nyanyushka, *tell* me, my dear], pro tovo, pro *buku strashnovo*" [about that *man*, about the *horrible ogre*].[8] The accents are exaggerated, as a child would make them, while the unaccented or half-accented syllables are more or less thrown away, in Russian as in English. For instance, *nyanyushka* and *mílaya* would normally take a first-syllable accent, but because they are routine incidents in the child's way of talking, they retain only a light emphasis. Above all, the accents are irregular, and Musorgsky makes no attempt to iron them out into a regular metric scheme, but instead lets the child sing in even crotchets, marking the accents by discreet melodic climaxes and hairpin crescendos. The result of all this is a constantly changing meter controlled by the verbal accents. The song starts off in 7/4 but is soon changing time signature on practically every bar, and since the child scarcely pauses for breath, rests are used mainly for emphasis (for instance, a quaver rest before "*strashnovo*"—"*horrible*"). At the end of the first section, after he has finished listing all the disagreeable things the ogre did to the children, the little boy at last pauses, then goes on more hesitantly and rather slyly: "Nyanyushka! Was that why the ogre ate them, those children, because they upset their old nyanya?" All this Musorgsky captures with wonderful precision; one pictures the child, hears his tone of voice, senses precisely his desire to tease, perhaps mildly irritate. Will he come and get *me,* is the unspoken thought, for being annoying about stories? "Is *that* why he ate them . . . *nya*-nyushka?"

The music's identification with the child is absolute, and this has some interesting consequences, of which the irregular meter is only the most obvious. The tune also to some extent follows the verbal accents, but it also responds to the child's expressive way of describing things. Thus on "pro tovo, pro buku strashnovo" the voice drops on the final syllables of each word, as if the ogre might be a dark secret, better mentioned in a hushed whisper. The prevailing melodic interval is, for the moment, the tritone, or augmented fourth, conventionally a nonvocal interval, used here and elsewhere to express horror. In general, Musorgsky pays little attention to the normal rules of well-formed melody, any more than he bothers about correct harmony. The harmony is essentially anecdotal, coloring the child's mental picture and his way of talking about it. Dissonance is used to enhance the picture, not always in a strictly grammatical way, though the writing is certainly not atonal; rather, the tonal design is extremely informal. The song starts in G-flat major, but tends toward B-flat (the key it ends in). But Musorgsky uses cadences like bookends, to brace a somewhat easygoing sequence of events in between. Sometimes the child sings what might be fragments of folk song: for instance, about the tsar and tsaritsa "who lived across the sea in a rich castle," an almost lyrical picture which he then spoils by remembering that the tsar had a limp, and wherever he stumbled a mushroom would grow. In this way, the music always reflects the imagery of the moment, which of course is just the way a child talks.

Analyzed in this way, "With Nyanya" might sound chaotic. In fact it is a crisp little scena which ends just soon enough, with a snatch of the opening music, a mock-dramatic cadence, and a soft piano coda, as if apologizing for the child's naughtiness. Above all, there is a mastery of timing and an instinct for character that reveal the born theatre composer. When Musorgsky performed the song at the Purgolds' at the end of April 1868, Dargomïzhsky is supposed to have remarked, "Well, that outdid me," though whether in a complimentary sense or in the sense "if nothing else" is not entirely clear. It certainly did, in any case. The novelty of *The Stone Guest* has always been overstated, as has its quirkiness. Technically, it did nothing much beyond what Wagner had been doing more brilliantly and on a far bigger scale in his as yet unknown *Ring,* and its vaunted realism was little more than the word-for-word setting of an existing play, which, if it had actually been offered as a libretto, would hardly have raised an eyebrow. "With Nyanya," by contrast, does seem to take Chernïshevsky's admonitions about art aspiring to the level of reality quite literally, though in so doing it also shows the limitations of the theory. After all, the piece has to succeed as a self-contained entity, an object with specific boundaries that enclose it within a virtual space. The idea that watching a child play for three or four minutes would be in any way a comparable (let alone a superior) experience is not so much obviously false as categorically absurd, which is of course why Chernïshevsky, when he talked about music, had to limit his idea of "reality" to the concept of folk singing as a natural phenomenon. Nevertheless, Musorgsky did for a time believe that the mere imitation of life could be a blueprint for worthwhile art, and it took a much bigger experiment than this one brief song to convince him that that was not in fact the case.

The logical next step was to follow Dargomïzhsky and compose an opera on an existing play. But the play would have to be in prose, like "With Nyanya," which effectively ruled out Pushkin or, for example, Griboyedov, whose famous *Woe from Wit* (*Gore ot uma*) was likewise in verse. The natural choice was Gogol, whose three completed plays are comedies in prose. Musorgsky later told Stasov that the idea of making an opera out of *Marriage* (*Zhenit'ba*)—the least well-known of the three—was suggested by Dargomïzhsky himself "as a joke," and backed up by Cui "not as a joke."[9] He duly started composing the first scene early that June and had soon written enough to play to the circle and get their opinion.[10] Three weeks later he went with his brother's family to their new dacha at Shilovo, near Laptevo, a hundred miles or so south of Moscow, and there, in a little over a fortnight, working in a wooden hut, and for the first time in his life without a piano, he composed the remaining three scenes of the opera's first act. Outside the rain poured down; inside the music poured forth. "So that the weather and I," he told Cui, "went in parallel."[11]

More even than in Gogol's *Government Inspector* (*Revizor*), the comedy in *Marriage* hinges on the deeply prosaic, corrupt, and above all indolent nature of the provincial Russian gentry class. The central character, a minor civil servant called Ivan Podkolyosin, has for some time been reluctantly contemplating getting married, not because of a sentimental attachment to any individual, but because, as he explains in his opening speech, it's something that at a certain point, and all things considered, one probably ought to do. A matchmaker (a woman by the name of Fyokla Ivanovna) is on the case, and has a suitable candidate, Agafya Tikhonovna, in view. Unfortunately there are not only rival suitors but also a rival matchmaker, in the person of Podkolyosin's friend Kochkaryov, himself a former client of Fyokla's, who in the course of the play's two long acts sees off Fyokla and the other suitors, sets up the wedding, complete with guests and reception, but is left in the lurch by Podkolyosin, who at the last minute loses his nerve and escapes through a first-floor window of Agafya's house.

It is easy to see why Dargomïzhsky, whose own "realist" opera had been elevated in its subject matter if not its treatment, was only half-serious in proposing this rambling farce as a subject for an opera. Mozart might have composed it brilliantly; but it was precisely the farcical-cynical element in Mozart's buffa subjects that the nineteenth century disliked (*Don Giovanni* was played, but without its deflating final sextet, *The Marriage of Figaro* much less, *Così fan tutte* hardly at all). For Musorgsky, on the other hand, the antiromantic tone suited his current needs like a glove, because it forced him to imagine a music that would come as close as possible to a simulacrum of everyday speech, without the intervention of the loftier aspects of romantic realism: the vivid portrayal of the fantastic or the extraordinary; the cultivation of the ugly and sinister; the idea of program music; the symphonic prose of Wagner, which Musorgsky knew about but did not know. Set verbatim, as Dargomïzhsky had set Pushkin's *Stone Guest*, *Marriage* gave even less opportunity for musical digression and was tailor-made for a music in which, as Musorgsky was soon explaining to Lyudmila Shestakova, the characters

speak on the stage, as living people speak, but withal so that the character and intonational force of the *dramatis personae,* backed up by the orchestra, which consists of a musical outline of their way of speaking, achieve their aim directly, that is, my music must be an artistic reproduction of human speech in all its finest shades, that is, *the sounds of human speech,* as the external manifestations of thought and feeling, must without exaggeration or violence turn into *music* that is truthful and precise, *but* (which means) artistic, highly artistic.[12]

By the time he concocted this somewhat elaborate explanation of what is, in fact, quite a simple idea, Musorgsky had essentially composed all the music he would ever compose for *Marriage.* He had set the entire first scene of the play, in all its prosaic, ribald detail, with only minor cuts, mainly of speeches that were too mundane even for his well-armed sensibilities: for instance, Podkolyosin's ruminations on how boots can give you corns, and Kochkaryov's shopping list of drinks for the wedding reception. He had written some forty minutes of music, covering approximately a fifth of the two-act play, and must have begun to realize that at that rate the finished opera would end up longer than *Ruslan and Lyudmila,* a notoriously lengthy work. It's true that he was telling everyone that he was thinking about his second act (Gogol's act I, scene 2), albeit in somewhat guarded terms. At the end of July, writing to Shestakova, he was "thinking over the second act"; but a fortnight later he was still—in a letter to Cui—thinking about it but had "not started writing it down. I feel I must bide my time."[13] "The second act," he told Rimsky-Korsakov on the same day, "exists only as an idea and a plan—it's still too early to compose it!"[14] But then he had already told Cui that "the first act will, in the end, the way I see it, be able to serve as an experiment in *opéra dialogué* [Dargomïzhsky's term for the straight setting of an existing play]." He was still at this point early in July working on the first act and hoping to "finish [it] by winter; then we'll be able to judge and ordain."[15]

The key word in all these equivocations is "experiment." He had suddenly become highly self-conscious about what he was up to, and had perhaps begun to realize that, like any experiment, this one might not work. The issue is clear from the very start of the first act. In the normal way planning an opera is a reasonably complicated process. A libretto has to be either invented or distilled from an existing story: in any case, it has to be worked out in advance, its structure, sequence of events, and characterization devised to meet specifically musical needs, which are obviously not remotely the needs of a spoken drama. One has only to think of the relationship between Glinka's *Ruslan* and the Pushkin poem on which it was based, or between Verdi's *Rigoletto* and its source, Victor Hugo's play *Le Roi s'amuse* (both of them operas Musorgsky knew well), to see how fundamental the change of medium is to the change of genre. By contrast, Musorgsky had only to take out a copy of Gogol's play, open the book, and start writing. It was as if he were simply to decide, on the spur of the moment, to read the play out loud, a decision hardly momentous enough in itself to guarantee a momentous result.

So, he turns to page 1, composes half a dozen bars of somewhat inconsequential introduction (for piano—he never got round to the orchestration), and brings the curtain up on Podkolyosin reflecting on the pros and cons of marriage-by-broker and nagging his manservant, Stepan, about his new tailcoat and the boot polish. As in "With Nyanya," the music is essentially subject to the text. Musorgsky pays careful attention to the contours of the words as they might be spoken, bearing in mind the element of caricature in Gogol's portraiture, which he brings out by enhancing the strong Russian tonic accent with sharp rises and falls in pitch and pointed dynamic emphases. The Russian habit of discarding weak end syllables is precisely caught: for example, "da ta*k*aya, *n*akonets, | *sk*vernost' stanovitsya" ("and in the end it's such a horror"), with a swell and chord on the accented high E of "ta*k*aya," fading triplet quavers on "*n*akonets" (unaccompanied) and "stanovitsya," on both of which the accents are actually misplaced, but so faintly as to escape notice (correct would be "nako*nets*" and "stano*vit*sya"). The effect, though, is clinical rather than arresting. In Gogol, Podkolyosin's languid indecisiveness and Stepan's resigned, monosyllabic replies are funny because of the sheer ludicrous irrelevance of the preoccupation with buttonholes and the obsession with rank ("Whichever way you look at it, a court counselor is equal to a colonel! Only without the epaulets"). But put to music, even *dialogué*, they are simply slower; and if the music aspires to the condition of speech, the listener is likely to wonder why not simply stick to speech. Later on, Musorgsky's answer would be (echoing the German theorist Georg Gottfried Gervinus) that since "human speech is strictly regulated by musical laws," it was logical for music to retrieve and reassert that dimension in its original, authentic form.[16] In 1868, though, it seems unlikely that he had read Gervinus, whose main contribution to the theory of music and language, a book called *Händel und Shakespeare: Zur Aesthetik der Tonkunst*, only came out in Leipzig that same year. The clear impulse for *Marriage* was still the quest for realism, or "truth," prompted by the discussions surrounding *The Stone Guest*, and as an extreme version of the vivid portraiture in Musorgsky's recent songs.

Theory aside, the main consequence of his way of working in *Marriage* is that the music is almost entirely anecdotal. It reacts to words and situations, but has little structure beyond what is provided by the often absurd action of the play. The dominating mode is accompanied recitative. Lyrical melody is almost entirely lacking. In its place is musicalized speech, cleverly and often wittily composed but seldom of actual musical interest. As Taruskin has pointed out, most of the music would be meaningless without the words.[17] The accompaniment occasionally throws in what one might call mood music: snatches of sentimental lyricism (for instance, when Fyokla is describing Agafya—"Like a sugar lump! White, rosy, the picture of health. I can't tell you how sweet"— the piano supplies an insinuating fragment that tells us, of course, that it's a lie and Agafya will be anything but a demure wallflower, though Musorgsky never got as far as composing her music); dissonant harmonies that touch in the characters' gestures but lead nowhere; scherzo flurries for Fyokla and for Kochkaryov, whose impatience to get Podkolyosin married off is in sharp contrast with the latter's procrastination. Here and there a figure will act as a reminiscence motive; the grumpy opening music comes back a few times, as a reminder of Podkolyosin's impenetrable bachelorhood. But these are references, not leitmotifs; of musical development as understood by Wagner, or even Balakirev, there is none.

When he finished what he called his act I, Musorgsky had been at Shilovo for just over two weeks. The weather had been bad, and he had spent most of the time indoors, composing. Now, with the act finished, the weather improved and the composer stepped out into the sunshine and looked about him. He began to roam the countryside and enjoy what he called the rustic life. He helped with the haymaking, made jam and pickles, and observed the local peasants. Perhaps for the first time, he began to write down his impressions, even made musical notes of the intonations of peasant speech. He studied their faces and imagined them as characters in books. One of them reminded him of Mark Antony in Shakespeare's *Julius Caesar,* "a very clever muzhik, malicious and original."[18] "How many fresh aspects swarm in the Russian nature, untouched by art," he exclaimed to Lyudmila, "oh how many! And what juicy, splendid ones . . . A small part of what life has given me I have portrayed in musical images for those dear to me, and talked my impressions with those dear ones. If God gives me life and strength, I shall talk something big."[19] And to Nikolsky—the infamous, drunken Pakhomich—he remarked gnomically:

Supposing a reproduction by artistic means of human speech with all its subtlest and most capricious nuances, a natural portrait, as a man's life and mentality commanded—would this come close to a deification of the human gift of the word? And if it were possible to clutch at the heartstrings by the simplest means, while strictly obeying one's artistic instinct in the quest for the intonations of the human voice, shouldn't one work at that? And if at the same time one could capture the intellect in a vice, then wouldn't it be right to devote oneself to such a task? Without preparation you can't boil a soup. Which means: in preparing oneself for this activity, even if it's Gogol's *Marriage,* the most capricious thing for music, won't one be doing something good, i.e. drawing nearer to life's cherished goal? To this one can say: why only ever preparing oneself—it's about time to do something. I've prepared myself with small things, I've prepared myself with *Marriage,* but when, finally, will something be ready? To this there's only one answer: *the force of necessity;* perhaps some day that will be ready.[20]

So *Marriage,* too, was merely a trial, a dry run, and in all probability by mid-August he was no longer seeing it as an ongoing project, even though, with a piano again at his disposal, he probably revised what he had already composed.[21] Concepts such as "the deification of the word," "clutching at the heartstrings," "capturing the intellect in a vice," hardly sound like Podkolyosin and his anxieties about tailcoats. They have an altogether grander, more abstract, but also more theoretical flavor. At the same time the sudden enthusiasm for the peasantry and their ways of thinking and speaking might seem a rather oblique offshoot from Gogol's play, whose characters are urban merchants, civil servants, and their hangers-on. We seem much closer to the world of Platon Karatayev in Tolstoy's *War and Peace,* the peasant soldier who restores Pierre Bezhukov's faith in the human spirit out of the shattering impact of his wife's infidelities and the vacuous response of Petersburg society to the French invasion. Whether or not Musorgsky had read the serialized parts of the first two books of *War and Peace* in the *Russkiy vestnik* a year or two earlier, there is a sense in his remarks to Nikolsky of a readiness for a project of comparable range, one that would set individual lives against a backcloth of momentous historical events.[22]

Musorgsky returned to St. Petersburg toward the end of August, and since his brother's family had stayed on at Shilovo, he now moved in with Nadezhda Opochinina and her brother Alexander in their apartment in the so-called Engineers Castle on the Fontanka Canal. As usual, he sidestepped any suggestion that he might set up house on some regular basis either on his own or with a friend. A month or so later *Marriage* was performed complete, as far as it went, at a soirée in the Cui apartment, with the composer himself as Podkolyosin, Sasha Purgold as Fyokla, Dargomïzhsky as Kochkaryov, and Nadya Purgold at the piano. The response was characteristic in a variety of ways. There was a good deal of laughter, Stasov recalled, "because the exact intonations of Gogol's comic genius were so truthfully caught at every turn."[23] Stasov liked the piece, he later claimed, for its "astounding truth of expression, that proximity to ordinary, everyday human speech, which cannot fail to be considered a great step forward in the matter of art."[24] But privately he called it "an unsuccessful thing, an exaggeration, a monstrosity and a blunder on Musorgsky's part."[25] The pure-minded Rimsky-Korsakov liked the recitatives but was "perplexed by certain chords and harmonic progressions."[26] Borodin reported to his wife (in Moscow) that the work was "an unusual thing, curious and paradoxical, full of novelty and in places very funny, but as a whole—*une chose manquée*—impossible for performance."[27] Balakirev (who was not present at the first run-through) and Cui himself "saw in *Marriage* a mere curiosity with interesting declamatory moments."[28]

In his heart of hearts Musorgsky probably agreed with them; but he retained a soft spot for the work and never rejected it entirely, though he equally never made the slightest attempt to complete it or even to orchestrate what he had written. Early in 1873 he presented the manuscript to Stasov as a fifty-ninth-birthday present. "Take my youthful work on Gogol's *Marriage*," he wrote, "examine this attempt at musical speech, compare it with *Boris* [*Godunov*], confront 1868 with 1871, and you will see that I am giving you myself irrevocably... I can't stand darkness and I think that for a connoisseur, *Marriage* will reveal much as regards my musical audacities. You know how *dearly* I value it—this *Marriage*... So take me, my dear, and do with me what you wish."[29]

CHAPTER 16

Outsiders

While Musorgsky had been passing his time with children and peasants, Rimsky-Korsakov had made his way from the bottom of the sea to the heart of the Syrian desert and the ruins of Palmyra. Having finished with the merchant Sadko, he turned to the adventures of a disillusioned Bedouin prince called Antar, as told in 1832 by the myth-making Polish-born Orientalist Osip Senkovsky (alias Baron Brambeus).

As with *Sadko,* the subject was passed on to him by Balakirev via Musorgsky, though in this case there is no sign of the original suggestion having come from Stasov in any form. Senkovsky's tale, after all, is not based on a traditional story but is an invention of his own, drawing vaguely on a romantic notion of old Arabic epic poetry but without specific models (it evidently has no connection with the sixth-century poet Antarah ibn Shadad). This was not quite Stasov's territory, though he seems to have been happy enough with the outcome. It coincided with at least two of his predilections: it offered a detailed program, and it was set in what, in the Russian mind, passed for the Orient.

Senkovsky's hero is an Arab chieftain who has abandoned his tribe in favor of a nomadic life in the desert. He "has taken leave of humanity forever. He has shed his blood for them, sacrificed his property, lavished his love and his friendship on them—and they have betrayed him!" Later we discover that he has been defrauded of his inheritance by those who were appointed his guardians when he was a child. But now a strange thing happens. He sees a gazelle and gives chase, intending to kill it; but suddenly a huge bird of prey appears overhead, itself pursues the gazelle, and is about to seize it when Antar, his protective instincts overcoming his blood lust, hurls his spear into the monster's throat. The gazelle turns out to be the beautiful peri Gul-Nazar in disguise. The Palmyra ruins are transformed into an exquisite palace, Antar awakes on a satin couch, waited on by slaves and eunuchs and "fifty maidens veiled in white," and Gul-Nazar, concealed by a richly patterned red curtain, offers him a reward of the three greatest pleasures of life: revenge, power, and (here, toward the end of the story, the curtain parts and she reveals herself) love. Antar tastes revenge but returns to Palmyra embittered by "the salt taste of human blood . . . and the aroma of death"; he tastes power, but returns "haunted by pale ghosts of suspicion, danger, and betrayal"; finally he enjoys the love of Gul-Nazar, but fears the poison at the bottom of the heart "when the sweetness evaporates." He implores her to end his life "the instant you perceive that bitterness has begun to creep into it." One day she indeed notices that his thoughts are wandering, that he is bored by her charms, and "with her last kiss the peri breathe[s] in his soul and unite[s] it with her own."[1]

There are certain striking parallels between this yarn and Lermontov's *Tamara*: the beautiful princess, the traveller trapped by her magic, the love-death motif. It is tempting to suppose that Rimsky-Korsakov may have expressed enthusiasm for some such topic, and that Balakirev duly obliged from the storehouse of his own researches. The differences are in the detail, and particularly the quantity of detail. Lermontov's poem is a vignette in a dozen short quatrains, whereas Senkovsky's tale is a twenty-page novelette, tricked out with narrative archaisms ("Fair is the desert of al-Sha'm, and fair are the ruins of Tadmur which lie therein," etc., etc.), but also replete with pictorial and conversational minutiae: the pursuit of the gazelle, the shooting of the terrible *unka* bird, the transformation of the ruins of Palmyra into the wondrous palace of Gul-Nazar, her lengthy account of the origins of the city of Tadmur, and the concluding story of Antar's love and death.

Rimsky-Korsakov duly embarked, in January 1868, on what was planned as a narrative program symphony in four movements, in the spirit of Berlioz's *Symphonie fantastique* and *Harold in Italy*. He pictured Antar, in a dark F-sharp-minor motto theme, morosely surveying the great ruins of the ancient city; he pictured the gazelle and the swooping bird, the flight of the arrow and the wounded bird's departure. Within a week he had composed an entire first movement, taking the story to Antar's awakening in Gul-Nazar's palace and her promise of the three great "sweetnesses" (*sladosti*). At this point one senses a momentary hesitation. The formal idea was to devote one movement to each of the pleasures. But it was by no means obvious how to handle the first one, revenge, since Senkovsky is vague about the objects and character of Antar's vengeance. We learn, for example, that he has "slain those who slandered me and then sat among them as the sand smoked with their blood, holding converse with them as with bosom friends." But narrative detail is suddenly, painfully lacking. Similarly with the second sweetness, power. Antar describes the pleasure of ruling over everyone and everything: "Nothing," he admits, "is more delightful than to see thousands upon thousands of creatures like yourself acting according to your word, drawing their will from the common spring of your will, gladly sacrificing their thoughts, property, and life to carry out your wishes." But once again, no details are vouchsafed. Both sweetnesses end in bitterness, in circumstances that are not revealed.

Perhaps blocked by this lack of focus in the story, Rimsky-Korsakov turned instead to the fourth movement, the third sweetness: love. Here Senkovsky touches in more detail, and of course the subject itself is more obviously up music's street. By mid-February this finale was complete and Rimsky-Korsakov was turning his attention back to the revenge movement. He swiftly composed a breezy, mildly sinister four-minute scherzo in B minor, based on swirling tremolo quavers with menacing versions of the motto theme on trombones. But the piece is thin; and when Rimsky-Korsakov played the three movements through one spring evening at Borodin's apartment, Musorgsky must have pointed out that he had unwittingly purloined the main quaver theme from his own *St. John's Night on Bald Mountain*. In his memoirs, Rimsky-Korsakov notes only that the movement "proved a total failure" with the circle, which it might well have done even without this rather glaring act of homage. The other movements, he insists, "earned the praise of my friends," though he admits that Balakirev liked them only "with reservations": what these may have been, we shall consider in due course.[2]

He seems all the same to have been discouraged, either by the general reaction or by the problems posed by these two somewhat abstract sweetnesses, and for the next three months he put the work to one side and concentrated instead on orchestrating Schubert's four-hand Grande Marche héroïque, D. 885 (composed, for some unknown reason, in 1826 "on the occasion of the coronation of His Majesty Nicholas I, Emperor of all the Russias"), for a concert Balakirev was conducting at the Mikhailovsky Manège in May. This was, Rimsky-Korsakov reports frankly, "a more difficult task than the orchestration of works of my own imagination," and "the instrumentation came out life-less, pallid and good for nothing."[3] But there were distractions. The soirée at Dargomïzhsky's in March, which included the first proper run-through of *The Stone Guest,* was Rimsky-Korsakov's first encounter with the Purgold sisters, as it was also Musorgsky's; and it would affect him more, and more directly. Later that month there was a still more momentous encounter for them all with a young composer from Moscow who turned up at a Balakirev evening and played through the first movement of his symphony in G minor.

Pyotr Tchaikovsky had been one of the first graduates from the new St. Petersburg Conservatory in 1865, but he had gone to Moscow to teach in the new conservatory there early in 1866 and had thus avoided close contact with the Balakirev circle at a time when he might easily have fallen under their influence. As a music student he must have been aware of the circle's activities. He attended the premiere of Rimsky-Korsakov's First Symphony in December 1865, and ten days later his own graduation cantata, *K radosti* (a setting of Schiller's "Ode to Joy"), had been premiered in a public examination concert in the conservatory and reviewed with acid contempt by Cui. But there is no evidence of any actual meeting. David Brown claims that Tchaikovsky met Stasov at the time of Berlioz's visit, but he is vague about the details.[4] The first certain contact was with Balakirev, who travelled to Moscow for the Berlioz concerts there in January 1868, met Tchaikovsky, and discussed with him the possibility of including his "Dances of the Hay Maidens" ("Tantsï sennïkh devushek") in an RMS concert in St. Petersburg. They were soon corresponding on this and other subjects. So when Tchaikovsky visited St. Petersburg at the end of March, it was natural that Balakirev should invite him to his evenings and encourage him to play some of his music.

The G-minor symphony was not wholly unknown in St. Petersburg; the central adagio and scherzo had been played at an RMS concert under Nikolay Rubinstein a year before. But the first movement was entirely new to the circle, and it took them by surprise. After all, its composer was a conservatory graduate, and therefore an object of suspicion among the Balakirev set. Any talent he might have possessed would obviously have been wrecked by all those Jewish pianists and German professors. Yet what did they hear? A beautiful, elegant melody, without preamble, flowing in the most natural, unaffected way into a no less attractive and interesting second subject: writing that transformed the sonata principle into an effortless lyrical outpouring. The circle liked it, Rimsky-Korsakov reports, and they liked its composer, "agreeable company and a sympathetic man who knew how to conduct himself simply and always speak with sincerity and warmth."[5] The feeling must have been mutual, since Tchaikovsky would continue to correspond amicably with Balakirev, and would often attend his soirées when he was in St. Petersburg. Now and then Balakirev would feed him subjects for musical treatment, as he did his *kuchka* friends, and they would correspond about the results and Tchaikovsky would often defer to his three-year-senior colleague. Artistically, though, he tended to look down on the *kuchka,* and to consider their admitted talents too inhibited by coarse or limited technique. His own bent was naturally toward the Western tradition; he would generally be working on a symphony or a concerto or a string quartet, or a ballet or opera based, as likely as not, on some non-Russian literary subject.[6] And he would usually (if not quite always) finish what he had started. It wasn't that he was uninterested in Russian materials: he would write operas on subjects from Pushkin or Ostrovsky, and he would sometimes borrow folk tunes or Orthodox chant. His many songs nearly all set Russian texts. But his Russianness would remain essentially a dialect of the great European musical language; and this suited his particular genius, which had no need of rejecting traditions or techniques or influences in order to define itself adequately. Tchaikovsky was one of those fortunate artists whose individuality is so natural that they never have to think about it. The *kuchka*'s perpetual agonizing about style and methodology was alien to him; he could not understand it, and to the extent that he was aware of it, he was apt to despise it.

The fluency of Tchaikovsky's symphony may well have troubled Rimsky-Korsakov, who was himself writing what he thought of as a symphony, but was apparently having difficulty reconciling symphonic procedures with the demands of his program. In June he tried again with revenge, and this time came up with a thematic figuration that was original and had the necessary venom, even if the movement was not in other respects essentially different from the discarded one: figuration alternating with motto, and a marked tendency to go round in circles rather than open out new territory. No doubt happy, all the same, to have solved one of his problems, he set off to stay with the Purgolds, who were spending the summer of 1868 at Lesnoye, in Tver province. Perhaps he was already attracted to the younger sister, Nadezhda. But curiously, the message of the two songs he composed at Lesnoye is that it was Sasha, the older sister, who for the moment held his eye. "Noch' " ("Night"), which he dedicated to Nadya, is an uncomplicated evocation of nocturnal sounds and scents, likable enough but in no way suggestive. On the other hand "Tayna" ("The Secret"), dedicated to Sasha, is a love song of a certain insistence, a setting of an anonymous Russian translation from Adalbert von Chamisso (the poet of Schumann's *Frauenliebe und -leben*).[7] "When, my dear friend, you kissed me on the mouth, the stars gleamed alone in the night ... Who gave away our secret?" Or was Rimsky-Korsakov himself engaging in a tactical deception?

Soon after his Lesnoye holiday, Rimsky-Korsakov spent three weeks on the Tver estate of a certain Ivan Lodïzhensky, the elder brother of the twenty-five-year-old composer who had started coming to Balakirev's evenings a few years before. Like Musorgsky, Nikolay Lodïzhensky had suffered the fate of many a younger brother in the ruinous conditions imposed on landowners by the emancipation. As a composer, to be sure, he was little more than a dabbler. He seems to have been a talented keyboard improviser; but not much got written down, and hardly anything got finished. In later years Nikolay became a respectable diplomat. But in the sixties he cut a somewhat eccentric, antiestablishment figure, sleeping on bare boards, going to confession in his filthiest old clothes, and generally behaving in an erratic, unpredictable way. One might see him as the ultimate failed archetype of a kuchkist: gifted, untutored, unmotivated, unfocused, also perhaps rather lazy. According to Rimsky-Korsakov, he improvised bits of at least one opera (*The False Dmitry*), one or more symphonies, and "musical fragments that simply had no home." "All of this," he goes on, "was nevertheless so graceful, beautiful, expressive, and even technically correct that it at once won the attention and sympathy of us all."[8] Alas, apart from one set of half a dozen songs, published in 1873, every note of it vanished without trace.

Borodin had also started writing songs again in 1867, after a hiatus of more than twelve years, and while his subject matter is closer in genre to Rimsky-Korsakov's than to Musorgsky's, he is noticeably less beholden to lyrical stereotypes. Like Musorgsky, he liked to write his own texts, but less in order to describe the observed reality that interested his younger colleague than to achieve a certain precision of form and imagery in the magical world that he wanted to inhabit. So (in 1867) he writes about a "Sleeping Princess" ("Spyashchaya knyazhna") whose Prince Charming never comes, and a dark forest that sings of ancient battles between freedom and force. Then, the following summer, there is a "Sea Princess" ("Morskaya tsarevna") who, Tamara-like, lures young travellers into deep waters; a setting of a poem that could almost be by Heine ("The False Note," "Fal'shivaya nota") about a false assurance of love; and finally one about a poisoned love ("My Songs Are Full of Poison"—"Otravoy polnï moi pesni") that actually is by Heine. The settings perhaps lack the freshness and vividness of Musorgsky, but they never lapse into the merely conventional. Dianin links the 1868 songs to Borodin's feelings for Lodïzhensky's unhappily married sister, Anna Kalinina, who had fallen in love with him during the summer and with whom, in the autumn, he had an intense relationship, described in agonized detail in long letters to his wife in Moscow.[9] But there is little in either the words or the music to support Dianin's claim that they "reflect what he was going through and reveal the slight element of tension in his relations with his wife."[10]

For some reason both princesses—the one who sleeps and the one who entices—prompted the same musical image: ostinato chords based on unresolved major seconds, a quietly disturbed sonority that might suggest the mystery of sleep or the magic of seduction, but was probably a straightforward musical obsession of Borodin's for which he simply wanted a pretext. "The Sleeping Princess" also makes much use of the whole-tone scale, but not, as one might expect, to portray the dissolution of unbroken sleep, but on the contrary to depict the activity around the sleeper that fails to wake her: the witches and goblins, the (false) rumor of an approaching hero. The one element of tension in "The Sea Princess," on the other hand, is the chord of the flattened sixth (D-flat in the key of F major), which alternates with the tonic chord, a reminder of Glinka's fondness for this harmony as an exotic device. But exactly the same chord (C-flat in the key of E-flat) opens the Heine song, where it presumably stands for the lover's bitter if unexplained resentment ("I bear many snakes in my heart, and have to bear you there as well")—a favorite Heine motif. Borodin's own poem for "The False Note" is itself a fairly obvious imitation of Heine: "She assured me of her love, I didn't believe her"—and here the harmonic tension is momentarily greater, though one might feel that the song reflects Yekaterina Borodina's (likely) feelings at least as much as her husband's.

The most unusual thing about these songs is their structure. Both "The Sea Princess" and "The False Note" seem incomplete, the one apparently for lack of a concluding verse to accommodate the music's return to the home key, the other as a Schumannesque rejection of the beloved's falsehoods; here, as so often in Schumann, the piano concludes the song on its own. "My Songs Are Full of Poison" is based on a three-bar phrase pattern, likewise rounded off each time by an extra piano bar. These rhythmic effects must have been a deliberate experiment, since Borodin wrote two of the poems himself, while the Heine—so brief and dismissive—has what one might regard as a built in ellipsis, the poet's characteristic refusal to inform us what exactly it is that he so bitterly resents in the woman he loves.

The most interesting of these songs, however, is the simplest. The "Song of the Dark Forest" ("Pesnya tyomnogo lesa") is an imitation folk poem of a somewhat bardic character, and Borodin sets it entirely in heterophony—the kind of unison in which the parts stray from one another but never quite lose touch. The divergence becomes greater, as one might expect, as the poem becomes more dramatic and the force overwhelms the freedom. The other striking feature of this song is the largely unvaried five-four meter, which, however, Borodin disguises by redistributing each set of three fives as 5 + 3 + 7. Later there are 5 + 6's that recall Musorgsky's "Little Feast," composed at roughly the same time (September 1867). But whereas Musorgsky is merely responding to the poetic meter, Borodin creates his irregularities by adding rests or by arbitrary barrings. This is essentially the difference between the realist and the idealist, or, if you like, the pragmatist and the theorist—though the latter term suits Borodin rather poorly. The point seems to be that Borodin has an idea of what might constitute bardic practice, and re-creates it; Musorgsky simply treats his material as he finds it.

Back in St. Petersburg in early August 1868, Rimsky-Korsakov at last put the finishing touches to *Antar.* The third movement, "Power," still remained to be finalized, and he was also planning a slow introduction to the fourth movement, modulating from the D-major ending of "Power" to the D-flat major of the finale. He described his work on the third movement in a letter to Musorgsky, still far away in Shilovo. "I am drawing the situation of an Oriental potentate rather than an abstract feeling," he explained. "The beginning which you know is played only by woodwind and brass with cymbals. The second theme in A major (the harem), with a quite original accompaniment on tamborines and cymbals, has a certain oriental *chic* of its own, after which Power (Antar's theme in F major with fanfares)."[11]

He must have played at least parts of the third movement at Borodin's before they had all gone off for the summer, and in true *kuchka* fashion there had been a good deal of discussion, and some disagreement, about the course the work was taking. Rimsky-Korsakov had told them he was writing a symphony, but Balakirev had evidently complained that it was not symphonic enough, and wanted him to compose "Power" "as a big *allegro* with a broad symphonic development of the themes."[12] Musorgsky, on the other hand, bridled at any such suggestion. Symphonic development, he said, was like German *Milch-suppe* or *Kirchensuppe,* "a calamity for us, but Germans love it. In short, *symphonic development, technically understood,* is manufactured by a German, like his philosophy, which has now been done away with by English psychologists and our own Troitsky. A German, when he thinks, starts by *analyzing,* then *demonstrates,* while our [Russian] brother starts by demonstrating, and only then amuses himself by analyzing."[13] By the same token, Musorgsky opposed Rimsky-Korsakov's idea of a modulatory introduction to the finale. "What could be more poetic," he inquired, "after a *forte* D major, *pomposo,* . . . than a melancholy D-flat major, directly, without any preliminaries? . . . Why do you want to borrow Love from the Germans? . . . Oh preliminaries! How much good you have ruined!"[14]

Poor Rimsky-Korsakov! By nature a conventional thinker whose instinct was to develop colorful ideas by traditional methods, he tumbled straight into the intellectual gulf that was already opening up between the different members of the circle. Balakirev had already shown in his Russian and Czech overtures that it was to some extent conceivable to pursue Glinka's style of folk-song treatment along symphonic lines. In due course, *Tamara* would show that a "national" style had nothing to fear from good conservatory practice, even if it did not adhere to it literally, and whatever its composer might say about conservatories. This, however, was something Musorgsky could never swallow. His artistic xenophobia remained impenetrable; he longed for his friends to share it and refused to see why they could not. For him music had become an empirical activity, and received forms and procedures no longer held the slightest interest. Not that he was careless about artistic refinement or form in a more general, pragmatic sense. His work on *Marriage* had probably taught him that you could not rely solely on natural phenomena to make fine art; you could start with the intonations of the world around you, but in the end everything hung on what the artist did with those intonations, how he selected them, cut them, and framed them, how he related one element to another. But Rimsky-Korsakov's worries about whether you could follow D with D-flat without going through tortuous modulations were to him quite alien, if not actually ridiculous. "Creation itself," he argued, "contains its own laws of refinement. Verifying them is internal criticism; their application is a matter of the artist's instinct. Without either of these, there is no creative artist; if there is a creative artist, there must be both the one and the other and the artist be a law unto himself."[15]

These arguments may or may not have impressed Rimsky-Korsakov, but it's clear that he gave them some thought. Whatever his opinion of Musorgsky's technique at that time, he respected his artistic judgment, and after toying with a deft slow introduction to the finale pivoting on a sustained horn A (the dominant of D) sideslipping to A-flat (dominant of D-flat), he scrapped the whole idea and instead brought in the solo cor anglais directly on the D-flat of his beautiful finale theme, which incidentally had been given him, complete with harmony, by Dargomïzhsky, who in turn had found it in a published collection of Arab melodies.[16] But the problem continued to bother him, and when he revised *Antar* in 1897 (by which time he was a composition professor at the conservatory) he reinstated the modulatory introduction, albeit in a slightly different form. He also took to worrying once again about the work's status as a symphony, until in his last revision, of 1903, he decided to abandon the designation altogether and rename the work a "symphonic suite"—the label he had meanwhile also attached to his *Sheherazade* (1887).

In his autobiography, he tried to explain: "I was wrong to call *Antar* a symphony. My *Antar* was a poem, a suite, a fairy-tale, a story, or whatever you like, but not a symphony." And he proceeded to elaborate the point that while the first movement was "a free musical representation of one episode of the story after another, unified in the music by the constant occurrence of Antar's own theme," the second movement was more or less monothematic, while the third movement, for all its contrasted themes, remained essentially an episodic march, with "a sort of middle section and light development of the two main themes." The finale was "a kind of simple rondo with one theme and subsidiary phrases ... [and] a long coda on Antar's and Gul-Nazar's themes." Withal, he adds the claim that "this form came to me without outside influences or indications," since after all the task was a narrative and lyrical one, allowing "complete freedom of musical structure."[17] A symphony, by implication, entailed no such freedom. Perhaps Balakirev would have agreed. And yet one feels that these complicated, not to say self-exculpating, observations come somewhat strangely from the erstwhile junior member of the supposedly maverick *kuchka*.

Whatever Balakirev's initial opinion of *Antar*, he programmed it at once for the coming RMS season, and duly conducted the first performance in March 1869. According to Rimsky-Korsakov, it went down well enough (including with Balakirev himself),[18] though Cui, reviewing the second performance three years later, remembered its reception in 1869 as "cold," and congratulated the audience on their "developed musical understanding" in the intervening years.[19] The crucial point, in any case, was that—as before—Rimsky-Korsakov was writing music that was fit and ready for performance while his older colleagues were still mired in unfinished, inchoate, fragmentary masterpieces that might gratify their sense of pioneering heroism but stood little chance of ever reaching the stage or the concert platform. Cui, admittedly, had at last finished *William Ratcliff* after seven years of difficult time management, and it was staged at the Maryinsky in February, a month before the *Antar* premiere. Musorgsky, meanwhile, had abandoned *Marriage* and was embarking on a wholly new, far more ambitious operatic project. Rimsky-Korsakov himself had for some time been toying with a similar project of his own. Balakirev's *Firebird* was at least theoretically still a going concern. Then, in April 1869, the full house collected its last card with Stasov's suggestion that Borodin compose an opera on the twelfth-century Russian epic *The Lay of Igor's Campaign.*

Anyone familiar with the *kuchka*'s past record of work completion might well have viewed these activities with dismayed incredulity. It would have seemed a classic case of running before they could walk. But opera was a huge temptation to the *kuchka,* as to nationalists elsewhere. It passed so many of their tests for a music that would be specifically Russian; it suggested a broad narrative canvas that could accommodate the ebb and flow of historical conflict, the clash of the personal and the public, the vivid portrayal of the ethnic or the mythic or the exotic, the color, the fantasy—all those things that, by identifying time and place, prompted a music that would be theirs rather than anyone else's, that drew on their materials, their forms or lack of them, their typologies, their language. If instrumental music was German by tradition and international by its nature, opera was the particularist genre par excellence. It helped, no doubt, that the Germans had never truly made it their own, notwithstanding some goodish attempts. Mozart, it should be remembered, was not highly regarded by the *kuchka,* and in any case his best-known opera was Italian. Wagner most of them knew only by reputation and from a few bleeding chunks heard in concert. They could, they thought, safely ignore or abuse him.

This situation suddenly changed early in October 1868, when for the first time a Wagner opera was presented on the St. Petersburg stage. According to Rimsky-Korsakov, the Maryinsky production of *Lohengrin* under Konstantin Lyadov "was greeted by us with utter contempt and by Dargomïzhsky with an inexhaustible torrent of humor, ridicule, and venomous cavilling."[20] Balakirev, who missed the first night but attended a later performance, complained that it gave him a headache and he dreamed of geese all night.[21] Cui duly reviewed the production in the *Vedomosti* but made no bones about his disdain for the work ("a more colorless and boring opera" he never had heard) or the composer ("completely without talent, no creative ability").[22] In general, though, the opera was well received in the press, and Serov predictably greeted it with enthusiasm in an open letter to Wagner in the French-language *Journal de St. Pétersbourg,* followed by a more conventional review in *Novoye vremya,* in which he claimed that *Lohengrin* had "scored a complete victory and met no opposition at all," adding that "this is a remarkable event in the chronicles of Slavonic art and has great significance for the fate of musical drama in Russia."[23] All this was more than Vladimir Stasov could bear, and he quickly penned a lengthy reply to Serov, including an extended critique of the Russian translation of Wagner's libretto (by Konstantin Zvantsev), but culminating in a violent denunciation of Serov's Wagnerism and a contemptuous dismissal of the whole idea of Wagner's importance for Russian composers. "At first," he wrote,

the public went to *Lohengrin* because curious to see an opera by a new composer about whom there had long been so much talk, and who they were persuaded was an art-reformer of genius; but then, when the initial curiosity passed, they began to go to *Lohengrin* more lazily and reluctantly, because it didn't suit anyone's taste. Boring! boring! Unimaginably boring! some say. Absurd subject, talentless music! say others. Well it's nothing much, only so-so, say a third lot, precisely those who are afraid of somehow missing out in their estimation of the great genius and appearing insufficiently up-to-date. So this is the sum of Petersburg opinion, its entire verdict on Wagner's *Lohengrin.* Perhaps besides there are still people like Messrs. Serov and Zvantsev, to whom Wagner's music seems the summit of human genius, and his operas the final thrust of contemporary creativity, intelligence and poetry ... Almost with tears in his eyes, Mr. Serov grumbles to Wagner that the performance of his opera on our stage was a little too *realistic* and *prosaic.* Poor unhappy Mr. Serov! What a model for us all of how far artistic coat-tailing can go with "a celebrated friend" (as Mr. Serov calls Wagner in his letter), and of the wax-like capacity for taking on the imprint of any old stamp.

No, no. Let Mr. Serov not ruin our artists with his notions and instructions, let him not confuse them with opinions picked up from some dreadful Germans whose word for him is law, and let him not think, in fact, that Wagner's music is capable of taking root with us, or, even more of a joke, that "the success of Wagner in Russia (!) is an event of huge importance for the fate of our music drama and the musical education of our public," that this success is "an event that will play a huge role in the history of Slavonic art and civilization." No, we don't need these ideas and oracles of Mr. Serov . . . [24]

The curious aspect of the kuchka's rage against Lohengrin is that in many respects it adhered to their own ideas about the way forward for Russian composers and for opera in general. A historical drama with big choral scenes and an explicit nationalist background (in the very first scene Heinrich calls on the Brabantians to "defend the empire's honor . . . ; Let any land that calls itself German assemble its troops, so that none shall ever again insult the German empire"), it also evolves ways of writing that to some extent fit in with kuchka ideas about the relation between words and music. For instance, Wagner's having written his own libretto, and his obviously careful integration of the text and the music, ought to have pleased Cui, the supposed operatic expert in the Balakirev circle, who had criticized Serov's Rogneda for its alleged inadequacy in this department, and who had argued for precisely the kind of "melodic recitative" (as he called it) that Wagner had composed to such powerful effect in the dialogue between Ortrud and Telramund at the start of his second act, and for Lohengrin's narration in his third. Cui ought also to have approved of Wagner's rich involvement of the chorus in the dramatic action, including complex passages where the chorus splits into antiphonal groups and responds to the situations contrapuntally. "The chorus in our [Russian] operas," he had written in 1864, "plays a more important role than in all others. It's no longer a mindless crowd brought together purely to sing; it's a collection of people who act consciously and independently; from this, music acquires a new element of depth and breadth of scope."[25] It is no longer, in other words, singing, marching scenery.

Above all Cui might well have praised in Lohengrin the handling of "an intense personal drama unfolding against a rich historical or genre background."[26] Of course, there was nothing particularly new about this idea. It was fundamental to Meyerbeer, as well as various operas of the Italian school that Cui routinely despised for other reasons. The truth is that Wagner could have composed The Stone Guest and he would still have been reviled by the kuchka, because their loathing (fear) of him—like their loathing (fear) of Serov—was an article of faith unconnected with actual taste or disinterested critical values. Fortunately, this meant that they could quietly take what they needed from his work—as also from Serov's—without moderating their abuse in the very slightest.

Exactly when Musorgsky decided to compose an opera on Pushkin's Shakespearean drama *Boris Godunov* is uncertain, but there are good grounds for supposing that it was after seeing *Lohengrin* that October. The idea seems to have come from Nikolsky, no doubt as a response to Musorgsky's cri de coeur—"When will something finally be ready?"— in his August letter from Shilovo. Nikolsky was a regular at Lyudmila Shestakova's evenings, and Shestakova herself was evidently involved in the discussions about possible opera subjects, since it was she who supplied Musorgsky with a copy of Pushkin's *Boris* with blank pages tipped in to enable him to compile his libretto directly from the play. This was probably toward the end of October.[27] By 4 November he had completed the first scene (in the courtyard of the Novodevichy Monastery) and ten days later the coronation scene was also complete. "The power of necessity," which he had told Nikolsky would be the trigger for whatever he had been preparing with *Marriage* and the recent songs, was suddenly asserting itself with a vengeance.

CHAPTER 17

History for the Stage

One might think it had taken the *kuchka* a surprising length of time to get round to composing operas on historical subjects since Balakirev and Musorgsky had raved about old Moscow in 1859 and Stasov had talked endlessly in the early sixties about the histories of Solovyov and Kostomarov and "our beloved Novgorod which you [Balakirev] and I have loved instinctively for so long."[1] To some extent it was probably a question of readiness, as Musorgsky himself had put it. To us now it seems obvious what form a historical opera would take that met the requirements of Stasovian realism and that elevated the Russian people to the level of the ruling classes as subject matter. We know the eventual solutions. But in the 1850s and '60s historical drama still meant the romantic epics of the French and Italian stage: the plays of Victor Hugo, the spectacular grand operas of Meyerbeer, and the singer-based quasi-historical operas of Donizetti and Verdi. It was true that Glinka had provided what looked like a better precedent in *A Life for the Tsar.* But for Stasov this was by no means a suitable model. Its image of the Russian people was the image of a sycophantic crowd of happy peasants; and as for Susanin himself, far from being a hero, he was a mere "low serf, loyal as a dog, narrow as an owl or a capercaillie, sacrificing himself for some urchin he has no reason to love, whom there is no need to rescue, and on whom it seems he has never even set eyes."[2]

Stasov's historical ideal was the medieval *veche,* the popular assembly which had acted as a kind of ad hoc parliament in the administration of independent cities such as Novgorod, Pskov, and Kiev. "In both pagan and Christian times," he had assured Balakirev in the same letter, "the *essential* Russia was democratic in its heart and nature, constantly fragmenting into millions of bits, families and precincts." Russians, he maintained, were as hostile to the single monarchical principle as they were (he likewise maintained) to a centralized despotism in matters of religion. It was symbolic for him that the *veche* in Novgorod and Pskov had been stamped out by the Muscovite proto-tsars of the late fifteenth and early sixteenth century, the ancestors—in title at least—of the autocratic tsars of his own day, who were still throttling independent thought and expression, whatever their feeble efforts at liberalizing the Russian economy and rural life. But there was not much suggestion at this stage that such ideas might form the basis for operatic or even symphonic treatment. He might even have agreed with Serov that "music, by virtue of its open, candid nature, is but a poor elucidator of political and diplomatic intrigue."[3] As musical subject matter, he apparently saw more future in Russian folk tales, with their color and magic, their aura of mystery and romance.

Meanwhile, the straight theatre in St. Petersburg was suddenly flooded with plays on Russian historical subjects, inspired no doubt by the steady publication of the volumes of Solovyov's history. In February 1867 Alexey Tolstoy's *Death of Ivan the Terrible* was staged for the first time, almost simultaneously with Alexander Ostrovsky's *Dmitry the Pretender and Vasily Shuisky*. Tolstoy swiftly followed up his play with two sequels, *Tsar Fyodor Ioannovich* (1868) and *Tsar Boris* (1870), the first of which was immediately banned from performance and was in fact never staged at all in the nineteenth century, while the second was simply blocked by the Imperial Theatres' directorate. Lev Mey's *Maid of Pskov* (*Pskovityanka*), about Ivan the Terrible's menacing but ultimately benign entry into Pskov in 1570, had been published in 1859 but was still, in 1868, under a stage ban. Pushkin's *Boris Godunov,* though published in its final form in 1831, had been cleared for performance only in 1866, and eventually reached the stage, reportedly in an atrocious production and heavily cut, only in 1870. One of the striking things about the *kuchka*'s almost unanimous decision to start writing historical operas in the late sixties is that they began by basing themselves on plays that either were or had until very recently been banned by the censorship. Another, more explicable, is that—like all of the plays mentioned above—they dealt exclusively with the pre-Romanov tsars. So long as historical drama, like school history, meant "kings and queens," this was unavoidable, because it was strictly illegal to represent members of the Romanov dynasty (to which the nineteenth-century tsars also belonged) on the stage.[4]

As it happened, it was not Musorgsky but Rimsky-Korsakov who first took the plunge and embarked, in the summer of 1868, on an operatic version of Mey's *Maid of Pskov*. He probably already knew the play, as he had set a lullaby from its first act as a separate song (op. 2, no. 3) two years before. Oddly enough, he says in his autobiography that the operatic idea—like the idea for *Antar*—actually came from Musorgsky and Balakirev, which if true may be significant, since it suggests that as late as the spring of 1868, Musorgsky was not himself thinking of composing such a work. Naturally this did not prevent him and the rest of the circle from interfering in the process of composition. From the start the project was the subject of discussion at group meetings, apparently with Rimsky-Korsakov's approval, since he notes the fact without the irony that creeps into his reports of Balakirev's "sharp paternal despotism," which he admits was beginning to get on his nerves at this same time.[5] With the opera, the initial issue lay with the libretto. Presumably, with *The Stone Guest* constantly in their eyes and ears, there was talk of setting the play as it stood. But there also existed an independent libretto, originally written by a certain Vsevolod Krestovsky for Anton Rubinstein, and passed on to Rimsky-Korsakov by Tchaikovsky, perhaps as a result of their meeting or meetings at Balakirev's in the spring.[6] Whether or not Krestovsky's version was considered by the circle is unclear from Rimsky-Korsakov's account, which asserts, ambiguously, that "The idea was that I would write the libretto myself as need arose!"[7] The exclamation mark seems to express incredulity, but in the end this is more or less what he did, using Krestovsky as a starting point, but basing himself more generally on Mey, with the inevitable cuts and compressions, and in due course incorporating folk-song texts supplied by Musorgsky for some of the choruses.

Mey's drama is historical in its setting and in the crucial events that serve as frame for an invented human tragedy which might, nevertheless, serve to explain certain puzzling aspects of the known history. In 1570, having laid waste the city of Novgorod and massacred thousands of its inhabitants as punishment for supposed conspiracy with Poland-Lithuania, Tsar Ivan the Terrible marched on Pskov with, its inhabitants not unreasonably feared, similar intentions. In the event, Ivan stayed for only a short time and left without incident, even though Pskov was closer than Novgorod to the Lithuania he so much feared, and closer still to Izborsk, where there had been clear treachery (and consequent reprisals) the previous year. Mey imagines a romantic explanation for the sparing of Pskov. On a visit to the city some years ago, Ivan had an affair with a certain Vera Sheloga, the sister-in-law of the city's governor, Prince Yury Tokmakov. Unbeknown to Ivan, Vera gave birth to a little girl called Olga who—after Vera's death—was brought up by Tokmakov as his own daughter. At the time of this second visit, Tokmakov is planning to marry Olga off to an elderly boyar by the name of Nikita Matuta, but she is passionately in love with the son of the *posadnik* (mayor), Mikhail Tucha. Alas, on Ivan's approach, while Tokmakov and the people decide to welcome him "with bread and salt," Tucha and a few young men opt for guerrilla tactics and make off into the surrounding forest. In Pskov, Ivan meets Olga and realizes, from Tokmakov's explanations, that she is his daughter. He at once declares, "Pskov khranit Gospod'!"—"Let God preserve Pskov!" But Tucha, unaware of the altered situation, attacks Ivan's camp outside the city, and in the ensuing gunfight is shot dead. Olga, in despair, commits suicide.

One can well imagine that the circle discussed the operatic possibilities of all this with a certain excitement. As a subject it was conventional enough for them to be able to relate it to existing Western operas that set powerful human dramas against a backcloth of historical events, while at the same time it had the added appeal of being purely Russian. Unlike the obvious precedent, *A Life for the Tsar,* it sets the people against the autocrat, showing them cowed and acquiescent, but only out of fear for their lives; and Tsar Ivan is made to pay the price of his habitual cruelty, since the daughter he is just beginning to love dies because of the actions of those who take it for granted that he will continue to behave in character. Perhaps it was the circle, in conclave, who decided that Olga should not commit suicide in the opera, but should be caught in the crossfire and accidentally shot. They certainly were responsible, as a group, for the decision to cut out Mey's first act, which dealt with Vera Sheloga at the time of Olga's birth (Krestovsky had also excluded this act).[8] Since the rest of the action takes place in Pskov at the time of Ivan's second visit, the effect was to impose a certain pseudo-Aristotelian unity of time and place on the drama, which at least suited its tragic outcome.

One remaining aspect of the play must have excited Stasov, and through him all the other members of the circle: the *veche* scene in the second act, in which the citizens meet to discuss how to respond to the tsar's impending arrival. Stasov knew perfectly well that the Pskov *veche* had been abolished by Ivan the Terrible's father, Vasily III, sixty years before (along with the rank of *posadnik,* supposedly held by Tucha's father). But just as Mey had evidently thought the idea far too good as theatre to be rejected on tedious historical grounds, so its musical potential will have been an irresistible attraction for the opera composer. Whether Rimsky-Korsakov, in his sublime inexperience of writing for the theatre, had any clear image at this stage of how he would handle such a scene might be doubted. It hardly mattered, in any case, since *Antar* still lay on his desk demanding completion; and meanwhile the fair maid of Pskov would have to wait her turn.

It came gradually and in typical kuchkist bits and pieces. He had just finished the new second movement of *Antar,* in the middle of June 1868, when Nikolay Lodïzhensky sent him a note inviting him to their Tver estate, and suddenly there welled up in his mind what he later called "a rush of indefinable love for Russian folk-life, for her history in general and for *The Maid of Pskov* in particular." He sat down at the piano and promptly improvised the main theme of the chorus of welcome in act 3 of the original version of the opera[9]—presumably just the theme, not the whole fairly elaborate movement. Serious composition only began after the completion of *Antar* in August. For some reason he started with the long duet for Olga and Tucha toward the end of the first act, then turned back to the earlier part of the act, the curious tale of Tsarevna Lada told by Olga's nurse, Vlas'evna (or rather, not told, as she is interrupted by the arrival of Tucha), and the preceding genre scenes, the game of *gorelki* (catch) and the conversation between the nurses about events in Novgorod, punctuated by verses of the chorus of girls picking raspberries and currants. He was able to play some or all of this music at Cui's one evening in late September, amid gasps of delight, no doubt, from his fellow kuchkists. "Well," Borodin reported to his wife, "I can tell you that this is something of such fragrance, such youthfulness, freshness, beauty—I was simply weak with pleasure. What a heap of talent this man has! And how easily he creates!"[10]

It was the same evening that Musorgsky played them *Marriage* and Cui the latest parts of *William Ratcliff.* But this was something quite different—neither an experiment, like the Musorgsky, nor a thumping piece of old-fashioned melodrama, like the Cui. Rimsky-Korsakov had obviously taken *A Life for the Tsar,* with its folk tunes and dance episodes, as his character model; and he had learned lessons about the setting of Russian in arioso style from Dargomïzhsky. Yet as a whole the flavor and dramaturgy of these *Maid of Pskov* fragments was new. No Russian composer, perhaps even no non-Russian, had ever integrated conversation, storytelling, and genre with quite such fluency and naturalness: the girls playing catch, the nurses discussing Olga's paternity and the horrors in Novgorod, while the girls accompany their fruit picking with a delicious setting of an actual folk tune, "Po malinu, po smorodinu," about the perils of tangling your long hair in the wild fruit bushes. When it came to the duet, Rimsky-Korsakov showed that he could effortlessly raise the temperature without essentially changing idiom. Tucha announces himself somewhat imperiously from offstage with a song about the cuckoo in the dark forest; and when Olga runs out to him they sing a duet that achieves what Dargomïzhsky neither managed nor seems to have wanted, a smooth progression from arioso (accompanied recitative) to lyrical song, so that from the start of the act to (nearly) its finish the focus sharpens from the proto-cinematic montage of the genre scenes to the intense, concentrated feeling of the distressed lovers on the edge of the forest, still expressed, though, in musical terms recognizably derived from the earlier folk elements, and incorporating as its main theme an actual folk song, "Uzh tï, pole moyo," no. 25 in the Balakirev collection.[11]

By January, Rimsky-Korsakov had completed the first act, with a final scene in which Olga's supposed father, Prince Tokmakov, confesses to her unwanted fiancé, the boyar Matuta, that she is not his daughter but his niece—at the same time revealing this fact to Olga herself, who is eavesdropping in the bushes. Who her father is, Tokmakov has no idea. At the end of the act the bells ring out, announcing the *veche* meeting, which in this original version will form the entire second act. (When he revised the work, Rimsky-Korsakov took the—one would think fairly obvious—step of running the two scenes together.) "They ring no good," Olga sings. "They are burying my happiness."

Unfortunately, they were also for the time being burying Rimsky-Korsakov's work on *The Maid of Pskov*. Early on 5 January 1869, Dargomïzhsky had at last died after a long struggle with heart disease, leaving his magnum opus, *The Stone Guest*, unorchestrated and even with some musical threads untied. The previous evening, Balakirev had conducted the first proper performance of Borodin's First Symphony (as well as the *Maid of Pskov* chorus of welcome, now fully composed and orchestrated), and Dargomïzhsky had "waited impatiently for news of how the concert had gone, but unfortunately none of us called on him after the concert for fear of disturbing a sick man so late at night ... By the following morning Dargomïzhsky was no more ... "[12] He had always said, "If I die, Cui will complete *The Stone Guest* and Rimsky-Korsakov will orchestrate it."[13] Such decrees from beyond the grave cannot be refused, however regrettable they may seem; so, for the first but by no means the last time, poor Rimsky-Korsakov had to down tools on his own work and muddy his hands with somebody else's. True, there had been minor precedents, including the Schubert arrangement of the previous May, and the orchestration of a wedding chorus from *William Ratcliff* for a summer concert at the Maryinsky, which Cui claimed he had no time to do. Both had given him trouble and the results, in his opinion, had been unsatisfactory. He now had to score, from scratch, an hour and a half of another man's masterpiece. It would be good practice—better, perhaps, than he knew. But it slowed his own work down, as he put it, to the pace of a snail.

By the time Musorgsky put pen to paper on his own new opera, late in October 1868, he had both *Lohengrin* and parts of the first act of *The Maid of Pskov* in his mind's ear. Wagner was perhaps a negative influence, a trigger rather than a model, but Rimsky-Korsakov's work must have set him thinking along musical lines, and may even have been a factor in his decision to compose *Boris Godunov*. The similarities were obvious enough. Here in Pushkin was a monarch obsessed with power, fearful and paranoid, with blood on his hands, a deep love of family in his heart. As in Mey, the personal factor played against a broad historical canvas, including a handful of crowd scenes, slender in content but suggestive for a composer prepared to take the hint and expand. This would mean, of course, departing from Pushkin's text, whereas it was a mere three months since Musorgsky had been explaining to Shestakova how, by setting *Marriage* as it stood, he would "fix Gogol in his place and the actor in his place, that is . . . say it musically such that you couldn't say it in any other way and say it as Gogol's characters wish to speak."[14] But then *Marriage* had, by his own admission, been an experiment, and one which—already in August—he had confessed to Rimsky-Korsakov ran the risk of "a monotony of intonation." The same day he had described it to Nikolsky as a "preparation."[15] One might see it as a necessary discipline, like life classes as a way of learning to draw; the student won't always be drawing human bodies, but the technical study is at once purifying and enriching, in due course enabling work not envisaged by the discipline.

In 1868 Pushkin's *Boris Godunov* had never been staged, and there were some who regarded it as unstageable. Though clearly modelled in some respects on Shakespeare's history plays, and poetically and linguistically rich in the same kind of way, it seems studiously to avoid crucial aspects of Shakespearean drama. For one thing, the title character appears in only six of the twenty-three scenes in the play as published, and in two of these his appearance is fleeting. Moreover, the dramatic texture is loose, not unlike a comic strip, in which the narrative is laid out in a series of discrete images, and the sequence of events can be hard to discern, unless, like Pushkin's presumably intended audience, you already know (from Karamzin's history) the salient details.[16]

You would know, for instance, that Boris Godunov was the brother-in-law of Ivan the Terrible's feeble-minded son, Tsarevich Fyodor, for whom he had acted as regent after Ivan's death; that Fyodor's half-brother, the nine-year-old Dmitry, had been found one day in 1591 with his throat cut, and that Boris was widely suspected of having ordered his murder.[17] At the start of the play (the year 1598), Fyodor himself has died and Boris is being urged to accept the crown, against his own presumably tactical show of reluctance. The monk Pimen has almost finished chronicling the history of Orthodox Russia, and describes to the young novice Grigory how he was himself present at Uglich, saw the corpse, and heard the murderers incriminate Boris. Grigory, travelling with the vagrant monks Varlaam and Misail, flees to Poland, intending to return as Tsarevich Dmitry back from the dead. At an inn on the border he narrowly escapes capture. In Krakow he secures Polish support and the hand of the ambitious Princess Marina (who is well aware of his imposture), on condition that he become tsar. Boris, meanwhile, though relaxed and authoritative in his family circle, is increasingly terrorized by accounts of miracles at Dmitry's grave and reports of his supposed return. Suddenly, inexplicably, he dies, passing the succession to his own son, Fyodor. But in the final scene Fyodor is murdered by boyars loyal to the Pretender.

Possibly with *kuchka* assistance, possibly without, Musorgsky compiled seven scenes from this complicated sequence, in some cases eliding elements from more than one, and drawing in all on ten of the scenes in the play. Most strikingly, he left out altogether Pushkin's four Polish scenes, and all the later scenes in which the Pretender appears, so that Grigory vanishes from the drama—except as an unseen threat—after jumping out of the pub window on the Lithuanian border in Musorgsky's scene 4. On the other hand, he retained the essential elements of all the play's scenes in which Boris himself figures, and by ending with the tsar's death (which Pushkin does not), he ensured a much sharper focus on the title role. He also engineered a crucial change in Boris's personality. Pushkin makes it obliquely clear that his Boris is guilty of the murder of Tsarevich Dmitry, but though shaken to the core by Shuisky's description of the child's undecayed corpse and by the patriarch's account of the miracle at the graveside, the tsar retains his composure, and his death is not directly linked to these revelations. For Musorgsky, by contrast, Boris is a character unhinged by guilt, who has hallucinations of the murdered child (not just Pushkin's metaphorical "bloody boys in the eyes"), appears deranged at the boyars' council, and collapses and dies on hearing about the miracle. In fact his treatment of Boris in this first version of the opera is the climax of his *opéra dialogué* experiment, transferred from Gogol's trivial comedy of manners to the epic ravings of a tragic ruler.

In general, Pushkin is as cool in his portraiture as he is easygoing in his dramaturgy; he treats his characters like pawns and pieces in a chess game. Now and then a deeper psychology emerges, in Boris's scene with his children or the scene of his death, or the scenes for the Pretender, or Shuisky, or the boyar Pushkin. But the psychological development is inhibited by a certain disjointedness in the action, whereby the different "regions" of the plot seem to exist independently of one another, and might even be interleaved in different sequences.

For Musorgsky this neutrality, so to speak, may well have been a particular attraction of the play as an opera subject. It meant that he could impose his own musical needs on the template supplied by Pushkin. This was certainly a change from his attitude toward Gogol in *Marriage*. There he had allowed himself to be limited by the text of the play, composing nothing but monologue and dialogue, and studiously avoiding the specific things that normally give music its point: song, aria, ensemble, chorus, movement, orchestral color. By contrast, his handling of *Boris Godunov* at once restores the primacy of music. The very first scene he composed—the people outside the Novodevichy Monastery being goaded by the police to implore Boris to accept the crown—is an amalgamation of two short scenes in the play, in the first of which three individuals refer briefly to Boris's refusal, while in the second the same individuals (presumably) describe the people (the *narod*) "howling, sinking down in waves, row on row, more and more," while the "people" themselves have only two lines of "weeping and wailing." For a composer it was too good an opportunity to miss, and Musorgsky duly turned it into a tremendous choral tableau. He invented byplay between individuals, and he introduced the figure of the brutal, whip-cracking *pristav,* the police officer, with whom the people seem to enjoy a curiously ambivalent, almost affectionate relationship. What in the play had been little more than spoken stage directions was converted at a stroke into a musical equivalent of a broad popular canvas, like the ones that would soon be painted by the nascent Wanderers (*Peredvizhniki*) group of realist painters.

Altogether, Musorgsky constructed three substantial scenes out of Pushkin's relatively casual images of the *narod*. In fact his coronation scene (scene 2), with its massive choral setting of the well-known "Slava" folk song, is based on a brief scene in the play in which Boris accepts the crown in the presence of the patriarch and the boyars, and the people do not figure at all. The third choral scene in the opera's first version, the so-called St. Basil's scene, is textually fairly close to Pushkin's scene 19, but again with the role of the chorus, and the individual characters who step out of it, considerably expanded. Musorgsky seems not to have contemplated any equivalent to Pushkin's final two scenes, where the author's namesake addresses the people in the name of the "lawful" tsar, Dmitry, and the death of Tsarevich Fyodor and his mother is proclaimed to the crowd in the Kremlin Square. Perhaps the composer was impressed by the final stage direction in the published version of the play, in response to the boyar Mosalsky's command that they shout for Dmitry: "The people are silent." Whether he would have accepted this neat balance to his opening scene if he had known that the play originally ended with the people shouting as instructed, we shall probably never know. More likely, given his general approach to Pushkin's work, he would have avoided tying threads in any such tidy fashion.

What clearly did interest him was how to translate his Gogol method of word setting into writing for chorus. Pushkin, as we saw, had used the device of individual voices on the fringes of the crowd describing its behavior. But for Musorgsky it was important to get inside the crowd and capture its vital flesh-and-blood energy: to represent its behavior, not merely describe it. And the way he managed this was a stroke of genius, one that stamped *Boris Godunov* from curtain-up as something entirely new and fresh and virtually without precedent in opera as it was known. At first the people, goaded by the *pristav*, fall dutifully on their knees and implore Boris to accept the crown, much as they might pray to God to save their souls. The style is essentially that of folk song, *protyazhnaya*, complete with irregular barrings shaped by the verbal accents, and simple block harmonies in root position (tonic in the bass). Soon the crowd fragments, and badinage replaces pious hymn singing. Now, however, the orchestra regulates the meter, and the voices fit into it, in groups of two, four, six (Musorgsky indicates the numbers), singing most of the time in even quavers, but erratically placed within each bar, so that a feeling of spontaneous conversation is achieved within a tautly structured frame.

But the most powerful discovery in this first *Boris Godunov* is in the writing for solo voice, where Musorgsky devised a procedure that retreated quite sharply from the verbal dialoguing of *Marriage.* The reason for this is obvious once one hears the result. In the Gogol opera the characters are drawn satirically; their essential existence is one-dimensional. They represent sloth, or venality, or officiousness, and they are funny because so absolute. They are like Parolles in *All's Well That Ends Well:* simply the thing they are makes them live. Music can give them very little more, beyond making fun of them, which is what a Rossini might have done brilliantly, or casting them in vignettes, like the simpleton in "Darling Savishna" or the distracted novice in "The Seminarian." Pushkin's characters invite a very different kind of musical treatment. Even when not fully developed, they are drawn psychologically; they are driven by confused motives and passions, their sins and terrors are grand, their ambitions outrageous. Their spiritual existence is intense. Here music is in its element, but it has to act as music; it can't just sit back and let the words tell it what to do. It has to peer into the characters and situations, and light up hidden areas of feeling where words, with all their power, fall short.

The first hint of this in *Boris* comes in the just-crowned tsar's brief monologue, aside, amid the celebrations in scene 2 of the opera. But as a technique, it comes fully into its own in the third scene, in the Chudov Monastery, which in the original version was composed exclusively for the solo voices of the monk Pimen and his acolyte, Grigory.[18] From the start of the scene, structural control is exercised by the orchestra, which sets and maintains the pace throughout, like a steady-flowing river on which the voices float like driftwood, sometimes catching the stream, sometimes bumping over rocks or shallows. Vocally, the writing is what is technically known as *recitativo stromentato:* "instrumented" or, better, accompanied recitative. The voice has to fit into the tempo and rhythm of the accompaniment, but can distribute its own phrases freely within that scheme. This might sound like a description of Wagner's technique as described in *Opera and Drama* or as implemented in *The Ring.* But Musorgsky's orchestral writing is not symphonic in the Wagnerian sense. There are themes and motives (recurrent themes), some of which act as leitmotifs representing characters or even concepts; but they are rarely treated discursively or developmentally. To abandon the image of the river, one might hear this accompaniment as a kind of rolling backcloth, as scenery which, miraculously, changes to reflect the mood and imagery of the libretto.

Section by section, then, it is the text that dictates the musical discourse, while the voice reacts phrase by phrase, word by word. In the case of the old monk, Pimen, this is a calm, reflective process. Only when recalling the terrible events at Uglich does he become agitated, reliving the horror of that night. The young monk, Grigory, is from the outset more excitable, his latent instability revealed in quick, snapped phrases as he suddenly wakes from his recurrent dream about surveying Moscow from a high tower. Then, as he observes Pimen still writing, he becomes calmer, more monkish, until he remembers hearing about Pimen's earlier career as a soldier in Lithuania and at the siege of Kazan, at which point a distinctly uncloistral note of exaltation invades his music. Such contrasts are the lifeblood of Musorgsky's method throughout this first version of *Boris*. They of course reflect his painstaking word settings in *Marriage*, but without the remorselessly verbal speech rhythms and melodic contours of that work. In fact the text in this scene, as well as in the following scene in the inn, is as close to Pushkin as *Marriage* was to Gogol. The enrichment is in the music.

One can trace the entire technique through the part of Boris himself in the brilliant Kremlin scene, which Musorgsky completely rewrote (including the libretto) when he revised the opera, but which in its original version remains a model of how *opéra dialogué* can be transformed into music that speaks both as music and as theatre. Here Pushkin's text is treated more freely, with various additions and compressions; for instance, Boris's "Dostig ya vïsshey vlasti" ("I have attained the highest power") has no equivalent in the play, which tends to avoid reflective soliloquies. Nevertheless, the setting is still essentially measured recitative. The vocal part is strictly mapped on to a metrically regular accompaniment, but with its own idiosyncratic internal rhythms which reflect the extreme strong-weak accentuation of the Russian language. In general, as before, the flow of musical ideas is governed by the orchestra; sometimes the voice leads, sometimes it travels the same road, often it takes a slightly different route, like one of those hill paths that, inexplicably, divide and rejoin, or even like the *podgoloski* type of folk polyphony.[19] This turns out to be an extraordinarily flexible form of *dramma per musica*. It can change character with mercurial speed: from the gentle, affectionate simplicity of Boris's words of comfort to his widowed daughter Xenia (mainly regular quavers), to the greater range and intensity of his monologue, and the near-hysteria of his interview with the wily Shuisky. These contrasts are achieved largely within a single tempo and meter through variations in the note values: the greater the stress, the greater the variation—*opéra dialogué*, but with strict musical controls.

Some of these controls are lyrical in character. The choral dialogue, as we saw, is interspersed with set pieces of a broadly expressive or ceremonious type, hinting at folk song or even liturgical chant, as in the beautiful entreaty of the crowd outside St. Basil's imploring Boris for bread ("Kormilets batyushka"—"Father benefactor")—needless to say the same crowd, the men at least, who five minutes before were muttering excitedly about the Pretender and baying for Boris's blood. This scene also contains the greatest lyrical moment in the entire opera, the wonderful lament of the Simpleton, set first to Pushkin's nonsense verse about the moon and the kitten (slightly extended), then to lines about the sorrows of Russia and her people—lines not in Pushkin. But the original *Boris* is not predominantly a lyrical work. The recitative settles often into brief songlike episodes, in and out of focus, so to speak. But solo song, as such, is largely absent. The one clear exception, the monk Varlaam's bibulous song about the attack on Kazan (at which he, unlike Pimen, was obviously not present), is a drunken outburst that opens a window on his character, but is quite devoid of lyricism; rather, it explodes out of a context almost entirely dominated by unadulterated musical dialogue: a real-life pub song in a real-life pub. In Pushkin, Varlaam breaks into song a number of times, and Musorgsky, too, gives him a second song ("Kak yedet yon"—"How he goes on"), tipsier and more nonsensical than the first, which serves, however, the dramatic purpose of covering Grigory's discreet inquiry of the landlady about the way to Lithuania.[20] This is one of only two actual folk tunes in the first version of the opera (the other is the "Slava" melody in the coronation scene). But of song as a decorative or genre element, without specific dramatic function, the first version is more or less innocent.

It took Musorgsky just over a year to compose and orchestrate the two and a half hours of the first version of *Boris Godunov*, which for a composer who had never previously managed to complete anything longer than the twelve-minute *Night on Bald Mountain* was a remarkable feat of concentrated effort. More significantly, in composing it he effectively discovered himself as a creative artist. Nearly everything he had written before had been either small-scale, or in some sense experimental, or theoretical, or else simply stylistically unformed, like the "Intermezzo in modo classico," or *Salammbô* (some of which he was able to incorporate in the final, death scene of *Boris*). His best songs, of course, were brilliant; but they were all to some extent style sketches, explorations of single images, rather in the manner of instrumental studies. *Night on Bald Mountain* had been an isolated exception, an indication rather than a fulfilment of a more extended and wider-ranging conception. On the other hand, *Marriage* was an essentially theoretical undertaking—music, that is, based on an idea of what music ought to be rather than a musical impulse as such: music, for instance, as a reflection of social reality, music as "a reproduction, in an artistic medium, of human *speech* with all its most refined and capricious nuances, a natural reproduction, as the life and mind of man demands."[21]

It is perhaps significant that Musorgsky did not regale his friends about *Boris Godunov* while and after writing it, as he had done about *Marriage.* He simply composed, and more than usual he kept himself to himself. "Musoryanin," Stasov wrote to Rimsky-Korsakov at one point, "obviously cannot be enticed from his lair with any kind of gingerbreads" (such as might be served by the Purgolds).[22] No letters of Musorgsky's survive from the period of composition, up to July 1869, and only one from the subsequent months when he was orchestrating the opera, and that letter (to Balakirev) is unconnected with the opera and doesn't even mention it.[23] Nevertheless, he sometimes appeared at circle evenings. He was at Dargomïzhsky's on 15 November for what its composer called the first complete run-through of *The Stone Guest* (though it was still not in fact quite finished), and sang the parts of Leporello and Don Carlos. He went to concerts, including one probably at the end of November, at which Stasov recalled giving him the text of Varlaam's Kazan song and remarked "with what avidity he began to skim through it then and there in the hall, during the music."[24] And he brought work in progress to the evenings, singing all the male parts himself while Sasha Purgold somehow deciphered the female roles. They were all, of course, in raptures over it. At the finish Stasov told his brother Dmitry that "Pimen's story [in the death scene] is so magnificent that it equals Finn's ballad [in *Ruslan and Lyudmila*], and the best places in the first and second acts of *Boris,* i.e. the popular scene with the weeping and wailing of the women under the knout, and the scene at the inn with the police officers."[25]

A good deal has been said and written about the supposed political tendencies of *Boris Godunov.* It is easy enough to interpret Musorgsky's sudden interest in popular speech and individualized crowds as motivated by a love of liberty, fraternity, and equality. The most comprehensive study of Musorgsky's aesthetics is tainted by the assumption (characteristic, of course, of Soviet musicology) that they were "exclusively conditioned by his socio-ethical views on social goals and musical problems."[26] But the evidence of the composer's own remarks on the subject, and of the music itself, is that his interest in people was more anthropological than ideological or sociological. He was inspired by types rather than theories. There is plenty in *Boris* to indicate a fascination with poor, ragged individuals as such, little or nothing to suggest a political program for feeding or clothing them. By and large his people are cowed and brutish, and they sometimes behave badly. They are ignorant, pious and superstitious. There are no noble peasants like Tolstoy's Platon Karatayev, and no saints like Dostoyevsky's Sonya Marmeladova. Even the *yurodívy* (holy fool), though pure in spirit, is harsh in manner, and he speaks, not for the people, but for God; he is an advocate of poverty, not its enemy. And if he laments over Russia, it is its spiritual desolation, not its political injustice, that grieves him.

What the first *Boris* shows clearly is Musorgsky's vision of art as the representation of human reality in all its varied colorings (the natural world interested him less: he was a portraitist, not a landscape painter). Above all, he had no time for received forms and procedures; *Boris* is almost wholly devoid of such things. But he had evidently realized, through *Marriage,* that reality, too, had its artistic forms, that it was not enough simply to reproduce what one heard and saw, it was necessary to distill it in ways that had their own kind of artifice. The image of Musorgsky as some kind of rustic amateur, struggling ineptly but with flashes of genius in a medium that he only half-understood—the image perpetuated after his death notably by Rimsky-Korsakov, from his professorial chair at the St. Petersburg Conservatory—will not survive a sympathetic and open-minded examination of his work on its own terms. On the contrary, he was astonishingly successful at perfecting what is arguably one of the most difficult kinds of art: art that is sui generis, that creates its own forms and procedures out of its subject matter. He quotes the Russian philosopher Matvey Troitsky on the virtues of observation as against the supposed Germanic love of abstract theorizing.[27] The extraordinary achievement of *Boris Godunov* was that it not only put these ideas into practice—something, after all, that Musorgsky had been doing successfully for some time in individual songs and choruses—but did so on the grandest possible scale, and with apparently unwavering confidence. The fact that the opera's completion, in December 1869, was by no means the end of its creative life is not necessarily a criticism of it as a work of art. Circumstances would force the composer's hand, and drive him to transform it into something in many ways different, whether or not superior.

CHAPTER 18

An Opera Performed, an Opera Abandoned

The first performance of Cui's *William Ratcliff* at the Maryinsky on 14 February 1869 shed a curiously oblique light on all this operatic activity. While Musorgsky was chiselling away at a purely Russian subject treated in a specifically Russian manner, and Rimsky-Korsakov had temporarily shelved his own Russian historical opera in order to orchestrate *The Stone Guest,* with its studiously idiomatic setting of Pushkin, the *kuchka* were represented on the stage for the very first time by a blood-and-guts romantic melodrama based on a German play set in Scotland. It was, of course, a relatively old project. But there was no sign of the *kuchka* themselves disowning it or in any way seeking to excuse it on these or any other grounds. On the contrary, they rallied behind it as if it were not only the very embodiment of their own thinking and aspirations, but on all counts a major contribution to world opera.

Rimsky-Korsakov reviewed the work in Cui's place in the *Vedomosti* and, perhaps inevitably, praised it to the skies with only a few minor qualifications, no doubt put in, as Taruskin suggests, for the sake of credibility.[1] The overture, he claimed, broke new ground by setting the dramatic scene rather than merely introducing the best tunes—as if the operas of Meyerbeer and Verdi (to say nothing of Serov) were completely unknown in St. Petersburg. The final love duet was without equal in any other opera, an opinion that Rimsky-Korsakov later tried to justify by moderating it to any "contemporary musical literature," which still looks a pretty tall claim in the shadow of Wagner's *Tristan,* a work not yet known in St. Petersburg in 1869, but perfectly familiar there by 1905, when Rimsky-Korsakov wrote the relevant chapter of his memoirs.[2] A few weeks later, Vladimir Stasov weighed in with an enormous article in the same newspaper, in which, after an extended and characteristically polemical survey of the press reaction to Cui's opera, he predicted that it would soon come to be recognized as one of the most brilliant products of the Russian school.

> True, not everything in this opera is yet valued at its real worth, and its profoundest, most precious details are still not fully recognized. Thus, for example, even the best section of the public have still not quite accepted that the scene at the Black Stone (Act 2 of the opera) is among the highest things in music; that in general there has never yet been in any opera an expression of the most mysterious, deep-lying heartstrings conveyed with more staggering force, passion, and fascinating beauty; that Douglas's narration is a wondrous specimen of pictorial description; that the roles of Mary and Margaret contain inexhaustible treasures of beauty and dramatic effect; that the scene of Ratcliff and Mary is the first love duet in the world; finally, that *William Ratcliff* occupies in Russian music a place in direct succession to the great works of Glinka and Dargomïzhsky.[3]

Needless to say, this was not the general opinion of the fourth estate, nor perhaps of those other sections of the public that Stasov would not have included among the best. From the audience point of view, *William Ratcliff* was a failure; it ran for only seven performances, after which (taken off at the offended Cui's own request) it vanished from the stage for more than thirty years. The press reaction was for the most part hostile or worse. But this of course has to be seen in the context of Cui's own bloodstained career as a music critic, which had included some of his composer-critic colleagues among its victims. Most prominent among these was the critic of *Golos,* Alexander Serov, whose *Rogneda* Cui had dismissed barely three years before as "a sequence of scenes . . . without the slightest organic connection between them," and who, like Stasov, came on the scene with a late review after the opera had ended its short run. Serov would have had to be a much grander spirit than it was reasonable to expect to resist the temptation to get his own back on the composer of *William Ratcliff.* After somewhat dangerously ridiculing his fellow critic's efforts at passing himself off as a composer, he launched into the work itself. "The most significant 'bravura' aria by Donizetti or Verdi," he suggested, "is a veritable colossus of dramatic truth—in its own way—beside this absurd jumble of syncopations and disharmonies expressive of nothing because they strive to express too much." Soon he was more or less admitting his parti pris: "With such exponents as Messrs. Stasov and Balakirev our musical maturation cannot get very far; we can already admire one operatic product of their camp. From there one could have expected nothing for the theatre except monstrosities and lo!—the monster is before us! It is a totally failed attempt, exuding overwhelming ennui, and it is therefore no wonder that after its sixth [*sic*] performance came the final death-throes."[4]

In general the press, though largely negative, avoided Serov's vindictive tone and concentrated on the perceived weaknesses in the work itself: "perceived" because, with reviewers as conservative as most of these, it is sometimes hard to distinguish between thought-through judgments and gut reactions to what still seemed, in sixties Petersburg, a disconcertingly modern approach to operatic form and musical style. One reviewer compliments Cui on his harmony and orchestration, but complains of the "predominance of rhythmic effects." Another grumbles that the voices are entirely sacrificed to the orchestra. The critic of *Notes of the Fatherland*, Rostislav (pen name of F. M. Tolstoy), accuses Cui of "harmonicide" (*ubíytsey garmonii*), on the strength of a few idiosyncrasies such as the occasional use of the whole-tone scale and a general richness of harmonic texture that actually scarcely goes beyond the norms of Western composers such as Schumann or even late Beethoven, whose music was perfectly well known in Russia.[5] Yet it was quite reasonable to criticize *William Ratcliff* on dramaturgical grounds. It was erratically paced and dramatically implausible, poorly characterized on the whole, and with an inadequate grasp of orchestral writing. It was, after all, a first opera (at least, on the public stage): an *Oberto* (Verdi), a *Die Feen* (Wagner). Tchaikovsky's own first completed opera, *The Voyevoda*, had had its premiere in Moscow a fortnight earlier and had flopped completely, running for a mere five performances. Tchaikovsky soon withdrew the work and destroyed the score.

The premiere of *William Ratcliff* was by far the biggest public manifestation to date of the work of the Balakirev circle, but it gave a very imperfect idea of what the rest of them were up to by this time. Borodin, for instance, had been so excited by the performance of his E-flat symphony in January that he embarked almost immediately on another one, this time in another favorite Balakirev key, B minor. However, he had barely had time in his overcrowded schedule to do more than sketch an outline for the first movement before Stasov's fertile brain produced *The Lay of Igor's Host* (*Slovo o polku Igoreve*)—yet another operatic subject from Russian history. No doubt there was a connection between these two projects. After the composer's death, Stasov reported that Borodin had explained the Second Symphony to him as a kind of bardic depiction of medieval Russian knights in battle. Stasov himself claimed that the first movement made him think of the "clashing of the swords of bogatyrs [heroic knights]," and he admitted that the whole idea had been Borodin's. So one assumes that Borodin was already talking about the symphony in these terms that spring, and that the opera-loving Stasov promptly tried to persuade him to do it for the stage, long before the symphony itself existed beyond a few jottings. "I've found more details in the chronicles (about Vladimir Galitsky and Konchak)," he writes in mid-April, "so that I've had to change one thing and add another."[6] With the letter he encloses a lengthy three-act scenario. "Your scheme is so complete and detailed," Borodin replies, "that everything comes out as clear as daylight; the only changes that may be needed will be shortenings . . . The subject is terribly to my liking. But will I have the strength? I don't know. If you're afraid of wolves, don't go into the forest. But I'll try."[7]

It was by no means his first operatic project. Apart from his satirical piece *The Bogatyrs,* he had also in 1867 toyed with setting another Mey drama about Ivan the Terrible, *The Tsar's Bride* (*Tsarskaya nevesta*), and had even composed what Stasov called some "first-rate scenes and choruses," but seems never to have written anything down.[8]

With *Prince Igor* his initial approach was quite different. He started by spending the summer of 1869 with his wife on the estate of a distant cousin, Prince Nikolay Kudashev, a few miles from Kursk, not far from the modern Ukrainian border. Just over the (at that time nonexistent) frontier was the small town of Putivl', from whose walls the Kievan Prince Igor of Seversk set out on his ill-fated campaign against the Polovtsian tribes of the southern Don in the year 1185. Back in St. Petersburg in September, Borodin composed, and wrote down, a first version of Igor's wife Yaroslavna's arioso in the opening scene—her anxiety at her husband's departure and her forebodings about the outcome, prompted by a terrifying nightmare. But his music soon once again fell prey to the circumstances of his life. As before, his wife was compelled by her chronic asthma to spend the winter in Moscow, while her husband settled back into his bachelor existence in the Academy of Physicians, taken up with lectures and administration, his own chemical research work, musical evenings when he could spare the time, and writing her long, newsy letters two or three times a week. Dianin asserts that he also found time for "serious work on his opera," and Rimsky-Korsakov says that he was studying *The Lay* and the *Hypatian Chronicle*.[9] But there was precious little to show for it in any finished form. A version of "Yaroslavna's Dream" (as he called it) he played to the circle, and they liked it. He also probably at least drafted a cavatina for Khan Konchak's daughter. Later, on a trip to Moscow, he composed a vividly dramatic ballad, "The Sea" ("Morey"), about a young man in a boat swallowed up in a storm with his young wife and all his worldly wealth. But *Prince Igor* made no further progress, and by the end of February 1870 he had made up his mind to abandon it altogether.[10] "After all," he asked his wife rhetorically,

> what's the point of my getting mixed up with opera? A lot of trouble and a huge waste of time; performance even more unlikely; and if they did perform it, where would I find the time for all that heap of petty troubles and unpleasantnesses with managements and performers and rehearsals and so forth? And meanwhile the subject, however well suited to music, is hardly likely to please the public. Not much dramatic effect, almost no stage movement. In the end, to do a libretto that meets both the musical and the scenic demands is no joke. I haven't the experience for it, or the ability or the time . . . I reached this conclusion after many attempts at several numbers from the materials that were ready. In the end, opera for me is not dramatic in the strict sense, and it seems to me something unnatural.[11]

For Stasov, he softened the blow by dedicating to him his latest song, perhaps himself feeling a bit like the young sailor and his wife, lost at sea.

Balakirev had long since rejected the latest attempt (by a certain Dmitry Averkiyev) at a libretto for his *Firebird*, and it must by now have been apparent that he had no real intention of ever composing this or any other opera. Of all the *kuchka* he was the one who would most have sympathized with Borodin's sudden—and in his case essentially defensive—hostility to the stage. Quite simply he disliked opera, and sometimes found his colleagues' obsession with the genre hard to accept. But his creative problems ran deeper than this. He had composed practically nothing since the Czech overture of May 1867. *Tamara* still hardly existed in written form, though bits of it were constantly in the air at circle gatherings, along with other improvisations that teased the ear but never seemed to find their way onto paper. Of course there were purely practical, as well as psychological, reasons for his unproductiveness. Since the beginning of 1868, when Lomakin resigned as director of the FMS, he had been in sole charge of the school and its concerts, as well as conductor of the Russian Musical Society. He had to plan the programs, organize rehearsals and publicity, and worry about the availability of performance materials, for works that were often far from mainstream. In fact his obstinate refusal to program standard repertoire—in a city where, after all, there were few opportunities to hear the great classical masterpieces—was the cause of more trouble than mere inconvenience. It probably cost him one of his posts, and it greatly increased the difficulties of the other one.

Exactly why the éminence grise of the RMS, Grand Duchess Yelena Pavlovna, turned against him in the course of 1868 is hard to establish precisely. But he had never been her man; when Rubinstein had first set up the society, Balakirev had been the opposition, and when he, Balakirev, took over from Rubinstein, it had been distinctly faute de mieux. Even so, had he been prepared in any way to moderate his programming, all might still have been well. In himself he was a more than adequate conductor, no showman, but musically authoritative in his way, respected by serious musicians and the amateur singers who formed the RMS and FMS choirs, and liked by audiences. Alas, his obsessive distaste for much of the standard German repertoire annoyed and eventually antagonized the conservative-minded musicians who made up the committee of the RMS, and who naturally had the grand duchess's ear. They included Nikolay Zaremba, Rubinstein's successor as director of the conservatory, a stickler for orthodox method and a confirmed enemy of modernism in all its forms, including, of course, the Russian variety; also the critic Alexander Famintsïn, who had written scathingly about *Sadko,* loathed the Russian school in general, and had probably been disappointed in his hope that Balakirev would program a work of his.

The machinations might have made a good subject for the opera Balakirev did not want to write. As soon as he left St. Petersburg for the Caucasus in the early summer of 1868, Yelena Pavlovna told the RMS board that she intended to invite a German conductor by the name of Max Seifriz to take over the RMS. Balakirev thought that Zaremba had put her up to this piece of jiggery-pokery, but he may not have known that Seifriz was a former teacher of Famintsïn's at Löwenberg, and incidentally a respected conductor of the Hohenzollern orchestra in that town, described by Liszt as "one of the most intelligent and

Mikhail Glinka from an etching
by V. Samoilov, Paris, 1853

Vladimir Stasov in 1873.
Portrait by Ilya Repin

1810—1848 г.

Vissarion Belinsky.
Portrait by K.A.Gorbunov

Alexander Dargomïzhsky

Nikolay Chernishevsky

Mily Balakirev, c. 1860

César Cui in 1890.
Portrait by Ilya Repin

Cl. Carl .mon (Mus k Verlag) edit. à Berlin
CHARGE DE RUBINSTEIN VIRTUOSE

Anton Rubinstein:
"Charge de Rubinstein
virtuose"

The Balakirev Circle, caricature by Konstantin Makovsky, 1871. Left to right: Cui, Balakirev, Stasov (with the sculptor Mark Antokolsky on his right shoulder and Viktor Hartmann as a monkey perched on his trumpet), Borodin (to the rear), Rimsky-Korsakov with the Purgold sisters as lapdogs, Musorgsky, and Serov as Jupiter, hurling thunderbolts

Borodin in the early 1860s

Musorgsky at the time of
Boris Godunov

АЛЕКСАНДРЪ СѢРОВЪ
ALEXANDER SEROFF
(1820-1871)

174

Alexander Serov

Nikolay Rimsky-Korsakov
at the age of twenty-eight

Boris Godunov: set design for the fountain scene, 1874

Paris Catacombs by Viktor Hartmann

Musorgsky and Pavel Naumov
in the late 1870s

experienced conductors in Germany"[12] and by Berlioz (who was there in 1863) as "a conductor and trainer of rare skill and thoroughness."[13] The grand duchess had duly requested references for Seifriz from Liszt and Berlioz, but also, less tactfully, invited Berlioz to provide a negative reference for Balakirev, which he categorically declined to do. Balakirev had been informed by Vasily Kologrivov—one of the directors favorably disposed toward him—that there had been a terrible quarrel, and that a majority of the board had refused to countenance his dismissal. The Seifriz idea faded away, and for the time being Yelena Pavlovna and her Germanophile directors had to face up to another season of Balakireviana: yet more Berlioz, Liszt, and Schumann, new works by Rimsky-Korsakov, Borodin, and Tchaikovsky (his symphonic poem *Fatum*), plus the usual bits and pieces of Glinka and Dargomïzhsky, and hardly a trace of Mozart or Haydn.

At the end of April 1869, after the final concert of the season, the grand duchess at last had had enough and summarily dismissed Balakirev, appointing the Czech-born Eduard Nápravník (who had also recently become principal conductor at the Maryinsky) in his place. It was the start of a difficult phase in Balakirev's life. The loss of the RMS post was a severe blow to his finances, shaky at the best of times; and to crown his misfortunes his father died in June. When the new season began in October 1869, he was forced to give more and more piano lessons to supplement his income, while at the same time, as Borodin reported to his wife, having to expend time and energy canvassing support in his ongoing guerrilla war with Yelena Pavlovna.[14] Yet he appeared to be in high spirits. Borodin described with some glee the scenes in St. Petersburg that autumn. The RMS had sold so few tickets for their opening concert that it had had to be postponed, while the first FMS concert of the season—conducted, of course, by Balakirev—drew a decent audience and was a fair success. This so enraged the grand duchess that she embarked on a policy of luring away the students who formed the ballast of the FMS chorus by offering them free RMS tickets and free classes with tea and sandwiches, all of which they accepted with relish, while nevertheless remaining loyal to the FMS.

Meanwhile, the eventual first concert of the RMS was more like a salon. Yelena Pavlovna had drummed up an audience of guards officers and courtiers, lawyers and headmistresses, assorted civil servants, "and other such musical connoisseurs," Borodin sneered; and to keep them happy she had brought in the coloratura soprano Désirée Artot from Moscow to sing some vocal potboilers—a Chopin mazurka arranged by Pauline Viardot, Pierre Rode's G-major variations, an aria from

Handel's *Alcina*—which for Borodin turned what was supposed to be a serious symphony concert into something more like *The Barber of Seville*. He consoled himself by totting up what it was costing the grand duchess to be horrid to Balakirev, including a fat honorarium for Artôt, even fatter payments for replacement conductors, a bribe for Serov, and the cost of tea and sandwiches for the FMS students. He had to admit that Nápravník, though somewhat cold and mechanical, was generally an improvement on Rubinstein as a conductor. But the most remarkable incident came after the RMS concert when the epaulets and impossible décolletages had departed, the hall was taken over by Balakirev himself for a late-night rehearsal of the FMS, and the fading echoes of the Moroccan March and Artôt's roulades were drowned out by "the mighty sounds of Berlioz's *Lélio*."[15]

Through all these tribulations, Balakirev was by no means without support, public or professional. Yelena Pavlovna's antics were even beginning to annoy the conservatory professors, who were far from natural friends of the *kuchka,* and Anton Rubinstein went so far as to forbid his students to accept the grand duchess's handouts. But Balakirev was clearly his own worst enemy when it came to professional success. His reluctance to program any kind of normal popular repertoire, his flat refusal to play the piano in public, his almost total silence as a composer, his constant willingness to sacrifice his own interests to the interests of others: all this exasperated his friends at least as much as his domineering attitude to their work and his tendency to sulk when they ignored his instructions. Stasov had heard that Balakirev was planning to hand over his teaching at the Maryinsky Institute for girls, and implored him not to do so, protesting at his "never satisfied need to do good to others and to stop at nothing in helping those who need your help—whether material or intellectual."[16]

Perhaps he had also heard that Balakirev had been using up his creative energies mapping out the future work of their Moscow friend Tchaikovsky. Balakirev had conducted Tchaikovsky's *Fatum* in an RMS concert in March, but he had formed a very low opinion of the work and had not hesitated to communicate this fact to the composer (though he *had* hesitated to send his first letter, and eventually rewrote and sent it in a softened form).[17] Then, when they met and spent time together in Moscow in August, Balakirev proposed a symphonic poem on Shakespeare's *Romeo and Juliet.* Tchaikovsky seems to have liked the idea and soon started work. But by early October he was telling Balakirev that "I'm completely played out, and not one remotely tolerable musical idea is coming into my head. I'm beginning to be afraid that my muse has flown off somewhere far away (perhaps visiting Zaremba)."[18] For Balakirev this was red rag to a bull, and he quickly fired off a lengthy reply describing in detail how he had set about composing his *King Lear* Overture and suggesting how Tchaikovsky might do the same with *Romeo and Juliet*—even offering a few bars of actual music as an opening idea.[19]

By a supreme irony, at almost exactly the same time, Stasov was doing his best to galvanize Balakirev into composing some major new work of his own and, by a worse irony, failing dismally. Since his Czech overture, Balakirev had completed only one work, the so-called "Eastern fantasy" *Islamey*, an eight-minute piano piece of such staggering virtuosity that when Nikolay Rubinstein played it at an FMS concert at the end of November, the audience cheered it to the rafters but, according to Borodin, were puzzled by it and unable (he seems to imply) to see the connection between the technical bravura and the thematic design, which in fact is essentially that of Glinka's *Kamarinskaya*: multiple repetitions of a pair of folk themes with elaborate variations in texture and color. Balakirev probably had been playing these or similar variations as improvisations at circle meetings for the past two or three years; the themes in question are Kabardian tunes that he had picked up on one of his trips to the Caucasus, most likely in 1863. But he seems to have written nothing down until his Moscow visit in August 1869, and it's even tempting to imagine that he may have been provoked into it by some response of Tchaikovsky's to his bullyings about his, Tchaikovsky's, compositional failures. One day that month, Balakirev heard a Tartar melody sung at Tchaikovsky's house by the Bolshoi singer Konstantin de Lazari, and soon afterward he wrote *Islamey* out, very rapidly, with a new, slower middle section based on the Tartar theme.

Whatever he may have thought of *Islamey*, Stasov had more ambitious ideas about the sort of music Balakirev ought to be writing. He reminded him of the subjects he had given him before. There was *King Lear* and there was the at first modestly titled Second Overture on Russian Themes, recently published for the first time with the resounding title *1000 Years*, a work they had supposedly thought of after reading Herzen's article "The Giant Awakens" ("Ispolin prosïpayetsya") in *Kolokol'* in 1861. "From all sides of our enormous fatherland," Herzen had written, "from the Don and from the Urals, from the Volga and the Dnepr a moan is growing, a rumble is rising—it is the beginning of a tidal wave which is boiling up, attended by storms, after a horribly fatiguing calm."[20] No doubt significantly, Stasov misremembered the title of the article as "Bogatïr' prosïpayetsya" ("The Knight-Hero

Awakens"). While Herzen's sense of Russian destiny combined a hatred of its present political structure with the expectation of its overthrow by sheer weight of numbers, Stasov's populism was more romantic in character and linked to a mystical idea of Russianness embodied in remote periods of history and myth. He admits to Balakirev that "you are a Slavophile, and I don't share your convictions. But to each his own, and anyone's strength lies only in that which constitutes the very roots of his soul." And he goes on to propose what might be the subject of a four-movement symphony that "breathes a passionate longing for the triumph of the Slav people, that breathes a passionate hatred of the German oppressor, and finally that breathes a fanatical renunciation of love, of peace, of the beauty of life—if only to achieve the apotheosis of the most tormenting and fulfilling idea."[21]

The subject in question is the early-fifteenth-century Hussite general Jan Žižka, who helped defeat the Teutonic Knights at the Battle of Grunwald in 1410 and subsequently led the Hussites to a succession of victories over the largely German forces of the Holy Roman Empire. The precise point about Žižka, of course, was that he was a Slav walloping Germans. Stasov lays out a detailed program for the imagined symphony, adding somewhat ambiguously that the subject "concerns not only the Czechs, but all peoples of the new Europe, where the majority go or want to go forward to freedom, and only the great individual renounces everything, in order simply to deliver the victory to others."[22] The proposal tells us a lot about Stasov's highly un-Tolstoyan view of popular movements. But as far as one can tell it drew no response from Balakirev. He still had the partly composed first movement of a C-major symphony in his bottom drawer; and as for program music, no doubt the lovely Tamara was still calling from the banks of a very different river from the ones listed by Herzen. Once or twice at circle gatherings during 1870, Balakirev would play through as much of Tamara as existed. But it would be many years before either work got finished, and meanwhile Balakirev lapsed into a more or less total creative silence.

The completion of Boris Godunov in December 1869, and its submission to the Imperial Theatres directorate the following April, left Musorgsky in an unfamiliar condition of creative fulfillment without any fresh project in view. Stasov, of course, had been active here too. Even before Boris was finished he had discussed with Musorgsky the possibility of an opera based on a short story called "Leshiy" ("The Wood Goblin") by Alexey Pisemsky, the author of the influential novel A Thousand Souls

(*Tïsyacha Dush*). Nothing came of this idea. Stasov next devised a whole libretto freely based on a novella called *Hans und Grete* by the German writer Friedrich Spielhagen, converting the sentimental original into a Gogolian comedy called *The Landless Peasant* (*Bobïl'*). Stasov described the plot in some detail in a letter to his brother, Dmitry (whose wife, Polixena, had provided the book), and added that "as you can see, the whole subject has now turned out very rewardingly, and since Musorgsky's talent is purely Gogolian, it fits his needs and abilities like a glove."[23] Perhaps for a time Musorgsky agreed with him. At any rate he swiftly composed music for the scene in the second act in which a crowd of people visit the fortune-teller, who arranges for them all to meet in the forest at full moon, where she intends to unmask the thief who has been poaching the local landowner's elks. But soon afterward he turned to other ideas, the fortune-telling music went into a drawer, *The Landless Peasant* was put on one side, and no more was heard of it.

Some months earlier, Musorgsky had been forcibly and somewhat painfully reminded that while he may just have completed a big, big opera, it was as a songwriter that he was becoming known to St. Petersburg music lovers, and in particular to the St. Petersburg press. After all, hardly anything of his had been performed in the concert hall. But his songs were beginning to be published, and in February 1870 the music journal *Muzikal'nïy sezon* had printed a lengthy review of the two sets of, in all, seven songs published thus far by Johansen. The review, by the doggedly anti-kuchkist Famintsïn, took what must have seemed a studiously asinine line on the more idiosyncratic elements in these songs. Famintsïn liked the "Jewish Song" and, guardedly, the early "Tell Me Why." Also, significantly, he thought the start of "Mushrooming" "very graceful and beautiful," but could not get on with the grating dissonances of the middle section or, apparently, understand why "graceful and beautiful" harmonies might lie oddly with a text about poisoning your grandpa. In the other songs, "Darling Savishna," "Gopak," "The Feast," and "The Billy Goat," he could detect little beyond "an inordinate desire to be, or at least seem to be, original in defiance of aesthetic feeling, to the detriment of musical beauty." He was outraged by Musorgsky's habit of ending his songs "not through the dominant as pieces usually end, but in some other way just so long as it isn't how other composers would end. People usually leave their houses," Famintsïn continued, "through the door, which in no way excludes the possibility of climbing out through the window ... Mr. Musorgsky, at the end of his songs, usually leaps out of the window." To Famintsïn, this was tantamount to musical suicide.[24]

It may have been this review, among other provocations, that gave Musorgsky the idea for another satire along the lines of his earlier Famintsïn parody, "The Classicist." Stasov later claimed that the original idea was his, and it's true that he had had his own go at Famintsïn in a *Vedomosti* article the previous year ("Musical Liars," "Muzïkal'nïye lgunï"), about the reporting in the newspaper *Golos* of Balakirev's relations with the RMS and the reasons for his dismissal. The article had characterized the various *Golos* critics as "a whole nest; ensconced there are Messrs. Famintsïn, Serov, and Rostislav, with a certain Mr. I, brooding on all the things they hold dear." And it was precisely this group (apart from the mysterious Mr. I), all of them composers as well as critics, together with the director of the conservatory, Zaremba, that Musorgsky took as targets for his poisoned arrows in "The Peep Show" ("Rayok").[25]

"The Peep Show" is a long and, for modern performers and listeners, largely pointless lampoon of a series of figures who were of some—albeit aggravating—importance on the St. Petersburg musical scene in 1870, but are now almost completely forgotten. It starts with the fairground caller's "roll up, roll up" routine (labelled by Musorgsky "I myself"—"Ya sam"), before launching into the parody of Zaremba and his pedantries by way of Handel's "See, the conquering hero comes," marked *piano* and "tainstvenno" ("mysteriously"). Next comes the *Golos* critic Rostislav (F. M. Tolstoy), notorious for his addiction to Italian opera and especially to the diva Adelina Patti. The main part of Musorgsky's Rostislav spoof is a "salon waltz" harping somewhat laboriously on the Patti motif ("Patti, Patti, O Papa Patti! Wonderful Patti, divine Patti," etc., etc.) and ending with a vocal cadenza written, it may be observed, in the bass clef. Famintsïn is portrayed this time through a studiedly boring slow song labelled "one of the pieces"—supposedly a piece by him. Last comes Serov, "shaggy, fearsome, on the Teutonic Bucephalus, the overworked Zukunftist," in the form of an extended spoof on themes from "the celebrated opera" *Rogneda*.

Musorgsky sang and played "The Peep Show" for the first time within a few days of completing it in mid-June, and it soon became a regular party piece of his within the circle. He was a gifted performer of such things: an easy, fluent pianist, and a singer who could do voices comic and serious. For those who knew the work's targets, it was an irresistible display, witty in detail and hilarious in its sheer excess. It undoubtedly had them rocking in the aisles, and Stasov claimed later that "even those ridiculed laughed till they cried, so talented and infectiously jolly and amusing was this original little novelty." Unfortunately, the musical content is almost zero, and since the satire is as dead as last year's market reports, the work now has no more than curiosity value. It reminds us, perhaps, of the difference between targeted and generic parody—between jokes about individuals and jokes about types and situations, like "Darling Savishna" and "The Seminarian."

One can readily see how talent for the one would go with talent for the other; so it is no great surprise to find Musorgsky treating "The Peep Show" as a launching pad for a new series of genre settings along the lines of "With Nyanya," his nursery song of two years earlier. In the last three months of 1870 he added four more songs, evidently with the intention of creating a cycle; and the five songs were duly published as the original version of *Detskaya* (*The Nursery*) eighteen months later.

Each one is a genre picture along the lines of the original song. In "In the Corner" ("V uglu") the child has unwound Nyanya's wool, dropped the stitches and spilled ink on the sock she was darning, so she puts him in the corner. He is at first piteous, then becomes spiteful ("Nyanya is mean and old and has a dirty nose"). Musorgsky divides the song in two: the brusque, angry Nyanya—quick, short phrases with big, emphatic leaps—and the child, crying (piano left hand), then vengeful, with snappier phrases (all quavers) and insistent final-word emphases, just like a sulky child, and ending "So there!" ("Vot shto!"). The next song, "The Beetle" ("Zhuk"), is the child's own account of being hit on the head by a large beetle while building a sand castle, then opening his eyes and finding, to his astonishment, that it's the beetle and not him that's dead. Here Musorgsky distinguishes between the child's breathless chatter ("Nyanya, what do you think happened?") and his vivid description of the beetle on the roof ("huge, black, and *this* fat"), where the mood becomes more secretive, faintly sinister, childishly overplayed. The last two songs are about bedtime. "S kukloy" ("With Dolly") is a lullaby sung by the little girl to her doll, an inspiration of striking simplicity and economy. Finally, in "Na son gryadushchiy" ("Time for Bed"), the child herself is put to bed but has first to say her prayers: God bless Mummy and Daddy (sincerely prayerful), Granny and Grandpa (slight harmonic pout), then a despairing rattle through the aunts and uncles and servants, until . . . "Nyanya, what else?" Then a sharp reminder and: "God have mercy on me, a sinner! Is that right? Nyanyushka?"

These verbal details are important, because Musorgsky's portraiture is so bound up with the exact turn of speech (always to his own texts) and the precise tone of voice. The songs are solidly made, and melodious in an unassuming way. Unlike "The Peep Show," they last not a second too long. But what makes them live, perhaps more than any other music ever written about childhood, is the penetration of mood, the power of images that are more truthful than casual observation, that hit off the character of the moment so vividly and unsentimentally that the listener finds himself actually laughing in recognition. To understand the technique involved, it helps to think of each song as a kind of revue sketch or vignette. The singer acts out the story in a way that freely mixes song and declamation, while the piano has the task of binding everything together, paying attention to the action, but keeping a hold on themes and motives. One could imagine that if Musorgsky had been asked to sing and play some anecdote or other off the cuff, the result might have been like this. In terms of musical manners, a certain informality—even irregularity—of harmony and rhythm would be a natural part of the proceedings. Where the songs in *The Nursery* differ from such a description is in the artistic precision with which the "informality" is handled. "Realism" becomes an artistic category like any other, subject to rules of balance, coherence, and well-formedness, but dependent like all art on (and there is no other word) inspiration. The idea that to write good music, all you had to do was follow the dictates of a good text, had been well and truly scotched by *Marriage. The Nursery* shows that, *pace* Chernïshevsky, truth is relative to the medium through which it is expressed. The medium cannot be reduced to some category of truth imposed from outside, without reference to its own particular nature.

Experience has proved that *The Nursery* is by no means easy to perform. Musorgsky himself, a baritone, was a talented vocal actor who not only sang and played his own songs to brilliant effect but also took leading roles in circle run-throughs of operas like *The Stone Guest* and *William Ratcliff*. But the cycle is problematical for the male voice in general, and particularly for basses of the heavy Russian variety, who can only imitate children in a style of comic mimicry. The songs are in fact notated in the treble clef, and were first sung—after the composer—by Sasha Purgold, herself a gifted character singer rather than a lyric soprano. Her sister, Nadya, wrote in her diary that "some of Musorgsky's pieces would never have been written were it not for Sasha. Without realizing it, he wrote his 'kids' only because of her and for her, because he knew very well that she was the only one who could perform them as they should be performed."

Sasha was at this period in love with Musorgsky, and Nadya thinks he was aware of the fact and allowed it to affect his behavior toward her sister. She observed that Modest was able to talk in a normal, serious way to her, but invariably adopted a jokey or even openly rude manner with Sasha—a sure sign of emotional unease and a repressed character. It went with his love of older women, his ease with children, above all his ability to empathize with invented or observed characters as compared with the difficulty he sometimes had behaving in a natural and open way with the people in his own circle. Hence, no doubt, the foppish, overcultivated drawing-room manner; hence the footloose, free-loading attitude to accommodation; hence, in the end, the addiction to drink. In his case a certain inability to confront reality was a bitter concomitant of his genius for representing it in his work. Finally, music's gain would prove to be his tragedy.

CHAPTER 19

A Shared Apartment . . .

In July 1872, Musorgsky wrote to Lyudmila Shestakova: "The circle's past is bright—its present is overcast: gloomy days have begun. I do not accuse any one of the members, 'because my heart holds no malice,' but thanks to my inborn good-natured sense of humor I can't help honoring the circle with a quotation from Griboyedov: 'Some have been pensioned off, others, you see, have been killed off'."[1]

Artistic circles, thought of as hives of creativity, rarely exist for more than brief periods, though they may survive much longer on a purely social level. As a rule they come together at times of shared artistic immaturity and when general ideas about the purpose of art or the forms it ought to take predominate over the compelling urgency of individual work. Once the members of the circle get immersed in their own projects, the identity of the group will at best begin to blur, at worst become a source of tension and disagreement, of accusations of betrayal and disloyalty. Alas, the work of art is an unruly beast, deaf to the dictates of theory, ideology, even friendship; and the artist himself must either be its slave or become its victim.

For Balakirev, as 1870 faded into 1871, this painful truth was growing harder and harder to ignore. For more than a decade he had dominated the *kuchka* by right, not of seniority, but of technical expertise backed up by an instinctively autocratic nature. He had guided his acolytes along the pathways that he himself, as a brilliant instrumentalist, had trodden. He had inducted them as best he could into the mysteries of instrumental composition and of effective—if not textbook—form;

where necessary, he had written or rewritten parts of their work for them, and when this no longer seemed appropriate, he had at least made clear to them his approval or disapproval of this or that aspect of what they had composed. He had disliked Musorgsky's *St. John's Night on Bald Mountain* and had refused to conduct it; he had disapproved of Rimsky-Korsakov's *Antar* in general and detested its second movement in particular, but had nevertheless conducted it and had the grace to change his mind. He had bullied Tchaikovsky into composing and recomposing *Romeo and Juliet,* leaving his only-just-younger and much-better-taught colleague in no doubt about what he did and did not like in the end product. All this vicarious activity had sapped his own creative energy; or perhaps it had merely provided him with the necessary explanation of its decline.

At the heart of the problem, from Balakirev's point of view, was the underlying weakness of St. Petersburg concert life. His battles with the RMS were an obvious symptom. He had tried to use his position as conductor of that institution to promote the kind of music he wanted his Russian colleagues to write; but there simply were not enough concerts, nor a strong enough native repertory, to justify such a policy in the face of the subscribers' understandable desire to hear the masterpieces of the Western classical tradition. After losing his RMS post, he had concentrated harder than ever on the FMS. But the school's finances were so precarious that by the end of the 1869–70 season the coffers were empty and for the following season no concerts could be slated at all. Balakirev's own position was no better. In June 1870 he gave a fund-raising piano recital in his home city, Nizhny-Novgorod, but hardly anybody came, and Balakirev returned to St. Petersburg practically destitute. For the 1871–72 season, the FMS announced five concerts, with the usual mixture of Liszt, Berlioz, Schumann, and an assortment of contemporary Russiana; but they too were so unsuccessful that the final concert had to be cancelled.

Meanwhile, Balakirev's fellow kuchkists had for some time been composing operas, a genre of which he was more than a little suspicious, and authority in which he had long ago ceded to the circle's official opera composer, César Cui. After abandoning *Prince Igor* early in 1870, Borodin started work on his Second Symphony, and soon afterward noticed a curious change in Balakirev's manner. "For a long time," he told his wife, "he has been offhand with me and openly cool, cross, and inclined to carp. I arrive at Lyudmila's—Mily unrecognizable: tender and soft, gazing at me with loving eyes, and in the end, not knowing how to express his affection, carefully took my nose between two fingers and gave me a smacking kiss on the cheek. I couldn't help laughing! You've naturally guessed the reason for this change: Korsinka has told him that I'm writing a symphony . . . ."[2] No wonder Balakirev had cooled toward Musorgsky, so preoccupied with *Boris,* and no longer attentive to the master's pronouncements. But there was something excessive in Balakirev's behavior, beyond the merely theatrical demonstration of an autocratic preference. One day in November 1870 at Shestakova's he suddenly remarked, in a malicious tone, that *Boris* had been rejected by the Imperial Theatres directorate. Yet *Boris* had not been rejected, was not in fact rejected for another three months. Balakirev must have heard some rumor, and chosen to stir up trouble over it rather than keep his peace until the facts were known.

Early in 1871 matters came to a head. Balakirev had been invited in December to conduct a concert in aid of a fund for the production of *The Stone Guest.* But two months later it was apparent that he had taken and was taking no steps toward organizing this event. Stasov wrote to him in despair, but Balakirev eventually replied only that "I am very busy at the present time with my own affairs and have absolutely no possibility of occupying myself with concerts."[3] This was an evasion. The truth was that he had become so depressed at the apparent futility of his existence, the failure of his FMS concerts, the decline in his creative impulse, and the loss of faith in his circle, that he had come close to suicide. He had sat at home on the anniversary of his mother's death in early March, a prey to bleak reflections; and at that very moment he had undergone some kind of religious experience, an experience he himself described, to his friend Vladimir Zhemchuzhnikov, as a "conversion." He implored Zhemchuzhnikov to keep this to himself. "I myself will tell only those I find necessary, and for the rest I'll stay as I was."[4] Stasov, a confirmed nonbeliever, he did not at first "find necessary." A few days later they met; Stasov observed him closely and noticed only something upsetting which reminded him of death. "In his appearance," he told Rimsky-Korsakov,

> it was as if everything were the same and nothing had changed: voice the same, figure, face, words—all the same, yes—but actually everything had changed, and of the past not one stone stands on another . . . Can you imagine, from time to time silence would suddenly set in and continue for several minutes . . . I tried, in this way and that, to begin anew, starting first from one end and then from the other, carefully skirting anything that might be unpleasant, such as the concert for *The Stone Guest*—nothing helped me; he would answer in a few words and again

silence. When has anything like this ever happened? Why, it's fifteen years that I've known him! No, this is an entirely different man; it was some sort of *coffin* before me yesterday, not the former lively, energetic, restless Mily . . . [5]

Somehow Balakirev pulled himself together. He conducted the FMS concerts of the 1871–72 season. But he began to absent himself from circle meetings, and to speak slightingly to outsiders about its members and their work. Borodin paid him a rare visit in October 1871 in order to retrieve the manuscript of his First Symphony, which Nadya Purgold intended to transcribe for piano; but Balakirev was reluctant to give it up, insisting that he would make the arrangement himself. When he finally handed the score over, Borodin found it marked up with corrections to alterations that he had made a few months earlier precisely at Balakirev's suggestion. It was pure arbitrary despotism. No longer able to control his erstwhile pupils, the master had acquired a new set of acolytes, who were completely under his thumb and whom he treated like a *nyanya* with her charges. Meanwhile, he disparaged *Boris Godunov* and *The Maid of Pskov* to anyone who would listen. "If he goes on like this," Borodin told his wife, "he could easily end up isolated, and that, in his condition, would be a kind of moral death."[6]

Musorgsky was hurt by the remarks that got back to him from Balakirev about *Boris*. Yet, curiously, he had been less upset than anyone expected about the opera's rejection by the directorate. No reason had been given, but it was variously supposed that the absence of significant female roles, the damaging portrait of the tsar, the satirical treatment of the Orthodox monks Varlaam and Misail, the generally unconventional idiom and design of the opera, even the unorthodox scoring, were to blame. In fact, since all these elements survived into the revised version except the gender problem, it looks as if all that was needed was a good, solid prima-donna role to reconcile the crusty members of the directorial panel to the oddities of this strange and suspiciously novel musical drama. Of course, arts committees are not necessarily so rational; they take to things or they don't. Next time, having made their point, they may take the opposite view. They may, like Pontius Pilate, have been set upon by enlightened wives; they may have received advice or instruction from some previously passive source. The most striking thing about all forms of censorship is the arbitrary power it places in the hands of mediocre, unproductive, and sometimes embittered individuals. Such people, unlike historians, are not necessarily motivated by strict considerations to which they adhere with scrupulous fairness and consistency.

Whatever the reasons for the opera's rejection, Musorgsky reacted with a sweeping energy that showed very clearly what improvements *he* thought necessary to his original conception. After all, the original *Boris* had been composed somewhat on the rebound from the essentially experimental *Marriage*. It had moved on from that work with astonishing assurance and inventiveness. It might seem practically certain that as work proceeded, Musorgsky would have continued to evolve as a composer, continued to understand his still emerging method in new ways. Just as the change from *Marriage* to *Boris* had entailed a measure of retreat from a doctrinaire, theoretical position, so he might well have gone on reinstating hybrid or corrupt ingredients previously outlawed by the purity of the doctrine. The self-confident artist can act in this way precisely because he no longer needs a dogma to argue his originality. He no longer needs to exclude things in order to prove his adherence to advanced thinking. Probably he no longer even needs advanced thinking. It so easily gets in the way.

At all events, Musorgsky proceeded to recompose *Boris* in a manner that transformed it into a significantly different kind of opera, and he did so with an alacrity that has led many to argue that he had already been planning some kind of revision for some time before the rejection was announced.[7] He almost immediately composed the first scene of an act set in Poland, at the castle of Sandomir, in the boudoir of the beautiful but unscrupulous Princess Marina Mniszek. The Pretender has arrived at the Polish court in the hope of drumming up support for his attempt on the tsarist throne, and Marina, egged on by the sinister Jesuit Rangoni, plans to seduce him, become his tsaritsa and, as Rangoni puts it, "proclaim the true [that is, Roman Catholic] faith to the Muscovite heretics."

There are a number of remarkable things about this new scene. For one thing, it has no real parallel in Pushkin, and in particular virtually the entire character of Rangoni and his interview with Marina is a pure invention of Musorgsky's.[8] Secondly, the scene launches at once into a chorus of maidservants of a conventionally decorative "operatic" kind as remote as can be imagined from the unadorned severity of the rejected score. It is almost as if Musorgsky had made up his mind to solve the gender problem and ditch his embargo on operatic set pieces all at a single stroke. The chorus is followed by an extended solo for Marina, in alternating mazurka and krakowiak rhythm à la

Glinka, again very much in the character of a set piece. Finally Rangoni appears, and in a tense duet terrorizes the princess into pursuing her ambitions on the church's behalf. Even this is more formal in its texture than any of the duologues in the original version of the opera. Musorgsky is naturally at some pains to distinguish the effete and (as he wants to insist) devious Polish court from the rough, if dangerous, honesty of the Moscow streets. Yet it remains hard to avoid the sense of an altered stylistic perspective, and this is to some extent borne out by subsequent changes and additions.

The first Polish scene is dated 10 April 1871 but was probably finished a week or so later. "I'm finishing the scene," Musorgsky wrote to Stasov on the 18th; "the Jesuit has given me no sleep for two nights running. That's good—I love it, that is I love it when composition goes like that."[9] He soon embarked on the next Polish scene, but was then for some reason sidetracked into rewriting the existing Kremlin scene, perhaps because he was still thinking about the gender question and had the idea of composing songs for the female characters in that scene, Boris's daughter, Xenia, her nurse, and Tsarevich Fyodor (a trouser role for a girl soprano). In fact Xenia did not get a song, but instead had her opening lament for her dead fiancé recomposed, so that by the time Musorgsky reached the point of adding songs for the Nurse and Fyodor he was in a new imaginative groove and more or less committed to redoing the entire long scene.

The final product, completed in September, is a radically different affair from the original, even though it incorporates a good deal of the same text and episodes, and some of the same music. There are not only new songs, but also new ideas. The Kremlin has now installed a chiming clock which, as Fyodor explains to his sister, strikes the hours and half-hours and out come people playing trumpets and drums. This is of course a setup by Musorgsky for the astonishing final episode, in which Boris, unhinged by Shuisky's insinuating description of the smiling corpse of the murdered Tsarevich Dmitry, mistakes the mechanical figures for the image of the bloodstained child. Thus an element of formal balance is introduced into what was previously pure episode-by-episode *opéra dialogué*. In the same way, as Taruskin has shown, what was originally a fairly relaxed two-part design—genre scenes followed by the political and psychological brass tacks of Boris's interview with Shuisky—is hardened into an emphatic contrast between the songs and games, the maps and clocks and the (alas) unimportant bereavement of the first part, and the melodramatic mental and moral disintegration of the second part, connected, however, by the single thread of the clock. Above all Musorgsky weakened the *dialogué* element by importing into Boris's monologue a whole further chunk of the temple music from *Salammbô*—music essentially lyrical in character, and conceived well before there was any idea of speech-music.

After finishing the new Kremlin scene, Musorgsky made a few changes to the cell scene in Chudov Monastery; he cut out Pimen's account of the murder and introduced the offstage choruses of monks. For the inn—probably at about the same time—he composed a little folk song for the Hostess and rewrote the start of the scene to fit. But once again his creative juices began working toward a new conception, this time to do with the treatment of the crowd, which had not of course been an issue where the gender problem was concerned (since the chorus women had always had plenty to sing), but which now somehow got caught up in the implications of his more spectacular—one might say more operatic—approach in the Polish and revised Kremlin scenes. The impulse was so strong that he was prepared to discard one of the most brilliant scenes in the original version of the opera—Boris and the *yurodívy,* the Simpleton or holy fool, outside St. Basil's Cathedral—in order to accommodate his new idea of a revolutionary scene in the Oryol countryside to the south of Moscow. It was to be a straight substitution. St. Basil's would be replaced by Kromy Forest—as the setting was called—and the opera would end, as before, with Boris's death.

Where St. Basil's had been a masterly example of the application of *dialogué* principles to a dynamic crowd scene taken straight from Pushkin, Kromy Forest was to be, rather, a series of large-scale set pieces like the more spectacular moments in Meyerbeer or, to take a more recent example, Verdi's *Don Carlos,* which had had its Russian premiere at the Maryinsky three years before. There was no equivalent scene in Pushkin, so Musorgsky had to write his own text, and the result was significantly different from anything in the original score, or even in the score as so far recomposed. Where the Pushkin scenes, however much altered textually, had retained the essentially unitary, snapshot character of the individual tableaux, Kromy turned out more cinematic in its dramaturgy, with a powerful forward thrust in the action toward what might have been a triumphant curtain had Musorgsky not decided to expose the emptiness of the whole popular charade by transferring the *yurodívy* and his lament for the poor, starving Russian people from the end of St. Basil's to the end here. When Musorgsky later accepted Nikolsky's suggestion that the Kromy scene should come *after* Boris's death, he effectively turned this lament into an epilogue for the entire opera.

Musically, Kromy is constructed as a series of evolving paragraphs driving toward a catastrophic climax at the appearance of the Pretender on horseback, in armor and a white cloak. The chorus, previously so passive, are suddenly galvanized into violent and destructive action. They capture the boyar Krushchov (Boris's envoy), tie him to a tree stump, and torment him, at first in the same style of choral dialogue as in the Novodevichy and St. Basil's scenes, but then in a mock glorification based on an actual folk song about a hawk in pursuit of a quail and set as a choral song in three verses. At this point Musorgsky inserts the first of the two *yurodívy* episodes from the St. Basil's scene, here something of a distraction in dramatic terms, but musically useful as respite from the relentless thrust of the choruses, and also because it will "explain" the reprise of the *yurodívy's* lament at the very end. Next, enter Varlaam and Misail, the bibulous monks from the inn scene, transformed into rabble-rousing demagogues who goad the people into the uncontrolled frenzy of the choral music from here to the entry of the Pretender. This is by far the most constructed sequence in the whole opera. The people respond to the monks in a headlong ternary-form chorus (with another folk song, "Zaigray, moya volïnka"—"Play on, my bagpipes"—from the Balakirev collection, as its central element), after which two Jesuits appear singing a Latin variant of Varlaam and Misail's opening chant, thereby completing what amounts to a broad five-part arch form—something previously quite alien to Musorgsky's dramaturgy. This whole section then flows effortlessly (via a brief episode in which the crowd sets about lynching the Jesuits) into the slow march of the Pretender and his retinue—another offshoot of the monks' chant, but also, as it happens, a further gift from *Salammbô*, where it accompanied the procession of the priests after the sacrifice to Moloch. Finally the *yurodívy* and his lament for Russia close out the whole intricate design.

How did it come about that Musorgsky ended his work on *Boris Godunov* (apart from completing the love duet in the fountain scene and orchestrating all the new music) with a scene so unlike its predecessors in style and conception? It has been argued that the switch from St. Basil's to Kromy embodied a change in the political aspect of the work. It made the people the real heroes of the opera, portrayed them as taking the destiny of Russia into their own hands, etc., etc. This was naturally an idea greatly favored by Soviet critics. But it hardly survives unbiased analysis. Musorgsky himself called the people in Kromy *brodyagi*—that is, "vagrants" or "tramps"; they are the down-and-outs who will latch on to any upheaval: the opportunist, semi-criminal element of the fourteenth-century Jacquerie troubles in France or the summer riots in London and Vancouver in 2011. They attack Krushchov, an emissary of the tsar (as they suppose, though Pushkin has him defecting to the Pretender); they next lynch the two Jesuits (foreign Catholics), but then side with the Pretender and his foreign Catholic army. To read this as political (not to say heroic) action is clearly to mistake the act for the motive. It's true that in Pushkin, the urban poor participate in, without actually committing, the murder of the tsarevich and his mother. But even there the people are portrayed as more or less passive instruments of renegade boyars. There is no sign of a Wat Tyler or a Stenka Razin to lend their behavior ideological direction.

As for the scene's musical design, what Taruskin calls its "new monumentality . . . its reliance on the kind of thing Serov had called 'musico-scenic frescoes,' and in particular its heavy reliance on folk song motives," it is plausible to hear all the new elements in the revision as simply the latest stage in Musorgsky's retreat from the doggedly theoretical positions of *The Stone Guest* and *Marriage.* But if so, the change was not without its external impulses. Almost on the very same April day that Musorgsky completed his first Polish scene, Serov's third and last opera, *The Power of the Fiend* (*Vrazh'ya sila*), had its first performance at the Maryinsky Theatre. The production was posthumous. Serov had died at the age of fifty three months before, and this may have made it easier for the *kuchka* to study it with an open mind, though there is not much evidence of any such frailty in Cui's venomous review of the premiere in the *Vedomosti*. Only later did he acknowledge the work as "an early attempt to present a people rather than a chorus," and in so doing admit its composer, however reluctantly, to the ranks of the New Russian School.[10]

For all its bloodcurdling title (which can simply mean *The Devil*), *The Power of the Fiend* is a kind of folk opera, based on a fantastic Gogolian comedy by Ostrovsky (*Live Not the Way You'd Like—Ne tak zhivi, kak khochetsya*) about a philandering young merchant who, during the Shrovetide carnival, falls temporarily into the power of a diabolical local blacksmith, but escapes just in time as the matin bell chimes. For various reasons, Serov transformed this tale into a tragedy which ends with the merchant murdering his wife. But he retained the folk elements that are a crucial part of the play, and tried to incorporate them as an organic aspect of the work's overall musical idiom, very much as (unbeknownst to Serov) Musorgsky was doing in the first version of *Boris Godunov.* In both cases, a certain aspiration to "realism" was a vital part of the concept. But it came out in fundamentally opposed ways.

Whereas with Musorgsky, realism—at least initially—meant abandoning the artificialities of conventional number opera and treating music according to the patterns and rhetoric of ordinary speech, Serov's idea was to reduce operatic formulae to the simplicity and naturalness of authentic folk song, as in the old Russian vaudeville, but with a greatly enriched harmonic and melodic palette. So *The Power of the Fiend* ended up as a number opera, carried along by songs and set pieces of one kind and another, in apparent defiance of the work's tragic theme, which had admittedly emerged only at a comparatively late stage and as one element in a terminal disagreement between the composer and the playwright, who up to that point had been acting also as librettist.

We can't be sure that Musorgsky was in any specific way influenced by Serov's highly unorthodox treatment of this subject. He certainly attended the first performance, but no opinion of his on the work has come down to us beyond a few guarded remarks about the libretto in a letter to Stasov written the day before the premiere. All we can say is that in all Serov's operas, there was a strength of conception and often an unexpected musical resourcefulness that one instinctively knows impressed the circle, even though it was virtually impossible, for reasons of pride and politics, for them to admit it directly to one another. Whatever they may, for instance, have thought of his somewhat primitive idea of setting Ostrovsky's rhyming couplets straight in the manner of folk poetry, they were surely struck by the originality of his expansion of this method in the Shrovetide celebrations of the fourth act, where he layers and imbricates his ethnic material in a way that clearly anticipates the richly overlaid textures and swift intercutting of Stravinsky's *Petrushka*. Taruskin calls this scene "one of the supreme evocations of urban folklore on the Russian stage," and he quotes Boris Asafyev's vivid description, which can almost be read as a description of the outer tableaux of *Petrushka*.[11]

We can be a little surer of another operatic influence on the revised *Boris Godunov*, that of Rimsky-Korsakov's *Maid of Pskov*, not only because the composers were close in the two or three years during which both operas were being written, and not only because both were frequently present at play-throughs of each other's work in progress, but above all because, for a crucial few months in the gestation of both works, they shared an apartment in (of all people) Zaremba's house on Panteleimonovskaya; and this "apartment" was in reality no more than a single large room in which the two composers Boxed-and-Coxed, Musorgsky composing at the piano in the mornings while Rimsky-Korsakov performed mechanical tasks such as copying or orchestrating, then

Rimsky having the room to himself in the afternoons when Musorgsky went off to work at the ministry.

In fact, by the time the two composers moved in together in August 1871, *The Maid of Pskov* was fully composed, and the first two acts were complete in full score. The attractive image of Musorgsky writing his Kromy scene in the mornings and Rimsky-Korsakov his *veche* scene in the afternoons is one of those neat scenarios beloved of romantic film directors, but unnecessary as an explanation of the workings of influence in real life. Musorgsky had heard and admired the *veche* scene more than a year previously, in June 1870, when Rimsky-Korsakov had played it to him before going off to his brother's house in western Finland, where he finished the orchestration of *The Stone Guest*. The point about their cohabitation is that any part of the draft score of *The Maid of Pskov* was available to be played through, studied or—in the evenings—talked about. Since it was their long-established habit to discuss each other's latest work, it would have been an odd turn of events for them not to do so when actually living in the same room. In the circumstances, one might suggest that the similarities between the two works are surprisingly few.

The *veche* scene already in any case shows ample signs of a familiarity with the choral scenes in the first version of *Boris Godunov*. The bells that announce the *veche* are, iconographically at least, those that proclaim Boris's coronation; the harmonies and scoring are different, but the idea of alternating unrelated dissonant chords over deep pedal notes is the same. Rimsky-Korsakov has also taken hints from Musorgsky's choral dialogue music in the Novodevichy and St. Basil scenes of his opera. The crowd's agitation at the summoning of the *veche* and its reaction to the messenger's news from Novgorod are brilliantly conveyed in snatches of conversation, a hushed chorale at his first bitter words of greeting from the ravaged city, and a distraught scherzo after the announcement that Ivan is on his way to Pskov. But in general Rimsky-Korsakov makes less than Musorgsky of the distinction between spontaneous exchanges between individuals and groups, on the one hand, and the expression of group emotion on the other. In Musorgsky's 1869 score the set-piece choruses are always moments of collective action: the regimented appeals to Boris in the opening scene, the coronation festivities, the cries for bread outside St. Basil's. In *The Maid of Pskov,* after the first *veche* exchanges, Rimsky-Korsakov tends mostly toward an oratorio-like treatment of the chorus without distinction between what one might call the public and the private. Of course, the dramatic situation is inherently public in this sense. Taken as a whole this fifteen-minute scene is a superb piece of musical theatre for a composer with no previous experience of the medium. From the ringing of the tocsin to the point at which Mikhail Tucha breaks into his revolutionary song (another tune from Balakirev's collection,[12] but of course with a new text, which was censored when the composer first submitted the opera for approval early in 1872), the alternation of solo, ensemble, and chorus has an irresistible impulse not equaled in *Boris* until Musorgsky composed *Kromy*, almost certainly under the impression of this *veche* music. The two scenes have the same accumulation of mass energy, fragmented at first, building up to a terrifying, terrified collectivity. By contrast, the crowd scenes in the 1869 *Boris* are more tableau-like in design, echoing the dynamic of Pushkin's individual scenes. In order to break this pattern, Musorgsky had finally to design a scene of his own.

After the *veche, The Maid of Pskov* has its disappointments. The third act (to stick to the numbering of the original version) is dominated at first by choruses of apprehension, as the crowd nervously awaits the tsar's arrival, and welcome, whose main theme Rimsky-Korsakov had improvised at the piano back in June 1868. Both are fine, if essentially static, pieces of choral writing, separated by a scene for Olga and her old *nyanya*, Vlasyevna, and followed by an extended scene between Ivan himself (at last) and the governor, Prince Tokmakov, Olga's supposed father. As in the first act, Olga is depicted in essentially lyric terms: a passionate young girl in love with a freedom fighter and uncertain of her parentage. The portrait is extremely touching and beautifully composed in a flowing style which, as before, moves freely between aria and arioso. But the character of Ivan remains indistinct. It is, after all, hard to find the right music for a tyrannical maniac in a rare mood of sweet reasonableness and, later, sentimental affection. Musorgsky, one feels, would have found it. But in Rimsky-Korsakov the character hangs fire; his conversation with Tokmakov and eventually Olga herself is long and somewhat featureless (apart from the chorus of maidens that Ivan, perhaps also a shade bored, commands in praise of his as yet unrecognized daughter: the folk text for this was supplied by Musorgsky).

Similarly, in the final act Rimsky-Korsakov's lyrical instincts prove a sure guide in the superb love duet for Olga and Tucha in the forest, before their kidnapping by Matuta's men, but less helpful in the again very long scene in which Olga, still unaware that she is the tsar's daughter, is brought to his tent and pleads with him for Tucha's life. On paper this is a moment of high psychological drama. Ivan is torn between his growing love for the girl he now knows to be his daughter and his determination to crush Tucha's insurrection; Olga very finely confronts him, not without warmth on her own part born of some obscure intuition of closeness to this historic monster. But the music just fails to ignite, so that the swift closing scene of Tucha's abortive attack on the camp and the accidental killing of Olga lacks the climactic force it needs if the tragic irony of Mey's drama is to be realized in musical terms. Rimsky-Korsakov revised this scene heavily on two occasions (in the mid-seventies and early nineties), but without really solving the problem. Here and elsewhere, the final revision would introduce elements from his later operatic experience, notably his encounters with the mature Wagner, still largely unknown to the *kuchka* in 1870. But the original score is in a sense sharper and more characteristic, and the work's essential strengths—the *veche,* the choral writing, the portrayal of Olga and Tucha—are already present.

Yekaterina Borodina was once again forced by her sickly lungs to spend the winter of 1871–2 in Moscow, while her husband sent her regular bulletins on his bachelor existence in St. Petersburg. In September he visits Rimsky-Korsakov and Musorgsky in their apartment and updates himself on their operatic work and their personal relationship. They are, he moralizes, "a wholesome influence on each other," and being "diametric opposites in musical values and methods, they as it were complement one another." *The Maid of Pskov,* he reports (not quite accurately), is finished; *Boris,* with all its changes (which he describes), is now "simply magnificent," and he notes with surprise that it seems to affect nonmusicians more powerfully than the Rimsky-Korsakov opera. *The Maid of Pskov,* he admits after hearing a complete run-through at the Purgolds', is "unimaginably beautiful, but somewhat chilly and passionless, apart from the *veche* scene, which is amazingly fine in power, beauty, novelty, and impact." He also reports on Cui's latest project, just begun: an opera based on Victor Hugo's play *Angelo, tyran de Padoue,* for which Cui has already composed an entire scene. The scene, it will transpire, is part of the work's fourth and final act, since Cui—true to the typical *kuchka* working method, if not to its characteristic idioms—has started at the end, perhaps out of some obscure superstition about finishing. Borodin also mentions a set of three "lovely" choruses Cui has written. Probably they include two early pieces (op. 4) written in 1860 but not previously put on show, together with a striking new Dante setting, "Chorus mysticus," for female chorus and orchestra—a piece adventurous in harmony and imaginative in texture beyond anything in Cui's operatic music to date.[13]

For a composer who has not long since abandoned his own operatic ambitions, Borodin is attractively enthusiastic about his friends' efforts in the genre. In his remarks there is no trace of envy or mean-mindedness, but genuine delight at their success as he sees it. His own musical activity is now firmly in the symphonic field. By October he has completed the first movement of his new B-minor symphony, at least in piano score, and it seems that the finale was also finished during that month. Musorgsky, Rimsky-Korsakov, and Lodïzhensky all came round to hear the not-quite-complete finale and raved about it, and when, two or three weeks later, it was actually finished, Cui impressed Borodin by calling on him specifically to hear the ending. Only Balakirev, Borodin reminds his wife, "stays aloof from this family of share-and-share-alike." There was the episode of the First Symphony score, which Balakirev tried to avoid giving back. And on the same visit, Borodin showed him the finished parts of the Second. It seems that Balakirev had seen the first movement in the spring, had insisted on various changes, but now—exactly as with the E-flat symphony—completely changed his mind and demanded that Borodin change everything back. Borodin charitably explained this as "eccentricity," but he knew in his heart of hearts that it was an advanced symptom of Balakirev's despotic nature thwarted by increasing distance from its targets.

Borodin would certainly still have been amenable to constructive criticism. Exactly how much of the symphony he had actually composed by this time is by no means clear, but what is certain is that its progress was blighted not only by his disorganized way of life but by the symphony's own confused origins. As we saw, he had abandoned *Prince Igor* with only the single scene of "Yaroslavna's Dream" composed. But there must have been other sketches as well, fragmentary no doubt, but with sufficient profile for Stasov to have "lamented the waste of the wonderful musical 'materials' already composed by him for *Igor*."[14] At the time Borodin had assured him that everything would go into the symphony. What the symphony took over above all from the opera was its historic, bardic atmosphere, its flavor of "Russian warrior-heroes . . . feasting to the sound of guslis and amid the exaltation of a great host of people";[15] and no doubt this flavor was carried over in specific musical ideas, including some that, in true *kuchka* fashion, Borodin had sketched for Stasov's epilogue, which describes a wedding banquet for Prince Igor's son in language taken from *The Lay of Igor's Host,* but which, in the end, was never composed. A few other ideas are actually shared with the opera as eventually written, or to be exact, as eventually left in a disordered state. Borodin may not have considered *Prince Igor* a dramatic enough subject for an opera. But the stage picture surely survived in his mind and laid its hand generously on his symphony.

The scene is set unmistakably by the pugnacious opening theme, in brusque unison (like the one in Beethoven's Fifth Symphony), but with an antique coloring supplied by the prominent flattened intervals—the Phrygian C natural, the D natural "correcting" the D-sharp, the descent through B-flat to A in the final phrase. Borodin also engineers punch-ups between string chords (F-sharp major, dominant of B minor) and fortissimo brass chords (G major/E minor). The whole opening is marked by brutal contrasts, abrupt changes of character and key; even the more fluid second subject, in the relative major, feels uneasy in its lyricism and never settles down harmonically, is always poised over expectant dominant pedals, waiting for the next outbreak of violence. Strange and interesting that the urbane, civilized, soft-natured Borodin was so taken with this turbulent imagery—imagery, admittedly, not without a certain celebratory ebullience, in which sword strikes on sword but blood is not shed.

Balakirev, as we saw, had had a hand in this movement. He had persuaded Borodin to change the key in which the second subject comes back in the recapitulation, from the already unorthodox G major to the still more irregular E-flat (then tried to make him change it back, which he declined to do). The very key of the work, B minor, is a Balakirev fingerprint, and so is the key of the andante, D-flat major; Balakirev had bullied Tchaikovsky into the same improbable relation in *Romeo and Juliet.* And according to Rimsky-Korsakov, Balakirev was also responsible for the brassy minor ninth chord which takes us from B minor to the remote F major of the scherzo. All this suggests (as Dianin points out) that these decisions were taken in 1871, while Balakirev was still on the scene and before Borodin visited him in the autumn. Probably the middle movements were only sketched, and possibly not fully composed for another two or three years. Instead Borodin carried on with the finale, a movement of even greater exuberance, if possible, than the opening allegro.

No wonder his friends were excited by what they heard of the symphony that October. By classical standards it is by no means a sophisticated work. It follows formal guidelines rather than processes, and looks analytically like a typical product of the circle's rather academic approach to textbook form. But in the face of such creative vigor, these things seem of trivial importance. As in the First Symphony, the sheer energy of the writing is irresistible, and in effect it braces the architecture. Moreover, the quality of the invention is superb. Whenever he needs a strong lyrical theme, he seems able to pull one out of the hat. The allegro material buzzes with invention. The ideas, it's true, have a family, rather than motivic, resemblance; for instance, the elegant second theme of the first movement draws on the same repertoire of notes as the sumptuous main tune of the andante: the six notes of the major scale (without the leading note), with a prominent descent to the lower relative—B-flat minor in the andante's key of D-flat—a tendency that Borodin may have derived from the folk-song device of *peremennost'*. Also folklike, in a way, is the floating, free-rhythmic character of these tunes, a faint memory, perhaps, of the flexible *protyazhnaya*. But this is not a folksy work. Its remoteness is that of heroic antiquity, symbolized above all by the bardic harp that introduces the slow movement and figures prominently throughout. This is the gusli of Glinka's Bayan in *Ruslan*, and it reminds us that the symphony started with *Prince Igor* and will eventually lead back to it.

. . . and a Shared Commission

While Balakirev was slowly removing himself from the circle of which he had been founder and presiding musical genius, its youngest member was taking a very different sort of step, one that might well, nevertheless, have had much the same general effect. In July 1871, Rimsky-Korsakov had been invited by Mikhail Azanchevsky, who had just succeeded Zaremba as director of the conservatory, to join its staff as professor of practical composition and instrumentation and conductor of the orchestra. To accept such an appointment might have seemed to run counter to everything that had ever been argued about such institutions within earshot of Balakirev or Stasov. A loathing of academic teaching and pedagogical authority had always been one of the cornerstones of Stasov's thinking about the nature of Russian music. When Rubinstein was setting up the conservatory ten years before, Stasov had gone so far as to assert that "academies and conservatories serve only as breeding grounds for talentless people and aid the establishment in art of harmful ideas and tastes." Now, according to Rimsky-Korsakov himself, his friends (presumably including Stasov) were in favor of his accepting the post, even though he must have pointed out to them how totally unqualified he was. Balakirev "insisted on my answering in the affirmative, with the main object of *getting one of his own men* into the enemy Conservatory."[1]

Barely twenty-seven, Rimsky-Korsakov was young for such a post. But more to the point, he was hopelessly untaught in the things that, for better or worse, it is usually assumed conservatory teachers will communicate to their pupils. His memoirs are superbly candid on this point. Of course, he had shown an instinctive grasp of musical procedures and method in his own works. But when it came to explaining or demonstrating such matters to young students, he was hamstrung by his ignorance of the most basic theoretical terminology or the logical structure of musical grammar and form. "To be sure," he acknowledges, "it is more important to hear and recognize an interval or a chord than to know what they are called . . . more interesting to compose an *Antar* or a *Sadko* than to know how to harmonize a Protestant chorale or write four-part counterpoint . . . . But it is shameful not to know such things and to find them out from one's own pupils."[2] He also admits that, after finishing *The Maid of Pskov,* he experienced a creative block which he attributed to his own technical deficiency, and which he maintains was eventually released precisely by the technique which he was forced to acquire in order to stay ahead of his students. Borodin, for one, seems to have grasped this at once. "Korsinka," he reported to Yekaterina, "is in seventh heaven over his new job . . . And actually his 'orchestra class' will be just as useful for him as for his pupils."[3]

Amid these new responsibilities, Rimsky-Korsakov managed to finish *The Maid of Pskov* that autumn, urged on, no doubt, by his new flatmate. The question then arose: what next? Just at that time a folk rhapsode (*bílína* narrator) by the name of Trofim Ryabinin visited St. Petersburg and gave a series of recitations, including probably the *bílína* of the bogatyr Dobrïnya Nikitich, a kind of Kievan St. George, who slayed the dragon and rescued Princess Zabava Putyashina. Musorgsky certainly attended one of these performances, and soon afterward conceived the idea of an opera based on the Dobrïnya story. But as with *The Maid of Pskov,* he seems not to have wanted the new subject for himself, but instead set to work devising a scenario for Rimsky-Korsakov. Meanwhile, Nadya Purgold, who had just got engaged to Rimsky-Korsakov and was taking his interests peculiarly to heart, had been reading Gogol and looking for new subjects in that somewhat more promising arena. She read "Sorochintsï Fair," one of the stories in Gogol's *Evenings on a Farmstead near Dikanka,* and thought it "good and even suitable for an opera, perhaps, but not for you, and not in general as good as 'May Night' [in the same collection] would be, for example." She was unimpressed with the *Dobrïnya* idea, and felt that "nothing very good will come out of all this cutting and remaking. In *Dobrïnya* there is so little of artistic value . . ." Nevertheless, she added magnanimously, "the main thing in this matter is that you have to follow your personal taste." Instead she persuaded her sister to propose "Sorochintsï Fair" to Musorgsky; but he, in his turn, was on another tack altogether. "I know the Gogol subject well," he responded, "I thought about it some two years ago, but the subject-matter doesn't fit in with the direction I've chosen—it doesn't sufficiently embrace Mother Russia in all her simple-hearted breadth."[4]

Just at that moment Vladimir Stasov came forward with an idea that might seem to have had the disadvantages of all these suggestions and the advantages of none. The idea had originated with the director of the Imperial Theatres, Stepan Gedeonov, who had devised a scenario based on the ancient Baltic Slav fairy tale of Prince Yaromir and the murdered Princess Mlada, a story neither Russian nor historical, yet no less fantastical than *Dobrïnya,* and hardly more coherent or vividly characterized. What Gedeonov envisaged was a mixture of opera and ballet, with spectacular stage effects, magical transformations, a witches' sabbath, and guest appearances by Morena, the goddess of darkness, the black god Chernobog, Attila the Hun, and assorted ghostly Kievan princes. His first intention had been to commission Serov to compose *Mlada* as a ballet. But Serov's death had put paid to that idea; and Gedeonov now presented the scheme to Stasov in the form of an opera-ballet which, in the absence—presumably—of an obvious, dependable single composer, he proposed as a joint project to be offered to the members of the *kuchka* as a collective. The libretto, based on Gedeonov's scenario, was by Viktor Krïlov, Cui's old librettist for *The Mandarin's Son* and *A Prisoner of the Caucasus,* and the ballet music was to be provided by the Imperial Theatres' official ballet composer, Ludwig Minkus. Rather curiously, one might feel, the four operatic (and available) kuchkists accepted this unlikely project without demur. There was a meeting at which the various parts of the libretto were allocated, then they all set to work, it seems, with little or no further discussion.

Nobody who has ever edited a collaborative publication of any kind will be surprised to learn that the *Mlada* project came to nothing, even though it inspired a significant quantity of music before it foundered, at least partly because Gedeonov himself was unable to find the cash needed to stage this complicated and extravagant spectacle. Rimsky-Korsakov later remembered *Mlada* as "a most grateful subject for musical treatment." Yet he himself got no farther with his contribution (a share of the second and third acts with Musorgsky) than a few sketches for choruses in the festival scene of act 2 and for the apparitions of the dead at the start of act 3, before deciding that the scenario was too vague to form the basis of properly considered work. Musorgsky achieved rather more, partly, it's true, by adapting existing music from works incomplete or as yet unperformed. For the second act he composed a vigorous market scene, partly based on traders' cries, and a strikingly individual march for the entry of the princes and (in a somber middle section) the priests. Between these two sections he seems to have planned what he called a "fistfight" (*kulachnïy boy*), based on his hard-worked *Oedipus* chorus. And for the Chernobog scene in the third act he made a major adaptation for chorus and orchestra of his *St. John's Night on Bald Mountain,* with extra material lifted from *Salammbô,* and a beautiful new ending as day dawns, a cock crows, and the evil spirits hurriedly disperse. Yet for all the brilliance of these musical images, Musorgsky soon wearied of what he called "the hired farm labor" (*batrachestvo*) of the collaboration. "My dear, kind friend," he wrote to Stasov,

> you know that I can't lug rubbish around inside me and care for it; accordingly I must switch to an active mode—it's both simpler, more direct, and better. I explained (as openly and delicately as I know how) to Korsinka and Borodin that in order to rescue the circle's maiden chastity, and to avoid their making a prostitute of it, I shall *in the matter of our labor* prescribe, not listen, I shall put the questions, not give the answers (and this of course only with Korsinka's and Borodin's permission) on their behalf and mine, and the contractor can please himself.[5]

He was working on his *Bald Mountain* adaptation, which, he admitted, was going well. But thereafter he seems to have put the project to one side, and only returned to it several weeks later and composed the market scene, after a run-through at Cui's at the start of May, when presumably he had to endure some teasing about his high-minded inertia.

The other two kuchkists were at least better organized in their approach to the commission, if with varying degrees of enthusiasm. Cui had been allotted act 1—a nice but presumably unintentional joke at the expense of his usual inability to begin anything at the beginning. He accordingly polished off act 4 of *Angelo* by the middle of April, then settled down to *Mlada.* We are among the ancient pagan Slavs in the Polabian city of Retra (on the river Elbe) in the ninth century; Prince Mstivoy and his daughter Voyslava have murdered Prince Yaromir's bride, Mlada, at their wedding, with the intention of arranging for him to marry Voyslava. Unfortunately for them, Yaromir is still in love with Mlada, so Voyslava sells her soul to the black goddess, Morena, to secure his love. But Mlada appears to Yaromir in a dream and reenacts her murder, thereby revealing to him its perpetrators. Yaromir is appalled by the vision, but at the end of the first act is called away to the hunt.

According to Rimsky-Korsakov, this was the most dramatic act in the work and was allocated to Cui on account of his supposed expertise as a dramatic composer. Rimsky's view may have been influenced by the fact that, by the time he wrote his memoir of this period, he had himself composed an entire opera based on an adapted version of Krïlov's libretto, and knew from personal experience what the dramatic demands of this scene were in relation to the rest of the drama. But why Cui should still have been regarded as the circle's dramatic specialist after the completion of *The Maid of Pskov* and *Boris Godunov,* both of which they all knew well from private run-throughs, is hard to imagine. More likely it was felt that the composer of *William Ratcliff* was the best qualified to find the right sort of music for the magical apparition of the dark goddess and Yaromir's vision of the murder, and perhaps also the most likely to produce a score in good time and get the opera off to a sound start. In the event Cui satisfied the latter requirement but hardly the former. His music is bland and conventional, and gives the impression of having been composed rapidly and without real engagement in the task. Most disappointingly of all, his treatment of the big melodramatic scenes is perfunctory at best, while the musical characterization is rudimentary, everyone having more or less the same kind of essentially lyrical music whether they are an evil princess, an elderly witch, or a tormented hero (the dream-Mlada herself was meant to dance but not sing).

None of this would call for particular comment, given the character of the project, if it were not for the fact that Borodin, with the task of composing the fourth and final act, was excited by it in a way that he had specifically not been by *Prince Igor.* Stasov would call on him from time to time that spring (1872) and find him "in the morning standing at his high writing-table, at the moment of creation, his face blazing and inspired, his eyes on fire, his physiognomy transformed." On one occasion "he had been slightly unwell, had stayed at home for the past two weeks, and the whole of that time he had hardly left the piano. It was during those days that he above all wrote the most capital and amazing things for *Mlada.*"[6] The middle acts had been dominated by ensemble tableaux: the Festival of Kupala (John the Baptist), and the witches' sabbath of St. John's Night (Midsummer Night). But the final act resolves the drama amid cataclysmic scenes of natural and supernatural intervention. Yaromir goes to the temple and asks the High Priest to interpret his dream; he is visited by a succession of spirits of ancient Slav princes, each of whom announces that Mlada was poisoned by Voyslava and must be avenged. Voyslava confesses and begs Yaromir to love her; but instead he draws his sword and kills her. In response the dark goddess Morena appears and sets off a *Götterdämmerung*-style climax in which a storm inundates the temple and the whole city, and Mlada and Yaromir are seen rising to the realm of light locked in each other's arms.

For some reason, Borodin was inspired by this hocus-pocus, and composed at high speed a quantity of brilliant music that in integrity of atmosphere and inventive richness far outstripped any of the other contributions, whatever might be said about this or that individual piece by Musorgsky. For once, Borodin wrote an entire score from start to finish, apparently uninhibited by the dramaturgical problems he had sensed with *Prince Igor*. No doubt it helped him that the situations and characters were given, having presumably been established and justified in the preceding acts. So he could treat the scene of the apparitions, for example, as a tableau vivant, a self-contained vignette, with mysterious, vagrant harmonies and an incantatory, quasi-ritualistic tone, as the four spirits repeat the same mantra: "Voyslava poisoned Mlada. Take your revenge!" He could compose a desperate, one-sided love duet for Voyslava and Yaromir, an inundation scene, and a romantic apotheosis for the genuine lovers, Mlada and Yaromir, as if they were set projects in a composition prize, without needing to worry about how these situations came about or what kinds of personage these characters really were. He also, of course, had at his disposal the music already composed for the abandoned *Prince Igor*. He probably at least worked the original version of Yaroslavna's arioso into the scene of Yaromir with the High Priest, though the state of the manuscripts makes this hard to establish beyond doubt.[7]

The irony of Borodin's *Mlada* was that his work was abortive partly because of the failure of others to fulfill their side of the commission. Its corresponding virtue was that it left him with a body of first-rate music and a number of bankable themes and motives that he was able to put to good use when he eventually returned to composing *Prince Igor*.[8]

Just when they were variously turning their minds to *Mlada*, *The Stone Guest* at last reached the stage of the Maryinsky Theatre, more than three years after its composer's death, its loose ends tied by Cui, its orchestration supplied by Rimsky-Korsakov. There had been difficulties bringing the performance to fruition, partly because of official restrictions on the amount of money permitted to be paid as a one-off royalty to the composer (or estate) of a new opera. But the production, when it came on 16 February 1872, was a first-rate affair, with leading singers in the main roles: Fyodor Komissarzhevsky as Don Juan, Yulia Platonova as Donna Anna, and Osip Petrov, the original Susanin and Ruslan, as Leporello. The performance was generally praised, but the work, predictably enough, divided opinion more or less along party lines. It was naturally understood as a manifesto of the Stasov tendency; Cui had made sure of that by plugging it in advance as "the first conscious experiment in creating contemporary opera-drama without the slightest concession, . . . dramatic truth brought to its highest expression, combined with intelligence, experience, and mastery of craft, along with a musical beauty that bears in many places the inimitable stamp of Dargomïzhsky's originality."[9] In fact, as we saw, and as Taruskin has argued at some length, *The Stone Guest,* whatever may be said about its musical quality, is by no means simply an arid experiment in unremitting recitative, and its advance apologists did it no favors by what Serov called their "comically inflated advertisements [which] sooner hurt the as yet unknown work than worked to its advantage."[10] *The Stone Guest* is better described as a conversation piece, whose "true domain," as Hermann Laroche, another hostile but highly intelligent critic, observed, "is the salon, its true orchestra, the pianoforte"—a remark that must have been read with mixed feelings by Rimsky-Korsakov and his betrothed, "our dear orchestra," as Musorgsky called her—"for which reason," Laroche continued, "there is no pretense to musical drama."[11]

It must in any case have been a strange experience to turn from this humble masterpiece of speech-song whose sole incursion from the other world is its living statue, to the apparitions, the devil worship, and supernatural cataclysms of *Mlada,* "this offspring of *delirium tremens,*" as Musorgsky described it to Stasov in a moment of exasperation.[12] *Mlada* had been one aspect of Stasov's enthusiasm for antique Slav culture; but there was another, very different aspect that was more and more claiming Musorgsky's attention. It may have been as a result of a play-through of *Boris Godunov* for the benefit of the historian Nikolay Kostomarov, in the early spring of 1872, that Stasov set himself the task of finding a new historical subject for a Musorgsky opera. "It seemed to me," he wrote subsequently in his biography of the composer, "that the battle between the old Russia and the new, the departure of the former from the stage and the entrance of the latter, was a rich soil for drama and opera, and Musorgsky shared my opinion."[13] This was an understatement. Musorgsky was soon obsessed with the whole subject of the power struggle in late-seventeenth-century Moscow between what Stasov called the "ancient, dark, fanatical, impenetrable Russia" of the old boyar families and the Raskolniki, the so-called Old Believers, on the one hand, and the various modernizing, Westernizing forces on the other, the followers of the regent Sofia and those of her young half brother, the future Peter the Great, the bicentenary of whose birth fell, as it happened, that very June. Not only did Musorgsky enthuse, in a series of long confessional letters to Stasov, he began speaking in tongues, expressing himself in circuitous, quasi-biblical language about "the power of the black earth" and "thunder over Mother Russia."

> Not for the first time I begin to plow the black earth, and I want to plow not the fertilized but the raw earth, thirsting not to know the people but to become their brother: terrible, but good! . . . The black earth's power will become manifest, when you plow it to the very bottom. One can plow the black earth with tools wrought of alien materials. And they did plow Mother Russia at the end of the seventeenth century with *such* tools that she did not immediately recognize with what they were plowing, and how the black earth *expanded* and began to *breathe*.[14]

Stasov's interest in the Raskolniki went back more than ten years to his reading of Kel'siyev and Kel'siyev's idea of the schism in the Orthodox Church as "a great pledge of the future development of Russia" and an image of the Russian people's perennial and confused strivings toward dimly glimpsed political goals.[15] In fact the schism had originated in the mid–seventeenth century as a conservative reaction to the church reforms of Patriarch Nikon, superficially trivial in themselves, but symptomatic of a broader attempt to centralize the power of the church hierarchy by reference back to the Greek origins of Orthodoxy. But as successive Roman Catholic and Protestant authorities had discovered in Western Europe in the sixteenth century, ordinary people were not so readily wooed from long-standing religious practices that they had been brought up to believe necessary for their personal salvation; and in the same way resistance to the reforms often took on an extreme character and swiftly came to be associated with anarchism and various brands of millennial politics. The so-called Old Believers, the most identifiable group of schismatics, adopted the ultimate form of resistance to Nikon's changes. They fled in large numbers into the remote Russian forests, nailed themselves up in coffins, and even committed mass suicide by self-immolation. When Peter I became sole ruler in 1696, and embarked on a policy of suppressing the outward manifestations of Orthodoxy, the Old Believers took him for the Antichrist, whose coming heralded the end of the world. Mass immolations increased; the sense of the Raskolniki as a politically, as well as spiritually, dissident group intensified.

For the different intellectual movements of nineteenth-century Russia, the Raskolniki offered a flexible model for their own various ideologies. The Slavophiles were sympathetic to them because they stood for opposition to the Westernizing reforms of Peter the Great and his successors. For liberals like Stasov, they were an interesting, if equivocal, example of systematic, organized opposition to autocratic government. For anthropological nationalists like Musorgsky, they were one manifestation of the soul of Russia, its spiritual essence, misguided perhaps, but untainted by foreign values. To be more exact, just as in *Boris Godunov* Musorgsky had avoided taking sides but had portrayed all his characters as human beings in the grip of forces beyond their control or comprehension, so in *Khovanshchina,* as the new project was called from the start, it was the collision of historic forces, rather than this or that faction or individual, that seized his interest. To adopt his own image, it was these forces that plowed the black earth so deep that they could no longer see their own tools; but as they plowed, the true nature of Russia was revealed, a nature that it was the task of those who would reassert a Russian identity to discover and embrace.

While Stasov saw the dramatic potential of this material, he did not immediately come up with anything approaching a detailed scenario. Even less than with *Boris* was there an obvious narrative. The dramaturgical problem was complicated by the legal impossibility of representing either Peter himself or the regent Sofia—both members of the Romanov dynasty—on the stage, and instead of trying to resolve this difficulty *ab initio* (simply assuming that Peter and Sofia would nevertheless appear), Musorgsky plunged into a program of study, compiling a list of sources on the accession of Peter the Great and the troubles that accompanied it, and presumably starting to read. "I am bathing in information," he informed Stasov, "my head is like a cauldron, just keep adding to it. Zhelyabuzhsky, Krekshin, Count Matveyev, Medvedev, Shchebalsky and Semevsky I have already sucked dry; now I am sucking at Tikhonravov, and then comes Avvakum—for dessert."[16] His enthusiasm for the subject led him to treat it as a research project rather than a drama. He spent many hours in the public library, reading up about the *Deeds of Peter the Great,* the *History of the Vygovsky Old Believers' Hermitage,* the archpriest Avvakum, who was burned at the stake in 1682 for his persistent opposition to the Nikon reforms, and so forth.

But still there was no sign of a coherent scenario, and certainly nothing remotely resembling a libretto. Musorgsky seems to have had in his mind a succession of episodes, rather than a structured narrative of the fate of individual characters against a historical backcloth, even to the extent that this had been the case with *Boris Godunov*. Episodes came and went, characters were inserted or removed. As yet there was no music; but when it began to flow, it did so more or less at random, so that even when he started composing, in late 1872 or early 1873, he seems to have had no very clear picture of the trajectory of the opera as a whole.

Grand projects evidently had a centrifugal effect on Musorgsky's brain; it was an aspect of his *rasseyannost'*, his mental tendency to stray. At first, thinking about *Khovanshchina*, he imagines for Stasov's benefit the Moscow of Peter the Great as the outcome of the *yurodivy*'s prophecy at the end of *Boris*: "Soon the enemy will come and darkness will descend: darkness, impenetrable darkness." The city is a children's work camp. Innocent boys exercise in the streets "with the help of carefully tooled muskets in the application of the Malthus theory"—that war is an effective means of controlling population. He next finds in one of his library sources a mythical account of the diabolical origin of the Teutonic race and the satanic birth of Peter himself, led from the womb by Lucifer during a thunderstorm at Epiphany. Envisaging a poor press reception for *Khovanshchina* when it eventually gets written, he identifies the usual critical suspects—the *Golos* critic, Hermann Laroche, Famintsïn, and the rest—with "the German musical guild," and from here proceeds to a disquisition on the matter of technique and the tendency of musicians toward a certain kind of academic pedantry in discussing their art. "Why, *tell me*," he asks, "when I hear a conversation of young artists—painters or sculptors . . . can I follow their train of thought, their ideas, aims, and seldom hear anything about technique—except when necessary? Why, *do not tell me*, when I listen to our musical brethren, do I seldom hear a living idea, but mostly stuff from the school-room—technique and musical vocab?" "Maybe I'm afraid of technique," he admits, "because I'm bad at it." But after all, when you eat a pie, you don't want to be told the ingredients, still less the conditions under which it has been cooked. One doesn't mind food, only cookery. "I'm not against symphonies, but only symphonists." And he lists some recent paintings and sculptures of the Wanderers school—works by Ilya Repin, Vasily Perov, and their sculptor friend Mark Antokolsky—and inquires why these works live, "and so live, that you get to know them and feel that 'you are what I wanted to see,'" whereas the latest music, however good, never has that effect.

Explain this to me, only leave out the boundaries of art—I believe in them only in very relative terms, because *boundaries of art* in the religion of the artist amount to *inertia*. What if someone's wonderful brains didn't come up with anything; but somebody else's brains did think and come up with something—where then are the boundaries? But relatively speaking—yes! sounds can't be chisels, brushes—well, of course, as *every best thing has its weakness and vice versa*—even children know that.[17]

Musorgsky, as we saw, got on well with children and understood childhood, and there certainly are aspects of his own mentality that remind one of the wayward, lateral, even naughty, tendencies of a very bright schoolboy. As it happened, his *Nursery* song cycle had just been published by the firm of Bessel, and perhaps it was this momentous event (by far his most significant publication to date), as much as the boys with their muskets or the child who could tell a hawk from a handsaw, that prompted him to turn aside from his operatic researches and compose two more songs that look like a deliberate supplement to the published cycle and that would, long after his death, find their way into an expanded version of it.[18]

The point about the first of these songs, "Sailor the Cat" ("Kot Matros"),[19] is that the little girl has hurt her hand and runs to her mother for a bit of emotional first aid. She was looking for her parasol when she saw the cat through the window, trying to get at the bullfinch in the cage. She ran out and roughly pushed the cat away, but hurt her hand on the cage. Naturally she blames the cat: "What sort of a cat is that, Mama—eh?" ("Kakov kotto, Mama—a?"). For Musorgsky the question is rather: "What sort of a child?" The answer is unmistakable: she is jolly and happy and ever so slightly dishonest. The damage seems not very severe. She tells the story like a nursery rhyme, simple and sprightly at the start, then piling on the harmonic agony when she gets to the juicy part: the bullfinch chirping pathetically in its cage, her tiptoeing up, then standing very still, pretending not to notice, then clouting Sailor just as he's about to grab the bird. Musorgsky handles these details in his now familiar graphic manner, but discreetly, without any more exaggeration than a child would give in the telling, and in a neat ternary form, plus a slow coda in which she suddenly remembers her hurt hand and grizzles softly, ending alone with the piano's final dissonance still hanging unresolved.[20]

In the other song, "Poexal na palochke" ("He Rode Off on a Broomstick," sometimes rather freely translated as "Ride on a Hobbyhorse"), a boy goes wild pretending that the broomstick is a galloping steed carrying him away for something urgent in the town. But he gets overexcited, falls off his "horse," and hurts his leg, and there is another short-lived episode of adult comforting, another rapid cure, and he's up and away once more, this time hurrying home for supper. Here Musorgsky lets the piano be the broomstick, with the boy's voice riding the brilliant accompaniment somewhat erratically, stopping to call out to his friend Vasya, then setting off again, then getting very audibly out of control and crash-landing with an "Oh, it hurts! Oh, my leg!" ("Oy, bol'no! Oy, nogu!"). As in the bedtime song that had ended the published cycle, the *nyanya* now appears and distracts his attention in one of the most beautiful episodes of the whole cycle—beautiful especially, it seems, because, like the final movement of Schumann's *Kinderszenen,* "The Poet Speaks," it supplies much-needed reassurance, to the listener as much as to the injured child, of refuge and solace in the dangerous childish world of heroic deeds and fatal disasters. But Musorgsky refuses the potentially sentimental ending and instead waves the boy off into the imagined distance, back on his broomstick. The Soviet editor of Musorgsky's works, Pavel Lamm, placed this song last for fairly obvious reasons: it does genuinely end, and happily, unlike "Kot Matros," with its painful doubts about feline morals. What is most telling, though, is the delicate subtlety of the conclusion, its complete avoidance of rhetoric or intrusive adulthood. This is the boy's coda, not the slightly patronizing grown-up smile that Rimsky-Korsakov tacked on to "Kot Matros" at the very end of the cycle as he arranged it.

All this work—the songs and the thinking around *Khovanshchina*—reveals an artist in love with humanity as a chaotic and seemingly unpredictable phenomenon. The whole idea of a classical art promoting an idealized, perfected image of man, the art of the Renaissance and the art of the Greeks on which it modelled itself, has become anathema. He has been reading Darwin's *Descent of Man,* and is obsessed with the richness of the world in which mankind finds itself, and enthralled by the idea that what may seem to be the prison of determinism is in truth the loving, violent embrace of a passionate, hot-blooded reality. This is the letter in which he compares man's situation to being clasped in the arms of a "strong, burning, loving woman." "The Lilliputians," he tells Stasov, "are compelled to believe that the classical school of Italian painting is the absolute, while in my opinion—it is deadly and as repulsive as death itself." He implicitly rejects that aspect of Chernïshevsky that sees art as an inferior representation of the beauty of the real world. "The artistic depiction of beauty alone," he asserts, "that, in its material sense, is sheer childishness—art in its infancy. *The finest traits in man's nature* and in *the mass of humanity,* tirelessly digging through these little-known regions and conquering them—that is the true mission of the artist." "Toward new shores!" ["K novïm beregam!"], he thunders, apparently echoing Herzen's *From the Other Shore* (*S togo berega*), a key document of the irrationality and randomness of history, written a decade before *The Origin of Species.*[21]

> "Toward new shores!"—fearlessly, through storm and sandbank and hidden rocks, "toward new shores!" Man is a social animal and cannot be otherwise; among men in the mass, just as in the individual man, it is always the finest traits that slip through the grasp, traits untouched by anyone: to notice and study them, by reading, by observation, and by conjecture, to study them with *one's whole being,* and feed humanity with them—what a healthy dish such as they have never yet tasted—there's a task! Delight and eternal delight!
>
> In our *Khovanshchina* we shall try, shall we not, my dear soothsayer?

CHAPTER 21

Three Tsars and a Tyrant

The Imperial Theatres directorate had finally, in their cautious, unenthusiastic way, removed their objections to the staging of Musorgsky's *Boris Godunov*. The relevant report, issued in March 1872, commented on the libretto's "mutilation" of Pushkin and its vulgarization of his historical characters. The opera's ending, it added (referring presumably to the scene of Boris's death, which still at this point concluded the work), "is incoherent and compressed to an extreme degree." "But in opera," it admitted in a resigned tone, "even a poor libretto, in the presence of good music, has its merits." The only possible barrier to a stage performance was Nicholas I's decree of 1837 against the portrayal of tsars onstage, and this the committee did not have the power to override. Instead it passed the buck to His High excellency, the Minister of Internal Affairs, who could, if he saw fit, solicit a waiver from Tsar Alexander. On 5 April, Alexander added the single word "agreed" (*soglasen*) to the report, and that—allowing for the necessary slow progress of the documentation back down the chain of command—was that, at least as far as the lèse majesté issue was concerned.

Exactly when *Boris* was actually, officially cleared for performance is a lot less certain. The soprano Yulia Platonova, who took the role of Marina in the early performances, claimed many years later that she had forced Gedeonov to put it on by demanding it for her benefit performance;[1] and it does seem that Gedeonov decided rather suddenly and inexplicably, as late as October 1873, to bring an end to the heel dragging and foot shuffling of his subordinates and order that the work be put on during the 1873–4 season. Whatever the truth of Platonova's memoir (written more than a decade after the event), the final decision to stage the opera was almost certainly not taken until the autumn of 1873. Meanwhile, various excerpts had been performed. Nápravník had conducted the coronation scene in an RMS concert in February 1872, and Balakirev had included the polonaise from the second Polish scene in what turned out to be his final FMS concert in April. Naturally there were several private run-through performances with piano, and—if Musorgsky's own autobiographical note is to be trusted—it was as a result of one of these, at the Purgolds' that autumn, that Gedeonov's assistant, Nikolay Lukashevich, agreed to stage three scenes from the work as part of a triple bill at the Maryinsky the following February. This could have been in spite of the lack of full clearance, since the scenes performed—the inn scene and the two scenes of the Polish act—were ones in which neither the tsar, the people, nor any Russian courtier or dignitary of the Orthodox Church appears (Varlaam and Misail were described as vagrants, and of course the Jesuit Rangoni didn't count). Nevertheless, it does seem that the late decision to stage the work was unconnected with problems of censorship or official clearance, all or most of which had been resolved by the end of 1872.²

Rimsky-Korsakov had also had his problems with the censorship over *The Maid of Pskov,* but they had been got over, he tells us in his memoirs, thanks to the intercession of the navy secretary, Nikolay Krabbe, a longstanding antagonist of his brother, Voyin, who, when Voyin died suddenly in 1871, went out of his way to help the young composer, presumably in some spirit of remorse. It was agreed with the directorate that Tsar Ivan could appear, in return for the expunging of all direct references to the proto-republicanism of the *veche,* Tucha, and his fellow freedom fighters. On these terms, *The Maid of Pskov* had been slated for performance in the autumn of 1872, but had been several times postponed because the tenor, Dmitry Orlov, had been ill. It finally reached the stage on New Year's Day 1873, only the second *kuchka* opera to be produced, and by far the most ambitious public statement thus far of the nationalist ideals of the Balakirev circle, in particular its preoccupation with Russian history, language, and folk culture, the plight of the Russian people, and the significance of the country's ancient political institutions.

In his memoirs, Rimsky-Korsakov paints a colorful picture of the rehearsals for his opera: the conductor, Nápravník, "impassive . . . but

his disapproval [making] itself felt even against his will," the singers "conscientious and amiable" but often irritated by the composer's
youthful unwillingness to make adjustments on practical grounds. But
the performance went off "marvellously" (*chudesno*), according to Cui,
Rimsky-Korsakov took a dozen bows from the conductor's box, and
the students were so taken with the freedom fighters' song at the end
of the *veche* scene (not, of course, so called) that they "bawled the song
to their hearts' content up and down the corridors of the conservatory."
Needless to add, the press was in the main carping and negative. Even
Cui, who reviewed the performance at great length in the *Vedomosti*,
managed to pick holes in the fabric of his praise. He found the music
monochrome, the recitatives incorrectly arranged as between the singers and the orchestra; and in tracking through the work scene by scene,
he as usual allocated marks, plus and minus, in the Balakirev manner.
But he found much to admire, especially the *veche* scene ("a step forward for art") and the orchestration throughout; and with all its shortcomings, he thought *The Maid of Pskov* "a most gratifying event in our
art, [enriching] our repertory with a solid and extremely talented work
[and serving] as new proof of the seriousness of direction, strength of
conviction, and significant future of the new Russian operatic school."[3]

Few agreed with him in print. Laroche, in *Golos,* even drew attention
to the fact that Rimsky-Korsakov's membership of the Balakirev circle
guaranteed him "the invariable and enthusiastic praises of the musical
feuilleton of the *Sanktpeterburgskiye vedomosti*" (that is, of César Cui). In fact
Laroche makes it clear that he regards the young composer as by far the
most gifted member of the circle, but one whose work is "infected with
all the deficiencies of the musical surroundings that bred him."

> The music in the new opera is all too esoteric in the harmonic sense, too
> full of choice dissonances and rarefied modulations, too rich in curiosi-
> ties, too highflown and precious for a drama taken from historical life
> and representing a coarse age with simple feelings and passions, and
> people not driven by reflection. In the extremes of harmony, in present-
> ing the sharpest and most abrupt dissonances, in unexpected combina-
> tions and chordal twists Rimsky-Korsakov has taken a significant step
> forward as against his previous works, and this is what gives the opera
> its extremely morbid character. Such music, to my mind, ought to have
> been written for an opera on Dostoyevsky's *Crime and Punishment.*[4]

Curiously enough many of the passages that Laroche grumbles
about are ones also singled out by Cui for complaint, a fact that says a

good deal about the Petersburg factions of the day. Laroche, one of the first batch of conservatory alumni, argues from the lofty position of the well-taught, well-groomed graduate thrown into unwilling contact with the artistically and technically unwashed, while Cui, himself a musician of extremely doubtful academic pedigree, is both anxious to conceal that fact and at the same time actually somewhat unsympathetic to the innovations that, as a matter of policy, he trumpets as the attributes of the New Russian School. Cui's own music reveals, as we have seen, a fundamentally conventional cast of mind wrenched into nonconformity, as Laroche might have said, by its own technical inadequacies. It would continue to be hard for the professor of fortifications to grasp the true merits of the work of his "fellow radicals."

Exactly five weeks after the *Maid of Pskov* premiere, on 5 February, Musorgsky's *Boris* at last had its first taste of the public stage. In the end, according to Stasov, it was the chief stage director of the Maryinsky, Gennadi Kondratyev, who persuaded Gedeonov and Lukashevich to include the three scenes as part of his benefit performance, alongside the second act of *Lohengrin* and act 2, scene 1, of Weber's *Der Freischütz,* knowing—Stasov remarks cynically—that the choice would bring in good money, since *Boris*'s problems with the censor had done wonders for its public profile, while the three scenes were chosen to avoid as far as possible reigniting those problems. The selection ignored questions of stylistic or narrative coherence. The inn scene emerged as a comic, satirical vignette; it provoked uninhibited laughter, and when the curtain came down someone shouted "Gogol in music."[5] Practically the only thing it had in common with the ensuing Polish scenes was the figure of the Pretender, sung by Fyodor Komissarzhevsky, whose friendship with Lukashevich may also have been a factor in the choice. In essence the scene in the inn was a product, little altered, of the *opéra dialogué* phase of the work's evolution, while the Polish act at least partly reflected Musorgsky's concern to regularize his work for the benefit of the directorate, and thus came appreciably closer to the popular idea of the "operatic."

Curiously enough, these inconsistencies, so obvious on a cool appraisal, seem to have bothered hardly anyone in the Maryinsky Theatre that night. At the end of the inn scene, and again at the end of the whole performance, the audience stood and cheered, in spontaneous reaction to the work's sheer theatrical brilliance, and untroubled by those aspects of the music that were either radical or inept, depending on your point of view. It was as usual the critics, guardians of artistic rectitude, who had to weigh up the awkward balance between stylistic novelty and techniques evolved and codified under quite different auspices. The problem was confronted by Laroche with startling candor. Contemplating Musorgsky's few published works—songs, piano miniatures, a short piece for chorus and orchestra—he set off for the Maryinsky "with the strongest prejudice against the new music that I was expecting to hear."

> For the most part [the published works] were series of tuneless cries, abstruse for the ear and uncomfortable for intonation, accompanied by some kinds of chord or chordal figurations whose cacophony, whether naïve or malicious and deliberate, surpass all description. In terms of musical technique this accompaniment offers a spectacle unheard of in the annals of art. The most elementary schoolboy blunders—parallel octaves, parallel fifths, unresolved dissonances, the appearance of new tonalities without modulation, spelling mistakes in sharps and flats, wrong barrings—all these things leapt to the performer's gaze . . . Playing through a work by Musorgsky I was always thinking of the need to open a reform school for musical juvenile delinquents.

But the *Boris* excerpts forced a sharp change of mind. Of course the same technical failings were apparent at every turn. "But the ratio between these shortcomings and the spiritual power that breaks out from under them is not at all what I saw in the romances." The first Polish scene Laroche found unremarkable. "But the other two excerpts from the opera—the inn scene and the scene by the fountain—amazed me with the brilliant musico-dramatic talent they proclaimed." He was particularly struck by Varlaam's Kazan song. "Both the melody and the multifarious instrumental variations of this song display immense power; the harmonic discourse is marked by an elasticity and brilliance which I least of all expected of Musorgsky, and there is something wild and terrible about the atmosphere of this whole number, which the composer conveys with poetic animation. The same animation reigns also in the scene by the fountain." And in observing that of the two composers whose new operas had just been staged Rimsky-Korsakov was by far the more finished and technically knowledgeable, Laroche made a judgment whose acuity seems to cut through the prejudices of the academic mind toward an instinctive, if grudging, recognition of the authority of genius.

> In offering my candid assessment of the merits and defects of Musorgsky's music, I have not the least idea of giving him any kind of advice. I

regard him as a *fait accompli,* and I suppose that for him to turn from his
wrong road and fill in the gaps in his education would be incomparably
harder than for Rimsky-Korsakov... The composer of *Boris*... possesses much greater imaginative individuality and originality, as a result
of which it must be more difficult for him to submit to any kind of
external discipline, for example the rules of strict contrapuntal style.
What is missing from Musorgsky's musical education can scarcely ever
be made up, and even if he himself should still have any doubts about
his artistic maturity, they must have been dispelled on the 5th February
by the brilliant reception given to his work.[6]

Similar distinctions might have been observed in the lifestyles of the
two composers. Rimsky-Korsakov, having become a professor of composition in 1871, had married Nadezhda Purgold in June 1872, and was
busy demonstrating his newfound regularity of existence by composing a third symphony, in C major (no flats or sharps), as if in conscious
rejection of the endless flats and sharps of Balakirev's favorite keys. As
for Musorgsky, his life was reaching a crisis. After Rimsky-Korsakov's
marriage (at which he was best man), he naturally had to find new
lodgings, and that September he moved into an apartment on his own,
but in the same house as César Cui and his wife, Malvina, close to the
Neva. At about this time his behavior began to cause concern among
his close friends. The first to notice something amiss was Stasov, who
wrote to his daughter Sofia Medvedeva six months later hinting enigmatically at trouble in store for Musorgsky, without quite specifying its
nature. The three scenes of *Boris* have been given, but there are still no
plans to stage the whole opera; Vasily Bessel's plan to publish the vocal
score in the autumn will produce income, but meanwhile its composer
is without means, and in danger (Stasov seems to imply) of stagnating
and losing the impulse to compose.

The fact was that Musorgsky was drinking more heavily than was
good for him. This had become common knowledge at least within
the Stasov family. A few weeks later Dmitry Stasov wrote to his wife,
Polixena (who was away in Salzburg), that Musorgsky had confessed
to recent fits of dementia—presumably *delirium tremens*—while empha-
sizing that he had not been drinking to excess, as Dmitry would presumably have supposed. But Musorgsky *was* drinking. He had taken to
frequenting a *traktir* (bar-restaurant) on the Bolshaya Morskaya called
the Maly Yaroslavets and drinking cognac in large quantities into the
small hours with a group of new arty friends, including an ex-naval officer called Pavel Naumov and the actor and storyteller Ivan Gorbunov.

The effects began to show in his appearance and perhaps also in his manner and conversation. Dmitry noticed that he looked drawn and thinner, and Polixena became so concerned at her husband's reports that she wrote to Musorgsky in motherly terms from Salzburg urging him tactfully to look after himself and not to allow whatever was troubling him—office work, promotion, finance, the failures of life—to undermine his health and destroy his creative spirit. One day that summer, Borodin reported to his wife, Musorgsky was seen in Pavlovsk blind drunk, and kicking up such a din that the police had to be called. "They tell me," he added, "that he's already drunk himself out of his mind and has begun to imagine all kinds of rubbish . . . This is horribly sad! Such a talented man and to sink so low morally. Now periodically he disappears, now reappears morose, untalkative, quite unlike his usual self. After a while he pulls himself together again—nice, jolly, amiable, and witty as ever."[7]

No doubt it was in the hope of disrupting this lifestyle that Vladimir Stasov tried to persuade Musorgsky to travel with him to Vienna that summer. "Such a man should certainly be given a sniff at Europe as soon as possible," he told his daughter Sofia.

> Apart from anything else, so much first rate *new* music will be played in Vienna, both in the theatre and in concerts, which at another time he couldn't see or hear anywhere else. It's impossible to let such an opportunity pass. Besides, he is already thirty-four years old; he is now at the peak of his talent and he is starting a new opera.[8]

Soon Stasov devised a more elaborate scheme, which involved taking Musorgsky to visit Liszt in Weimar. It may have reached Stasov's ears that Vasily Bessel was himself planning to call on Liszt in order to show him some Russian scores, and it will have struck him that this would be a good moment to present the most talented of their composers in person at the fountainhead of new music. Alas for Stasov's plans, Musorgsky resisted all attempts to tear him away from his routine. Even after Bessel's brother had stopped his cab and run after him down the street in order to tell him about Liszt's enthusiastic response to *The Nursery,* he insisted that his duties in the Forestry Department prevented him from leaving St. Petersburg, and when Stasov wrote from Vienna in early August urging him to come anyway, he concocted what looks like a cock-and-bull story about his office chief having eye trouble and the inhumanity of abandoning him at such a moment. Stasov wrote to his sister Nadezhda Stasova in a rage:

I sent Musoryanin a demand that he come here *immediately,* using for the journey the cash reserves I left behind in St. Petersburg. But already on Saturday evening 4/16 August a telegram arrived from him saying that it was "impossible, since the illness of some chief or other meant that he was running his department on his own." What! Because of some idiotic head of department, such a marvellous thing as a visit to Liszt, playing with him and listening to him, has to go by the board! Yes, and Musoryanin's a fool, he doesn't know how to lie, how to invent, how to get his way.[9]

But Musorgsky presumably *was* inventing, or at least exaggerating, as a cover for some sense of inadequacy or inferiority, the fear that he, the untutored composer of an ambitious grand opera, would be shown up in front of Europe's most famous musician and his no doubt highly competent retinue. For Stasov, a seasoned traveller who made no special claim to musical ability, it was another matter. He could discuss music with Liszt in an intelligent and sufficiently deferential way without invasion of his own professional competence. For Musorgsky, who had never travelled outside Russia, it was one thing to ridicule German musical expertise from the safety of a St. Petersburg drawing room, quite another to confront it on its home ground and in the person of its, in a sense, greatest representative. He might have been bolder had he known that Liszt had particularly remarked on the freshness of works like *Sadko* and *William Ratcliff,* as well as *The Nursery,* which he put down to their freedom from outside influence, "their energetic defense against foreigners," as his acolyte Adelheid von Schorn expressed it in her account of the episode to Bessel.[10] But there was something else that would probably have kept Musorgsky at home in any case. He was bathing, as he put it in his next letter to Stasov, "in the waters of *Khovanshchina.*"[11] "I realize," he wrote a month later, "that I *had* to find a free minute to have a talk with you, my dear *généralissime, had* immediately to answer your new urgent call to *Europe*—to *Liszt.* But at the same time I realize that I *had,* finally, to get down to *Khovanshchina,* as its time has come."[12]

If he had said he was drowning in the waters, it would have been not much farther from the truth. "None of us," Rimsky-Korsakov wrote twenty years later, "knew the real subject and plan of *Khovanshchina,* and from Musorgsky's accounts, extremely florid, elaborate, and involved (as was his habitual way of expressing himself at that time), it was hard to grasp its subject as something whole and consistent."[13] This remained the case. Throughout July and August 1873, Musorgsky was writing long, rambling letters to various members of the Stasov family, pouring out his obsession with different episodes of the history that he hoped to turn into a viable music drama but whose eventual shape was still, it seems, shrouded in mystery.

What we have, at this stage, is situations: the battle between, on the one hand, the modernizings of the young Tsar Peter and, on the other hand, tradition, represented by the old boyar family of the Khovanskys and the so-called streltsy militia, originally founded by Ivan the Terrible as a tsarist guard, but by the late seventeenth century a dangerous, freebooting element that took sides in the succession struggles, had opposed Peter's accession, and at the time of Musorgsky's opera was acting more or less as a private Khovansky militia. Peter has removed his older half-sister, Sofia Alexeyevna, from her position as regent, but she is still in correspondence with her former chief minister (and perhaps lover), Prince Vasily Golitsïn, an unscrupulous opportunist, Westernizing and modernizing in tendency, but above all hungry for power. From the convent to which Peter has consigned her, Sofia machinates against the Khovanskys; her agent the boyar Shaklovity invents a Khovansky plot against the throne and, later, engineers the murder of old Ivan Khovansky. Meanwhile, Tsar Peter moves against the streltsy, first condemns them all to death, then pardons them on condition that they disband. Through all these events runs the thread of the Old Believers, in the persons of the elder Dosifey and the complex figure of his acolyte Marfa, opponents not only of Tsar Peter's threatened repressions against the Orthodox Church, but of recent reforms within the church itself. Musorgsky's chronology, as it eventually emerged, is a considerable distortion of the actual history; but as a picture of the times and of the issues and personalities that shaped them, it seems reasonably accurate.

Of clear narrative there is as yet little sign. Musorgsky talks mostly about the opera's ending, in which the Old Believers, led by the formidable Dosifey, are to commit mass suicide on a funeral pyre rather than wait to be massacred by Tsar Peter's guards. But he also contemplates the opening of the first act, in which the sinister boyar Shaklovity forces the Scribe to write out a denunciation of the Khovanskys, father and son; to Stasov he describes in some detail the scene (eventually act 2) between Prince Golitsïn and the dissentress Marfa and the ensuing row between Golitsïn, Khovansky, and Dosifey, and in great detail the confrontation in act 3 between Marfa and the embittered spinster Susanna. Some of the music for these scenes he claims is "in hand" but that it is "too early to transfer it to paper."[14] The only hint of any music on paper is his remark to Stasov that "I prepared the scene of Marfa with Mother Susanna, which (that is, the scene) I have just presented, together with the instrument [*sic*], to Dmitry Vasilevich [Stasov]: we're to try out the said scene today . . . "[15] The dates on the manuscript scores of Marfa's song at the start of act 3 (18 August) and the scene with Susanna, up to the entrance of Dosifey (5 September), confirm the hint, though curiously the text as set is a great deal less elaborate than the version Musorgsky describes, in considerable poetic detail, in his letter to Stasov. It is as if the drama is evolving in his mind quite independently of its musical setting, a drama distilled from his extensive reading and profound cogitation, and uninhibited by the fierce demands of music. No wonder it cost him so much in sheer artistic discipline to bring the opera to even the sprawling near-completion that it reached before his death. "How people can get things done," he lamented to Nadezhda Stasova, "I don't know; but I can't and it's probably because of this that I try to outdo Sisyphus himself."[16]

He might well have been thinking of Rimsky-Korsakov as an example of such people: steady, married, a full-time professional musician, disciplined, an effective time manager. For Musorgsky, life was entropic, tending toward disorder. Rimsky-Korsakov was a kind of closed system, his energy always directed efficiently toward the task in hand. At the start of 1873 he was still nominally an officer in the Russian navy. But in the spring of that year he was appointed to the civilian post of inspector of navy bands, which meant not only that he was able to hang up his uniform for the last time, but also that, with his new income added to his modest emolument as a conservatory professor, he was for the first time what he called "a musician officially and incontestably."[17] His conservatory appointment had forced him into a close study of harmony and counterpoint; now his new post inspired, if it did not actually force, him to familiarize himself with the musical instruments in the bands he was going to inspect. He had always laid claim to a sharp ear for orchestration, and on the whole his orchestral works had proved it. But he also admitted to a certain ignorance of the mechanics of the different instruments, their ranges, their strengths and weaknesses, their technical possibilities and limitations. He now set about remedying this defect with the same thoroughness that he had brought to his theoretical studies two years before. He even planned a textbook on instrumentation, but soon realized that this was beyond him and, in a rare leakage of the closed system, quickly abandoned the idea.

The C-major symphony, which he orchestrated that summer while working on the textbook, is a better expression of the organized mind anxious to demonstrate the virtues of study. The first movement, for example, works on the principle that strict symphonic writing is a form of economy, a process whereby a small amount of material is made to serve a grand purpose, with the help of various technical devices: fugue, imitation, free motivic working, augmentation (the theme played slower), or diminution (the theme played quicker). This is all quite impressive, but unfortunately the material itself is colorless, and nothing in the treatment suggests that the composer's juices were stimulated by these worthy processes in the way they had been by the exotic imagery of *Antar* or the historical drama of *The Maid of Pskov*. Listening to this music, as well as the slow third movement and the very fast finale, one remembers the stern ticking-off Rimsky-Korsakov gave himself in his memoirs for ever having called *Antar* his "Second Symphony." "Only its form of four separate movements," he wrote, "approximated it to a symphony. Berlioz's *Harold en Italie* and *Symphonie fantastique*, despite being program music, are indisputably symphonies; the symphonic working out of the themes and the sonata form of the first movements of these works remove all doubt about the correspondence between their content and the requirements of symphonic form."[18]

Leaving aside the circularity of a symphony being symphonic, and the begged question about the "requirements of symphonic form," there remains something deeply unedifying about this kind of taxonomy, as if a musical genre were a kind of navy manual or a passport application. The slow movement and finale of Rimsky-Korsakov's C-major symphony pass his test with flying colors: they work their motives efficiently and noticeably, use respectable contrapuntal techniques, and even form family relations between movements (the main first-movement theme pops up at the end of the finale, in the most natural way imaginable). They never for a minute stir the blood. The five-four-time scherzo, which Rimsky-Korsakov took from his abandoned B-minor symphony of 1866, is livelier and fresher. But the trio, which he tells us he wrote on an Italian lake steamer on his honeymoon in 1872, is disappointingly short on radiance or joie de vivre. One hopes they were a jollier couple than this. But of course, being a symphonic movement, it had no business with the catching of moods; its sole task was to be a trio.

Surveying these two works, the first hesitant sketches for *Khovanshchina* and the far from hesitant first version of Rimsky-Korsakov's symphony, one might well wonder what had become of the *kuchka* as a creative or even theoretical entity. There was surely no reading of kuchkism—or probably any other -ism—that could subsume two such fundamentally disparate concepts. What was more, the group itself

was visibly disintegrating. Balakirev had entirely abandoned composition and conducting, had gone into a deep depression, and had taken to
religion, to Stasov's intense dismay, not only because of his own agnos-
ticism, but because he was well aware of Balakirev's defining role in the
circle's activities. In his gloomier moments, he could more or less write
its epitaph. After a thinly attended musical evening at his apartment
in March 1874, at which Anton Rubinstein had played Schumann's
Carnaval, Stasov told his brother that

> in spite of the incomplete company, Rubinstein made an unusually big
> impression on me . . . Musorgsky and Rimsky-Korsakov lost out terribly
> by their absence, but we—I think not. In their present condition, they
> would scarcely have added a thing! And what has that spineless creature
> Borodin contributed? Scarcely one word, scarcely an idea, hardly any
> sign of life—has he actually got anything to say? No, they've gone to the
> bad without the whip and spur and the rousing voice of Balakirev. He
> alone among them had energy, strength of spirit and initiative.[19]

Only Cui escapes the lash of Stasov's scorn, perhaps because while
he, like Musorgsky, was engaged on an opera for which Stasov had supplied both subject and scenario, he, unlike Musorgsky, was showing
signs of working systematically toward a decisive end product. With
Angelo there was slow but definite progress; with *Khovanshchina* there was
merely enthusiastic digression. By the end of 1873, Cui had completed
the final (fourth) act of his opera, a substantial part of the third act,
and at least two scenes of the first, to judge by a letter of early August
from Musorgsky to Stasov, which refers specifically to the scenes and
quotes the main theme of one of them.

Hugo's play, *Angelo, tyran de Padoue,* is a characteristically long-winded
and elaborate sixteenth-century love story masquerading as political
drama, somewhat similar in this respect to his *Le Roi s'amuse,* on which
Verdi had based *Rigoletto* twenty years before. It had already supplied
Mercadante with a subject for his opera *Il giuramento* and would soon be
the base of Poncielli's *La Gioconda.* Angelo has a wife, Catarina, and a
mistress, an actress called Tisbe, but he is troubled more by fear of the
Venetian Council of Ten, under whose aegis he governs Padua, than
by passion for either woman. Tisbe meanwhile is in love with a certain
Rodolfo (the alias of Ezzelino da Romana, the scion of a former ruling, but now exiled, family of Padua), who, however, is in love with
Catarina, though he has not set eyes on her for seven years. All this we
learn through a device whereby a Venetian spy by the name of Homo-

dei proves to Rodolfo that he has the power to help him gain entry to the governor's palace and see Catarina. It transpires that Homodei is himself in love with Catarina and is devising her meeting with Rodolfo in order to incriminate her in Angelo's eyes. But there is one crucial aspect of Catarina's history that Homodei does not know. Many years before, she had successfully pleaded for Tisbe's mother to be reprieved from execution for some petty indiscretion, and Tisbe has long been seeking her unknown benefactress in the hope of repaying her. After recognizing Catarina in Angelo's chambers, she arranges a deception whereby (as in *Romeo and Juliet*) Catarina swallows what Angelo believes to be poison but is in fact a sleeping draught. She also arranges for horses to be waiting for Catarina's and Rodolfo's escape. But Rodolfo, who has killed Homodei and now believes Catarina dead by Tisbe's hand, stabs Tisbe, who dies as Catarina revives.

Cui and Stasov managed to include a surprising proportion of this farrago of complexities in their scenario, and even introduced some genuine political action in the form of a revolution scene (act 3) in which Rodolfo is revealed as a conspirator and freedom fighter (inspired perhaps by the role of Tucha in *The Maid of Pskov*), but Homodei, renamed Galeofa by Cui, is killed not by Rodolfo but by the crowd, after Rodolfo has denounced him as an informer. This scene, dominated by choral action of one kind and another, is obviously modelled on Rimsky-Korsakov's *veche* and perhaps also Musorgsky's Kromy Forest (so far heard only in the drawing room with piano). But Cui was unable to overcome a certain timidity of style in the portrayal of popular unrest, and the scene comes out tame by comparison with its models, square in phraseology and conventional in harmony.

More interesting and revealing is the way in which the character portraiture and the lyric and dramatic writing in the solo scenes is left far behind by *Boris Godunov* and even by *The Maid of Pskov*, both of them works that Cui knew perfectly well by this time. The exact reason for this quickly becomes obvious. The basic problem that Cui never managed to overcome was short-windedness. Like many moderately talented but untrained composers, he had good ideas but found it hard to extend simple phrases into complex musical sentences and paragraphs. He could deploy rich chromatic chords with the best; his harmonic language is compounded of higher dominant preparations of one kind and another, the sort of thing that hotel pianists have at their fingertips and can use to enrich any tune, from a nursery rhyme up to a twelve-note row by Schoenberg. But as with hotel pianists, the preparation is followed at regular intervals by the expected resolution, with the result that what ought, on dramatic grounds, to be an intricate, developing fabric constantly lands with a thud on the musical equivalent of a full stop. The general effect of this habit is to trivialize the characters and the drama. What should be psychologically involved and evolving is reduced to a mosaic of emotional utterances, affecting in their way, but limited in reach, like those of an adolescent. At times we seem almost to be in the land of Gilbert and Sullivan, whose *Trial by Jury* was on the stocks at much the same time as *Angelo*. But whereas Sullivan was parodying the clichés of romantic opera, Cui was taking them seriously and in constant danger of being trapped by them.

The strange thing is that most other members of the circle seem to have been unaware of any shortcomings in Cui's manner. *Angelo* is largely innocent of significant Russianisms or notable individualism of any kind. Yet Musorgsky was at first enthusiastic: "Kvey [Cui]," he told Stasov, "has done a very good scene for Rodolfo with Anafesto [Galeofa] and a *marvellous* narration for Tisbe to Angelo about her mother."[20] And when Borodin heard the first two acts at Rimsky-Korsakov's a year later, he was beside himself with delight: "beyond charm, beyond beauty," he described it to his wife.[21] No doubt there was an element of wishful thinking or simple loyalty in such remarks. Stasov himself, though, was more equivocal. A lot of the first act, he told Dmitry's young daughter Zinaida, was "so-so," though Tisbe herself was "splendid!!"[22] To Dmitry himself, on the other hand, he observed three months later that Musorgsky still "believed in Cui stupidly and blindly." But the most trenchant judgment on *Angelo* was penned very early in its career in a diary entry at the end of 1871 by Sasha Purgold, after singing Tisbe in a run-through of (probably) part of act 4 at her parents' house. "I have no sympathy for this piece," she wrote; "it is terribly stilted, complicated, and not very talented."[23]

Angelo would have to wait another two years for its first stage test; but for those with ears to hear, it was already becoming apparent that, if kuchkism meant *Boris Godunov, The Maid of Pskov,* Borodin's B-minor symphony, and Balakirev's longed-for *Tamara,* whatever these works might add up to as a coherent national or reform program, Cui no longer had anything of substance to contribute to it.

CHAPTER 22

Toward New Shores

At long last, on 27 January 1874, Musorgsky's *Boris Godunov* reached the stage of the Maryinsky Theatre as a complete opera, conducted by Eduard Nápravník. As one would expect of a work so unlike anything to which either the singers or the orchestra were accustomed, the first performance was preceded by a large number of rehearsals, all or nearly all of which Musorgsky himself attended. His participation was important, and not only for reasons of musical style and interpretation. It guaranteed his approval of the way the work was presented. From start to finish he acquiesced to Nápravník's suggestions, which included cuts and also, one may surmise, modifications of detail, since Nápravník, though painstaking as ever in his preparation and rehearsing, was unenthusiastic about the music and inclined to be dictatorial about ways of showing it in the best possible light. Stasov, for one, was infuriated at the sight of Musorgsky lamely giving in to whatever butchery Nápravník saw fit to visit on his opera. "Our poor Modest," he wrote to his daughter Sofia Fortunato after the premiere, "is drinking more and more this year, and now is so fogged by wine and by the fear that they will remove his opera from the theatre that he slavishly listens to Nápravník and all the Maryinsky Theatre singers, is halfway distanced from our circle, cuts from the opera whatever they tell him to, and, in general, seems as much a *wet rag* as if he were Al. Nik. Serov, of blessed memory. If he continues to be such a cowardly, shallow, and small-minded person, I've definitely made up my mind to break with him."[1]

Musorgsky had agreed to the complete omission of the scene with Pimen and Grigory in the Chudov Monastery and a number of less substantial cuts, including the tsarevich's parrot song, both chiming-clock episodes, and various passages from the two Polish scenes and the Kromy Forest scene. Apart from the Chudov scene, this was all, as it happened, music added in the revision. It was long supposed that Chudov had been cut because of the censor's actual or anticipated objection to the representation of monks onstage. But the equivalent scene in Pushkin had been included in the production of the play in 1870, and in any case Pimen appeared later on in the opera in the scene of Boris's death.[2] So it seems that the cuts were made on Nápravník's insistence, either on grounds of artistic taste or simply because of the work's inordinate length. Done in full, it would play for well over three hours of music, plus the numerous intervals demanded by scene changes between the acts. All the same, the choice of cuts seems curiously damaging. In particular, the loss of Grigory's initial motivation must have made the work's already somewhat casual dramaturgy more impenetrable than ever. Yet this scene was cut from all performances of *Boris* during Musorgsky's lifetime; it was first heard, on its own, in 1879 in a concert performance by the FMS conducted by Rimsky-Korsakov, but was not staged until the premiere of Rimsky's version of the opera in 1896.

Withal, the production was by every account a spectacular success, visually stunning, musically persuasive. The sets, taken over from the play (apart from Kromy, which of course had to be newly designed), were sumptuously realistic to a degree that may be hard for the modern reader, accustomed to stark, geometric stage designs and symbolic or updated costuming, to comprehend. The two Kremlin interiors, the Terem and the Granovitaya Palace, were authentic and detailed reproductions of richly painted, vaulted sixteenth-century Muscovite chambers; the fountain scene was a leafy glade in a densely wooded garden through which could be glimpsed the steps and buttresses of Sandomierz Castle. The singers were, of course, costumed accordingly.[3] The intervals, four of them, must have been lengthy. As for the music, the cast could hardly have been stronger. Ivan Melnikov, the first Ratcliff in Cui's opera five years earlier, stepped up as the first in a long line of great Borises, most of whom have taken his melodramatic parlando style (with attendant cries, gasps, and moans—a style that, as we saw, probably originated with Mikhail Sariotti in Serov's *Judith*) as an automatic element in the vocal technique required to convey the hysteria that overtakes the guilt-wracked tsar in his great act 2 and act

4 monologues. The tenor Fyodor Komissarzhevsky (the Pretender), the venerable Osip Petrov (Varlaam), and the soprano Yulia Platonova (Marina)—whose benefit it was—all repeated their roles from the three scenes of the previous year. Nápravník, though out of sympathy with the music, conducted conscientiously, as ever, and won plaudits on all sides for the clarity of his reading and the quality of the orchestral playing.

The audience loved it. They loved the spectacle, they responded to Musorgsky's astonishing grasp of character and his unfailing instinct for the stage, and they apparently liked his music, even though it had few of the attributes that normally appeal to an operatic public weaned on Italian bel canto and Gallic lyricism. They called the composer onto the stage over and over again—eighteen or twenty times, according to Stasov. They were noisy in their appreciation of this huge opera by a composer most of them had scarcely heard of until a year ago and whose biggest previous work on public view was a chorus lasting barely seven minutes. Of course they were reacting intuitively, as audiences will. They apparently did not notice the defects in Musorgsky's technique, his failure to observe the most elementary rules of good harmonic and contrapuntal behavior, his "wrong notes" (as one critic called them), and his deplorable lack of respect for Pushkin's text. But fortunately, a band of well-read music critics was on hand to explain why this audience reaction was incorrect, to point out that in fact (as another critic put it) "on the technical side . . . Mr. Musorgsky is weak to the point of absurdity," that his "lack of artistic instinct, coupled with ignorance and the desire always to be 'new,' results in music that is wild and ugly," and that his orchestration, when bearable, was like Rimsky-Korsakov's (that is, by the book), but at other times was "repulsive and monstrous." In general, this same critic insisted in a later review, every aspect of the work bore "the stamp of incompetence." But then, in discounting the first-night success, he concluded that "we consider it a real success [only] when operas attract good audiences over a period of several years," after which, presumably, the "incompetence" ceases to matter.[4]

Even the most cursory glance at the many and lengthy reviews that *Boris Godunov* attracted exposes the remarkably low intellectual standard of music criticism in St. Petersburg in the 1870s. By and large, the critics were simply bemused by the originality of Musorgsky's style, and preferred to see it as a product of his well-known lack of training rather than of an exploratory genius that simply did not fit their preconceptions. Here and there the work was praised for its dramatic qualities but damned for its lack of music in the "normal" sense. The word "cacophony" crops up with monotonous regularity. It never seems to occur to these reviewers, a number of whom were professors at the St. Petersburg Conservatory, that the rules and conventions by which they earned their daily bread had not been brought down by Moses from Mount Horeb but had been distilled ex post facto by theorists like themselves from the works of creative geniuses who, in many cases, had made their own rules and broken them to suit themselves. All that can be said in defense of such critics is that greater musical minds than theirs sometimes reacted in a similar way. The conservatory-trained Tchaikovsky, for instance, told his brother, Modest, after studying the score that "Musorgsky's music I send to the devil; it is the most vulgar and vile parody on music."[5]

The only reviews of the first *Boris* that are seriously worth reading today—and even these less for their acuity of judgment than for what they tell us about the musical context in which Musorgsky was working—are those of Tchaikovsky's friend and ex-fellow student Hermann Laroche and Musorgsky's close friend and kuchkist colleague César Cui. Laroche, as we saw, had surprised himself the year before by finding a "brilliant musical and dramatic talent" in the inn and Polish scenes. Now, after witnessing the complete opera, he still finds talent; but the praise is more muted and judicial. He manages, in effect, to explain away Musorgsky's gifts as a product of a progressive spirit and a kind of studious method, which knows how to feed its artistic ambitions by opportunistically tapping into a range of contemporary resources while endeavoring to rise above them all. "Such personalities," he remarks with mild condescension, "are well known to experienced observers of Russian life: a man who has learned 'gradually, something, and somehow,' but feels constrained by his surroundings and is unconsciously striving toward the light, toward freedom, is a sympathetic phenomenon." Laroche might be thinking, one imagines, of Pierre Bezhukov in *War and Peace,* or even Raskolnikov in *Crime and Punishment.* He analyzes how this liberalism, as he calls it, affects Musorgsky's treatment of Pushkin, compelling him to coarsen and disfigure the "soaring poetry" of the play on the grounds that "the real Boris, the real Pretender and the real Marina, in the opinion of such liberals, did not speak at all as beautifully as Pushkin has them speak." With more than a touch of irony, he suggests that it is only the folk-song element in Musorgsky's style that prevented him from writing like the hyper-realist novelists Nikolay Pomyalovsky and Fyodor Reshetnikov (both, incidentally, alcoholics who had died in their twenties). Then, Laroche sneers, his language "could have been made more real than

reality itself." Yet he seems to praise the composer's talent for repro-
ducing the characteristics of speech. "We have seen a man here who
can observe how people speak and who is gifted with a sensitivity that
perceives the special accent of the moment and the individual accent
of the person."[6]

In all these observations Laroche shines an acute intelligence on
music whose power he plainly recognizes but is unable, at bottom, to
comprehend. One way of evading this dilemma is to trace what he
calls Musorgsky's borrowings from the recent operas of other composers whose work there are good reasons to despise. Musorgsky may, for
instance, ridicule Serov in his "Peepshow," but this doesn't prevent him
from copying aspects of Serov's style and method. Fyodor's clapping
song (Laroche thinks) is an obvious derivative of Yeryomka's song in
the third act of *The Power of the Fiend* and generally of a number of things
in that work and *Rogneda*. Musorgsky's habit of piling up dissonant
chords over long bass pedals is learned from the carnival scene in *The
Power of the Fiend,* though never, Laroche adds, "have the crudest model
works reached such naïve coarseness as we see with this imitator." And
if not Serov, then Dargomïzhsky, the influence of whose *Kazachok* and
Finnish Fantasy Laroche finds in the more general folk-montage elements of *Boris* (rather, he adds, than that of Glinka's *Kamarinskaya*; but
then, "in this method of variation, Dargomïzhsky himself is nothing
other than an impoverished and motley dressed Glinka"). Finally, the
conservatory-trained, theoretically solid critic notes with thinly veiled
contempt that Musorgsky writes his music at the piano. "Remove his
piano today," Laroche insists, "and tomorrow he would no longer be a
composer . . . It can generally be said that the imagination of this musical realist is tremendously influenced by the position of his own ten
fingers on the black and white keys . . . The selection of tonalities, the
modulation, and the voice-leading [part-writing] of this strange composer are so pianistic that one can only explain them as an incessant
noodling with an abundant use of the right pedal." As a critical observation this is shrewd and suggestive; as an insult it hardly merits serious
consideration.

Cui's notice in the *Sanktpeterburgskiye vedomosti,* like his review of *The
Maid of Pskov* the year before, is essentially an elaborate and extended
mark sheet. This scene is good, that not; this detail pleases, that is inef-
fective. He objects to the fact that in the opening chorus of the Polish
act, "the note F-sharp fails from too frequent repetition." He likes Marina's mazurka, especially the "charming episode" in the middle section,
though even here "the note D-sharp fails from too frequent repetition."

As before, one is irresistibly reminded of Rimsky-Korsakov's report on Balakirev's teaching method. The review is by no means wholly negative, but the laundry-list approach gives equal prominence to the praise and the blame, whereas one might reasonably have expected that in writing about a major work by a fellow kuchkist, Cui could have congratulated him more generously on an astonishing achievement while presenting the negative points (such as might have been unavoidable) as the wholly understandable symptoms of Musorgsky's inexperience at composing on this vast scale. Instead he dwells, finally, on the opera's flaws, which result, he alleges, "from the fact that the author is not strict or critical enough with himself, and from his undiscriminating, complacent, hurried way of composing."[7] Musorgsky was outraged. "The tone of Cui's article," he wrote to Stasov, "is odious . . . This reckless assault on the *complacency* of the composer! . . . *Complacency!!! Hurried composition! Immaturity! . . .* whose? . . . whose? . . . I should like to know."[8]

It would be easy to suggest that Cui was simply jealous of his younger colleague's popular success, so much greater than the at-best-tepid reception of his own *William Ratcliff.* He probably was genuinely uncertain how to respond to this curious musico-dramatic hodgepodge, so lacking in coherent narrative or musical process in any traditional sense. His own concurrent work on *Angelo* is enough to show where his own sympathies lay in the matter of musical drama. And as for the remorseless impartiality of the distinguished columnist, that was simply the standard journalistic tone in the dangerous little aquarium of St. Petersburg music, where it was always a case of eat or be eaten, and where the time-honored Russian habit of compensating extreme approval with extreme reproof was fully on display.

Cui was not the only one of Musorgsky's circle who found it hard to swallow the more eccentric aspects of his originality. Some time in 1873 he had formed a close friendship with a twenty-five-year-old poet by the name of Count Arseny Golenishchev-Kutuzov. In June of that year he had written to Stasov recommending the young man as a poet in whom "almost everywhere, sincerity gushes up, almost everywhere you can smell the freshness of a fine, warm morning, with a superlative inborn technique." He went on to explain that Kutuzov was not at all a man of the sixties, writing poetry of a socially motivated type, but on the contrary an introspective kind of writer who "forged into verse those thoughts that occupied *him,* and those longings peculiar to *his* artistic nature."[9] At one of the circle's evenings that summer Musorgsky had performed his "Peepshow" for the umpteenth time, as usual to hoots of laughter from the assembled company. Kutuzov, however, was baffled, not knowing any of the musical references, and afterward, walking home with the composer, he confronted him with his difficulty. Surely, he suggested, "The Peepshow" could not be regarded as a work of art; it was merely a private joke, "witty, wicked, talented, but still no more than a joke, a prank." That night they stayed up till dawn while Musorgsky went through his repertoire of works that he thought would please the earnest Kutuzov. When at last they parted, they left each other, Kutuzov records, "with the realization that we had much more in common than we had supposed a few hours earlier and that we would be seeing each other rather more often."[10]

The two did become close for a time, as is clear from Musorgsky's letters, gushing, affectionate, at times emotionally indiscreet. Some have read them as evidence of some kind of homosexual relationship or impulse at least, but this is surely to make too much of that extreme intimacy of tone which occurs elsewhere in Musorgsky's correspondence and which goes with the romantic artist's tendency to blur the boundary between emotional and artistic confession. Musorgsky thought highly of Kutuzov's gifts and wanted to encourage him. Probably in November 1874, the young poet took rooms next door to Musorgsky's on Shpalernaya, where the composer had been living for the past year and a half, and for the next few months—except for several occasions when Kutuzov visited his mother in Tver—they lived in close proximity, at first on Shpalernaya, then for a month or so in the summer of 1875 in an apartment Kutuzov had taken on Galernaya, near the Admiralty.[11] Early in August 1875 Kutuzov left in unclear circumstances, locking the apartment and, according to one account, leaving Musorgsky's belongings on the doorstep. A few months later, to the intense annoyance of the composer, who like many confirmed bachelors disliked his close friends tying the knot, Kutuzov married the fifteen-year-old Olga Gulevich.

At the time of his intimate friendship with Musorgsky, Kutuzov attended circle gatherings and by his own admission completely accepted their ideas and prejudices about art. But soon after Musorgsky's death in 1881, he produced a lengthy memoir which painted a very different picture of the composer's work and its relation to Stasov's doctrines. In essence, Kutuzov maintained that the progressive tendencies in *Boris Godunov* and in songs like "Darling Savishna," "The Seminarian," and "The Billy Goat" were in fact artificial, put on to please Stasov and his circle, but that by nature Musorgsky was a lyricist whose best and most personal work was to be found in romances like the Pushkin setting "Night," the lyric-dramatic "King Saul," and the more conventional romantic scenes in the Polish act of *Boris*. Kutuzov reports that when Musorgsky sat at the piano and improvised, the result was always more spontaneously beautiful than when he wrote it down, at which point it would take on the attributes required of it by the kuchkist circle.

> The fact is that Musorgsky the artist improvised, but the Musorgsky who wrote was a member of the circle, a musical innovator who above all took account of his mentors' opinions, whose tastes he knew and whose approval he sought. Above all, whenever possible one had to confuse and conceal the beauty and tunefulness of a theme in order to avoid the accusation of "sugariness and sticky sweetness," as was their usual expression at that time, and meanwhile simplicity would vanish, to be replaced by "harmonic originality." The breadth of theme and organic consistency of sound that had flowed naturally in the original act of creation also suffered reworking, since that organic consistency of sound and breadth of theme needless to say represented in the aggregate something correct, which smelt of the "classicism" of the "conservatory." It was necessary at all costs to exterminate this "retrograde spirit."[12]

About *Boris Godunov* Kutuzov was of two minds. That it contained "many good musical points," as he condescendingly put it, he did not deny. But on the whole he found it regrettable that Musorgsky chose to accept the enthusiastic popular verdict, rather than the generally negative opinion of the "competent judges" (that is, the newspaper critics). "Such a hastily accepted view on Musorgsky's part was a great and regrettable mistake," he argued. "Not only did it for a long time hold back the development of his talent and impede his inward labor of artistic self-improvement, it alienated Musorgsky from his fellow composers, who, for all their ardent sympathy for the composer of *Boris Godunov,* could not credit this work with the perfection demanded by its mentors, and in many respects agreed candidly and honestly with the critics."[13]

One would hardly give this analysis a moment's consideration if it were not for the fact that Musorgsky himself was probably, for a short while at least, influenced by the personality behind the opinions, whether or not the opinions themselves were, at the time, openly expressed. Kutuzov's judgment on the *kuchka* is, after all, understandable. There is no particular need to accuse him, as his Soviet editors have done, of systematic lying.[14] He was, simply, a minor poet of limited vision. His preference for Musorgsky's romance style is that of a conventional mind, not a mendacious one. And if he sometimes remembers Musorgsky agreeing with him about the defects in *Boris,* we may recall that Musorgsky himself had bent over backwards to accommodate Nápravník's cuts, and later, when the opera was revived in October 1876, even apparently consented without protest to the omission of the entire Kromy Forest scene. As Stasov, who did protest, pleaded: "Ah, don't talk to me about 'consent'! What does an author's consent mean? When you have an author in a vise, in your power, he'll probably consent to anything you like, he has no defense, no protest; and you'd consent willy-nilly if they could simply strike out your entire opera with all its performances. Not everyone has the courage of a Beethoven or a Schubert, and would rather withdraw his work than agree to its mutilation."[15] Yet it does also seem to have been an aspect of Musorgsky's personality to agree too readily, in conversation, with other people's opinions, even to express opinions himself that he supposed congenial to his interlocutor. So, while it seems unlikely that he "fully agreed," as Kutuzov claimed, "that this last act was obviously superfluous to the course of the whole drama and had the character of something stuck on in haste," it is less unlikely that he said as much to Kutuzov, simply out of a desire not to disoblige a fellow artist for whom he felt deep affection, whatever he may have thought of his views on music.[16]

He was soon, at all events, turning to Kutuzov for poetry to set to music, and the music he wrote does undoubtedly mark out a new direction in his work, as compared with his most recent things since (and including) *Boris*—admittedly a rather unfocused bunch of pieces, some fragments of *Khovanshchina* (notably Marfa's song in act 3, the vocal score of which had actually been published in the autumn) and a new middle section for the "Destruction of Sennacherib" chorus, which Rimsky-Korsakov had orchestrated with Musorgsky's approval, and conducted in a famine-relief concert three weeks after the *Boris* premiere. The Kutuzov songs, begun in May 1874 and completed in August after a break for other work, formed a cycle of six with the somewhat forbidding title *Bez Solntsa* (*Without Sun,* or *Sunless*). Musically they are essentially unlike anything Musorgsky had written before. When he performed five of them at Rimsky-Korsakov's in September, Borodin heard them as a by-product of *Boris* "or the fruit of a purely intellectual inventive process that makes a highly unsatisfactory impression."[17] But for once Borodin, who was at the same time busy admiring the first two acts of *Angelo,* missed the point. *Sunless* owes comparatively little to *Boris,* and hardly anything to brain work. Unusually for Musorgsky, it is the direct response, not to a visual impression, but to an imagined state of consciousness. Exactly as in Schubert's *Winterreise,* the dark-ened mind conjures up a series of images to reflect its own bleakness of spirit. Unlike in *Winterreise,* however, the imagery remains for the most part intangible and, with a few exceptions, lacks the picturesque or narrative dimension of the earlier masterpiece. If the triple sun of Schubert's "Die Nebensonnen" stands for his hero's fading grip on life, Musorgsky's absent sun is the ultimate blackness of accidia, that nega-tivity which denies the purpose of everything, including death.

What inspired him to write in this way? The Soviet musicologist Vera Vasina-Grossman thought that *Sunless* was a direct expression of his personal loneliness, and an indirect projection of the despair felt by thinking Russians in the 1870s after the collapse of the liberal hopes raised by the reforms of the early sixties.[18] Gerald Abraham argued that Musorgsky was affected by "the hostile and uncomprehending criticisms of *Boris,* and by the boredom of the work in the Forestry department."[19] But great music is not composed in a state of depres-sion; and in any case, after interrupting work on *Sunless* to compose *Pictures from an Exhibition,* a score of surpassing vitality, Musorgsky was able to return to the song cycle and recapture its atmosphere of languid negation apparently without difficulty, just as Schubert could hap-pily sandwich the joyous, beatific "Lied im Grünen" between the two books of *Winterreise.* One might suggest, instead, that the new friend-ship with Kutuzov prompted him to look at the young poet's work, most of it lyrical in manner and modest in scale; that Kutuzov, who was unsympathetic to Musorgsky's character-sketch style, encouraged him to set some of these lyrics as conventional romances; and that Mus-orgsky, no longer very interested in the romance as a genre, looked for a way of capturing the lyrical essence of Kutuzov's poetry by adapting his speech-melody technique to simple, scanned verse. In this sense the first song, "Within Four Walls," feels like an experiment. The short poem's regular scheme of internally rhymed dactylic tetrameters is rigorously echoed by the music until the very last line, where the final two feet are briefly drawn out to form a rhythmic cadence. At the same time, the melody studiously reflects the contour and accent pat-tern of the spoken verse. But the point is not just a technical one. The relentless musico-poetic scheme is an image in sound of the "cramped little room" and the enclosing darkness of the poet's "lonely night." The image is achieved without the usual nocturnal graphics: no growl-ing dissonances or scurryings in the musical undergrowth, nothing but a slow procession of soft, mysterious chords over a persistent D pedal (another discreet image of entrapment), with some unobtrusive

crotchet movement here and there in an inner voice of the accompaniment—interior music in every sense.

Having set this tone of dark quietism, far from counteracting it,
Musorgsky persists with it. The second song, "You Didn't Know Me in
the Crowd," is in the same D major and at virtually the same andante
tempo. Its meter is more relaxed, though still regular, but Musorgsky
now uses the scansion against itself, so to speak, speeding up the second and fourth lines, in which the poet seems to accuse his uncaring
lover: "Your look expressed nothing" (dismissive triplets); "but I felt
strange and fearful when I observed it" (triplets again); then prolong-
ing the accent on the words "no ver' mne"—"but believe me." But the
key to the song lies in the opening chord and its relation to the home
tonic. The chord is an augmented sixth (German form), which is like
a dominant seventh with a different resolution or exit. The previous
song having ended in D major, the new one starts with what sounds
like an oddly laid out dominant chord in E-flat, a semitone up. But
read as a sixth chord, it resolves back to D major, with the pedal D acting not as the leading note of E-flat but as a D-major anchor. In this
way Musorgsky undermines any sense of progress or upward motion,
and throughout the song he equivocates superbly between the two
implications, even combining them in a wonderfully vagrant series of
descending chords to the words "in it [that moment] I endured the
delight of all our past love," before ending, with brutal tenderness, on
the opening sixth chord, *pianissimo,* without its dissonant G-sharp (the
actual augmented sixth in the original chord), but still with the pedal
D at the bottom.

These technicalities are hard to describe in bearable language. The
crucial point is Musorgsky's lordly disregard for normal harmonic procedure in the interests of emotional precision, a method he originally
evolved in the context of musical portraiture. To suggest he was too
untaught to understand the "mistakes" he was making is simply ridiculous. A clever child can learn such things in a week. It may, however, be
true that having missed out on the formal study of theory, Musorgsky
was less indoctrinated with the virtues of good practice, and was more
prepared to trust his own ear and his own hands on the keyboard. This
he did to marvellous effect in the much longer third song of *Sunless,*
"At an End Is the Futile, Noisy Day." The poet—still, it seems, in his
lonely, darkened room—broods sleeplessly over long-lost hopes and
joys, "as if once again inhaling the poison of passionate spring dreams";
and the memory drifts past in a sequence of slowly oscillating descending chords so haunting that they were subsequently copied both by

Debussy (to suggest drifting clouds in "Nuages") and by Stravinsky (to set a nocturnal forest scene in *The Nightingale*). Later the poet seems to reject these memories, "bored with their dead throng and the noise of their ancient chatter"; but for the composer the shadow of past love brings a momentary radiance and a passionate surrender to it "in silent tears." Suddenly this is music that does briefly recall *Boris Godunov,* especially the *Boris* of the monologues, though it is not particularly close in detail.

Musorgsky composed one more *Sunless* song before breaking off in early June to write *Pictures from an Exhibition.* This is the brief "Be Bored" ("Skuchay"—the hard-to-translate imperative of the Russian verb meaning "to be bored"). The eccentric chord sequence in the opening two bars—mainly simple triads (B minor, D minor, B minor, A major, E major, G minor, B minor, but with all their flats spelled as sharps as if they were passing dissonances in B minor)—makes a curiously listless, inconsequential, but hardly tragic effect. The cadences are nearly all major, which might imply that true boredom undercuts misery as much as happiness. But when he returned to the cycle in late August, he rounded it off with a pair of more substantial and in some ways more conventional songs. Both "Elegy" and "On the River" support the voice with piano figuration that at least looks on paper as if it might descend from the Schubert of the late Heine settings in *Schwanengesang,* though it takes only a few seconds of each song to undermine the comparison. "Elegy" even yields here and there to pictorialism, of a kind largely avoided by the preceding songs. We picture the night "slumbering in the fog" (rocking piano chords), the silent, twinkling star, the tocsin of "cheerless death." But the most telling image is that of the night clouds that drift above the poet's head like his own changeable, uneasy thoughts, in the form of a vagrant quaver melody in piano right-hand octaves (incidentally the only quick music in the cycle), winding its way "without goal or purpose" from memory to memory, idea to idea: the face of the beloved, the "noise of disorderly life," the "insidious murmur of hatred and worldly trivia." Here at last the piano has a chance to color in a musical picture.

Piano figuration is just as crucial to "On the River," whose deep, nearly motionless waters conceal every secret of the heart, every passion, every dark fear. Like a sluggish river, the accompaniment is turbid and muddy-bottomed, stuck fast on a persistent C-sharp pedal articulated by deep left-hand triplets that vary their form but never their anchorage. Above it the voice sings the most purely lyrical melody in the whole cycle, somehow finding in the key of C-sharp major all kinds of chromatic byways without at any point breaking the steady tetrameters of the poem, which give more space than those of "Within Four Walls" since they rhyme alternate whole lines rather than every half-line. At the end, the poet considers suicide, but in an oddly dispassionate, insouciant way, very different from Schubert's journeyman rocking himself to sleep in the brook of *Die schöne Müllerin*. Like Eliot's hollow men, he stands on the beach, too passive to cross to death's other kingdom.

Something of the same air of hopelessness infects one other Kutuzov song Musorgsky wrote in the early stages of work on *Sunless*. That March the war artist Vasily Vereshchagin had exhibited a series of paintings of Konstantin von Kaufman's Turkestan campaign the previous year, including a number of images that General Kaufman, when he saw the exhibition, pronounced unpatriotic and insisted on their removal from the exhibition. One of them, entitled *Forgotten* (*Zabïtïy*), depicted a dead Russian soldier lying unburied in the Asian sands, his body pecked at by crows. Kutuzov's eponymous poem, evidently prompted as much by the Kaufman incident as by the actual subject matter, overinterprets in the direction of pathos and adds a young widow at home in Russia, nursing her baby son and promising him that "Daddy will come home and I'll bake a pie."

The poem may have been written at Musorgsky's request, since one on the same subject by Nikolay Shcherbachev (a minor composer in the Balakirev circle) survives among Kutuzov's papers, decorated with ironic marginalia in Musorgsky's hand. His Kutuzov setting was made soon after "Within Four Walls" (the start is actually on the back of the manuscript of that song); but that is no reason to suppose that it was meant as part of the cycle, which anyway may not yet have been in the composer's mind. For all its melancholy E-flat-minor tone, "Forgotten" would not have suited *Sunless* as it turned out, being much more in Musorgsky's objective-realist vein, a sinister dead march with augmented seconds in the melody hinting at the poor soldier's Eastern resting place. *Sunless,* moreover, though a work of negation, is predominantly in major keys. Even sorrow, it seems to assert, is not worth the candle. As for "Forgotten," a late Schubertian model once more suggests itself, the Heine song "Ihr Bild" in *Schwanengesang,* with its image of loss in a dark unison opening and hesitant dotted rhythms.

Although things seen had figured prominently among Musorgsky's sources in the past, "Forgotten" is his first work directly inspired by a painting. Within a few weeks, however, it was joined by another, altogether more ambitious, and a still more direct response, for piano solo without the mediation of words. The exhibition in *Pictures from an Exhibition* was a memorial show for the painter and architectural designer Viktor Hartmann, a close friend of Musorgsky's, who had died suddenly at the age of thirty-nine in July 1873. Hartmann had first been introduced to the circle a few years before by Stasov, who was interested in Hartmann's work, not so much for its architectural significance as for its character as design. Hartmann was not only or even primarily a functional architect. He was at his best drawing monumental fantasy buildings that might never be built or utilitarian objects transformed into richly elaborate or grotesque objets d'art. There are parallels between his work and that of William Burges and William Morris in England, or Christian Jank—the original designer of Neuschwanstein—in Germany. He combined a talent for showcase building projects with a fascination for peasant artifacts and idioms, which he would transform into contexts or onto a scale apparently quite alien to their original purpose. For instance, his design for the Russian Naval Pavilion at the Vienna World Exhibition in 1873 resembled nothing so much as a glorified peasant izba, richly decorated, framed by Russian naval standards and crowned by a fantastically ornate imperial eagle. His design for a ceremonial gate to the city of Kiev was topped off by a peasant woman's hat (*kokoshnik*) and a cupola in the shape of a Slavonic helmet. He drew a clock in the form of the witch Baba-Yaga's hut and a nutcracker in the form of a misshapen gnome. These references were a foretaste of what soon became a nationalist movement quite distinct from the socially conscious realism of the sixties to which, in part at least, the *kuchka* had subscribed. Hartmann's work in a small way prefigured the neonationalism associated with art patrons such as Savva Mamontov (whose house at Abramtsevo he designed) and with the World of Art movement—a nationalism focused on design and the revival of rural arts and crafts, and only peripherally, if at all, concerned with social questions and the plight of the peasantry.

So far as one can judge from the few exhibits that survive, the drawings and paintings in the memorial exhibition that opened in February 1874 at the St. Petersburg Architectural Association were remote even from the world of *Boris Godunov*. By no means all the subjects were Russian, and those that were seem to have been of the fantasy variety, devoid of realism in any conventional sense. Nevertheless, they caught Musorgsky's imagination, no doubt partly because of his grief over Hartmann, but surely also because there was in his idea of Russianness an instinct for the grotesque and exotic, for the magical and superstitious, and for images of heroism and terror. On one level *Pic-*

tures is all the same a realist work. Its primary subject is the composer visiting the exhibition. "My physiognomy," he told Stasov, "is to be seen in the intermezzi."[20] We hear him, see him, enter the gallery, stop in front of the first picture, ponder, move on to the next one, and so on until the ordinary considerations of well-formed art decree that the "Promenade," as he called the introduction and, by implication, each intermezzo, should retreat into the pictures and reappear as part of *their* subject matter, rather than his.

As for the pictures themselves, they remain cool images, pieces of music hung on the wall: the hobbling, bow-legged gnome; the old castle with (according to Stasov) a troubadour singing before the gate; the children squabbling in the Tuileries gardens in Paris; the Polish cart drawn by oxen ("Bydlo" = cattle); the ballet of young chicks in, literally, shell suits; the rich and the poor Jew (a montage by Musorgsky from two separate paintings which Hartmann had given him early in their acquaintance); an argument about a cow in Limoges market; the Rome catacombs with Hartmann and (in a mysterious sequel) the "physiognomy" of the composer himself; Baba-Yaga circumnavigating her hut in a mortar (using the pestle as a propeller); and finally the Kiev gate, a very grand translation of Hartmann's somewhat quaint façade.

For all its anecdotal appearance, *Pictures from an Exhibition* makes a surprisingly integrated impression in performance. This is partly thanks to the linking "Promenade," which comes five times, much varied each time, before vanishing into the pictures: the second part of "Catacombs," where Musorgsky seems to join Hartmann inspecting the skulls ("Con mortuis in lingua mortua," the subtitle reads, in somebody's, if not Musorgsky's, bad Latin);[21] and "The Great Gate" whose main theme is a kind of abstract of the "Promenade" motif, which itself then rematerializes in the clanging of bells toward the end.

No less important, though, is the key sequence, obviously planned with care, using the device of linking or adjacent pitches. Thus, for instance, the "Promenade" ends on a B-flat chord; "Gnomus" starts on C-flat, a semitone up, in the key of the subdominant, E-flat minor; and the second "Promenade," in A-flat major, has E-flat as its second note, which in turn, respelled as D-sharp, is the first note of "Il vecchio castello"; and so on. The model for these various mechanisms is probably the piano suites of Schumann, which adopted similar devices to bind together loose assemblages of character sketches. Stylistically, too, Musorgsky is more indebted to Schumann than he might have cared to admit, whatever the circle's general admiration for that particular German master. Several of the individual pictures seem to echo the capricious imagery and figuration of pieces in *Carnaval* or the *Davids-bündlertänze,* without imitating them in any specific way. There is, at any rate, nothing overpoweringly Russian about Musorgsky's "Tuileries," or his "Ballet of Unhatched Chickens," or his "Limoges Marketplace"—and why, after all, should there be?

But these pieces, with their orthodox harmonies and regular phrasing, stand in deliberate contrast with the overtly Russian "Promenade," as is plainly indicated by the marking *nel modo russico* at the start of the work.[22] The main theme is a Musorgskian folk song, by its nature unbarred, but barred for convenience in fives and sixes, and harmonized, after a solo opening, in the manner of the opening chorus of *A Life for the Tsar,* in block chords as if it were an Orthodox liturgy. Later "Promenade"s vary these elements but retain their essential character. The third and fourth intermezzi, for example, introduce some modest polyphony, suggestively colored minor-key harmony, and (in the fourth) metric irregularities so deviant as to make nonsense of the actual barrings. Here no two consecutive bars have the same number of beats (the sequence is five, six, seven, six, five, seven, five, six, five, three); yet on a coolly rational view the piece could be barred in four-four, with the exception of a single six-four bar. Needless to say, this is not a serious suggestion. Musorgsky's barrings are obviously designed precisely to undermine the strict metric accent, and particularly to weaken the sense of upbeat, which he will surely have associated with the highly regimented and directed character of German music. We first saw this weakening in vocal music, in *Marriage* and *The Nursery;* but although those are not folk-song-based works, the idea undoubtedly originates in folk singing, as is evident from the barrings in Balakirev's 1866 collection, which sometimes struggle to fit the melodies into halfway-regular meters. The humble "Promenade" of *Pictures* may, however, be the first in a long line of Russian instrumental pieces that treat meter as a function of an imaginary verbal syllabication, rather than as an abstraction from the dance, the march, or the work song.

Taken as a whole, *Pictures from an Exhibition* is a rare example by a *kuchka* composer of an effective synthesis of strong Russian and strong Western elements, in which respect it echoes Hartmann's own work, much of which has non-Russian subjects and was executed outside Russia. As a gallery of visual images turned into music, it perfectly reflects the circle's ideas about realism; in fact, it draws on Musorgsky's own technique of portraiture through song. What, after all, are "Bydlo" or "Samuel Goldenberg and Schmuyle" but piano portraits akin to "Darling Savishna" or "The Seminarian," either of which one might imagine rethought as drawings by Hartmann? At the same time, Musorgsky must have recognized that in an instrumental work on this scale, thoughtful construction was de rigueur. Even in the casual-sounding "Gnomus," with its graphic montage of the stumbling, shambling, scrabbling dwarf, there is a careful balancing, though very little integration, of the different musical elements. Several of the pictures are cast, Schumann-like, in ternary form. The two Jews enter separately, then combine, after which Musorgsky adds a melancholy little coda— the poet speaking, perhaps: one of the most beautiful moments in the whole cycle.

But compositionally the most impressive part of the work is the final series, from "Limoges" onward, which achieves a powerful sweep of continuity through the solemnities of "Catacombs" and the mystery of the "lingua mortua," by way of the violent "Baba-Yaga," to the grandiose "Great Gate," with its clanging bells and its imaginary choir chanting a free version of the Orthodox hymn "As you are baptized in Christ," a reminder that Kiev was the tenth-century cradle of Russian Christianity (though, as Michael Russ points out, Musorgsky's chorale-like treatment has a somewhat Lutheran flavor).[23] These are also the most original pages. Stasov compared "Great Gate" (unfavorably) with the final scene of A Life for the Tsar but still, without deliberate paradox, called it "a beautiful, mighty and original thing . . . in an entirely new manner."[24] As for the sepulchral harmonies of "Catacombs," familiarity with the famous Ravel orchestration is apt to obscure the extraordinary boldness of these slow, heavily pause-marked chords as writing for piano, an instrument that cannot sustain long notes or crescendo or diminuendo on notes once struck. Musorgsky may have had Schubert's "Doppelgänger" in the back of his mind as he sat at the piano composing this music; the piano texture and spread of the hands are similar. But how did he expect the hapless pianist to execute the drastic crescendos and diminuendos that he placed over almost every chord in the first line of music? The answer must be that he didn't, but that he wanted the player to *think* them, and in thinking them to create an illusion of slow progress, as the guide's lantern swings from side to side, illuminating the skulls at random, and making them—in what follows—glow.

Although Musorgsky must have played *Pictures* in whole or part at circle evenings at Stasov's or Borodin's or Lyudmila Shestakova's, he never played it in public, and there is no record of a performance by any other pianist, nor was the work published, in his lifetime. Perhaps he thought of it as an orchestral piece that awaited scoring. That

would explain why, though he was a fluent pianist, the writing sometimes lies awkwardly on the instrument; but the same is true of other
piano works by him. Stasov referred to the "purely orchestral chords" in
"Catacombs,"[25] but that might simply be a way of describing them. Not
the least oddity is that the so easily distracted Musorgsky composed
this half-hour masterpiece—by far his biggest instrumental work—in
a matter of three weeks of June 1874.[26] It's almost as if he regretted
finishing it with such ease and feared that it might not withstand the
scrutiny of the kinds of pianist (most probably the Rubinstein brothers) who might be expected to perform it. Had Balakirev still been on
the scene, things might have been different. But just as likely, Balakirev
would have tried to make him rewrite it; and that would not have gone
down well.

CHAPTER 23

Distractability

Whatever Stasov might say about Musorgsky's drinking habits, he had to admit that they had no very obvious adverse effect on his composing. A thirty-minute piano suite and a fifteen-minute song cycle would be a good one-year tally for the most professionally minded composer; and there was more: not only the Goleniscev-Kutuzov song "Forgotten" but also a revised version of the old "War Song of the Libyans," retitled *Jesus Navin* (the Orthodox name for the biblical Joshua), and with a new middle section derived from Mathô's lament in act 4 of *Salammbô*. Musorgsky had even, at Stasov's suggestion, tinkered with a new satire, in the general vein of "The Peepshow," but this time aimed at the critics of *Boris Godunov*, especially Laroche. Oddly enough, Musorgsky's new friend Kutuzov, the scourge of "The Peepshow," seems to have provided the text for this piece, which went by a mysterious pair of alternative titles: "Nettle Mountain" ("Krapivnaya gora") and "The Crab" ("Rak"). But hardly any music got written, and when Kutuzov inquired about the work's fate, Musorgsky replied that "I had a lot of fun with 'Peepshow,' and that's enough! I can find something more serious to do."[1]

That, at least, was an understatement. In July 1874, with *Khovanshchina* in fragments and *Sunless* still wanting its last two songs, he had started contemplating yet another opera subject, the very one that the Purgold sisters had suggested to him the previous year, Gogol's *Sorochintsï Fair*. This comic tale, he wrote to Karmalina, would be "good as an economy of creative strength" since "two heavyweights, *Boris* and

Khovanshchina, in a row might weigh me down."[2] At the same time he was struggling with a song in memory of his beloved Nadezhda Opochinina, who had died at the end of June at the age of fifty-three. This "Graveside Letter" ("Nadgrobnoye pis'mo"), for which Musorgsky himself composed the text, is an intensely personal cri de coeur, if not quite a confession. "Oh, if only those to whom, I know, my wild cry makes no sense could comprehend your soul; if only people could hear you in conversation, in heated debate, perhaps I could sketch for them your bright image, lit by your love of truth, your questing mind, your calm way of observing people." The simple directness of the words is an assurance of sincerity if not much else. But the music Musorgsky composed, before abandoning the song with some unknown proportion unwritten, is very far from simple. Suddenly, for this master of the graphic, unexpected dissonance and the vivid response to words and character, musical language has become an intensely concentrated expression of inner feeling, melodically and harmonically cohesive and process-driven, as if he had undertaken a crash study of Wagner's *Tristan und Isolde* or Liszt's "Vallée d'Obermann." As it stands, the song is in two parts, a dark, grief-stricken *lento lamentabile* in a highly chromatic E-flat minor, and a somewhat lighter, but still slow, section in G major (triggered by the "bright image" and the "love of truth"), ending on the dominant of that key. Probably Musorgsky intended a quasi-reprise of the *lento* but had difficulty envisaging a strong, as opposed to morose, conclusion. Or perhaps he became uneasy about the confessional aspect of the text. But even in its incomplete state, the "Graveside Letter" is one of his most moving, committed songs, and an intriguing complement to the not-yet-finished *Sunless* and its despairing lovelessness.

"The year 1874," Rimsky-Korsakov later wrote, "may be considered the start of Musorgsky's downfall."[3] It was, all the same, comparatively speaking an annus mirabilis for his music. He seemed to have acquired focus and an ability to work in a concentrated way. The same was hardly true of his fellow kuchkists. Rimsky-Korsakov was taken up with his new post inspecting navy bands; he spent the summer in Nikolayev in the southern Ukraine redesigning the port band and the spring and autumn teaching and pursuing his study of counterpoint and fugue. In Bakhchisaray, the ancient capital of the Crimean Khanate, he "first got to know so-called Oriental music in its natural state ... [and] was particularly struck by the apparently random beats of the big drum, out of time, which produced a marvellous effect."[4] But all year he composed hardly anything of his own until, at the very end of 1874 or early in 1875, he lost patience with fugal study and gave vent to a string quartet (in F major) which demonstrated, with a certain laborious self-satisfaction, his newfound mastery of imitative counterpoint, a technique that dominates every one of the four movements.

Not surprisingly, this work went down badly with Stasov and company. It must have justified their worst fears about Rimsky-Korsakov's various kinds of institutionalization: not only his newfound obsession with formal counterpoint, but even the (as one might suppose) harmless decision to write a string quartet, something that no member of the *kuchka* had ever risked before, and dangerous evidence of a capitulation to the Germanic tendencies of the conservatory. Borodin, who had also had a practically blank 1874, was probably only half-joking when he told Lyubov Karmalina that he had sketched a string quartet of his own "to the horror of Stasov and Modest [Musorgsky]."[5] But unlike Rimsky-Korsakov, whose quartet was completed long before its first performance at an RMS concert in November 1875, Borodin made only spasmodic progress on his A-major quartet and only finished it in 1879. His difficulties were the same as before. His administrative duties at the Academy of Science were, if anything, more arduous than ever after the retirement of the professor of chemistry, Nikolay Zinin, in 1874; he had his own teaching, and constantly took on gratuitous extra work, for instance the organizing of courses in medicine specifically for women, who were still not admitted as regular students. The decisive obstacle to his composing, however, had been his wife's, Yekaterina's, presence in St. Petersburg for the entire winter and spring of 1874. As usual, she kept her husband up half the night, ate supper at midnight, and slept till the middle of the afternoon, while he, of course, had to be at his academy desk at a normal time every morning. This timetable, moreover, can have done his health little good. He was twice ill in the early part of 1875, and the only good thing about that, as he told Karmalina, was that it gave him spare time to compose a little, and the act of composing made him feel better.[6]

In spite of this lifestyle, he had suddenly in October announced to Stasov his intention of resuming work on *Prince Igor,* nearly five years after definitively abandoning it. Stasov later reported that he had been talked into this decision by one of his music-loving academy pupils.[7] But perhaps he was in an operatic mood in any case after hearing and liking the first two acts of *Angelo* at Rimsky-Korsakov's a month or so earlier; or possibly he had been to hear the revival of Tchaikovsky's *Oprichnik* at the Maryinsky early in October, six months after its premiere in that same theatre. There is some perceptible common ground between Tchaikovsky's rich blend of lyrical arioso and ethnic Russiana in an epic historical context and what Borodin eventually made of Stasov's scenario for *Prince Igor.* One could add that Tchaikovsky's sometimes ramshackle dramaturgy would have made a questionable model for Borodin's. But alas, *Prince Igor* was not destined to achieve dramaturgy even in this specific, rounded sense.

The scenario that Stasov had handed over in 1869 was a detailed and reasonably coherent distillation from *The Lay of Igor's Host,* a typically rambling bardic poem rich in brothers, cousins, ancestors, lamenting wives, abducted maidens, blood-stained soil and rivers, and assorted birds of the air and beasts of the forest. At the core of the scenario is the tale of Igor, son of Sviatoslav, prince of Novgorod-Seversk, who sallies forth from the city of Putivl against the Don tribes, is defeated and captured together with his son, Vladimir, but in due course escapes (without Vladimir, who has fallen passionately in love with the daughter of their captor, Khan Konchak), and returns in somewhat qualified triumph to his grieving wife, Yaroslavna, who, in his absence, has had to endure the abuse of her debauched but ambitious brother, Vladimir Galitsky, and his henchmen.

From the composer's point of view, the beauty of this plot was that it offered a number of strong individual portraits, especially of Yaroslavna and of Konchak—an intriguing mixture of civility, fraternal warmth, and sheer bloody barbarism—against a broad backcloth of Russian history in both its epic and exotic modes. Its difficulty lay in a certain narrative vagueness and an almost total absence of dramatic stage action. In the lay, Igor's defeat and escape are culminating events in a long history of triumph and disaster amid the feuding of Russian princes and the incessant to-and-fro of battle, carnage, and rapine. But in Stasov, Igor has already departed on campaign, and the first time we meet him he is already a prisoner reduced to hanging his head and declining Konchak's offer of freedom on the unacceptable condition that he promise not to attack the Polovtsï any more. Even in escape, Igor is essentially a beaten character, and one who, unlike Musorgsky's Boris, lacks the psychological prehistory that might have given his defeat an authentically tragic meaning. The "triumph" of his return to Putivl is empty, not least because he has left his son in the arms of his enemy's daughter. To get round this problem, Stasov contrived an epilogue in which Vladimir and Konchakovna are married with spectacular operatic ceremony in Putivl. Borodin eventually discarded this idea, but without it the ending seems provisional and dramatically perfunctory. Vladimir is forgotten, Galitsky unpunished, the pagan Polovtsï victorious. Borodin might in due course have found a way of solving these problems. But his lifestyle and working method made that unlikely, and his sudden death at a fancy-dress ball in 1887 finally ruled it out.

Unlike Musorgsky composing *Boris Godunov*, Borodin seems never to have imagined *Prince Igor* as a whole. He made changes to the scenario as he went along. He devised a prologue in Putivl, in which Igor's departure on campaign is interrupted by an eclipse of the sun, throwing the city into a darkness that is at once interpreted as a divine omen, though whether good or evil no one can tell (in Stasov these events are merely related to Yaroslavna by a party of merchants bringing news of Igor's defeat). He introduced a comic element, along the lines of Musorgsky's vagrant monks, in the form of the gudok-players, Skula and Yeroshka, who support Galitsky but adroitly change sides on Igor's return.[8] But he never wrote or commissioned a libretto; he merely compiled text, number by number, as he needed it. And since his way of composing the music was to seize on individual characters or situations that happened to excite his interest at this or that moment, regardless of narrative sequence, it is hardly surprising that his legacy was a mess of incomplete and disconnected scenes, uncertain intentions, and amorphous drama. The remarkable fact is that, despite these apparently insuperable obstacles, what he did write includes some of the most brilliantly conceived, most superbly executed, most sheerly beautiful and thrilling music in any nineteenth-century opera, Russian or otherwise.

It had been like this almost from the outset. In opting to compose "Yaroslavna's Dream" in 1869 he had begun at the beginning of Stasov's scenario: Igor's wife brooding on her anxiety at his absence, on the menacing behavior of her brother, and on a frightening dream she has just had in which Igor is beside her, beckons her to follow him, but then fades away out of sight. But after this he had turned to the start of Stasov's second act in the Polovtsian camp and invented a song for Konchakovna, a call to her Russian lover, similar in idea but not style to the Pretender's invocation to Marina at the start of Musorgsky's second Polish scene. Clearly he was drawn by the emotional concentration of these two utterly different situations and personalities. Yaroslavna's song in its revised form of 1874–5 (based on material from Yaromir's scene with the High Priest in *Mlada*, itself possibly, though not certainly, derived from the now inaccessible Yaroslavna original) is a free-flowing, lyrical arioso, syllabic in setting, but of a character very different from the parlando style of *The Stone Guest* or *Boris Godunov*.[9]

The vocal line is effortless, tender, devoid of rhetoric, but carefully constructed around two or three simple melodic figures which seem to arise out of the nature of the voice at least as much as from the contours of the language. The harmony is flexible, mobile, but conventional; it converses with the voice, so to speak, but never imposes on it, never gesticulates.

Yaroslavna's femininity is distinct but unselfconscious. Konchakovna, by contrast, is entirely the Oriental seductress of the Western imagination. Her line is sensuous, chromatic, ornate, twisting and turning like the body of a snake dancer to the accompaniment of insinuating woodwind solos—oboe, then clarinet, then flutes (the orchestration here is by Borodin himself). This is the purest form yet of Stasovian Orientalism—purer, certainly, than anything in *Ruslan* (apart from a few woodwind swirls in the lezghinka), purer even than *Antar* or (so far as it yet existed) *Tamara*. Borodin's instant picture had been the drastic contrast between Western and Eastern sensibilities, and when he took the work up afresh in 1874 he pursued this idea. He wrote a chorus for the Polovtsian girls in Konchakovna's retinue, sinuous in melody like her cavatina, and rich in those augmented seconds which, in Western music, serve as an insignia of the mysterious East. He also wrote them a dance, wild and untamed, like some kind of Scythian tarantella, and then followed this up by sketching a sequence of choral dances for the girls and the men, music of such startling originality and vitality that it was destined to become perhaps the single most famous icon of Russian musical barbarism before Stravinsky's *Rite of Spring*. Finally, there is a brisk march for the victorious returning Polovtsian army, plainly modelled on Chernomor's march in *Ruslan and Lyudmila*.

This is all act 2 music in Stasov's scheme, but the precise order of composition is hard to establish, not least because Borodin still appears to be thinking in terms of set images, tableaux vivants, rather than dramatic narrative. He imagines Khan Konchak himself upbraiding Igor, in his rough, generous way, for declining to accept his captivity as a form of hospitality; Konchak's aria (largely based on the duet of Voyslava and Yaromir in *Mlada*) is a masterly portrait of offended masculine clubbability. But the composer also, a few months later, imagines Igor brooding on his captivity in a superb introspective monologue, also based on *Mlada*, especially the scene of the visitation of spirits (what Borodin called his *teney*, his "shadows" or "phantoms"), with its mysterious chromatics and bold vocal declamation. Unfortunately, Borodin allowed himself to be swayed by Stasov and company, who told him, as he reported to his wife, that the shadows "took on a completely different character in the new version, to the music's detriment."[10] So he dutifully discarded this whole monologue, and in due course replaced it with the more brilliant, extrovert aria that found its way into the eventual published score.

Meanwhile, there is a beautiful lament for Yaroslavna, intended for the start of the final act before Igor's unexpected reappearance in Putivl, and introducing for the first time the elegant tune that will later form the second subject of the overture and a vital component of Igor's aria in act 2, earlier in the work but several years ahead in the sequence of composition. Many of these items are listed by Borodin, in a letter of April 1875 to Lyubov Karmalina, as work composed or at least drafted while officially off sick. "But I'm at a loss as to when I'll manage to complete it all The summer's my only hope. But in the summer I have to finish orchestrating the second symphony, which I promised to deliver ages ago and, to my shame, haven't done so yet." He is also supposed to be making a piano reduction of the symphony for the publisher, Vasily Bessel. And then there's the string quartet . . .[11]

Under all these circumstances, it is hardly surprising that *Prince Igor* was, and was to remain, an episodic work, vivid in its portraiture of emotional moments and its colorful, spectacular tableaux, but largely devoid of narrative coherence or psychological development. Igor is the sorrowful chieftain, Konchak the violent, openhearted barbarian, Yaroslavna the abandoned queen in her tower, Galitsky the incorrigible scoundrel, and so forth. Skula and Yeroshka change, admittedly; but changeability is their set character. Even within individual acts, it is possible to arrange the musical numbers in a variety of orders without noticeably damaging their continuity. Borodin did not think through or forward. He responded to flashes of inspiration; and certainly inspiration hardly ever failed him. The consistent quality of the music is astonishing. How was it possible for a man clever and gifted enough to do original research in a field as complex as organic chemistry, and sufficiently focused to run a major scientific faculty in one of Europe's main capital cities, also to compose music on an ambitious scale that regularly meets the highest standards of invention and often, indeed, of method? For we should not pretend that Borodin's amateurism extended to his technique. Within the demands of what he wrote, he wrote well, with style and a certain polish, a fine ear, and unfailing good taste. He seems to have understood his own limitations; whether from choice or circumstance, he avoided complexities in the way he conceived his music. His symphonies are direct, incisive, strongly gestural works, rather than profound or in any sense "difficult." His string quartets, as we shall see, are lyrical, beautiful but in the best sense weightless, even when they venture, as the first does, into fugal territory. None of this is work that embraces the late-classical German concept of instrumental music as an intellectual or profoundly spiritual exercise; nor does his writing for voice explore the borderlands of human experience, as Musorgsky's does. Radical elements there are. The violent ostinato writing of the Polovtsian Dances may hark back to the Glinka of *Kamarinskaya* or the Oriental dances in *Ruslan,* but it goes far beyond him in sheer Dionysian power. The Orientalisms in *Prince Igor* may be essentially decorative, but for as long as they last they involve the whole music, not just one component of it. In the end, though, what Borodin composed of his opera shows that he was driven, not by any theory of what kind of music a Russian composer ought to be writing in the year of grace 1874, but by the simple desire to create artistic beauty. In the end this is, after all, a classical impulse, and at bottom somewhat remote from the kuchkist enthusiasm for the real, the eccentric, the ugly, and the true.

Musorgsky, meanwhile, had been turning his attention once again to *Khovanshchina* and was at last beginning to think in terms of a coherent scenario, though, like Borodin, he seems not to have thought of writing anything of the kind down on paper. In true *kuchka* fashion he had told Polixena Stasova back in the summer of 1873 that "the opening moments of the action are ready, but not written down," while filling his letters—to her and Vladimir Stasov—with reflections on the immolation scene in the final act, and actually composing music for Marfa and Susanna in act 3. Now, however, in 1874, he starts to think through the first act as a whole, and by the summer of 1875 he is able to announce to Stasov—far away in Paris at a geographical congress—that "the first act of *our Khovanshchina* is finished."[12] If so, it was no mean achievement. Audiences have always had difficulties with the narrative thread of this opera; but the difficulties were there from the start and were clearly felt by the composer.

The key figure in the drama is Peter the Great; but he, as we saw, could not be represented on the stage, nor (for the same reason) could the other controlling character, Peter's half sister, Sofia, who acted as regent for seven years (1682–9) of the dual sovereignty of Peter (who was ten in 1682) and his older, but feeble-minded, half brother, Ivan. It was as if Handel had had to compose *Giulio Cesare* without Julius Caesar, or Mozart *Don Giovanni* without the Don. In spite of the law, there had been an intention to include the two rulers; but in the end practical good sense prevailed.

The main *dramatis personae* in Musorgsky's opera relate to one another by way of the throne or its agents, and their behavior is hard to understand in its absence. To recapitulate: at the start of the first act we meet various members of the imperial guard, the so-called streltsy, and later we meet their commander, the brutish, reactionary but popular Prince Ivan Khovansky. The streltsy were technically in the service of the crown, but with two tsars and a regent they had assumed what might euphemistically be termed a roving commission. They had supported the diarchy of Ivan and Peter and had set Sophia up as regent. But there was a subtext. The Orthodox hierarchy had wanted the intelligent Peter as sole ruler, and Khovansky's support of Ivan went with a rooted opposition to the church reforms of Patriarch Nikon. Khovansky was hardly an Old Believer of the self-immolating variety, but rather, perhaps, a Russian seventeenth-century equivalent of the twentieth-century defenders of the Latin mass, who resented having to abandon the religious practices of a lifetime. At the end of Musorgsky's first act, he meekly accepts the elder Dosifey's authority, like a schoolboy obeying his headmaster, but only for as long as he is in his sight.

Before Khovansky, we meet the boyar Shaklovity, who commissions the official Scribe to write out a proclamation denouncing the Khovanskys (Ivan and his son, Andrey) as agitators and traitors. Shaklovity is a shadowy figure in Musorgsky's drama. He seems to act (like his historical self) on behalf of the regent, who in fact had Khovansky executed in 1682 on the pretext that he sought the crown and was using the streltsy in support of that aim. But Shaklovity also appears, later in the opera, as the voice of suffering Russia, like the *yurodivy* in *Boris Godunov,* which would, if anything, argue support for Peter, who was widely regarded as the best hope for political stability.

In all this one detects the influence of the historian (Stasov) more than the dramatist (Musorgsky). The amount of open-ended factual detail, though vivid and fascinating in itself, constantly threatens to choke the narrative. Before the end of the first act we have also encountered Andrey Khovansky, a young Lutheran girl called Emma, and the ambiguous invented figure of Marfa, an Old Believer whose piety is colored from start to finish by a blighted passion for Andrey. The fact that Musorgsky made Marfa a contralto has sometimes led to her representation as a dowdy middle-aged woman. But Stasov had thought of her as "a Potiphar's wife," youthful and passionate, and Musorgsky had imagined her as a boyarina—Princess Sitskaya, "who has run away from 'the top,' that is from the stuffy incense and the feather-beds of the terem," a character reminiscent of the boyarina Morozova in Vasily Surikov's famous painting.[13] In another letter to Stasov he describes her as "a complete, strong, and loving woman [we perhaps recall Musorgsky's own preference for women of a certain age] . . . an extremely sensual but at the same time passionate alto."[14] Stasov had grumbled about Marfa and Dosifey (Prince Mïshetzky) "being *downgraded aristocrats.*"

> What is this in the end but *an opera of princes,* while you were always specifically planning an opera of the *people.*[15] Who finally out of all your characters will not be a *prince* or an *aristocrat,* who will be directly *from the people?* No, no, I strongly protest with all my might and . . . I implore you that they should both of them abhor every kind of aristocracy and remember it with due hostility. Let them both be *genuine people from the soil,* from the izba, from the village and the field, from the plow and the distaff, from hard, oppressive labor and with callused hands. That's what will be more interesting and better!"[16]

Musorgsky agreed, rather lamely. But he made no significant change, and while Marfa and Dosifey ended up untitled, they are also, one feels, uncallused.

Despite the eventful and somewhat diffuse nature of the first act, work on the music was at last, in the early part of 1875, going well. In fact it was probably for this reason that by April Musorgsky was announcing to Karmalina that he had given up the idea of a Gogol opera, though he told her (and may actually have believed) that it was because of "the impossibility of a Great Russian posing as a Little Russian [that is, a Ukrainian], and consequently the impossibility of mastering of the Little Russian recitative."[17] *Khovanshchina* was turning out in many respects like a continuation of the Kromy scene in *Boris.* It had the same proto-cinematic character, the same swift sequencing, the same skillful manipulation of small and large blocks of people, the same sharpness of portraiture, the same rough violence. As in *Boris,* the chorus sometimes splits up into groups who converse with each other and discuss courses of action; at other times they come together and sing as a collective. Musorgsky's handling of this kind of discourse is as brilliant as ever. The whole scene in which the newly arrived settlers from Muscovy bully the Scribe into reading the pillar inscription, with its string of denunciations, then systematically dismantle his booth, is a masterly example of the kind of choral montage that Musorgsky had first invented for the Novodevichy and St. Basil's scenes in the original *Boris*. At the climax of this scene, the chorus (all male at this point) come together in what amounts to a chorale, as in a Bach Passion, reflecting on the sufferings of Mother Russia from internal strife, just as the distant trumpets of the streltsy announce the approach of Khovansky, one of the chief engineers of that strife.

Splendid as such moments are, both as music and as dramatic spectacle, they cannot altogether make up for the lack of a clear narrative thread in the libretto of this act as a whole. Shaklovity's scene with the Scribe is an exciting vignette, but since the subject of their conversation (the proclamation against the Khovanskys) leads nowhere without the character of the tsar or the regent, it remains dramatically unexplained. Khovansky's entrance is likewise a thrilling set piece; but one needs expert knowledge of Russian history to grasp the basis of his popular support, and when his son bursts on to the stage, not as a participant in the "Khovansky trouble"—the *Khovanshchina* of the title—but in crude pursuit of the young Lutheran girl, the audience may well begin to wonder where the focus of the drama is meant to lie. Finally the appearance of Marfa adds one further layer of narrative and psychological complexity to an already sufficiently intricate weave. Stepping between Andrey and Emma, she upbraids him for his infidelity to her, yet talks in mystic language about her aching heart "divining the pronouncement of fate" and seeing "in the heavens a marvellous dwelling radiant with light." With Marfa we understand that physical passion has transmogrified into a metaphysical impulse; but again the context is ambiguous, since Andrey is presented as a young man of uncontrolled sexual appetite prepared to have his way, if necessary, through extreme violence. This conflict of motivation will remain a problem to the very end of the opera. Here it is resolved temporarily by the calming influence of Dosifey, the third solo bass in the act (after Shaklovity and Khovansky). But Dosifey is not only a moderating force, as we shall discover in the second act.

By the end of July 1875 Musorgsky had composed the whole of act 1 in piano score (he never orchestrated any of it), and was soon hard at work on act 2. This brought a complete change of tone. We are in the house of Prince Vasily Golitsïn, chief minister to the regent Sofia and also her lover, as is revealed by the letter from her that he is reading as the curtain rises. Unlike the Old Believers and reactionaries of the first act, Golitsïn is a self-consciously modern thinker, a Westernizing sophisticate, social reformer, enemy of serfdom. The suave introduction seems to portray him as a gentleman of cosmopolitan taste and good breeding, but this is soon exposed as a mere cloak for a rough Russian temper and a manner scarcely less bullying than that of the Khovanskys or Shaklovity. He receives a series of visitors. A Lutheran pastor comes to complain about Andrey Khovansky's harassment of Emma and to ask Golitsïn to permit the building of a new church in the German quarter. Next Marfa appears and, for no clear reason, offers to tell the prince's fortune, a piece of mumbo-jumbo that seems out of tune with her Christian piety, but was presumably included so that Musorgsky could use up the one piece of music he had composed for his abortive Gogol opera *The Landless Peasant* five years before. To both these visitors Golitsïn reacts with a degree of violence. "Have you gone mad?" he yells at the pastor. "Do you want to build over the whole of Russia with your churches?" And Marfa's somewhat negative view of Golitsïn's future provokes a still more poisonous response; as she leaves, he instructs his servant to follow her and drown her in the marsh. It is no surprise, therefore, that when Khovansky arrives to discuss Golitsïn's recent annulment of certain aristocratic privileges, the conversation rapidly becomes a quarrel, a quarrel into which Dosifey himself soon intrudes and to which he contributes with an attack on Golitsïn's "foreign schooling" and an invitation to "lead your Teutons against us with their diabolical army" (a sentiment that no doubt came straight from Musorgsky's own heart). Eventually the quarrel is interrupted by Marfa, who has somehow escaped murder with the help of a troop of the tsar's youth guard, and by Shaklovity, announcing an attempted coup by the Khovanskys in the nearby estate-village of Izmaylovo.

Throughout 1875 one has the impression of an intense labor of composition, the outcome of which was more than an hour of high-quality music, whatever the dramatic problems encountered—and to some extent left unsolved—along the way. Musorgsky had even found time to write what turned out to be most of a superb new song cycle to words again by Kutuzov. By the end of the year he claimed to have completed the opera's second act (of five), and to be embarking on the third, which, he told Stasov, was "in waiting [and] will be easy now." But that proved unduly optimistic. True, the first part of the act, with Marfa's love song and her altercation with Susanna, was already written (the song was even in print). But after composing the chorus of Old Believers that precedes the song, the intervention (yet again) of Dosifey—this time defending Marfa against Susanna—and Shaklovity's aria lamenting Russia's fate at the hands of her enemies within and without, he found his attention drawn back to certain unresolved difficulties in act 2. The scene with the pastor was, it seems, as yet unwritten or for some reason unsatisfactory. Above all, the final scene lacked an ending. Musorgsky now wanted it to be a quintet for Marfa, the tenor Golitsïn, and the three basses, but was balking at the intractable combination of voices. He eventually planned to write it "under Rimsky-Korsakov's supervision." But in the end he never wrote it at all.

These problems, in any case, were as nothing to the objections Stasov suddenly came up with in a long, painstaking, and deeply dispiriting letter he wrote to his younger colleague in May 1876.[18] He was, he said, very happy with the first act of *Khovanshchina,* but profoundly unhappy with act 2. Marfa's two appearances, he said, were completely pointless, and the quarrel between Golitsïn and Khovansky utterly irrelevant to the rest of the opera. To tell the truth, he remarked with an almost sadistic lack of sensitivity, "this whole act (*us libretto*) might as well be thrown out, and the opera would lose nothing by this in terms of plot." He took equal exception to act 3 as it stood, where he admitted there were "choruses and songs . . . and superb music, but neither action nor interest of any sort." There was also, he added, "no connection of any kind with the rest of the opera." Being Vladimir Stasov, he naturally had concrete alternatives to propose. He produced a completely new scenario for these two acts which would have enabled Musorgsky to recycle a good deal of the existing music, albeit in a radically reorganized and to some considerable extent recomposed form. An act he had regarded as near enough finished, and another that was quite fully planned, would suddenly have to be rethought. Stasov's criticisms were of course correct (though it might be argued that his alternative version was only marginally an improvement). But what seems not to have occurred to him, well though he knew Musorgsky, was the ease with which the wind could be taken out of those merrily flapping but all too loosely rigged sails. After a longish pause, the composer replied humbly and with only the faintest hint of an epistolary pout. "For some while," he confessed, "but long enough, Musoryanin has been subject to certain doubts, misgivings, suspicions and all these *tutti quanti* of one's leisure time . . . *Khovanshchina* is too big, too unusual a task. You, *généralissime,* I'm convinced, did not suppose that your remarks and suggestions had been taken by me in any un-Musoryanin way. *I have suspended work—I have taken thought,* and now, and yesterday, and weeks ago, and tomorrow are all thought."[19]

Somehow work on act 3 staggered on. Excerpts were played at Stasov's and Shestakova's, plans were announced, suggestions made. But not till the last year of his life did Musorgsky again achieve the intensity of work on the opera that, had he kept going in 1876, might have brought this ramshackle masterpiece to a proper and early conclusion. And, whatever he may have told Stasov, he adopted none of his suggestions.

The eventual failure to complete *Khovanshchina* was nearly as great a disaster as Borodin's failure with *Prince Igor*: at least in the end Musorgsky composed most of his piano score, and left the work in more or less comprehensible shape as a whole. There was no need for the frantic shuffling of bits of paper, the desperate speculation about what music went with what action, the ransacking of memories of play-throughs, and the composing of whole scenes "in the style of" that were necessary to make Borodin's work even remotely stageable. It's true that Rimsky-Korsakov did in fact compose whole stretches of music for *Khovanshchina,* did in fact change almost every bar of Musorgsky's score, as well as performing the essential task of orchestrating (or, less essential, reorchestrating) it all. But this was because of his opinion that Musorgsky, for all his undoubted genius, was incompetent to the point where his artistic intentions were constantly blocked by his lack of technique. "A lot had to be redone, shortened, and extended," he reported in his memoirs. "In Acts I and II there turned up much that was superfluous, ugly as music, and a drag on the action."[20] The idea that these two acts were musically on so consistently high a level that to change them at all amounted to a kind of sacrilege would have been beyond the comprehension of this brilliantly gifted but at bottom conventional-minded musician.

In *Sunless,* Musorgsky had evolved a new kind of lyrical style that drew on the realist manner of *Boris* and *The Nursery* but adapted it to the requirements of poetry that was inward and reflective rather than visual or theatrical. *Khovanshchina* continues this exploration in a variety of different ways. "I'm working," he told Stasov, "on human speech [and] I've arrived at a melody created by this speech, I've arrived at an embodiment of recitative in melody . . . I should like to call it intelligent justified melody."[21] And he cites an example from the third act: Marfa's confession to Dosifey of her "sinful" love for Andrey ("The terrible torment of my love"—"Strashnaya pïtka lyubov moya"), which he claims to be "something alien to classical melody (so much loved), but at once understandable by each and every one."[22] On the face of it the distinction might seem rather fine. The prose text is laid over a metrically regular melody, with the aid of some discreet melismatic ornamentation, which helps stretch the words to the bar lengths, a normal enough classical procedure, but one usually applied to verse texts. The melody moves by step, while the harmony at first reflects the torment in Marfa's soul (tense diminished-seventh chords in a very unsettled E-flat minor), then relaxes into the static calm of D-flat major as Marfa pleads for release in death, at which point the two-plus-two structure of the phrases expands into a more generous three-plus-three. All this is beautifully managed, but hardly seems likely to cause the river Neva to burst its banks. In fact there are similar things even in the original, austere *Boris,* notably the *yurodivy*'s song, but also Xenia's lament at the start of the first version of the Kremlin scene. Meanwhile, there is still plenty in *Khovanshchina* that employs the arioso style of its predecessor—for instance, much of Shaklovity's scene with the Scribe in act 1, or the Scribe's altercation with the Muscovite settlers just afterward, a scene that Rimsky-Korsakov thought "extremely unmusical" and removed bodily from his edition.

The difference is essentially a matter of emphasis. *Boris* had been cast mainly as a series of relatively compact tableaux, whereas *Khovanshchina* has at the outset more the feel of a grand opera with stage spectacle mixed in with confrontations of individuals. The first three tableaux of *Boris* last, between them, about as long as act 1 of *Khovanshchina,* and it may be partly for this reason that the discourse in the later opera seems wider-ranging and more varied, not always, it must be said, to its advantage dramaturgically. Musically, though, this sense of elongation goes with a noticeable enrichment of the lyrical element, which, after all, had been largely absent from the original *Boris.* In the revised version of that opera a change is already noticeable, not so much in the extra songs, which are charming but add nothing much to the language, as in the music for Marina and the Pretender in the Polish act. Kromy is not lyrical in this sense (apart from the *yurodivy,* pasted in from the old St. Basil's scene), but it does, as we saw, foretell the broad, cinematic sequencing of events that characterizes much of *Khovanshchina* but not, to the same extent, the rest of *Boris Godunov.*

The ingredients, though, are not dissimilar. The *Khovanshchina* chorus still chatters polyphonically, then breaks periodically into collective prayer or lamentation or greeting, couched in the form of harmonized chant or folk song. Compare the people's pleading for bread in the St. Basil's scene of *Boris* with the Muscovites' lament for Mother Russia in the first act of *Khovanshchina,* or the chorus of pilgrims in the prologue of *Boris* with the chorus of Old Believers at the end of act 2 of *Khovanshchina.* A change in discourse is more noticeable in the big choral greeting of Khovansky in act 1, which not only has a broader sweep than anything in *Boris* outside Kromy but also expands by way of clear thematic connections into the music for Khovansky himself and then a ceremonious choral version of that music. This is followed by a most un-*Boris*-like trio for Emma, Andrey, and Marfa, culminating in a brief but very grand ensemble reprise of the Khovansky music. All this has a Meyerbeerish feel that we noticed also in Kromy and that will eventually color the later acts of *Khovanshchina* as well.

As for the more conversational act 2, from the start an intimate, almost lyrical note is struck in Golitsïn's reading of the regent Sofia's letter with its recollections of their past love. But this is still within the compass of the arioso style, involving mainly syllabic word setting and the voice part laid out freely over a metrically regular accompaniment. The genius of this style is shown by the way Musorgsky adapts it to characterize the different personages who enter Golitsïn's drawing room, even to depict different sides of his and their personalities. The music of this act has been considered dull; but as the dramatization of conflict between individuals it is anything but dull. Notice, for instance, Golitsïn's proneness—for all his supposed cosmopolitanism—to outbursts of embittered patriotism (a motivic element much weakened by the cuts often made in this act); notice, too, the difference of pace between the mercurial, quick-tempered Golitsïn and the rougher, earthier Khovansky, and also how Musorgsky underlines Khovansky's barrack-room simplicity by frequently accompanying him in bare unison octaves, just as he outlines Dosifey's cloistral placidness in *religioso* block harmony, at least until the old Raskolnik is goaded into sarcastic mockery by Golitsïn's dismissal of "the old ways."

The biggest anomaly of this act is that Golitsïn, having been set up as such a strong figure, effectively vanishes from the opera hereafter. The next biggest is Marfa herself. Stasov wanted to make her Golitsïn's mistress, no doubt in the same spirit as certain stage directors who have wanted to imply that she has been Dosifey's. But we may feel relieved that Musorgsky ignored the former suggestion (and perhaps never thought of the latter). Marfa is nevertheless the most interesting figure in the whole opera, and the hardest to pin down. Her music does have a certain mournful sensuality, and it could be from this quality that Musorgsky drew his concept of intelligently justified melody, which might just as well be thought of as speech-song rendered poetic. Unfortunately the difficult gestation of the work's later acts may have prevented him from developing this intriguing idea into a fully evolved operatic language. As it stands, in Marfa's music and, perhaps, in Shaklovity's act 3 aria, it looks not much different from well-formed lyrical writing of the kind that came spontaneously to Borodin, with the one, perhaps important, qualification that, as previously in *Marriage,* Musorgsky was working with a prose text, something that was still rare on the operatic stage.

There will be more to say about both *Khovanshchina* and *Prince Igor,* but nothing more will happen that will turn either of them into a complete or satisfactory entity. Both remained dramaturgically disordered works, with characters who come and go, scenes that make no sense, confrontations that hang in space, unmotivated and unresolved. Both have powerful situations that might belong to the greatest operas ever written. And both have music of such brilliance that merely to think about them is to feel excitement tinged with a painful regret. If *Boris Godunov* and *Maid of Pskov* had shown the kuchkist ideal as an authentic route to great music, these two successors reveal the depressing consequences of what Musorgsky had called *rasseyannost',* distractability, a quality that was, alas, ingrained in the kuchkist mentality.

CHAPTER 24

Dances of Death

The circle had continued to meet, at Shestakova's, at Borodin's, or at the Stasovs' city apartments or their dacha at Pargolovo, among the lakes and low hills to the north of the capital. But it was more and more difficult to see it as a coherent group. Part of the trouble now was Rimsky-Korsakov's defection to academe, and his typically uncompromising attempts to fill the gaps in his technical equipment and theoretical knowledge by spending most of the summer of 1875 composing fugues. Musorgsky, in particular, was scathing about such activities.

> *Oh that his ink had dried up quite,*
> *Before it helped the quill to write!*

he versified viciously to Stasov.[1] Then, a month later to Kutuzov: "Artistic truth can't tolerate predetermined forms; life is varied and often capricious."[2] "Is it possible," he eventually demanded of Stasov, "that remembering the *past* will fail to disturb his [Rimsky-Korsakov's] log-like slumber; if only one living thought were to slip into the cerebellum (that needs it) and down as far as the heels (that need it). Repentance is a great thing. The trouble is that repentance is inaccessible to Talmudists, they are too strong on the dead letter of the law, too soullessly enslaved."[3] But Rimsky-Korsakov was no longer his sole target. As a member (ironically enough) of the music panel convened to report to the Imperial Theatres directorate on Cui's *Angelo* in the spring of 1875, he had written with loyal enthusiasm about its "remarkable musical charms" and the "astounding impression" likely to be produced by its act 2 and act 3 finales. But privately he reacted coolly when Cui played the third act over at Shestakova's in September. "It's so-so; it'll do," he remarked laconically to Kutuzov; and to Stasov, "when will these people, instead of their *fugues and obligatory* third acts, glance into sensible books and converse in their pages with sensible people?" Even *Prince Igor* was not completely spared. "In the amalgam of Borodin's very sympathetic, dramatic work," he assured Kutuzov, "there's a lecture: you, as an artist, will sense this in a flash. I hope you've understood me: Borodin instructs his heroes to form conclusions from a collision of facts and accidents—as you like, it's all the same. However likeable the composition—the listener has no option, but only: 'roll up, gents, and see the wild beasts.'"[4]

Amid all the obscurities and periphrases, one detects a problem that is at least partly Musorgsky's own. Up to the time of *Boris Godunov*, his musical thinking had essentially been driven by circle doctrine, by Stasov's theories of Russianness and Balakirev's negative attitude to the music profession and musical convention in general. In *Boris* itself he had, almost without noticing, begun to pursue his own course, ungoverned by other people's (or his own) theories or polemical ideas; and since *Boris* he had moved farther away, and in a direction that could scarcely have been predicted under the tenets, such as they were, of kuchkism. Suddenly his sense of the thrust of his own art has made him acutely aware of its difference from the art of others. After all, it is unbelievable that, in the sixties, he had simply failed to notice that Cui was a limited composer of a fundamentally orthodox gift, that Rimsky-Korsakov was a hardworking, methodical craftsman for whom productivity came before aesthetic posturing, and that Borodin's was a lyrical, melodic talent that would stand or fall on its response to emotion and the exotic, and was hardly suited to the meticulous psychological portraiture that Musorgsky wanted to cultivate. The only big thing these composers had ever had in common was that at a certain time, they had cleaved to one another as Russian musicians to whom Russia did not cater. Now suddenly this all became clear to him, and casting around for an explanation, he found it in Balakirev's disappearance. "Held by Balakirev's iron gauntlet," he fantasized to Stasov,

> they began to breathe with his mighty lungs (if not with all his powerful chest), and set themselves tasks that would have troubled great men. Balakirev's iron gauntlet was released, and they felt weary, in need of rest; where to find this rest? In tradition, of course ... The "Mighty

Heap" have degenerated into soulless traitors; the "lash" has proved to be a child's whip. Anyone more indifferent to the essence of life, more unnecessary to contemporary creativity than these artists, I think you will not find anywhere *in the Celestial Empire*.[5]

What, though, had been these heroic tasks? An opera or two, a symphony here, an overture there, a few songs, some piano pieces. The real heroism, surely, was here and now, in *Khovanshchina,* in the Gogol opera he was half-planning, and in the settings of Kutuzov's verse, which were presenting new challenges for which neither kuchkism nor Kutuzov's own somewhat blinkered view of Musorgsky's art offered much guidance. Suddenly he seems afflicted by artistic loneliness. It shows in his complaints; and it shows in his behavior.

The Maly Yaroslavets provided him with one form of escape. But there were others. He began to appear frequently in concerts, especially charity evenings, as a piano accompanist, often in music that, in his moments of aesthetic moralizing, he would have regarded with contempt. Unfortunately, he was an excellent pianist, a quick and adept sight reader, and a responsive partner who seemed able to pick up the nuances of a singer's interpretation at a moment's notice. Various stories were told about his ability to perform competently, without rehearsal, even when far gone in drink. As a result he was in constant demand, and seems rarely to have refused. "Generally speaking," the physician Vasily Bertenson recalls, "no charity concert took place without Musorgsky. The musical evenings in the seventies that were organized annually by the students of all the institutions of higher education for the benefit of their needy comrades, were unthinkable without his participation. Modest Petrovich was a superb accompanist of singers. Himself as poor as Job, where charity concerts were concerned he would never accept money for his work."[6]

Then there was his employment at the Forestry Department, which occupied a substantial part of each day, however much or little of his mental energy it may have absorbed. In March 1875 he was promoted to "senior chief of Section III," a very doubtful distinction which landed him with the task of looking after the office in the not infrequent absence of his immediate superior, a man called Voluyev (promptly corrupted by Stasov into "Kholuyev"—"the lackey"), who seems to have been the worst kind of rule-bound bureaucrat and who was perhaps behind what Musorgsky, at the end of the year, called "a vulgar little intrigue [that] has been got up against me at the Ministry."[7] One can well imagine the mixed feelings, of boredom, dread, and relief, with which he put away his manuscripts every day at noon and departed to push a pen and shuffle papers for several hours in his government office.

Finally, there was the issue of his accommodation. After being shut out of Kutuzov's apartment at the end of July, he turned up at five o'clock in the morning at the apartment of his Maly Yaroslavets friend Pavel Naumov on Vasilevsky Island, and effectively billeted himself on him and his common-law wife, Maria Fyodorova. "As you know," he explained to Kutuzov, "I am afraid to stay *alone*." "I've liked very much being at Naumov's," he went on, "particularly in the summer: the garden, the wide street, the Neva nearby. Visitors . . . good conversation, sometimes music; all kinds of news, gossip, and chitchat—you live, breathe, and work."[8] Naumov was famously good company, a bon vivant living on a naval pension and that of a deceased, rich wife (Maria's sister), art- and music-loving, and generally free and easy in his ways, as is borne out by his openly living with his sister-in-law after his wife's death. Musorgsky got on well with them both, and even dedicated to Maria Fyodorova a song "Misunderstood" ("Neponyatnaya") that seems to defend her against the aspersions and even, perhaps, ostracism of Naumov's respectable friends. Unfortunately, the song is nondescript and does the lady no very notable favors.

Naumov himself was in many respects an agreeable distraction. And for the same reason his influence was feared, no doubt rightly, by those who set store by Musorgsky's ability to concentrate on his composition. Three years later, when he was still living with Naumov and was causing his musical friends extreme anxiety, Lyudmila Shestakova confided in Vladimir Stasov: "It's too bad about Musorgsky, he's such a wonderful person! If there were only some way to pull him away from Naumov, I think he might be rescued definitely . . ."[9]

In 1875, few yet understood the depth or extent of this danger. Musorgsky was drinking and easily distracted from his music, true enough; but the music he was actually producing seemed to belie the ill effects of his lifestyle. At Naumov's he rapidly finished off the first act of *Khovanshchina,* and by the end of the year he had also completed the first draft of act 2. But even before the move, he had composed a set of songs that, in retrospect, show his music to be moving into a new and powerful phase that might, had he lived longer, have led on to operatic work of even greater range and power than *Boris Godunov.*

At this stage there were only three *Songs and Dances of Death,* as the cycle was eventually christened. But in scale and emotional weight they were the equivalent of twice that number. It's worth comparing these six-minute pocket dramas with the music being written by Musorgsky's colleagues. Rimsky-Korsakov had spent the year studying counterpoint and composing fugues and canons. He described his activities in a letter to Tchaikovsky:

> Having gone through all the species of counterpoint during the winter, as well as imitation and a bit of canon on a cantus firmus, I have gone on to fugue and canon. This summer I wrote 61 fugues (long and short, strict and free, in 2, 3, 4, and 5 voices, with and without chorales), 5 canonic variations on one chorale, 3 variations on another, and several embellished chorales.[10]

This was not quite like the study of Bach famously made at certain stages of their careers by Mozart or Beethoven or Schubert, the effects of which are immediately and powerfully apparent in their own music Rimsky-Korsakov's contrapuntal studies were, it seems, strictly directed toward teaching. He understandably disliked the idea of a professor of composition who did not know the mechanics of his art, just as he disliked the thought of a professor of instrumentation who did not know instruments. Accordingly he set out to correct both deficiencies in himself. That he did not regard this work as artistically significant is apparent from the pieces he allowed to be published; for instance, the Six Piano Fugues, op. 17, are, as he claims in his autobiography, "successful," but only in the sense that they are proper fugues expertly worked. Musically they are quite impersonal and without profile.[11] And the same can almost be said, as we saw, of the F-major string quartet, which is so cluttered with imitative counterpoint that one might be listening to a demonstration rather than a piece of music.

Cui, on the other hand, since finishing *Angelo,* had been writing songs. There are two sets of six, settings of Heine, Pushkin, Alexey Tolstoy, and others. But while some of the songs are attractive, they scarcely step outside the range of the conventional drawing-room romance (in a few cases in the first set, op. 9, they barely even aspire that high); and the rare instances of harmonic daring are apt, as before with Cui, to look like poor judgment, the product of an imprecise ear rather than an adventurous mind. Looking at these songs, Rimsky-Korsakov's fugues, and the character—if not the quality—of much of *Prince Igor,* one might be forgiven for wondering what was so special about the *kuchka,* at a time when Wagner was finishing *Götterdämmerung,* Brahms his C-minor symphony, Bizet his *Carmen.* Verdi's *Aïda* appeared on the Maryinsky stage for the first time in November 1875 and earned mildly ironic praise from Musorgsky for "[outdoing] everything, everyone, even himself. He has done for *Trovatore*, Mendelssohn, Wagner—practically Amerigo Vespucci. The spectacle is wonderful, and fabulously impotent in the personification (with reminiscences!) of the tooth-grinding African blood."[12] For the psychologist of *Boris, The Nursery*, or, now, the quarrel at Golitsïn's house, this was an empty kind of splendor. But if he was struggling with the ensembles in *Khovanshchina* (the trio in act I, and the unwritten quintet in act 2), a genre at which Verdi excelled, he could show his dramatic mettle in a form of songwriting that went beyond anything in the recent Western concert repertoire and would hardly be out of place on the operatic stage.

The *Songs and Dances of Death* in fact draw to some extent on an earlier Western model, cultivated by Schubert and Loewe, among others: the narrative ballad. Musical storytelling, with or without reflective interludes, was of course an ancient tradition, linked to the public recounting of heroic tales or topical news or propaganda. The ballad singer was essentially a channel for the information he conveyed. Graham Johnson has described Schubert's approach to the ballad in terms that might well be applied also to Musorgsky: "It seems," he writes, "that in composing ballads Schubert enjoyed playing the somewhat distanced role of camera operator (also responsible for lighting, costumes and crowd scenes) as opposed to leading man, as in his own lieder productions (where the poet is of course co-director)."[13] In its original incarnation, moreover, ballad singing was often associated with dance, as the name suggests (the root is the same as for "ballet"). Schubert's ballads tend to be very long, rambling affairs, recitative interspersed with lyrical song, and with frequent changes of mood and angle, like the different emotions and voices one puts on when telling a fairy story to a child. But there are compact examples, of which the most famous by far is "Erlkönig," a dance of death if ever there was one. When August von Gymnich sang "Erlkönig" and other songs at a private concert in Vienna in 1820, a reviewer observed that Schubert "knows how to paint in sound, and these songs surpass in the truthfulness of their characterization anything else in the world of Lieder."[14] He, too, might have been talking about Musorgsky.

Like "Erlkönig," each of Musorgsky's ballads (the description is mine, not his) tells a story that ends in a death, or, in one final case, celebrates multiple deaths: the sick child lulled into a sleep from which there is no awakening; the dying girl serenaded by Death in the person of "an unknown knight with miraculous powers"; the drunken peasant who falls asleep in a snowstorm; the battlefield patrolled by Death as a military commander whose troops are the dead soldiers. The poems, like those of *Sunless,* are by Kutuzov, but the idea was Stasov's, or so he claims in his biography of the composer.[15] The beauty of the concept, of course, was that it was open-ended. Kutuzov had listed the project as "Dances of Death: Scenes from Russian Life"; and you could imagine a whole series of different scenes ending in death: the monk in his cell, with distant bells; the returning political exile drowning in sight of his home shore; and any number of others. Kutuzov wrote out a list of twelve topics, of which Musorgsky composed and wrote down three, though he certainly composed at least two others that he never put on paper. The fourth surviving song, "The Commander" ("Polkovodets"), added in 1877, is not on Kutuzov's list of topics.

In his valuable study of the composer, David Brown calls the first song, "Lullaby" ("Kolïbel'naya"), "Musorgsky's last truly realist song." While true in a sense, this seems to me to miss a point. The obvious difference between "Lullaby" and the other three songs is that it is not a dance, but a ballad in the Schubert manner, in many sections and many tempi, alternating recitative with the songlike lullabying, not of the mother (who spends her time trying to push Death away), but of Death himself. The picture, certainly, is vividly truthful in the same way that the songs in *The Nursery* are truthful. But realism is by no means absent from the other songs. Instead, they locate the objective image in a musical genre that is highly specific to the narrative context: a serenade for a beautiful girl; a rough trepak for a drunken peasant tottering home in a blizzard; an imperious march for Death on the battlefield. In this way Musorgsky imports the Chernïshevskian concept of "reality" into a formal language close to that of the lied and remote from the simple lyricism of the typical Russian romance. We might almost be witnessing the birth of a Russian lieder genre which, like Schubert, fuses the simple songlike and descriptive styles of earlier writing into a new form richer in dramatic and expressive possibilities. "Almost," because the *Songs and Dances of Death,* by a tragic irony, had no successors in Musorgsky's or, it seems, anyone else's work until the Fourteenth Symphony of Shostakovich.

"Lullaby" specifically reverts to the anecdotal discourse (and perhaps setting) of *The Nursery,* except that the atmosphere is no longer light, but somber. The introduction depicts the dying child and his mother, a frozen candlelit tableau; but as the door cautiously opens and Death enters, the scene comes to life in an unequal dialogue between the terrified mother and Death, portrayed as something between a doctor and an undertaker, chillingly calm in speech and manner, black clad no doubt, with top hat and leather bag. With such a scene Musorgsky is in his element. As Death tiptoes to the child's bedside, the music recalls another narrative episode involving the death of a child, Pimen's account of the murder of the tsarevich in the first act of *Boris Godunov*. It then brilliantly—and to tell the truth, beautifully—parodies the conventions of the lullaby style, robbing it of its soothing effect by ending, every time, on a minor chord and with a perfunctory, dismissive quaver on the last syllable. The mother, by contrast, pleads with increasing agitation for her son's life, as she might beg a doctor to do something—anything—to save him. Musorgsky handles this rapid montage of tempo and figuration with the easy virtuosity of the born storyteller. For the singer, though, especially the kind of bass who often finds himself singing this music, the task is less straightforward and can easily be botched by overcharacterization. The character is already in the music, and needs only nuanced help to make its effect. Musorgsky himself was famously gifted at this kind of performance, and no doubt in his case the ability to think it went with the ability to do it.[16]

The remaining three songs abandon the dialogue method, and instead explore the narrative possibilities inherent in the genres being parodied. Thus, for example, the second song, "Serenade," is cast as a languid siciliano—the same basic rhythm as Don Giovanni's serenade in the second act of Mozart's opera. First Musorgsky sets the scene, using conventional romance imagery: gentle semiquaver figures (in E minor) for the "magical languor of blue nighttime in the trembling dusk of spring," except that the restless harmonies and searching melody warn us that the girl who might—even would—enjoy the promise of such a night has a lover whose kisses will be fatal. Death serenades her a semitone lower in a funereal E-flat minor, offering her a freedom from decay every bit as mendacious as Don Giovanni's promise of marriage to Zerlina, and perhaps in its way no less seductive. The extraordinary power of this slow dance must lie, precisely, in its grasp of the psychological truth that destruction can have an irresistible beauty of its own, and that charm often teeters on the edge of evil because it disturbs the balance of the mind. As usual with Musorgsky, the scene materializes out of the music. The girl rises from her bed with shining eyes and calls out softly to her lover; she descends the staircase, goes out to him, and perishes in the *petite mort* of his embrace. Death's melody has a grandeur and nobility that seem to belie its deadly intention, until we recognize that our usual concept of nobility is about as limited as the image of nature in the average moon-and-June romance.

"Trepak," the third song, makes a similar point in a less somber way, if one can speak about death in such terms. The peasant in this tale is not sick but drunk, so his death in a snowstorm is tragicomic, and almost as agreeable (the poet seems to argue) as the oblivion that came in bottled form. The old man is "hounded by grief, sorrow, and indigence," but he dies smiling, or so Death assures us, to the rhythm of the dactylic dance that, in Rimsky-Korsakov's *Sadko,* had created frenzy in the sea kingdom and set off a storm that sank the ships. Musorgsky's trepak, like his siciliano, is essentially slower than the folk model, though it lurches somewhat from tempo to tempo, and is itself affected by the weather, as Death calls up a blizzard, vividly portrayed in the piano part, to "weave a snowy, downy shroud to wrap the old man in like a child." But the real comedy of the song, in the richest sense, lies in the derivation of the trepak melody from the penitential requiem hymn, the Dies Irae. The opening figure of the dance is an inversion of the first three notes of the plainsong tune, while the next four are a modally altered version of the next four in the plainsong. Musorgsky's version first emerges in the scene-setting introduction, to the second line of Kutuzov's poem, about the blizzard that "weeps and moans" (cf. the penitent in the Dies Irae's "Ingemisco," "Guilty, now I pour my moaning, / All my shame with anguish owning; / Spare, O God, thy suppliant groaning!"). It then forms almost the entire basis of the actual dance.

The composer may or may not also have noticed the parallel between the opening of his tune and one of the folk songs in the Balakirev collection, "U vorot, vorot, batyushkinïkh," with the same trepak rhythm (the tune is famous for its later appearance in Tchaikovsky's *1812 Overture*). Then, as the snow gradually covers up the sleeping peasant, Death lulls him with a beautiful countermelody, alternating with snatches of trepak, the whole passage anchored by a pedal D beneath wistful, sliding chromatic harmonies. Finally the piano intones a solemn amen over the frozen corpse.

"Trepak" was in fact the first of these songs to be written, in February 1875. At that time the cycle seems to have been without a clear plan, but when he had completed "Serenade" in May he grouped the three songs in their eventual order, titled them, added dedications, but then announced to Kutuzov that "the first installment of the second album is ready," which was certainly untrue but at least indicated a definite intention to add further songs. At the end of the year he was contemplating the theme of the returning exile, but probably wrote no music, while the following year he played fragments of "The Monk" to Stasov, who pronounced it "very good" in a letter to Rimsky-Korsakov and mentioned that Musorgsky was also starting a fifth song on the subject of the legendary bogatyr Anika the Warrior, who recklessly challenged Death to a duel but was defeated and killed. Alas, not a note of either song was ever written down.

Not until 1877 did he fully compose a fourth song, "The Commander," to complete the cycle as we know it. The battle rages throughout the day, but as the sun goes down the armies retreat, leaving the Commander in sole possession of the battlefield with his army of the dead. As with the other songs, the piece starts with scene setting: the thunder of battle ("Vivo—alla guerra"), the setting sun, the retreat. Death appears on his warhorse and surveys the terrible scene by the light of the moon, and gradually the march that constitutes the "dance" in this particular song takes shape, as the Commander takes stock of his triumph. Like "Serenade," the piece is in two distinct parts, somewhat in the manner of a recitative and aria, if less clear-cut in the division. And it follows the same tonal path, dropping down by a semitone for its second section (E minor down to E-flat minor in "Serenade," E-flat minor down to D minor in "The Commander") Since D minor is also the key of "Trepak," and the first song, "Lullaby," had moved from F-sharp (= G flat) minor to A minor, the minor dominant of D minor, the whole cycle has a kind of tonal coherence, though Musorgsky's way with harmony generally is so unorthodox that the listener probably responds to the connections as a matter more of architecture than of process. More noticeable, perhaps, is a certain family resemblance in the thematic and metric character of the four songs. This may partly be an accident of style. But essentially it must be deliberate. In the dance sections especially, Musorgsky invents striking figures based on melodic commonplaces, often involving simple rising or falling scales clinched by fifths or fourths in the opposite direction: compare the fully formed tune of "Serenade" at the words "Slukh tvoy plenilsya moey serenadoy" ("Your ear is captivated by my serenade") with the main "Trepak" melody or the march theme in "The Commander" (at "Konchena bitva!"—"The battle is over!"—based on a Polish hymn, "Z dymem pozarów"), and then notice how Musorgsky has regularized their meter, dance-fashion, even though the poetic rhythm and meter are different in each case.

This genius for the defining melodic and rhythmic figure once again recalls Schubert; and it's true that the *Songs and Dances of Death* are the closest thing in Musorgsky—perhaps in any Russian music—to that fusion of folk simplicity with richness of thought and imagery that is the mark of the German lied in the hands of its greatest exponents.

What they have that lieder for the most part lack is an almost tangible element of theatre. In Schubert or Schumann the image, with occasional exceptions ("Erlkönig" is one), is a vehicle, sometimes a metaphor, for emotional reflection. In Musorgsky we are in the presence of something like a tableau vivant. The mother pleading with Death for her son's life is just that: a pleading mother faced with Death in person. She is not a metaphor, and we are not invited to reflect on her feelings, any more than a child listening to a fairy tale is aware of anything except the story and the characters in it, however much grown-ups may theorize after-the-fact about its hidden psychological or atavistic meaning. It is no doubt significant that the great nineteenth-century lied composers (with the solitary late exception of Strauss) either did not write for the theatre or did so unsuccessfully. Musorgsky, by contrast, was a theatrical genius who knew how to transfer that talent to the miniature scale of the song, a born storyteller with a flair for character and situation. Perhaps his distractability was what constantly drew him back to the compact, self-contained form of the song. Meanwhile, his operatic work, though driven by the same flair, continued diffuse and unplanned, sprouting new elements, discarding old, but seldom, if ever, glimpsed as a whole, and doomed, alas, to incompletion.

Rimsky-Korsakov, on the other hand, had been finding new ways of avoiding original composition altogether. Toward the end of 1874 he had added the directorship of the Free Music School to his conservatory and navy-band posts; and a year or so later he complemented his obsessive work on fugal counterpoint with a sudden enthusiasm for the collecting and arranging of folk songs.

Exactly why, at that specific moment, he should have felt drawn to a subject so seemingly remote from his academic and technical studies is a little hard to divine. Perhaps he simply felt the need for fresh air. In his autobiography the question pops up in the same paragraph as his somewhat weary description of the board meetings of the FMS, an activity he loathed and for which he admits he had no talent. At first, he implies, the idea of making a collection of his own came from nowhere in particular. Then Tyorty Filippov, a music-loving civil-servant friend of Balakirev's with a particular knowledge of Russian folk songs and an ability to sing them from memory, suggested that Rimsky-Korsakov write the tunes down at his dictation, provide piano accompaniments, and publish the result. Eventually the composer took down forty songs in this way. But he was disappointed to find that some of the songs had been corrupted by what he calls "military and factory elements," and more especially that there were no songs of the kind he was specially interested in: that is, "ritual and game songs," being "the most ancient to have come down to us from pagan times and to have been preserved in essence in the most inviolate form." Accordingly, he made up his mind to make a collection of his own, partly from his own memory of songs that he had heard as a child from the mouths of his mother and uncle, partly from songs remembered by close friends such as Musorgsky, Yekaterina Borodina, and others "in whose musical ear and memory I had confidence," and partly from the published but long-out-of-print collections of Lvov/Prach and Stakhovich. He worked on this collection with typical application during 1875 and 1876, and the result was published in 1877 by Bessel under the title *Collection of 100 Russian National Songs* (*Sbornik 100 russkikh narodnikh pesen*).[17]

Like Balakirev ten years earlier, Rimsky-Korsakov took considerable pains to write down the songs in authentic versions and to compose accompaniments that fitted their native character. By a curious irony, it didn't occur to him to think polyphonically, though it turned out not long afterward, in the work of Yuliy Melgunov, that the peasant way of enriching folk tunes was, precisely, to accompany them with variants of themselves—the heterophony, or *podgoloski*, mentioned previously.[18] But the real clue to the relevance of this work to his academic studies lies elsewhere. Unlike his predecessors, he approached his collecting in a taxonomic spirit—in the spirit, that is, of a scientific researcher wanting to classify and catalog his findings. Specifically, he was interested in the purpose of each song. There were *bilini*, dance songs, game and ceremonial songs relating to the different seasons of the pagan or folk-Christian year. There were songs for Shrovetide, Whitsun, Trinity, Ascension, wedding songs, "glory" songs (*velichal'niya*), and many others. In a way his attitude to this material was not so very different from his attitude to the instruments in the bands he was inspecting, or the procedures in the fugues he was writing. He wanted thorough, organized knowledge. He wanted to know not only the character of the tunes he was assembling, but their history and cultural significance. Soon he would find a way to use this knowledge in a creative, musicianly way. But for the time being he was content, it seems, with the study for its own sake.

Needless to say, all these varied activities effectively blocked out serious composition altogether. Apart from a few short piano pieces and a number of choruses rather obviously tied in with the counterpoint exercises, he wrote nothing during this time, and none of what he did write displays the slightest spark of individuality. Instead, he occupied himself—in what must have been his few free moments—with revising and editing existing work. He took down the manuscript of *Antar,* which was still unpublished, reorchestrated it, in his own phrase "harmonically purified" it, and conducted the new version at an RMS concert in January 1876.[19] Not long afterward he got involved in editing the full scores of Glinka's two operas for publication, a process that involved a certain amount of instrumentation of stage music for which Glinka had given only general indications, and also the correction of a large number of mistakes in the manuscript. And this arduous labor seems to have inspired in him the desire to revisit his own solitary opera, *The Maid of Pskov,* substantially rewrite it, and compose a new prologue and additional music later on.

The meticulousness of all this editorial work is simply astonishing, not least because it involved so much more than the regularization of an existing text. Starting with his own music, Rimsky-Korsakov, the young composition professor, clearly saw it as his task to recompose in the light of his newfound theoretical knowledge, to smooth out the humps and hollows of his own untutored youth, to rethink the music as he might have thought it after years of studying harmony, counterpoint, and fugue. That was no doubt his prerogative with his own work. It was when he turned his attention to the work of others that he began to invade a territory where he was not, as the Russians say, *u sebya*: not in his own home.

CHAPTER 25

A Chaos of Operas

The first performance of Cui's *Angelo* at the Maryinsky on 1 February 1876 was a moment of truth for the *kuchka* comparable to that of *William Ratcliff* seven years earlier. In their different ways they had reacted positively, even warmly, to the various scenes the composer had presented at circle gatherings. Stasov had a qualified admiration for the work, though he had come to dislike its composer.[1] But faced with the work's four-act totality, it was more difficult to see it as a significant contribution to their collective agenda, however vaguely that might be defined. "How intolerable are the *old-believer* artists," Musorgsky grumbled to Stasov a few days after the premiere, "stagnating in their closet labor and their four-walled dreams. O *Angelo*!" And a week or so later there was a confrontation at one of Shestakova's evenings, the exact cause of which is uncertain but may have been some remark of Musorgsky's to the same effect. Afterward Lyudmila herself must have written him a sympathetic letter, siding with him over the issue of truth and falsehood in art. He replied bitterly:

You are right, golubushka! Among people, there *must* remain *genuine* people, when "playing false" weighs you down and makes you ill. Everything (almost) "plays false" in our enlightened age in which whatever you like progresses except *humanity*. Not behind one's back, but right before one's eyes has been perpetrated an impertinent treason *à bout portant* [point blank] of the best, vital, omnipotent conceptions of art in that very home where, *once upon a time*, boiled new life, where new powers of thought were united, where new tasks of art were discussed and evaluated. But let's not bother about C. Cui and N. Rimsky-Korsakov: "the dead do not feel shame."[2]

Rimsky-Korsakov's "death," needless to say, was his continuing obsession with technical study and his (consequent?) failure to produce work of creative value or interest since (as Musorgsky probably felt) *The Maid of Pskov* or since—as he may have felt but will hardly have said—getting married. Musorgsky had been struggling to reconcile himself to Kutuzov's marriage only a few weeks before, and with his candid views on the incompatibility of wives and art he may well have been tempted to equate the study of fugue with the compilation of shopping lists and all those other horrors of domesticity that he himself had managed so effectively to dodge. At this very moment, Nadezhda Rimsky-Korsakov was bedridden after an agonizing labor with her second child, Sofia Nikolayevna. It was not her fault, of course, but it was just the kind of distraction that marriage tended to throw up; and when recently wedded men showed signs of organizing their lives, it was often a case of cherchez la femme.

Borodin was a different matter. You could accuse his wife of many things, but not of trying to impose order on his existence. In any case, he was inclined to be sympathetic to Musorgsky's point of view; at least he refused to take sides against it. "Borodin mustn't betray us," Musorgsky insisted; "it's too late and there's no reason. *Oh, if only Borodin could get angry.*"[3] But the great chemist in his laboratory was the least factious and doctrinaire of men. Thank God we all have our individuality, he would say, and can work in our own way without falling out as human beings. Perhaps it was easier for him. He had his scientific work, and for him music was a private matter, "a relaxation, a diversion, a caprice that takes me out of my actual work," while "for others it's a goal of life."[4] Since his prime occupation was the blending and separation of chemical elements and the study of their effects on one another, he liked the idea that his musical compositions had become a kind of nexus of everything that the *kuchka* stood for. "It's curious," he remarked to Karmalina,

> that in my *Igor* all the members of our circle meet: both the ultra-innovator-realist Modest Petrovich [Musorgsky] and the innovator in the field of lyrical-dramatic music César Antonovich [Cui] and the strict in outward forms and musical traditions Nikolay Andreyevich [Rimsky-Korsakov] and the violent champion of the new and strong

in everything Vladimir Vasilyevich Stasov. For the time being they're all pleased with *Igor,* though where other things are concerned they strongly disagree.

He himself had never really got on with what he called the "pure recitative style."

> I lean toward song and cantilena rather than recitative, though in the opinion of knowledgeable people I don't handle this badly. I also tend toward more finished, rounded, more extensive forms. My own way of dealing with operatic material is different. In my opinion, in opera, as in design, trivial forms, details, small change, have no place. Everything must be written in bold strokes, clear, vivid, and as far as possible practical for performance, both for the voice and for the orchestra. The voice must be in the foreground, the orchestra in the background. Insofar as I achieve my aim—this I can't judge—but by intention my opera will be closer to *Ruslan* than to *The Stone Guest,* more than this I can't guarantee.[5]

In fact he could guarantee next to nothing where composing was involved. It wasn't as if he resented the demands of his scientific work; on the contrary, he loved it all—the research, the teaching, the students, even the desk work—and he was even a little scared of his musical talent for its ability to distract him from what he saw as his main task in life. As a composer, he had always wanted to keep a low profile. But alas for any intention he might have had to keep *Prince Igor* out of the public gaze, he had acquiesced to a performance of what he called the "Chorus of Glorification" ("Khor slavleniya"), which opens the work in the published score but which he had originally planned as its epilogue, at an FMS concert conducted by Rimsky-Korsakov in March 1876. And now the world knew that he was writing an opera, and would naturally start expecting its completion and a fully staged performance. He suddenly felt like "a young girl who has lost her innocence and reputation, and has thereby gained for herself a notorious kind of freedom." The implication that completing the opera despite the demands of his regular calling might be a form of prostitution was perhaps more than he intended by the image. But the freedom was clearly a temptation as well as a threat; and like many an unwanted temptation, it could rapidly become a compulsion.

As usual, he had composed the chorus while ill in bed (with influenza) during the Christmas holidays. But there is nothing in the least sickly about its inspiration. Stasov's original idea for the epilogue was, as we saw, to tie the blatantly dangling threads of the narrative by having Vladimir Igorevich marry Konchak's daughter in a spectacular ceremony in Putivl, which he probably envisaged as a grand tableau along the lines of the final scene of *A Life for the Tsar.* Borodin's chorus, with its stark parallel chords and bold block rhythms, is plainly meant to invoke a rougher, more primitive, if not more warlike, time than the Time of Troubles. We are in the year 1185, the era of the bogatyrs in their chain mail and spiked helmets (as in the paintings of Viktor Vasnetsov). The melodies, of both the main section and the middle section, are the most basic type of folk tune, somewhat in the manner of the "Song of the Volga Boatmen," "Ey, ukhnem!," which Balakirev had picked up in Nizhny-Novgorod a dozen years before. Dianin suggests a parallel with the *protyazhnaya* "You Hills, My Sparrow Hills" ("Uzh' vï gorï moy gorï Vorob'evskiya") in the recently published collection of Vasily Prokunin (1872). But there are also significant connections with the chorus of idolaters in *Mlada,* where the context is pagan rather than proto-Christian. And over the whole piece hangs the shadow of the Second Symphony, which was on Borodin's desk as he composed *Mlada* and, for that matter, was still on his desk when he transferred so much of *Mlada* to *Prince Igor.* So even this fairly short, straightforward chorus is a microcosm of the confused, confusing working methods of this great composer who could not find time to compose. One can only assume that his work as a professor of chemistry was better regulated.

Exactly when he conceived the idea of a prologue to precede and explain the opening scene of Stasov's scenario is likewise unclear. Perhaps it was as late as 1883, the date usually given. But there are circumstantial reasons for suggesting 1876. For one thing, he seems to have composed the G-major chorus that eventually replaced the original epilogue in or soon after that year.[6] Then there is the question of the eclipse, which darkens the stage like an evil omen just as Igor and his retinue are about to set out on their campaign against the Polovtsï. In Stasov, this portent is merely described to Yaroslavna by a group of merchants who have witnessed the battle and Igor's defeat. But Borodin did away with the merchants by 1879 at the latest; and to accompany the eclipse in the prologue he used material from the apparitions scene in *Mlada,* material that had also cropped up in the first ("monologue") version of Igor's aria, but which came available once again when that version was discarded at the end of 1875. On the principle of Occam's razor, it looks as if these various decisions were all taken at the same time, even if Borodin was as usual unable to implement them all at once.

The one other piece we can be certain that he composed in 1876 is the duet for Yaroslavna and Igor on Igor's unexpected return to Putivl in the fourth act, and the beautiful recitative for Yaroslavna that precedes it. Miserably she contemplates the devastation in the countryside around the city, laid waste by the victorious Polovtsian army. Yekaterina Borodina recalled that her husband composed this music at the end of their summer holiday in the village of Staraya Ruza, not far to the west of Moscow, after being unable to cross the Moscow River on his way home to St. Petersburg, and having been forced to wait on the riverbank and watch "the rushing torrent, and the gray dreary waves leaping and surging."[7] "How cheerless is everything around," sings Yaroslavna, to an exquisite melody that might well have come out of the Balakirev or Prokunin collection. Borodin went back to Staraya Ruza and improvised this piece on the piano there.[8] The rest of the number Yaroslavna's excited dotted-rhythm *più mosso* to a hesitantly major version of the recitative tune, and the brilliant duet that follows—was probably composed that autumn in St. Petersburg. Like almost everything else in the opera, they were written without much concern for the dramatic trajectory of the action as a whole, but with a vivid image of the situation. Like the pieces in a child's jigsaw puzzle, they fitted perfectly into the space marked "recognition duet." As for the adjacent pieces, they would no doubt turn up in good time.

As if all this random operatic composition were not enough to fill his almost nonexistent spare time, Borodin now encountered a fresh aggravation. His Second Symphony was slated for its first performance at an RMS concert in February 1877, and suddenly the orchestral scores he had made of the first and last movements were nowhere to be found. Then, just when he needed to produce the material for a meeting with Nápravník at the end of November, he fell ill once again and had to take to his bed. In despair he pleaded with Rimsky-Korsakov to help him with the rescoring and recopying. Then, within days, the scherzo and andante also vanished without trace. Luckily, Stasov remembered seeing them on Shestakova's piano, covered up by a poster, and Borodin sent his adoptive son-in-law, Alexander Dianin, to collect them, relieved that they had not, as he had feared, got mixed up with a shopping bag of sausages and vegetables and dropped in the street. In the end, still under the weather but with Rimsky-Korsakov's help, he somehow managed to rescore the missing outer movements and have the parts copied in time for the rehearsals.

So haphazard was this whole train of events that one inevitably wonders whether the slightly clumsy scoring of some parts of the symphony had anything to do with the sense of panic that attended its birth. Rimsky-Korsakov reports that in their work together (he admits to consultation rather than contribution), they got very excited about the brass instruments, under the influence of Rimsky's inspectorial expertise, and as a result Borodin overwrote badly for that section. Nápravník, Rimsky claims, had to conduct the scherzo well below the proper tempo, simply because the brass players could not manage the rapid chord changes required. The performance as a whole was a noisy failure: noisy not only because of the heavy orchestration but because, as Alexander Dianin noted, "the audience created a proper racket, reminiscent of a cat's concert."[9] Another friend remembered that "the first movement was received very coldly and when somebody started clapping you could hear hissing. The whole work was received in this way, and the composer wasn't called out."[10] Borodin revised the orchestration for an FMS concert under Rimsky-Korsakov himself two years later (February 1879), and this time the performance went off well enough; but problems remained, and remain to this day, with a work of such stunning originality and inventive flair, mitigated here and there by a certain awkwardness of facture, especially in its rhythmic and orchestral detail.

By the time of the symphony's premiere, a good deal of *Prince Igor* existed in one form or another. But the chaos of Borodin's working methods is glaringly apparent from a simple inventory of the movements composed thus far. In terms of the numberings in the eventual score, and in approximate order of composition, they were: nos. 3, 9, 7, 18, 15, 25, 8, 2 (part), 17, 21 (part), 27, 29, 1 (part). And even this list flatters the coherence of the actual material. Only two or three pieces were orchestrated, and some were in draft form or in other ways incomplete. There was still no libretto and no proper scenario apart from Stasov's original, from which Borodin had significantly deviated. The composition of Yaroslavna's "Moscow River" recitative, on an impulse and apparently without any prior plan, was entirely typical. In the same way, in 1877 he composed a recitative and cavatina for Vladimir Igorevich, and the following duet with Konchakovna (nos. 11 and 12), supposedly under the influence of an aborted relationship with a young girl who fell in love with him and whom, according to his wife's tactful account, he had great difficulty "in treating . . . as a daughter."[11] Such connections may be nebulous; but the mere fact that they can plausibly be made is suggestive enough in itself. Without these sudden impulses Borodin might not have composed even as much as he did; but they were not helpful to the planning regime. When Rimsky-Korsakov and

Glazunov started editing the work after his death, they often found themselves adding passages or vocal parts; they had to orchestrate (a process that would involve filling out textures), and they sometimes had to speculate on the exact placing of this or that number in the overall plan of the opera. To this day *Prince Igor* is a "mobile," an endless work in progress, that will surely never come wholly to rest.

Khovanshchina, by comparison, was a model of good order. By the start of 1876 Musorgsky had composed act 1, act 2 apart from the final quintet, and a planned scene between Golitsïn and the Lutheran pastor, and was starting act 3 in the happy knowledge that most of its opening scene, Marfa's song and her confrontation with Susanna, was already in existence. He embarked on the recitative and aria for Shaklovity (his *yurodivy*-like lament for the fate of Russia) and would very soon have the third act half done. Then came the cold douche of Stasov's May letter about the second and third acts. None of its suggestions were adopted, but Musorgsky was sufficiently perturbed by it to go back to his second act and rethink certain aspects, especially the quarrel. But even before any of this could happen, a mere twenty-four hours after writing his pained reply on 15 June (St. Modestus's Day), he went to Stasov's apartment on the Nadezhdinskaya, played all evening to him and their friend the sculptor Mark Antokolsky, and prompted a very different reaction from the one in the letter. "I will say," Stasov wrote to Polixena, "that he's now composing the *best* things he's done so far in *Khovanshchina*." And he mentions a scene in which the streltsy wives enter "howling at their husbands and lying down beside the execution blocks and axes, while in the distance the poteshny [Petrine guards] approach" (an early version combining the streltsy scene after Shaklovity's aria in act 3 with the scene in act 4 in which the streltsy enter carrying their own execution blocks and halberds). But, ominously for *Khovanshchina*, Stasov continues: "What struck me even more forcibly was the beginning and ending he has attached to *Chernobog* [*Night on Bald Mountain*]: he wants to insert this number into his future opera *Sorochintsï Fair*, and it's one of the most marvellous things he's done so far in his entire life."[12] Musorgsky must have led Stasov to believe that he would be composing the Gogol opera once *Khovanshchina* was finished. In fact he was in the process, not for the first time, of shelving the latter work in favor of the former.

Sorochintsï Fair had now been floating around in Musorgsky's mind as an operatic subject for at least two years, but as far as is known he had written no music for it. Stasov reports in his biography of the composer that he had first thought of it in 1875 (actually 1874) as a way of creating a Ukrainian role for Osip Petrov, who was himself Ukrainian by birth. Petrov had been an acquaintance at least since 1870, and a close friend since creating the role of Varlaam in the *Boris* excerpts of 1873. Recently he had been much in Musorgsky's thoughts, as 1876 was his jubilee year, the fiftieth anniversary of his début as a professional singer, and the composer had been helping Shestakova plan aspects of the ceremony on the stage of the Maryinsky, at which Petrov once again sang the role of Susanin in *A Life for the Tsar* and a series of grand presentations were made to him between the acts. By this time Musorgsky was a frequent guest of Petrov and his wife, Anna, herself an operatic contralto of some distinction; and he would sometimes accompany "Grandpa," as he called him, in his public and private performances.

Although Petrov continued performing until his death at the age of seventy-one in 1878, the idea of his ever appearing in a new opera by Musorgsky must always have seemed somewhat fanciful. It is just as likely that the great bass—an enthusiastic admirer of *Boris Godunov* and of what he knew of *Khovanshchina*—encouraged Musorgsky to compose *Sorochintsī Fair* in the hope of tying him down to the completion of both works in progress. It was impossible to be close to Musorgsky in the mid-seventies and be unaware of his unfocused way of working or its various causes. A definite commission might be as good a way as any of concentrating his mind. "The Little Russians [the Petrovs]," Musorgsky tells Kutuzov in November 1877, "fervently beg me to bring *Sorochintsī* quickly to the stage." The fact that it caught him at a moment of difficulty with *Khovanshchina* may have been chance or it may have been part of the motivation. At all events, the Petrov connection was obviously crucial. The jubilee event took place on 21 April 1876, and within two months he had made his preliminary adaptation of his *St. John's Night on Bald Mountain* and was talking about *Sorochintsī Fair* in the same breath as *Khovanshchina*. By the end of the year, *Khovanshchina* has virtually disappeared from his correspondence, not to resurface until the summer of 1878. He starts gathering material for the new opera (a girls' chorus, various Ukrainian folk songs); he draws up a scenario; and he composes pieces, apparently at random: some music for the Gypsy who engineers the "supernatural" events as part of a deal on a cow; a song for the heroine's crosspatch stepmother; and a significant part of a middle act, starting with the *Bald Mountain* intermezzo (in the guise of a dream sequence) and continuing with scenes for the stepmother with her husband and with her lover. But of serious dramatic continuity, such as he had been laboriously developing in *Khovanshchina,* there is little trace. The process is much closer to that of *Prince Igor,* and it is hardly surprising that the outcome was in general terms much the same.

On the face of it Gogol's story was a curious choice for Musorgsky at this stage of his career. Its whimsical tale of a young man who falls in love with the carter Cherevik's daughter at the village fair, and strikes a deal with a Gypsy to sell him a cow at a bargain price if he can persuade the carter and his wife to agree to their marriage, is a million miles from any previous Musorgsky subject—even Gogol's *Marriage,* which, as Taruskin points out, is a genuine, if grotesque, comedy of manners, whereas *Sorochintsï Fair* is a fantastical folk tale, in which, admittedly, the fantasy element is for once fake. The fair is supposed to lie under the curse of a red jacket, pawned by the devil to a Jewish pawnbroker who sold it on and was then attacked by a herd of pigs on stilts; but the pigs' heads that burst through the windows and terrorize Cherevik and his friends are a trick played by the Gypsy in order to soften the carter up and persuade him to let his daughter marry. There was only one sensible way to set such a plot in the 1870s, and that was with extensive use of folk song, something Musorgsky had hitherto largely avoided.

Admittedly there were recent precedents. Serov's *Power of the Fiend,* though not based on Gogol, was similarly a village-fairground tale with diabolical trimmings and much use of folk material. In 1876 Tchaikovsky's *Vakula the Smith,* based on another of Gogol's Dikanka tales, "Christmas Eve," and freely enriched with authentic folk songs, had its premiere at the Maryinsky; but that was in late November, some months after Musorgsky's own decision to write a Gogol opera. It's hard to believe, in any case, that he was suddenly influenced by such models. Had he not told Sasha Purgold: "I know the Gogol subject well. I thought about it some two years ago, but the subject matter doesn't fit in with the direction I've chosen—it doesn't sufficiently embrace Mother Russia in all her simple-hearted breadth."[13] Simple-hearted, perhaps; but broad, in the historical sense of *Boris* and *Khovanshchina,* hardly. Above all it offered little to the keen student of psychology, the sharp observer of human motivation and dark eccentricity, the master of *The Nursery,* of Boris himself, of Golitsïn and Khovansky. Perhaps it was the very absence of these elements that appealed to him, making it, as he had told Karmalina, "good as an economy of creative strength."[14]

Above all, he may have felt that he could write *Sorochintsï Fair* quickly, then come back refreshed to *Khovanshchina.* From the start he planned to incorporate his revised *Bald Mountain,* originally as a dream intermezzo at the beginning of the second act (though it could in truth have fitted in anywhere, being entirely irrelevant to the action); also probably the existing market scene from *Mlada,* though he seems not to have worked this up until 1880. In less than three months after compiling the scenario, he composed a large part of the second act, starting with the scene in which Khivrya, Cherevik's wife, manages to wake him up and get him out of the house so that in the next scene she can receive her paramour, the priest's son, Afanasy Ivanovich. Between these two scenes, she sings a lengthy solo of anticipation: "Come soon, my darling" ("Prikhodi skorey, moy milen'kiy"). But the crucial final scene of the act, in which Cherevik returns with his drinking buddies, Afanasy hides in the attic, and one of the buddies tells the story of the red jacket, gave Musorgsky trouble, and in fact he never managed to compose it. Here the pigs' heads smash the windows and thrust their snouts into the hut where Cherevik and his friends are drinking. It would be nice to suppose that Musorgsky balked at this scene on grounds of taste. But the real problem was no doubt its sheer intricacy, the long, convoluted narrative, and the violent yet somehow ludicrous climax which, he may have sensed, would be hard to make plausible onstage. The scene is close in dramatic structure to the inn scene of *Boris Godunov.* But its farcical tone is obviously another matter.

Richard Taruskin suggests that from a technical point of view, the challenge of the earlier scenes in this second act was "just the same" as the challenge of the inn scene (and, he adds, of *Marriage* as well).[15] All three are made up of "uninterrupted dialogue." The inn scene, it's true, works a couple of folk songs into the conversation; but they are strictly part of the action, aspects of Varlaam's tipsiness. The Khivrya scenes in *Sorochintsï Fair* are treated somewhat differently, with authentic Ukrainian folk tunes providing a significant proportion of the actual dialogue music. The normal *kuchka* idea was that characters in opera could sing songs (whether or not folk songs) if the plot required it; so Varlaam's Kazan song, or his "Kak yedet yon," or Tucha's revolutionary song in *The Maid of Pskov,* would be justified, but Marfa's song in the third act of *Khovanshchina* not. Khivrya's and Cherevik's music in *Sorochintsï Fair* goes still farther in that the folk song is absorbed, as if it were the natural speech of these rustic characters, while retaining its scanned, versified, sometimes rhyming formality. The effect is in fact quite remote from the naturalistic intention of *Marriage* or the original *Boris Godunov,* or even from those moments in the revised *Boris* when the children play clapping games or tell stories in song form. There is about these scenes from Gogol a kind of folksiness that at times comes dangerously close to vaudeville. The quality is superior; Musorgsky always finds nuances in his folk material that lift it out of the ordinary. And yet there remains some indissoluble element of condescension in this urban view of country ways that he had always avoided in his songs about (or sung by) idiots, or children, or distracted seminarians, or the dead.

Stasov hated much of this music, perhaps not only because it had displaced *Khovanshchina* in Musorgsky's nonexistent schedule of work. He remarked to Kutuzov that "Musarion . . . has written a lot of rubbish for *The Fair at Soroch.* this summer, but after everyone's attacks (especially mine), has now decided to throw it all away, leaving only the good stuff."[16] Even the faithful Lyudmila was cool. She had told Stasov that Musorgsky had "written some scene for Khivrya and something else, but that it was all terribly mediocre and bloodless, like this whole unfortunate Little Russian undertaking so far."[17] Musorgsky himself reports the circle's reaction to Kutuzov in different terms but to similar effect:

> During the first reading of the 2nd act of *Sorochintsï* I became convinced of a radical lack of understanding of Little-Russian humor on the part of the musicuses of the crumbling "heap": such a frost emanated from their looks and demands, that "the heart went cold," as Archpriest Avvakum says. Nevertheless I have come to a halt, taken thought, and tested myself more than once. Having rested from this hard work on myself, I shall resume work on *Sorochintsï.* I can't have been completely wrong in my aspirations, I simply can't . . .[18]

Stasov's remarks about *Khovanshchina* had stopped him in his tracks; now his colleagues' opinion of *Sorochintsï Fair* had the same effect. For a year he wrote almost nothing for his Gogol opera. And while there were other causes of the loss of impulse (chief among them Osip Petrov's death in March 1878, which upset him terribly and deprived him of a vital father figure), the true reason was surely the too-freely expressed reservations of the circle. The conductor Mikhail Berman was present on one occasion when Musorgsky played excerpts from *Khovanshchina.* "It was pitiful to observe," he recalled, "the way those present (especially Cui) would incessantly pester him with demands for all kinds of cuts, changes, abbreviations, and so on . . . To worry and poke at a newborn piece like that, and not just face to face but in public, is not only the height of tactlessness, but an out-and-out act of cruelty. But the poor, modest composer keeps still, assents, makes the cuts."[19] No doubt they treated *Sorochintsï Fair* in much the same way.

If, however, one can agree that the Ukrainian opera was in some respects a wrong turning for Musorgsky just at that stage of his work, there is other evidence of uncertain drift in his music in 1877. Early in the year, before compiling the Gogol scenario, he had written a series of songs, mainly to texts by Alexey Tolstoy, the author of *The Death of Ivan the Terrible* and its still unperformed sequels, and the co-creator of Koz'ma Prutkov, the fictional civil servant and poet whose career as a government pen pusher must have struck a chord with Musorgsky, even though, sadly, he never set any of Prutkov's poems. The poems he did set are a moderately bland collection of lyrics, the most piquant of which is "Is It Right for a Young Man to Spin Flax?" ("Oy, chest' li to molodtsu lyon pryasti?"), which includes, among its catalogue of activities unworthy of a real man, the all-too-pertinent image of "the minstrel-singer awaiting his orders and idling his life away." But Musorgsky ignored the polemical slant of these questions and instead treated the poem as a series of images, including rolled chords and arpeggios for the minstrel and his gusli, and soft tremolos for the vision of the stream and the nightingale and the shady garden where, in the poet's opinion, the young man should be feeding his romantic soul.

In general, though, these songs are not notable for their musical imagery. Musorgsky seems to have been at pains to "recite" Tolstoy's verse in an even, measured way, without the kind of volatile response to verbal incident or narrative that had made *The Nursery* or, in their different way, the *Songs and Dances of Death* so vivid. "Not with divine thunder did grief strike" ("Ne bozheem gromom gore udarilo") runs one first line, and Musorgsky composes, so to speak, the negative: no thunder and a very subdued grief. In another song ("Rassevayetsya, rasstupayetsya grust' poddumami"), "the melancholy in my thoughts disperses and parts, breaking into my dark soul like the sun through clouds," but the stately piano chords notice neither spiritual nor meteo-rological change. The tone is literally that of *Sunless,* but without the intensity of experience. There is one other Kutuzov setting of this year (apart from "The Commander," composed in June, after the sce-nario): this is "The Vision" ("Videniye"). Here the personification of night as a young woman in black who seems to be enticing the poet, summoning him "to love and delight," does have a certain intensity of atmosphere, which, however, Musorgsky fails to capture with his slow opening of vagrant piano harmonies or the curious final page, where the poet walks on ahead of the "magical creature," his voice doubled by heavy left-hand tremolo octaves. After all, we have just learned about the girl's "light and transparent figure," and the "inviting murmur of her invisible lips." It may seem pedantry to criticize a song on such anecdotal grounds, as if one were Cui or Balakirev. But Musorgsky was usually so punctilious in this way; it was his specialty. With him, more than with others, one notices the disjuncture.

In any case his failures mark out the growing differences within the circle almost as clearly as his successes. Taken together, these songs and the two operas that were vying for his attention in 1877 are a virtual conspectus of everything the *kuchka* had ever stood for.[20] They offer history and folk legend and song, realism and dramatic "truth," naturalistic, syllabic word setting, deviant harmony and meter; and above all they at no point so much as hint at a learned or taught method. Even Borodin was unable to continue to evade good practice as comprehensively as Musorgsky at this time. As for Rimsky-Korsakov, he seemed to have given up the struggle altogether. His theoretical studies had most recently borne fruit in some choral settings of Lermontov and Pushkin (op. 16), dominated by imitative techniques of various kinds, including fugue, canon, and variation. Then in the summer of 1876 he composed in rapid succession a string sextet and a quintet for piano and wind, and entered both works in a chamber-music competition organized by the RMS. History doesn't relate what Stasov and Musorgsky thought of these pieces; but the composer himself was quite pleased with them, and irritated that they failed to win the prize, which went to a piano trio by Nápravník.

Both works are lively, likable, skillfully written, but limited in reach and rather impersonal in character. The five-movement sextet, which has a fugal rondo as its second movement and another fugue in the trio of its scherzo, is otherwise quite unsophisticated, full of simple, square-cut melodies, and distinctly formulaic in its approach to the mechanics of classical form. Its most beautiful moment is the cello solo that forms the main theme of the andante fourth movement, an inspiration worthy of (and perhaps indebted to) Schumann. But it never approaches—or attempts—the richness of texture or subtlety of development of the two Brahms sextets, which Rimsky-Korsakov had surely studied. The problem is essentially one of organic continuity. Rimsky has good, attractive themes, but they tend to fall into neat, symmetrical phrases that, at their plainest, suggest the jaunty scansion of nursery rhymes—not a good recipe for extended musical discussion. This is notably true of the first-movement second subject of the quintet and also of the main theme of its finale, which, in the nature of rondo form, comes much too often to survive its insistent tone of light-headed whimsy.

The quintet is, however, superbly written for the ensemble, with a fine ear for the blend and balance of these disparate instruments. So much listening to wind bands had had its effect, though one wonders why Rimsky-Korsakov, who must have known Mozart's great E-flat quintet, K. 452, substituted a flute for Mozart's oboe, and thereby effectively ruled out his work being programmed on the rare occasions that wind and piano are brought together in concert. In the next year or so he added three more works to his tally of wind scores: a trombone concerto, a set of variations for oboe (on Glinka's song "Shto krasotka molodaya"), and a *Konzertstück* for clarinet, all three works with band accompaniment, and conducted them at the band concerts on the naval island of Kronstadt. These are all pièces d'occasion, and their only real interest lies in the mere fact of their having been written at all. They mark Rimsky-Korsakov's arrival as a professional composer, and as such effectively signal his departure from the spiritual ambience of the *kuchka,* though by no means, as we shall see, from their physical or musical presence.

CHAPTER 26

Drowning in the Waters

By the late seventies the *kuchka* were an established presence in St. Petersburg music, but only in the largely negative sense that they were known about and regarded, at least in professional circles, with disdain bordering at times on open hostility. In general, the press favored them with varying degrees of vituperation or at best damned them with faint praise. Hermann Laroche, in an article in *Golos* of June 1876, had ironically thanked the composers of the *kuchka* for "so favourably align[ing] your creative activity with my critical strengths," then proceeded to bombard Musorgsky's *Sunless* from the fortress of the conservatory graduate who knows the rules and can monitor their breach. "There is nothing special here," he remarked of the third song, "At an end is the futile, noisy day." "But everything is nice and euphonious while there is no composer. The composer appears and, as if with a magic wand, the scene changes. From the keys of the accompanying piano there flows a kind of stream of musical sewage, as if a girl in a boardinghouse were trying out a new piece without having noticed how many flats there were in the key signature."[1] And a good deal more in the same, wild metaphorical vein. He even managed a fresh sideswipe at *Boris Godunov,* music "such as only Mr. Musorgsky is able to write: music of Bedlam," while the work itself continued to be revived, tickets sold, curtain calls demanded by the composer's fellow inmates, apparently out of Laroche's field of vision.

Others, not burdened with the reviewer's theoretical baggage or his professional dignity, were better able to adjust their critical compass.

Turgenev, for example, had been rude about Glinka in *Smoke,* and had reacted with derision to the so-called Russian School at the concert he attended with Stasov in 1867. Later he had told Stasov that "among all the 'young' Russian composers there is some talent, to be sure: in Tchaikovsky and Rimsky-Korsakov. But all the rest of them—not as people, obviously (as people they are charming, but as artists)—in a bag and into the water! The Egyptian king Rampeinit XXIX is not as neglected now as they will be in 15–20 years."[2] But after attending a soirée at Petrov's in May 1874 he had changed his tune. He reported on the evening to Pauline Viardot:

> Dined with Petrov . . . who still adores you, as in the past. He has a bust of you crowned with laurels, still a good likeness. I also saw his wife, who is sixty and has not a single tooth in her upper jaw. Well! After dinner she sang two romances, quite odd but touching, by M. Musorgsky (author of *Boris Godunov,* who was present), in a still adorable voice, youthful in timbre, expressive, charming! I was open-mouthed and moved to tears, I assure you. This Musorgsky played to us and, I wouldn't say sang, but groaned some fragments from his opera and from another that he's writing, and this struck me as characteristic, interesting, upon my honor! Old Petrov sang his drunken, scurrilous old monk (Varlaam . . .) to perfection. I begin to believe there's a future in all this. Musorgsky is misleadingly like Glinka, but with a completely red nose (unfortunately he's an alcoholic), pale but fine eyes, and small lips squeezed into a large face with flabby cheeks. I liked him; he's very natural and unaffected. He played us the introduction to his second opera. It's a bit Wagnerian, but fine and pointed. On, on, the Russians![3]

Turgenev, of course, had no musical axe to grind, but was merely caught in the toils of the operatic and musical conventions in which, in her way, Viardot had ensnared him. On the other hand, he had an instinctive sympathy with the quest for an authentic Russian speech, and once this particular penny dropped he had no difficulty responding to a music that had little in common with anything he encountered on the Viardot circuit. "I am mainly a realist," he told Mariya Milyutina, "and what interests me above all is the living truth of human physiognomy."[4]

For trained musicians like Laroche or his fellow graduate Tchaikovsky, this sort of thing was much harder to swallow. But Tchaikovsky's assessment, though severe, was at least devoid of the blockheaded arrogance of his erstwhile colleague. In fact, with due allowance for the natural bias of the well-schooled, his portrait of the group for the benefit of his patroness Nadezhda von Meck is remarkably perceptive, and worth quoting at length:

All the newest Petersburg composers are very talented, but they are all infected to the core by the most awful self-importance and a purely dilettante conviction of their superiority to all the rest of the musical world. A recent exception is Rimsky-Korsakov. He is self-taught, like the others, but in his case there has been an abrupt reversal. His is a very serious, very honest, and conscientious nature. As a very young man he fell in with a group who, first, convinced him that he was a genius, and then secondly told him that it wasn't necessary to study, that schools kill inspiration, dry up creativity, etc. At first he believed this. His earliest works are evidence of a strong talent devoid of any theoretical development. In the circle to which he belonged, they were all in love with themselves and with each other. Each of them tried to imitate one or other product of the circle that they regarded as wonderful. As a result the whole circle soon sank into a uniformity of method, into impersonality and affectation. Korsakov is the only one of them to whom it occurred, five years ago, that the ideas preached by the circle were without any foundation, and that their contempt for the schools, for classical music, their hatred of authority and models, were nothing but ignorance. I have kept a letter of his from that time. It both touched me deeply and shook me. He had gone into deep despair on seeing how many years had gone by without any benefit, along a path that led nowhere. He asked what he should do. The obvious answer was that he had to study. And he did begin to study, but with such zeal that academic technique soon became his necessary atmosphere. In one summer he wrote an incalculable number of contrapuntal exercises and sixty-four fugues, of which he at once sent me ten to look over. The fugues seemed faultless in their way, but I noticed at the time that the reaction had produced in him too sharp an about turn. From contempt for the schools, he had gone over at a stroke to a cult of musical technique. Soon after that, his symphony and quartet appeared. Both works are full of a multitude of tricks, but as you so rightly observe they are imbued with a character of dry pedantry. At this moment he is obviously going through a crisis, and how this crisis will end is hard to predict. Either he will emerge as a great master or he will get terminally bogged down in contrapuntal trickery. Cui is a talented dilettante. His music is devoid of originality, but elegant and graceful. It is too coquettish, too smarmy, so to speak, so that it pleases at first hearing, but quickly palls. This comes from the fact that Cui is not a musician by trade but a professor of fortifications, very busy with a mass of lectures in practically every military academic institution in Petersburg. By his own admission to me, he can't compose without picking out tunelets at the piano, with background chords. When he comes across a nice little idea, he fiddles about with it, takes it to pieces, adorns and greases it in every conceivable way, and all this takes a long time, so that, for example, it took him ten years to write his opera *Ratcliff*. But I repeat, he has talent all the same; at least he has taste and flair. Borodin is a fifty-year-old professor of chemistry at the Academy of Medicine.[5] He, again, has talent, even great talent, but a talent that has died from lack of attention and a blind fate that took him to a chair in chemistry instead of to a vital musical activity. On the other hand, he has less taste than Cui, and his technique is so weak that he can't compose a single line without somebody's help. Musorgsky you are quite right to call unteachable [*otpetïm*]. In terms of talent he is perhaps superior to all the above. But he has a narrow nature, devoid of the desire for self-improvement, with a blind faith in the absurd theories of his circle and his own genius. In addition it's some sort of low nature that loves the coarse, the uncouth, the rough. He is the direct opposite of his friend Cui, who swims in the shallows but is always decorous and graceful. By contrast, Musorgsky flaunts his illiteracy, prides himself on his ignorance, botches any old how, blindly trusting in the infallibility of his genius. But with him there are flashes of real, as well as not unoriginal, talent. The outstanding personality of the circle is Balakirev. But he has gone silent, having done very little. He has a colossal talent that has perished because of some kind of fatal circumstances that made him go all pious after having long taken pride in complete atheism. Today he never leaves church, he fasts for the sacrament, genuflects to the relics, and nothing else. Despite his great gifts, he has done a lot of harm. For example, he ruined Korsakov by convincing him that study did damage. In general he is the architect of all the theories of this strange circle, which unites so many untouched, misdirected, or prematurely blighted powers.[6]

In fact Balakirev had begun to resurface some time before Tchaikovsky wrote this letter. It was true that he had become something of a religious recluse, had taken to vegetarianism and various forms of strict Orthodoxy, not to mention an element of pure mumbo jumbo. The few friends who called on him found him depressed and unresponsive. He seems to have suffered what would later have been called a nervous breakdown. As we have seen, he allowed his conducting posts to lapse and completely abandoned composition and attendance at circle gatherings. To supplement his paltry income from teaching he took a job as a clerk in the goods section of the Central Railway Company, but soon gave that up as well, on some unexplained pretext. The one member of the circle who retained any influence with him was Lyudmila Shestakova, who persuaded him to lodge his musical manuscripts with her, while at the same time seeing to it that her brother's piano, which had been in Balakirev's possession, was moved to the conservatory for safe keeping. The composer of *King Lear* became in certain respects a poor copy of his Shakespearean hero, disposing of his worldly goods and abandoning his family and titles. But in his case, the condition turned out to be temporary.

Already in 1876 there were signs of his emerging from purdah. After conducting the *King Lear* Overture in his FMS concert that March, Rimsky-Korsakov had taken the trouble to drop its composer a letter of appreciation, with added greetings from Borodin and Stasov. Balakirev was touched, and told Lyudmila so, adding a definite promise to at last write out his much-considered, long-awaited *Tamara*. "It means," Stasov told Borodin, "that he's not yet a complete corpse, and I haven't yet lost all hope of his resurrection."[7] Borodin may merely have been reporting this letter when he told Karmalina a few weeks later that "on the insistence of the ever energetic and passionate Lyudmila Ivanovna, Balakirev has begun to write down his unfinished *Tamara*."[8] But by January 1877 the picture is more sharply drawn. "Balakirev," he told the singer, "dear, gifted Balakirev, is rising again for music! He's again almost the same Mily Alexeyevich, passionately disputing and fighting over every D-flat major and B minor and the smallest details of musical works that previously he didn't want to hear."[9] He was now once again to be seen at Shestakova's and the Stasovs'. One day at Christmas 1877 he played fragments of *Tamara* to Dmitry Stasov, then soon afterward called on Vladimir Stasov, in vain, to wish him happy birthday (2 January), which prompted what seems to have been Vladimir's first letter to him for almost five years. "So you haven't completely forgotten me," he wrote, "haven't entirely shut me out of your heart." In Balakirev's absence, he has been listening to his music: *Islamey* (which Nadezhda Rimsky-Korsakov has been learning), the "Georgian Song," and "The Dream," sung by a good new tenor, Pyotr Grigoryev. "But it was particularly bitter for me to think yesterday, one more time, how long I've gone without hearing your marvellous *Tamara*. And you see I not only could but must hear it. No one loves both you and it more than

I do. If others have been able to hear it today, then I have deserved to a hundred thousand times more."[10]

With this, their correspondence takes up again, almost as if it has never been interrupted. *Tamara* is mentioned from time to time. "If you don't hear *Tamara*," Balakirev writes, "it's only because I wouldn't want to present it to you in bits, as it is at present, still less to play some kind of paste-up of a few bars or figures, as I did for your brother."[11] Stasov hears from Rimsky-Korsakov that "*Tamara* is under way, and even whole pages have been newly composed!"[12] At last, in March, he hears Balakirev play, presumably, substantial excerpts. But somehow the work still does not get finished. Balakirev is preoccupied editing *Ruslan and Lyudmila,* with the help of Rimsky-Korsakov. He transcribes Berlioz's *Harold in Italy* for two pianos, and Stasov, in Paris for the 1878 World Exhibition, acts as his go-between with the publisher, Brandus & Cie. Meanwhile the indefatigable Stasov starts proposing subjects for new works, just like old times. He sends Balakirev the great vision-ary poem of chapter 6 of the book of Isaiah ("In the year that King Uzziah died, I saw also the Lord sitting upon a throne"), together with Pushkin's free paraphrase ("The Prophet"—"Prorok"). "Who knows," he muses, "maybe you will do something on this wonderful, incompa-rable subject, to which, in my opinion, nobody is so suited as you!"[13] Later he proposes Raphael's great Vatican fresco of the "Meeting of Pope Leo with Attila the Hun."[14] But Balakirev is concentrating on the *Ruslan* proofs, ignores the Isaiah idea, then elaborately rejects the Raphael as "not even a serious picture, but rather a Roman Catholic scherzo—an edifying vignette, fit for an illustrated volume of improv-ing works on the Ravenna Fathers, which, elegantly bound and illus-trated, might make a suitable impression as a reference book on a nice little table in [Nikolay] Shcherbachev's mummy's boudoir."[15] And still *Tamara* remains unfinished.

If Tchaikovsky was wrong about Balakirev, he was right enough about Cui, who had added more songs to his op. 9 and op. 10 sets, without apparently any greater desire to go beyond their bland charm. His *Thirteen Musical Pictures* (*Trinadtsat' muzikal'nïkh' kartinok'*) precisely fit Tchaikovsky's picture of the composer fussing over pretty little ideas, adorning and embellishing them, but never breaking out of the pat-tern imposed by the childlike imagery of what are apparently Cui's own poems: the little hare hopping around in the fir tree, the swallow arriving as herald of spring, the cockerel with his golden comb. Even where the poems have a genuinely folkish quality, the music does not, but remains firmly in the parlor of tonic-dominant harmony and two-

or four-bar phrases. Here and there the next set of romances, op. 11, attempt something more challenging. Most striking is Alexey Tolstoy's "To the Bell, Peacefully Dozing" ("V kolokol', mirno dremavshiy"), a poem that briefly recalls the *veche* scene in *The Maid of Pskov*, with its clamor of bells summoning the people to war. Within his limits, Cui achieves a certain vividness of sonority in response to the poet's crashing bombs and brazen bell peals, even if the potential horror of the scene escapes him. Settings of Adam Mickiewicz and Heine have the instant charm that Tchaikovsky identifies as characteristic of Cui; but as he also indicates, they lack personality, and might for the most part be by Schumann on a slightly off day.

As for Musorgsky, Tchaikovsky's assessment differs from Laroche's only in its avoidance of colorful imagery. And it seems unlikely that he would have moderated it in any way if he had been aware of the parlous condition of Musorgsky's personal life and health in the early months of 1878. Since working on act 2 of *Sorochintsï Fair* (at Naumov's dacha at Tsarskoye Selo) the previous August Musorgsky had composed nothing. In concert after concert he appeared as accompanist, invariably unpaid, rarely in music of his own: concerts in aid of working girls, concerts in aid of needy students, or wounded soldiers, or indigent artists. He accompanied Darya Leonova (the original Hostess in the *Boris* excerpts of 1873) on two or three occasions in April, and spent several weeks of the summer at her dacha in Peterhof, without—probably—producing anything more demanding than a vocal score of the fortune-telling scene from his old *Landless Peasant* draft for act 2 of *Khovanshchina*.

Petrov's death in March undoubtedly hit him hard—more, one might say, than was entirely natural. All his life he had depended to an abnormal degree on father and mother figures, and this dependency seems if anything to have grown more marked as his psychological condition worsened. The new closeness to Leonova, whether or not sexual in character, suggests an exceptional need of the moral support of an older woman (he was thirty-nine, she forty-nine and apparently happily married). And this need could sometimes emerge in the form of behavior that, in a disagreeably adult way, could only be described as infantile. Since the previous autumn, his drinking and its effects had grown worse. He would talk about "strange ailments" or—the old euphemism—"nervous fever." The condition would come in phases. After Petrov's funeral he calmed down for a while, and Lyudmila reported to Stasov that he had been to see her "completely straightened out and almost like a decent person."[16] At the end of July he and

Balakirev met at Lyudmila's for the first time since Balakirev's resurrection, and Balakirev was "pleasantly surprised by him as a person. No self-promotion or any kind of self-worship, on the contrary he was very modest, listened seriously to what was said to him, and didn't protest at all against the necessity of knowing harmony and even had nothing against working at it with Korsinka."[17] But within days the amenable façade had cracked. Several days running he appeared at Lyudmila's "looking dreadful and stayed quite a long while; seeing that things were getting worse, I felt I had to do something, and in order to save him and to protect myself, I wrote him a letter, asking him not to call on me when suffering from his nervous irritation (as he calls it)."[18] This ultimatum, from a woman he adored, had a sobering effect, and the next day he appeared at her apartment "in *complete* order." But Stasov, to whom she related all this, was not convinced.

> Before our eyes [he told Balakirev] one of the best, most talented of our comrades and brothers—Musorgsky—is quietly sinking into the water, down, down to the very bottom, like a ship in which damned worms are, day in day out, chewing a hole. Maybe all is not yet lost and he can be saved. He's surrounded by appalling drunkards and scoundrels of the worst, grossest variety: all his drinking companions at the Maly Yaroslavets—they're the ones who've dragged him down and ruined him, with his weak and impressionable nature. But you exert a strong attraction on all the best people, who include Musoryanin . . . It seems to me that if you want to, Mily, you can do, if not everything, then a lot. What's needed is to detach and remove him from his low drinking crowd and their whole vacuity. Ask him round often, see him often, smother him with work and jobs, with your kindness and gentleness and fatherly protection and helpfulness, don't leave him alone—it will be a self-sacrifice on your part, but you will be doing, perhaps, one of the greatest and noblest deeds of your entire life: you will be saving a human soul.[19]

Balakirev did his best. Musorgsky had brought his "Witches," as Balakirev still called *St. John's Night on Bald Mountain,* for his old mentor to look over, and Balakirev had sent him away with the usual instructions about how to remedy its defects. Whether or not he saw the revised *Mlada/Sorochintsï Fair* version and its beautiful new ending with chiming bells and dawn breaking is not altogether clear, though one suspects not, since he makes no mention of this striking and important change. Later there were meetings to discuss progress. But one evening in October Musorgsky failed to turn up, and Balakirev reacted with irritation. "So much for your talk about my beneficial influence," he grumbled to Stasov. "On the whole I've no hope of making a lively, energetic human being and composer out of Musorgsky. He's too physically damaged to be anything but the corpse he now is."[20]

Balakirev had also been trying to talk Borodin into giving more attention to composition, but had come to the conclusion that Lyudmila was to blame for distracting his attention by inviting too many irrelevant people to her evenings, instead of treating them as a species of night school in which the renascent Balakirev could offer instruction to the disorientated members of his former circle. But Borodin needed no help in the gentle art of self-distraction. Early in 1877 he had expressed to Karmalina the faint hope of finishing *Prince Igor* by the 1877–8 season. But he had then proceeded to spend a good part of the summer—theoretically his best time for composition—on a trip to Germany, escorting two students who were going to complete their studies in Jena, and paying a series of visits to Liszt in Weimar—visits that produced a sheaf of wonderful letters and a set of reminiscences, gave a great boost to Borodin's confidence, but seem to have done little to concentrate his creative energies. Later, holidaying with Yekaterina in the village of Davidovo in Vladimir province, east of Moscow, he tinkered with the string quartet he had sketched two or three years before, but otherwise spent most of his time walking in the pine forests and breathing in the wonderfully fresh, resinous air. Of *Prince Igor*, as far as we know, not a note was composed.

The following winter, as we have already seen, he composed Vladimir's act 2 cavatina and the duet with Konchakovna, but nothing much else apart from four short pieces for a collaborative piano work called *Paraphrases*. Once again he and Yekaterina holidayed at Davidovo, and this time the distraction was altogether more spectacular. One night the whole village caught fire, and they had to flee for their lives and spend the rest of the night in a field, where the nervy Yekaterina promptly had a fit of agoraphobia. Poor Borodin! Much as he adored his wife, he must sometimes have wished her on some remote planet where she could be an object of loving contemplation rather than an all-too-present destruction of the tranquility of his days and nights. According to Dianin, Yekaterina would never thereafter go to bed before dawn, and would insist, as before, on everyone else staying up until her bedtime. Nevertheless, soon after the fire Borodin went to Moscow, bought a piano, had it installed in the undamaged Davidovo house to which they had soon moved, and on it composed a substantial part of the scene in act I of *Prince Igor* in which a group of young girls plead unsuccessfully with Yaroslavna's brother, Vladimir Galitsky, to release one of their number who has been abducted by his retainers, and the retainers themselves—including the comic villains Skula and Yeroshka—sing a drunken song in praise of Galitsky. The composer seems to have had no difficulty thinking himself into this dazzling and chaotic tableau, and the music has an effortless brilliance of movement and portraiture that makes a complete mockery of Tchaikovsky's remarks about Borodin's supposed technical ineptitude. Liszt had been more perspicacious. "Please don't listen," he had urged after playing through Borodin's B-minor symphony, "to those who hold you back from your direction; believe me, you are on a true path, and you have so much artistic flair that you have nothing to fear in being original; remember that exactly the same advice was given to Beethoven and Mozart and others in their time, and they would never have become great masters if they had thought of following such advice."[21]

As for the *Paraphrases,* this was one collaborative work that actually got written and published. It had started some years previously as a polka that Borodin had composed for a little girl (his future adopted daughter, Ganya) who had asked to play a piano duet with him. Since it turned out that all she could play was the two-finger piece known in Russia as "Tati-tati" (a version of "Chopsticks"), Borodin had simply composed a polka that fitted that piece played over and over as an ostinato, or a kind of "ground treble," with ingenious harmonic digressions in the grown-up part. Later Rimsky-Korsakov suggested a set of pieces written in the same way. So Borodin, after an initial show of reluctance, added a "Funeral March" and a "Requiem" (with mock organ introduction and phantom voice parts), and there were other pieces by Cui, the young Anatoly Lyadov, and Rimsky-Korsakov himself, whose contribution, unsurprisingly, included a "Fugue grotesque" and a "Fughetta on B-A-C-H." The young pianist was simply required to repeat "Tati-tati" for the entire duration, pretty much as children have rattled away at "Chopsticks" ever since Euphemia Allen first had the infuriating idea at about the time that *Paraphrases* was conceived. The collection was published in 1879, and a copy was sent to Liszt, who liked it so much that he wrote a fragment of his own which was duly included in facsimile—along with a piece by Shcherbachev and a new mazurka by Borodin—in a second edition of 1893.[22]

Meanwhile, Rimsky-Korsakov's work with Balakirev on the editing of Glinka prompted him to take another look at *The Maid of Pskov,* and soon afterward it inspired him to set about composing a new opera. He seems to have recognized early on that this was a decisive moment in his career. "Work on Glinka's scores," he wrote fifteen years later, "was an unexpected schooling for me." He had allowed himself to become bogged down in schoolroom studies of a conventional kind, and suddenly here he was confronted by the sheer freshness of a genius who had never known a lecture theatre, who had learned all he needed to know by direct encounters with music and musicians, and who had merely taken a few months of crash instruction by a German theorist in order to knock all these different influences into some kind of cohesive style. "I greedily lapped up all his methods," the ever-studious Rimsky-Korsakov reports. "I studied his handling of the natural brass instruments, which give his orchestration such unspeakable transparency and lightness; I studied his elegant and natural part-writing. And this for me was a salutary discipline, leading me out as it did onto the path of contemporary music, after my vicissitudes with counterpoint and strict style."[23]

For a start, he looked on *The Maid of Pskov*, and found it wanting. It was altogether too unbalanced, too rich in harmonic extravagances, too poor in counterpoint, too roughly structured, too obviously the product of an untutored method. With characteristic thoroughness he embarked on a root-and-branch revision. What was there he rewrote bar by bar, enriching the texture, regularizing the harmony, expanding some scenes, contracting others, adding counterpoints, and generally making a respectable woman of the poor maid. Above all he composed an entirely new prologue, taken from Mey's original play (and including the lullaby he had composed eleven years before), about Olga's mother, Vera Sheloga, her confession to her sister, Nadezhda, of how she had fallen in love with a boyar who rescued her when she was lost in the forest and had given birth to his child, and how this boyar turned out to be Tsar Ivan himself. At the end of the prologue, Vera's husband returns from the wars, and Nadezhda, to save her sister, claims the child, Olga, as her own. Apart from this thirty-minute scene, Rimsky-Korsakov added a number of new episodes, including a confrontation between the tsar and a *yurodivy* called Nikola the Simpleton, all too obviously modelled on the St. Basil's scene in *Boris Godunov*, and a (partly fugal) chorus of wandering pilgrims based on a folk tune called "Poem About Alexey, Man of God," which Rimsky included, he tells us, on Balakirev's insistence "in view of the beautiful tune and because of his penchant for saints and the religious element in general."[24]

This 1877 *Maid of Pskov* turned out in every respect better written and more substantial than the original. But alas, no one liked it. The circle gave it routine endorsement but without warmth; even the composer's wife was tepid, and to tell the truth the composer himself found it hard to prefer it to the original. "I also felt that in its new form my opera was long, dry, and rather heavy, in spite of its improved design and noteworthy technique."[25] He offered it to the Imperial Theatres for production, but Nápravník was as unenthusiastic as everyone else, and nothing happened. The second version of the opera was neither performed nor published, and in the end Rimsky-Korsakov was reduced to plundering it for other works. He extracted the "Alexey" chorus and published it separately; he took the short overture to the prologue and four of the entr'actes and turned them into a suite of incidental music for Mey's drama, likewise neither performed nor published as such. And many years later he made yet another, final version of the opera—without the prologue, which he worked up and published as a separate one-acter called *The Boyarina Vera Sheloga.*[26] Suddenly, having belonged to a group of composers who seldom finished a single work, he had become a sort of magician who could turn one work into five without obvious effort. This facility might partly account for his friends' cool reception of what had once been a model kuchkist artifact. It certainly explains Tchaikovsky's muted admiration, and his uncertainty as to whether Rimsky-Korsakov would "turn out a great master" or be "completely swallowed up in contrapuntal complexities."

In the event, release from this latter fate came through the composition of a completely new opera, based on a Gogol story to which his attention had been drawn by his then fiancée, Nadezhda Purgold, more than six years before. This was "May Night" ("Mayskaya Noch' "), in the same collection—*Evenings on a Farmstead near Dikanka*—as contained "Sorochintsï Fair." At the time that he and Nadezhda read this story together he had just been appointed to the conservatory, and his thoughts were turning toward the technical demands that, one way or another, had preoccupied him ever since. But by 1878, when virtually all his *May Night* was composed, his studies had taken a fresh turn. Putting together his folk-song collection, he had taken an interest not only in the tunes and the words for themselves, but also in their specific ceremonial or seasonal associations. *May Night* offered the possibility of incorporating this kind of material in an actual drama, making sure that the songs sung at particular points of the tale were the right ones in the right place and at the right time.

Gogol himself tells us only the month in which his story happens, but this is quite enough of a clue for Rimsky-Korsakov to color in the rituals for that time of year in rural Ukraine, where all the Dikanka stories take place. For Gogol, spring is the best time for the flowering of love on warm nights when "the earth . . . is suffused with silver light; the marvellous air is cool and heady, full of sweetness, and awash with an ocean of fragrance."[27] It is a time for serenading, but also a time for all kinds of strange and sinister manifestations, genuine magic, not just the counterfeit sorcery of the Gypsy in "Sorochintsï Fair." Levko, Gogol's hero, is in love with the fair Hanna, but his father, the village mayor, who also has designs on her, is forbidding their marriage. Levko tells Hanna the story of a strange house by a nearby lake whose owner had married a witch after the death of his first wife, and the two of them had driven his daughter out of the house. The girl (Pannochka) had thrown herself into the lake and turned into a *rusalka*—a water nymph—dragging her evil stepmother into the water after her. That night Levko is walking near the old house, singing and strumming his bandura (Ukrainian archlute), when suddenly the drowned girl appears, the *rusalki* all play a game of raven, and the unhappy girl implores Levko to identify the stepmother, who continues to haunt her while herself disguised as a nymph. When he does so, she rewards him with a letter for his father, purporting to be from the Commissar, and instructing him to permit his son's marriage. Gogol locates this jiggery-pokery clearly as genre within actual village life—the unpopular mayor and his sister-in-law, the drunken charcoal burner, the distiller who now lives in the old house, the village lads and lasses—and he positively begs for the whole thing to be turned into an opera, so plentiful is its musical imagery:[28] Levko with his bandura, the young villagers "pouring out their cheerful souls in song," the charcoal burner and his tipsy *gopak*, the boys' song about the Mayor, the round dance of the *rusalki*. The composer had only to follow Gogol and his libretto fell into place, song, dialogue, and all.

Whether or not he was in any way influenced by Musorgsky's current on-off engagement with *Sorochintsï Fair*, there is obvious common ground between the two operas, starting of course with Gogol's own inimitable style of storytelling, his wonderful sense of place and character, his particular way of mixing down-to-earth reality with flashes of magic and witchcraft. Both works have a folksy air, derived from the unconcealed use of authentic folk songs; both employ folk tunes as a basic material also for arioso and even recitative. Both seem now to embody what Taruskin calls "not a progressive but a retrograde tendency,"[29] even if one confines oneself to questions of musical and narrative style, and avoids discussing the somewhat ambiguous politics of aligning oneself in the troubled, populist 1870s with the increasingly right-wing and antiprogressive author of *Dead Souls,* who had died in 1852. They belong, rather, to some pre-*kuchka* epoch of folk vaudeville, or the early operas of Weber or Lortzing, or (in the case of *May Night*) the multitude of early-romantic water-sprite operas, from Hoffmann's *Undine* to Wagner's *Die Feen* and, of course, Dargomïzhsky's *Rusalka.* Of the novel elements of *Boris Godunov* or *The Maid of Pskov* they are largely innocent. *May Night* is a pretty opera with atmospheric moments, some effective orchestration, but, in operatic terms, mostly stock characters. An obvious (and much-cited) parallel is with Smetana's *Bartered Bride,* composed in the early sixties and first staged in St. Petersburg in 1871. But Smetana's work sounds much deeper psychological tones than Rimsky-Korsakov's, and even for a time veers toward tragedy, of which there is no real trace in *May Night.*

Apart from its easy charm, the main interest of *May Night* lies in its careful placement of its folk materials, their precise application. *Sorochintsï Fair* has as many authentic tunes, but their use is nonspecific in relation to ceremony or ritual. By contrast, Rimsky-Korsakov's method tends toward a kind of ethnographic purity, with folk materials entirely taken from an unimpeachable source, Alexander Rubets's collection of *216 Ukrainian Folk Songs,* published in 1871. His opera starts, after the overture, with a millet-sowing game for two "teams" (double chorus); later he combines two songs for Trinity Sunday (in the chorus "I wind garlands on every feast day," "Oy! Zav'yu venki na vsye svyatki"—*svyatki* is Christmastide, but here it refers to Trinity, the so-called "Green Christmas"); and in the final scene, the offstage chorus approaches singing a *rusal'naya pesnya* (connected with the fast days between Whitsun and St. John the Baptist's Day) and another song about the Green Christmas, the *zelonïye svyatki.* There are other, less specific folk songs, and there are beautiful melodies that are pure Rimsky-Korsakov: Levko's first aria, for instance, is a Ukrainian folk tune out of Rubets, but his song by the lake in act 3 is original, pentatonic to be sure (you can play its main theme, transposed, on the black keys of a piano), but too rangy to be a folk song. In general the tenor, Levko, has the best solo music in the whole work. But the most touching moments are the folk choruses, especially the offstage *rusal'naya,* which counterpoints and, so to speak, reprimands the comic scene of the reading of the "Commissar's" letter with its "Dust on the road, commotion in the oakwood, a father is murdering his daughter." Rimsky-Korsakov was proud of the counterpoint in *May Night,* which he felt at last escaped from the schoolroom and became simply one element in a sophisticated compositional technique. He also claimed that he had written *podgoloski*—Russian folk heterophony—a year before Melgunov described the phenomenon in his folk-song collection of 1879.[30] In the Trinity song in act I of *May Night* the chorus sopranos and altos sing different variants of the same melody in two-part harmony that sometimes is, and sometimes is not, actually in two parts. No doubt *podgoloski* in its natural habitat was less elegant and well-bred than this; but the idea is right.[31]

Thus this attractive but unremarkable opera turns out to mark a significant stage in its thirty-four-year-old composer's development. Just when folk-song collecting was becoming scientific, and taxonomy was starting to replace beautification, Rimsky-Korsakov showed that art, too, could be precise about the reality on which it drew. At least in one aspect of his work he acts like a photographer, recording the living environment even while his drama is acted out by pasteboard figures such as never walked a real street or a forest path. From now on, for him, opera would be a realism of context rather than narrative, a trawl through ancient customs and rituals and their associated tales, poems, and music, often attached to stories as remote as could possibly be imagined from the kind of historical or contemporary truth espoused by Belinsky or Stasov. Day-to-day realism ceased to appeal. "It's wearisome somehow," he complained to Vasily Yastrebtsev years later, "to listen to these fools—the Mayor, the Scribe, and the rest—after the *rusalki* and Pannochka, whom I love and will always love as much as I do Snegurochka [the Snow Maiden], Mlada, and the Sea Queen."[32]

May Night reached the stage quickly, in January 1880, and, being tuneful and easily grasped, it went down well with the audience, badly with the press. Cui grumbled in his *Vedomosti* review that the only decent ideas were the borrowed folk tunes, and Rimsky-Korsakov reports that when he ran into Malvina Cui soon afterward she sneered at him: "Now you've learned how to write operas."[33] He understood the remark as a stab at the opera's popular success. But perhaps it was also adding opera to the inventory of techniques that Rimsky-Korsakov, in defiance of best circle practice, had mastered by study. If so, it was a curious complaint to level at *May Night*, whose weaknesses, whatever they may have been, hardly included erudition.

CHAPTER 27

The Chemist in His Laboratory

In the early months of 1879 it was suddenly possible to hear some of the latest, and some of the not so latest, music by the *kuchka. Boris Godunov* was still in repertory at the Maryinsky, though now even more heavily cut than when first put on. On the other hand, the FMS was once again able to mount a concert series in January and February, after a silence of almost two years for lack of funds, and Rimsky-Korsakov seized the opportunity to program the cell scene from *Boris,* which was still excluded from stage performances of the opera and in fact had never been heard in any form in public. He also conducted excerpts from *Prince Igor* and *May Night* (a complete novelty, of course), Bala-kirev's Czech overture, and Borodin's B-minor symphony with its revised scoring. A casual visitor, unfamiliar with the history of these various works, might well have formed the impression of a hyperactive group of composers. He might have been struck by the power of the symphony, the dramatic intensity of the cell scene, the sheer brilliance of the Polovtsian Dances and the Rimsky-Korsakov choruses. Stasov, though, had his own slightly eccentric preference, influenced, perhaps, by the demands of renewed friendship. "I was literally driven mad with delight," he wrote to Balakirev, "by your Czech overture. And I wasn't alone . . . . It's simply a masterpiece of beauty, strength, energy, and fan-tasy."[1] Even Balakirev, who was still not attending concerts, must have blushed at such praise of what he certainly knew to be a minor, if effec-tive, work. "They say the Czech overture went splendidly," he remarked modestly to Rimsky-Korsakov, but then quickly switched to Liszt's

Hamlet, which Rimsky had called "a headache, mechanistic, and heavily scored." "Even Liszt's weakest things should be performed at least once," Balakirev insisted, "since listening to them is extremely instructive for Russian composers, and no less necessary for the public."[2]

Musorgsky, who had assiduously attended Maryinsky *Boris* rehearsals, also put in an appearance at Rimsky-Korsakov's rehearsal of the cell scene. But he was of strictly limited usefulness. He was either drunk or acting drunk, and "often made," Rimsky recalled, "obscure and involved speeches.

> At the rehearsal in question, he listened with great intensity to what was being played, for the most part carried away by the performance of individual instruments, often in the most ordinary and indifferent musical phrases, now pensively hanging his head, now haughtily raising it and shaking his mane, now lifting his hand with the theatrical gesture that he had often made in the past. When at the end of the scene the tamtam representing the monastery bell sounded pianissimo, Musorgsky made it a deep and deferential bow, with his arms crossed on his chest.[3]

But the critics, of course, had their own brand of irony. "I am not in the least exaggerating," one wrote, "if I say that the best place in this music is the blows on the beautiful tamtam. Just imagine, Mr. Musorgsky could not find anything wittier for this scene than to give the orchestra a figure from everyday five-finger exercises," as if, he muses, Pimen were doing his piano practice.[4] Hermann Laroche was more direct. "A very tender love is necessary," he asserted, "to give the inspirations of [Musorgsky's] muse a place on a concert program between Weber and Beethoven . . . I do not hear any spark of poetry in this declamation, so extolled by the composer's adherents."[5]

The composer himself was still acting as unpaid accompanist for every kind of charitable concert, while composing little or nothing of his own. He apparently wrote no music at all before late June, when he signed and dated a fragment of Marfa's scene with Andrey before St. Basil's—in act 4, scene 2—of *Khovanshchina.* Exactly when he composed the rest of this scene, in which Dosifey and Marfa decide that self-immolation is the only recourse for the Old Believers, while the streltsy enter the square carrying their own execution blocks, only to learn that Tsar Peter has reprieved them, is not known. Meanwhile, in March, he had accompanied Leonova in a mixed concert of Russian music including, for once, music of his own (the song "Gopak"

and Marfa's song from act 3 of *Khovanshchina*); and three weeks later
he played at an "artistic evening" which included readings by Fyodor
Dostoyevsky from *The Brothers Karamazov* and a performance by Fyodor
Stravinsky of Musorgsky's song "King Saul." Early in July he again
moved into Leonova's Peterhof dacha, and there he composed the heroine Parasha's song (her so-called dumka) in the final act of *Sorochintsï
Fair,* and possibly also the scene of Marfa with Andrey in the final act
of *Khovanshchina*, before the self-immolation.[6]

But it was a brief interlude. A fortnight later he and Leonova set
off on a three-month concert tour of southern Russia that would take
him farther from St. Petersburg than he had ever previously travelled,
would leave him weakened in health and little if at all strengthened in
his finances, and would ensure that work on both operas ground to a
complete halt until the end of the year.

Needless to say, Stasov was in despair over this tour. "Our poor
Musoryanin," he grumbled to Borodin, "your Siamese twin in point of
originality, is quite lost.

> On 21 July he went off on a tour of Russia, imagine who with—with
> Leonova, in the guise of her accompanist!! Useless to argue with him
> or try to dissuade him from this servile, lackey role as stooge to our
> Gypsy Patti. No, he digs in his heels and won't understand. He says,
> "Rubinstein also accompanies; he also goes and gives concerts!" What
> a comparison!!!!! Of course, instead of the 1000 rubles he hopes for to
> pay his debts, he'll scarcely get a few kopeks, and he'll get more drunk
> than ever, entertaining all those merchants and vice-governors. Poor
> ex-Prometheus![7]

The Gypsy and her ex-Prometheus were heard in Poltava and Eliza-
vetgrad, in Nikolayev and Kherson, in Odessa, Sevastopol, Yalta,
Rostov-on-the-Don, Novocherkassk, in Voronezh, Tambov, and Tver.
Their programs were hybrid. There would be a song by Schubert, a
song or two by Musorgsky himself, some Dargomïzhsky or Serov or
Glinka, perhaps a group of folk songs. And in between vocal items,
Musorgsky would play a solo or two. But though he had been a good
pianist in his time, these days he was little more than a keyboard func-
tionary. He had, Rimsky-Korsakov notes, "no repertory whatsoever."
Drunk or sober, he could sight-read in musicianly fashion anything
you cared to put in front of him, but he could not play you a Beethoven
sonata or a Chopin study remotely to a concert standard. His Leonova
solos, therefore, had to be knocked up mainly from his own music,

or even out of his head on the spur of the moment. He would play excerpts from *Khovanshchina* or *Sorochintsï Fair* (including the recently composed gopak) in piano reduction, or the coronation scene from *Boris* ("with the Great Pealing of Bells") or a piano arrangement of *Jesus Navin*. Doubtless he modified these pieces to suit his technique or even his whim of the hour, since the music must have been mostly quite unknown to his audiences. Occasionally he improvised from scratch. In Odessa he played a fantasy on Jewish melodies heard that same day in the local synagogue; but not a note of any such music ever got written down. Two somewhat juvenile pieces that he did eventually manage to get down on paper—"On the Southern Shore of the Crimea" ("Na yuzhom beregu Krïma") and "Near the Southern Shore of the Crimea" ("Bliz yuzhogo berega Krïma")—plainly began life in the same way, and there was another piece, "a rather long and extremely confused fantasy that was meant to depict a storm on the Black Sea," which he played at a Rimsky-Korsakov soirée but apparently never did write down.[8] Anyone who has ever had to extemporize at the piano (as opposed to the organ in church) will recognize the signs at once: the babyish themes, the simple, repetitive figuration, the elementary harmonies, the total absence of counterpoint.

What the provincial audiences thought of such stuff is not recorded by any objective observer. Musorgsky's own letters home, to a skeptical readership, are naturally inclined to present everything in the most glowing terms. The audiences are not large, but they are "representative" or "select"; the takings "good, but less than we expected"; the artistic triumph is "unquestionable," "tremendous"; Leonova herself is "beyond comparison," and her voice "not only has lost none of its force and freshness, but has gained in power." He talks about the significance of their tour as a service to art. "Ukrainian men and women," he tells Stasov (who dislikes the whole idea of *Sorochintsï Fair*), "have recognized that the character of the *Sorochintsï* music is thoroughly national." "Life calls for new musical labors, broad musical work," he enthuses to Lyudmila Shestakova; "further, still further on the good road; what I am doing is understood; with great vigor *toward the new shores* of art, which so far is limitless!"

It is hard to relate such biblical pronouncements to the reality of Leonova's scrappy, potpourri programs or the likely character of her audiences, which consisted mainly of provincial civil servants and their wives, stiffened by military families from the local garrisons. The landowners were for the most part away on their estates. In the home of a certain Captain Yurkovsky, in Nikolayev, they were greeted "with sincere cordiality," and Musorgsky sang his *Nursery* cycle to the captain's children. Nothing so substantial figured in Leonova's public concerts. Nor were they always so well received. In Yalta, which they reached from Sevastopol in a springless, horse-drawn tarantass, they were set down "in some mud-hut [in fact, an ill-kept private house] along with centipedes that bite and a kind of snapping beetle, which also bites, and other insects that justify their earthly existence by an ideal of making life nasty for people." By some miracle, in Yalta lived Vladimir Stasov's daughter Sofia Fortunato, and by an even greater miracle she owned and managed a clean, comfortable, well-run hotel (the Rossiya: "a large house, with baths and a garden, on the harbor"),[9] into which she promptly moved them as her guests. But her own account of the circumstances is revealing.

> When I arrived at the concert, I saw to my chagrin a very small number of concertgoers, although at that time the highest society from the capital and other towns, so to speak, converged on Yalta . . . In the first interval I rushed to the green room. M.P. was sitting in an armchair, disheartened, like a wounded bird. The lack of audience and the failure of the concert had obviously had a serious effect on him.[10]

In this particular case, though, steps could be taken. The Rossiya "had a magnificent, large hall with a decent grand piano, and, moreover, the hotel was full of people whom it would be possible to interest in the forthcoming concert. This time the concert was a great success."

But as in Nikolayev, the best music-making was in private. "We managed," Madame Fortunato explains, "to listen to many of Musorgsky's wonderful songs performed by the composer himself and Leonova, but above all several scenes from *Boris* and *Khovanshchina*. Is it necessary to say how great and powerful the experience was for those listeners, including the young and the old who had almost never or not at all listened to music, and were shaken to the depths of their being?"[11] These were the tour's best moments; but Yalta (perhaps among other places) also witnessed some of the worst. We can imagine the details all too well from a letter Stasov wrote to his daughter a day or two before the travellers' return to St. Petersburg.

> I was vexed by only one thing that I learned from your letter, namely that he continued with the same outrageous behavior as here. It was impossible for us to discover this from anyone previously—and it's specifically what interested us: we all hoped that perhaps the change of

scene and company and the unexpected novelty of travel would bring about some kind of revolution in him, would set him to rights. Vain hope—everything has remained as before.[12]

Amid the general gloom of this strange episode in Musorgsky's life, one small light shines. At some point on the tour he made a setting of Mephistopheles' song in Auerbach's cellar from Goethe's *Faust*: the so-called "Song of the Flea." Exactly when and for what reason he composed this song is hard to establish; it was certainly written for Leonova and is dedicated to her, but she seems not to have performed it until they were back in St. Petersburg.

At first sight, the piece sits oddly among Musorgsky's realist songs, and it certainly does not belong with his romances. But the mistake is to see the text in isolation.[13] Mephistopheles's absurd tale of the king who loves his flea so much that he has him fitted with an expensive outfit, appoints him minister of state, and forbids his courtiers to scratch when bitten, is a satire, not on royalty, but on the coarseness and futility of tavern life, as symbolized by Brander's only slightly less stupid song about the poisoned rat who believes his affliction to be unrequited love. It is this exaggerated absurdity that is the real subject matter of Musorgsky's song. Of course, Russian and Russianist basses from Chaliapin on have tended to test the self-parody to destruction, with their demonic laughter and their heavy insinuations on the repeated word *blokha* ("flea": the creature is for some reason feminine in Russian). But this is not wholly alien to Musorgsky's image of a Mephistopheles who is showing Faust that no matter how vulgar or fatuous the entertainment, it will go down well with the mindless and the drink-sodden. One hopes that the composer's brilliant re-creation of this vignette was not inspired by his own condition. The song's immaculate workmanship seems to suggest that it was not.

While Musorgsky was trekking round the Ukraine, Borodin had returned for the summer to Davidovo, despite unhappy memories of the previous year's fire, and despite the fact that the house he would be staying in had other occupants, no beds, a broken stove, and chairs that gave way when you sat on them.[14] His piano, though, had been moved in, along with various papers, which (characteristically, one fears) included sketches for *Prince Igor* that he had forgotten about. The first music he worked on, though, was the string quartet he had started five whole years before and that still lacked its scherzo. In essence, the work dated from the winter of 1874–5, at a time when Rimsky-Korsakov had also been writing a string quartet as an escape from his fugal studies, but had ended up filling the quartet with fugues after all. Borodin's A-major quartet is also quite generously supplied with fugue, and may well originally have been the outcome of conversations with Rimsky about the desirability of proving oneself in the kind of chamber music not much favored by the Balakirev circle. But there is no doubt which of these two works is the more successful and characteristic. Rimsky-Korsakov's work is patently an experiment in applied technique; Borodin's is a minor masterpiece.

Probably the real model for the fugal elements—in every one of the four movements except the scherzo—was in any case not Rimsky-Korsakov but late Beethoven. On the title page of the original edition, published in Hamburg in 1884, Borodin added a note: "angeregt durch ein Thema von Beethoven" ("prompted by a theme by Beethoven"), the theme in question being the second subject of the substitute finale of the B-flat quartet, op. 130, which is practically quoted as the allegro first subject of Borodin's first movement. Roger Fiske once suggested that the reference was accidental and the acknowledgment a face-saving recourse after the fact.[15] But if so, the discovery was made early on, since Borodin pointedly repeats the theme in Beethoven's key (A-flat) in his development section, which would be unlikely in an A-major movement without the conscious allusion. But Borodin had used this kind of starting point before, in his early Cello Sonata, based on a Bach theme overheard from the next-door flat in Heidelberg. He seems not to have felt apologetic about such borrowings; in fact one suspects he was rather proud of them.

In any case, his quartet writing is fundamentally unlike Beethoven's. Where Beethoven had used the equality of the four instruments as pretext for the intense working of themes and motives, Borodin's approach remains essentially lyrical, with fugal episodes as conscious intrusions of formal counterpoint. When he wants to complicate the texture, he simply enriches the accompaniment, sometimes spectacularly so, as in the rolling arpeggio embroideries of the second subject in the development section and the first subject in the recapitulation. A cellist himself, he may seem to be chancing his arm in such passages, which can sound laborious in performance, though technically unproblematic on paper. But there are few things more exquisite, even in Beethoven, than the trio section of the scherzo, a wonderful tapestry of high violin and cello harmonics supported by semiquaver figures in the alto register, *con sordino*. There might be a faint memory of the musette trio in the scherzo of Beethoven's A-minor quartet, op. 132. But really Borodin's piece is a completely original find, made perhaps with cello in hand.

Indeed the whole scherzo, largely composed at Davidovo in 1879, is one of his most brilliant and stylish inventions, and one that makes nonsense of his supposed inability to compose without help. Borodin's problem was not technique but time and mental space. Given those rare commodities, he could write with fluency and flair.

The result, admittedly, belongs to a straightforward classical quartet tradition. Hardly anything in the work would identify it as Russian, except possibly the andante theme in F-sharp minor (Aeolian mode), which Dianin traced to the same "Sparrow Hills" folk song that had formed the basis of the "Chorus of Glorification" he had composed almost four years earlier, a few months after the initial drafts of the quartet.[16] This is Russian, though, in the same way as the slow movement of Tchaikovsky's first quartet of 1871, which Borodin must certainly have known: a modal folk tune harmonized like any ordinary tonal melody, then twisted into a fugue subject with a chromatic headpiece. Apart from this, Borodin's A-major quartet is if anything less folksy than Tchaikovsky's D-major. Its Russianness has to be teased out of certain minor devices of harmony and melody that the *kuchka* tended to copy from one another or from their historic mentor, Glinka.

It is worth comparing this andante with the beautiful chorus of peasants that Borodin inserted, during these same months at Davidovo, between Yaroslavna's lament and her reunion duet with Prince Igor in the final act of the opera. Here again the key is F-sharp minor and the mode Aeolian (the mode of the piano white notes starting on A); but now the music is genuinely modal, with hardly a single note outside the scale. Moreover, the chorus is partly composed in *podgoloski* style, like Rimsky-Korsakov's Trinity song in *May Night*, and with *peremennost'* (the tendency to switch to a lower keynote, in this case from the F-sharp to the unison E on "gore naveval"—"that blew sorrow [down on us]"). It's as if, with a string quartet, Borodin had been conscious above all of writing in a Western tradition, whereas with Russian operatic peasants he was positioning himself no less consciously within a nationalist tradition defined, romantically, by thinkers like Stasov and, ethnographically, by recent collectors of folk song, from Balakirev to Prokunin and even Melgunov, whose collection came out precisely in 1879.

During the summer, though, he composed a swath of music for the opera's first act that shows him adopting folk idioms on a much broader platform, as a way of defining all kinds of people, as groups, and even—in particular cases—as individuals. In 1878 at Davidovo, as we saw, he had composed the scene in which the girls plead in vain with Galitsky to release their abducted friend, after which Galitsky's retinue (including Skula and Yeroshka) sing his praises and call for him to take over as ruler. Now he completes this scene with Galitsky's own apostrophe to fun, drink, and sex as a recipe for good governance (just before the girls come to plead, so that we know their chance of success is not high), then continues with the remainder of the act, in which Yaroslavna (after her arioso) hears the girls' complaint against Galitsky, confronts him with it, then receives the boyars who report the defeat of the Russian army and the capture of Igor and his son. This whole act forms a complete dramatic entity full of action and color and rich in portraiture of a psychologically rounded type. If only Borodin had been able to continue his work on this level, what an opera *Prince Igor* would be! But the fact is that at this stage he still had no finished scenario but was still working from hand to mouth dramaturgically. And so it would continue.

Not the least remarkable feature of this act is the powerful continuity that is able to embrace so many characters and episodes, and such a wide range of musical materials. The pacing, for an act compiled at such intervals, is amazingly assured. The tone is set by the opening "Slava" chorus (composed 1875), then swiftly taken up by Galitsky himself in his recitative and song (1879). The mood is rough and unruly. The men, patently, are buoyed up by alcohol, and what they sing is essentially street music: coarse, rowdy, and suggestive. As a crowd they are what police sometimes nowadays call "good-natured": that is, to be avoided. And Galitsky is as bad as the rest, expressing the most unsavory sentiments in a loutish, foursquare drinking song distantly reminiscent of Varlaam's Kazan song in *Boris Godunov*, but without even Varlaam's pretense at heroism. When the girls appear, they plead with Galitsky in the style of a folk lament, with chromatic inflections, still at a tempo that implies a certain urgency (1878); but his response is lazy, mock-reassuring: "What are you women howling about? Your sister will be well looked after . . . " This comes twice, in the manner of a verse and refrain, at the end of which Galitsky shoos the girls away. Then enter the so-called gudok-players, Skula and Yeroshka, who act as rabble rousers for Galitsky's retinue in what Borodin, with nicely placed irony, christened "Knyazhaya pesnya" ("Princely Song," or "Song About the Prince": 1878), again essentially a wild drinking chorus, with solo repartee for the tenor Yeroshka and the bass Skula in the manner of a rhyming party game: "bring us bitter—brew it [*navari*]; bring us sweet—fill it [*nasiti*]; bring us vodka—still it [*nakuri*]," and so on. Finally, in an orgy of drunken celebration, the men name Galitsky as their chosen leader, before reeling away into oblivion in a well-modulated musical fade-out.

The scene now changes to Yaroslavna's quarters, and the frenzied mood gives way to anxious calm and a general atmosphere of genteel femininity (1869). The rough folkishness that dominated the previous scene is replaced by a flexible, free-flowing arioso, eloquent but restrained, as befits a princess of the blood. But when the girls come in (1879), they revert to the folk character of their scene with Galitsky, albeit in a gentler, more respectful tone (until, that is, they turn to describing the behavior we ourselves have just witnessed, which they do in a breathless five-four chatter not unlike that of Musorgsky's "Dearest Savishna"; this passage was probably not composed until 1880). The scene that follows between Yaroslavna and Galitsky (1879) is a superb piece of confrontational music drama, the two utterly different personalities maintained against one another, while the progress of their dispute is carefully charted by the musical pacing. Yaroslavna is at first reproachful but dignified (arioso, allegro moderato); but Galitsky's tone is cheeky from the start, adapting the motive of his first entrance ("It would be a sin to hide that I dislike boredom") to what now becomes an insolent, indolent brush-off: "It's none of your business, and curtsey when you speak to me." He even borrows a musical phrase from Yeroshka's party game: "I keep what I seize, I seize what I want, and what I have seized I neither know nor wish to know." Yaroslavna flies at him—*agitato* but contained—with the threat of Igor's return, referring to the main theme of her arioso on this precise topic, but Galitsky only repeats his mocking song—"What is your Igor to me?"—and when she rebukes him for threatening her with retribution when he takes over as ruler, he repeats it once more, a semitone down, with the ultimate masculine sneer that "I was only joking; I wanted to see you get angry." Borodin thus turns their argument into a kind of refrain form in which it really is hard to see how Yaroslavna, with all her grandeur of personality, can get the better of this ruthless and dissolute brother. In the end, she dismisses him from her presence, but shaking with emotion and weary at heart. And the music trembles and sinks down with her.

The complicated finale (1879) starts with the arrival of the boyars as messengers of Igor's defeat and capture, to music of great solemnity, matched by Yaroslavna's restored arioso of dignity. Like their Muscovite confreres in *Boris Godunov*, the Putivl boyars are a sturdy but bovine crew, qualities that Borodin captures in unison choral writing of an impressive, lumbering stolidity, against which Yaroslavna's growing agitation and random interventions stand out for their warmth and immediacy of feeling. Such contrasts, so often treated as stereotypes in romantic opera, Borodin seems to have been able to imagine in vividly human terms, and everything in this scene is truthful and touching.

In the second part the boyars, having informed Yaroslavna that the army has been destroyed and her husband and son taken prisoner by a tribe of godless barbarians, cheerfully reassure her that the city walls are sound and have always withstood attack. She is doing her best to look happy at this news when the tocsin booms out warning that the city is indeed under attack, the fortress in flames and the people fleeing. This was the sequence of events left by Rimsky-Korsakov when he edited the act from the confusion of Borodin's papers. But there survives also a brief but highly dramatic scene before the tocsin (1879), in which Galitsky breaks in with his retinue, shouting that the Polovtsï are at the gates, and threatening to seize power there and then himself. Why Rimsky-Korsakov (or Borodin) excluded this passage is unclear. The music is crude, certainly, like the participants: a violent five-four solo and chorus are answered by the boyars rebuking the intruders in their bluff, monometric style, and insisting on their loyalty to the absent Prince Igor. But dramatically the episode is important, because it confirms Galitsky not just as a repellent wastrel but as a serious political threat.

Unfortunately Borodin was never able to pursue the implications of this marvellous act, much of which is left hanging by what survives of the later Putivl scenes. Galitsky, so menacing at this point, plays no further part in the drama; Skula and Yeroshka reappear at the very end in time to assert their undying loyalty to the throne. We are left with the frustrating sense of having witnessed a great musical dramatist at work, but without the finished product of his labors. The torso of *Prince Igor* may lack the consistent power and originality of Musorgsky's best work, but in quality of idea and in its sense of character and the stage picture, it is scarcely inferior. Its realism is the natural instinct of the intelligent, humane dramatist, not the hard-won truthfulness of the ex-theorist. Its barbarism is superbly unconstrained, as barbarism must be but, in nineteenth-century opera, seldom is. Had Borodin ever completed the work, it would surely have ranked with *Boris Godunov* among the great music dramas of the age. As it is, like *Khovanshchina,* it remains a potential, sometimes vivid, sometimes shrouded in uncertainty, never less than exciting: a Venus de Milo among operas, as intriguing for what is not there as beautiful for what is.

One day in December 1879, Musorgsky reported to Arseny Golenishchev-Kutuzov that for the past few months he had been suffering from "some kind of strange illness, which broke out with such force in November that my doctor, who knows me well, gave me only two hours to live."[17] No doubt it was the old trouble, and the doctor, Lev Bertensson, knew Musorgsky well enough to know that only the direst threats could be expected to influence his behavior. Whether even they did so in this case seems open to question. Musorgsky had already, more than a year before, effectively lost his job in the Forestry Department, and had only been rescued from complete indigence by Balakirev's friend Tyorty Filippov, who held a senior civil-service post in the Government Control Office and arranged for Musorgsky to be transferred there as a junior inspector. The position carried few if any duties; according to another close friend, Nikolay Lavrov, the composer's sole obligation was to collect his monthly salary. He "did nothing at work and would arrive drunk after a sleepless night," but Filippov "never reprimanded him for such behavior, and permitted Musorgsky such indulgence by saying, 'I am a servant to the artists.' "[18] Eventually, however, even the warmhearted, music-loving controller could no longer keep up the pretense, and at the end of 1879 Musorgsky was finally and irrevocably dismissed from the government service.

Three days into the new year Stasov wrote to Balakirev in alarm. Musorgsky, he announced, "is *on the way out*—from the 1st January he's been left without a job and without any means!!! There'll be even harder drinking! Can't you do something, and very soon if possible. There's no time to lose."[19] Stasov seemed to believe that Balakirev still had some kind of paternal influence over the prodigal son. But it was Filippov, once again, who came up with the best idea. They would all club together to pay Musorgsky a monthly retainer of one hundred rubles, by way of a commission for him to complete *Khovanshchina*. Balakirev, who was himself practically penniless, would not contribute. But Stasov, Filippov himself, and two or three other friends would between them make up the amount; and with luck *Khovanshchina* would get finished quickly. What Stasov did not yet know was that another group of Musorgsky's friends, headed by his old Preobrazhensky colleague Fyodor Vanlyarsky, had had or would soon have a similar inspiration with a different goal. In mid-February Stasov wrote again to Balakirev: "Mily, it seems that another company is giving Musorgsky assistance at eighty rubles a month, but on the sole condition that he complete his opera *Sorochíntsï Fair* within a year or so. This is why he is so determinedly resisting writing *Khovanshchina* at the present time." The coincidence is striking, and knowing the devious tendencies of the serious addict, one is tempted to suspect manipulation on Musorgsky's own part. In January he had written, in his orotund way, to thank Stasov for his "good news." "In spite of small misfortunes, I have not and will not give way to faintheartedness. My motto, which you know: 'Dare! Forward to new shores!' has remained unchanged. If fate allows me to broaden the well-trodden path toward the vital goals of art, I shall be delighted and exult: the demands of art on its practitioners today are so huge that they are capable of swallowing up the whole man."[20] After all, if *Khovanshchina,* why not *Sorochíntsï Fair?* There were those who had always had a predilection for his Ukrainian opera, not least Anna Petrova, for whose husband it had been intended from the start. Musorgsky could happily trust to his ability to finish both operas, relieved as he was of his daily visits to the ministry. Why not broaden the well-trodden path in this essentially practical fashion?

The small misfortunes could not be wholly discounted. Some were behavioral, others circumstantial. Soon after returning home from the Leonova tour he had had at short notice to orchestrate Marfa's song and the first part of the streltsy chorus from act 3 of *Khovanshchina* for an FMS concert that Rimsky-Korsakov was conducting at the end of November. (Rimsky also conducted the Persian dance from act 4, but had to orchestrate it himself, time being short: typically he "corrected" the harmony and part writing, without, he claims, Musorgsky's noticing.)[21] The next "misfortune" was a commission to provide a piece for a gala spectacular in the Bolshoi Theatre in St. Petersburg celebrating the silver jubilee of Tsar Alexander II. The performance, on 19 February, was to take the form of a series of tableaux vivants representing various triumphs of the reign. Borodin, for instance, would compose a brief symphonic poem, *In Central Asia* (*V sredney Azíí*), portraying Russian expansion to the East; Rimsky-Korsakov would provide a choral-orchestral setting of the well-known "Slava" tune (as in the coronation scene of *Borís Godunov*); Tchaikovsky would write a piece about Montenegro; and so forth. Musorgsky's topic was the capture of the city of Kars, in Kurdish eastern Turkey, a rare success in the Crimean War which had conveniently happened soon after Alexander's accession in 1855.

Taruskin sees this whole event (which never took place, on account of the disappearance of the would-be promoters) as one more sign of the *kuchka* "being unmistakably drawn into the establishment." But this is to make a great deal out of a minor paying commission for a composer who had just lost or was about to lose his salaried job. It isn't as if Musorgsky took a great deal of trouble over his *Capture of Kars.* On the contrary, he simply took the unused "Procession of the Princes and Priests" from his music for *Mlada,* scrapped the middle (priests') section, and composed a new so-called *trio alla turca,* a distinctly tired piece of snake charmery with the regulation crop of augmented seconds and diminished fourths and little or no connection with the main march, based on a Russian folk song from Balakirev's collection. With this done, he could return to his juggling act with the two operas and their respective sponsors.

At first he seems to have concentrated on *Sorochintsï Fair,* exactly as Stasov had feared. The main reason for this was that his Vanlyarsky agreement required him to publish individual movements as he went along, which made it hard for him to pretend he was composing when he was not. It also meant, of course, that he had to take time making fair copies for the printer, copies which from time to time the publisher, Nikolay Bernard, managed to lose, so that Musorgsky had to make them again. Under this compulsion, he worked ostensibly on the adaptation of the *Bald Mountain* music to fit the improbable scenario of the hero Gritzko's dream of the Black God (Chernobog) and the witches' sabbath. But when Rimsky-Korsakov visited him early in May, he saw that it was the same old *Mlada* version of the original symphonic poem, not even recopied. He also found Musorgsky still in bed at midday and vomiting at frequent intervals, as if it were a perfectly normal function. He tried to persuade him to spend the summer in the country with him and his family, but to no avail. Meanwhile, *Khovanshchina* was being deferred until 1881.

In fact Musorgsky was not wholly fabricating when he told Stasov in early August that "all that's left to be written of *Khovanshchina* is a little bit of the self-immolation scene." Spending the summer at Leonova's dacha in Oranienbaum, he had just, at last, completed the violent first scene of act 4 in Khovansky's house, with the Persian dance and the painfully beautiful setting of the "Ladu, ladu" folk song (to a Belorussian melody he had got from the Maryinsky's lighting engineer), leading up to Khovansky's murder. He had finished the third act with the scene of the streltsy and their wives, Kuzka's song with balalaika, and Khovansky's last-minute instruction to the streltsy not to take on Tsar Peter's guards. And he had written the fifth act up to, but not including, the final chorus of Old Believers, for which he wrote out the theme but composed nothing more. The quintet at the end of act 2, with which he had wanted Rimsky-Korsakov's help, remained unwritten. And the whole work, apart from the scenes he had scored for the November 1879 concert, still had to be orchestrated. "As for *Khovanshchina,*" he wrote to Stasov at the end of August 1880, "it is *on the eve* of completion: but the instrumentation—O ye gods!—time."[22] It was the last time that he mentioned the work, and it seems likely that not another note of it was composed.

Death by Sunlight

Borodin's contribution to the ill-fated gala was a six-minute tone poem depicting the passage through the central Asian desert of an Oriental caravan of horses and camels with an escort of Russian soldiers. The image was apparently meant to be patriotic and Russo-centric. Borodin's program note for the eventual first performance (in a concert put on by Leonova in April 1880) talks about the caravan being "under the protection of the formidable military power of the conquerors," and only for an RMS performance in Moscow in August 1882 was this discreetly changed to "under the protection of the military power of Russia," with "the peaceful songs of the Russians and the natives [merging] into one common harmony."[1] The idea of conquest, no doubt, had been germane to the gala in praise of Alexander II. By August 1882, alas, the conquering tsar had gone the way of many would-be liberalizing rulers down the ages and been blown to pieces by a revolutionary's bomb on his way to the Mikhailovsky Manège on 1 March 1881.

Borodin's visual concept is an extension of Musorgsky's idea for his Polish oxcart in *Pictures from an Exhibition,* which had set off in the foreground but then gradually receded into the distance.[2] Borodin's caravan starts far away, draws (rather suddenly) near, then more gradually recedes again. The effect is of an exaggerated perspective, as in certain paintings by the realist Wanderers (for instance, Repin's *Barge Haulers on the Volga,* or Perov's *Troíka*), whose annual exhibitions had become a feature of the late-winter months in St. Petersburg. The musical means

are simple. A solo clarinet is the first to appear, playing what is supposed to be a Russian folk song in A major, soon taken up by a solo
horn in C major, as if slightly more distinct. Next we glimpse the caravan itself, in the form of plodding bass string pizzicati, soon joined by
a melancholy A-minor tune on the cor anglais. This melody is the Oriental element, winding its way sinuously across the steppe in the manner of the Polovtsian girls at the start of the second act of *Prince Igor*.
But as Dianin points out, the version here is less "Oriental" than the
operatic version; it lacks the chromatics and augmented seconds and
of course the insinuating quality of the soprano voices, partly because
Borodin wrote it specifically to fit the Russian tune when they come
together as the caravan starts to recede. One could, perhaps, interpret
this as emblematic of the closeness of Russia to its eastern provinces.
Or it might suggest that the Stasovian "East" was simply Russia with
bare tummies and pointed shoes. Either way, *In Central Asia* remains a
small masterpiece sui generis, like Glinka's *Kamarinskaya,* which in procedural terms it somewhat resembles.

After composing this elegant piece, Borodin went back into his scientific shell for many months. In the summer he completed the act I
finale of *Prince Igor,* including the episode of the mutiny and some other
fragments that were subsequently discarded, and probably composed
the brief five-four chorus in which the girls describe the ghastly behavior of Galitsky's retinue. But otherwise worldly cares took precedence.
In May he had told Balakirev that he was busier than he had ever been.
"There's never been a year," he wrote to another friend, "when I have
had so much urgent and essential work as now. It has happened quite
often that I've gone to bed at two or three in the morning, and got up
at four or five."[3]

Thus the *kuchka* worked away at ancient concepts, or at nothing
much at all. Since *Angelo,* Cui had written only songs, his contribution
to *Paraphrases,* and an attractive but derivative suite in six movements
for violin and piano (op. 14), a work that violinists in search of repertoire might still find useful, but that makes few waves artistically.
Balakirev was working on *Tamara* but still using his editing of Glinka as
an excuse for not finishing it. Only Rimsky-Korsakov, as usual, worked
steadily on substantial compositions, even though he, too, had been
editing Glinka as well as orchestrating Musorgsky and at least offering
to help Borodin "revise" *Prince Igor* (though the offer was at this stage
declined). He was also teaching and conducting. Balakirev had not
forgotten his important role as adviser to his young colleague. On one
occasion he turned up at an FMS rehearsal of his Overture on Three

Russian Themes and started instructing Rimsky-Korsakov on how to conduct, "which," its object not unreasonably thought, "at a rehearsal, in the presence of the whole orchestra, was wholly inappropriate."[4] When it came to the teaching of music theory, though, Balakirev was pleased to acknowledge Rimsky-Korsakov's greater competence, and would pass his pupils on to him for instruction in that subject. In January 1879 he had asked him to take on a thirteen-year-old gymnasium pupil by the name of Alexander (Sasha) Glazunov, a boy "very talented and extremely interested in orchestral music, forever writing out scores, and constantly getting his mother to ask me things like how to write for triangle or double bass."[5] For various reasons it was nearly a year before Rimsky-Korsakov made Sasha's acquaintance, but he at once recognized his brilliant gifts, his "superior ear" (which obviated the need for him to study elementary theory or the basic aural training known as solfeggio), and his enthusiasm for self-education. "His musical development," Rimsky-Korsakov informs us, "advanced not by the day, but by the hour."[6]

Perhaps it was his acquaintance with the young Glazunov that provoked Rimsky-Korsakov's scathing judgment, in a letter to Semyon Kruglikov, about his fellow kuchkists: "Owing to inadequate technique, Balakirev writes little, Borodin with difficulty, Cui in a slipshod way, Musorgsky sloppily and often absurdly . . . Believe me, although, speaking perfectly frankly, I consider that they possess far more talent than I have, yet I don't envy them a penny's worth."[7] Glazunov was the living proof that genius properly and systematically guided would swiftly rise above the limitations of even the most brilliantly gifted amateur. Rimsky-Korsakov would probably have regarded himself as an intermediate case: gifted, if not brilliantly, self-taught and a rapid learner from a poor start, in which he was hampered by the obscurantist attitudes of a group of untaught ideologues. The danger of such an argument was that it was too much predicated on quality of product. What if the systematically guided genius turned out to be a *petit maître*, a fluent stylist who simply did what his predecessors had done, but updated? Would that prove that Stasov was right after all to claim that conservatory teaching stifled the imagination, or merely that the initial assessment of the individual's talent had been overoptimistic? Was it even sensible to make such judgments on so little evidence?

Rimsky-Korsakov himself was daily demonstrating the virtue of disciplined method. After finishing *May Night* he had cultivated a growing enthusiasm for folk mythology and pagan ritual. In the summer of 1879 he had started an orchestral tone poem called *Fairy Tale*

(*Skazka*), prompted by Pushkin's prologue to the narrative poem *Ruslan and Lyudmila,* which was in his mind, presumably, because of his work on Glinka's opera; and he had composed a four-movement string quartet on Russian folk themes. Alas, Balakirev immediately took against *Fairy Tale* when its composer—unwisely, one might feel—showed him the draft that autumn; and as for the quartet, it went down badly with the members of the Davïdov Quartet (including Leopold Auer) when they played it over for his benefit. He promptly withdrew the quartet and abandoned *Fairy Tale*; instead he embarked on a revision of his old Overture on Russian Themes. Then, in the late spring of 1880, he set to work on a new opera, based on Ostrovsky's play *The Snow Maiden* (*Snegurochka*). Within three months he had composed a complete draft of this long opera, and in less than a year, by the end of March 1881, the score was complete and ready for performance. As light relief from the opera, he had taken up his *Fairy Tale* again in late July 1880, and polished it off, orchestration and all (a nineteen-minute work), within a couple of months. At the same time, he had started turning the string quartet into a twenty-minute Sinfonietta for orchestra. A more telling illustration of his remarks to Kruglikov, made while at work on the score of *The Snow Maiden,* would be hard to imagine.

Exactly what Balakirev had objected to about *Fairy Tale* Rimsky-Korsakov does not say. But he may have disliked its lack of a clear program. Pushkin's prologue (which is printed as an epigraph to the score) is a mildly ironic list of possible fairy-tale subjects which he imagines told by "a learned cat" tethered by a golden chain to a green oak tree by the sea. From the cat's repertoire, Pushkin chooses *Ruslan and Lyudmila.* Rimsky-Korsakov chooses instead to compose a musical tale whose plot, purely and simply, is the music itself. It annoyed him, he tells us, that people tried to find in his work a depiction of the physical elements of the prologue; they wanted to hear the cat prowling up and down on the end of its chain, the mermaid in the branches, Baba-Yaga in her hut, and the thirty beauteous knights who emerge one by one from the clear waters. But *Fairy Tale* is its own fairy tale.

Admittedly Rimsky-Korsakov slightly undermined his position by referring to the 1879 draft, in a letter to Kruglikov, as "the musical tableau *Baba-Yaga*,"[8] added to which the highly episodic form seems positively to invite pictorial interpretation: the *larghetto* introduction with its mysterious chromatics and fluttering violins; the D-minor allegro, *pesante* and menacing, the solo flute weaving a magic spell, and the curious allegretto theme, played first by solo clarinet, which the composer for some reason bars in duple time though its meter is unequivocally triple—a sure sign of hocus-pocus. Although the work is in some kind of sonata form, with all the main themes recapitulated and ending with a curtailed repeat of the introduction, there is no real attempt to integrate them into an organic entity. They keep their distinctive profiles, like the pictures in a child's storybook. In itself this is hardly a weakness, and the main problem with *Fairy Tale* is that its harmonic texture is somewhat unvaried and the melodic material unremarkable. There is color in the orchestration and contrast in the instrumental texture; but this is not quite enough to carry such a substantial score.

The Sinfonietta, eventually completed in 1884, is a much simpler, more candid piece of work, directly based on the first three movements of the abandoned string quartet, probably somewhat expanded, to judge from the composer's own description of the quartet. In general character it resembles the early overtures of Balakirev and Rimsky-Korsakov himself in being made up of a medley of folk songs worked up in quasi-symphonic style, with motivic development, some unobtrusive thematic cross-referencing, and even, in the slow movement, a rather self-conscious fugal episode. The tunes themselves are nearly all taken from Rimsky-Korsakov's own 1877 collection, including one later made famous, in modified form, by Rimsky's most illustrious pupil, Igor Stravinsky, in the "Round Dance of the Princesses" in his *Firebird*. In fact Stravinsky took more than just the theme from his teacher; the surrounding figuration also suggests an acquaintance with the Sinfonietta, short of actual theft; he knew, in any case, that the work was unknown in the West and so could safely be plundered. But then, as is often the case, Stravinsky's version is better than its model. And in general the Sinfonietta is a well-made, dullish piece, at best the sum of its borrowed parts.

The Snow Maiden is altogether another matter. It was already apparent from *May Night*, with all its limitations, that opera would be Rimsky-Korsakov's best avenue of escape from the aridities of his contrapuntal studies, which had gone on draining the sap from his instrumental and choral music. Even with *Fairy Tale*, one senses in its lack of subject matter a certain straitlaced reticence about imposing a story on a serious piece of music. With an opera there could obviously be no such constraint. We don't know why, in the winter of 1879–80, he reread Ostrovsky's play, having first read it without much pleasure soon after it came out in 1873. But probably the search for a subject that would provide a platform for his growing interest in folk mythology stirred some memory of the play. In fact the piece is quite undramatic compared with Ostrovsky's realist or genre pieces such as *The Storm* or

Live Not the Way You'd Like. Its strength is in its atmosphere and poetic charm, the charm of invented worlds; but atmosphere was precisely what Rimsky-Korsakov was looking for at that moment. Suddenly, he tells us, his "warmth towards ancient Russian custom and pagan pantheism, which had manifested itself little by little, now blazed forth in a bright flame." He became obsessed with Ostrovsky's characters: Snegurochka herself, the shepherd Lel, Tsar Berendey, and the various anthropomorphisms—Spring, Shrovetide (Maslenitsa), and Grandfather Frost. The following year he and his family spent the summer at an estate village called Stelyovo, in the flat, wooded, lakeland country south of Luga, and here the whole environment and landscape fed his obsession: "Everything somehow particularly harmonized with my pantheistic mood at that time ... Some thick, gnarled branch or a stump overgrown with moss appeared to me the wood demon or his dwelling; the forest Volchinyets, a forbidden forest [as in act 3 of the opera]; the bare Kopytyets hillock, Yarilo's [the Sun god's] mountain; the triple echo heard from our balcony seemed the voices of wood-goblins or other wonders."[9]

To the modern way of thinking, these excitements seem essentially those of a child, and very curious indeed in a hard-nosed rationalist like Rimsky-Korsakov, a man whose mind was much later described by Stravinsky as "closed to any religious or metaphysical idea."[10] One has, though, to remember the connection for Russians of his generation between pagan ritual and magical fairy tales, on the one hand, and ethnic Russianism and *narodnost'*, on the other: what Stasov, raving about the tale of Sadko, had labelled as "tableaux of Russian nature on the island of the Sea King ... themes of pagan antiquity, of ancient worship, of our ancient life."[11] Also, by a peculiar twist of mentality, these atavistic mysteries could become an object of scholarship and taxonomy. In his autobiography, Rimsky-Korsakov describes Yuli Melgunov, whose first collection of folk songs "transcribed directly from the voices of the people" had come out in 1879, as "a dry theorist and compiler of a barbarous collection of Russian songs."[12] But he himself, as we saw in connection with *May Night,* was starting to interest himself in the correct classification and application of the tunes he included in his compositions. You could share the pagan wonder at the forest and the bird life and the seasons and at the same time take careful note of the ritual practices, their timings and purposes, associated with these phenomena. You could be, at one and the same moment, primitive man and modern anthropologist. The combination seems to have appealed to Rimsky-Korsakov (though whether or not his musical attributions are correct is another matter).[13]

The Snow Maiden, on this reading, is a fairy tale that might take its place in some monumental treatise about seasonal customs in pre-Christian Russia. We are in the land of the Berendey people and their Tsar Berendey, a wise and soft-hearted old ruler. In the nearby forest, winter is almost over, Spring is freeing herself from the grip of Grandfather Frost; but their quarrel is an annual event, and in fact they have a daughter, Snegurochka, whom they plan this year (like well-constructed bourgeois parents) to place for the summer with a good family, Bobyl' Bakula and his wife, Bobylikha, a childless (and presumably landless) Berendey couple. Snegurochka is beautiful, gentle-natured, but, of course, cold. She makes friends with the villagers, and especially the herdsman Lel; she loves his songs but cannot return his affection. When her friend Kupava's fiancé, Mizgir, catches sight of her, he is so enraptured that he instantly throws Kupava over, and meanwhile the same thing happens to every engaged couple in the land, so that Tsar Berendey's plan to propitiate the sun god, Yarilo, by marrying them all on Yarilo's day looks like coming to grief. But if any man can win Snegurochka's love, Yarilo will be appeased. On the eve of Yarilo's day Mizgir makes passionate advances to Snegurochka, but only succeeds in frightening her, until, in the final act, Spring responds to the snow maiden's prayer and enables her to fall in love with him. Alas, at the mass wedding ceremony the next day, the hot rays of the sun melt Snegurochka; in despair, Mizgir drowns himself in the lake. But the Berendeys rejoice at the death of winter and sing a hymn of praise to Yarilo.

The resonances of this tale are various, some obvious, some perhaps less so. They belong to a land where winter is an extreme, frightening event, and spring is scarcely less violent: destructive as well as creative, but in any case not responsive to human cares. All we people can do is perform ritual acts that will appease the elements, remind them, perhaps, of our presence and our needs, and reassure ourselves that we too are participants in the natural cycle, constant like the birds and the trees, even if, like them, we perish as individuals. For Rimsky-Korsakov such matters were of vital interest. His score is punctuated by songs and choruses that mark out the natural cycle of winter, spring, and summer. Even the birds have a ritual dance in the form of a musical game, in which the feathered creatures are classified by rank: "Who among us birds is the greatest, who is the least? Eagle the chief, quail the scribe; owl the deputy chief," and so on. At the end of the prologue in the forest, the natural scene is invaded by the townspeople, bidding ceremonial farewell to Maslenitsa, the Orthodox equivalent of Shrovetide, but in pagan mythology the last week

of winter. In a brilliant medley of folk songs, Rimsky-Korsakov con-
structs a ceremony of his own, proceeding from the surly, almost mocking "Hey, holy Maslenitsa" ("Oy, chestnaya Maslenitsa!" to a fragment
of a melody from his own collection, no. 32), through the joyous "The
cocks crowed very early" ("Ranïm-rano kurï zapeli"), to the solemn,
heraldic "Happy to meet you, greet you" ("Veselen'ko tebya vstrechat',
privechat'," based on Rimsky's no. 42, which is actually about waiting
for Maslenitsa), and ending with the hushed "Come back to us in three
short days" ("Vorotis' k nam na tri denyochka"), which plainly refers
to the Resurrection. Rimsky-Korsakov explains that the short, chantlike fragment that intrudes at this point—"Maslenitsa mokrokhvostka"
("Soggy-tailed Maslenitsa")—is "a scoffingly sacrilegious reminder of
the Orthodox Mass for the dead," which seems to confirm a Christian
subtext to the whole chorus.

Sequences of this kind can make a brilliant spectacle on the stage.
At the start of the third act, the people celebrate the eve of Yarilo's day
to a sparkling, Glinka-like setting of the folk song "Hey, in the Field
a Lime Tree" ("Ay, vo pole lipen'ka," no. 54 in Rimsky's collection)—a
tune Tchaikovsky had also used in his incidental music for the original production of the play. In the final scene, just before Snegurochka
melts away, the brides and grooms approach Tsar Berendey singing
two variants of a millet-sowing song from Balakirev's collection (no.
8). Here the stage direction specifies that "during the singing the two
sides [girls and boys] approach with slow steps in the time of the song."
And there *is* something balletic about this kind of tableau. The setting
is ceremonial, pageant-like, and frames an action that is more often
decorative than dramatic. The prologue, for instance, contains many
beauties of a "forest murmurs" variety (though Rimsky-Korsakov's
knowledge of Wagner still probably stopped at *Lohengrin*).[14] The orchestral texture, especially the woodwind scoring, is a constant delight, and
the harmonic language, both here and in the Berendey acts, is just rich
and chromatic enough to suggest a magical, fairy-tale world, without
ever straying beyond what Rimsky would have permitted his advanced
composition students. At such times, the Glinka of *Ruslan and Lyudmila*
is never far away, and is sometimes distinctly close, for instance in the
bardic chorus that opens the second act, or Berendey's processional
soon afterward.

As drama, too, *The Snow Maiden* has a good deal in common with *Ruslan*. As in a fairy story, its characters are largely emblematic. They have
no psychology and they seldom change except by magical intervention,
as when Snegurochka is allowed to fall in love with Mizgir by fiat of

her mother, Vesna-Krasna (Spring-Beautiful). And as usual in fairy land, such change, reluctantly conceded, brings rapid disaster. The human characters, with the marginal exceptions of Tsar Berendey and Lel (who sings three attractive, somewhat folksy arias), are ciphers. We know nothing about Mizgir or Kupava except that they have just fallen in love. Mizgir switches to Snegurochka for no reason (her astounding facial beauty is a fairy-tale reason, not a real one). Kupava complains to the tsar, then the next time we see her she is in Lel's arms. When Snegurochka melts, Mizgir jumps into the lake, but nobody minds much. As Tsar Berendey explains, "The sad death of Snegurochka and Mizgir's terrible end cannot alarm us. The daughter of Frost, chilly Snegurochka, has perished. For fifteen years the sun has been angry with us; now with her miraculous death, Frost's interference is at an end." In other words, the Snow Maiden and her lover are seasonal events. The cold is defeated by a human sacrifice, and all combine in a hymn of praise to the Sun god, Yarilo.

The opera's sheer length (over three hours of music) and its flat dramatic and psychological surface will probably always militate against its acceptance on the non-Russian stage, for all its musical charms. It remains, though, a work of some historical significance. As Musorgsky struggled with the final stages of *Khovanshchina* and Borodin tried, on the whole successfully, to bring the epic personages of *Prince Igor* to emotional life, the era of realism as an artistic rallying cry was discreetly drawing to a close. One might instead see Ostrovsky's play, and Rimsky-Korsakov's better-known opera, as the pursuit of a different strand in nationalist art: authenticity not in the history and language of Russians, but in their mind and their art. *The Snow Maiden* is many things, but realistic it is not. It harks back, however artificially, to ancient mythologies, and transports the Russian peasant with his smock and his folk song out of the historical world and into a timeless antiquity of magic and ritual. It was fitting that, after its Maryinsky premiere in February 1882, it would be one of the first operas staged, in 1885, by the Chastnaya Opera (Private Opera) at Abramtsevo, where Savva Mamontov had established a colony of artists, including several of the Wanderers, dedicated to the revival of Russian folk design in costume, furniture, architecture, ceramics, and book illustration. The decorative aspect of fairy tales was one element in all this. The parallel with the English Arts and Crafts movement and the Pre-Raphaelites is obvious and has often been made, though in the Russian version the social element—always a strong factor in pre-emancipation realism and a powerful motive in the English rural revival—is much less evident. On the contrary, Mamontov's most notable successors, the magazine *Mir iskusstva* and Serge Diaghilev's Ballets Russes, held aloof from any kind of social concern and dedicated themselves instead to pure design, the rule of beauty or fantasy, the "making strange," art for art's sake. Thus, by a curious twist of fate, the gentle Snow Maiden turns out to be a direct ancestor of the Chosen One who dances herself to death to propitiate the vernal gods in the most famous ballet of Rimsky-Korsakov's most famous pupil.

In Oranienbaum, that summer of 1880, Musorgsky had composed, and composed well. Without the distraction of *Sorochintsi Fair,* he might even have finished *Khovanshchina* properly, whereas there was little chance of his completing the Gogol opera that year, even without *Khovanshchina.* The material was too fragmented, too inchoate, and it seems probable that his mind was no longer capable of imposing a coherent structure on such a large-scale work. He was observed by an eleven-year-old boy who was living at the same dacha with his parents.

> Once a week at Leonova's there was a reception followed by a dinner. Usually Musinka was in charge of the dinner. From the room in the rear one could hear the clatter of dishes and the uncorking of bottles. Each time Musorgsky came out he was more and more "in his cups." After dinner the concert would begin. Musorgsky played the piano (by now quite "ready") as accompanist and soloist. He performed his own works with amazing perfection, producing a "shattering effect" on the listeners.[15]

Leonova had decided to start singing classes in her St. Petersburg apartment on the Kryukov Canal, and recruited Musorgsky to act as her assistant. She prided herself on her "totally new methods of teaching," which somehow included having him write exercises in two, three, and four parts as a basis for practicing solfeggio. Rimsky-Korsakov records with dismay the "horrible part writing" in these exercises and the very idea of Musorgsky teaching elementary theory; but above all he laments the time that Musorgsky devoted to a collaboration that he, Rimsky-Korsakov, regarded as demeaning and unproductive. Leonova was an aging opera star whose sense of her enduring vocal qualities far outstripped the reality, and while she claimed that "Musorgsky was astonished at my success in the training of voices," Rimsky remembered her as untrained herself, and "so hardly capable of teaching vocal technique."[16] As for Musorgsky, he kept himself going with a constant supply of wine and mushrooms, to the despair of Leonova, who minded the interruptions and recognized them as a symptom of decline.

Some time in 1880, Musorgsky had left the Naumovs and moved into a room on Ofitserskaya, not far from Leonova's and the Maryinsky; and there, during the autumn, he composed in somewhat desultory fashion a series of short, insipid piano pieces: "Meditation" ("Razdum'e"), a childlike "album leaf" mostly in two parts or with pedal notes in the left hand; "In the Village" ("V derevne"), an extended fantasy on what Musorgsky labels, for some reason, a "canto popolare"; and finally "A Tear" ("Sleza"), shed, we may suppose, for the premature demise of a mighty creative gift. On 3 February 1881, Rimsky-Korsakov conducted "The Destruction of Sennacherib' in a concert of the FMS, and Fyodor Stravinsky sang Musorgsky's song "Forgotten." It was the last written music of his to be heard in public during his lifetime. But the next evening he himself presided at the piano for a literary evening in memory of Fyodor Dostoyevsky, who had died a week before. As a black-framed portrait of the great novelist was brought into the hall, Musorgsky improvised "a funeral knell, similar to that heard in the last scene of *Boris.*" It was one of those unrepeatable historic moments, like Beethoven's legendary *Weihekuss*—his consecrating kiss—on the child Liszt, except that in this case there was no passing of the flame, only a dying flicker, shared, but soon to be extinguished.

A week later Musorgsky arrived at Leonova's in "a nervous and irritable state"—presumably of the usual kind—and suddenly announced that he was homeless and without means of any sort. No doubt this was not strictly true. Later in her account of the episode, Leonova explains that she decided to give him a room "knowing that if anything were to happen to him again in his lonely apartment, he might be left without help."[17] In certain moods, as we know, Musorgsky was afraid of being on his own. But this time it was something more than a mood. That evening he and Leonova attended a party in the house of a certain General Sokhansky, the father of one of Leonova's vocal pupils, who sang during the evening to Musorgsky's accompaniment; but afterward, during dancing and cards, he suffered what seems to have been a mild stroke. That night he slept in a chair in Leonova's apartment. The next morning he appeared much better, but when she asked him how he was, he replied that he felt well, then immediately swivelled round and crashed to the floor. "My fears were not unfounded," Leonova remarks; "had he been alone he would certainly have suffocated; but we at once turned him over, took care of him, and sent for the doctor. Before evening he had two more, similar, attacks . . . "[18]

With the help of Dr. Bertensson, they got him into the Nikolayevsky Military Hospital on Suvorovsky Prospekt (near the Smolny Convent). For this highly irregular arrangement—since these days he was a civilian—he had to be listed as "the hired civilian orderly of intern Bertensson." He had a quiet, spacious, sunny room, his own nurses and ancillaries, excellent food, and frequent visits. Naturally, alcohol was forbidden. But in all other ways, Stasov thought, "it was just as if he were in his own home, surrounded by his own family and by the fondest of attention." The reality, as he knew, was more sinister. "The doctors now say," he told Balakirev two days after Musorgsky's admission, "that they weren't strokes that he had, but the onset of epilepsy.

> I was with him yesterday and today (Borodin and Korsakov were there yesterday and the day before, and a lot of other friends as well): he looks as if *nothing was wrong with him*—now he recognizes everyone, but talks the devil only knows what nonsense and tells a stream of fantastic stories. They say, too, that, quite apart from the epilepsy and the strokes, he's also gone a bit mad. As a person he's done for, though he may live on (say the doctors), perhaps for a year, perhaps for a day.[19]

He lived, in fact, for a month. Sometimes he seemed to be recovering, under the strict but beneficent hospital regime. He wrote to Shestakova that he was feeling so well that he was thinking of discharging himself and paying her a visit. In the final stages of his illness, like Violetta in *La traviata,* he told everyone that he felt his vitality returning. His appearance improved, and with it his mood and outlook. The day after the assassination of Tsar Alexander (1 March), Ilya Repin came to paint his portrait, and found him "in an especially healthy, sober condition," whatever the eventual portrait may suggest to the contrary.[20] When Arseny Kutuzov visited him, they talked projects. "You know," Musorgsky said, "I should like something completely new, something I haven't yet touched. I'd like to take a rest from history, and in general from any kind of *prosiness,* which in life, too, doesn't let one breathe . . . And I'll tell you something else—up to now you and I have concentrated only on trivia. Let's work instead on something big—you write a fantastic drama and I'll clothe it in sounds."[21] Perhaps he was, not for the first time, telling Kutuzov what he wanted to hear; or perhaps Kutuzov—as his Soviet critics alleged—was simply making it up. But it was easy enough for Musorgsky to fantasize. He must have known, in his heart of hearts, that it would not happen.

On 9 March, a Monday, he celebrated his forty-second birthday. Soon afterward there was a sudden and rapid deterioration. His arms and legs became paralyzed, and the paralysis started working its way through his entire body. By the following weekend his condition was hopeless. According to the music critic Mikhail Ivanov, there was some slight improvement on the Sunday. He was helped into an armchair, saying, "I have to be polite, ladies are visiting me; what are they going to think of me?" But when Ivanov called in the next morning, 16 March, he was met at the door by Kutuzov. "You want to see Musorgsky?" he inquired. "He's dead."[22]

CHAPTER 29

Heirs and Rebels

In the immediate aftermath of Musorgsky's death, Vladimir Stasov's pen was active. The next day *Golos* printed a short, largely factual obituary including an account of the ebb and flow of the composer's health in his last days, a brief biography referring to his most important works, a mention of the Repin portrait, and an assessment. "Musorgsky was one of those few who direct their activity among us toward distant and magical, unprecedented and incomparable 'new shores.' And people sensed this. The musical conservatories and reactionaries honored him with their persecution, but at the same time the mass of incorruptible, fresh, right-minded youth sustained him with their love."[1] Stasov's account of the funeral on 18 March appeared in *Golos* on the 19th: the procession from the hospital to the Alexander Nevsky Cemetery; the wreaths and their inscriptions; the impressive list of those taking part—the surviving kuchkists, naturally; the conservatory director, Karl Davïdov; Nápravník; the leading Maryinsky singers (Ivan Melnikov, Fyodor Stravinsky, and others); members of the orchestra; and a whole crowd of musical amateurs and music lovers "who deeply sympathized with Musorgsky's original and nationalist talent."[2] The May and June issues of the *Vestnik Evropï* carried Stasov's much longer and more considered biography, a vital source of primary information on Musorgsky's life and work.[3] Finally, at the end of 1882 there began, in the *Vestnik,* the serial publication of his immense *Twenty-five Years of Russian Art,* culminating in the section on music, "Our Music in the Last 25 Years," itself a sixty-page study apparently prompted by the twenty-fifth anniversary of the death of Glinka.[4]

Stasov's entire view of Russian music had long been predicated on the central tradition of what he called the New Russian School, descending directly from Glinka himself by way of Dargomïzhsky and the Balakirev circle, to the recent emergence of certain younger figures, pupils—by an irony that he preferred not to dwell on—of Rimsky-Korsakov at the conservatory. "The lofty activity of the 'comrades,' " he insisted, "continues to this day. Only one of them is no longer with us—Musorgsky, carried off by an early death. All the others, now in their maturity, are continuing, perfecting themselves, along the path already marked out for them in their youth."[5] The remark is a spectacular tribute to Stasov's Housmanesque ability to see the world as the world's not. Of the four chief surviving members of the circle, Rimsky-Korsakov had notably deviated from the youthful path and was now a respected professor of the hated conservatory; Balakirev had composed nothing for the past dozen years; Borodin was still struggling with an opera of similar vintage; Cui had written nothing but salon pieces since finishing his own latest opera seven years before. As a functional, not to say historic, group, in fact, the *kuchka* had long ago ceased to exist.

As for "perfecting themselves" in the 1880s, the list of works is both unimpressive and devoid of any but the most trivial coherence. Balakirev at last completes *Tamara*, but then retreats into his shell and in the entire decade does nothing but revise early works and compose two or three Chopinesque piano pieces and a handful of choruses.[6] Rimsky-Korsakov is superficially more active. After the first performance of *The Snow Maiden* in January 1882, he composes a compact, somewhat Lisztian piano concerto, a number of songs and choruses, and some occasional instrumental pieces. But none of it amounts to much artistically until, in the late eighties, he suddenly produces a set of brilliant orchestral works—the *Capriccio espagnol*, *Sheherazade*, and the *Russian Easter Festival* Overture—that will largely define him for a posterity preoccupied with Russian glitter, but that are hard to reconcile with Stasov's vision of "lofty activity." Throughout this time César Cui—whose main qualities, according to Stasov, are "poetry and passion, combined with an unusual sincerity and heartfeltness that go to the deepest recesses of the heart"[7]—composes salon pieces of one kind and another, at their best music of genuine charm, but hardly ever marked by noticeable individuality or even Russianness. A Suite concertante for violin and orchestra, and a couple of purely orchestral suites, at least stray beyond the confines of the drawing room, in scale if not technique or aesthetic reach. Of the four survivors, only Borodin produces new work of the front rank until, to be generous, Rimsky's *Sheherazade* of 1888.

The chemistry professor's Second String Quartet, in D major, composed, for once, entirely in the single summer of 1881, is a lyrical pair to its predecessor, but if anything still stronger and more distinctive in the quality of its material, of which the lovely melody of the nocturne is by far the best known but by no means the sole example. In music of this kind, Borodin's method is simple and effective. He balances his movements carefully as regards texture and rhythmic contrast, attempts nothing overambitious in terms of counterpoint or motivic development, and writes effortlessly for the instruments, whose melodic character, after all, suits his own gifts to perfection. Like Schubert, Borodin makes chamber music sound like a natural emanation of the heart and the body: in this sphere he is, to tell the truth, Stasov's description of Cui made flesh. His later music bears out this comparison. On the face of it, the seven-movement *Malenkaya syuitai* (Little Suite) for piano solo is not unlike Cui's various sets of salon pieces from the mid-eighties. But with Borodin a distinctive idea invariably surfaces to lend individuality to even the most conventional imagery. As usual with him, the main problem lies with the lack of continuity, which, in the suite, he tries to conceal by an artificially concocted program (artificial because three of the pieces were actually composed at some time in the 1870s, while the suite was assembled only in 1885 as a gift for his new patroness, the Belgian Comtesse Louise de Mercy-Argenteau). The work is subtitled "Petit poème d'amour d'une jeune fille," which Dianin speculates may be a reference to some incident in the comtesse's youth.[8] It certainly has little direct bearing on the music, which is for the most part sentimental in the best sense, but without narrative shape (of the kind supplied by the texts in, for instance, Schumann's *Frauenliebe und -leben*). The one exception to this tone is the first piece, "Au couvent" ("Under the vaults of the cathedral one thinks only of God"), which experiments interestingly with bell chords in unusual spacings as a frame for the simple chanting of the choir. It's a striking musical picture, but its connection with young girls in love is, to say the least, oblique.

During the eighties Borodin worked spasmodically on *Prince Igor,* but never came within sight of finishing it or even leaving it—like *Khovanshchina*—in a clearly articulated form. Soon after composing the D-major quartet, he wrote a completely new version of Igor's aria to replace the "shadows" monologue, discarded under pressure from circle colleagues in 1875. Later he settled finally on the form and content of the prologue, and he revised and reformulated much else that he had already composed. But of new material there is precious little: a chorus here (part of the act 3 finale), a recitative there (Konchak and Igor, before the Polovtsian Dances). To some extent the opera had become an albatross round his neck, a compulsion that he could neither avoid nor confront. One day early in 1887, he dined with his medical friend Alexander Dobroslavin and his wife, and they talked about *Prince Igor.* But "as usual this was disagreeable for him, and he began to lose his temper. 'Look,' he said, 'I've come to play you something, but because you torment me with *Igor,* I shan't play.' "⁹

What he did eventually play was the variation slow movement of a third symphony, which he had been writing, on and off, for the past three years. It was an intense piece in C minor, based on a hymn tune Borodin had unearthed in the village of Pavlovsky, near Moscow, where he spent the summer of 1884. Alas, though the movement was complete, Borodin never got round to writing it down. Nor did he write down the symphony's first movement; but in this case Glazunov felt able to reconstruct music that he had heard the composer play and for which sketches existed. He also assembled a scherzo movement from a D-major scherzo in five-eight time that Borodin had composed for string quartet in 1882, adding a trio section based on music originally intended for the merchants' scene scrapped from the opera's first act. This all seems to have been in accordance with Borodin's known intentions. And yet one can hardly regard the two movements of the A-minor symphony, deeply attractive though they are, as strictly representative; too much of Glazunov's memory is involved. At least with *Prince Igor* there were large swaths of authentic music that only needed tidying up, and some that barely needed that much. For a lot of the time Borodin's voice is clear. Of course, the opera's provisional state is a tragedy; but it is a tragedy with consolations.

Borodin died in February 1887. For the past few years his life had proceeded in the same disorderly fashion as before. His wife's health had continued to deteriorate, and in 1885 he himself went down with what his biographer, Serge Dianin, calls "a mild form of cholera [*cholerine*]" which, paradoxically, was "so severe that the patient was only saved by an injection of a physiological solution of culinary salt."¹⁰ The key to his general condition was clearly exhaustion, mental as well as physical. The pressure of his professorial duties, anxieties about his beloved Yekaterina, her destructive, self-centered lifestyle, his own inability to refuse help or favors to others, above all his dedication to two demanding and mutually hostile vocations, destroyed his health as surely as it undermined his music. That February he had organized a fancy-dress dance in one of the academy lecture rooms, and appeared himself as a Russian peasant in baggy trousers, high boots, and a red woolen shirt. He was in conversation with Marya Dobroslavina and one of his fellow professors when his speech suddenly became indistinct, he started to sway, then crashed to the ground, striking his temple on the corner of the stove. He had suffered a rupture of the aorta, an event that, the autopsy revealed, might have happened at any time, so thin was the artery wall. He was fifty-three years old.

A year almost to the day after Musorgsky's death, on 17 March 1882, a symphony in E major by the now sixteen-year-old Glazunov received its first performance at a concert of the FMS conducted by Balakirev, who had resumed the directorship of the school after Rimsky-Korsakov's resignation the previous September. The symphony made an extraordinary impact on audience, critics, fellow composers alike. It took César Cui back to 1865, the year of Glazunov's birth and the year of the premiere of Rimsky-Korsakov's own First Symphony. "Then as now a young Russian artistic débutant has embarked on a musical career; then as now there has fallen to the lot of the critic the gratifying task of welcoming a remarkable new-born talent and wishing him the furthest possible development, maturity, and success." But Glazunov was even younger than Rimsky-Korsakov had been, and in Cui's opinion his symphony was more mature and still more gifted. It was technically strong and accomplished. It was inventive and even original. Of course, Cui had his reservations. Glazunov was too wedded to the repeated four-bar phrase, and this led him into a certain prolixity of form, a tendency to drag things out longer than strictly necessary. The slow movement was attractive and poetic but inclined to drift. Still, the symphony as a whole was "a fine, remarkably talented work with the most serious musical virtues notwithstanding Glazunov's youth. Taking into account its composer's seventeen [sic] years, it's an exceptional phenomenon."[11]

Also in the audience that evening was a very different kind of music lover from the normal patrons of St. Petersburg concerts, a rich timber magnate by the name of Mitrofan Belyayev. Belyayev belonged superficially to a class of Russian society known as the kupechestvo—that is, the merchant class, but with a much more specific and self-contained identity than that of the business class in Western Europe at that time. Because of the general rigidity of Russian society and the backwardness of Russian trade even as late as the mid-nineteenth century, the kupechestvo had preserved a character of their own, a character derived from their peasant background but somehow culturally intensified toward a profoundly conservative, inward-facing, atavistic view of life, dress, speech, and education. By the 1850s the gradual emergence in Russia of a fully fledged capitalism had started to generate fantastic wealth in the trading community. And these nouveaux riches, as Taruskin calls them, began to emerge from their mercantile ghetto, to acquire education and a taste for the rich things of life, the entertainments, both high and low, the style and the ostentation. They bought and built, they sponsored and patronized. But they never completely shed their aura of old Russia, their Slavophilia and religious Orthodoxy, and for that reason, Taruskin explains, "merchant patrons were more inclined than the aristocracy to lend their support to native talent." So Nadezhda von Meck, the widow of a Baltic railway tycoon, supports Tchaikovsky; the textile millionaire Pavel Tretyakov collects and commissions Russian paintings and builds a gallery in Moscow (in the style of a Russian fairy-tale palace) to house them; Savva Mamontov, another railway tycoon, founds an arts colony at Abramtsevo and fills his house with peasant designs and fabrics and with artists who base their work on such things. Belyayev had derived his money from a family timber business (which also probably to some extent meant railways), but he was fundamentally better educated than most of his industrial peers, and in particular he was more musically literate. He was a decent violinist who played chamber music and in good amateur orchestras, and who held regular string-quartet evenings on Fridays at his St. Petersburg home. Borodin probably composed the scherzo that eventually found its way into his A-minor symphony for a Belyayev Friday in 1882.[12]

Belyayev was so impressed by Glazunov's symphony that when it was premiered in Moscow in August of that same year he travelled there specially to hear it again. At the concert he introduced himself to Rimsky-Korsakov, and either then or soon afterward he broached the idea of publishing the symphony at his own expense. It was a suggestion that would have consequences far beyond anything any of them could have foreseen. In effect, Belyayev was setting up a publishing house, and he did so like an instinctive *kupets*. By establishing the business in Leipzig, he bypassed the lack of copyright protection in Russia and at the same time ensured German quality of production, which went with his determination to print immaculate full scores, properly and thoroughly edited, together with all individual orchestral parts, and four-hand piano transcriptions. Likewise in true *kupechestvo* spirit, he proposed to publish only works by Russian composers, starting with Glazunov and Rimsky-Korsakov. It was a resolution he kept. Two years later he paid for run-through performances of Glazunov's symphony and his D-major orchestral suite, and this in turn led in 1885 to the initiation of the Russian Symphony Concerts, an annual series like those of the RMS, but devoted, like the publications, exclusively to Russian music, much of it, in the nature of things, newly composed.

Richard Taruskin has shown, in an exhaustive and riveting account of the environment from which Igor Stravinsky emerged, the extent to which Belyayev's initiative overlaid St. Petersburg music with a rigid template of what did and did not conform to the training and aesthetic preconceptions that lay behind Glazunov's own early work. Glazunov appeared as a kind of well-taught kuchkist, able to write symphonies that no longer sounded like exercises written to meet Balakirev's requirements but were nevertheless stylistically indebted to the circle. They reflected Rimsky-Korsakov's growing contempt for the lack of application and craftsmanship in the work of the *kuchka,* but they also echoed his distaste for the wilder shores of (in particular) Musorgsky's imagination, which he was at that very moment doing his best to tame by editing and smoothing out what he regarded as the music's artistic absurdities. Bearing in mind that Belyayev invariably asked Rimsky-Korsakov's advice on the acceptance or otherwise of new works for publication or performance, and eventually constituted him and his two star pupils, Glazunov and Anatoly Lyadov, into a formal committee for that purpose, it is not hard to imagine how difficult it would have been for any sort of maverick composer (say, a Russian Debussy or Hugo Wolf, not to mention Schoenberg) to make headway in the Petersburg of the 1880s or 1890s. It would perhaps be too much to argue that the system of regulation that survived into Soviet times and eventually ossified into the concept of socialist realism was essentially a reconstitution of the Belyayev-Rimsky regime. Yet it is a fact that several of the most influential composition teachers in the early decades of the Soviet Union were former pupils of Rimsky-Korsakov, including Stravinsky's contemporary Maximilian Steinberg, who would torment *his* pupil Dmitry Shostakovich with "the sacred traditions of Nikolay Andreyevich [Rimsky-Korsakov]."[13]

Thus, at the very moment that Stasov was issuing what masqueraded as a progress report on the work of the Balakirev circle, what was left of the circle was being displaced by a highly professional tendency that drew on aspects of its work but echoed little if anything of its spirit. Glazunov and Lyadov were only the most gifted of an expanding dynasty of conservatory-taught composers, pupils of Rimsky-Korsakov himself or, in due course, of his pupils, who accepted without question the authority of the master, adhered to the values that he had espoused so assiduously when first appointed to his professorship, and aspired to nothing grander or more challenging than to be published by Belyayev, performed in his Russian Symphony Concerts, or, after his death in 1903, awarded the Glinka Prize established under his will and under the stewardship, specifically, of Rimsky-Korsakov. "From Glinka on," Stasov wrote in 1882, "all the best Russian musicians have put very little faith in academic learning, and have not at all regarded it with the servility and superstitious awe with which it is still regarded to this day in many parts of Europe."[14] It was pure bunkum. For more than a decade Rimsky-Korsakov had been instilling into his students the very opposite view. As for Stasov's ideas about nationalism, they were not entirely submerged, but merely lost their radical thrust. "In order to be national," he asserted, "in order to express the spirit and soul of a nation, [music] must be directed at the very roots of the people's life."[15] And on what he called "the Oriental element": "The new Russian musicians . . . shared the general Russian love of everything Eastern. This is not surprising, since so much of everything Eastern has always been an integral part of Russian life and all its forms, and has given it such a particular, characteristic coloring."[16] The musical insignia of the Orient, the snake-charmer aspect, the sinuously ornamented melodies and hip-waving chromatic harmonies, are still there, but they no longer breathe the alien, perfumed air of *Antar* or *Prince Igor.* Folk song, folk legend, ritual, and myth all raise their heads from time to time; there are ancient modes and strange scales. But the danger has gone out of these ingredients; they are merely so many stylistic resources, part of the repertoire of the well-bred, well-taught composer. A good example is the *gamma ton-poluton*—the tone-semitone, or octatonic, scale—which Rimsky-Korsakov first used in his *Sadko* tone poem of 1867 to suggest the suspension of the laws of nature as Sadko descends to the Sea Kingdom. By the 1890s this scale has become such a standard expedient with Rimsky and his pupils as to amount to a shibboleth—a passport of group membership. It no longer registers as a disruptive force. It draws our attention to an oddity we might otherwise not notice.

Rimsky-Korsakov himself was a big enough artist to survive this general drift into academicism. The dozen or so operas he composed after *Sheherazade* have never entered the repertoire outside Russia, with the possible exception of the last one, *The Golden Cockerel* (*Zolotoy petushok*). On any count, they are an uneven body of work. But at their best they are the only significant pan-Russian heirs to kuchkism before the early ballets of Stravinsky, which are inconceivable without Rimsky's influence but which, as dance works (a genre he despised) written for performance abroad by a company dominated by artists rather than musicians, elude his direct authority. Musically the Rimsky operas are full of interest; they are colorful, inventive, often witty, and they even here and there hark back to Belinsky's ideas on the social significance of the artwork, though the political connotations of, for instance, *The Tale of Tsar Saltan* and *The Golden Cockerel* (both based on narrative poems by Pushkin) are not always easy to disentangle from the frequently ludicrous goings-on on the stage. As dramas, though, they are often sluggish when not actually obscure, the characterization is flat, and the music patchy: at times dazzling, melodious, vital, at other times routine and foursquare. Stravinsky found Rimsky *sans reproche,* regretting that he was not more "reproachable"—that is, artistically adventurous.[17] And indeed there *is* something a shade too respectable about Rimsky, a slightly self-satisfied correctness of musical deportment which shouts out as a limitation. One thinks of J. Alfred Prufrock, who measured out his life in coffee spoons. Listening to the beautiful but slightly too comfortable opening of *The Legend of the Invisible City of Kitezh,* Rimsky's penultimate opera, one wonders if this can have been quite what Musorgsky had in mind when he issued his perennial clarion call "Toward new shores!"

What Stasov would have thought of *Kitezh,* with its curious mixture of pantheism and Christianity, is matter for speculation, since he died in October 1906, four months before its premiere. But he would probably have approved of it. He had adored *The Snow Maiden,* which has more discreet elements of the same mixture. The more one looks at Stasov's musical judgments, the more one feels that they were under the sway of general ideas at least as much as good taste: or rather, that they tended to emerge from a somewhat eccentric reconciliation of those very different criteria. On what other grounds could he have praised Balakirev's attractive but irretrievably minor overtures or his *King Lear* music or a moribund project like Musorgsky's "Nettle Mountain" so extravagantly while obstinately refusing to see any merit in Verdi or Wagner? Behind such hierarchies lies a straightforward agenda. Stasov wanted Russian music to do well on its own terms, in the way that a mother wants her children to shine with their own light and will loyally, lovingly refuse to see them as the world sees them. All his geese were swans. But it was also a question of ideology. Stasov, as we have noted, saw Russian music in terms of categories: historical subject matter, legend, folk song, geography (East versus West), rejection of the academy. But he was factious, and could decline to notice these categories in the works of composers of whom, for whatever other reason, he disapproved. All this is naturally a poor basis for durable artistic judgments, and while, of all the Balakirev circle, Stasov was beyond question the most broad-minded, in that he never sought refuge in convention when confronted with the new or the radical, it seems very doubtful whether he had a clear picture of the lasting artistic differences between the various works that, on ideological grounds, he chose to praise.

From our distant point of view, we can distinguish the landmarks more clearly. They are not particularly numerous. *Boris Godunov* stands out as a masterpiece by any reckoning, and a handful of other finished works by Musorgsky confirm the quality of his genius while hardly adding up to the rounded or consistent output of a great master. Borodin had a God-given talent, yet produced scarcely any completed work of the front rank: one symphony, a short tone poem, a pair of string quartets, and a few songs. Balakirev eventually wrote more, but only a single large-scale work, *Tamara,* plus two or three songs of unquestionable stature. Cui wrote a few operas and many salon pieces, all of which have faded—for the most part rightly. Only Rimsky-Korsakov produced what looks, on paper, like a respectable harvest of finished, high-quality music, much of which is still regularly played in Russia, though mostly unknown in the West. Of course, there are circumstantial reasons why the *kuchka*'s work is not much performed abroad. Their most characteristic music is vocal, and non-Russian singers tend to be put off by the unknown language and the Cyrillic script. Much of Borodin's best music, and some of Musorgsky's, is in unfinished operas whose performance involves compromises of an inhibiting kind. At bottom, the crude fact is that these interesting composers talked a lot but composed rather little; and often what they composed does not measure up to what they said about it.

The basis of their interest lies nevertheless, of course, in the sheer brilliance of their finest works, however meager their quantity. *Boris Godunov* and *Prince Igor,* in its fragmentary state, would be landmarks even if their composers had written nothing else. But isolation of this kind is unhistorical. Musorgsky, Borodin, and the rest belonged to a process that took the halting character it did specifically because of the conditions under which it evolved. Glinka wrote two utterly disparate operas and a lot of second-rate work because his enormous talent fought a mostly losing battle with circumstances that encouraged idleness and devalued technique. Dargomïzhsky went through long periods of creative silence and eventually struggled to complete a work whose main impulse was theoretical because there was little or no practical compulsion on him to write at all. If it had not been for Stasov's ideological tendencies and Balakirev's bullying nature, the young composers in their circle might well have vanished without trace. Even when they did not strictly, or even approximately, reflect the circle's ostensible motivating ideas in their work, they thought of themselves as doing so, and this sustained them through those difficult times for an artist when inspiration languishes and technique serves as an engine to keep the car on the road. But the key to all these composers' music is precisely the lack of compulsion, the feeling that in the end nobody minded what, or whether, you wrote, nobody outside your own small group was waiting for the next product of your genius. One has only to compare the profile of their music in the sixties and seventies with the steady productivity of the conservatory-taught Tchaikovsky or of Rimsky-Korsakov in his years as a conservatory professor to understand the importance of preparedness and expectation in the work of the creative artist.

But if the tempo of the *kuchka*'s writing stuttered, its focus shifted from side to side like that of the leisurely traveller who does not have to get to any particular town by nightfall. And such wayfarers notice and are drawn to things that the regular tourist or the commercial traveller is likely to reject or overlook. The waywardness of much of the Balakirev circle's work has often been put down to plain incompetence. But as I have argued earlier, ineptitude is a weak explanation of artistic originality. A stronger account would suggest that the absence of compulsion—both of the kind imposed by good schooling and of the kind imposed by other people's expectations—freed them to follow their ideas into terrain not mapped by conventional theory, and in turn forced them to evolve their own methodologies to deal with the situations that arose when they got there. Here, though, one must be selective. Cui, whatever his intellectual interest in the circle's ideas, derived hardly anything from them creatively; his music (like his criticism) is simply that of a limited mind. Balakirev composed with flair but soon lost heart; his period of withdrawal, followed by a protracted "old age" spent revising early works and composing piano miniatures, suggests a psychological inability to confront the perils of absolute freedom. It is in the work of the other three composers that one finds the gems of originality that not only in themselves justify all the theorizing about Russian history and the people, all the tirades against the conservatory and German professors, all the backbiting at Serov, Rubinstein, Tchaikovsky, and the rest, but also lead on toward new shores, as Musorgsky dreamed, in the work of their successors.

Some but by no means all of these beneficiaries were themselves Russian. Musorgsky was a political hero in the Soviet Union on account of his supposed populism; but his musical influence seems to have been spasmodic at best, perhaps because his unorthodox style was hard to take further without infringing the narrow criteria of Soviet arts policy. It comes out most clearly in the darker vocal works of Shostakovich, his *From Jewish Folk Poetry* and the Thirteenth and Fourteenth symphonies. Under socialist realism, Rimsky-Korsakov was an easier path to follow. He naturally influenced his pupils, not always for the better. Many of them, from Lyadov and Glazunov onward, were as inhibited as he became by excessive regard for correct procedure. But nearly all of them profited from his brilliant grasp of the orchestra; Prokofiev, one of Rimsky's last pupils, was impatient of his teaching but admired his late operas and learned lessons from them that are hard to detect amid the fire and fury of his early piano works but are more noticeable in his lush student opera, *Maddalena*. None of this, however, would have given Rimsky-Korsakov more than passing significance in one particularly murky phase of twentieth-century Russian music. His great claim to more than parochial influence is through the work of a pupil who specifically did not study at the conservatory but whom Rimsky-Korsakov took on as a private student and to whom he never gave formal tuition in theory but taught only by precept and through direct engagement with musical scores—his own and the pupil's.

This was Igor Stravinsky. It was Stravinsky's good fortune never to be subjected to the grind of conservatory course work or examination, never to be surrounded (and probably crushed) by what he himself later called "these ephemeral, prize-winning, front-page types" who tend to dominate musical academies in all countries. In a sense Stravinsky was the negative proof of Stasov's theory that conservatories destroy creative talent. Rimsky seems to have taught him much as Balakirev might have done, by setting him graded tasks, going through his scores with him, tinkering with them, adding details in his own hand. But the *kuchka*-like appearance was deceptive. Rimsky-Korsakov in old age was a systematic, well-organized teacher who did not encourage his pupils in dilettante habits of work.

His musical influence on Stravinsky was almost painfully evident from the start. The young man imitated Rimsky's orchestral method, which he had studied at close quarters in working on the scores of the master's late operas *Pan Voyevoda* and *The Legend of the Invisible City of*

Kitezh. His first mature orchestral works, the *Scherzo fantastique* (1907–8) and *Fireworks* (1908), are orchestrally chips off the late-Rimskian block, with much the same glitter and wizardry of scoring that Rimsky himself was deploying at that very time in *The Golden Cockerel.* More importantly, the harmonic language of these sparkling works is no less derivative. Both make heavy use of the octatonic (*ton-poluton*) scale that had been a standard device with Rimsky for depicting magical or supernatural events for the past forty years, and both adopt the slithery chromaticism of his portraits of evil sorcery in another recent opera, *Kashchey the Immortal,* and of the weird, lunatic court of King Dodon in *The Golden Cockerel.* Stravinsky's own Kashchey work, his ballet *The Firebird* (*Zhar ptitsa*) composed for the Ballets Russes just after Rimsky-Korsakov's death, derives a good deal from the same works, though it takes ideas from other Russian sources as well. In any case, much of the idiom of *Firebird* goes back to Glinka, the magical writing in *Ruslan,* and the folk-song variation treatments in *Kamarinskaya.*

None of this would be of particular interest if the influence had been confined to Stravinsky's early works. But though the Rimsky sound quickly vanishes from his music, the effects of the method remain. Stravinsky continued to use octatonic harmony in one way or another for the rest of his life, particularly (but by no means exclusively) in works with a traceable Russian angle. *Petrushka,* his second ballet, has long stretches of pure octatony, again standing for the magical, transformational aspects of the story—the coming to life of the puppets—exactly as in the original *Sadko.* In *The Rite of Spring,* the complex inner structures of the octatonic scale underlie the peculiar layered texture of the score (something that can be seen on the page as well as heard in performance). Later—in works like the Symphony of Psalms and the Symphony in Three Movements—the scale loses its magical associations altogether and instead often seems to hark back more generally to the composer's Russian origins. At the same time what started as an essentially coloristic device with a particular dramatic symbolism turns out to be a powerful resource with far-reaching implications for a modern harmonic palette.

Stravinsky's harmony, however, like that of any well-organized composer, cannot be understood in isolation from the linear (melodic) and rhythmic aspects of his music. As a melodist, Stravinsky starts out as a true kuchkist. In *Petrushka* there are so many folk songs—both urban and rural—that Russian musicians and even audiences tended to regard it as a set of arrangements, and were astonished by the Western view of it as an original masterpiece. *The Rite of Spring* is likewise heavily dependent on folk song, but more disguised and fragmented, and with irregularities that lead in turn to the sorts of rhythmic convulsion that are perhaps the most famous thing about the work. Stravinsky was soon investigating these kinds of irregularity in smaller, more intimate works—songs and choruses—as well as in dance works with sung texts. He had discovered, he tells us, that "one important characteristic of Russian popular verse is that the accents of the spoken verse are ignored when sung," and "the recognition of the musical possibilities inherent in this fact was one of the most rejoicing discoveries of my life."[18] But the idea that the manipulation of textual accent might have interesting musical consequences was not Stravinsky's discovery. It was another kuchkist idea, and it had first cropped up in the songs and operas of Musorgsky.

Of all the *kuchka* composers Musorgsky was the most inclined to ignore the normal rules and procedures of textbook composition. Rimsky-Korsakov had always been a systematic worker who wrote as correctly as he knew how, which he admits was not very correctly until he became a conservatory professor and embarked on a serious program of theoretical study. Borodin was neither a pedant nor a natural innovator, but a gifted, civilized musician who saw no reason not to explore unusual colorings within a broadly conventional discourse. But Musorgsky had a naturally exploratory mind and no special brief for best practice. His songs, in particular, often go their own way in search of what he regarded as the true or the real. Sometimes they model themselves on ordinary speech rhythms and contours; sometimes they mimic the eccentricities of the child, the simpleton, the drunkard, or the merely distracted. His songs can be obsessively even in their values, like "Darling Savishna" or "The Seminarian," or they can be almost anarchically free, like "With Nyanya," where the bar lines are determined by wayward verbal accents. Always his harmony reflects the mood or context. It can be perfectly regular and by the book, or it can be volatile and unpredictable, or it can be a wonderful, disconcerting combination of these qualities.

As for the floating accent exploited by Stravinsky in his Russian songs and the ballet *Les Noces* (among various other works), this is already a feature of the folk choruses in *Boris Godunov*. In the very first chorus, Musorgsky sometimes moves the verbal stress onto a weak beat of the bar, usually with a melodic accent of some kind, while placing the bar line counterintuitively on an unaccented syllable; for example:

The actual barring of course reflects the fact that folk song knows no such boundaries, but moves freely according to its own internal melodic and verbal patterns.[19] But even these often do not coincide with each other, perhaps because over the years different words have been fitted to the one tune without too much concern for anything as inhibiting as correct scansion or prosody. On the whole, Musorgsky's way of handling this device feels quite relaxed and natural, whereas Stravinsky treats it more self-consciously, accenting the one word in different ways, and adding multiple metric patterns in the instrumental accompaniment. In fact one might even argue that the so-called polyrhythms of *The Rite of Spring* (a work that preceded the "rejoicing discovery") are in part a product of this kind of floating accent, though their direct origin lies in the habit—also folk-song based—of shortening and lengthening individual figures in a given melody. Behind this, in turn, lies the idea of endless repetition, which is such a feature of peasant music, with its singing games, its verse-after-verse storytelling, and its dance-till-you-drop fiddle tunes. Mechanical repetition is a feature of all folk-based music, and Russian music is no exception. From Glinka (the wedding chorus and Finn's aria in *Ruslan,* as well as *Kamarinskaya*), through the Polovtsian Dances, *Pictures from an Exhibition, Tamara,* the finales of *Sheherazade* and Tchaikovsky's Second Symphony, up to the final scene of Stravinsky's *Firebird,* the device is more or less routine. Stravinsky himself transformed it into a new form of rhythmic discourse by applying to it the mobile accents and the shortenings and lengthenings he found in Russian folk poetry: hence the "Danse sacrale" and the whole of *Renard* and *Les Noces,* and on from there to music of his that no longer has anything to do with ethnic culture, but cannot shed its Russian ancestry.[20]

All the three main kuchkists have had their admirers and imitators both in and out of Russia. But it is Musorgsky who has been most praised and studied by composers who have found themselves consciously at odds with the conservatory and its routines. Of these by far the most significant is Debussy. As a young man in the early 1880s Debussy had spent consecutive summers in Russia as pianist to Tchaikovsky's patroness, Nadezhda von Meck, and a few years later he borrowed, but probably did not study, a vocal score of *Boris Godunov* that Saint-Saëns had brought back from St. Petersburg. But his close acquaintance with Musorgsky's music probably dates from the 1890s. He perhaps heard the first French performances of various songs, including *The Nursery,* in Paris in February 1896, and five years later he published a short article on *The Nursery.* "It is," he wrote, "a masterpiece . . .

> Nobody has spoken to that which is best in us with such tenderness and depth; he is quite unique, and will be renowned for an art that suffers from no stultifying rules or artificialities. Never before has such a refined sensibility expressed itself with such simple means: it is almost as if he were an inquisitive savage discovering music for the first time, guided in each step forward by his own emotions. There is no question of any such thing as "form," or, at least, any forms there are have such complexity that they are impossible to relate to the accepted forms—the "official" ones. He composes in a series of bold strokes, but his incredible gift of foresight means that each stroke is bound to the next by a mysterious thread. Sometimes he can conjure up a disquieting impression of darkness so powerful that it wrings tears from one's heart.[21]

To trace Musorgsky's effect on Debussy's music is by no means easy, because stylistically they have rather little in common. One can say that the free declamation in *Pelléas et Mélisande* was influenced by *Boris Godunov,* but in the end the fundamental differences between the accent structures of French and Russian—the one accent-light and even, the other heavily accented, with clusters of discarded syllables—inevitably mean that the flavor of the two works differs radically even before one considers the contrasts in sensibility. One has to remember, too, that even as late as 1902, when *Pelléas* was first performed, Debussy had heard not a note of *Boris,* whether or not he had seen the score.

Where he can be said to have used Musorgsky, if not as a model, at least as an excuse, is in precisely those areas that he singles out in his *Nursery* article: the willingness to avoid "official" forms, to compose in a seemingly episodic, fragmentary way that nevertheless creates its own intricate forms sui generis. Such forms are a particular feature of Debussy's piano music: for instance, "Hommage à Rameau" in the first book of *Images,* or "Et la lune descend" in the second book, or several of the preludes. Elsewhere in the article he makes pointed observations about harmony. "For Musorgsky," he notes, "one chord is often sufficient (although it would have seemed poor to M. What's-his-name). Or else he uses a modulation so individual that it wouldn't even have been in the books of M. So-and-so." These remarks not only suggest Debussy's own harmonic practice, they also recall a series of conversations he had had with his old Conservatoire professor Ernest Guiraud at the end of the eighties, before he had more than glanced at any music of Musorgsky's. At one point, Debussy had gone to the piano and played a series of intervals. "What's that?" Guiraud asked. "Incomplete chords, floating," Debussy replied. "You have to drown the tonality. One can travel where one wishes and leave by any door." "But when I play this [he plays a dissonant, French sixth chord] it has to resolve." "I don't see that it should. Why?" Finally, Guiraud tries out a string of parallel triads (as if anticipating Debussy's own "Sirènes" or "La Cathédrale engloutie"). "Do you find this lovely?" "Yes, yes, yes!" In the end the broadminded Guiraud concedes: "I would agree with you in regard to an exceptional person who has discovered a discipline for himself and who has an instinct which he is able to impose. But how would you teach music to others?"[22] As a description of Musorgsky and a catalogue of his harmonic methods, by a musician who had probably never heard of him, this would be hard to beat.

Certain things in Debussy's early songs suggest, not Musorgsky, but Borodin: for instance, the clashing whole tones at the start of the late-eighties Baudelaire setting, "Le Jet d'eau," a memory perhaps of Borodin's "Sleeping Princess," a song Debussy may have found himself accompanying during his von Meck summers. But one finds much more undigested Russianism in the music of Debussy's younger contemporary Maurice Ravel. Ravel, like his great compatriot, was susceptible to the naturalism of the word setting in The Nursery, which seems clearly to have had an impact on his Histoires naturelles (1906) and the opera L'Heure espagnole (1907–9), though as with Debussy the effect is blunted by the more liquid character of the French language, just as Musorgsky's brusquely dissonant harmonies translate into something smoother and more insinuating under the Gallic touch. Ravel, of course, famously made a brilliant orchestration of Musorgsky's Pictures from an Exhibition (1922), and he also orchestrated two large chunks of Khovanshchina (in collaboration with Stravinsky) for Diaghilev's Paris production in 1913. But the technique he brought to these exercises owed more to Rimsky-Korsakov than to Musorgsky, whose less showy orchestral manner would have been largely unknown to him at that time. On the whole, Ravel was more inclined than Debussy to appropriate elements of style or technique that happened to take his fancy. For instance, his *Rapsodie espagnole* of 1907–8 unashamedly borrows orchestral effects from Rimsky-Korsakov's opera *Christmas Eve,* excerpts from which the composer had himself conducted at the Paris Opéra the previous May; and the influence of the finale of Rimsky's *Sheherazade* on the concluding "Danse générale" of *Daphnis et Chloé* is overt to the point of plagiarism. Yet curiously, Ravel is able to absorb these thefts into his own style without disrupting it. As with Stravinsky, there was a streak of kleptomania in his creative process. But the stolen objects sit happily on his musical mantelpiece like the objets trouvés of the world traveller (which, as it happens, Ravel was not).

Echoes of the *kuchka* have been heard in many other corners of twentieth-century music. It is a critical commonplace that Leoš Janáček was influenced by Musorgsky, both in the dialogue character of his operatic word setting and in the fact that he derived his technique partly from a field study of demotic speech. But though a passionate admirer of Russian literature and lover of all things Russian (he wrote two operas on Russian subjects), he seems to have been ignorant of Musorgsky before 1910, and did not hear *Boris Godunov* until 1923, five years before his death. A year later he told the *New York Times* critic Olin Downes that he "admired it very much," but denied any influence.[23] Oddly enough, he had always displayed more enthusiasm for precisely those Russian composers least admired by the *kuchka*: Tchaikovsky and, of all people, Anton Rubinstein. His biographer John Tyrrell argues that the late emergence of Janáček's individual manner in the late nineties was a direct outcome of a trip he made to Russia in the summer of 1896. But specifically of the *kuchka* there is no sign. As for the circle's impact on English music, I have noted a similarity between the early orchestral music of Balakirev (specifically his *King Lear* music) and certain works of the English ruralists, Vaughan Williams in particular. But Vaughan Williams was already writing in this style before he can have known any of the folk-song-based works of the *kuchka,* so the resemblance must be largely coincidental.

In any case, to judge an art by its influence, supposed or otherwise, is a vain exercise. The detectable traces are almost by definition the most superficial, whereas the way in which an artist of any subtlety will process those experiences that touch him most deeply is an impenetrable question of creative psychology. At best we can know what the artist wants us to know, which is about as likely to be the whole truth as any other confession of the inner soul, even assuming that the artist himself has much idea of what actually makes him tick. The surest external evidence of the power that resides in the spasmodic, often unsatisfactory, and frustratingly incomplete work of this extraordinary group of dilettante geniuses lies in the sheer quality of their admirers, at least as much as in what the admirers made of their admiration. To have enabled a Stravinsky (as Rimsky-Korsakov palpably did, and the others did by example); to have been praised and copied by a Debussy or a Ravel: these would be accolades that would take most composers to their graves happy.

But their true monument remains their own music, which, amid much that is fragmentary, poorly considered, or frankly second-rate, also includes some of the most powerfully original and brilliantly executed works by any nineteenth-century composer. As already suggested, if Musorgsky had written nothing but *Boris Godunov* he would still be a towering figure; but in fact he also composed more than sixty songs, of an inventive richness that has gone substantially unrecognized because their texts are in (and depend on) a language strange to Western singers and audiences. Partly for the same reason, Rimsky-Korsakov's fifteen operas are largely unknown in the West, even though their musical and dramatic interest is at least the equal of that of some operas that are regularly staged here. For *The Maid of Pskov* or *The Legend of the Invisible City of Kitezh* not to have been mounted by any professional British company since the Second World War is a sad comment on the limited view of repertory planners. Few, certainly, would argue the same way for Cui's *William Ratcliff* or *Angelo*. Yet many worse pieces have been staged by fringe companies of the Opera Rara type and have proved to be as bad as their neglect has implied. *Prince Igor* and *Khovanshchina* are problematical, of course, but even in their scaffolded state they contain whole stretches of music—even whole acts—that one longs to experience more often in the theatre. Balakirev's *Tamara* is a masterpiece, seldom programmed. His songs, and Borodin's, are not numerous, but they include some of the most beautiful and refined lyrical utterances by any nineteenth-century composer.

Vladimir Stasov no doubt harmed his case by overstating it. But the battle he fought is one we can recognize. "Who knows," he asked at the end of his 1882 essay, "perhaps in a few years the ideas, taste and sympathies of the public and its spokesmen, the music critics, will also change from top to bottom itself, with a corresponding change in their attitude toward our new school, the heirs of Glinka."[24] The attitude he complained about was hostility. Today it is indifference or trivialization: the mentality of the "Russian Spectacular" or the "White Nights Prom."

The Survivors

Stasov died in 1906, eighty-two years old but still at his desk at the St. Petersburg Public Library, still fighting old battles as the clash of arms receded into the past. Russian art had long since moved into a new phase. *Mir iskusstva*—the *World of Art* magazine—had come and gone; symbolism and art for art's sake had displaced Stasov's beloved realism as the vehicles for innovation and the war on academicism. Though for some reason sympathetic to the heady musical vapors of Alexander Skryabin, and, more understandably, the writings and personality of the young Maxim Gorky, he loathed most of the new art. He described Diaghilev's second World of Art exhibition in January 1898 as "utterly idiotic, outrageous, antiartistic, and repulsive." He told the artist Yelizaveta Boehm that "I am generally very much discouraged with all our artistic affairs, with the victory of falsehood, filth and stupidity. It seems that I would be better off keeping quiet and no longer interfering with anything. What's the point in fighting two or three mosquitoes, bedbugs, or lice—even a whole hundred—if the *general dirtiness* and *wretchedness* multiply them more and more with each passing minute!!"[1] He did, nevertheless, keep writing. His final article was a defense of an old love, Schumann, against press attacks on the fiftieth anniversary of his death in July 1906. The article came out on 28 September. A fortnight later he himself was dead.

Rimsky-Korsakov, though twenty years his junior, outlived him by less than two years. He had become disillusioned in a different way. After reading Stasov's "Twenty-five Years of Russian Art," he had suggested to the critic Alexander Ossovsky that he write "an article called 'Fact and Fiction on the "New Russian School." ' "² And one day in 1904, at a dinner after a Belyayev memorial concert, he had turned to Stasov with a tragic look on his face and blurted out:

> Do you know what it is that, amid all these festivities, toasts, congratulations, and speeches, is secretly tormenting and tormenting me, deep down, relentlessly? Do you know? Today I'll tell you. Look over there, that one sitting opposite us with his napkin tucked into his collar, and who is making all these wonderful, wise, pithy little speeches (*that was Glazunov himself*)—he is the last of us. With him Russian music, the whole New Russian period ends!!! It's horrible!³

Stasov had replied that he himself had long thought the same. But he may have overlooked—deliberately or otherwise—the implied criticism of Glazunov himself, the suggestion that the end, the failure of promise, was embodied not just in the lack of successors, but in Glazunov's own limitations. There was, in any case, a streak of pessimism, even fatalism, in Rimsky-Korsakov's makeup. Of all the *kuchka,* he—not Stasov—was the most politically minded, the most apt to feel the inertia and futility of Russian public life at the start of the new century. In 1905, at the time of the student demonstrations and the forced closure of all academic institutions in the wake of the disturbances of January and February that year, he sided openly with the students and was dismissed from his conservatory post in consequence. Three years later, mortally sick with angina pectoris, he confided to his friend and chronicler Vasily Yastrebtsev that his heart was weak and his body worn out. "As you see," he added stoically, "everything is proceeding normally; it's all moving toward a single end."⁴ Three months later, in June 1908, he died at his dacha at Lyubensk, not living to witness the Moscow premiere in 1909 of his final opera, *The Golden Cockerel,* with its ludicrous Tsar Dodon and his inept generals, nothing but "delirium, daydream, a pale specter, emptiness," as the Astrologer's epilogue informs us. Nor can he have had much presentiment of the spectacular success of his least conventional pupil, Igor Stravinsky, with his *Firebird* another two years in the future. But that was on another stage, and in another country.

Balakirev also died without knowing about Stravinsky's success with the subject he himself had for so long contemplated as an opera. He died of pleurisy in May 1910, four weeks before the Paris triumph of *The Firebird.* But for a long time before that he had been a marginal figure in

St. Petersburg's musical life. His seventieth birthday, in 1906, had been virtually ignored, and a concert of his music in February 1909 had been cancelled for lack of ticket sales. By 1910 only César Cui, of the original circle, survived to remind the world, in a brief obituary in the *Birzheviye vedomosti*, of Balakirev's crucial role in the emergence of the *kuchka* half a century before.[5] Talking to a reporter, he recalled their first meeting in 1855, Balakirev's subsequent dominant position in the circle, his critical methods and curious judgments:

> God, how disrespectful we were to Mozart and Mendelssohn, how crazy about Schumann, then Liszt and Berlioz, but above all stood Chopin and Glinka. [Balakirev] nursed us like a broody hen with her chicks. All our early works passed through his strict censorship. He wouldn't let anything be printed until he had looked it over and approved it. Soon each of us left the circle, but to his dying day Balakirev would insist that only what we had written under his wing was any good.

"The history of Russian music," Cui went on,

> will assign to Balakirev one of the highest, most honored, places I realize he could have done much more than he did. At one time all music was in his hands. He could have been director of the conservatory or the Imperial Opera. He conducted symphony concerts, fussed over the Free Music School. The powerful of the world were prepared to sponsor him. But Mily Alexeyevich's character was far from public. He was a person of an independent disposition, not very sociable, and at all events obstinate.... What he wrote is very fine, elegant and superbly worked. I should even say too superbly worked. Without doubt he could have composed much more and left huge musical riches. But his character prevented it.

And finally Cui reflected on his own situation.

> So I'm the last one left. It's a little frightening, but I haven't lost my mind. I sit and rummage through the pile of thematic material I've accumulated. I'm getting something ready to bring into the world. As you see, I remain custodian of the New Musical School.

The custodianship lasted eight more years; it embraced children's operas, songs, piano pieces, music of a charm almost ridiculously discordant with the events of those most violent years in Russia's history.

Cui's final performance was a production of his completion of Musorgsky's *Sorochintsï Fair* at the Petrograd Music Drama Theatre on 13 October 1917. Twelve days later the Bolsheviks seized power. When Cui died the following March, the new Soviet Union had been out of the war for three weeks. The civil war inside the country had scarcely begun.

Notes

CHAPTER 1   Arrivals

1. See for instance Taruskin, *Defining Russia Musically*, 29.
2. Glinka, *Memoirs*, 36, 68.
3. Sargeant, *Harmony and Discord*, 15.
4. D. Brown, *Mikhail Glinka*, 279–80. See also S. M. Lyapunov and A. S. Lyapunova, "Molodïye godï Balakireva," in Kremlev and Lyapunova, *Miliy Alekseyevich Balakirev*, 7–71, especially from 47 onward.
5. Letter to Vladimir Stasov, 3 June 1863, in *BSP1*, 211.

CHAPTER 2   The Father Figure

1. Glinka, *Memoirs*, 82–3.
2. *Askold's Tomb* is the first of a number of Russian operas whose reputation seems to thrive on ignorance of its music. Verstovsky himself resented Glinka's preeminence, but acquaintance with his music quickly rules out serious comparison.
3. Taruskin, *Defining Russia Musically*, 29.
4. See Swan, *Russian Music and Its Sources*, 25–6, for a clear, nontechnical definition of this folk heterophony, known to Russianists as *podgoloski*.
5. Glinka, *Memoirs*, 101.
6. This is an example of *peremennost'*, the "variable mode" characteristic of Russian folk tunes and Orthodox chant. See, for instance, Taruskin, *Defining Russia Musically*, 132–3.
7. Ibid., 36.
8. V. F. Odoyevsky, "Letter to a music lover on the subject of Glinka's opera *A Life for the Tsar*," in Campbell, *Russians on Russian Music*, 2–3.
9. Quoted in D. Brown, *Mikhail Glinka*, 88–9; also 44–5.
10. Glinka, *Memoirs*, 136. Glinka may have been consciously or unconsciously exaggerating the dilettante way in which the scenario was created. A scenario survives in Glinka's hand that cannot be much, if at all, later than the Bakhturin plan, which has not survived. See D. Brown, *Mikhail Glinka*, 185–6.
11. Swan, *Russian Music*, 68.
12. Exactly what Glinka meant by the glass harmonica is obscure. It may have been a keyboard instrument in which, presumably, the hammers struck glass strips or plates. See del Mar, *Anatomy of the Orchestra*, 493. Today a celesta is normally used, as it is also for the *campanelli* (bells) in the Magic Dances in act 4. The stage music was orchestrated by Balakirev and Rimsky-Korsakov for the publication of the full score in 1878.

13. It was published only in 1845 and not played outside France before 1842. Glinka first visited France in 1844. He may have known Liszt's transcription for solo piano, published in 1834.
14. Anonymous critic in the *Russkiy invalid,* quoted in Orlova, *Glinka v Peterburge,* 169.
15. Glinka, *Memoirs,* 172.
16. Ibid., 234.
17. Lakond, *The Diaries of Tchaikovsky,* 250–1 (entry for 27 June 1888). Emphases in the original.

CHAPTER 3   The Lawyer-Critic

1. See Sharp, *Heine in Art and Letters,* 44.
2. Ibid., 1.
3. Quoted in Karenin, *Vladimir Stasov,* 140.
4. Ibid., 134.
5. "The Idea of Art," in Belinsky, *Selected Philosophical Works,* 168. "Images" translates the word *obraztsakh,* strictly "types," "patterns." See, for instance, Taruskin, *Musorgsky,* 11.
6. Belinsky, *Selected Philosophical Works,* 149.
7. Letter of 1 January 1844, quoted by Gerald Abraham in his introduction to Jonas, *Vladimir Stasov: Selected Essays,* 9–10.
8. "Liszt, Schumann and Berlioz in Russia," in ibid., 121.
9. "Muzïkal'noye obozreniye 1847," in *SSM1,* 23–38; translated as "Review of the Musical Events of the Year 1847" in Jones, *Vladimir Stasov: Selected Essays,* 15–37. Stasov had contributed a few brief reviews of foreign books, as well as short anonymous pieces on art, architecture, and music, to the same paper earlier in the year.
10. Letter of 18/30 April 1852, quoted in Karenin, *Vladimir Stasov,* 184. Emphases in the original.
11. See Lebedev and Solodovnikov, *Vladimir Vasil'yevich Stasov,* 50.
12. Letter of 21 March 1861, in *BSP1,* 128–30. For further information on Kel'siyev, see Herzen, *My Past and Thoughts,* 101–16 (the passage is not in the abridged version).
13. "Nasha muzïka za posledniye 25 let," in *SSMIII,* 168.
14. "Pis'ma iz chuzhikh krayev," in *SSMII,* 209. The article is an account of the circumstances surrounding the first performance of Wagner's *Das Rheingold* in Munich in 1869.
15. Letter of 18/30 November 1853 to Glinka, in Karenin, *Vladimir Stasov,* 211. See also Stasov, *L'Abbé Santini.*
16. Letter of 24/25 July 1861, in *BSP1,* 153–4.
17. *Journal des débats,* 16 April 1845, quoted in D. Brown, *Mikhail Glinka,* 315.
18. Introduction to Jones, *Vladimir Stasov: Selected Essays,* 6–7.

CHAPTER 4   The Officer and the Doctor

1. Quoted in Dianin, *Borodin* (1960), 39–40; cf. Dianin, *Borodin* (1963), 18.
2. Ibid., 2. Stasov indicates that "Herke prepared [the work] for publication with pleasure," information he probably had from Musorgsky himself. *MBO,* in Ogolevets, *V. V. Stasov,* 32.

3. Dianin, *Borodin* (1960), 41; *Borodin* (1963), 20.
4. Ibid.
5. See his "Prosheniye ob otstavke" ("Request for discharge"), in *MLN*, 270–1.
6. See "Little Star: An Etude in the Folk Style," in Taruskin, *Musorgsky: Eight Essays*, 38–70.
7. The term "pedal" derives from the pedal board of the church organ, on which the organist can hold a note indefinitely with his foot while improvising freely with his hands. The pedal note has the effect of bonding the upper harmonies, regardless of their character. The piano cannot, of course, sustain in this way, but can suggest the effect by repetition.
8. Letter of 19 October 1859 to Balakirev, in *MLN*, 46; *MR*, 21–2.
9. Letter of 10 February 1860 to Balakirev, in *MLN*, 48; *MR*, 23–4. This later Soviet edition omits the reference to "onanism," but it is in the earlier Russian text edited by Andrey Rimsky-Korsakov. See Rimsky-Korsakov, *M. P. Musorgskiy*: 55.
10. Ivan Turgenev, *The Diary of a Superfluous Man and Other Stories*, trans. Constance Garnett (London: William Heinemann, 1894).
11. Stasov wrongly dates the meeting with Dargomïzhsky to the winter of 1856–7, so has Glinka still alive, but abroad. See *MBO*, 35–6.
12. Letter of autumn 1856, quoted in *ODR*, 258. I am indebted to Taruskin for much of the information in this paragraph.
13. *MBO*, 34.
14. Letter of 9 December 1857 to L. I. Belenïtsïna (Karmalïna's maiden name), in Pekelis, *A. S. Dargomïzhsky*, vol.1, 53.
15. See his letters to M-D. Calvocoressi, in Montagu-Nathan, "Balakirev's Letters," 347–60.
16. *LMMZ*, 24–5; *MML*, 28–9. (Unless otherwise stated, the translations from the work are my own.) But according to Cui, in his obituary of Balakirev, Chopin was highly regarded by the circle: "Ts. A. Kyui o M. A. Balakireve," *Birzheviye vedomosti*, 18 May 1910, reprinted in Gusin, *Ts. A. Cui: Izbrannïye stat'i*, 548–50.
17. Letter of 18 June 1858, in Gusin, *Ts. A. Cui: Izbrannïye pis'ma*, 46; also *MDW*, 66–7.
18. See his letters of 12 July and 13 August 1858 to Balakirev, in *MR*, 9–13. *MR* translates *rasseyannost'* as "absentmindedness"; but Musorgsky is not talking about forgetfulness.
19. Letter of 10 February 1860 to Balakirev, in *MLN*, 48; *MR*, 23.

CHAPTER 5   On Aesthetics and Being Russian

1. I am indebted to Walicki, *A History of Russian Thought*, 191–4, for much of the present discussion.
2. Letter to V. P. Botkin and N. A. Nekrasov, 25 July 1855, in Turgenev, *Polnoye sobraniye sochineniy i pisem*, vol. 2, 300–301.
3. Quoted in Walicki, *A History of Russian Thought*, 192.
4. Karenin, *Vladimir Stasov*, 162.
5. Lebedev and Solodovnikov, *Stasov*, 62–3.
6. Olkhovsky, *Vladimir Stasov*, 139.
7. Belinsky, *Selected Philosophical Works*, 86.
8. "Nasha muzïka za posledniye 25 let," in *SSMIII*, 151.
9. Letter of 18 November 1858, in *BSP1*, 84–5, referring to Marx, *Ludwig van Beethoven: Leben und Schaffen* (Berlin, 1859). A note to the published text explains that Marx's book, though dated 1859, actually came out in 1858, and was already listed in the

St. Petersburg Public Library's register of acquisitions for that year. As far as I am aware, there is no authority in Beethoven for Marx's interpretation.

10. Letter of 19 July 1858, *BSP1*, 63–9. Stasov's emphases.
11. *SSMIII*, 147; cf. Glinka, *Memoirs*, 60.
12. Belinsky, *Selected Philosophical Works*, 86.
13. Ibid., 111.
14. Ibid., 112, 114.
15. Letter to Balakirev, 12 June 1860, in *BSP1*, 106.
16. Letter to Balakirev, 20 August 1860, in *BSP1*, 114–5. But Stasov's arithmetic is adrift. There are either six modes (or seven, including the purely theoretical Locrian mode), or twelve, if the so-called hypo-modes are counted. The major scale is the same as the Ionian mode, but the minor scale has three versions, of which two (the harmonic minor and the rising melodic minor) have no modal equivalent. The descending minor scale is the Aeolian mode. So Stasov might have allowed Balakirev as many as fourteen scales, or even—with the Locrian and Hypolocrian—sixteen.
17. *SSMI*, 231. See Richard Taruskin's detailed analysis of the article in *ODR*, 6–13. Stasov's emphases.
18. Letter to Balakirev, 13 February 1861, in *BSP1*, 121–4.
19. Belinsky, *Selected Philosophical Works*, 112–3 (translation adjusted).
20. Karenin, *Vladimir Stasov*, 306–7.

CHAPTER 6   New Institutions

1. Anton Rubinstein, "Die Componisten Russland's," *Blätter für Musik, Theater und Kunst* (Vienna: 11 May, 25 May, 8 June 1855).
2. Quoted in Ridenour, *Nationalism, Modernism and Personal Rivalry*, 83.
3. See ibid., 28, for an English version of the complete conversation.
4. Letter of 15 October 1852, quoted in Taylor, *Anton Rubinstein*, 38.
5. Quoted in ibid., 30.
6. Rubinstein, "O muzïke v Rossii," *Vek* (1861, no.1); English translation in Campbell, *Russians on Russian Music*, 64–73.
7. Letter of 1 March 1861, in *BSP1*, 125–6.
8. "Konservatorii v Rossii: Zamechaniya na stat'yu g. Rubinshteyna," *Severnaya pchela*, 24 February 1861, reprinted in *SSMII*, 5–10; English translation in Campbell, *Russians on Russian Music*, 73–80.
9. Letter of 13 January 1861, *MR*, 31.
10. Quoted in Campbell, *Russians on Russian Music*, 82.
11. Letter of 23 January 1867, *MLN*, 80; *MR*, 76. "Tupinstein" was one of various corruptions of Rubinstein's name with which the *kuchka* amused themselves. *Tupoy* is Russian for "dull."

CHAPTER 7   First Steps

1. Letters of 18 and 19 October 1859, *MLN*, 46–7; *MR*, 20–22.
2. Gordeyeva, *M. P. Musorgskiy*, 179; cf. Orlova, *Musorgsky Remembered*, 39.
3. Letter of 25 July 1858, in *BSP1*, 72.
4. As reported by Musorgsky in a letter of 12 July 1858 to Balakirev; *MR*, 10.
5. Musorgsky subsequently worked on two further *Oedipus* choruses, according to a

letter to Balakirev of 26 September 1860 (*MR*, 25–6), but nothing is known of them for certain. Gerald Abraham has plausibly identified them with other music in *Salammbô*. See Calvocoressi, *Mussorgsky*, 97.

6. See Stasov to Balakirev, letter of 19 July 1858, in *BSP1*, 63–9. According to Edward Garden, Stasov's source was William Chappell's *Collection of National English Airs* (1838–40, expanded as *Popular Music of the Olden Time* [1855–59]). Garden speculates that Balakirev may have taken his act 4 tune either from Chappell or from a previous, lost Stasov letter. See Garden, *Balakirev: A Critical Study*, 42 and 46, note 16.

7. Letter of 7 July 1858, in *MDW*, 66 (but wrongly dated to June).

8. Rimsky-Korsakov lists the *Oedipus* chorus as "the only work of Musorgsky's acknowledged by the [Balakirev] circle," when he, Rimsky, first came on the scene (*LMMZ*, 27; *MML*, 31). But that was in 1861.

9. *MBO*, 42.

10. *ODR*, 341, 343. The work's brevity in its original two-act form may also have been a problem. See Gusin, *Ts. A. Cui: Izbranniye pis'ma*, 533, note 4.

11. Taruskin's assertion that she drowns herself in the opera, as in the poem, is a curious and uncharacteristic mistake. See *ODR*, 354.

12. See N. Basmajian, "The Romances," in M. H. Brown, *Musorgsky in Memoriam*, 38.

13. Letter of 31 December 1860, in *MR*, 28.

14. Undated letter postmarked 25 December 1860, in *MLN*, 51; *MR*, 27. "Voice" in this context is a technical term for "part"; voice leading is the technique of writing music in several parts, and does not refer specifically to the human voice.

15. The Mengden play is not known. Georgiy Mengden was a school friend of Musorgsky's, but the Mengdens were a well-known family of aristocratic Balts, and the playwright may have been Georgiy's father or one of his Mengden-Altenwoga cousins. See *MLN*, 50; *MR*, 25.

16. See *MDW*, 71, entry for 25 December 1858, for a somewhat confused account of this discussion. A clearer source is Calvocoressi, *Musorgsky*, 20.

17. See, for example, Turner, "Musorgsky," 153–75, for a theory about the composer's supposed homosexuality and sadomasochism. As an example of theorizing on flimsy evidence, the diagnosis of homosexuality from a pair of extravagantly affectionate letters to Arseny Golenishchev-Kutuzov is something of a prize exhibit.

18. *MR*, 15, note 32.

19. Letter of 12 May 1859, in *MLN*, 42–3 (where it is—probably wrongly—dated 12 June), *MR*, 15–16.

20. Letter of 13 February 1861, in *BSP1*, 121. Stasov's emphases. Lyadov (father of the composer Anatoly) had cut this entr'acte from the performances of Glinka's opera.

21. Letter of 19 January 1861, in *MLN*, 56–7; *MR*, 34–5.

22. Letter to Vladimir Stasov, 18 October 1872, in *MLN*, 140–1; *MR*, 198–200; emphases Musorgsky's.

23. The letter has not survived, but its contents can be deduced with some precision from Musorgsky's reply of 19 January 1861, in *MR*, 34–5.

CHAPTER 8 The Third Rome

1. Letter of 5 July 1858, in *BSP1*, 62–3.

2. Letter of 23 June 1859 to Balakirev, in *MLN*, 43–4; *MR*, 17–18.

3. Quoted in Figes, *Natasha's Dance*, 162.
4. "Nasha muzïka za posledniye 25 let," in *SSMIII*, 159.
5. *SSMI,*, 231.
6. "Nasha muzïka za posledniye 25 let," in *SSMIII*, 149.
7. Letter of 3 June 1862 to Alexander Arseniev, quoted in the introduction to *BSP1*, 26.
8. Letter of 25 June 1862, in *BSP1*, 188–9.
9. Letter of 10 July 1864 to Stasov, in *BSP1*, 229–30.
10. See, for instance, Taruskin, *Defining Russia Musically*, 17–24. Something comparable happened in eighteenth-century Hungary, leading to confusion in the following centuries over what was and what was not "authentically" Hungarian.
11. Of the most prominent Slavophiles, Ivan Kireyevsky had died in 1856, and Konstantin Aksakov and Alexis Khomyakov both died in 1860.
12. See Raeff, *Russian Intellectual History*, 197, on Kireyevsky.
13. Herzen, *My Past and Thoughts*, 301–2.
14. Lebedev and Solodovnikov, *Stasov*, 50–57; see also Karenin, *Vladimir Stasov*, passim.
15. Letter of 9 August 1888, in Karenin, *Vladimir Stasov*, 598, note 1; emphases Stasov's.
16. Private communication, 29 May 2009. Dr. Kelly answered my inquiries about the relationship in generous detail, and the observation about the absence of significant references is hers.
17. Letter of 22 June 1863, in *MLN*, 70–1; *MR*, 55–7. Musorgsky's emphases.
18. Letter of 10 June 1863, in *MLN*, 70; *MR*, 54. Musorgsky's emphases.
19. See Novikov, *U istokov velikoy muzïki*, 158. For more details on the conditions of the Toropetz peasantry at the time of emancipation, see Obraztsova, "Faktï k biografii Musorgskogo," 83–88. She depicts them as living in extreme poverty, poorly housed, fed and clad, and with no local medical center. When, after the emancipation decree, the peasants refused to pay their *obrok* (quit rent) or do the corvée (labor in lieu), "the disturbance was harshly put down." She finds it "hard to believe that the Musorgskys did not know about this, and . . . were not disturbed by these events." As always with Soviet historians, it is necessary to bear in mind a possible parti pris.
20. Letter of 10 June 1863, in *MLN*, 70; *MR*, 54.
21. *LMMZ*, 13; *MML*, 17.
22. *LMMZ*, 25; *MML*, 29.
23. *LMMZ*, 18; *MML*, 22.
24. *LMMZ*, 21; *MML*, 25.
25. *LMMZ*, 18; *MML*, 23.
26. Letter of 13 April 1863, quoted in *TDM*, 105; *MDW*, 106.
27. *LMMZ*, 20, *MML*, 24.
28. *MR*, 46.
29. Letter to Stasov, 11 October 1862, in *BSP1*, 191–2.
30. Balakirev started writing them down only in 1906, and even then failed to complete the task before his death in 1910. The completion is by his pupil Sergey Lyapunov. See Garden, *Balakirev*, 254.
31. See Dianin, *Borodin* (1963), 41, note 2.
32. But one has to be cautious. The sonata was completed from Borodin's sketches and drafts by the Soviet composer Mikhail Goldstein, who had form as a counterfeiter of "old" music. In the late forties he had invented a "Symphony no. 21" allegedly composed in 1810 by a (real) Ukrainian by the name of Ovsyaniko-Kulikovsky. The Borodin material is said to be complete in sketch form, but I have not myself seen it.

CHAPTER 9   Wagner and His Acolyte

1. *MBO*, 48.
2. Letter of 22 April 1863, in Gusin, *Ts. A. Cui: Izbrannïye pis'ma*, 57.
3. *MBO*, 47–8.
4. Letter to Balakirev, 31 March 1862, in *MLN*, 61; *MR*, 40–43. Musorgsky's emphases.
5. For more details on Musorgsky's stay at Volok, including his piano-teaching of Natalya's children (one of whom was later a prominent revolutionary and associate of Karl Marx), see Obraztsova, "Faktï k biografii Musorgskogo"; also Novikov, *U istokov velikoy muzïki*, 158–61.
6. By far the best source of information on Wagner's Russian visit and reception is Bartlett, *Wagner and Russia*.
7. Letter of 5 May 1863, in Gusin, *Ts. A. Cui: Izbrannïye pis'ma*, 58; Cui's emphases. He does not mention that Wagner achieved his successes facing the orchestra, a novelty for conductors in Russia at the time. See Bartlett, *Wagner and Russia*, 1. One wonders whether Stravinsky was remembering this opinion of Cui's, whom he knew, when he remarked that Britten was "a vonnnderrful . . . accompanist." See Stephen Walsh, *Stravinsky: The Second Exile* (New York: Knopf, 2006), 620, note 7.
8. See his letter to Balakirev of 26 February 1863, inviting him to come round and "listen to what I've sketched about Richard"; Gusin, *Ts. A. Cui: Izbrannïye pis'ma*, 56.
9. Letter of 17 May 1863, in *BSP1*, 206.
10. "Mikhail Ivanovich Glinka," *Russkiy vestnik*, nos. 20, 21, 22, 24 (October–December 1857), reprinted in *SSM1*, 175–351.
11. Quoted in *ODR*, 16. Taruskin's account of the dispute is detailed and authoritative.
12. "Muchenitsa nashego vremeni," *Russkiy vestnik* (April 1859), reprinted in *SSM1*, 389–98.
13. "Nasha muzïka za posledniye 25 let," in *SSMIII*, 163.
14. Herzen, *My Past and Thoughts*, 241–2.
15. Letter of 3 May 1858, in *BSP1*, 57.
16. Letter of 16 January 1860, in *BSP1*, 100–101.
17. Letter of 10 June 1863, in *MLN*, 64; *MR*, 48.
18. Letter of 17 May 1863 to Balakirev, in *BSP1*, 202.
19. *ODR*, 36. Taruskin's brilliant chapters on Serov in this volume are almost the only English-language source that does the composer justice. But see also Gerald Abraham, "The Operas of Serov," in Westrup, *Essays Presented to Egon Wellesz*, 171–83. According to Abraham (quoting the composer's Russian biographer, V. S. Baskin), Serov also completed an operetta, *La Meunière de Marly*, in 1845, but this too has vanished apart from the overture, which was supposedly published, and "some *valse-couplets*," which Nikolay Findeisen reproduces in his life of Serov.
20. Serov, "Podlinnaya avtobiographicheskaya zapiska A. N. Serova," in *Serov Izbrannïye stat'i*, 69.
21. "Spontini i ego muzïka," in ibid., 371.
22. Ibid., 373.
23. *ODR*, 46–7.
24. Letter to Varvara Yefimovna Zhukova, quoted in *ODR*, 72, 69. Taruskin, a shade simplistically, blames Stasov's relentless polemics after Serov's death for the subsequent neglect of his work.
25. "Spontini i ego muzïka," 380.
26. Letter of 10 June 1863 to Balakirev, in *MLN*, 64–70; *MR*, 48–55. The final two sentences are a marginal note in the original.

27. Letter of 17 May 1863, in *BSP1*, 203.
28. Letter of 3 June 1863, in *BSP1*, 208–12.
29. Letter of 22 June 1863, in *MLN*, 71–2; *MR*, 56.
30. Ibid.
31. Two years earlier, Balakirev had considered Saul as a possible subject for an opera. See his letter of 14 February 1861 to Stasov, in *BSP1*, 124.
32. A suggestion made by David Brown; see D. Brown, *Musorgsky*, 46.
33. Musorgsky seems always to have intended to orchestrate the song, since the manuscript of the original version already contains indications for scoring.
34. See *ODR*, 66–7, for more on this.

CHAPTER 10   An African Priestess and a Scottish Bride

1. This idea is Nancy Basmajian's; M. H. Brown, *Musorgsky in Memoriam*, 43–4.
2. Boris Schwarz has identified the tune as an eighteenth-century Hasidic *niggun*. See "Musorgsky's Interest in Judaica," ibid., 89–92.
3. See D. Brown, *Musorgsky*, 35–6.
4. Gerald Abraham, "The Mediterranean Element in *Boris Godunov*," in Abraham, *Slavonic and Romantic Music*, 188–194.
5. Letter of 10 June 1863, *MLN*, 69; *MR*, 53.
6. *LLMZ*, 59; *MML*, 64.
7. Quoted in Orlova, *Musorgsky Remembered*, 4–5.
8. Cf. chapter 2, note 6.
9. *ODR*, 341–403.
10. Cui, "Pervïye kompozitorskiye shagi," quoted in *ODR*, 359.
11. *ODR*, 420, note 40.
12. Letter of 28 October 1869, in Kremlev and Lyapunova, *Milïy Alekseyevich, Balakirev*, 140–1.
13. *Sanktpeterburgskiye vedomosti*, 26 January 1865; English translation in Campbell, *Russians on Russian Music*, 145–51.
14. Quoted in *ODR*, 395.
15. Letter to Semyon Kruglikov, quoted in Taruskin, *Stravinsky and the Russian Traditions*, 33.
16. Letter of 20 July 1864, in Gusin (ed.), Gusin, *Ts. A. Cui: Izbrannïye pis'ma*, 498; *MDW*, 118.

CHAPTER 11   Home Is the Sailor

1. *MBO*, 71.
2. Ibid., 73.
3. *MML*, 41–2. The tune is very freely adapted.
4. "Pervïy kontsert v pol'zu besplatnoy muzïkal'noy shkolï," in *Cui: Izbrannïye stat'i*, 66–71. Cui himself was probably also in uniform.
5. Dianin, *Borodin* (1960), 63; *Borodin* (1963), 44.
6. *LMMZ*, 53; *MML*, 57–8.
7. Undated letter from the period 1864–7. See *PB1*, 62.
8. *ODR*, 105–6. Taruskin's entire chapter on *Rogneda* (78–140) is a unique mine of information on this fascinating episode in the history of Russian music in the 1860s.

9. Letter of 30 March 1865, in *BSP1*, 240–1. Several excerpts from *Rogneda* had been performed in concert during 1864, including the "Dance of the Skomorokhi."

10. Letter of 15 July 1867 to Rimsky-Korsakov, in *MLN*, 92–3; *MR*, 96–7.

11. 9 November 1865, quoted in *ODR*, 94.

12. *LMMZ*, 64; *MML*, 69–70.

13. *MML*, 116–7.

14. Letter of 15 July 1867.

15. Information on *The Bogatyrs* is in Dianin, *Borodin* (1963), 47–53, and in *ODR*, 121–4 and 450–90, with Taruskin's usual generous music examples.

16. *ODR*, 262. The author is not named.

17. Ibid.

18. *LMMZ*, 66; *MML*, 72.

19. Serov, *Izbrannïye stat'i*, vol. 1, 102.

20. Letter of 30 January 1866, in *BSP1*, 245.

21. Letter to Balakirev, 17 May 1866, in *BSP1*, 245–6.

22. Letter of 30 January 1866.

23. Letter of 9 April 1868 to Lyubov Karmalina, quoted in *ODR*, 263.

24. Letter of 27 July–15 August 1863 to Balakirev, in *BSP1*, 219–20.

25. Letter of 29 May 1865, in *BSP1*, 243.

CHAPTER 12   Life Studies

1. Chernïshevsky, *Selected Philosophical Essays*, 346.

2. Pleshcheyev's "Ah, why do your eyes gaze at me at times so seriously" ("Akh, zachem tvoy glazki") and Heine's "Ich wollt' meine Schmerzen ergössen."

3. *MBO*, 74.

4. Letter of 11 August 1858 to Balakirev, in *BSP1*, 78.

5. Ibid. Cui's intended was in fact called Malvina (Bamberg), and they did not split up.

6. Letter of 20 April 1866, in *MR*, 66–7.

7. Liszt had completed his final revision of *Totentanz* the previous year.

8. Rimsky-Korsakov even recalled that the original version of Musorgsky's work was, like Liszt's, for piano and orchestra. But there is no piano at all in the score as completed in 1867, and no other evidence that a solo part was intended. See *MML*, 73.

9. Letter of 5 July 1867, in *MR*, 85–8.

10. Letter of 18 August 1870, in *MLN*, 118–9; *MR*, 152.

11. Richard Hoops, "Musorgsky and the Populist Age," in M. H. Brown, *Musorgsky in Memoriam*, 278. A more sophisticated study is Igor Glebov (Boris Asafyev), "Muzïkal'no-esteticheskiye vozzreniya Musorgskogo," in Keldïsh and Yakovlev, *M. P. Musorgskiy*, 33–56.

12. "The Idea of Art," in Belinsky, *Selected Philosophical Works*, 168.

13. Hoops, "Musorgsky and the Populist Age," in M. H. Brown, *Musorgsky in Memorium*, 283.

14. Ibid., 280.

15. Letter of 16/28 June 1866 from Prague, in Kremlev and Lyapunova, *Miliy Alekseyevich Balakirev*, 79.

16. Letter of 28 December 1866/9 January 1867, quoted in Garden, *Balakirev*, 72–3.

17. Letter of 11/23 January 1867, in ibid., 73.

18. Clapham, *Smetana*, 34–5.
19. 30 January 1867, in Gusin, *Ts. A. Cui: Izbrannïye pis'ma*, 501–2.
20. Letter of 10/22 February 1867, in *BSP1*, 247–50.
21. Letter of 6/18 February, quoted in Garden, *Balakirev*, 75.
22. Letter of 10/22 February.
23. Ibid.
24. Knight, *The Empire on Display*, 1.
25. "Slavyanskiy Kontsert g-na Balakireva," in *SSMII*, 110–12. The Russian for "mighty heap" appears in the genitive case as *moguchey kuchki*. For some reason the commonest English translation has always been "mighty handful." It perhaps also needs stressing that Stasov originally applied the term to a group of composers that included Glinka and Dargomïzhsky, but not Borodin, Cui, or Musorgsky.

CHAPTER 13   Symphonic Pictures and an Abstract

1. Turgenev, *Smoke*, 117–8.
2. Petrova and Fridlyand, *I. S. Turgenev*, 102. Stasov had sat down after the interval in the row behind Turgenev, who seems to have made these remarks over his shoulder during the performance of the *King Lear* Overture.
3. Letter of 5/17–6/18 March 1867, in Granjard, *Quelques lettres d'Ivan Tourgénev*, 138 (original in French).
4. "Kontsert besplatnoy shkolï," in Gusin, *Ts. A. Cui: Izbrannïye stat'i*, 88–93.
5. Ibid, 91.
6. In his memoirs, Rimsky-Korsakov claims that the B-minor allegro was composed only as far as the development section, but was then abandoned in the face of criticism by Balakirev and others. See *MML*, 85. Andrey Rimsky-Korsakov, the editor of the original Russian edition of the memoirs, cites a letter to Borodin as evidence that the allegro was in fact completed, but subsequently destroyed. The E-flat scherzo was used in the Third Symphony.
7. *MML*, 65–6.
8. Garden, *Balakirev*, 54–5.
9. *PB1*, 89, and 343, note 3.
10. Quoted in D. Lloyd-Jones, preface to the Eulenburg miniature score.
11. *LMMZ*, 61; *MML*, 66.
12. Letter of 17 June 1879, in Diannin, *Borodin* (1960), 216.
13. Letter of 24 September 1867, in *MLN*, 93–5; *MR*, 98–100.
14. Letter of 12 July 1867 to Vladimir Nikolsky, in *MLN*, 89; *MR*, 90.
15. *LMMZ*, 218; *MML*, 249.
16. Letter of 24 September.
17. Letter of 12 July 1867. *Shashni* are naughty pranks of any variety, but at a witches' sabbath it seems fair to assume they were not simply pulling each other's hair.
18. "Le coeur a ses raisons que la raison ne connaît point." *Pensées*, IV, 277.
19. Letter of 5 July 1867, in *MLN*, 86–7; *MR*, 85–7.
20. Letter of 10 July 1867, in *RKP*, 291–2; *MR*, 91.
21. Letter of 15 July 1867, in *MLN*, 90; *MR*, 94.
22. Letter of 10 July 1867, in *MR*, 91–3.
23. Letter of 15 July 1867, in *MR*, 95–6.
24. Letter of 8 October 1867, in *RKP*, 302; *MR*, 102.
25. Letter of 10 July.

26. Taruskin, *Stravinsky and the Russian Traditions*, 266–9. Taruskin's is the most detailed exegesis of Liszt's technical infuence on the *kuchka*.
27. *LMMZ*, 73; *MML*, 78–9.
28. Ibid., 79–80. The passage is incomplete in the first Russian edition.

CHAPTER 14 A French Guest and a Stone One

1. See Taylor, *Anton Rubinstein*, 118–22, and Ridenour, *Nationalism, Modernism and Personal Rivalry*, 145 et seq., for these and other details.
2. Letter of summer 1867, quoted in Ridenour, op. cit., 145.
3. *MML*, 81.
4. *LMMZ*, 74; *MML*, 82.
5. Quoted in Cairns, *Berlioz: Servitude and Greatness*, 763.
6. Ibid.
7. "Chetvyortïy i pyatïy kontsertï Russkogo Muzïkal'nogo Obshchestva. Gektor Berlioz," in Gusin, *Ts. A. Cui: Izbrannïye stat'i*, 118–26.
8. Lyapunov, quoted in Garden, *Balakirev*, 82.
9. "Sed'moy kontsert Russkogo Muzïkal'nogo Obshchestva," in Gusin, *Ts. A. Cui: Izbrannïye stat'i*, 126–8.
10. *Muzïka i teatr*, no. 15 (1867), quoted in Campbell, *Russians on Russian Music*, 186–90.
11. Quoted in Ridenour, *Nationalism, Modernism and Personal Rivalry*.
12. Letter of 3 June 1874, in Zviguilsky, *Ivan Tourgénev: Nouvelle Corréspondance inédite*, 211–12.
13. *LMMZ*, 68; *MML*, 74.
14. Letter of 26 April 1868, Stasov to Balakirev, in *BSPI*, 254.
15. Letter of 24 January 1868, quoted in *TDM*, 148, *MDW*, 160.
16. Letter of 9 April 1868, quoted in *ODR*, 263.
17. *LMMZ*, 80; *MML*, 86.
18. Letter of 26 January 1867, in *MR*, 78.
19. *MBO*, 82.
20. *LMMZ*, 80; *MML*, 87.
21. *MBO*, 81.
22. Lang, *Music in Western Civilization*, 947; partially quoted in *ODR*, 267.

CHAPTER 15 A Child and an Aborted Wedding

1. Gordeyeva, *M. P. Musorgsky*, 96. Musorgsky's explanation of his colorful nose may well have been for the ladies.
2. *MR*, 154.
3. *MR*, 155.
4. Ibid.
5. Gordeyeva, *M. P. Musorgsky*, 97.
6. Ibid., 109–15.
7. According to Novikov, "With Nyanya" was inspired by a brief visit to Musorgsky's old family estate at Karevo in late March 1868. See Novikov, *U istïkov velikoy muzïki*, 141–2.
8. The Russian genitive singular ending *-ogo* is invariably pronounced *-ovo*, and in this instance it seems helpful to indicate the sound rather than the spelling.

9. Letter of 2 January 1873, in *MR*, 203–4.
10. P. Lamm, preface to *Zhenit'ba*, in Musorgsky, *Complete Works*, vol. 23 (New York: Edwin F. Kalmus, n.d.). What their opinion was at this stage is not known.
11. Letter of 3 July 1868, in *MLN*, 98; *MR*, 109.
12. Letter of 30 July 1868, in *MLN*, 100; *MR*, 111–2. Musorgsky's emphases. The word "but" in the final phrase was triple-underlined by Musorgsky and asterisked to a footnote (the phrase bracketed here: "which means").
13. Letters of 30 July to Shestakova, in *MLN*, 101; *MR*, 111; and of 15 August to Cui, in *MLN*, 105; *MR*, 118.
14. Letter of 15 August 1868, in *MLN*, 106; *MR*, 119.
15. Letter of 3 July 1868, in *MLN*, 97–8; *MR*, 108.
16. Musorgsky, *Avtobiograficheskaya zapiska* (June 1880), in *MLN*, 270.
17. *ODR*, 314.
18. Letter of 15 August 1868 to Cui, in *MLN*, 105; *MR*, 118.
19. Letter of 30 July 1868, in *MLN*, 100; *MR*, 111.
20. Letter of 15 August 1868, in *MLN*, 102–3; *MR*, 122.
21. Two separate manuscripts survive, of which the later shows many changes of detail, especially to the accompaniment. See Ye. Antipova, "Dva varianta *Zhenit'bï*," *Sovetskaya Muzïka* 28, no. 3 (March 1964), 77–85, for a detailed discussion with music examples. Antipova asserts that the revisions were undertaken "partly on the advice of Dargomïzhsky and Cui." But she cites no evidence. Musorgsky told Cui, in his letter of 3 July 1868 from Shilovo (misdated by Antipova to 3 June) that, as he was composing without a piano, he would "put everything in order" back in St. Petersburg. He also mentions some changes made at Dargomïzhsky's and Cui's suggestion. But these can only have applied to the first scene, whereas the revisions in the later manuscript cover the entire act. Probably the full revision was made in late August and early September as a result of Musorgsky's own physical experience of the music at the piano. See *MR*, 108.
22. The first books of *War and Peace* were serialized in 1865–6, but the remaining books (including the Karatayev sections) only came out when the novel was published complete in 1869.
23. Gordeyeva, *M. P. Musorgsky*, 39.
24. *MBO*, 92.
25. Letter of 1901 to A. M. Kerzin, quoted in *ODR*, 325.
26. *LMMZ*, 91; *MML*, 100.
27. Letter of 25 September 1868, in *PB1*, 108–9.
28. *LMMZ*, 92; *MML*, 100.
29. Letter of 2 January 1873, in *MLN*, 144; *MR*, 203–4. 1871 was the year of the revised version of *Boris Godunov*.

CHAPTER 16   Outsiders

1. Osip Senkovsky, "Antar: An oriental tale," in Korovin, 229–50.
2. *LMMZ*, 82; *MML*, 90.
3. *LMMZ*, 83; *MML*, 90–1.
4. D. Brown, *Tchaikovsky: A Biographical and Critical Study*, vol. 1 (London: Gollancz, 1978), 124–5.
5. *LMMZ*, 69; *MML*, 75.
6. At this particular moment, however, he was composing an opera on Ostrovsky's

play *Son na Volge* (*Dream on the Volga*), which would end up as *The Voyevoda*. Tchaikovsky destroyed the score, but it was reconstructed from surviving parts and published in the collected edition of his works. His next operatic venture, *Undina* (after La Motte-Fouqué), never got beyond fragments. But Tchaikovsky soon got over this early infection of kuchkism.

7. The poem, "Verratene Liebe," is not by Chamisso, but was translated by him into German from a French translation of an anonymous modern Greek poem. Schumann himself set the poem as op. 40, no. 5. See Sams, *The Songs of Robert Schumann*, 148–9.

8. *LMMZ*, 70; *MML*, 76.

9. Dianin, *Borodin* (1963), 55. Dianin calls it an "affair," but there seems no reason to doubt Borodin's own assertion that his feelings for Anna were essentially platonic, protective, and devoid of sensuality or passion. "She is absolutely not," he insists, "a mistress to me" (letter of 25 October 1868, in *PB1*, 134–5).

10. Dianin, *Borodin* (1963), 55.

11. Letter of 7 August 1868, in *RKP*, 308; *MR*, 116.

12. Ibid.

13. Letter of 15 August 1868, in *MLN*, 106–7; *MR*, 120–1.

14. Ibid.

15. Ibid.

16. The dominant, being unstable (it assumes a resolution on the tonic), makes a better pivot note than the tonic itself.

17. *LMMZ*, 85–6; *MML*, 92–4.

18. *MML*, 103.

19. "Vtoroy kontsert besplatnoy shkolï" (11 January 1872), Gusin, *Ts. A. Cui: Izbrannïye stat'i*, 191–3.

20. *LMMZ*, 92; *MML*, 101.

21. Letter of 3 November 1868 to Stasov, in *BSP1*, 258–9. Balakirev's goose, presumably, was Wagner's swan.

22. "*Loengrin*, muzïkal'naya drama R. Vagnera," *Sanktpeterburgskiye vedomosti*, 11 October 1868.

23. Quoted in Bartlett, *Wagner and Russia*, 38.

24. "Kompozitorskoye pis'mo," *Sanktpeterburgskiye vedomosti*, 4 December 1868, reprinted in *SSM2*, 142–3.

25. "Opernïy sezon v Peterburge," Gusin, *Ts. A. Cui: Izbrannïye stat'i*, 37.

26. The formulation is Taruskin's, in *ODR*, 346.

27. *MDW*, 177, specifies the 26th, but without saying why. Musorgsky's own note on this copy merely mentions the month.

CHAPTER 17   History for the Stage

1. Letter of 21 March 1861 to Balakirev, in *BSP1*, 128.

2. Ibid., 130. This whole question is discussed in great detail by Taruskin in his long essay "The Present in the Past," in *Musorgsky: Eight Essays*, 123–200. See also Taruskin, *Defining Russia Musically*, 38.

3. Letter of August 1866 to O. Novikova, quoted in Taruskin, *Musorgsky: Eight Essays*, 128.

4. This is, of course, why Mikhail Romanov makes no appearance in Glinka's opera about the saving of his life, and also, incidentally, why Catherine the Great

remains offstage at the moment of her arrival at the ball in Tchaikovsky's *Queen of Spades.*

5. *LMMZ*, 82; *MML*, 90.

6. See Abraham, "*Pskovityanka,* 58; also Taruskin, *Musorgsky: Eight Essays,* 151 and note 69. Nobody seems to know how or why Tchaikovsky came by the libretto.

7. *LMMZ*, 82; *MML*, 89.

8. Ibid.

9. Act 2, tableau 1 of the revised (1895) score, which is the version invariably performed now. See *LMMZ*, 89; *MML*, 97.

10. Letter of 25 September 1868, in *PB1*, 293.

11. In revising the opera in the late seventies and again in the mid-nineties, Rimsky-Korsakov changed many details in these early scenes. The present discussion is naturally based on the original version, rarely if ever performed now, even in Russia, but published as the very first two volumes of the Collected Edition.

12. Letter of 8 December 1888, Balakirev to Stasov, in *BSPII*, 142–3.

13. *LMMZ*, 92; *MML*, 100.

14. Letter of 30 July 1868, in *MLN*, 100; *MR*, 112.

15. Letter to Rimsky-Korsakov, 15 August 1868, in *MR*, 119; to Nikolsky, 15 August, in *MR*, 122.

16. Emerson and Oldani, *Modest Musorgsky and Boris Godunov,* 30.

17. This is no longer the case, but of course that has no relevance to Pushkin's drama. See Taruskin, *Musorgsky: Eight Essays,* 186, for details.

18. The offstage choruses were added in the revised score.

19. See chapter 2, note 4.

20. On the complicated question of the sources of Pushkin's and Musorgsky's texts for these songs, see Taruskin, *Musorgsky: Eight Essays,* 291–6; also Dunning et al., *The Uncensored "Boris Godunov,"* especially p. 472, note 90.

21. Letter of 15 August 1868 to Nikolsky, in *MLN*, 102; *MR*, 122.

22. Letter of 11 November 1868, quoted in *TDM*, 167; *MDW*, 177.

23. Undated letter [27 September 1869], explaining his refusal to act as accompanist at a rehearsal for an FMS performance of Schumann's *Scenes from "Faust"; MR,* 131–2.

24. *MBO*, 98.

25. Letter of 18 July 1869, *SPR,* 46; quoted in *MR*, 131.

26. Igor Glebov (Boris Asafyev), "Muzïkal'no-esteticheskiye vozzreniya Musorgskogo," in Keldïsh and Yakovlev, *M. P. Musorgskiy,* 34.

27. See his letter of 15 August 1868 to Rimsky-Korsakov, in *MR,* 120–1; also Glebov, in Keldïsh and Yakovlev, *M. P. Musorgskiy,* 43.

CHAPTER 18   An Opera Performed, an Opera Abandoned

1. *ODR*, 104.

2. *LMMZ*, 96; *MML,* 105. Rimsky-Korsakov admits that the original panegyric sprang "from a pure heart, but a small critical mind."

3. "Ratklif," *Sanktpeterburgskiye vedomosti,* 7 May 1869, reprinted in *SSMII*, 169–84.

4. Quoted in *ODR*, 395.

5. For these and other opinions, see "Ratklif," *SSMII*, 178–81.

6. Letter of 18 April 1869, in Dianin, *Borodin* (1960), 193.

7. Letter of 20 April, in *PB1*, 142.

8. Dianin, *Borodin* (1963), 53.

9. Ibid., 64; *MML*, 85 (although Rimsky-Korsakov gives the wrong year).
10. There remains disagreement about how much of *Prince Igor* Borodin composed in this first phase. For instance, A. N. Dmitriyev's suggestion that a first version of Igor's aria in act 2 was sketched in the winter of 1869–70 is questioned by Marek Bobéth in his major study of the work, in the absence of clear evidence. See Bobéth, *Borodin und seine Oper "Fürst Igor,"* 28. See also Dmitriyev, "K istorii sozdaniya operï A. P. Borodina *Knyaz' Igor,"* in Dmitriyev, *Issledovaniya stat'i nablyudeniya,* 138–9 (the article first appeared in the journal *Sovetskaya Muzïka* in 1950); and Gaub, *Die kollektive Balett-Oper "Mlada,"* 378–9.
11. Letter of 4 March 1870, in *PB1*, 200.
12. Quoted in Williams, *Franz Liszt: Selected Letters,* 969.
13. Cairns, *The Memoirs of Hector Berlioz,* 492–3.
14. Letter of 24 September 1870, in *PB1*, 234–5.
15. Letter of 3 November 1869, Borodin to his wife, in *PB1*, 161–2.
16. Letter of 12 November, in *BSP1*, 273.
17. The first letter, not sent, but kept by Balakirev, is dated 18 March 1869. The letter that he sent is dated 31 March. See Kremlev and Lyapunova, *Miliy Aleksegevich Balakirev,* 127–32.
18. Letter of 2 October 1869, in ibid., 135.
19. Letter of 4 October, in ibid., 136–9.
20. Quoted in Maes, *A History of Russian Music,* 66.
21. Letter of 11 October 1869, in *BSP1*, 270–2.
22. Ibid.
23. Letter of 29 July 1870, in *SPR*, 60.
24. *Muzïkal'nïy sezon,* no. 13, quoted in *TDM*, 182–3; *MDW*, 194–5.
25. Stasov's article is reprinted in *SSMII*, 186–96. A *rayok* is a small *ray* ("paradise"), hence the occasional translation of Musorgsky's title as "Penny Paradise." The fairground peepshow was like a magic lantern, a box with moving pictures, which you watched through an eyeglass to the accompaniment of *pribaoutki,* bawdy comic poems. According to wikipedia (http://en.wikipedia.org/wiki/Rayok), one of the favorite subjects for the *rayok* was the biblical fall—hence the name.

CHAPTER 19 A Shared Apartment . . .

1. Letter of 11 July 1872, in *MLN,* 133; *MR,* 188. The internal quotations are from Alexander Griboyedov's comedy *Woe from Wit (Gore ot Uma):* Colonel Skazolub is explaining to the civil servant Famusov how he has risen so quickly in the ranks.
2. Letter of 6 May 1870, *PB1,* 221–2.
3. Letter of 24 April 1871, in *BSP1,* 279.
4. Undated note of 12 April 1871, in Kremlev and Lyapunova, *Miliy Aleksegevich Balakirev,* 105.
5. Letter of 17 April 1871, in *RKP,* 34.
6. Letters of 17 and 24–25 October 1871 to his wife, in *PB1,* 305–13.
7. See, for example, "Musorgsky versus Musorgsky," in Taruskin, *Musorgsky: Eight Essays,* 201–90.
8. Pushkin's equivalent scene is a brief conversation between Marina and her maid, Ruzia, who in fact does most of the talking but takes no part in the opera. In the previous scene, the Jesuit Father Czernikowski has one speech to the Pretender, invoking St. Ignatius in his aid.

9. Letter of 18 April 1871, in *MLN*, 121–2; *MR*, 162–3. Taruskin argues that this refers to the second Polish scene, but his reasoning is questionable and includes a complicated point about the Russian word for "scene" (*stsena*), whereas the actual word used is *kartina*, which almost certainly relates to the whole tableau—i.e., act 3, scene 1. The second scene, as we shall see, was not finished until December. See *Musorgsky: Eight Essays*, 253–4, note 114.

10. See *ODR*, 141–239, for a comprehensive study of *The Power of the Fiend*. Cui's reviews are quoted at 228–38, passim.

11. *ODR*, 199.

12. No. 27, "Kak pod lesom, pod lesochkom."

13. Letters of 20 and 21 September 1871, in *PB1*, 291–5. That these are the Cui works in question is my deduction. The editor of Borodin's letters, by contrast, assumes that he is referring to choruses for *Angelo*. But the fourth act of that opera contains no choral music except for a twenty-bar monks' chorus at the very end, and there is no evidence that Cui was working on the earlier acts, where there are plentiful choruses, at this stage.

14. Quoted in G. Abraham, preface to the Eulenburg miniature score, p. II.

15. Ibid.

CHAPTER 20 . . . and a Shared Commission

1. *LMMZ,*, 103; *MML*, 116. Rimsky-Korsakov's emphases; see also Campbell, *Russians on Russian Music*, 78.

2. *LMMZ*, 105; *MML*, 117.

3. Letter of 21 September 1871, in *PB1*, 293.

4. Letter of 3 January 1872, in *MLN*, 126; *MR*, 176–7. Nadya Purgold's letter to Rimsky-Korsakov is quoted in *TDM*, 233; *MDW*, 251.

5. Letter of 31 March 1871, in *MLN*, 129–30; *MR*, 181–2.

6. Stasov, *Borodin*, quoted in Dianin, *Borodin* (1960), 93; *Borodin* (1963), 77.

7. This question is discussed in exhaustive detail in Gaub, *Die kollektive Balett-Oper "Mlada,"* 376–84. Gaub questions, on what seem good grounds, the standard assumption that the 1869 arioso ("Yaroslavna's Dream") was the same as, or even close to, the final version. Unfortunately, the original manuscript was obliterated by Borodin's subsequent adaptations.

8. Borodin's *Mlada* music, unlike Cui's and Musorgsky's, has never been published in any authentic form. The final scenes, including the inundation and the apotheosis, were arranged for orchestra by Rimsky-Korsakov after Borodin's death and published in 1892 by Belyayev. The other scenes were all plundered, in various ways, for *Prince Igor*.

9. *Sanktpeterburgskiye vedomosti*, 28 March 1868, quoted in *ODR*, 298–300.

10. Quoted in ibid., 337–76.

11. Quoted in ibid., 303.

12. Letter to Stasov, 31 March 1872, in *MLN*, 129–30; *MR*, 181–2.

13. *MBO*, 122.

14. Letter of 16 & 22 June 1872, in *MLN*, 131–2; *MR*, 185–6.

15. See his letter of 21 March 1861 to Balakirev, in *BSP1*, 129. See also chapter 3 of the present volume. Vadim Kel'siyev's *Sbornik pravitel'stvennikh svedenniy o raskolnikakh* (part 1) had been published in London in 1860.

16. Letter of 13 July 1872, in *MLN*, 134–5; *MR*, 189.

17. *MLN*, 137; *MR*, 93. Musorgsky's emphases.

18. The new songs were intended for a new set, to be called *At the Dacha* (*Na dache*), but no songs were added, and the pair were eventually appended to *The Nursery* by Rimsky-Korsakov when he made his edition of the cycle. Musorgsky quotes *Hamlet* in his letter of 13 July, Hamlet's mad-play with Polonius about clouds shaped like camels, weasels, or whales (act 3, scene 2, line 400 et seq.). Hamlet's "When the wind is southerly I know a hawk from a handsaw" is to Guildenstern in act 2, scene 2, line 403.

19. Not, as often given, "The Cat Sailor," which suggests a puss in a sailor suit aboard a toy ship. "Sailor" is simply the cat's name.

20. The rather banal piano coda sometimes heard in this song (resolving back to the home key) is by Rimsky-Korsakov, who placed this song last in his edition of the cycle.

21. Letter of 18 October 1872, in *MLN*, 141; *MR*, 198–200. See also Kelly, *Toward Another Shore*, 10.

CHAPTER 21   Three Tsars and a Tyrant

1. Quoted in *MR*, 253–4.

2. See Oldani, "*Boris Godunov* and the Censor," 245–53, for an authoritative account of this whole issue.

3. *Sanktpeterburgskiye vedomosti*, 9 January 1873, in Gusin, *Ts. A. Cui: Izbrannïye stat'i*, 215–24; see also Campbell, *Russians on Russian Music*, 207–17.

4. *Golos*, no. 10 (1873), in Gozenpud, *G. A. Larosh: Izbrannïye stat'i*, 105–12; see also Campbell, *Russians on Russian Music*, 217–24.

5. "City Notes," *Peterburgskaya gazeta*, quoted in *MDW*, 297.

6. *Golos*, 14 February 1873, in Gozenpud, *G. A. Larosh: Izbrannïye stat'i*, 119–24; see also Campbell, *Russians on Russian Music*, 224–30.

7. Letter of 25 October 1873, in *PBII*, 63–4.

8. Letter of 17 March 1873 to Sofia Medvedeva, in *SPR*, 102; *MDW*, 309.

9. Letter of 9/21 August 1873, in *SPR*, 146.

10. Letter of 19 May 1873 [NS], in *MR*, 209.

11. Letter of 6 August 1873, in *MLN*, 164; *MR*, 239.

12. Letter of 6 September 1873, *MLN*,, 166; *MR*, 247. Musorgsky's emphases.

13. *LMMZ*, 127; *MML*, 144.

14. Letter of 2 August 1873 to Nadezhda Stasova, in *MLN*, 163; *MR*, 237.

15. Letter of 6 September, in *MLN*, 166; *MR*, 239. The instrument in question was a piano.

16. Letter of 2 August 1873.

17. *MML*, 136. The passage is not in *LMMZ*.

18. *LMMZ*, 85; *MML*, 92. See also chapter 16, note 17 and related text.

19. Letter of 28 March 1874 to Dmitry Stasov, in *SPR*, 215–6.

20. Letter of 2 August 1873, in *MLN*, 160; *MR*, 233.

21. Letter of 25 September 1874, in *PB2*, 80–1.

22. Letter of 21 May 1873 to Dmitry Stasov's daughter Zinaida, in *SPR*, 110.

23. Quoted in *TDM*, 233; *MDW*, 251.

CHAPTER 22   Toward New Shores

1. Letter of 2 February 1874, in *SPR*, 206–9.

2. See Oldani, "*Boris Godunov* and the Censor," 249.

3. For monochrome reproductions, from lithograph originals, of all the sets transferred from the play, see Oldani, "Mussorgsky's *Boris* on the Stage," 75–92.

4. Nikolay Solovyev, *Birzheviye vedomosti*, 29 January and 2 February 1874, respectively, in *MDW*, 362, 376. The "wrong notes" were diagnosed by Hermann Laroche, *Golos*, 29 January 1874, in *MDW*, 364.

5. Letter of 29 October 1874, in Galina von Meck (ed.), *Pyotr Ilyich Tchaikovsky: Letters to His Family* (London: Dennis Dobson, 1981), 89.

6. *Golos*, no. 44 (1874), quoted in *TDM*, 365–9; *MDW*, 388–91.

7. *Sankt-Peterburgskiye vedomosti*, n. 37, quoted in *TDM*, 355–60; *MDW*, 378–83.

8. Letter of 6 February 1874, in *MLN*, 175–6; *MR*, 266–7.

9. Letter of 19 June 1873, in *MLN*, 149; *MR*, 217–8.

10. A. A. Golenishchev-Kutuzov, "Vospominaniya o M. P. Musorgskom," in Gordeyeva, *M. P. Musorgsky*, 136–7.

11. The duration of their cohabiting has been questioned by the Soviet scholar Alexandra Orlova, but there are gaps in her datings. On the whole there seems no reason to doubt Kutuzov's claim that he and Musorgsky shared accommodation from the autumn of 1874. See *Musorgsky Remembered*, 95, and 174, note 20. As for the reason for Musorgsky's being shut out of the apartment when Kutuzov departed for the country, he himself alleged (letter of 7 August 1875 to Stasov, in *MR*, 301) that Kutuzov had inadvertently gone off with the key; but how would he have got into the apartment in the small hours even if Kutuzov had left the key behind? The explanation has all the hallmarks of a face-saving formula.

12. A. A. Golenishchev-Kutuzov, "Vospominaniya o M. P. Musorgskom," in Gordeyeva, *M.P.Musorgsky*, 137.

13. Ibid., 142–3.

14. See, for instance, Alexandra Orlova's preface to *Musorgsky Remembered*, xi–xii, quoting the editor of Golenishchev-Kutuzov's memoirs, P. Aravin.

15. Letter to the Editor of *Novoye Vremya*, 27 October 1876, in *SSMII*, 309.

16. A. A. Golenishchev-Kutuzov, "Vospominaniya o M. P. Musorgskom," in Gordeyeva, *M.P.Musorgsky*, 17.

17. Letter of 25 September 1874 to his wife, *PB2*, 81.

18. *Russkiy klassicheskiy romans XIX veka*, cited in Walker, "Mussorgsky's *Sunless* Cycle," 382–91.

19. Calvocoressi, *Mussorgsky*, 85. The book was unfinished by its nominal author, and the relevant chapter on the songs was written by Gerald Abraham.

20. Letter of [?12] June 1874, in *MR*, 271; see also Rimsky-Korsakov, *M. P. Musorgskiy: pis'ma i dokumenti*, 302.

21. The subtitle is only in Russian in the manuscript and the Latin version was presumably added by Stasov or Rimsky-Korsakov before the work's first publication in 1886, perhaps in response to Musorgsky's marginal note: "A Latin text would be good. The creative spirit of the dead Hartmann leads me to the skulls, and apostrophizes them; the skulls slowly start to glow." The Latin for "with" is not *con* but *cum*.

22. Michael Russ, in his Cambridge Handbook on *Pictures*, finds octatonic harmony in "Tuileries." But there is nothing very unusual about the harmonic progressions as such, and the phrase structure is regular. See Russ, *Musorgsky: Pictures at an Exhibition*, 68–9.

23. Ibid., 55–6.

24. Letter of 1 July 1874 to Rimsky-Korsakov, quoted in *TDM*, 395–6; *MDW*, 419.

25. Ibid.

26. Letter of 18 June 1858, quoted in *MDW*, 66–7.

CHAPTER 23   Distractability

1. Golenishchev-Kutuzov, "Vospominaniya o M. P. Musorgskom," in Gordeyeva, *M. P. Musorgsky*, 149. Stasov gave a detailed account of the intended content of "Nettle Mountain" in his letter of 1 July 1874 to Rimsky-Korsakov, who expressed sharp disapproval. See *MDW*, 420, 422.

2. Letter of 23 July 1874, in *MR* 278; see also A. N. Rimsky-Korsakov (ed.), *M. P. Musorgskiy: pis'ma i dokumenti*, 306.

3. *LMMZ*, 130; *MML*, 147.

4. *LMMZ*, 132; *MML*, 149.

5. Letter of 15 April 1875, in *PB2*, 88–9.

6. Ibid.

7. See Dianin, *Borodin*, 85.

8. The gudok was a three-stringed lute played, however, with a bow in the manner of the medieval rebec.

9. See chapter 20, note 7.

10. Letter of 26 September 1875, in *PB2*, 101. As we shall see, Borodin later used some of the ideas in the scene of the solar eclipse in the opera's prologue. The monologue itself has been reinstated in the opera as staged at the Maryinsky Theatre, and is included in the recording conducted by Valery Gergiev.

11. Letter of 15 April 1875.

12. Letter of 7 August 1875, in *MLN*, 196; *MR*, 300 (Musorgsky's emphasis).

13. Letter of 15/27 August 1873, Stasov to Musorgsky (from Vienna), in Rimsky-Korsakov, *M. P. Musorgskiy: pis'ma i dokumenti*, 179; see also *MR*, 244–5; letter of 6 August 1873, Musorgsky to Stasov, in *MLN*, 164–5; *MR*, 239.

14. Letter of 6 September 1873, in *MLN*, 166; *MR*, 247.

15. Musorgsky had described his new work as "a people's musical drama" ("Narodnaya muzïkal'naya drama") in a letter of 13 July 1872 to Stasov (*MR*, 189), and it retains that subtitle in the published score.

16. Letter of 15/27 August.

17. Letter of 20 April 1875, in *MR*, 296 (translation slightly modified).

18. Letter of 18 May 1876, in Rimsky-Korsakov, *M. P. Musorgskiy: pis'ma i dokumenti*, 483–5; *MR*, 333–7.

19. Letter of 15 June 1876, in *MLN*, 219; *MR*, 338.

20. *LMMZ*, 226–7; *MML*, 259.

21. Letter of 25 December 1876, in *MLN*, 227; *MR*, 353. Musorgsky wrote the words "intelligent" and "justified" ("osmïslennoyu" "opravdannoyu") one above the other, like an arithmetical fraction.

22. See Taruskin, *Musorgsky: Eight Essays*, 361, on the question of identification.

CHAPTER 24   Dances of Death

1. Letter of 7 August 1875 in *MLN*, 197; *MR*, 302. The couplet is quoted direct from *MR*, but Musorgsky's version does not rhyme.

2. Letter of 6 September 1875, in *MLN*, 200 (dated 3 October); *MR*, 308.

3. Letter of 19–20 October 1875, in *MLN*, 202–3; *MR*, 312.

4. Letter to Kutuzov, 6 September 1875, in *MLN* ("3 October"), 199–200; *MR*, 307–9. Letter to Stasov, 7 August 1875, in *MLN*, 197; *MR*, 303.

5. Letter of 19 October 1875, in *MLN*, 202–3; *MR*, 311–12.

6. Gordeyeva, *M. P. Musorgsky*, 154.

7. Letter of 17 December 1875 to Shestakova, in *MR*, 321.

8. Letter of 17 August 1875, in *MR*, 303–4.

9. Letter of 9 August 1878, in *MR*, 371.

10. Letter of 5 September 1875, quoted in Taruskin, *Stravinsky and the Russian Traditions*, 30.

11. *MML*, 157.

12. Letter of 23 November 1875 to Stasov, in *MR*, 319.

13. Graham Johnson, "German Song," in entry *Ballad*, "The 19th- and 20th-century art form," in Stanley Sadie (ed.), *The New Grove Dictionary of Music and Musicians* (London: Macmillan, 2001), 2:549.

14. Quoted in Fischer-Dieskau, *Schubert: A Biographical Study*, 139.

15. *MBO*, 120.

16. Apart from Musorgsky himself (a baritone), one of the first singers of any of these songs was the tenor Pyotr Lodi. Musorgsky praised his singing of "The Commander" in a letter of 15 August 1877 to Kutuzov, and added: "You can't possibly clearly imagine, dear friend, the amazing distinction of your scene when it is rendered by a tenor!" See *MR*, 361.

17. *LMMZ*, 144–5; *MML*, 164–5.

18. See, for instance, chapter 2, note 4. Not long afterward, however, Rimsky-Korsakov would compose music that he later claimed had *preceded* Melgunov's description of this technique. See below, chapter 26, note 29 and related text.

19. *LMMZ*, 138; *MML*, 156.

CHAPTER 25   A Chaos of Operas

1. See his letter to his sister Nadezhda, 7 February 1876, in *SPR*, 279–80.

2. Letter of 28–9 February 1876, in *MLN*, 213–4; *MR*, 328.

3. Ibid.

4. Letter to Karmalina, 1 June 1876, in *PB2*, 107–10.

5. Ibid.

6. See Dianin, *Borodin* (1963), 96. The chorus was first performed at an FMS concert in February 1879.

7. Dianin, *Borodin* (1960), 110; *Borodin* (1963), 95.

8. According to Bobéth, this text originally figures in Yaroslavna's arioso, no. 3. See Bobéth, *Borodin und seine Oper*, 110.

9. Quoted in Dianin, *Borodin* (1960), 111; *Borodin* (1963), 97.

10. "Reminiscences of Mariya Vasil'evna Dobroslavina," in Dianin, *Borodin* (1960), 345.

11. Dianin, *Borodin* (1960), 116; *Borodin* (1963), 102.

12. Letter of 9, 17 June 1876, in *SPR*, 285.

13. Letter of 3 January 1872, in *MLN*, 126; *MR*, 176.

14. Letter of 23 July 1874, in *MR*, 278; also Rimsky-Korsakov, *M. P. Musorgskiy: pis'ma i dokumenti*, 306.

15. Taruskin, *Musorgsky: Eight Essays*, 367.

16. Letter of 7 November 1877, in *MR*, 362.

17. As reported by Stasov to Kutuzov in a letter of 22 August 1877, in ibid.

18. Letter of 10 November 1877 to Kutuzov, *MR*, 362–3.

19. As told to Ilya Tyumenev. Quoted in Taruskin, *Musorgsky: Eight Essays*, 357 (see also *MDW*, 622–3).

20. Three operas, if we include another project to which there is tantalizing reference

in Stasov's Musorgsky biography. This was a project for an opera based on Pushkin's novella about the Pugachev rebellion of 1774, *The Captain's Daughter*. Stasov claims that the subject was discussed at some length, and there is an echo of it in a letter of 14 November 1878 (or possibly 1879) to Kutuzov, where Musorgsky suggests a play—to be turned into an opera—about the so-called "life campaigners," a company of the Preobrazhensky Guards that had helped put down the Pugachevshchina. But apart from a single notation of a folk tune marked "for the last opera, Pugachev's Men" in Musorgsky's hand, no music seems to have been composed, and indeed it's hard to see how any could have been. See *MR*, 354 and 372–3.

CHAPTER 26   Drowning in the Waters

1. *Golos*, 9 June 1876, in *TDM*, 467; *MDW*, 495.
2. Letter of 15/27 March 1872, in *MDW*, 260–1.
3. Letter of 3 June 1874 (NS), in Zviguilsky, *Ivan Tourgénev. Nouvelle Corréspondance inédite*, 211–12.
4. Letter to M. A. Milyutina, 22 February/6 March 1875, in Turgenev, *Polnoye sobraniye sochineniy i pisem*, 31.
5. Borodin was forty-four.
6. Letter of 24 December/5 January, from San Remo, in *Chaikovskiy i Nadezhda Filaretovna von Meck: Perepiska* (Moscow: Zakharov, 2004), 160–5. See also *MR*, 364–7.
7. Letter of 30 March 1876, in Dianin, *Borodin* (1960), 203.
8. Letter of 1 June 1876, in *PB2*, 108.
9. Letter of 19 January 1877, in *PBII*, 123.
10. Letter of 3 January 1878, in *BSP1*, 288–9.
11. Letter of 6 January 1878, in *BSP1*, 289–90.
12. Letter of 23 February 1878, in *BSP1*, 291–2.
13. Letter of 4 July 1878, in *BSP1*, 299–300.
14. Letter of 18/30 August, from Paris, in *BSP1*, 307–9.
15. Letter of 8 October 1878, in *BSP1*, 315–6.
16. As reported by Stasov to Kutuzov, letter of 1 April 1878, in *MR*, 368.
17. Contribution to joint letter of 28 July 1878 from Musorgsky, Balakirev, and Shestakova to Stasov in Paris. See *MR*, 369–70; *BSP1*, 301–2.
18. Letter of 9 August 1878 to Stasov, in *MR*, 371.
19. Letter of 18/30 August.
20. Letter of 13 October 1878, in *BSP1*, 317.
21. Letter of 3 July 1877, Borodin to his wife, in *PB2*, 133.
22. Balakirev would have nothing to do with the project; Musorgsky composed "a galop or something of the kind," but missed the point by changing the cantus firmus at whim, then declined to modify what he had written. His attempt is apparently lost. See *LMMZ*, 179; *MML*, 204.
23. *LMMZ*, 152; *MML*, 175.
24. *LMMZ*, 153; *MML*, 175.
25. *LMMZ*, 156; *MML*, 179.
26. The original prologue consisted of the overture, the lullaby, Vera's narration, and the return of the prince. For the separate work, Rimsky-Korsakov composed the opening scene for Nadezhda and the nurse, Vlasyevna, and the conversation of Vera and Nadezhda leading up to the narration. See the introduction to volume 8 of the Collected Edition.

27. Gogol, "A Night in May," trans. Christopher English, *Village Evenings near Dikanka and Mirgorod* (Oxford and New York: Oxford University Press, 1994), 57.
28. Taruskin calls it "an opera in search of a composer." Taruskin, *Musorgsky: Eight Essays*, 331.
29. Ibid., 332.
30. Yastrebtsev, *Reminiscences of Rimsky-Korsakov*, 69.
31. As Taruskin remarks, "Rimsky's '*podgoloski*,' it hardly needs to be added, follow conservatory rules of voice leading." Taruskin, *Stravinsky and the Russian Traditions*, 725, note 136.
32. Yastrebtsev, *Reminiscences of Rimsky-Korsakov*, 118.
33. *LMMZ*, 194; *MML*, 222–3.

CHAPTER 27   The Chemist in His Laboratory

1. Letter of 24 January 1879, in *BSP1*, 320.
2. Letter of 26 January 1879, in *RKP*, 125.
3. *LMMZ*, 185; *MML*, 211.
4. Nikolay Solovyev, quoted in *TDM*, 525; *MDW*, 557.
5. Quoted in *TDM*, 526; *MDW*, 558–9. The program, on 16 January, had included Beethoven's "Pastoral" Symphony and Weber's Polonaise brillante (arr. Liszt) for piano and orchestra.
6. Letter of late December 1879 to Kutuzov, in *MR*, 400. See below, note 15.
7. Letter of 8 August 1879, in Dianin, *Borodin* (1960), 230–1.
8. *LMMZ*, 199; *MML*, 227–8.
9. Karl Baedeker, *La Russie* (Leipzig: Karl Baedeker, 1902), 364. The correspondence and repertoire are set out in detail in *MR*, 376–95.
10. Gordeyeva, *M. P. Musorgsky v vospominaniyakh sovremennikov*, 181.
11. Ibid.
12. Letter of 19 October 1879 to Sofia Fortunato, in *SPR*, 352–3. Sofia's letter has not surfaced.
13. As David Brown, for instance does, when he calls the poem a "satire on royal favoritism." See D. Brown, *Musorgsky*, 307.
14. Dianin, *Borodin* (1963), 108.
15. See Alec Robertson (ed.), *Chamber Music* (London: Penguin, 1957), 133–4.
16. Dianin, *Borodin* (1963), 237–41.
17. Letter of December 1879, *MLN*, 241; *MR*, 398–400. The letter is undated, and *MLN* and other sources give December 1878. The later dating is, however, supported by references to the publication of Kutuzov's play *Shuisky*, which was only passed by the censor in January 1879.
18. Orlova, *Musorgsky Remembered*, 116 (reminiscences of Nikolay Lavrov).
19. Letter of 3 January 1880, in *BSP1*, 332; excerpt in *MR*, 401.
20. Letter of 16 January 1880, in *MLN*, 259; *MR*, 401–2.
21. *MML*, 223.
22. Letter of 27–28 August 1880, in *MLN*, 261–2; *MR*, 406.

CHAPTER 28   Death by Sunlight

1. Dianin, *Borodin* (1960), 180, 185; *Borodin* (1963), 114, note 1, 129, note 3.
2. The approach-and-recede pattern of the well-known orchestral version is Ra-

vel's idea. The first published edition of 1886, edited by Rimsky-Korsakov, has no dynamic marking of any kind at the start of the movement.

3. Dianin, *Borodin* (1960), 125; *Borodin* (1963), 115. See also letter of 19 May 1880 to Balakirev, in S. A. Dianin (ed.), *Pis'ma A. P. Borodina*, vol. 3 (Moscow and Leningrad: GMI, 1949), 100.

4. *LMMZ*, 196; *MML*, 224–5.

5. Letter of 22 January 1879, in *RKP*, 123–4.

6. *LMMZ*, 202; *MML*, 231.

7. Letter of 9 November 1880, quoted in *MML*, 242, note 7.

8. Letter of 6 October 1879, quoted in *MML*, 216, note 22.

9. *LMMZ*, 203–4; *MML*, 233.

10. Stravinsky and Craft, *Memories and Commentaries*, 55.

11. Letter to Balakirev, 13 February 1861, in *BSP1*, 121–4. See chapter 5.

12. *LMMZ*, 225; *MML*, 257.

13. See, for instance, Taruskin, *Stravinsky and the Russian Traditions*, 698, for a "correction" of one of his usages in *The Snow Maiden*.

14. It will be recalled that Rimsky-Korsakov had been away on his naval cruise at the time of Wagner's St. Petersburg concerts in 1863, the only time any of *The Ring* had yet been heard there. The vocal scores, of course, had long been available.

15. Reminiscence of S. V. Rozhdestvensky, as recorded by Ivan Lapshin, in Orlova, *Musorgsky Remembered*, 119.

16. Gordeyeva, *M. P. Musorgsky v vospominaniyakh sovremennikov*, 183; *LMMZ*, 196; *MML*, 225.

17. Gordeyeva, *M. P. Musorgsky v vospominaniyakh sovremennikov*, 184.

18. Ibid., 126.

19. Letter of 15 February 1881, in *BSPII*, 10; excerpt in *MR*, 411.

20. Quoted in *MR*, 412–3.

21. A. A. Golenishchev-Kutuzov, "Vospominaniya o M. P. Musorgskom," in Gordeyeva, *M. P. Musorgsky v vospominaniyakh sovremennikov*, 151.

22. M. M. Ivanov, "Iz nekrologa," in ibid., 195.

CHAPTER 29   Heirs and Rebels

1. "Nekrolog M. P. Musorgskogo," *Golos*, 17 March 1881; in *SSMII*, 45–7.

2. "Zametka o pokhoronakh Musorgskogo," *Golos*, 19 March 1881; in ibid., 47–8.

3. "Modest Petrovich Musorgskiy: Biographicheskiy ocherk," *Vestnik Evropi*, May 1881, 285–316; June 1881, 506–45; reprinted in *SSMII*, 51–113. References in the present volume are to *MBO*.

4. "Nasha muzïka za posledniye 25 let," *SSMII*, 143–97.

5. Translated direct from *SSMII*, 193–4. Jonas, *Vladimir Stasov: Selected Essays* gives a later text that takes account of the death of Borodin in 1887.

6. The big C-major symphony, begun in 1864 and shelved in 1866 with its first movement half-written and a scherzo and finale only sketched, was eventually taken up again in the 1890s, and completed only in 1897. By this time, alas, its Russianisms (chromatic devices, Oriental colorings, harp flourishes, tarantella rhythms, etc.) have the slightly uncomfortable flavor of self-parody.

7. "Nasha muzïka za posledniye 25 let," in *SSMIII*, 177.

8. Dianin, *Borodin* (1963), 250, note 1.

9. Marya Dobroslavina's memoirs, quoted in Dianin, *Borodin* (1960), 153; *Borodin* (1963), 150–1.

10. Ibid., 145, 142.

11. "Poslednyaya kontsertnaya nedelya," in Gusin, *Ts. A. Cui: Izbrannïye stat'i*, 306–9.

12. Dianin, *Borodin* (1963), 130. For much of the information in this and the following two paragraphs I am indebted to Taruskin, *Stravinsky and the Russian Traditions*, 41–71.

13. Fay, *Shostakovich: A Life*, 24.

14. "Nasha muzïka za posledniye 25 let," in *SSMIII*, 146–7.

15. Ibid., 149.

16. Ibid., 150.

17. Stravinsky and Craft, *Memories and Commentaries*, 57. Craft's wording in fact accidentally reverses the paradox, but the point is clear enough.

18. Stravinsky and Craft, *Expositions and Developments*, 121.

19. It is instructive to compare Musorgsky's score with the Rimsky-Korsakov edition in this passage. Rimsky smooths out all the irregular meters, even in one or two places accepting false verbal accentuations and generally destroying the fluidity of the original.

20. For more on this subject see Taruskin, *Defining Russia Musically*, 117 et seq., and *Stravinsky and the Russian Traditions*, 669 and 923.

21. *La Revue blanche*, 15 April 1901; English translation in R. Langham-Smith (ed.), *Debussy on Music* (London: Secker & Warburg, 1977), 20–21.

22. The complete conversation in English is in Edward Lockspeiser, *Debussy: His Life and Mind*, vol. 1 (London: Cassell, 1962), 204–8.

23. Tyrrell, *Janáček: Years of a Life*, vol. 2, 485.

24. "Nasha muzïka za posledniye 25 let," in *SSMIII*, 197.

EPILOGUE The Survivors

1. Letter of 5 August 1900, quoted in Olkhovsky, *Vladimir Stasov and Russian National Culture*, 128.

2. Quoted in Taruskin, *Stravinsky and the Russian Traditions*, 28.

3. As reported by Stasov in a letter of 27 February 1904 to his brother Dmitry, quoted in ibid., 70–1.

4. Yastrebtsev, *Reminiscences of Rimsky-Korsakov*, 445, entry of 6 March 1908.

5. 18 May 1910, in Gusin, *Ts. A. Cui: Izbrannïye stat'i*, 548–50.

Bibliography

PRINCIPAL SOURCES

BSPI   A. S. Lyapunova (ed.). *M. A. Balakirev–V. V. Stasov: Perepiska*, vol. 1, 1858–1880 (Moscow: Muzïka, 1969).

BSPII   A. S. Lyapunova (ed.). *M. A. Balakirev-V. V. Stasov: Perepiska*, vol. 2, 1881–1906 (Moscow: Muzïka, 1971).

LMMZ   N. A. Rimsky-Korsakov. *Letopis' moey muzikal'noy zhizni 1844–1906* (St. Petersburg: Tipografiya Glazunova, 1909). English translation as *My Musical Life*, trans. Judah A. Joffe (London: Eulenburg, 1974) [MML].

MBO   V. V. Stasov. *Modest Petrovich Musorgskiy: Biographicheskiy ocherk*, in A. S. Ogolevets (ed.). *V. V. Stasov: Izbrannïye stat'i o Musorgskom* (Moscow: GMI, 1952).

MDW   A. Orlova (ed.). *Musorgsky's Days and Works*, trans. R. J. Guenther (Ann Arbor, Michigan: UMI Research Press, 1983).

MLN   A. A. Orlova (ed.). *Modest Petrovich Musorgskiy: Literaturnoye naslediye: pis'ma, biograficheskiye materiali i dokumenti* (Moscow: Muzïka, 1971).

MML   N. Rimsky-Korsakov. *My Musical Life*, trans. Judah A. Joffe (London: Eulenburg, 1974).

MR   J. Leyda and Sergei Bertensson (eds. and trans.). *The Musorgsky Reader* (New York: Da Capo Press, 1970).

ODR   R. Taruskin. *Opera and Drama in Russia as Preached and Practiced in the 1860s* (Ann Arbor, Michigan: UMI Research Press, 1981).

PBI   S. A. Dianin (ed.). *Pis'ma A. P. Borodina*, vol. 1 (Moscow: GMI, 1927–8).

PBII   S. A. Dianin (ed.). *Pis'ma A. P. Borodina*, vol. 2 (Moscow: GMI, 1936); also vol. 3 (1949).

RKP   A. S. Lyapunova (ed.). *N. Rimskiy-Korsakov: Polnoye sobrianïye sochinenniy*, vol. 5: *Literaturnïye proizvedeniya i perepiska* (Moscow: GMI, 1963).

SPR   Yu. V. Keldïsh and M. O. Yankovsky (eds.). *V. V. Stasov: Pis'ma k rodnïm*, vol. 1, part 2 (Moscow: GMI, 1954).

SSMI   V. Protopopova (ed.). *V. V. Stasov: Stat'i o muzïke*, vol. 1 (Moscow: Muzïka, 1974).

SSMII   V. Protopopova (ed.). *V. V. Stasov, Stat'i o muzïke*, vol. 2 (Moscow: Muzïka, 1976).

SSMIII   V. Protopopova (ed.). *V. V. Stasov: Stat'i o muzïke*, vol. 3 (Moscow: Muzïka, 1976).

TDM   A. Orlova, *Trudi i dni M. P. Musorgskogo* (Moscow: GMI, 1963).

SECONDARY SOURCES

Abraham, G. *Borodin: The Man and His Music* (London: William Reeves, [1927]).

———: "*Pskovïtyanka:* The original version of Rimsky-Korsakov's first opera," *Musical Quarterly* 54, no. 1 (January 1968), 58–73.

———: *Rimsky-Korsakov: A short biography* (London: Duckworth, 1945).

———: *Slavonic and Romantic Music* (London: Faber and Faber, 1968).

———: Preface to miniature score of Borodin, Symphony no. 2 (London: Eulenburg, [n.d.]).

Antipova, Ye. "Dva varianta *Zhenit'bï,*" *Sovetskaya muzïka* 28, no. 3 (March 1964), 77–85.

Bartlett, R. *Wagner and Russia* (Cambridge: Cambridge University Press, 1995).

Belinsky, V. G. *Selected Philosophical Works* (Moscow: Foreign Languages Publishing House, 1948).

Bobéth, M. *Borodin und seine Oper "Fürst Igor"* (Munich and Salzburg: Berliner musikwissenschaftliche Arbeiten, 1982).

Brown, D. *Mikhail Glinka* (London: Oxford University Press, 1974).

———: *Musorgsky: His Life and Works* (Oxford: Oxford University Press, 2002).

Brown, M. H. (ed.). *Musorgsky in Memoriam, 1881–1981* (Ann Arbor, Michigan: UMI Research Press, 1982).

Cairns, D. (ed.). *The Memoirs of Hector Berlioz* (London: Gollancz, 1969).

———: *Berlioz: Servitude and Greatness* (London: Allen Lane, 1999).

Calvocoressi, M. D. *Mussorgsky* (London: Dent, 1946).

Campbell, S. (ed.). *Russians on Russian Music, 1830–1880* (Cambridge: Cambridge University Press, 1994).

Chernïshevsky, N. G. *Selected Philosophical Essays* (Moscow: Foreign Languages Publishing House, 1953).

Clapham, J. *Smetana* (London: Dent, 1972).

Cui, César. *La Musique en Russie* (Paris: Librairie Sandoz et Fischbacher, 1880).

del Mar, N. *Anatomy of the Orchestra* (London and Boston: Faber and Faber, 1981).

Dianin, S. A. (ed.). *Borodin: Zhizneopisaniye, materialï i dokumentï* (Moscow: GMI, 1960).

———: *Borodin,* trans. R. Lloyd (London: Oxford University Press, 1963).

Dmitriyev, A. N. *Issledovaniya stat'i nablyudeniya* (Leningrad: Sovetskiy Kompozitor, 1989).

Dunning, C., et al. *The Uncensored "Boris Godunov"* (Madison: University of Wisconsin Press, 2006).

Emerson, C. *The Life of Musorgsky* (Cambridge: Cambridge University Press, 1999).

Emerson, C., and R. Oldani. *Modest Musorgsky and "Boris Godunov": Myths, Realities, Reconsiderations* (Cambridge: Cambridge University Press, 1994).

Fay, L. E. *Shostakovich: A Life* (Oxford: Oxford University Press, 2000).

Figes, O. *Natasha's Dance: A Cultural History of Russia* (London: Allen Lane, 2002).

Fischer-Dieskau, D. *Schubert: A Biographical Study of His Songs,* trans. Kenneth S. Whitton (London: Cassell, 1976).

Garden, E. *Balakirev: A Critical Study of His Life and Music* (London: Faber and Faber, 1967).

Gaub, A. *Die kollektive Balett-Oper "Mlada"* (Berlin: Ernst Kuhn, 1998).

Glinka, M. I. *Memoirs,* trans. R. B. Mudge (Norman: University of Oklahoma Press, 1963).

Golovinskiy, G. L. *M. P. Musorgskiy i muzïka XX veka* (Moscow: Muzïka, 1990).

Gordeyeva, E. M. (ed.). *M. P. Musorgskiy v vospominaniyakh sovremennikov* (Moscow: Muzïka, 1989).

Gozenpud, A. A. (ed.). *A. Larosh: Izbrannïye stat'i,* vol. 3 (Leningrad: Muzïka, 1976).

Granjard, H. (ed.). *Quelques Lettres d'Ivan Tourgénev à Pauline Viardot* (Paris: Mouton, [1974]).

Gusin, I. L. (ed.). *Ts. A. Cui: Izbrannïye stat'i* (Leningrad: GMI, 1952).

———. *Ts. A. Cui: Izbrannïye pis'ma* (Leningrad: GMI, 1955).

Herzen, A. *My Past and Thoughts,* trans. C. Garnett, vol. 5 (London: Chatto & Windus, 1926).

———. *My Past and Thoughts,* abridged edition, trans. C. Garnett (Berkeley: University of California Press, 1982).

Jonas, F. (ed.). *Vladimir Stasov: Selected Essays on Music* (London: Barrie & Rockliff, 1968).

Karenin, V. *Vladimir Stasov: Ocherk ego zhizni i deyatel'nosti* (Leningrad: Mïsl', 1927).

Keldysh, Yu, and V. Yakovlev (eds.). *M. P. Musorgskiy k pyatidesyatiletiyu so dnya smerti* (Moscow: GMI, 1932).

Kelly, A. *Toward Another Shore* (New Haven and London: Yale University Press, 1998).

Knight, N. *The Empire on Display* (Washington DC: National Council for Eurasian and East European Research, 2001).

Korovin, V. (trans. and ed.). *Russian 19th-Century Gothic Tales* (Moscow: Raduga, 1990).

Kremlev, Y. A., and A. S. Lyapunova (eds.). *Miliy Alekseyevich Balakirev: Vospominaniya i pis'ma* (Leningrad: GMI, 1962).

Lakond, W. (ed. and trans.). *The Diaries of Tchaikovsky* (New York: W. W. Norton, 1945).

Lamm, P. Preface to *Zhenit'ba,* in Musorgsky, *Complete Works,* vol. 23 (New York: Edwin F. Kalmus, [n.d.]).

Lang, P. H. *Music in Western Civilization* (London: Dent, 1963).

Langham-Smith, R. (ed.). *Debussy on Music* (London: Secker & Warburg, 1977)

Lebedev, A. K., and A. V. Solodovnikov. *Vladimir Vasil'yevich Stasov: Zhizn i tvorchestvo* (Moscow: Iskusstvo, 1976).

Lloyd-Jones, D. Preface to Borodin, Symphony no. 1 (London, Eulenburg, [n.d.]).

Lockspeiser, E. *Debussy: His Life and Mind,* vol. 1 (London: Cassell, 1962).

Maes, F. *A History of Russian Music,* trans. A. J. and E. Pomerans (Berkeley: University of California Press, 2006).

Montagu-Nathan, M. (ed.). "Balakirev's Letters to Calvocoressi," *Music and Letters* 35 (1954), 347–60.

Neef, S. *Die Russischen Fünf* (Berlin: Verlag Ernst Kuhn, 1992).

Novikov, N. *U istokov velikoy muziki* (Leningrad: Lenizdat, 1989).

Obraztsova, I. "Faktï k biografii Musorgskogo," *Sovetskaya Muzïka* 1982, no. 4, 83–88.

Ogolevets, A. S. (ed.). *V. V. Stasov: Izbrannïye stat'i o Musorgskom* (Moscow: GMI, 1952).

Oldani, R. W. "*Boris Godunov* and the Censor," *Nineteenth-Century Music* 2 (1978–9), 245–53.

———. "Mussorgsky's *Boris* on the Stage of the Maryinsky Theater," *Opera Quarterly* 4, no. 2 (1986), 75–92.

Olkhovsky, Y. *Vladimir Stasov and Russian National Culture* (Ann Arbor, Michigan: UMI Research Press, 1983).

Orlova, A. A. *Glinka v Peterburge* (Leningrad: Lenizdat, 1970).

———. (ed.). *Musorgsky Remembered,* trans. V. Zaytzeff and F. Morrison (Bloomington and Indianapolis: Indiana University Press, 1991).

Pekelis, M. S. (ed). *A. S. Dargomïzhskiy: Izbrannïye pis'ma* (Moscow: 1952).

Petrova, S. M., and V. G. Fridlyand (eds.). *I. S. Turgenev v vospominanyakh sovremennikov,* vol. 2 (Moscow: Izdatel'stvo Khudozhestvennaya Literatura, 1969).

Raeff, M. (ed.). *Russian Intellectual History* (New York: Humanity Books, 1999).

Ridenour, R. C. *Nationalism, Modernism and Personal Rivalry in Nineteenth-Century Russian Music* (Ann Arbor, Michigan: UMI Research Press, 1981).

Rimsky-Korsakov, A. N. (ed.). *M. P. Musorgskiy: pis'ma i dokumentï,* (Moscow and Leningrad: GMI, 1932).

Rubinstein, A. "Die Componisten Russland's," *Blätter für Musik, Theater und Kunst* (Vienna), 11 May, 25 May, 8 June 1855.

——. "O muzïke v Rossii," *Vek,* 1861, no. 1.

Russ, M. *Musorgsky: Pictures at an Exhibition* (Cambridge: Cambridge University Press, 1992).

Sams, E. *The Songs of Robert Schumann* (London: Methuen, 1969).

Sargeant, L. M. *Harmony and Discord: Music and the Transformation of Russian Cultural Life* (Oxford: Oxford University Press, 2011).

Serov, A. N. *Izbrannïye stat'i,* vol. 1 (Moscow, 1950).

Sharp, E. A. (ed. and trans.). *Heine in Art and Letters* (London: Walter Scott, n.d. [1895]).

Stasov, V. V. *L'Abbé Santini et sa collection musicale à Rome* (Florence: private publication, 1854).

Stravinsky, I., and R. Craft. *Memories and Commentaries* (London: Faber and Faber, 1960).

——. *Expositions and Developments* (London: Faber and Faber, 1962).

Swan, A. J. *Russian Music and Its Sources in Chant and Folk-Song* (London: John Baker, 1973).

Taruskin, R. *Musorgsky: Eight Essays and an Epilogue* (Princeton: Princeton University Press, 1993).

——. *Stravinsky and the Russian Traditions* (Oxford: Oxford University Press, 1996).

——. *Defining Russia Musically* (Princeton and Oxford: Princeton University Press, 1997).

Taylor, P. S. *Anton Rubinstein: A Life in Music* (Bloomington and Indianapolis: Indiana University Press, 2007).

Turgenev, I. S. *Polnoye sobraniye sochineniy i pisem* (Moscow and Leningrad: Izdatel'stvo Akademii Nauk SSSR, 1961).

——. *Smoke,* trans. N. Duddington (London: Dent, 1970).

——. *"First Love" and Other Stories,* trans. R. Freeborn (Oxford and New York: Oxford University Press, 1989).

Turner, J. "Musorgsky," *Music Review* 47 (1986–7).

Tyrrell, J. *Janáček: Years of a Life,* vol. 2 (London: Faber and Faber, 2007).

Walicki, A. *A History of Russian Thought from the Enlightenment to Marxism* (Oxford: Clarendon Press, 1980).

Walker, J. "Mussorgsky's *Sunless* Cycle in Russian Criticism," *Musical Quarterly* 67 (1981), 382–91.

Westrup, J. (ed.). *Essays Presented to Egon Wellesz* (Oxford: Clarendon Press, 1966).

Williams, A. (trans. and ed.). *Franz Liszt: Selected Letters* (Oxford: Clarendon Press, 1998).

Yastrebtsev, V. V. *Reminiscences of Rimsky-Korsakov,* trans. and ed. F. Jonas (New York: Columbia University Press, 1985).

Zorina, A. P. (ed.). *A. P. Borodin v vospominaniyakh sovremennikov* (Moscow: Muzïka, 1985).

Zviguilsky, A. (ed.). *Ivan Tourgénev: Nouvelle Corréspondance inédite,* vol. 1 (Paris: Librairie des Cinq Continents, 1971).

Index